DATE DUE

Library Use Only
Over Night Reserve

APR 1 '92
ILL#165080
6/27/94
NOV 02 '94

DEC 1 2 1994

Fashion Merchandising

AND Marketing

FASHION

Macmillan Publishing Company
New York

MERCHANDISING AND MARKETING

MARIAN H. JERNIGAN
Texas Woman's University

CYNTHIA R. EASTERLING
University of Southern Mississippi

Production Supervisor: Charlotte Hyland
Production Manager: Richard C. Fischer
Text and Cover Designer: Sheree L. Goodman
Fashion Illustrations: Julie Johnson
Endsheets and Opening Art: Fine Line Illustrations Inc.

This book was set in Horley by Ruttle, Shaw & Wetherill Inc., printed and bound
by Halliday Litho. The cover was printed by Lehigh Press.

Macmillan Publishing Company
866 Third Avenue, New York, New York 10022

Collier Macmillan Canada, Inc.

Library of Congress Cataloging-in-Publication Data

Jernigan, Marian H.
    Fashion merchandising and marketing / Marian H. Jernigan and Cynthia R.
  Easterling.
        p. cm.
      Includes bibliographical references.
      ISBN 0-02-331350-1
        1. Fashion merchandising—United States. 2. Retail trade—United
  States. I. Title.
  HD9940.U4J47 1990
  687'.068'8—dc20   89-48108
                      CIP

Printing: 1 2 3 4 5 6 7   Year: 0 1 2 3 4 5 6

PREFACE _____

Fashion Merchandising and Marketing is an introductory text designed to provide students with an overview of the competitive businesses that design, produce, distribute, and sell fashion goods. The text includes theoretical and practical concepts required to prepare students to enter a variety of fashion careers.

Fashion merchandising has become a growing area of study for students majoring in business or clothing and textiles. Many colleges and universities offer degree programs in fashion merchandising or retail marketing. One of the most common courses in a merchandising program is "Introduction to Fashion Merchandising." This text is designed for such a course.

Merchandising graduates seek careers relating to the production and distribution of fashion goods. A basic knowledge of the workings and interrelationships of the various industries and services that make up the fashion business is essential for individuals planning to enter these fields. This book emphasizes the complexity of the enterprises involved in the design, production, distribution, and selling of fashion-oriented merchandise. Considered part of the fashion industry are apparel and accessories for men, women, and children as well as cosmetics and home furnishings.

Organization and Content _____

Fashion Merchandising and Marketing is divided into four sequential parts: Part I, "The Business of Fashion"; Part II, "The Production of Fashion"; Part III, "Fashion

Marketing Centers"; and Part IV, "Retail Distribution of Fashion." Appropriate trade terminology is emphasized throughout the text, and industry profiles are used to illustrate successful fashion businesses, designers, or concepts. Each chapter concludes with a summary of key points, a listing of key words and concepts, and discussion questions or topics. A glossary and a bibliography are incuded ·at the end of the book.

Part I: The Business of Fashion

The first three chapters introduce the student to the fashion business and describe the fundamentals of fashion and the basic principles that govern fashion movement and change. In this section basic fashion terminology is defined, and an overview of career opportunities is presented.

Chapter 1, "Introduction to the Fashion Business," defines the fashion industry, introduces fashion terminology, and discusses career opportunities. Chapter 2 explains the principles of fashion movement and presents the theories of clothing origin and fashion adoption. Also discussed are fashion cycles and leadership. Stressed are the importance of understanding consumer motives and accurate prediction of fashion trends for continued success in the industry. Chapter 3 introduces the various enterprises within the fashion industry that assist retailers and manufacturers by providing information and support services.

Part II: The Production of Fashion

Chapters 4 through 7 describe the development, organization, and characteristics of industries producing the raw materials and finished products of fashion.

Chapter 4 presents the industries that produce the raw materials of fashion including textiles, leather, and furs. Chapter 5 discusses the role of the designer in the production of apparel and explains the production process. Included are profiles of prominent American designers. Chapter 6 traces the development of ready-made apparel and describes the characteristics of today's apparel industry. Discussed are women's apparel, menswear, children's wear, and intimate apparel. Chapter 7 presents a discussion of the operations of the industries that produce fashion accessories, cosmetics, and home furnishings.

Part III: Fashion Marketing Centers

In this section, Chapters 8, 9, and 10 describe both domestic and foreign fashion markets. Chapter 8 presents the reasons retail buyers attend markets and why manufacturers show at markets. The major U.S. fashion market centers are described and compared. Chapter 9 explores the primary foreign fashion centers, tracing the development of French haute couture and discussing the current status of couture design. Profiles of selected foreign designers are presented. Chapter 10 emphasizes the global market for fashion goods. Discussed are the growing penetration of foreign-made fashion merchandise into the United States, the methods of importing merchandise, and the attempts by governments and industry to control imports.

Part IV: Retail Distribution of Fashion

The final section includes seven chapters emphasizing the retailing of fashion. Chapter 11 discusses the historical development of retailing and describes the major types of retail businesses that distribute fashion goods to the consumer. Chapter 12 details the various organizational structures of retail stores and describes the key functional areas of retailing, including merchandising, financial control, store operations, personnel, and sales promotion. Also presented are the primary store ownership groups. Chapter 13 acquaints the student with the position of retail buyer and explains the basic responsibilities of buyers employed by different types of stores and buyers who work for resident buying offices. Chapter 14 shows how the buyer analyzes customer demand and determines what to buy. Emphasized are consumer buying motives and the sources of information that assist buyers in determining customer preferences. Also discussed are the tools used by the buyer in planning the merchandise assortment. Chapter 15 deals with how the buyer identifies sources of supply and the activities involved in buying the merchandise. Discussed are how the buyer makes contacts with suppliers and decides from whom to buy, the steps in making a market trip, and selecting merchandise at market. Chapter 16 examines the creation of a fashion image and describes the methods used to promote fashion merchandise. The final chapter presents recent developments and trends in retail merchandising.

The book includes a glossary of more than 400 industry terms. The development of an industry vocabulary is important to any student seeking a fashion career. Correct use of commonplace industry terminology should assist students in interviewing for positions in fashion merchandising. Understanding and speaking the "language" is important to anyone entering a fashion career.

Accompanying the text is the *Instructor's Manual,* which presents answers to the discussion questions, suggested supplementary assignments, and special learning activities. Sample objective examination questions with a key are included for each unit of study.

Acknowledgments

We are indebted to many who contributed to the development of this text. Our thanks and appreciation are extended to the following:

to our many students who have shown us the need for a text and have often served as a testing ground,

to our fellow faculty members for their continued support and encouragement,

to the many professionals in the fashion industry who provided ideas and illustrations for the book,

to the reviewers for their many helpful criticisms and suggestions: Emilie Duggan, Grossmont College, El Cajon, California; Ann E. Fairhurst, Indiana University; Lucille Golightly, Memphis State University; Shelly S. Harp, Texas Tech University; Terri S. Lynch, Centenary College, Hackettstown, New Jersey; Margery McBurney, Ashland College, Ashland, Ohio; Marcia A. Morgado, University of Hawaii at Manoa; Elaine L. Pederson, University of Nevada, Reno; Carmel Repp, Carmel Repp, Ltd.; Pamela V. Urich, Auburn University, Auburn, Alabama; and Janet Wagner, University of Maryland, and

to our editor at Macmillan, Julie Levin Alexander, for her special encouragement throughout the project.

Marian H. Jernigan
Cynthia R. Easterling

CONTENTS

FASHION MERCHANDISING
AND MARKETING

PART I _____

THE BUSINESS OF FASHION

FASHION today is a complex multibillion-dollar industry that includes the many designers, producers, and distributors of fashion products. Also part of the fashion business are the auxiliary enterprises that promote fashion, disseminate information, and assist the other segments of the fashion industry. To understand the nature and scope of the exciting, dynamic, and multifaceted business of fashion, one must begin by exploring the concepts that answer the following questions:

What is the nature of fashion? What part does fashion play in our lives? How is fashion defined, and how does it operate? What is the basic terminology of fashion?

What are the component parts of the fashion business, and what fashion career opportunities are available? What personal qualities are necessary for successful fashion careers? What are the advantages and disadvantages of a career in fashion?

How does fashion move, and what factors influence its movement? How do different groups of consumers initiate and lead the movement of fashion?

How can the fashion industry forecast the direction in which fashion is moving and predict what styles will be accepted by the majority of consumers?

What enterprises within the fashion industry assist retailers and manufacturers by providing information and support services?

Understanding the dynamics of fashion is important to anyone entering this field whether at the wholesale or the retail level. A knowledge of vocabulary is particularly important for success. The three chapters in Part I introduce the fashion business and describe the fundamentals of fashion and the basic principles that govern its movement and change. Basic fashion terminology is defined and an overview of career opportunities is presented in Chapter 1.

Chapter 2 explains the principles of fashion movement and the theories of clothing origin and fashion adoption. Also discussed are how fashion moves in visible patterns or cycles and how consumer acceptance of new fashions is influenced by economic, political, social, and technological factors. Because fashion is a product of change, predicting fashion movement is important at all levels of the industry. Fashion producers and distributors must successfully forecast the direction in which fashion is moving and predict what styles will be accepted by consumers even before consumers know what they want. How changing fashions are forecast is emphasized in this chapter.

Chapter 3 introduces the enterprises within the fashion industry that assist retailers and manufacturers by providing information and support services. Among these enterprises are fashion consulting and reporting firms, resident buying offices, the fashion press, advertising agencies, publicity and public relations firms, trade associations, and professional organizations.

CHAPTER 1 _____

INTRODUCTION TO THE FASHION BUSINESS

FASHION is a major force in our daily lives. It affects every aspect of our lives, influencing what we see, do, and wear. We are influenced by fashion from the time we get up in the morning until we go to bed at night. Fashion affects the clothing and accessories we wear, the environment in our homes and offices, the cars we drive, the food we eat, and the entertainment we enjoy. Fashion is everywhere, and it is unavoidable. Fashion is so integrated into our lives that we often are unaware of its impact. Some people say that they are not concerned with fashion. However, even these people are influenced by fashion even if only by trying to avoid it.

Men, women, and children all feel the effect of fashion in the clothes they wear as well as in other aspects of their appearance. Fashion extends even to the family pet, which may wear a fashionable collar or sweater and eat from an appropriately decorated bowl.

Fashion encourages women to wear their hair short or long, curly or straight, blond or brunette. Fashion influences the colors, the fabrics, and the styles of women's clothing. It also determines the types and colors of cosmetics worn. Men, as well as women, feel the impact of fashion. Fashion leads men to grow beards or be clean shaven, to wear wide or narrow ties, to choose single- or double-breasted suits. In recent years fashion has encouraged men to add more color to their wardrobes. At one time white was the only acceptable color for a man's dress shirt. Today the dress shirt is available in a variety of solid colors and stripes. Men's sportswear, too, has become almost as colorful and fashion-oriented as women's sportswear.

Children also respond to fashion. Clothing designed for toddlers and pre–school-age children often follows the fashion for adults. Children are influenced by their peers beginning at an early age to dress as others dress. They are often teased and ridiculed if their way of dressing is different from that of their peers. The influence of fashion grows stronger as the teen years approach. Wearing the right brand-name clothing is often very important to the teenager.

Fashion is a complex concept. It involves much more than apparel, accessories, cosmetics, and hairstyle. Almost any industry producing consumer goods considers fashion when designing products. The automobile industry is concerned with styling and color, factors often as important to the consumer as the technology under the hood. Fashion is also very important today in the home. It affects the selection of all home-furnishings products such as furniture, decorative accessories, housewares, household textiles, appliances, and home electronics. Customers want products that look right as well as products that are serviceable.

Today, many items that used to be available in a limited selection are now found in a tremendous variety of colors and styles. At one time all bed sheets and bath towels were white; today colors and prints are available to suit any taste. Home electronics, referred to in the industry as **brown goods,** used to be made of wood or synthetic materials that looked like wood. Today, television sets, radios, and telephones are designed to match any decor, in colors ranging from neutrals to pastels to vibrant primary colors. Telephones and radios have even been designed to look like many other items, including footballs, teddy bears, and cartoon characters such as Mickey Mouse, Snoopy, and Garfield.

Some people criticize fashion for encouraging people to buy things they do not need and for encouraging the replacement of items before they are worn out. It should be noted, however, that fashion does much to stimulate our economy. In fact, many retailers and manufacturers would not exist if it were not for fashion. If consumers purchased only to satisfy basic needs for food, shelter, and clothing and to replace worn-out goods, the number of retailers and manufacturers would be greatly reduced. Many are successful in business because the desire to keep current with fashion encourages consumers to purchase goods to fulfill wants as well as needs. Retailers and manufacturers recognize that fashion meets a basic desire that people have for change, and they know that consumers buy to satisfy emotional wants as well as physical needs.

The Fashion Business

The **fashion business** includes all of the industries necessary to produce and market **fashion goods** to the consumer. Fashion goods include apparel and accessory items for men, women, and children as well as home furnishings. The fashion industries can be organized into five different areas of specialization:

1. The producers and suppliers of raw materials for fashion goods

2. Designers and manufacturers of fashion goods

3. Wholesale distributors of fashion goods

4. Retail distributors of fashion goods

5. Auxiliary fashion enterprises

Many raw materials are used in the production of fashion goods. The apparel industry creates finished products from textiles, leathers, furs, metals, and plastics. Also needed to produce apparel and accessories are findings, which include zippers, thread, buttons, and decorative trims. The home-furnishings industry uses many of the same raw materials as the apparel industry; woods, plastics, and metals are important in addition to textiles in the furniture and home-accessories industries. Industries that produce and market any items needed to manufacture apparel, accessories, and home furnishings are part of the fashion industry. For example, the textile industry includes fiber producers, textile mills, converters, and finishers. Fiber producers make the basic unit used in the production of textile yarns and fabrics. Some firms specialize in making yarns, which are fibers that have been combined to form a continuous strand. Textile mills produce fabric by interlacing yarns or fibers together by such methods as weaving, knitting, felting, fusing, lacemaking, or braiding. Converters apply to a fabric finishes that change the appearance, the hand (feel), or the performance of the fabric. Some finishes are applied to the fiber or yarn before they are made into fabrics. Other finishes are applied to unfinished fabric called gray (greige) goods.

Once the raw materials are produced, the next step in the flow of the industry is to design and manufacture finished products. The fashion industry concerns the production of all apparel and accessory items for men, women, and children. Apparel includes both outerwear and innerwear. Accessories are items used to complete a fashion look. In the apparel industry accessories include hats, gloves, jewelry, scarves, belts, handbags, small leather goods, footwear, and hosiery. Cosmetics and fragrances are another segment of the fashion business. The home-furnishings industry includes furniture, window treatments, floor coverings, and decorative accessories such as lamps, pictures, and artificial flowers.

The various producers of apparel, accessories, and home furnishings market their goods to retailers through selling agents. In the fashion industry, goods are marketed through sales representatives located in fashion market centers, through manufacturers' own sales personnel who call on **retailers** in their stores, and by wholesalers who buy goods for resale to retailers.

The final link in the fashion industry flow chart (see Figure 1.1) is the retail distributor. Retailers provide the direct link to the ultimate consumer through stores or direct marketing. Retailers are persons or businesses that purchase finished goods and then sell these goods directly to the ultimate consumer. Many types of retailers sell to consumers—department stores, specialty stores, boutiques, off-price stores, discounters, manufacturers' outlets, mail-order firms, and direct marketers, for example.

In addition to the various producers, manufacturers, and retailers, the fashion business includes many auxiliary enterprises that promote fashion, disseminate in-

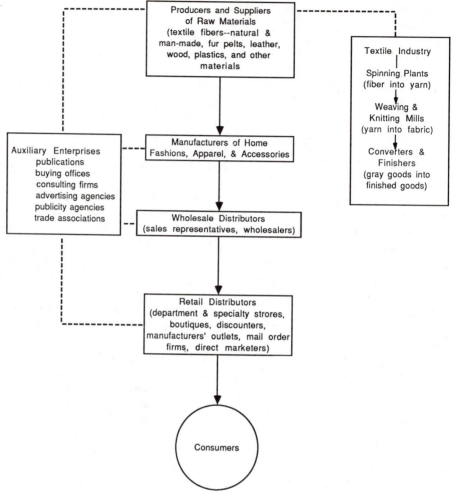

FIGURE 1.1
Fashion industry flowchart.

formation, and assist the other segments of the industry. Included among these auxiliary firms are many fashion-related services, trade associations, consulting and advising firms, advertising agencies, public relations and publicity firms, resident buying offices, consumer fashion magazines, trade publications, and modeling agencies.

The scope of the fashion business is broad and diversified. All segments of the business are interrelated, and all have the same ultimate goal—to identify what goods the consumer will want to buy and to make a profit by producing and selling those goods. Ultimately it is the consumer who determines the success of the fashion business. Through acceptance or rejection of the goods offered, the consumer decides which items will be in fashion.

Fashion Terminology

As with any business or industry, the fashion business has its own terminology. In order to communicate effectively, the student must understand the language of fashion. The most basic term is, of course, *fashion.*

Fashion

The definition of fashion by the economist Dr. Paul Nystrom is the most widely used and simply stated. According to him, "Fashion is nothing more or less than the prevailing style at a given time" (Nystrom 1928).

From the perspective of the fashion industry, fashion is what the majority of people are purchasing and using at a particular time. The retailer views fashion as what is selling. The styles that are currently most popular are said to be "in fashion." Such styles are widely accepted by consumers at one or more levels of the market. What is in fashion constantly changes; therefore, a basic characteristic of fashion is change. As stated in *The Dictionary of Retailing,* "Since styles constantly change in response to consumer demand for the new, it may be said that fashion is, in fact, change—that fashion is not some thing so much as it is an on-going process" (Ostrow and Smith 1985).

Retailers classify their merchandise as fashion merchandise or **basic merchandise.** Basic merchandise, also called staple merchandise, has a highly predictable sales history. Customer demand for basic merchandise remains stable for a long period of time; thus it is easy for the retailer to determine the amount of this merchandise to purchase. In apparel, examples of basic merchandise include certain styles of blue jeans, underwear, hosiery, and men's dress shirts. Fashion merchandise is defined by the retailer as goods with strong current customer appeal. Fashion goods are often purchased by customers on impulse. Such goods have a shorter life span than basic goods. Sales of fashion goods involve greater risk for the retailer and are less predictable because of changing consumer demand. Because consumer demand is more difficult to predict, the retailer makes more mistakes in the purchasing of fashion goods, and it is more likely that the goods will have to be lowered in price to encourage their sale before the end of the fashion's popularity.

Two levels of fashion apparel are available to the public: **high fashion and mass or volume fashion.**

High Fashion

High fashion is designed for the small percentage of consumers who want to be fashion leaders and are the first to accept fashion change. These individuals like to stand out from the majority. High fashion is characterized by designs that are innovative and often high-priced. Such fashions are produced and sold in small quantities by well-known designers or manufacturers and are targeted at fashion-conscious, trendy consumers.

Mass Fashion

Most apparel and home furnishings can be described as mass fashion or volume fashion because they are designed to appeal to the majority of consumers. These goods are mass-produced in high volume and are widely distributed at popular to moderate prices. Mass fashion is what the majority of consumers purchase. Such consumers want to be in fashion but are not fashion leaders. They want to fit in with rather than stand out from the majority.

Style

The word **style** was used in our definition of fashion. Sometimes, one hears the words *style* and *fashion* used interchangeably, but they do have different meanings and should not be considered synonymous.

Style is a particular characteristic or feature that distinguishes one object from another. In apparel, a style is a particular characteristic of design, **silhouette,** or line. Skirts and pants are examples of different styles, and each comes in different designs that may also be considered styles. For examples, skirts are designed in many styles, such as A-line, tubular, dirndl, flared, and pleated. Pant styles include trousers, Bermuda shorts, pedal pushers, and bell bottoms. Examples of various jacket and coat styles are the trench coat, Chesterfield, blazer, safari jacket, and Norfolk jacket.

Styles remain the same, whereas fashions change. A style is always a style, but it is in fashion only as long as it is purchased and worn by a significant number of consumers. The distinctive cut or style of a blazer jacket remains the same, but it will not always be in fashion. The shift, a straight dress without a waistline seam, was the most popular dress style in the 1960s. The shift remains a style, but it is out of fashion now. The miniskirt was the fashion rage in 1967 but ceased to be the fashion of the majority in the early 1970s. Fashion designers reintroduced the miniskirt in 1987, but the style was not widely accepted by a majority of consumers. Because of this rejection, sales in many stores were lower than predicted, and large price reductions were taken by retailers in an attempt to sell the goods.

Home furnishings also are available in different styles. Basic areas of furniture styles are traditional, country or provincial, and contemporary. There are variations within each general style; for example, traditional styles include Georgian, Queen Anne, Victorian, and French Empire. Each style has distinctive characteristics that set it apart from other styles. As in apparel, the styles that are fashionable change, but each remains a style even though it may no longer be in fashion.

Style is also used to describe people. Certain individuals are said to have style, meaning that they have a distinctive manner setting them apart from others. Some well-known individuals considered to have distinctive styles include Jacqueline Kennedy Onassis, Katharine Hepburn, and Princess Diana.

The word *style* has yet another meaning within the fashion industry. A manufacturer uses a style number to identify each item in his or her line. When retail buyers order or reorder an item in a manufacturer's line, the style number is listed on the order form. Thus in this usage the word *style* refers not to the particular style of the item but rather to the number given each item in the line.

Design

A **design** is a unique version of a style. For example, a shirtwaist is a specific dress style, but it can be interpreted in numerous ways. Each interpretation or version is

The three basic silhouettes are the straight or tubular, the bell-shaped or bouffant, and the bustle or back-fullness.

a design. Fashion design involves the manipulation of four basic elements: form or silhouette, detail, color, and texture. By changing these elements, one develops a new style that may become a fashion.

Silhouette is the overall outline or shape of a costume. It is also referred to as contour or form. Three basic silhouettes have been worn by women throughout the history of fashion. These three basic silhouettes are (1) the straight or tubular, (2) the bell-shaped or bouffant, and (3) the bustle or back-fullness. Many variations of each of these silhouettes are possible.

Details are the various components within a silhouette such as collars, sleeves, shoulder and waist treatments, and length and width of skirts and pants. Trims used to decorate the garment are also part of the detail. Trims include buttons, top stitching, lace edging, piping, appliqués, embroidery, and belts. Great variety in designs can be achieved through varying the detail.

Texture refers to the look or feel of a fabric or other construction material. It creates surface interest and effects the sensuous element of design. Texture greatly influences the appearance of the silhouette and changes the mood of the garment. The drape of the garment can change significantly with a change in fabric texture. A dress made in a soft flowing fabric such as silk chiffon will look very different from the same dress style constructed in a stiff taffeta fabric.

Color is often the most important element in a design. Highly influenced by both fashion and customer preference, color is usually the first factor the customer considers when selecting a garment. A change in color obviously makes a considerable change in the appearance of a garment. Color can make the garment and its wearer look larger or smaller. Color can also affect the mood of a garment, making it appear informal or dressy.

The Chanel suit is an example of a classic style.

Classic

A **classic** is a style that continues to be popular and remains in general fashion acceptance over an extended period of time. Such styles are less subject to the fluctuations in fashion and, therefore, are considered fashion basics by the retailer. The consumer may view classics as an investment purchase because they will be wearable for a long period of time. A classic serves as a standard or guide within a merchandise category. Examples of classic styles in apparel include the shirtwaist dress, the Chanel suit, blazer jacket, cardigan sweater, polo shirt, and loafers. Such classic styles seem to remain in fashion almost indefinitely. Minor changes may be made in the design of classics in order to update them, but such styles still retain their distinctive styling.

Fad

Some styles enjoy a sudden burst of popularity and disappear very quickly. These fashions are called **fads.** Such short-lived fashions are often popular only with a specific group of consumers such as high school or college students.

Nearly everyone can remember fads from their school days. A fad often sweeps through a junior high or high school very quickly and may be isolated within a certain school. Almost as soon as everyone has the fad item, it suffers sudden death, and few will wear it. Fads are associated most strongly with adolescents, but anyone at any age can be susceptible to a fad. The chemise or sack dress of 1957 is a classic example of a fad in women's fashions. It enjoyed a short burst of popularity and passed from the fashion scene very quickly. Jellies, plastic shoes in jelly bean colors, were a fad in the mid-1980s, as were animal necklaces and pins. Wearing torn jeans was a fad on many college campuses in the late 1980s.

Ford

A **ford** is a fashion item that sells in great quantities and is widely copied at a variety of price levels. A ford is also called a best-seller or a **runner.** It consistently will sell through a season or a year at full price. Another similar term is **winner,** which denotes a quick-selling item. Unlike a runner, however, a winner may not have a long period of acceptance.

Fashion Look

A **fashion look** refers to the total accessorized costume. The term was introduced in 1947 with Christian Dior's "New Look," which was a radical change from the fashions worn during the World War II period from 1940 to 1945. The New Look marked a return to more feminine styles with long, full skirts and fitted waistlines (Calasibetta 1986).

Fashion looks may be introduced by several means. Many fashion looks since 1947 have been introduced by young people protesting against society. The hippie look of the 1960s and the punk look of the 1980s were such examples. Other looks have evolved from stage, movies, and television. Movies that popularized fashion looks in the 1970s and 1980s include *Annie Hall, Saturday Night Fever, Flashdance,*

Christian Dior's New Look marked a return to more feminine styles with long full skirts and fitted waistlines.

and *Out of Africa*. The fashion for pastel colors and unconstructed linen suits in menswear was introduced by television's "Miami Vice." Some looks evolve from celebrities and public officials. First Lady Nancy Reagan, for example, popularized the color red and influenced a return to greater femininity and formality in dress. Some designers, too, such as Laura Ashley and Ralph Lauren, have developed distinctive looks in both apparel and home furnishings. Some fashion looks are adopted only by a few, whereas others are accepted by the majority and thus become mass or volume fashion.

Accessories

Within the apparel industry, **fashion accessories** are items that accompany items of wearing apparel to complete the total fashion look. Accessories include hats, gloves, jewelry, scarves, belts, handbags, hosiery, shoes, artificial flowers, and hair ornaments. Such items are closely tied to the prevailing fashions in outerwear. Accessories must be correlated with fashion apparel for the total fashion look. Obviously colors must be related, but changes in the fashion silhouette strongly influence accessories. When skirts are long or pants are important fashion styles, hosiery becomes less important. Some silhouettes require a belt; others eliminate belts. When pants are popular for women, belts are usually in demand. Thus, when changes occur in the fashion silhouette, the accessory business declines or expands.

Within the home-furnishings industry, accessories are decorative items that complete the look of a residential interior. **Home accessories** include lamps, pictures, and tabletop merchandise. **Tabletop** refers to china, glassware, flatware, and textile products such as tablecloths and napkins. Other decorative items such as vases, candle holders, ashtrays, and art objects may also be considered tabletop merchandise. **Domestics,** which are textile products for the home such as bed and bath linens, pillows, and kitchen linens, are also a necessary part of home accessories and add to the decorative look of an interior.

Fashion Trends

A **fashion trend** is the direction in which a fashion is moving. A number of trends are present at any given time. Trends include those fashions gaining in popularity and acceptance in the marketplace. Such fashions are the incoming trends. Those fashions diminishing in popularity are the outgoing trends.

To succeed in the fashion business, retailers and manufacturers must be able to forecast fashion trends with relative accuracy. How fashion trends are predicted is discussed in Chapter 2.

Fashion Season

In retailing, a **fashion season** is a selling period. The year is commonly divided into two seasons—spring, the twenty-six weeks of February through July; and fall, the twenty-six weeks of August through January.

In the fashion industry, new lines or collections are designed for each selling season. The number of seasons depends on the merchandise category. For example, accessories such as shoes and handbags may have only two seasons: spring and fall. In women's apparel four or five seasonal lines are produced a year: spring, summer, fall 1 or transitional, fall 2, and holiday or resort.

What Is Marketing?

Marketing includes all of the activities involved in conceiving a product and directing the flow of goods from producer to the ultimate consumer. Activities of marketing include product development, pricing, promotion, and distribution. The objective of marketing is to make a profit. If a retailer or producer is to make a profit, the firm must have a product that consumers perceive as desirable, and the product must be presented to potential customers in a way that makes them want to buy it. For a firm to do this, the organization must be marketing-oriented at all levels of the business. A firm that is marketing-oriented plans all of its operations around satisfying consumer wants and needs.

At one time most retailers and manufacturers followed a product-oriented approach to business. With this approach the focus is on the product, not on the consumer. The product is designed and produced with no attempt to identify the preferences of the consumer before the product is developed and manufactured. The marketing-oriented approach focuses on the consumer even before the product is manufactured. A company plans its entire operation around satisfying the consumer. The first step is to define a company's **target customers,** those persons the company most wants to attract as customers. Next the company identifies these customers' needs and wants. Products that will meet the needs and desires of target customers are then developed or selected. Most manufacturers and retailers today recognize that following a consumer-marketing approach leads to a profitable business. Firms that do not recognize this are likely to find themselves out of business.

What Is Fashion Merchandising?

Merchandising by its most basic definition is the buying and selling of goods for the purpose of making a profit. The American Marketing Association defines *mer-*

chandising as "the planning involved in marketing the right merchandise at the right place at the right time in the right quantities at the right price." Merchandising is concerned with all of the activities necessary to provide a store's customers with the merchandise they want to buy, when and where they want it, and at prices they can afford and are willing to pay. This involves making buying plans, understanding the customer, selecting the merchandise, and promoting and selling the goods to the consumer.

Merchandising is done by both manufacturers and retailers. For manufacturers merchandising begins with estimating customer demand in terms of styles, sizes, colors, quality, and price. Merchandising also involves designing the goods and selecting the fabrics and findings, designing the packaging, pricing, determining advertising and other sales promotion activities, directing the sales division, and the actual selling of the goods.

For retailers merchandising also begins with forecasting customer wants and desires. The retailer must first project sales in terms of dollars and units of merchandise. Also, the retailer must know what type of merchandise in terms of colors, sizes, styles, prices, and other selection factors the store's customers want to purchase. After planning what and how much to buy, merchandising for the retailer includes determining resources from which to purchase, selecting, and purchasing the goods. Once the goods are purchased the retail merchandiser must receive, mark, and prepare the goods for sale. Part of merchandising is presenting the merchandise attractively and effectively to the customer and promoting that merchandise so that the customer wants to buy it. Furthermore, the retail merchandiser may be responsible for training salespeople, selling the goods, and handling any merchandise returns and adjustments.

The goal of merchandising for both manufacturer and retailer is to sell merchandise at a profit. This requires careful planning and coordinating of all of the activities of merchandising. The merchandiser must consider the cost of the merchandise as well as all of the costs involved in receiving, handling, promoting, and selling the goods in order to achieve a profit.

Fashion merchandising presents a special problem because of the ever-changing nature of fashion and the difficulty of predicting consumer demand. Both retailers and manufacturers must adapt their products and services to what consumers want. Consumers determine fashions by selecting from the merchandise that is available the styles that they prefer.

Is the Fashion Business for You?

Fashion merchandising is an exciting and challenging field that offers many career opportunities, but it is a field about which many misconceptions exist. Those who are unfamiliar with the fashion industry often view fashion as a glamorous business involving beautiful merchandise and beautiful people. Although some aspects of the field are glamorous, fashion is a demanding field requiring hard work, long hours, and dedication. Students may visualize themselves working with elegant merchandise, traveling to exciting places, and making decisions in an elegantly appointed office.

In reality a career in fashion involves endless problems to solve, deadlines to meet, the tremendous pressure to make a profit. At executive levels work hours frequently extend beyond forty hours a week and often include weekends and holidays. In retailing, for example, Christmas vacation usually begins after 6:00 P.M. on Christmas Eve and ends at 8:00 A.M. the day after Christmas. Fashion is a cyclical business with periods of long hours and hard work followed by slower periods that may even become boring. Some fashion jobs involve travel—this sounds exciting, but such travel is for business, not pleasure. The business travel day is likely to be long, and often there is no time to sightsee because of the rushed pace of the trip. Except for the highest-level executives, offices are seldom elegant. In fact, office space is frequently cramped and unattractive. A buyer's office, for example, may be a desk in the corner of the stockroom, or it may be a partitioned space in a large area where many other buyers and their assistants work with telephones ringing constantly. Sometimes a junior fashion executive does not even have an office or a desk.

Many students choose a major in fashion merchandising or retail marketing because they want to become retail buyers. They often make this decision because they like clothes or because they like to shop. Such decisions are likely to be made without being aware of the skills and qualifications necessary for success in the fashion business or without knowing the wide range of career opportunities available within the field.

The student must first understand that one does not graduate from college and immediately assume an executive-level position. It is customary in the fashion business to learn the business from the ground up. One does not, for example, become a buyer, a designer, or a store manager immediately out of college. The beginning level in retailing may be as a salesperson, assistant buyer, assistant manager, clerical assistant to a buyer, head of stock, or executive trainee. The aspiring young designer is likely to begin as a pattern maker, sample maker, assistant designer, or as a "gofer" who runs miscellaneous errands.

Theories and concepts learned in the college classroom help the student learn company procedures and policies and may enable him or her to advance to a higher level position more rapidly than an employee who does not have an educational background in fashion. In the fashion business, however, much can be learned only on the job. Each company has its own policies and procedures that must be learned before an individual is ready to advance to an executive position. A student who has already acquired work experience in the field prior to graduation has a head start over the individual who has not worked. Work experience in the form of an internship, cooperative education position, or part-time job is helpful in obtaining a position and assists the student in climbing the career ladder after entering the fashion business.

Executive Training Programs

Most large companies operate formal training programs, which usually include both classroom training and on-the-job experience. The executive trainee may be required to write papers and present projects to fellow trainees and company executives as part of the training program. Thus classroom experiences do not end when the student graduates from college. There is much to learn before the trainee is ready to assume an executive position.

Often the first assignment for the retail trainee is in a sales position. All retailing is based on sales, and the new trainee must first learn the store's selling systems and understand the store's customer. The best way to learn about customers and their merchandise preferences is by direct contact with customers on the sales floor. In some stores the trainee begins as an assistant manager in a department or small store, or as an assistant to a buyer, but all trainees literally learn the business "from the floor up."

Executive training programs vary considerably in terms of activities and length of the program. Typical retail training programs provide orientation to the total store through rotating job assignments in all operational areas. When management judges the trainee to be ready, he or she is placed in an appropriate position.

Training programs enable the trainee to be exposed to all aspects of the business. A trainee often changes career direction after experiencing different areas of the business. A trainee may decide that management is the direction to follow rather than merchandising. Management is concerned with the operation of the business, whereas merchandising is concerned primarily with buying the goods to be sold. Through experience both the trainee and the employer learn more about the trainee's capabilities and where he or she best fits into the business.

The graduate does not have to enter the fashion business as a trainee. The student may also enter a company in an entry-level position and work up. Many retailers start as retail salespeople and advance into management or buying positions. Many designers begin as assistant designers or even as receptionists or models. The first step is to get a job with a company. This may mean lowering expectations for a beginning position. The student should not expect to begin in a top position. It is important to realize that one has to learn the business before one can run the business. No student, no matter how intelligent or how well-educated, is qualified to be an upper-level executive immediately after earning a degree.

Career Opportunities

The fashion business offers a wide variety of challenging and exciting career opportunities in the general areas of manufacturing, retailing, and promotion. The fashion business is concerned with fibers, textiles, sales promotion, public relations, manu-

The fashion business offers career opportunities in the areas of manufacturing, retailing, and promotion.
Source: Reprinted with permission of Macy's, Gitano, The Catco Corporation, Christian Dior N.Y., Barney's New York, and The Gap, Inc.

facturing, wholesaling, and retailing. Within each of these areas are many opportunities for someone with the necessary knowledge, skills, and interests.

Retail Opportunities

Many positions related to fashion merchandising are available with retail stores. The beginning level in retailing is often sales. The backbone of retailing is, in fact, sales. The primary goal of retailing is to sell merchandise to the ultimate consumer at a profit. Retailing includes all of the business activities necessary to acquire and to sell goods to the ultimate consumer. The activities of retailing involve buying goods from suppliers, receiving the goods, arranging them in a convenient store location, and selling the goods.

Retail careers are found in the areas of store operations, financial control, sales promotion, personnel, and merchandising. Although merchandising is only one of the functional areas of retailing, it is the function around which all of the others revolve. Merchandising is concerned with selecting, buying, and selling the merchandise. All of the other retail functions support the merchandising division. In order for merchandising to function, people must be hired and trained by the personnel division. The store's physical plant must be maintained and managed by the operations division. The goods purchased by buyers must be advertised and promoted so that the public knows what the store has for sale. Finally, the financial control division must manage the finances of the store, seeing that invoices are paid and monies due the store are collected. All of these divisions offer employment opportunities. An individual may begin retail employment in one division but may move into other areas of retailing after gaining experience.

Positions available with retail stores include the following:

1. *MERCHANDISING POSITIONS:* salesperson, personal shopper, assistant buyer, associate buyer, buyer, general merchandise manager, divisional merchandise manager, comparison shopper, fashion coordinator, fashion director, quality assurance technician, and product developer.

2. *PERSONNEL POSITIONS:* personnel interviewer, training supervisor, executive recruiter, and personnel director.

3. *SALES PROMOTION POSITIONS:* advertising layout artist, advertising copywriter, visual merchandiser, publicist, public relations director, advertising director, and promotion director.

4. *STORE OPERATIONS POSITIONS:* receiving and marking supervisor, warehouse manager, service manager, department manager, assistant store manager, and store manager.

5. *FINANCIAL CONTROL POSITIONS:* credit manager, statistical researcher, computer programmer, and controller.

Some positions, such as those in financial control, require specialized technical training and education. Many of the positions in retailing, however, require training that can be obtained on the job. Many people begin their careers in one area of retailing and then move to other areas as their careers advance.

Many begin their fashion careers in retailing and later change to careers in other areas of the fashion business. Retail sales experience is valuable to anyone entering the fashion industry because it is the best way to learn about consumers. All aspects of the fashion industry rely on the consumer for their success. It is the consumer who ultimately determines what merchandise items become fashion. Through their buying behavior consumers often determine the success or failure of a fashion business.

Retail Merchandising Careers

Most careers in retail merchandising start with sales. The next step upward may be as a department manager or an assistant buyer. One of these two positions is often where the trainee begins upon completion of an executive training program.

The department manager is responsible for supervising the salespeople in a department and serves as a liaison between the buyer and the salespeople. The manager is responsible for selling the merchandise and maintaining the department. Typical responsibilities include scheduling and supervising sales personnel, arranging the merchandise in the department, taking inventory counts and markdowns, handling customer complaints, and selling merchandise.

The assistant buyer is a buyer in training. As the buyer's understudy, the assistant works closely with the buyer in order to learn the job of buying. The assistant performs whatever duties the buyer requests and usually spends a great deal of time doing paperwork. The assistant buyer may write orders for basic stock items, calculate markdowns, fill out reports, and return damaged merchandise to suppliers.

Some stores have a position called associate buyer. It entails more responsibility than does the assistant buyer's position. The associate buyer, who is often given the responsibility of buying a merchandise classification, is close to becoming a buyer for a full department.

Buyers plan what to buy, select and purchase the merchandise, and determine what merchandise is to be advertised and promoted. Sometimes the buyer is directly responsible for selling. This involves training salespeople or seeing that the department manager has the necessary information to do this. In some single-store operations, the buyer also performs the duties of the department manager.

Much of the buyer's time is spent with paperwork—studying last year's figures and anticipating changing needs. Merchandise must be priced, markdowns taken, stock maintained, and records kept. Many of these tasks involve a thorough knowledge of merchandising arithmetic and an understanding of how profit is determined.

Many buyers today work with computers. The application of computer systems to retail merchandising has made statistical information readily available to buyers. Such information helps the buyer make decisions regarding merchandise purchases and stock management.

Communication is an important aspect of the buyer's job. A buyer writes numerous reports to notify others about activities involving the department and selling the merchandise. Reporting is especially important in multistore operations.

A buyer's job varies greatly depending upon the size, type, and location of a store. The buyer in a small, one-unit store has a very different job from that of the buyer in a multiunit operation. In a large store the buyer works closely with many people. Employees in all of the other divisions of the store assist the buyer in performing the functions of buying. The small store buyer must perform more functions independently. These buyers may even spend time working on the floor, selling to the store's customers.

The buyer's job also varies depending upon the type of merchandise being purchased. Visiting the wholesale market where goods are sold is part of the buyer's job. The market location may be close to the store or may involve long-distance or even foreign travel. Some buyers go to market frequently; others go only twice a year. Fashion buyers may need to visit a market once a month or even more frequently. Some buyers travel abroad and may be gone for several weeks at a time. The principles of buying are the same regardless of the type of merchandise being purchased. A buyer who understands the job of buying should be able to adapt quickly to buying different price lines or types of merchandise.

The next step up from the buyer's position in a departmentalized store is divisional merchandise manager (DMM). A divisional merchandise manager supervises a group of buyers and is responsible for coordinating efforts of several departments to maximize profits. Above the DMM is the general merchandise manager (GMM), which is a top management position responsible for policymaking.

Another merchandising position is that of **fashion coordinator** or **fashion director.** This job demands an understanding of fashion trends and fashion show production and staging techniques. The fashion coordinator is responsible for identifying fashion trends for seasonal purchases and promotion in order to project the store's fashion image. Fashion shows may be planned by the coordinator to project the store's fashion image to the public and to introduce fashion trends to sales personnel.

The responsibilities of the fashion coordinator vary greatly with different companies. In some stores the coordinator is responsible only for planning fashion shows. In other stores the coordinator or fashion director is an experienced buyer and merchandiser who is responsible for coordinating the overall store fashion image. The fashion director may hold a top-level executive position and be involved in determining store policies. These positions are few in number and are difficult to obtain.

Merchandising Jobs Outside of Retailing

Merchandising jobs are also available in areas of the fashion business other than retailing. Manufacturers need merchandisers to assist designers in assembling and promoting apparel lines. Personnel are needed to manage wholesale showrooms and to sell goods to retailers. Sales representatives are needed to sell at markets and to travel to sell directly to retail buyers.

Private **fashion consultants** and resident buying offices offer merchandising services to retailers. Advertising agencies, trade associations, textile manufacturers, and fiber companies all need merchandisers to plan, coordinate, and distribute products. The trade press and consumer fashion publications also have positions available for merchandisers.

Qualities Necessary for Success in Merchandising

To be successful in the fashion business requires physical stamina and good health—the jobs are often physically demanding. One must be capable of working under pressure and be stimulated by deadlines. One also needs the ability to work with people, as fashion merchandising is a people-oriented business.

Other qualities necessary for success include ingenuity, enthusiasm, aggressiveness, and decisiveness. A merchandiser has to be able to make quick decisions. An artistic sense may also be helpful as one needs to present merchandise in an appealing way. Most important of all is the ability to work with figures and to understand profit. Merchandising is a business, and a business succeeds or fails based on making a profit.

Excellent opportunities exist for men and women in merchandising. Women have long held a relatively higher percentage of executive positions in the industry. With hard work and determination, however, both men and women can move into rewarding and responsible positions in the fashion industry.

Manufacturing Opportunities

Producers of the raw materials of fashion and manufacturers of the finished products offer many varied employment opportunities. Fashion specialists are needed to design, produce, promote, and sell products.

Career positions in design are not as plentiful as those in retailing and merchandising. Designers are needed for fabrics, apparel, accessories, and home furnishings. Design positions require technical and artistic skills. Designers must be able to predict fashion trends and produce designs that consumers will want to buy. They must also understand production procedures and produce designs that can be manufactured within cost levels that permit the company to make a profit. For many designers in budget and moderate price levels, the designer's job involves adapting rather than creating designs. The designer may update successful styles from the previous season or may "knock off" (copy) styles produced by other firms. Employment of designers is not limited to manufacturers. Retailers also hire designers to design products to be sold under the retailer's private label.

Manufacturers hire merchandisers who assist designers in selecting fabrics, assembling lines, and promoting and selling finished products. Personnel are also needed to manage wholesale showrooms and outlet stores. Sales representatives are needed to sell at seasonal markets and to call on buyers at retail store locations.

Operations and production jobs are available for those interested in supervising and managing manufacturing processes, office management, overseeing warehousing and distribution of products, and handling customer service.

Sales Promotion Opportunities

Careers in sales promotion are found with retailers, manufacturers, advertising agencies, and public relations firms. Sales promotion includes advertising, visual merchandising, special events, and publicity. Most sales promotion positions require creative ability and special skills, such as writing or drawing. Training in journalism is needed for some sales promotion jobs.

Preparation of advertising requires copywriters, illustrators, layout artists, and supervisory personnel. Visual merchandising offers career opportunities for display artists, store and showroom interior designers, and sign artists. Public relations firms assist companies with developing publicity to assist in projecting the firm's image. Publicists are needed to write press releases and to plan promotion campaigns.

Auxiliary Opportunities

There are many career opportunities in auxiliary industries that are part of the fashion business. Jobs for fashion specialists exist with fashion consulting firms, resident buying offices, trade associations, and the fashion press. These auxiliary industries are discussed in later chapters.

Entrepreneurship Opportunities

One possible career route is to go into business for oneself. Owning a business is the goal of many students and professionals. Many **entrepreneurs** in the fashion business open a retail store, start an apparel design firm, do **freelance** fashion work, or become fashion consultants.

The most common type of fashion business is the retail store. Opportunities for stores exist anywhere people are located. An independent store owner must be interested in all aspects of the business. The small store owner is a generalist who must assume the responsibilities of buying, receiving, marking, selling, and promoting the merchandise in addition to store operations and maintenance. The small store owner must enjoy variety and be willing to work exceedingly hard to establish a business.

Going into business for oneself is demanding but rewarding. One must be dedicated to the business, willing to work long hours, and do whatever job needs to be done. Usually it takes two or three years to see a profit. The entrepreneur must be able to financially sustain him- or herself through this period. The reward for establishing a business is the expression of individuality and independence. Considerable ambition and drive are needed to succeed, and one must be willing to take risks. The entrepreneur must be highly motivated to succeed.

Most business failures are due to lack of experience, inadequate planning, and undercapitalization. Gaining experience by first working for an established firm before going into business for oneself is the best route to success.

Many opportunities exist within the fashion business for experienced specialists to do freelance work, where they work independently for an individual or on a contractual basis for several clients. Designers may sell their designs to manufacturers. Freelance promotion specialists advise retailers or small manufacturers and assist with preparing promotional campaigns, preparing advertisements, or writing publicity. Other freelance opportunities are found with store planning and interior design, window trimming and display design, fashion coordination, and fashion show presentation. Freelance specialists can seek jobs with retailers, manufacturers, and shopping malls, all of which use the assistance of outside specialists on an occasional basis or may contract with an outside individual to do a job on a continuing basis. Many display artists, for example, contract with several stores to design and install window displays.

Some fashion specialists work with consumers, advising them on wardrobe coordination, makeup application, or color analysis. Wardrobe consultants will visit a client's home and give advice concerning wardrobe coordination and planning. These consultants may also shop for the client, selecting appropriate clothing and accessories to complete the customer's wardrobe. Other consumer fashion consultants do individual color and figure analysis, telling clients what colors and styles are most becoming for them.

Advantages and Disadvantages of Fashion Careers

Both advantages and disadvantages are found in fashion careers. In many cases, one's personal viewpoint determines whether an aspect of a certain position is an advantage or disadvantage. What one person likes about a job, another person may dislike. It is important for students to have a clear understanding of both the advantages and disadvantages of the fashion business before deciding on a career path.

One of the major disadvantages found in fashion jobs is the low beginning pay for college graduates in comparison with many other fields. Pay increases occur as a person gains experience and exhibits dedication to the job, but young people may become discouraged and quit just as they are on the verge of advancement. For those who remain and work hard, the fashion business can be financially rewarding. Although starting salaries are often low, there are excellent opportunities for financial advancement within a few years of college graduation. In retailing, people often gain responsibility quickly and are given the chance to prove themselves after being employed only a short period of time. People are rewarded for success, and success is determined by sales figures and profit realized.

The long hours required, especially in retailing, are perceived by many as a disadvantage. It is often difficult to maintain a family or social life when working weekends and nights. Both manufacturing and retailing are somewhat seasonal, leading to heavy work periods followed by slower periods. In retailing the busiest time of the year is before and immediately following Christmas. Many find it difficult to accept the fact that Christmas vacation begins late on Christmas Eve and ends early the morning after Christmas.

Some companies require employees to relocate in order to advance. Moving can be viewed as a disadvantage, but in many companies relocation may be essential for promotion. Also, as noted earlier, some positions involve considerable travel. Travel is viewed in two ways: It may interfere with home life and be considered a disadvantage, or it may be viewed as a fringe benefit.

Opportunities in fashion are more plentiful in cities although certainly not limited only to metropolitan areas. Large fashion markets are limited to a few major cities, and apparel manufacturers' design offices are concentrated in a few large cities such as New York, Los Angeles, San Francisco, Chicago, and Dallas. Some specialized fashion jobs are found only in major cities, whereas others are located almost anywhere. Any community with retail stores offers some employment opportunities for the fashion major.

Fashion careers offer many advantages to an ambitious person who is willing to work hard. The fashion business gives people with imagination the opportunity to express their creativity. By nature, fashion means constant change, and many people enjoy the variety offered by fashion jobs.

Summary of Key Points

1. Fashion is an important force that affects every aspect of our lives. It impacts the production of many products related to personal appearance and the environment.

2. The fashion business includes all of the industries necessary to produce and market fashion goods. The areas of specialization among the fashion industries include: (a) the producers and suppliers of raw materials, (b) designers and manufacturers, (c) wholesale distributors, (d) retailers, and (e) related fashion enterprises.

3. An understanding of fashion terminology is important for effective communication within the industry.

4. The key objective of marketing and merchandising is to make a profit. If fashion manufacturers and retailers are to operate profitable businesses, they must be consumer-oriented.

5. Fashion careers are many and varied. They offer opportunities and challenges but require dedication and hard work for success.

Key Words and Concepts

Define, identify, or explain each of the following:

basic or staple merchandise	fashion season
brown goods	fashion trend
classic	ford
design	freelance
details	high fashion
domestics	home accessories
entrepreneurs	marketing
fads	mass or volume fashion
fashion	merchandizing
fashion accessories	retailers
fashion business	runner
fashion consultant	silhouette
fashion coordinator	style
fashion director	tabletop merchandise
fashion goods or merchandise	target customers
fashion look	texture
	winner

Discussion Questions and Topics

1. Explain how fashion is an important force in our everyday lives. Give several examples of current fashion in merchandise other than apparel.
2. How does fashion stimulate business?
3. Name the five areas of specialization within the fashion industry.
4. Explain what is meant by the following statement: "Today the fashion business is marketing-oriented."

5. Explain the difference between (a) high fashion and mass fashion, (b) style and fashion, and (c) a classic and a fad. Give current examples of each.

6. Name several apparel styles in fashion today that are considered classics.

7. Fashion design involves the manipulation of four basic elements. Name and describe each of these elements.

8. Discuss the advantages and disadvantages of a career in fashion merchandising.

Notes

Charlotte ManKey Calasibetta. *Essential Terms of Fashion*. New York: Fairchild Publications, 1986, p. 100.

Paul H. Nystrom. *Economics of Fashion*. New York: Ronald Press, 1928, p. 4.

Rona Ostrow and Sweetman R. Smith. *The Dictionary of Retailing*. New York: Fairchild Publications, 1985, p. 88.

CHAPTER 2 _____

FASHION DEVELOPMENT AND MOVEMENT

FASHION denotes change—something new and different from what existed before. Fashions are constantly changing, and the changes occur at different speeds, depending on acceptance by consumers.

Acceptance implies that a large number of people buy and use an item, which makes it a fashion. Different groups of people accept and adopt different fashions. Whereas one fashion appeals to one group, another may receive greater acceptance by a different group. Designers plan styles to appeal to certain consumer groups, and the development of a style into a fashion is determined by the extent to which consumers accept the styles.

Fashion changes are encouraged by both consumers and the fashion industry. Consumers desire change and variety in their environments and activities, and often the easiest change to make is in personal appearance. By purchasing new apparel or accessories, for example, the consumer enjoys a change. The fashion industry encourages fashion change by offering new lines of merchandise several times a year. Through advertising and promotion, consumers are moved to want to purchase the new items. Without such ongoing change in available styles, the fashion industry would cease to be an important business.

This chapter is a discussion of how fashion moves and what influences fashion change. Basic principles of fashion that serve as the foundation for fashion identification and movement are presented. The chapter includes an examination of the theories of clothing origin, and fashion motives and adoption, and defines fashion cycles and fashion leadership. The discussion stresses the importance of understanding consumer motives and accurately predicting fashion trends for the continued success of the fashion industry.

Principles of Fashion Movement

Five fundamental principles of fashion serve as a foundation for fashion identification and movement. These fashion principles remain constant; fashions change, but these principles do not. They are a solid foundation for identifying and predicting fashion trends. The basic principles of fashion movement include the following:

1. *Fashion movements are usually evolutionary in nature and are rarely revolutionary.* Fashions usually evolve gradually from one style to another—**evolutionary fashion**—rather than changing rapidly. This is often illustrated in the changing length of women's skirts. Seldom is a major change in skirt length accepted in one season. Instead, skirt length usually inches up or down gradually over a period of several seasons or even years. In the late 1950s and during the subsequent decade, skirt length began moving upward approximately an inch a year until skirts reached the mini style of the late 1960s. Throughout the 1970s skirt length gradually became longer.

Exceptions to this principle do occur, and occasionally a change becomes **revolutionary fashion.** For example, Dior's "New Look" was accepted rapidly by women following its introduction in 1947. The New Look appeared shortly after the end of World War II at a time when women were eager for a fashion change. During the war, fashion had changed little. The fashion silhouette had been slim, short, and somewhat masculine. When the men returned home, women were ready for the longer, more feminine style of the New Look. The lifting of wartime restrictions on the amount of fabric that could be used in a dress made this new look possible.

2. *The consumer makes fashion.* It is the consumer, not the designer or manufacturer, who determines what will be in fashion by accepting one style and rejecting another. Although designers, producers, and retailers can encourage or retard the progress of new fashions, it is consumers who ultimately determine fashion acceptance. An example of an unsuccessful attempt by the fashion industry to promote a radical change in fashion was the **longuette** or **midi** of fall 1969–1970. This style, with its mid-calf skirt length, was much longer than what women were currently wearing. Consumers were not ready for such an extreme change, and the style was rejected except by a small group of fashion-forward women. In spite of the encouragement by *Women's Wear Daily* and advertising by fashion retailers, the majority of consumers rejected the midi and continued to wear their skirt length near the knee. Many consumers avoided the skirt length issue by wearing pantsuits.

3. *Price does not determine fashion acceptance.* The acceptance of fashion does not depend on price. Although a new style may originate at a high price, it can quickly be made available at various prices. A custom-made designer dress may be priced at several thousand dollars; however, once the style is copied in ready-to-wear, a variety of prices are available to consumers. Sometimes copies are mass produced so quickly that they reach the stores even before the original designs. The trimmings and fabric may be different and the workmanship may not be equal in quality, but the dress style is basically the same.

4. *Fashion movement is not dependent on sales promotion.* Promotional activities, such as advertising, fashion shows, and window displays, cannot sell merchandise that consumers do not want to buy. Although advertising and other promotional efforts by manufacturers and retailers help to generate sales, they do not dictate what styles will be accepted by consumers. Once a fashion trend is established, however, promotional efforts do aid development of the trend. As noted earlier, the fashion industry has made unsuccessful efforts to promote radical changes in fashion, as they did with the "longuette" or midi length, a fashion that failed in spite of extensive advertising. Designers and manufacturers again miscalculated consumers' willingness to change skirt length in the spring of 1988 when skirt lengths above the knee dominated fashion offerings. The fashion industry ignored the needs and opinions of the professional woman who refused to adopt the short skirt. Working women voted with their pocketbooks and just wore their existing wardrobes for another season. Another example is the wearing of foundation garments. In the late 1960s many women replaced girdles with pantyhose, and increased promotional activities by the intimate apparel industry could not force them to wear what they no longer wanted to wear. After the comfort of pantyhose, women refused to wear girdles. No promotional effort can be effective enough to make consumers buy styles in which they have no interest.

5. *Fashions often end in excess.* Paul Poiret, a well-known French high-fashion designer of the 1910s, noted that "all fashions end in excess." This saying is true for fashions today as well. Once a fashion has reached an extreme in styling, a new and different look will occur. For example, in the late 1960s women became tired of bouffant hairstyles and sought new looks. Another example is the fashion silhouette of the mid-1980s, which emphasized shoulder width. When shoulder pads began to make women look like football players, the fashion for extreme padding ceased. And once the miniskirts of the late 1960s rose to the micro-minis of the early 1970s, short hemlines began to decline in popularity and longer skirt lengths were adopted. Skirt length is an excellent example of how a fashion trend can go only so far in one direction and must reverse if change is to occur.

Theories of Clothing Origin

What motivated human beings to begin to wear clothes? Social scientists have long sought the answer to that question. The explanations most often cited by the experts are protection, modesty, and self-adornment. Each of these theories bases the development of clothing on the desire to satisfy a single human need or want. A fourth explanation, "the combined-need theory," contends that dress cannot be traced back to a single need but was devised to satisfy several human wants and needs at the same time (de Paola and Mueller 1980).

Protection Theory

A simple and practical explanation for why human beings adopted clothing is the need for protection from the elements of their environment. However, because humans are believed to have originated in tropical climates, most experts consider protection a secondary motive for wearing clothes. Animal skins and vegetation used as body coverings were probably the first examples of protective clothing.

Physical protection is undoubtedly one reason that people wear clothing today. Many apparel and accessory items are designed to offer protection from the weather, for example, raincoats, umbrellas, rain hats. Many styles of coats provide warmth and protection from climatic elements. Various styles of visors, hats, and sunglasses protect the eyes from the sun. Elements other than the weather also call for protection. Clothing items such as diving suits, helmets, fire protective clothing, bulletproof vests, and the ultimate protective garment, the space suit, protect the wearer from harmful elements.

Clothing has also been used to offer protection from supernatural elements. In primitive societies clothing was worn to protect the wearer from evil spirits and other psychological dangers. Today's bride who wears something borrowed and something blue during the wedding ceremony reflects that belief in the protective powers of clothing. Other articles, such as a rabbit's foot, a Saint Christopher's medal, or a lucky clothing item, are modern-day evidence of belief that one can be protected by wearing certain apparel or accessory items.

Related to wearing clothing for physical protection is today's concern for comfort in dress, especially for casual activities. The consumer demands clothing that does not restrict movement and fabrics that feel good next to the skin and provide warmth in winter and coolness in summer. The sight of jogging suits and athletic shoes everywhere indicates how important comfort is to today's consumer.

Modesty Theory

The modesty theory states that the primary purpose of clothing is to cover the naked body. This theory is based on the idea that people want to cover their bodies because of a sense of shame or embarrassment when naked. The theory implies that by wearing clothing one can conceal or divert attention from certain parts of the body.

The modesty theory has been discounted by most scholars because ideas of modesty are not the same in all cultures, and it is not a universal notion; it is a habit and not an instinct; and one's degree of modesty changes with age. The traditions, customs, and mores of a culture influence what parts of the body must be hidden to avoid a feeling of embarrassment or shame. Whereas the members of one culture may be ashamed to show their naked bodies in public, those in another culture may see nothing indecent in, for example, both sexes bathing together in public baths.

The modesty theory is considered a secondary explanation of the development and origin of clothing. Modesty is, however, one reason why many people in our society today wear clothes. In our society modesty depends to a great extent on where the clothes are worn or the activities engaged in while wearing the clothes. Today's bathing suits are acceptable at the beach or by the pool, but they expose too much of the body to be worn elsewhere.

The urge toward modesty has been considered a culturally induced habit. Hoebel (1958), a noted anthropologist, expressed the idea that a "sense of modesty is merely a habit not an instinct." The idea is supported by the lack of a sense of modesty in young children. They must be taught to cover up certain parts of their bodies and do not develop any sense of modesty until taught that exposure of certain body parts is "not nice" and, therefore, unacceptable by society.

Self-Adornment Theory

The explanation accepted by most experts to explain the origin of clothing is the self-adornment theory. Flugel (1930, p. 86), in *The Psychology of Clothes,* supports the theory that people were first interested in clothing or body ornamentation as a way to enhance their attractiveness. He commented that narcissism, the love of one's own body, can be observed in many children as they indulge in "nude dancing and prancing."

Most scholars agree that clothes originated in the human desire to play up one's own physical charms and to make oneself more attractive to others, especially the opposite sex. Clothing can be used by individuals to stimulate sexual attractiveness. According to Flugel (1930, p. 26), "The ultimate purpose of clothes, and often indeed their overt and conscious purpose, is to add to the sexual attractiveness of the wearer and to stimuate interest of admirers of the opposite sex and the envy of rivals of the same sex."

Adults, especially women, seem to transfer their exhibitionistic urges to clothes. Clothing can be used to enhance one's body structure. Tight-fitting or low-cut garments emphasize the figure and give the wearer an opportunity for self-exposure. Present-day bathing suits, miniskirts, and revealing evening wear allow women to emphasize their physical charms.

Even before people wore clothing, they enjoyed decorating their bodies. The urge for self-adornment was satisfied by such techniques as body painting, tattooing, piercing, and body deformation, or by wearing decorative elements such as stones, shells, feathers, and bones. These adornment practices of primitive societies can be found in modified versions in the modern world. Today, people pierce their ears, pluck their eyebrows, and undergo plastic surgery to enhance their personal attractiveness.

Combined-Needs Theory

The combined-needs theory contends that the origin of clothing was multidimensional, filling several human needs at the same time. According to this theory, the origin of clothing cannot be traced to one single need but rather draws elements from all previous theories. Clothing, in other words, satisfied several needs concurrently.

Undoubtedly, people today wear clothing for a multitude of reasons. For most people interest in dress goes beyond adornment, protection, and modesty. Clothing contributes to the attainment of certain desires. It may provide physical comfort, prestige, or conformity. People also receive aesthetic pleasure from their clothes and find in clothes a way to project their own personalities and to use their creative abilities.

Theories of Fashion Adoption

Successful marketers of fashion realize that it is important to understand how new fashion ideas are disseminated and how they are adapted to fit the tastes, lifestyles, and budgets of different consumer groups. Three theories describe how different groups of consumers initiate and lead the movement of fashion: trickle-down theory, trickle-across theory, and trickle-up theory. These theories explain the course that a fashion travels or is likely to travel. Each theory identifies consumers who are first to adopt a style and explains how each style is diffused from these leaders to other consumers.

Trickle-Down Theory

The **trickle-down theory** is the oldest theory of fashion adoption. It assumes the existence of a social hierarchy in which lower classes seek identification with levels above them, and those at the top seek disassociation from those they consider inferior. This theory suggests that fashion trends start at the top of the social pyramid and gradually win acceptance at progressively lower social levels. The trickle-down theory implies that fashions are accepted by lower classes only if, and after, they are accepted by upper classes. Fashions are rejected by upper classes once they have disseminated or spread to a lower social level. According to the German social philosopher Georg Simmel (1957), "The fashions of the upper stratum of society are never identical with those of the lower; in fact, they are abandoned by the former as soon as the latter prepares to appropriate them."

The trickle-down theory implies that the upper class adopts a new fashion to symbolize its superior position. When the lower class shows its social equality by adopting the fashion, the upper class will then discard the fashion and adopt a new one to reassert its superior position. This type of class competitiveness contributes to the frequent adoption of new fashions.

Trickle-Across Theory

The **trickle-across theory** claims that fashion moves horizontally between groups at similar social levels. This theory suggests that each class or social group has its own fashion leader. With the availability of rapid communications and mass production, new styles at various price levels are exposed to fashion leaders of all social groups at approximately the same time. European fashions, for example, are copied for mass production at fast speeds, providing customers with similar styles at a variety of prices. Once fashions have been adopted by fashion leaders, the styles are spread through the groups simultaneously. The trickle-across theory implies that fashion diffusion can start at the same time within several social classes. Members within each class or social group look at leaders of their own group for fashion trends instead of watching unknown leaders from higher social classes or groups.

Trickle-Up Theory

The **trickle-up theory** is the opposite of the trickle-down theory. It maintains that fashion adoption begins among the young or with lower income groups and then moves upward. According to Greenberg and Glywn (1966), fashions filter up, not merely from youth to older age groups, but from lower to upper economic classes.

During the 1960s and early 1970s, young people influenced several fashion trends. Typical of fashions initiated by the young and less affluent are coveralls, khaki pants, fatigues, and blue jeans. Each of these trends began among the young members of lower income groups and then moved upward into higher income groups. In the 1970s many of these items began to carry designer labels and were sold at high prices. Calvin Klein brought designer jeans to the fashion forefront in the 1970s. It became fashionable to have the designer's label or signature prominently displayed on the exterior of clothing. The highest prices for these fashion items develop at the maturity stage rather than when the fashions are first introduced.

Other fashion trends have been inspired by minority groups. Black Americans started the fashion trend for African fabrics and dashiki dresses in the late 1960s and early 1970s. American Indians influenced the wearing of silver jewelry set with turquoise and coral stones. Native Americans have also influenced design motifs popular in home furnishings, such as blankets, rugs, and pottery. These fashions, which often begin as part of a young and/or lower income lifestyle, are soon diffused upward to more mature consumers with different lifestyles and higher incomes.

Fashion Cycles

Fashion moves in visible patterns that follow definite directions. These patterns of movement are referred to as fashion cycles. Each fashion moves in a cycle that includes several stages, from the introduction of the fashion through its decline in popularity. A **fashion cycle** is often depicted as a bell-shaped curve reflecting how a fashion moves from acceptance by a few to acceptance by the majority. The fashion cycle can demonstrate consumer acceptance of one specific style or acceptance of a general style, such as shirtwaist dresses, athletic shoes, or T-shirts.

Although the shapes of fashion cycles may be similar, no two cycles are exactly alike. Some cycles rise quickly; others take a longer time to reach their peaks. Generally, fashion cycles evolve gradually, but not always. A fashion fad may have a quick rise, short staying period, and abrupt fall. Fashion producers and marketers analyze the movement of fashions in order to interpret and analyze consumers' preferences.

Stages of the Fashion Cycle

Every fashion follows a life cycle reflecting the various stages of its life span, from the time the fashion is introduced until it is obsolete and no longer popular. All products that are subject to changes in fashion, such as apparel and home furnishings, have life cycles. The fashion cycles of apparel and accessories are often more easily traced. As illustrated in Figure 2.1, fashion life cycles consist of five stages: introduction, rise, culmination, decline, and obsolescence.

Introduction

The first stage of the fashion cycle is the introduction. At this beginning stage the product is first introduced and is accepted by only a limited number of people. During this stage, a fashion is worn by fashion leaders, the people who like to be first with what is new. Fashions are often introduced at a high price level and are referred to as "high fashion." Production costs are high for fashions in the introduction stage because they are produced in small quantities. Considerable risk is involved in the production of high fashion; therefore, because of the strong possibility of consumer rejection, a producer often sells new innovative styles at higher prices to cover losses on those fashions that may not be accepted. The retailer is likely to have to take big markdowns (price reductions) to sell some of the merchandise in this stage of the fashion cycle. Because of the high initial price tag common for fashions in the introduction stage, few people can afford these fashions.

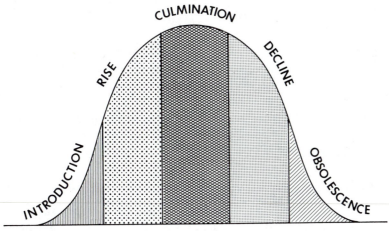

FIGURE 2.1
Stages of the fashion cycle.

Rise

The second stage of a fashion cycle is referred to as the rise. During this stage, the fashion becomes accepted by more people. As consumer interest increases, manufacturers copy the new looks or adapt some of their dominant features, making simpler styles in preparation for rising sales expectations. These copies or adaptations are often made of less expensive materials and produced with less meticulous or less detailed workmanship than were the original styles. Because production is on a larger scale, a decline in the selling price of the fashion often occurs. Mass production allows the merchandise to be distributed at prices affordable by many consumers. This decline in price also serves to further stimulate sales during the rising stage. As more people purchase and use the fashion, it becomes more visible and begins to gain widespread acceptance.

Culmination

During the culmination stage, fashions are at their height of popularity and acceptance. By the time the cycle reaches the culmination stage, the fashion is in great demand and is mass-produced and distributed. The prices for fashions at this stage vary and are within the reach of most consumers. The styles are also produced in many variations. The length of time that a fashion stays in the culmination stage depends, of course, on how long the fashion remains popular. This period could be short, especially if consumers become bored with the fashion quickly and decide to replace it with another look. The length of this stage can also be extended if the fashion becomes a classic or if interest is kept alive by updating or adding new details of design, color, or texture to the look.

Decline

The decline is the stage of the fashion cycle where consumer demand has decreased. During this period, many consumers will still be wearing the fashion, but they are no longer willing to purchase it at regular price. Consumers begin to tire of the style and want something new once many copies are being mass-produced, especially if they are widely available at a lower price point. Because demand for the style decreases, retailers reduce prices to sell the goods and make room for new looks. While these fashions are in the declining stage, newer fashions are moving through earlier stages of their cycles.

Obsolescence

Once the obsolescence stage is reached, merchandise is no longer desirable to consumers at any price. In this last phase of the life cycle, the style is rejected by almost all consumers. While some styles are becoming obsolete, new looks are being accepted by consumers.

Length of Fashion Cycles

Although all fashions follow cyclical patterns, the pattern and rate of movement vary with each fashion. A fashion cycle has no specific measurable duration or length of its life span. The length of time that a particular fashion remains in any of the phases of its life cycle depends upon the degree to which it is gaining or losing public acceptance.

Today, fashions tend to complete their life cycles faster than those of several decades ago. One reason for this increased rate of change is that rapid technological developments tend to make current fashions become obsolete more quickly. Also, increased competition among manufacturers and retailers constantly provides consumers with a multiplicity of new styles from which to select. As some fashions reach their peak or height of acceptance, their successors are already gaining acceptance in the rising stage.

Whereas all fashions have life cycles and all can be depicted by a bell-shaped curve, the shapes of the curves are different for each fashion. No two curves drawn to illustrate fashion cycles will be the same shape. The rise and fall may be gradual or sharp, and the phases where the styles gain full acceptance may be sharp peaks or long plateaus. The major factors that vary are the speed of passing from one phase to the next and the time it takes to complete the life cycle. Men's, women's, and children's apparel and accessories all have life cycles. Furniture, household appliances, and home electronics also have life cycles. Factors that influence the movement of fashions through their cycles include the level of technological development, existing lifestyles, and psychological reactions to prevailing social and economic conditions. These factors are discussed later in this chapter.

Cycles for Long-Lived Fashions

The time it takes for a fashion to follow through the different phases of a fashion cycle also varies with different types of merchandise. A fashion that takes a long time to complete its cycle is referred to as a **long-lived fashion.** The extended time of the cycle may be accounted for by a slow acceptance period, a longer stay in popular demand, and/or a slow period of decline. Fashions with more details tend to become dated faster than simple styles. In furniture styles, certain historical period furnishings remain in fashion almost indefinitely; however, even these styles have changing popularity of certain colors, fabric designs, or wood finishes.

Fashion silhouettes often have long-lived cycles. The silhouette or shape of women's apparel in particular is long-lived. Most silhouettes do not change drastically from one season to another but dominate several years while gradual changes in design details progress to a definite change in silhouette or overall new look.

Classics are an example of long-lived fashions. By definition, classics remain in general fashion acceptance for an extended period of time. Because classic fashions are usually practical and simple in design, they are not easily dated. Certain characteristics such as the fabrication, detail, and color, may change, but a classic style remains clearly recognizable and continues to be accepted as being in fashion. The shape of the life cycle for a classic is different from most fashion cycles since the curve never falls completely into obsolescence. The shirtwaist dress, which peaked in fashion during the late 1950s, has been popular for many years. The color, fabric, and trim may change, but the basic style remains the same. Another example of a classic style that remains popular is the basic cardigan sweater.

The shirtwaist dress, a classic style, is a long-lived fashion.

Cycles for Short-Lived Fashions

Short-lived fashions are popular for a short period of time, usually only one season. Fads are short-lived fashions. Often very simple in design and inexpensive to copy, fads rise in popularity at a fast rate and quickly saturate the market. People tire of a fad quickly, and its life cycle comes to an abrupt end.

Many accessory items are classified as short-lived fashions. The price of accessories usually contributes to their short life cycle. Their prices are often lower than for other categories of fashion merchandise, so consumers can afford to purchase accessories more often. The addition of a new belt or scarf may give an old garment a new look. The more expensive accessories, such as leather handbags and fine jewelry, usually have longer life cycles. Pearls enjoyed a long span of popularity during the 1950s and 1960s, losing popularity in the 1970s, then regaining fashion acceptance during the 1980s.

Specific features of fashion goods have their own life cycle. The life span of popular colors, for example, can be illustrated by a bell-shaped curve. Some merchandise characteristics such as color and texture usually have life cycles that last one season. The lightweight, bright fabrics popular during the summer often change for the fall season to heavier, darker fabrics. The trend in recent years, however, has been for some fabrics and colors to last from season to season and to be popular for three or four years. Clearly, some colors and textures are becoming less seasonally oriented. For example, pastel-colored and black patent leather shoes, once associated with only spring-summer wear, are now worn all year.

Breaks in Cycles

Several factors can cause a fashion cycle to change directions. The curve of a fashion curve can be broken or stopped because of such influences as a change in the weather, the occurrence of a natural disaster, or a change in group acceptance. Social and political unrest and wars also affect fashion and can retard fashion change, causing styles to remain relatively stable. The development of new fashions was limited during World War II because of fabric shortages and government restrictions placed on apparel production. During the war, producers, of course, directed their attention to the manufacturing of uniforms, parachutes, and other war supplies. As discussed earlier, when the war ended, consumer interest in fashion was revived and new fashions became popular. The short skirts and narrow silhouette that dominated fashions throughout the war years were thrown aside for Dior's New Look, with its more feminine style of longer, fuller skirts and a pinched waist.

Recurring Fashions

Recurring fashions are styles that enjoy popularity, decline, and once again gain consumer acceptance. Fashions do not usually reappear exactly as they were previously. Occasionally an entire look will return, and nostalgia will influence fashions in both apparel and accessories. Young people in the mid-1980s were intrigued by the fashions of the 1950s and the 1960s. Looking like Marilyn Monroe became a popular way of dressing. Successful fashions of the 1950s that returned during the 1980s included crinoline petticoats, strapless dresses, tapered pants, bobbie socks, and loafers.

Many times a single clothing component or a minor detail that has become obsolete will return to fashion again. Sometimes a single article of clothing will reappear, such as the miniskirt popular in the late 1960s and reintroduced by fashion designers in 1987. Sometimes accessories, makeup, and other fashion-related articles resurface and regain popularity. Home-furnishings styles also become obsolete and reappear. For example, the 1980s also saw the return of the art deco decorative style of the 1920s and 1930s.

Fashion Leaders and Followers

While a fashion is moving through its life cycle pattern, the fashion comes in contact with different consumer groups. At the beginning stage of the cycle, fashion leaders buy and wear a new style. When the followers begin to wear it, the leaders will have already accepted another new fashion. Because of the differences in taste among consumer groups, what is in fashion for one group may be out of fashion for another.

Fashion Leaders

Fashion leaders make up a small percentage of all consumers. They are usually members of higher income groups who can easily afford high fashion, which is often expensive. Many fashion leaders hold prominent positions, which allow them the opportunity to be seen frequently and to influence the dress of others. A fashion leader does not usually create the fashion, but launches new fashions by discovering and wearing a certain style. A fashion leader is an individualist who is confident of his or her own tastes. Fashion leaders do not need the approval of others when selecting fashions; they enjoy discovering and wearing unique and different new styles. They are people who like to stand out in the crowd.

    At one time most fashion leaders were members of royalty. In the late eighteenth century Marie Antoinette was known for introducing new fashions in the royal court of France. Empress Eugenie set French fashions in the mid-nineteenth century. Although Princess Diana of England has influenced fashion adoption in recent years, few members of royalty have served as fashion leaders in the twentieth century. Today most fashion leaders are people of social, political, and economic importance.

The miniskirt, a recurring fashion, was popular in the late 1960s, and it resurfaced in 1987.

Many are members of the entertainment industry, and some are from the fashion industry.

Many fashion leaders are followed closely by the press and have much exposure in the media. The general public is interested in them so the media keep the general public informed on what fashion leaders are doing and what they are wearing. Fashion leaders are seen frequently on television, at public events, or in the movies. Television and movie personalities strongly influence fashions in apparel. Religious leaders, politicians, sports figures, entertainers—all may be fashion leaders. Because they are the focus of much attention, people seek to imitate these leaders by copying their dress. Serving as trendsetters, fashion leaders are watched closely by designers and others in the fashion industry.

Certain fashions can be directly traced to society leaders and other newsworthy people. First Lady Jacqueline Kennedy influenced the wearing of the simple A-line black dress and pillbox hat during her husband's presidency. Nancy Reagan popularized the wearing of red, and her successor, Barbara Bush, the multiple-strand pearl necklace. Some fashion leaders appeal to certain age groups, as the entertainer Madonna, for example, has influenced her young fans to copy her sexy style, as have many other rock musicians. Michael Jackson popularized a whole look for students of all ages in September 1984 with his multizippered jackets, pants of polyurethane, white socks, and black loafers. Some students even copied the wearing of one white rhinestone-studded glove, Jackson's trademark.

Wallis Simpson, the Duchess of Windsor, influenced fashions from the 1930s into the 1960s. Her influence was felt again following her death when her jewelry was sold at auction in 1988, and items from her collection were copied or imitated by jewelry designers. The jewelry was then advertised as "inspired by the Duchess of Windsor" or "in the mood of the Duchess of Windsor's jewelry." The Duke of Windsor also had a strong influence on menswear. One of his lasting contributions to fashion is the oversized Windsor knot used to tie a four-in-hand tie.

Sometimes fashions are influenced by and associated with people who are not considered to be fashion leaders. For example, Charles Dana Gibson, a popular illustrator in the 1890s, influenced the Gibson Girl fashion through his illustrations. This look consisted of a high-necked, tucked shirtwaist with leg-of-mutton sleeves, belted wasp waist, and long skirt fitted over the hips and flared at the hem. The

The "Gibson Girl" fashion was influenced by Charles Dana Gibson in the 1890s.

hair was dressed in a high pompadour style and topped by a flat sailor hat banded in black. Another example is the Eisenhower jacket, a short battle jacket, bloused to the waistband with large patch pockets, worn by General Dwight D. Eisenhower during World War II.

Some retailers and designers are also fashion leaders, especially those who market high fashion and cater to customers who want to be in the forefront of fashion. Bergdorf Goodman, Saks Fifth Avenue, and Bloomingdale's are retail stores that project strong fashion images and have many customers who are also fashion leaders. These stores have "discovered" many fashion designers and helped to make them financially successful and well known by the general public. Fashion designers such as Calvin Klein, Ralph Lauren, and Bill Blass have become fashion leaders not only through their designs but also through their own personal style of dressing.

Fashion Followers

The largest group of consumers are the followers. **Fashion followers** are important to the fashion industry because they make economical mass production possible. Without fashion followers, there would be no need for mass production and mass distribution, which is vital to the success of the fashion ready-to-wear industry. A large number of consumers feeds the fashion industry's success.

Consumers are fashion followers for several reasons. Some people prefer to follow rather than to lead, perhaps because of feelings of insecurity, admiration of others, lack of interest in fashion, or ambivalence about new styles. Some people are uncertain about their own tastes and find security in conforming to standards established by others. These people tend to follow the fundamental human impulse to imitate people they admire or envy. By copying the appearance of such fashion leaders, followers display their admiration. In the 1950s Audrey Hepburn and Doris Day were followed; Twiggy in the 1960s; Farrah Fawcett in the 1970s; Linda Evans and Joan Collins in the 1980s. Others who are not fashion leaders may dress in a certain way out of habit or custom. These individuals do not develop a strong interest in fashion and need a greater time to adjust to new styles before accepting them. Other people lack the time or the money to devote to being a fashion leader. These individuals may have little fashion interest and may not even be fashion followers but may be fashion laggers.

Individuals vary in the rate they respond to the acceptance of new fashions. Some follow in the rising stage, others not until culmination. Especially when dramatic fashion changes occur, fashion followers need time to adjust and adopt new ideas. Although fashion leaders provide excitement in the fashion industry, followers assure its continued success. Because most consumers are fashion followers, most fashion designers and manufacturers copy, adapt, or update previously accepted fashions.

Factors Influencing Fashion Movement

Consumer acceptance of fashion is influenced both by the availability of technically feasible products and by the broad influences in the environment that affect consumer attitudes about fashion merchandise. Economic, political, social, and technological factors affect fashion interest and demand. Producers and retailers of fashion merchandise must be aware of these environmental conditions and their influence on consumer acceptance because outside factors strongly influence fashion demand. Some factors promote a rapid change in fashion movement, whereas others retard change. Learning to be observant of these influences helps producers and retailers forecast fashion trends.

Factors Accelerating Fashion Movement

Environmental factors that can accelerate the movement of fashion and influence consumer acceptance include economic conditions, technology, changing roles of women, increased leisure time, social and physical mobility, increased education, and seasonal change. These factors not only influence the rate of acceptance but also the direction that fashion takes.

Economic Conditions

Economic conditions play a vital role in the growth of the fashion industry and in turn affect the rate of fashion movement. Certain economic conditions such as the availability of resources, consumer income, and the value of the currency have a direct impact on the rate of fashion change. An upturn in the economy can encourage fashion change, whereas a declining economy often retards fashion change.

When consumers have less money to spend, they often turn to buying accessories as a means of creating a new fashion look for less money. Accessories, such as scarves, belts, artificial flowers, and costume jewelry, can economically update a fashion look. During poor economic periods, the ready-to-wear business may decline while the fashion accessories business increases.

Technology

New technological developments and improvements have made an impact on the acceleration of the fashion process. As technological advances have increased both the variety and availability of new products, the demand for new fashions has increased.

The introduction of specialized machinery in production has given impetus to fashion by increasing the speed with which products can be made. As machinery improves, manufacturers are able to quickly produce clothing at a variety of prices, making fashion goods available to more people in a shorter time.

New developments in the textile industry also speed up the fashion process. Fiber producers have developed new blends of manufactured and natural fibers, providing improved use, appearance, and quality. New fibers and chemical finishes have improved the wear of fabrics and made the care of garments and household textiles easier. Production of new and improved fabrics at a variety of prices encourages customers to make more purchases, and thus contributes to fashion acceleration.

Technological advances in communication and travel have affected the fashion industry. Improved transportation methods help to speed up the process of delivering fashion goods to retailers and consumers. Modern communications have increased culture contact, making people more aware of lifestyles and trends from throughout the world. Movies, television, magazines, and newspapers quickly bring new fashion ideas from many sources into the homes of consumers. Seeing the latest fashions, especially those worn by fashion leaders, consumers are stimulated to buy similar styles, resulting in the acceleration of fashion change.

Changing Roles of Women

The changing status of women has influenced the movement of fashion considerably in the twentieth century. Women's lifestyles have changed significantly since 1900. Only since the early 1920s have the majority of women been able to vote, own property, and pursue a career outside the home. As women gained new political and economic freedom in the 1920s and 1930s, their lifestyles changed and in turn changed fashions. Women discarded the constricting garments fashionable for many years. For their more active lifestyles, women adopted shorter skirt lengths and looser fitting dresses. They even began to wear one-piece bathing suits and engage in active sports.

Women's needs and wants in fashion have changed as they have become better educated, better employed, and more exposed to new ideas. The number of working women in the United States has increased significantly during the twentieth century. In 1950, 30 percent of women sixteen years of age and over held jobs, whereas in 1980, 50 percent were employed. By the 1990s, approximately 70 percent of all women from ages eighteen to sixty-four will hold jobs outside the home. With more women in the work force, more businesslike career clothing has been needed. As more women moved into executive positions in the business world in the 1970s, the "dressing for success" fashion of a tailored suit and blouse became popular for career women. The business dress style for women in the mid-1980s became less tailored as women gained greater confidence in their careers.

Women's desire to participate in sporting events has added active sportswear to their wardrobes. Because of the growing emphasis on health and exercise throughout the 1970s and 1980s, active sportswear has enjoyed increased demand. The physical fitness movement has brought about the need for such exercise clothing as jogging suits, aerobic outfits, and dance clothes.

During the past two decades, women have made progress toward equal employment opportunity and equal pay for equal work. Women enjoy more discretionary income than at any point in the past, which also increases the speed of fashion change. All of these changes in women's lifestyles contribute to changes in their fashion and buying habits.

Increased Leisure Time

A drastic decline in working hours each week has come about in the last century. In 1850 a typical work week averaged seventy hours. By 1950 the average work week was reduced to forty hours, usually consisting of five 8-hour days. Increased leisure time corresponds with the significant decline in the number of hours in the work week of Americans today. In addition to a shorter work week, most companies offer employees paid holidays and vacations and retirement plans.

Many people use their leisure time for traveling, participating in sports activities or other social activities, and/or relaxing at home. These increased activities have brought about consumer demand for a variety of types of clothing, leading to larger wardrobes. Not only do people have more time to think about fashions, but more leisure time encourages them to purchase at-home wear, sportswear, travel clothing, and casual wear.

The "dressing for success" fashion became popular for career women in the 1970s.

Social and Physical Mobility

Changes in the rate movements can be affected by social and physical mobility. Sociologists have long related fashion change to social mobility. In the United States society is characterized by a relatively high degree of upward mobility. Since social class is based largely upon occupation, income, and education, many Americans have moved upward to a higher income and social level through improved education.

With this rise often comes increased interest in fashion. People often show their improved status by wearing more expensive, fashionable clothing, redecorating their homes, or driving a status automobile.

The United States is known for having a large middle class. A direct relationship exists between the size of the middle class and fashion change because members of the middle class tend to be fashion followers rather than fashion leaders. As these middle-class followers accept new fashion ideas, the fashion leaders are encouraged to seek new and different styles to adopt. Thus the middle class stimulates fashion change. The size and the buying power of the American middle class have provided continued growth for the fashion industry.

Physical mobility also encourages demand for fashion. As people move around, they are exposed to many new fashion influences, and they develop the desire to adopt new ideas in their dress or living environments. Physical mobility can involve daily commuting, shopping at retail stores, traveling for business or pleasure, or changing residence. The private automobile and jet airplanes have made travel easier, faster, and more commonplace. The automobile, coupled with modern expressways, has made it possible for people to live a suburban lifestyle and work in the city. No longer are people restricted to shopping and engaging in activities close to where they live and work. Modern transportation has widely increased mobility and led to greater fashion exposure.

Increased Education

The increasingly higher level of education in the United States has accelerated fashion change. With more education, consumers can increase their earning power, allowing them to satisfy more of their wants and needs. Education gives consumers a more sophisticated taste level and often increases their desire for fashionable appearance and a fashionable environment. Knowledge also adds confidence in consumer decision making. Better-educated consumers are likely to be more willing to try new fashions, so all of this serves to accelerate fashion change.

Seasonal Change

Consumers demand fashion change with the seasons. Although central heating and cooling systems have made seasonal changes in clothing less necessary, most people still change their wardrobes with the seasons. They do so even in areas such as Florida and southern California where there is little change in temperature. Clothing for the summer months tends to be made of light colors and lightweight fabrics, whereas winter apparel is darker and heavier. The need or desire for seasonal change encourages fashion demand and accelerates fashion change.

Factors Retarding Fashion Movement

Certain forces tend to restrict or retard fashion change. Retarding factors discourage people from adopting new styles and encourage them to continue to wear styles that might be considered out-of-date. Factors that tend to work against fashion change include religion, customs, laws, and government restrictions.

Religion

Religious beliefs may be a restraining influence on fashion change. Some religious groups believe that certain fashions lead to temptation and corruption. Although most religious groups today have little influence on the dress of their members, some groups still demand that their followers avoid modern fashion trends. An extreme example is the Amish, who do not believe in using modern equipment or machinery and who demand that their people dress in a simple style similar to that of their ancestors.

Customs

Customs are manners or practices of dress that continue to appear in modern clothing and are established over a long period of time. Nystrom (1928, p. 123) notes that in fashion "people imitate their contemporaries, while in custom they imitate their elders, their parents, or past generations."

National costumes such as the Indian sari, Japanese kimono, and Scottish kilt are examples of custom in dress. Other clothing customs include traditional forms of dress such as bridal gowns, academic regalia, and judicial robes. Style of traditional garments has been transmitted from one generation to another and continues to be used in modern dress. National costumes and traditional attire slow fashion movement by preserving existing forms of dress.

Laws and Government Restrictions

At one time sumptuary laws prohibited excessive and lavish dress by regulating personal expenditures on extravagant attire. During the Renaissance (c. 1350–c. 1650), sumptuary laws regulated the length of pointed-toe shoes, the height of headpieces, and the width of sleeves that could be worn by people of the lower classes. Only members of nobility were allowed to wear certain items of apparel.

Historically, sumptuary laws were intended to maintain social order by restricting a person's dress or clothes according to an individual's class, rank, or status. For example, during the reign of Charles IX in France (1550–1574), only ladies of high rank were allowed to wear dresses of silk and to carry fur muffs. Queen Elizabeth I of England (r. 1558–1603) established sumptuary laws to regulate the size of her subjects' neck ruffs, the color of their gowns, and the length of men's hair and beards.

Although sumptuary laws are rare in today's modern society, they are still found in some countries where class distinctions are recognized. Sumptuary laws inhibit the movement of fashion since they regulate and/or prohibit the wearing of various items of apparel.

Today laws have been passed to regulate the use of certain furs and skins from animals that are in danger of extinction. The United States forbids the importation of furs from the cheetah and leopard. Until recently alligator skins were protected, but the increase in the number of alligators in the wild has led to a lifting of the ban on selling their skins.

When sources of raw materials are limited, the government may set legal regulations to assure that an equitable distribution of the supply will be available. For example, during World War II fabric usage was restricted because fabric production was needed for uniforms and other war supplies. Such shortages of raw materials obviously inhibit fashion change. Even in peacetime, governments may restrict certain fashion goods by imposing heavy excise taxes. Some countries partially or fully restrict the import of certain foreign goods, thus slowing fashion movement.

Prediction of Fashion Movement

Because fashion is a product of change, predicting its movement is important at all levels of the fashion industry. To successfully merchandise fashion, one must have a sense of timing and follow the movement of consumer preferences. One must successfully forecast the direction in which fashion is moving and predict what styles will be accepted by the majority of consumers to operate a profitable fashion business.

Sources Used to Predict Fashion Trends

Producers and retailers of fashion goods use several methods to forecast or predict fashion trends. They look at past experiences to seek clues for the future. By analyzing past fashion movements, they are able to see that most movements emerge with a predictable regularity and sometimes in a predictable sequence. Examining current activities of consumers also enables projections of fashion trends. Such projections based on studies of consumer preferences are important so that fashion goods can be produced in large quantities in advance of when consumers will make merchandise purchases. Predicting fashion trends is especially important to the producers of textiles and leather goods who must work one to two years ahead of the consumer's decision to purchase. Manufacturers of apparel and accessories also seek to successfully project fashion trends since they work almost a year ahead of the consumer's wearing season. Retailers of fashion merchandise study and evaluate fashion movements to make buying decisions three to six months in advance of when the customer buys.

To successfully predict fashion trends, much study and evaluation are necessary.

Various information sources are used in analyzing consumer activities and making fashion predictions. Sales records, designer collections, and observations of consumer behavior are all important data sources for predicting fashion trends.

Sales Records

Sales records are important data used in forecasting fashion trends. Most producers and retailers of fashion goods collect and analyze data concerning customer purchases. Largely because of the use of computers, methods used in collecting sales records are becoming more accurate and faster. Many retailers use computerized cash registers at the point of the sale. Small retailers may utilize computer services to analyze data on customer purchases.

Computers also provide instant inventory updating that enables the retailer to spot fast and slow-selling merchandise quickly. Increasing availability of such statistical information, as provided by electronic data processing, gives the retailer a greater ability to accurately forecast for the next season, having both sales trends and their consumer population more clearly in focus. Large chain stores are able to analyze sales by geographical region. Sales records provide facts about style numbers, fabrications, sizes, color, and other important selection factors. These statistics, available on a day-to-day basis, make it possible for the retailer to spot fast-moving trends. From these records, retailers can detect sudden or gradual changes in customers' preferences.

The information gathered from sales records concerning customer purchases is disseminated to all levels of the fashion industry. Retailers inform manufacturers about customer preferences through the placing of reorders. Manufacturers inform producers of textiles and other raw materials of the demand for certain colors and fabrications. Both retailers and producers need the evidence of sales figures to show current trends.

Sales figures alone do not give enough data to accurately evaluate trends. Although sales records indicate popular and desirable goods, they do not show what merchandise customers might have purchased had it been available.

Analyzing New Collections

Many retailers, producers, and members of the fashion press and fashion reporting services travel to major fashion centers throughout the world to attend showings of new designer collections. While viewing the showings, they evaluate and analyze the new styles presented. Trend directions are often suggested by these showings. Fashion forecasters single out the styles that they feel are prophetic. These interesting new styles, still in the introductory stage of their fashion cycles, are called **prophetic styles.** If adopted by the fashion leaders, they may become trends. Some will be adopted by fashion followers and will become volume fashion. Many times, analyzing the offerings of high-priced designer fashions is beneficial to establish directions that may affect other price levels.

Observing What Consumers Wear

For many years retailers and producers have obtained ideas about their customers by observing what they wear. Nystrom recognized in 1928 that observation should be used to predict fashion trends. It continues to be a valuable method today.

Changes in fashions may be checked and their trends determined by the simple process of making successive periodic counts of the same classes of people, comparing the results from one period to another, and taking note of the change [Nystrom 1932].

To determine future fashion trends, many retailers observe what is currently being worn. Retailers not only watch what their customers are wearing but consult outside sources to identify the fashion preferences and buying behavior of customers other than their own. The movement of fashion varies in different age, income, and interest groups. It also varies in different sections of the country. Once information is gathered, the retailer analyzes the data in terms of the company's own target customers. Retailers must know their own customers' lifestyles and economic status well enough to determine when in a fashion's life cycle their customers will accept or reject it.

Fashion and Human Behavior

The movement of fashion is affected by consumers' wants and needs. The fashion industry is concerned with the "whys" or motives of human behavior in relationship to selecting and purchasing merchandise. Many people realize that they desire more than the necessities of life and that the process of "needing" and "wanting" is an ongoing one. Needs represent a longing for or a lack of something. Needs can be physiological or psychological, conscious or unconscious. Needs exist in everyone but are not put to use until activated by internal or external forces called "drives." When this happens, needs become "wants" and can be handled concretely. Fashion marketers are interested in the needs of their customers and want to satisfy these needs.

Maslow's Fundamental Needs

Abraham Maslow, a noted psychologist, proposed an organization of human motives referred to as **Maslow's hierarchy of needs.** He suggested that humans exist in a perpetual state of "wanting" and that their behavior is determined by a priority of needs. According to Maslow, once a person's basic physiological needs, such as those for food and water, are met, the person will advance up the ladder or hierarchy of needs after each preceding need has been at least partially fulfilled. As shown in Figure 2.2, Maslow's list characterizes basic needs as follows (Maslow 1943):

1. *PHYSIOLOGICAL NEEDS:* Biological in nature, these include the need for food, water, sleep, and sex.

2. *SAFETY NEEDS:* Based on the human need for physical safety and security, these needs show a preference for what is familiar rather than unfamiliar.

3. *LOVE NEEDS:* Included here are the needs to love and be loved, to give and receive affection and approval, and to belong to a common interest group such as a fraternity or sorority.

4. *ESTEEM NEEDS:* The needs for self-confidence and self-respect, achievement, prestige, and independence are at this level.

5. *SELF-ACTUALIZATION NEEDS:* Ultimate personal fulfillment rests here with the creative aspects of accomplishment and acquiring knowledge; the "I've made it" phenomenon.

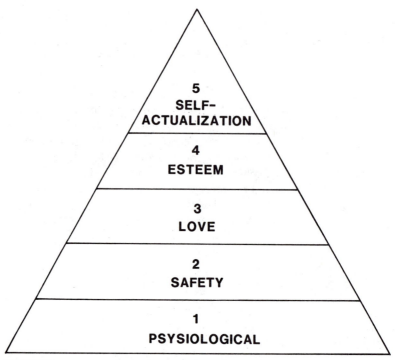

FIGURE 2.2
Maslow's hierarchy of needs.

THE BUSINESS OF FASHION

People often strive to meet more than one need at a time and are sometimes working on several needs at different stages. Similar needs are satisfied in various ways by different people in comparable behavioral circumstances.

Maslow's principles can be applied to consumer purchasing behavior. When considering the different needs, it is important to evaluate where a person is in the hierarchy with each situation. For example, a person who has little money and is in need of warmth during a cold winter season would satisfy his or her physiological need with an inexpensive blanket or cloth coat. However, a person who is financially secure and is status conscious would fill the need for both warmth and admiration by purchasing a designer brand or possibly a fur coat.

Nystrom's Principles of Human Needs

To explain what motivates people to follow fashion, Paul Nystrom in *Economics of Fashion* compiled an extensive list of fundamental human motives or needs. Although his book was written in 1928, **Nystrom's principles of human needs** are relevant to the needs and wants to today's consumers. Nystrom includes in his list several of the same needs noted by Maslow, such as the needs for food, drink, and sex and the desire to live free from danger and discomfort. Nystrom (1928, pp. 57–66) characterizes basic motives as follows:

1. *THE DESIRE FOR EXISTENCE:* The will to live and the desire to live free from danger and discomfort; also necessary are the hungers for food and drink.

2. *LOVE OF THE OPPOSITE SEX:* Sexual hunger is one of the most powerful and compelling forces in human nature.

3. *COMPANIONSHIP:* A desire to be with others and to have a feeling of belonging to a group. To secure sympathy, many people want to be like people of the group or society to which they belong.

4. *DESIRE FOR RECOGNITION:* Many people like to do things differently, think differently, talk differently, and dress differently from others. This desire for recognition varies from hunger merely for a response, to hunger for influence, for prestige, for freedom from control of others, and even for hunger for power over others.

5. *CURIOSITY:* Most people are inquisitive and naturally interested in many things. Curiosity is stronger in some people than it is in others. In its simplest form, curiosity appears to be merely a desire for new sensations and for change. However, curiosity can also take the form of a spirit of adventure, in daring to see what will happen under unknown or untried circumstances.

6. *DESIRE TO PLAY AND TRAVEL:* The desire to play is common to all children and adults, and it takes the form of adventure. To travel, move, migrate, or run away is an exceedingly fundamental human hunger. This desire brings with it the rich merchandising possibility of the sale of travel goods.

7. **DESIRE FOR BEAUTY AND HARMONY:** This desire is evident in all sorts of efforts at adornment, not only personal, but also in surroundings. The desire for beauty and harmony is universal and explains varying degrees or gradations of desire for orderliness.

8. **DESIRE TO MANIPULATE, CONSTRUCT, AND BUILD:** This desire varies greatly in different people. It is closely related to the desire for curiosity, but it goes further in that the manipulation proceeds to construction, putting things together, making changes and adaptations.

Nystrom also suggested several specific psychological motives for fashion. He noted that, "if we can successfully point out those inner human conditions which are responsible for fashion, we shall be able to understand fashion more clearly, and we may also be able to direct our business efforts with less waste and greater efficiency through the adaptation of fashion to human demands" (Nystrom 1928, p. 66). According to Nystrom, one of the simplest explanations of fashion change is the human tendency to become tired of sensations that are experienced constantly. Consumers tire of garments after wearing them for a season and because of this boredom, they develop a desire for something new to wear.

Nystrom believes that the curiosity factor is a key motivational component. Curiosity is related to the spirit of adventure, the thrill of breaking away from convention, the hunger for praise, and the excitement of creating an element of shock. It is this curiosity factor, not the decision of manufacturers to saturate the market with something new, that offers a chance for a new style to be successful.

No simple explanation can be given for what motivates people to purchase fashion. Maslow's hierarchy of needs and Nystrom's fundamental human motives indicate that a multiplicity of wants and needs determine which fashion goods are preferred and purchased by consumers. Producers and retailers in the fashion industry must consider these needs and motives if they are to successfully fulfill the wants and needs of their target customers.

Summary of Key Points

1. The five fundamental principles of fashion that serve as a foundation for fashion identification and movement are (a) fashions are usually evolutionary, (b) consumers make fashions by their acceptance or rejection of styles, (c) price does not determine a fashion, (d) promotional activities cannot sell merchandise consumers do not want to buy, and (e) fashions often end in excess.

2. Several theories explaining the origin of clothes are protection, modesty, and self-adornment. A fourth theory states that dress cannot be traced to a single theory but was devised to satisfy several human needs at once.

3. Three theories describe how different groups of consumers initiate and lead the movement of fashion: (a) trickle-down theory, (b) trickle-across theory, and (c) trickle-up theory.

4. Each fashion moves in a cycle that includes the following stages: introduction, rise, culmination, decline, and obsolescence. The rate of movement varies for each fashion.

5. Only a few people are fashion leaders. Most consumers are fashion followers. It is the followers who make economical mass production and distribution possible.

6. Fashions today change at a rapid pace. Many factors accelerate the rate of fashion movement, including economic conditions, technology, changing roles of women, increased leisure time, social and geographical mobility, education, and seasonal change. Changing roles of women have had a strong influence on fashion during the twentieth century.

7. Fashion movement can be predicted with reasonable accuracy by analyzing sales records, evaluating designers' new collections, and observing consumer behavior.

Key Words and Concepts

Define, identify, or explain each of the following:

evolutionary fashion	Nystrom's principles of human needs
fashion cycle	prophetic styles
fashion followers	recurring fashions
fashion leaders	revolutionary fashion
long-lived fashion	short-lived fashion
longuette or midi	trickle-across theory
Maslow's hierarchy of needs	trickle-down theory
	trickle-up theory

Discussion Questions and Topics

1. List and explain the five basic principles of fashion movement.

2. Discuss the theories explaining the origin of clothing. Which theory best explains what motivated human beings to begin wearing clothes?

3. Name and explain the five stages of a fashion's life cycle.

4. What can cause a disruption in the normal movement of a fashion through its life cycle?

5. Explain the difference between short-lived and long-lived fashions.

6. Explain the importance of the prediction of fashion by all levels of the fashion industry.

7. What are some of the methods used to predict fashion trends?

8. Why are fashion followers important to the fashion industry?

9. How does "Maslow's Hierarchy of Needs" relate to fashion?

10. Explain why fashions tend to complete their life cycles more quickly today than in the past.

11. Explain the three theories of fashion adoption.

12. Discuss the factors that accelerate fashion movement and the factors that retard fashion movement.

Notes

Helena de Paola and Carol Stewart Mueller, *Marketing Today's Fashion*. Englewood Cliffs, N.J.: Prentice-Hall, 1980, p. 23.

John Carl Flugel, *The Psychology of Clothes*. London: Hogarth Press, 1930.

Allen Greenberg and Mary Joan Glynn, *A Study of Young People*. New York: Doyle, Dane and Bernbach, 1966.

E. A. Hoebel, *Man in the Primitive World: An Introduction to Anthropology*. New York: McGraw-Hill, 1958, p. 248.

Abraham H. Maslow, "A Theory of Human Motivation," *Psychological Review* (July 1943), pp. 370–396.

Paul H. Nystrom, *Economics of Fashion*. New York: Ronald Press, 1928.

Paul H. Nystrom, *Fashion Merchandising*. New York: Ronald Press, 1932, p. 84.

Georg Simmel, "Fashion," *American Journal of Sociology*, 62, (1957), 543.

CHAPTER 3 _____

SUPPORTING FASHION ENTERPRISES

A NUMBER of enterprises within the fashion industry assist retailers and manufacturers by providing information and support services. The size and diversity of the fashion business make it almost impossible for one individual or company to keep abreast of fashion and business trends. Instead of trying to do everything independently, fashion firms frequently subscribe to the services of outside agencies. Among these enterprises are fashion consulting and reporting firms, resident buying offices, the fashion press, advertising agencies, publicity and public relations firms, trade associations, and professional organizations. These auxiliary firms act as advisors, information sources, and promoters of fashion.

Fashion Consulting and Reporting Services

A fashion consultant is an individual or a firm that assists fashion retailers and manufacturers with analyzing and interpreting fashion trends or providing other merchandising-related services. Such firms give advice and provide another point of view to assist in understanding and projecting consumer demand.

One of the oldest and best-known fashion consultant firms is **Tobé Associates,** founded in 1927 by Tobé Collier Davis. Tobé Associates was established to service

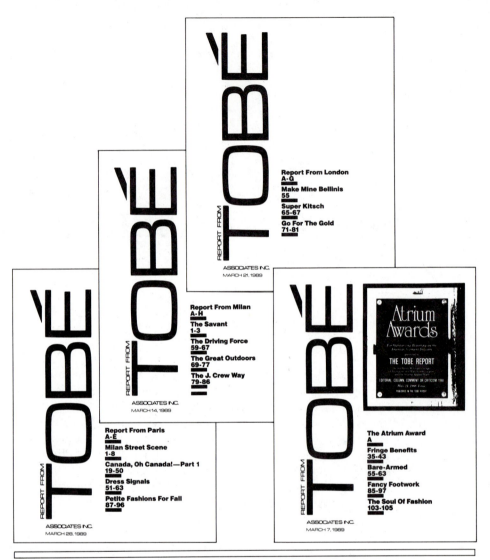

The Tobé Report *is published by Tobé Associates, a well-known fashion consultant firm.*
Source: *Reprinted with permission of Tobé Associates.*

retailers by reporting and interpreting fashion trends and to analyze the social, economic, and political events influencing those trends.

Tobé Collier Davis died in 1962, but her company continues to operate under the direction of Marjorie S. Deane. The *Tobé Report,* published weekly, covers the major fashion markets, reporting trends and naming manufacturers as resources for those trends. Retail clients pay a fee based on dollar volume of the store. Tobé also produces videotapes called *Tobé on Tape* for the five major market seasons.

Many other consultants provide services to retailers and producers on a fee basis. Consultant agencies cover fashion at each level of the industry, providing reports and informational materials. Other services of such agencies include holding clinics and seminars for clients and advising clients concerning their merchandising activities. Most of these services are designed for the retail level of the fashion industry, but services are also utilized by apparel manufacturers, fiber and textile producers, and various promotional organizations.

A fashion information service provides clients with information on fashion trends. Fashion producers and retailers subscribe to these outside sources of information in order to get another viewpoint. Information from outside services is compared with companies' own analyses of trends and conclusions.

A number of fashion information agencies or reporting services forecast trends far in advance to assist producers of raw materials of fashion and manufacturers of men's, women's, and children's apparel and accessories in designing their products. Examples of these firms are IM International, Nigel French, Promostyl, Prism, and Color Projections Inc. New firms are constantly being added to those already available.

IM International

One of the largest forecasting firms is **IM International,** founded in 1967 in London by Leigh Rudd and Nigel French. Their first activity was to sell sketches of British street fashions to American retailers and manufacturers. In 1975 the firm moved its headquarters to New York. Today Leigh Rudd heads IM International, and Nigel French has opened a separate firm under his own name.

IM prepares publications that forecast colors, fabrics, and silhouettes from eighteen months to two years in advance. IM, which stands for Imaginative Minds, covers all of the major apparel markets throughout the world, reviewing collections in Paris, Milan, London, New York, and the Orient. Also covered are the wholesale European fabric fairs such as Interstoff and Ideacomo. Trends are reported and evaluated for clients. IM gives advice on how to modify trends for immediate use in manufacturers' lines. In addition to covering markets, IM also visits retail shops around the world to select the hottest items and sketch them with exact details and measurements.

Various reports are sent to clients in the form of written reports, samples, slides, and videotapes. The primary publication for IM is *Action Report,* a lengthy spiral-bound monthly report featuring fabric swatches, photos, and sketches.

IM's clients range from mass manufacturers and retailers to better designers and manufacturers. The firm is considered an important information source by many designers and manufacturers. Individual clients pay annual fees ranging from $1,500 to over $4,000. Consulting fees for companies range from $20,000 to $40,000 a year.

GIRLSWEAR

ATTN: GIRLS' 7-14
December 4, 1987

A RECOGNIZABLE LABEL IS INTRODUCED
INTO THE GIRLSWEAR MARKET

A new resource: **HANG TEN KIDS**

HANG TEN Juniors recently acquired the
license for Girlswear.

Their concept is to offer the newest and
trendiest capsule fashion groups every
15-20 days, thus keeping a continuous
flow of exciting young looks within
the girls' department at all times.

Goods are all domestically manufactured
and are all cotton.

#8K240 - $8.50 - SML
Crop peasant top. Gauze w/woven
"Hang Ten Summer" patch.

#8K244 - $12.50 - SML
"Cha Cha" (3) tier skirt (interlock yoke -
gauze tiers).

Both styles shown: 100% cotton. Multicolor
of periwinkle/pineapple/watermelon.

(Also available, not shown)
#8K248 - $15.00 - SML
Elastic waist romper: Henley tank top with
ruffle side, short in gauze.

Delivery: 4/30 C.
FOB: L.A.
Terms: 8/10 EOM
Mkt. Rep.:   Lindy Cobb

ARKIN *California*

Resident Buyers • 206 East Ninth Street • Los Angeles, California 90015 • (213) 624-9714

Resident buying offices provide client stores with information such as this bulletin from Arkin of California.
Source: *Reprinted with permission of Arkin Resident Buyers.*

Resident Buying Offices

Resident buying offices are found in major domestic market centers such as New York, Los Angeles, Dallas, and Chicago as well as in international market centers. These offices act as market representatives for client stores. Resident buyers, also called market representatives, daily shop the market in which they are located to provide information to the stores they represent. Such service organizations cover the market, reporting back to their clients about general conditions, fashion trends, new resources, and supply conditions. When requested, a resident buyer will place orders for a retail store. They perform work that supplements but does not replace that of store buyers. The types of resident buying offices and the services they offer are discussed in detail in Chapter 13.

Promotion Agencies

Various agencies and individuals offer advertising, public relations, publicity, and other promotional services to retailers and manufacturers. These agencies provide expertise that many fashion firms cannot furnish on their own. They plan sales promotion activities; design, produce, and place advertisements in the media; devise public relations programs; and write press releases.

Some firms are highly specialized and deal with only one aspect of promotion. Other agencies are diverse and provide services in several or all aspects. Some large agencies service all types of businesses, whereas others specialize in fashion accounts.

Fashion retailers and producers use the print and broadcast media in two ways to communicate with consumers or with the trade: advertising and publicity. Advertising is the paid use of space or time in any medium, such as newspapers, magazines, radio, or television. Publicity is the free use of time or space to communicate a message about a firm or its products. With advertising, the firm sponsoring the message has purchased the media space or time and controls the content of the advertisement. With publicity, the message must earn the media space or time by its newsworthiness. Publicity is often written by the firm the message is about; it is always subject to the mercy of the editor who determines whether or not it will appear in the medium and in what form.

Advertising Agencies

The original function of the **advertising agency** was to prepare and place ads in magazines or newspapers for clients. The job of the advertising agency today has expanded to encompass much more than this. An advertising agency will assist a client with researching the consumer market and planning a total promotional campaign. Such agencies prepare and place ads in broadcast and print media, develop selling aids and packaging, and perform market research.

Advertising agencies derive approximately 65 percent of their revenue from commissions paid by the media from which they purchase advertising space or time. This rate is customarily 15 percent. The balance of their income comes from clients who pay fees for special services received such as market research or production of an advertisement. Advertising agencies are most often used by large manufacturing firms or national retail chains. J. C. Penney, for example, uses N W Ayer Inc. Other accounts held by N W Ayer include American Telephone & Telegraph Co., Burger King, and DeBeers Diamonds.

In preparing ads an advertising agency frequently becomes involved with fashion, even for nonfashion accounts. Ads for many products will feature a fashionably dressed person showing or using the product. A fashion stylist is responsible for pulling together the clothing and accessories used in the ad as well as planning makeup and hairstyles to project an appropriate image for the product being advertised.

Most medium-to-large retailers have their own in-house advertising departments that handle print advertising. Retailers are more likely to use an agency for preparation of television advertising because of the special expertise necessary to produce this kind of advertising. Small retailers may use advertisements prepared by manufacturers.

Publicity and Public Relations Firms

Publicity and **public relations firms** specialize in assisting companies with the projection of their public image. Image is the way a firm is perceived by its various publics. Both fashion retailers and producers are concerned with how they are viewed by their customers. Retailers want their target customers to believe that their store is the best place to shop. A manufacturer wants both consumers and retailers to have a favorable opinion about the firm and its products.

Publicity is the basic tool used by publicity and public relations firms to get information out to the public about their client firms. Publicity is editorial news about a company or a product. It is an unsponsored and nonpaid message about a firm in the public information media. The client pays a fee for the services of the publicity or public relations firm, but the space or time in the media is free.

A publicity firm looks for or creates news about a client. Press releases are written and sent to appropriate media having an audience interested in the news about the client firm. The person who writes the press release is called a **publicist.** The publicist seeks to place spot news items and feature stories with newspapers, magazines, and radio and television stations. The publicity firm attempts to get the fashion firm's name better known by the public. Many publicity agencies or individual publicists specialize in fashion accounts. Three well-known New York publicity firms that serve textile and apparel manufacturers are Eleanor Lambert, Ruth Hammer Associates, and Rosemary Sheehan.

Public relations is a broader term than *publicity*. A public relations firm is concerned with assisting a client in the development and projection of the company's public image through a planned program of activities. A public relations program is often aimed at the business community as well as at the consuming public. Public relations includes evaluating public attitudes, identifying the company's goals, and executing a program of communications to enhance the goodwill or prestige of the company. A public relations firm writes press releases about the client's company and also assists with developing ideas of new ways to get publicity for the client. A number of fashion industry firms have used fashion awards as a means of getting publicity. Coty cosmetics developed the annual Coty Fashion Award given to an outstanding fashion designer to promote American fashion and creativity worldwide. Stores such as Neiman-Marcus, headquartered in Dallas, and Marshall Field, head-quartered in Chicago, have also presented annual fashion awards that have brought the stores publicity.

Some large fashion firms have their own publicity or public relations departments responsible for developing public information material about the company. Such departments write press releases and distribute them to appropriate media. They may plan overall public relations and promotional programs for their firms.

The Fashion Press

The **fashion press** assists the fashion industry by presenting and interpreting news about the industry and by publishing paid advertising messages. The fashion press includes newspapers and magazines. These publications provide a means of communication between the fashion industry and the public as well as among the members of the fashion industry itself.

Consumer Periodicals

Fashion is considered news, and many consumer publications devote space to covering it. Stories about fashion trends and the fashion industry can be found in many kinds of periodicals, such as news magazines, general interest magazines, women's and men's interest magazines, and special interest magazines. Even *Sports Illustrated* publishes an annual issue featuring women's swimwear, and fashion advertisements and articles appear in news magazines such as *Time* and *U.S. News and World Report*. Fashion is, after all, of interest to almost everyone.

Newspapers

Most newspapers have a fashion editor or someone designated to cover fashion as part of his or her duties. Some major city newspapers devote a weekly section to fashion as well as covering fashion daily in their lifestyle section. Much fashion information comes to newspapers by way of press releases prepared by publicists. Other articles are researched and written by a newspaper's own reporters.

Fashion Press Week is one way for the fashion industry to get the news reported to the public. Fashion Press Week, Inc., was organized in 1931 to bring newspaper fashion editors throughout the United States to New York City for the showing of better women's apparel firms. Held twice a year in June and January, Press Week has done much to encourage fashion editors to feature American designers and manufacturers in their newspapers. Much nationwide publicity for apparel manufacturers and designers has been generated by Press Week.

The *New York Times* is noted for its fashion coverage. Reporters cover the major fashion showings and publish fashion articles. Twice a year special magazine sections entitled "Fashions of the Times" appear in the Sunday edition of the newspaper. Separate magazine sections feature men's and women's fashions.

Fashion Magazines

Fashion magazines have been an important means for disseminating fashion information to the consumer in the United States since the mid-1800s. Two of the early magazines featuring fashions were *Godey's Lady's Book* and *Burton's Gentleman's Magazine*. *Godey's*, published from 1830 to 1898, was the leading woman's magazine of its time and set the pattern for many other magazines to follow (see the profile on *Godey's* on page 74).

In 1868 **Ebenezer Butterick** started a magazine, the *Metropolitan Monthly*, designed to sell his dress patterns. The magazine was replaced in 1875 by the *Delineator*, which continued in publication until 1937. *The Delineator* called itself "A Journal of Fashion Culture and Fine Arts." In addition to featuring Butterick patterns, it emphasized etiquette and behavior.

Harper's Bazaar was founded in 1867 and *Vogue* in 1892. Neither of these high-fashion magazines was very influential until about 1913. Both featured expensive fashions that appealed to upper-income, fashion-conscious women. The first fashion magazine designed to appeal to a younger audience was *Mademoiselle*. Established in 1937, it was targeted toward the eighteen- to twenty-nine-year-old market and featured popular-priced fashions. *Glamour*, also targeted to a younger audience, appeared in 1939.

Seventeen, designed for the teenage girl, began publication in 1944. *Gentlemen's Quarterly*, a true fashion magazine for men, started in 1957. *W*, a women's fashion newspaper published every two weeks, was introduced in 1971. Three men's fashion magazines appeared in the 1980s: *M, The Civilized Man* in 1983; *MBM* (Modern Black Man) in 1984, and *MGF* (Men's Guide to Fashion) in 1985.

Fashion magazines serve as a means of disseminating fashion information to consumers.
Source: *Reprinted with permission of* Glamour, Mademoiselle, Gentlemen's Quarterly, *and* Vogue.

The fashion magazines most widely read in the United States today are *Glamour, Seventeen, Vogue, Mademoiselle,* and *Harper's Bazaar. Vogue* and *Harper's Bazaar* still feature expensive designer fashions aimed at the sophisticated high-fashion consumer of any age. *Glamour* and *Mademoiselle* emphasize fashions for the young career and college markets. *Seventeen* is still appealing to the teenage market.

As fashion has become more international in scope, foreign fashion magazines have become increasingly important in the United States. The English edition of *Elle,* a French publication, is now widely available in the United States and is popular among young women. Many foreign fashion publications are oriented toward high fashion and have smaller circulations because of their high cost and more limited appeal. Nonetheless, these publications are important reading for professionals who need to be aware of fashion trends. Table 3.1 lists some foreign fashion periodicals.

Harper's Bazaar and *Vogue* also have foreign editions. *Harper's Bazaar* publishes in Italian and Spanish; *Vogue's* seven foreign editions are: Argentine, Australian, Brazilian, British, French, German, and Italian.

Certain fashion magazines are aimed at very specific markets. *Essence* is designed for the fashion-oriented black woman. *Big Beautiful Woman Magazine* appeals to the large woman. *Brides* and *Modern Bride* are obviously targeted toward the woman who is planning a wedding or contemplating marriage. Two periodicals in addition to *Seventeen* target the teenager: *Teen* and *Sassy.*

Many women's interest magazines also feature fashion news. *Working Woman* and *Savvy* are aimed at career women and often present articles concerning appropriate business dress. *Town and Country,* which gives extensive coverage to American and international fashion designers, and *Vanity Fair* are society magazines that also emphasize high fashion.

Almost all women's general-interest magazines carry some fashion advertising and feature articles on apparel and personal appearance. Examples are *Family Circle, Good Housekeeping, Ladies' Home Journal, McCall's,* and *Woman's Day.* For many women these magazines are important sources of information on what is in and what is out of fashion.

Circulations for fashion magazines are lower than for the general-interest wom-

Table 3.1. Foreign Fashion Publications

Publication	Language	Frequency of Publication
Burda Moden	*German*	*monthly*
Depeche Mode	*French*	*6 times a year*
Elle	*French*	*weekly*
High Fashion	*Japanese*	*bimonthly*
Lina Italiana	*Italian*	*monthly*
Linea Uomo Sport	*Italian*	*6 times a year*
Modasport Vacanze	*Italian*	*quarterly*
L'Officiel De La Couture Et De La Mode De Paris	*French*	*10 times a year*

en's magazine. *Family Circle,* which is distributed through grocery stores, has a circulation of 6,661,956. *McCall's* circulation is 6,312,403; *Good Housekeeping,* 5,203,000; and *Ladies' Home Journal,* 4,100,000. The highest circulation for a fashion magazine is 2,300,807 for *Glamour. Seventeen* has the next highest with 1,750,513. Circulation figures for other fashion magazines are listed in Table 3.2. Information concerning periodicals and their circulations may be obtained through directories such as *Ulrich's International Periodical Directory, Standard Rate and Data Service,* and *IMS/Ayer Directory of Publications.*

Men's fashion magazines include *Gentlemen's Quarterly, M,* and *MGF* (Men's Guide to Fashion). Examples of foreign fashion magazines for men are *L'Officiel Hommes, L'Uomo-Linea Italiana, L'Uomo Vogue,* and *Vogue Hommes.* In addition, men's general-interest magazines, such as *Esquire* and *Playboy,* present fashion articles and ads.

A number of consumer magazines feature home-furnishing and fashion trends for the home. Some are specialized as to decorating style; others have a wider appeal. Examples include *Architectural Digest, Better Homes and Gardens, House Beautiful, HG* (formerly *House and Garden*), *Colonial Homes, Country Living, Metropolitan Home,* and *Southern Accents.* Many women's general-interest magazines also feature home decorating articles.

Role of the Fashion Press

The influence of the fashion press is far greater than periodical circulation would indicate. Consumer fashion publications serve an important communications role within the fashion industry. Through their activities, they provide direction to all

Table 3.2. Consumer Fashion Publications

Publication	Date Founded	Circulation
Brides	1934	342,912
Elle	1945	436,912
Essence	1970	800,248
Gentlemen's Quarterly	1957	633,501
Glamour	1939	2,300,807
Harper's Bazaar	1867	769,369
M, The Civilized Man	1983	133,600
Mademoiselle	1935	1,236,392
MGF (Men's Guide to Fashion)	1985	200,000
Modern Bride	1949	293,188
Seventeen	1944	1,750,513
Vogue	1892	1,179,339
W	1971	175,000

Source: *Ulrich's International Periodicals Directory 1987–88.* New York: R. R. Bowker, 1987.

levels of the industry as well as providing consumers with information concerning fashion trends.

Fashion editors visit the fashion markets, attend major shows, and report the fashion news. The role of the editor is to educate by providing information to both consumers and to all levels of the fashion industry.

Fashion editors fulfill the following functions:

1. Shop markets worldwide to select newsworthy styles to feature in their magazines.

2. Work with manufacturers to create merchandise that they believe will be successful; thus editors may influence the production of apparel and accessories.

3. Participate in distribution by encouraging retailers to carry items featured and endorsed by magazines.

4. Communicate fashion information to consumers.

5. Give **editorial credit** to retailers and manufacturers. Editorial credit is given by fashion editors when they select the styles and accessories that they feel best exemplify fashion trends. These styles are presented in their publications and names are given of designers, manufacturers, and retail stores where these fashions may be purchased. Listing such sources is a service and encourages sales within the industry. Retailers are encouraged to purchase the items that are featured editorially because they know that customers are likely to visit their stores and ask to see specific garments or accessories they have seen in a fashion magazine. Sometimes customers approach a retailer and ask for a "look" they saw featured in a magazine. In either case, editorial credit given by a fashion periodical encourages the sale of fashion merchandise. Listing these sources is a service for readers.

6. Publish advertisements for retailers and manufacturers.

7. Provide point-of-sale advertisements to retailers, such as posters of magazine blowups and garment hangtags.

8. Hold fashion shows and seminars for store customers.

9. Provide stores with information on how to sell, sources for merchandise, projections of fashion trends, and suggestions for promoting merchandise.

10. Serve as a general clearinghouse for information within the industry.

11. Sometimes perform market research to find out about consumers and their merchandise preferences. For example, *Seventeen* conducts an annual survey of teenage female consumers that is available to retailers and manufacturers. *Glamour* periodically surveys its readership to compile information about their interests, opinions, and fashion preferences. Such surveys provide valuable information to the entire fashion industry.

Trade Periodicals

Trade periodicals are available that specialize in each division of the fashion industry. These publications are not written for the consumer but rather are addressed to the

Trade publications are a good source of research for professionals in the fashion and home-furnishings industries.
Source: *Reprinted with permission of* Furniture World, Visual Merchandising and Store Design, Stores, Executive Chain Store Age, Body Fashions Intimate Apparel, *and* Advertising Age.

professionals within the industry. Some publications are general in subjects presented, whereas others are limited as to merchandise category or industry specialty covered.

Trade periodicals aimed at the retail manager that provide overviews of business conditions and retail trends include *Stores, Chain Store Age, Discount Merchandiser, Discount Store News,* and *Shopping Center World.* Publications dealing with advertising are *Advertising Age, Madison Avenue,* and *NRMA AD/PRO. Visual Merchandising and Store Design* covers window and interior display techniques as well as trends in store layout and decor.

Typical examples of trade publications dealing with one aspect of the fashion apparel and accessories industries are *Body Fashions/Intimate Apparel, Earnshaws* (children's wear), *Fashion Jewelry Review, Footwear News, Men's Wear, Knitwear Fashions,* and *Product Marketing* (beauty industry).

The home-furnishings industry has its trade publications as well. Some examples are *Contract Magazine, Decorating Retailer, Furniture Today,* and *Furniture World. Gifts and Decorative Accessories* describes itself as the international business magazine of gifts, tabletop merchandise, gourmet foods, home accessories, greeting cards, and social stationery.

Fairchild Publications

A major publisher of trade periodicals for the fashion industry is **Fairchild Publications,** located in New York City at 7 East 12th Street. Among the fashion newspapers published by Fairchild are three daily papers, each considered the "bible" in its division. *Women's Wear Daily* covers the women's and children's industries; *Daily News Record* is its counterpart in the men's wear industry; and *HFD Retailing Home Furnishings* presents news of furniture, decorative accessories, and household textiles.

Fairchild Publications dates back to 1890, when Edmund Fairchild bought an interest in the *Herald Gazette,* a trade paper for the men's wear industry in Chicago. He was joined in this publishing endeavor by his brother Louis. In 1900 the two brothers moved the *Herald Gazette* to New York, where it evolved into *Men's Wear,* a biweekly trade magazine. Soon they added the *Daily News Record,* covering the men's wear and textile industries.

Women's Wear Daily had its beginning in 1910 when the Saturday edition of the *Daily News Record* began devoting a single page to the women's garment industry. *Women's Wear Daily* today is the leading trade paper in the fashion industry. With a circulation of 62,094, *WWD* is read by more people in the industry than any other trade publication. The circulation for the *Daily News Record* is 24,238 and for *HFD Retailing Home Furnishings,* 35,000 (*Ulrich's* 1987).

In the late 1960s so many upper-income, fashion-conscious women began reading *Women's Wear Daily* for the fashion news that Fairchild decided to add a newspaper for consumers. In 1971 *W* began publication; by 1985 it had a circulation of 175,000.

Professional Organizations and Trade Associations

Trade associations represent every division of the fashion industry. Some are highly specialized as to area of interest; others are more general, dealing with a total industry such as retailing. Many trade associations conduct research and report information concerning consumer preferences, fashion trends, and market conditions. Each trade association is interested in promoting the aspect of the fashion industry it represents. Trade associations are found in all areas of the industry: apparel and accessories, beauty culture, media, retailing, textiles, and home furnishings. Examples of trade associations include the following:

Apparel and Accessories Trade Associations

> American Apparel Manufacturers Association (AAMA)
>
> American Cloak and Suit Manufacturers Association (ACSMA)
>
> American Fur Merchants Association
>
> American Home Sewing Association
>
> Associated Corset and Brassiere Manufacturers
>
> Clothing Manufacturers Association of the United States (CMA)
>
> Headwear Institute of America
>
> Infants, Childrens and Girls Sportswear and Coat Association
>
> Jewelry Industry Council
>
> The Men's Tie Foundation
>
> National Association of Blouse Manufacturers (NABM)
>
> National Knitwear and Sportswear Association (NKSA)
>
> United Better Dress Manufacturers Association

Beauty Culture Trade Associations

> Cosmetic, Toiletry, and Fragrance Association (CTFA)
>
> Intercoiffure America

Media Trade Associations

> American Association of Advertising Agencies
>
> American Newspaper Publishers Association

Magazine Publishers Association

Newspaper Advertising Bureau (NAB)

Public Relations Society of America, Inc.

Radio Advertising Bureau (RAB)

Television Bureau of Advertising (TBA)

Retailing Trade Associations

Association of General Merchandise Chains

Direct Marketing Association

Direct Selling Association

International Council of Shopping Centers (ICSC)

Mail Order Association of America

Men's Merchandising Association, Inc.

Menswear Retailers of America

National Mass Retailing Institute (NMRI)

National Retail Merchants Association (NRMA)

National Shoe Retailers Association, Inc.

Textile Trade Associations

American Fiber Manufacturers Association

American Printed Fabrics Council

American Textile Manufacturers Institute (ATMI)

American Yarn Spinners Association (AYSA)

Cotton, Incorporated

Embroidery Council of America

International Linen Promotion Commission

International Silk Association

Knitted Textile Association

Linen Trade Association

Textile Information Council

Wool Bureau

Furniture and Home Furnishings Trade Associations

American Furniture Manufacturers Association

Contract Furnishings Council

National Association of Bedding Manufacturers

National Association of Decorative Fabrics Distributors

National Home Fashions League, Inc.

National Wholesale Furniture Association

Southern Home Furnishings Association

National Retail Merchants Association

The primary trade association for department, chain, and specialty stores is the **National Retail Merchants Association** (NRMA). It provides many services to its member stores and is dedicated to research and education in general merchandise retailing. Of the 50,000 stores that are NRMA members, 45,000 are located in the United States, and the remaining 5,000 represent fifty foreign countries. Included among the services provided by NRMA are conferences designed for executive development, an annual convention and equipment exposition, professional publications, and professional advisors.

Numerous NRMA conferences, seminars, and workshops are held in various cities to provide retailers with a way to keep up-to-date with happenings in the industry, solve common problems, and exchange information with other retailers. Conferences deal with every phase of retailing, including general management, management information systems, credit and finance, store operations, sales promotion, and personnel.

In mid-January approximately 15,000 retail executives attend the annual NRMA convention held in New York City. The convention presents sessions dealing with all aspects of retailing. The National Retailers Business and Equipment Exposition is held in conjunction with the annual convention. This exposition provides retailers with an overview of current equipment, services, and supplies for store operations and sales promotion. Exhibits range from computers and other electronic equipment to display fixtures and merchandising aids. Exhibitors include consulting and service firms, publishers of trade publications, and equipment manufacturers. Attending the NRMA annual convention is an excellent way to find out about new technology, trends, and concerns within the retailing industry.

NRMA publications include books, periodicals, and checklists on subjects of interest to retailers. *Stores,* a general-topics magazine, is written to provide senior retail executives with a monthly review of current issues and trends in all areas of retailing. Special features include *Stores'* annual ranking of the "Top 100 Department Stores" and the "Top 100 Specialty Chains," published in the July and August issues.

Other NRMA periodicals are *Creditalk, Employee Relations Bulletin, NRMA AD/ PRO, Profitmaker, Retail Control, Retail Operations News Bulletin,* and *Traffic Topics.* Each of these publications deals with a specific area of retailing.

Two annual NRMA publications present statistical data concerning retail department and specialty stores in the United States. *Merchandising and Operating Results of Department and Specialty Stores,* referred to as **MOR Results,** presents a summary of merchandise statistics by merchandise category and store size. Information is given by selling department and includes gross margin, markdowns, turnover, stock shortage, and newspaper and selling costs. *Financial and Operating Results of Department and Specialty Stores (***FOR Results***)* provides expense data by function for all major expense categories by store volume, size, and type. Included are expenses for payroll, real estate costs, supplies and merchandise control, receiving, marking, selling, delivery, accounting, and buying office expense. Retailers use the statistical data provided by *MOR Results* and *FOR Results* for comparative purposes.

Also available to NRMA members are experts on all retailing subjects. Members may contact these experts to seek information or advice on retailing problems or concerns. The offices of the NRMA are located at 100 West 31st Street, New York, New York 10001.

The Fashion Group International

The **Fashion Group International** is a nonprofit professional organization of more than 6,000 women executives representing all segments of the fashion industry and related fields. Members are employed in apparel, cosmetics, and home-furnishings industries. They work in such fields as design, manufacturing, retailing, public relations, advertising, and education. International headquarters for the Fashion Group are in Rockefeller Center, New York City. Regional groups are found in forty-two cities worldwide, with thirty-one in the United States and ten elsewhere. Foreign locations include Johannesburg, London, Melbourne, Mexico City, Montreal, Paris, Seoul, Sydney, Tokyo, and Toronto.

The Fashion Group provides members with information on emerging industry directions and fashion and industry trends and offers valuable professional contacts and exchanges for members. The Fashion Group describes its mission as "to keep its members in touch with all aspects of the rapid changes in the volatile fashion business" (Fashion Group 1987).

Membership is limited to women in executive or administrative positions concerning the creation, production, distribution, and merchandising of fashion and fashion-related products; in publishing, public relations, publicity, research, advertising, teaching, and fields related to fashion work. Applicants for membership must be sponsored by a member of the organization who has known the applicant professionally for at least one year and must be recommended by two additional members.

The original purpose of the Fashion Group was to increase the opportunities for women at executive levels within the fashion industry. Today the organization provides members a wide range of services and opportunities to network with other professionals. Through slide programs, fashion shows, and lectures, members and guests are presented information on fashion and industry trends. A quarterly bulletin reports Fashion Group events and programming and features a guest editor addressing an area of common fashion interest. The organization also offers career counseling sessions to assist members in dealing with job loss or change. Many of the regional groups hold annual career-day programs for fashion students and offer scholarships for fashion study.

The Fashion Group was founded in 1930 by seventeen women. The organization was created to offer executive women a means to exchange ideas and resources in the fashion business. Among the original founders were such notables in the fashion business as Dorothy Shaver, president of Lord & Taylor and the first female president of a major department store; Edna Woolman Chase, editor-in-chief of *Vogue;* Carmel Snow, editor-in-chief of *Harper's Bazaar;* Tobé Collier Davis, founder of Tobé Associates, fashion consultant firm; and Estelle Hamburger, vice president of Jay-Thorpe, a New York specialty store, and a fashion marketing consultant.

Miscellaneous Supporting Enterprises

Many other types of firms or individuals provide information and support services to specific segments of the fashion industry. Individual specialists provide their services or expertise to appropriate businesses on a fee basis. Examples include freelance display artists, sales promotion specialists, fashion show coordinators, fashion writers, and publicists. Such individuals may be hired to assist a retail store, a manufacturing firm, a shopping center, or some other type of fashion support firm with completing a particular assignment. For example, the manager of a shopping center might hire a fashion coordinator to plan and present a seasonal fashion show, or a small apparel designer might hire a publicist to write press releases about the designer and distribute them to the press.

Marketing research firms may be hired to conduct consumer or industry surveys for retailers, manufacturers, or trade associations. Many fashion firms lack the time or the expertise to conduct such research for themselves. Sometimes a firm wants an unbiased outside firm to conduct research or analyze an existing problem and recommend solutions. Many firms are available to offer support and service to the fashion industry. Specialists exist who offer almost any imaginable service.

Summary of Key Points

1. Because of the complexity of the fashion industry, it is impossible for any one individual or firm to be aware of all business and fashion trends. Numerous advisory and consulting services provide retailers and manufacturers with information and assist with analyzing and interpreting trends.

Godey's Lady's Book

Louis Antoine Godey began publishing a woman's magazine called the *Lady's Book* in Philadelphia in 1830. In 1837 he purchased another woman's periodical called the *Ladies Magazine,* which had been started in Boston in 1828 by **Sarah Josepha Hale.** The two magazines were combined under the title *Godey's Lady's Book* with Sarah Hale as editor and Louis Godey as publisher. Together they built the magazine with the highest circulation of its time and one that had tremendous influence on Victorian women. Although famous for its hand-colored fashion plates, *Godey's Lady's Book* was much more than a fashion magazine. It featured articles on many women's interests, including home architecture and interiors, child care, nutrition, and health.

Sarah Josepha Hale, a widow with five children, was a remarkable woman, and as a working woman she was an exception for her times. Mrs. Hale was editor of *Godey's Lady's Book* from 1837 to 1877. During her forty years as editor, she used Godey's to promote equal opportunity for women as well as to influence tastes in fashions in clothing and home decorating.

The contributions of Sarah Josepha Hale were so outstanding that one writer called her "the greatest woman in the history of our country" (Helen Woodward, *The Lady Persuaders.* New York: Ivan Obolensky, 1960, p. 5). Mrs. Hale was a feminist who used Godey's and her social influence in Boston and Philadelphia to promote many causes to better the position of women. In relation to fashion, she denounced the tight lacing of women's waists but was unsuccessful in convincing women to abandon this unhealthful fashion. To encourage better hygiene, she wrote in support of the weekly bath at a time when baths were rarely taken. When the home sewing machine became available in the 1850s, she gave it enthusiastic support and free advertising. She saw the sewing machine saving women many hours of drudgery sewing the family's clothing by hand. She encouraged women not to follow blindly European styles but to adapt costumes to their own figures and individual personalities. In 1852 she introduced the French word *lingerie* to her readers, and in the same year she instituted the first shopping service. *Godey's* offered to choose for readers and forward to any part of the country "bridal wardrobes, bonnets, dresses, jewelry, cake boxes, envelopes ... with a view to economy as well as taste" (Ruth Finley, *The Lady of Godey's: Sarah Josepha Hale.* Philadelphia: J. B. Lippincott, 1931, p. 157).

Some of her many other contributions include the following:

- She promoted the establishment of Thanksgiving as a national holiday.

- She was an early champion of elementary education for girls equal to that of boys and of higher education for women.

- She helped Matthew Vassar organize Vassar College, the first U.S. college for women (1861).

- She was the first to advocate women as teachers in public schools. (Women had been looked on as mentally unfit to teach.)

- She demanded for housekeeping the dignity of a profession and put the term "domestic science" into the language.

- She began the fight for the retention of property rights by married women.

- She founded the first society for the advancement of women's wages, better working conditions for women, and the reduction of child labor.

- She started the first day nursery.

- She was the first to stress the necessity of physical training for women.

- She was the first to suggest public playgrounds for children.

- She was among the earliest to recognize health and sanitation as civic problems and the first to crusade for remedial measures.

- She organized the Seaman's Aid and established the first Sailors' Home.

- She sent out the first women medical missionaries.

- She raised the money that finished Bunker Hill Monument.

- She rescued the movement to preserve Mount Vernon as a national memorial.

- She was the author of two dozen books and hundreds of poems, including "Mary Had a Little Lamb" (Finley, p. 17).

2. Promotional assistance is available from advertising, public relations, and publicity firms. Advertising agencies assist with developing and placing advertisements in the media. Publicity and public relations firms specialize in assisting companies with the projection of their public image.

3. Periodicals serve as an important communication tool by reporting and interpreting fashion news to the industry as well as to consumers.

4. General and specialized trade associations represent every division of the fashion industry. Trade associations actively promote the segments of the industry that they represent.

Key Words and Concepts

Define, identify, or explain each of the following:

advertising agency

editorial credit

Ebenezer Butterick

Fairchild Publications

Fashion Group International

fashion press

Fashion Press Week

FOR Results

Sarah Josepha Hale

IM International

MOR Results

National Retail Merchants Association (NRMA)

public relations firm

publicist

publicity firm

resident buying office

Tobé Associates

trade associations

trade periodicals

Discussion Questions and Topics

1. What services are offered by fashion consulting and reporting firms?

2. Explain the difference between an advertising agency, a publicity firm, and a public relations firm.

3. Who was Sarah Josepha Hale, and what were her contributions to fashion?

4. What functions are performed by the fashion editor?

5. Differentiate between editorialized merchandise and advertised merchandise. Find an example of each from a consumer fashion magazine.

6. Discuss the role of the fashion press within the fashion industry.

7. What services does the NRMA provide to member stores?

8. How does one gain membership in The Fashion Group, International?

Notes

Fashion Group, *Annual Review,* 1987.

Ulrich's International Periodicals Directory, 1987–88. New York: R. R. Bowker, 1987.

PART II _____

THE PRODUCTION OF FASHION

ANYONE entering a fashion career should have an understanding of the interrelated roles played by the producers of fashion products. Part II presents an overview of the enterprises that produce the raw materials and finished products of the fashion industry. Fashion products begin with raw materials such as fiber, fabric, leather, and fur. The industries that produce these materials are the primary suppliers to the fashion industry and are discussed in Chapter 4.

After the raw materials are produced, they must be turned into finished products by the secondary suppliers. Products must be designed and produced to meet the needs and preferences of consumers. The American designer has played an increasingly important role in gaining worldwide recognition for American fashion products. Chapter 5 presents a discussion of the role of the designer in the production of apparel and includes brief profiles of prominent American designers.

Chapter 6 traces the development of ready-made apparel and describes the characteristics of the industries that produce apparel for men, women, and children. Also part of the fashion business are the industries that produce intimate apparel and fashion accessories such as shoes, handbags, hosiery, and jewelry. Although apparel and accessories make up a major part of the fashion business, today many consumer products are produced and sold with a fashion approach. The industries that produce accessories, cosmetics, and home furnishings are discussed in Chapter 7.

CHAPTER 4 _____

RAW MATERIALS OF FASHION

THE producers of fashion goods are categorized by two levels: (1) the primary markets and (2) the secondary markets. The **primary markets** produce the raw materials of fashion, which include fibers, textiles, leathers, and furs. The **secondary markets** are industries that manufacture the finished products of the fashion industry from the raw materials of the primary markets.

This chapter is a discussion of the primary markets, the suppliers to apparel and accessories manufacturers. Presented are the textile, leather, and fur industries and their relationships to the secondary markets. The primary markets play important roles in the fashion industry. They must be attuned to consumers' needs and to current fashion trends. These suppliers plan and produce earlier than any other area of the fashion industry because their products require numerous and complicated production processes. Planning within the primary markets begins as much as one to two years before the goods are available on the retail market.

The Textile Industry

The **textile industry** is the largest segment of the primary markets. It is one of the oldest manufacturing industries in the United States and plays an important role in the national economy. The United States produces over $25 billion each year in textile products, and almost one out of every ten manufacturing jobs is in textile and apparel production. In 1987 these industries had a combined employment of approximately 1.8 million. Whereas the textile industry employs approximately 700,000 workers, several hundred thousand others work in support industries, including fiber producing, machinery manufacturing, and the production of dyestuffs and fabric finishes (Standard and Poor's 1988). Textiles are used more than any other material in the production of apparel and are also important in the production of home furnishings. Table 4.1 lists many of the end-uses for textiles.

The textile industry includes four segments: (1) fiber producers, (2) yarn producers, (3) textile mills, and (4) finishers. Fiber producers make the basic unit used in the production of textile yarns and fabrics. Yarn producers specialize in making yarns, which are produced by spinning or twisting fibers together to form a continuous strand. Textile mills produce fabric by interlacing yarns or fibers together by various methods such as weaving, knitting, felting, fusing, knotting, and braiding. **Finishers** apply finishes to a fabric that change the appearance, the hand (feel), or the performance of the fabric. For example, special finishes can be applied to make a fabric crease-resistant, water-repellent, or shrink-resistant. Some firms specialize in a single phase of the textile industry, whereas others operate in all four phases.

Table 4.1. Classifications for Textile End-Uses

Apparel (womenswear, menswear, childrenswear, and infants)	Home furnishings

Sportswear
  tops
  bottoms
	Furniture
	  upholstery
	  slipcovers

Swimwear and beachwear	Window treatments draperies

Activewear
  jogging suits
  leotards and dancewear
	curtains
	  shades

Intimate apparel
  foundations (bras and girdles)
  daywear (slips, panties)
  sleepwear (nightgowns, pajamas)
  loungewear (robes, loungewear)
	Domestics
	  sheets and pillowcases
	  pillows
	  bedspreads
	  comforters
	  blankets and throws

Maternity wear	mattress pads bath towels

Outerwear
  jackets
  sweaters
	Linens
	  tablecloths
	  napkins

Coats and suits	kitchen towels

Accessories
  scarves
  belts
	Floor coverings
	  carpets
	  rugs

gloves
  handbags
  ties
  handkerchiefs
	Miscellaneous
	  lamp shades
	  decorative pillows

hosiery millinery	
Footwear	

Fiber Producers

Every textile product begins with **fibers.** Composed of fine hairlike substances, fibers are the fundamental unit used in the production of yarns and fabrics. Most fabrics are constructed of yarns that are made by combining fibers into continuous strands. Fibers play a vital role in the color, weight, texture, and care qualities of finished textile products.

Fibers are divided into two broad categories: natural and man-made (manufactured). **Natural fibers** come from plant, animal, or mineral sources, whereas man-made fibers are manufactured from either natural materials or chemicals. The term **synthetic** is sometimes loosely applied to all man-made fibers; however, it is not applicable to all such manufactured fibers. True synthetic fibers are synthesized completely from chemical substances. For example, rayon and acetate are not synthetics because they are made from cellulose, a plant source. In the development of textile products, both man-made and natural fibers go through similar basic processes. Included in these processes are yarn making, fabric construction, and finishing.

Natural Fibers

Ancient civilizations used mainly four fibers that served the world's primary textile needs until the twentieth century. Of the early great civilizations, Egypt is associated with flax, India and Peru with cotton, China with silk, and Mesopotamia with wool. Natural fibers have been used for thousands of years dating back to the Stone Age (8000 B.C. to 6000 B.C.). Garments woven of flax are known to have been worn as early as 6000 B.C. by Swiss lake dwellers, and flax was cultivated extensively in the Mediterranean region at least 6000 years ago. Cotton fiber may be as old as flax, but archaeological evidence of cotton dates to around 3500 B.C. in India and 3000 B.C. in Peru. Silk dates from about 2700 B.C. in China, and the secret of silk production was not known in the West until about A.D. 450. Wool was probably the last of the major fibers to be spun and woven into cloth. Sheep were first domesticated in Mesopotamia prior to 2000 B.C., and wool was mentioned frequently in the Old Testament. Spinning and weaving of wool were extensive in the Holy Land and Asia Minor by about 1000 B.C.

Today the most important natural fibers are still cotton, wool, silk, and flax. In 1985 cotton comprised 49 percent of the total fiber used by the world's textile industry; wool use was 5.5 percent and flax, 2.7 percent (*Textiles* 1986). Other examples of natural fibers include jute, sisal, ramie, and hemp. In the apparel industry, cotton, wool, and silk are most often used in production, whereas linen and ramie are used to a lesser extent. Jute, sisal, and hemp are used in the home-furnishings industry, as are the other natural fibers.

Cotton, a vegetable fiber made from the boll of the cotton plant, is the most widely used of all natural fibers. The production of cotton fiber and fabric in the United States is concentrated in the South. The cotton plant is grown in a fourteen-state region of the southeast and southwest; fabric production is located primarily in the Carolinas and Georgia. The United States has long been a major cotton-producing country, but in 1982 China surpassed the United States and became the world's leading cotton producer. The Soviet Union is the world's third largest cotton producer. India and Pakistan are other major cotton-producing countries.

Growing consumer interest in natural fibers has stimulated an increase in the consumption of cotton and cotton blends in the U.S. market for apparel and home textiles. U.S. textile mills significantly increased their use of cotton in the 1980s; 5.3 million bales were used in 1981 and 7.8 million bales in 1987. One of the reasons for this increase is that cotton has become more competitively priced. In 1980 cotton cost 27 percent more than polyester; in 1985 it cost only 6 percent more because of large supplies and cost-saving innovations in manufacturing. Although cotton accounted for only 29.1 percent of total U.S. mill consumption in 1987, it is still the most widely used fiber worldwide, making up 49 percent of the total fiber used in the world's textile industry. Cotton is widely used in apparel production as well as for household linens, furniture upholstery, and draperies. Especially when treated to help prevent staining or soiling, cotton is the most widely used of the natural fibers for upholstered furniture.

Wool is a fiber that comes from the fleece of animals, most commonly sheep. Specialty wools, such as cashmere, mohair, angora, camel hair, alpaca, and vicuna, are obtained from animals in the goat, rabbit, and camel families. The production of wool in the United States occurs mostly in the mountain states of Utah, Nevada, and Colorado, but the Northeast also produces a considerable amount. U.S. wool production has declined consistently for the past 40 years. In the early 1940s the United States produced approximately 11 percent of the world's wool. Today it produces only 1 to 2 percent of the world's wool. Most of the world's wool is produced in the Southern Hemisphere and is then exported to the main wool-processing and consuming countries in North America, Europe, and Japan. Australia, New Zealand, and the Soviet Union are the three leading wool producers, accounting for approximately 58 percent of world output (Piercy 1987). Wool is a versatile fiber with a variety of end-uses. Approximately two-thirds of global wool consumption goes into apparel, with the remaining one-third consumed in other textile products such as blankets, mattresses, carpeting, rugs, and upholstery. Because wool fibers retain body heat, wool is traditionally used for fall and winter wearing apparel, including knitwear and tailored suits and coats. Other end-uses for wool include hand knitting yarn, underwear, socks, and accessories such as hats, gloves, and scarves. Wool fabric is comfortable to wear since it is soft and resilient. Because wool fibers have natural crimp, they are frequently used in insulated garments. Wool's natural flame-retardant qualities make it an important fiber in the home-furnishings industry. In fact, the major nonapparel use of wool is for carpets, where wool has 12 percent of the market. Wool is also used for upholstery fabrics.

Silk is an animal fiber made from the cocoons of silkworms. The silkworm spins silk to form its cocoon, the shell that protects it during its transformation from caterpillar to moth. Approximately 1,000 yards of continuous yarn come from one cocoon. According to legend, in 2640 B.C. a Chinese princess discovered silk when she dropped a silkworm cocoon in her tea. The hot tea caused the fiber to separate into a delicate tangle that was a continuous filament. The princess realized that this continuous filament could be woven into cloth.

All silk used in the United States is imported, mostly from Japan, Thailand, and China, the major silk-producing countries. Silk is considered a specialty fiber. Because of high production costs and limited durability, silk remains at a low production level. In spite of its increased fashion popularity in recent years, silk still accounts for less than 1 percent of the world's textile consumption. Consumers purchase silk garments because of the fabric's aesthetic appeal and luxurious feel. Although garments of silk are beautiful, they require considerable care and usually must be dry-cleaned. However, new washable silks provide the consumer with comfortable, easy-care garments. Primary end-uses for silk include suits, dresses, blouses, men's ties, and scarves. Because of its high cost, silk is used in home furnishings only to a limited extent.

Flax, a vegetable fiber from which linen is made, comes from the stem of the flax plant. The oldest of the textile fibers, flax was the world's most important textile fiber until the eighteenth century. It was replaced by cotton during the Industrial Revolution because cotton was easier to raise and process. The production of flax has never been a commercial success in the United States, and the flax fiber used in textiles in the United States is imported. Russian and Eastern bloc countries grow the largest amount of flax, approximately 80 percent of the world's total. In western Europe, France is the predominant producer of flax, followed by Belgium and Holland.

End-uses for flax include apparel, wall coverings, upholstery, draperies, towels, bed sheets, and tablecloths. Flax, like cotton, absorbs moisture very rapidly and transmits heat, which makes linen clothing, bed linens, and furnishing fabrics ideal for hot, humid conditions. Because flax will hold up to 20 percent of its weight in water without feeling wet, it is the ideal fabric for dish towels, napkins, and handkerchiefs. Linen has a tendency to crease and wrinkle, so its popularity in wearing apparel decreased with the development of wrinkle-resistant, man-made fibers in the 1950s. However, renewed fashion interest in natural fibers in the 1980s and the application of wrinkle-resistant finishes to linen revived consumer demand for linen and linen blends. In recent years apparel has been the biggest growth area for linen fabrics, growing from 5 percent of total linen production in 1976 to 40 percent in 1985; however, linen still comprises less than 3 percent of the total fiber used in the world's textile industry (Hamilton 1986).

Marketing Natural Fibers

Because of their usually small size, natural fiber producers work together on marketing procedures. The impact of man-made fibers on the apparel industry has led natural fiber producers, especially of cotton and wool, to make united efforts to be more aggressive and to develop new marketing strategies. The need to compete with man-made fibers has forced producers of natural fibers to improve the desirable properties of their fibers and to make extensive use of advertising, publicity, and market research. This has led to the development of blends and finishes that make natural fibers more wrinkle-resistant and provide for easier care.

Natural Fiber Trade Associations. One of the major ways natural fiber producers promote their product is through promotional activities of trade associations, each representing the producers of a particular fiber. Examples of trade associations for natural fibers are Cotton Incorporated, the Wool Bureau, the Mohair Council, and the International Linen Promotion Commission.

The natural **fiber trade associations** promote the favorable characteristics of their fibers to all levels of the fashion industry. The trade associations disseminate information about new fiber developments and their application to fashion apparel and home-furnishings products. They also offer fashion advice and information to the textile industry, retailers, and the public. Publicity kits, fashion styling reports, and educational materials are developed as ways to promote their fibers. Trade associations also make cooperative advertising programs available for use by textile producers and retail stores. They produce educational films and other visual aids for use by the trade and by schools and consumer groups. Furthermore, fiber associations provide assistance to textile and apparel producers in locating sources of supply. Some trade associations conduct seasonal clinics and workshops for all segments of the fashion industry, presenting fashion projections and trends through visual presentations such as posters, fashion shows, and videotapes.

Fabric libraries are another important service provided by fiber trade associations. Fabric libraries contain samples of fabric currently available or scheduled for production for an upcoming season. Manufacturers, retailers, and members of auxiliary fashion industries use fabric libraries to get information on new fabrications and color trends, locations of fabric suppliers, cost of fabrics, and new developments in fiber and fabric production. The libraries also offer product swatches, color cards, and fabric specifications. In addition, designers, producers, and retailers visit the fabric libraries to inspect new fiber blends, yarns, and fabrics.

Cotton Incorporated is the research and promotion company, headquartered in New York City, of U.S. cotton growers. It distributes information about fabrics made of cotton or cotton blends to members of the fashion industry. Cotton Incorporated makes long-range forecasts of consumer trends in apparel and home furnishings. It promotes cotton by several methods, including design awards, newsletters, television commercials, consumer print advertising, videotape presentations, and press kits. In 1980 Cotton Incorporated initiated a cotton textile design contest. Open to textile mills and converters, the annual contest requires submission of one to three fabrics representing innovative stitching, construction, and/or weave. Publications distributed by Cotton Incorporated provide information on fashion trends and new cotton products. Cotton Incorporated's "The Cottonworks" fabric library provides fabric samples and extensive information about sources of cotton and cotton blend textiles.

The Wool Bureau is the U.S. branch of the International Wool Secretariat, which has its headquarters in London. The International Wool Secretariat is sponsored by wool growers of the Southern Hemisphere, including Australia, New Zealand, South Africa, Uruguay, and Brazil. It works worldwide to increase the demand for wool.

The Wool Bureau offers a variety of services to the fashion industry in the United States. Its monthly newsletter, "The Wool-Flash," provides information on fashion trends and new developments relating to wool fabrics. Additionally, the Wool Bureau offers staged fashion events, personal consultations, and audiovisual presentations to promote wool use. The advertising division of the Wool Bureau works with the marketing division, providing advertising and promotional activities for retailers and manufacturers.

The Mohair Council of America, established in 1966, serves as a promotional organization for mohair producers in the United States. The Mohair Council provides advice and information to both users and producers of mohair. The Council's executive offices are located in San Angelo, Texas, at the edge of the primary mohair production area in the United States. Workshops and seminars for mohair growers are held at the Texas office. The promotional activities of the Council are coordinated through a New York office, which publicizes mohair through fashion presentations, press kits, and design competitions, and maintains a library of mohair yarns and fabrics from domestic and foreign sources. The Council also performs market research on trend developments and new blends.

The Mohair Council of America promotes the use of mohair yarns and fabrics.
Source: *Reprinted with permission of the Mohair Council of America.*

The International Linen Promotion Commission promotes linen fibers to all segments of the fashion apparel and home-furnishings industries. The Commission is a branch of the International Linen Confederation, a Paris-based organization of linen growers, spinners, and weavers from Austria, Belgium, France, Germany, Holland, Italy, Japan, Switzerland, and the United Kingdom.

The International Linen Promotion Commission in New York offers educational

Linen Today *is one of several publications that the International Linen Promotion Commission uses to promote linen appropriate for apparel, interior furnishings, and household products.*

materials and literature on the history and production of linen. The New York office also has a resource library of western European linen fabrics appropriate for apparel, interior furnishings, and household products.

Fiber Symbols. Trade associations such as those noted above have made major contributions to the promotion of natural fibers. For example, because of these organizations' efforts, many consumers recognize the symbols designed for wool and for cotton (see Figure 4.1). Such logos or symbols for specific fibers easily identify a fiber and bring it to the consumer's attention. The woolmark of the Wool Bureau was created in 1964 to identify 100 percent wool yarns and products for the consumer. In 1972 the wool blend mark was developed to certify that various blends of wool and other fibers contain at least 60 percent wool. Cotton Incorporated encourages the use of its logo, the seal of cotton, in the advertising of all cotton merchandise. In 1980 Cotton Incorporated introduced a symbol for the home fashion area. This symbol placed the outline of a house around the original cotton seal logo. The new symbol was developed for an advertising campaign, "Come Home to Cotton," which promoted the use of cotton products in home furnishings. These logos are also used on hangtags attached to merchandise and displayed on posters used at the point-of-sale in stores.

Man-Made Fibers

A man-made fiber (also called a manufactured fiber) is defined by the Textile Fiber Products Identification Act as "any fiber derived by a process of manufacture from any substance which, at any point in the manufacturing process, is not a fiber." The majority of man-made fibers are produced by large multinational chemical companies with less than a third of their business done in fibers. Although these fibers account for approximately 40 percent of the world's fiber production, in the United States man-mades make up nearly 70 percent of fiber production. Because of imports of natural fibers, man-made fiber's share of total U.S. fiber consumption is lower than production figures suggest; in 1986 it was approximately 62 percent.

PURE WOOL
The sewn-in Woolmark label is your assurance of quality-tested products made of the world's best...Pure Wool.

FIGURE 4.1
Examples of natural fiber logos. (Source: Courtesy of the Wool Bureau, Inc. and Cotton Incorporated.)

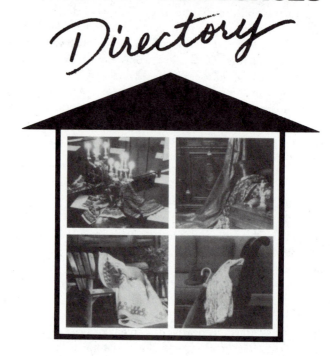

The cover of The Home Products Resources Directory *illustrates the symbol used to promote cotton products in home furnishings.*
Source: *Reprinted with permission of Cotton Incorporated.*

Development

Before 1880 several scientists tried unsuccessfully to develop manufactured fibers; however, their efforts led the way to the discovery of rayon, the first successful such fiber. Rayon was developed by Count Hilaire de Chardonent, a French chemist, who created a fiber from cellulosic substances in 1883, which he called artificial silk. He built the first commercial "artificial silk" plant in France in 1891. Later "artificial silk" became known as rayon. In 1910 the first rayon fiber plant opened in the United States in Marcus Hook, Pennsylvania, and in 1924 acetate, the second man-made fiber, also made with cellulose, was introduced in the United States.

Nylon, the first noncellulose man-made fiber, was developed by E.I. du Pont de Nemours & Co. in 1938, and was exhibited at the 1939 New York World's Fair, where visitors saw coal, water, and air enter a machine and nylon stockings exit the other end. Women's nylon hosiery was test marketed in the United States in late 1939 and early 1940, and "nylons" became a true marketing success story. Well-planned advertising campaigns launched national sales of nylon stockings on May 15, 1940; on that day four million pairs of nylons were sold. "Nylons" were an immediate success as women quickly substituted them for less durable silk stockings. Although temporarily absent from the consumer market during World War II, nylon stockings had no difficulty regaining their popularity following the war. In the immediate postwar period, the bulk of all nylon produced went into hosiery, but by the end of the 1940s, nylon was being used in carpeting, intimate apparel, and outerwear as well.

In the late 1940s and during the 1950s several other man-made fibers were developed and marketed. Among them were vinyon, saran, modacrylic, acrylic, polyester, olefin, anidex, and novoloid. During the 1950s and 1960s, man-made fibers revolutionized the textile industry. *American Fabrics and Fashions* magazine hailed the advent of man-made fibers as a "liberation from domestic slavery" (De Llosa 1985). Before man-made fibers, upkeep for clothes cost much more in time and money than their original purchase price. Natural fibers had to be dry-cleaned or required time-consuming washing and ironing. Man-made fibers freed homemakers from hours of household drudgery, and the fiber most responsible for this freedom was polyester.

Mass production of Dacron polyester was begun by du Pont in 1953. Polyester was first blended with wool in men's suits but was soon blended with cotton in men's shirts and women's blouses as well. Polyester began to affect every cotton producer in the textile industry. Between 1954 and 1967, for example, Burlington's Galey & Lord division shifted 90 percent of its production from all-cotton to cotton/polyester blends. Consumers quickly accepted the wash-and-wear qualities of polyester blends in men's shirts, slacks, and suits, as well as in women's dresses and blouses.

In 1965 permanent-press finishing greatly improved the wrinkle resistance of polyester fabrics blended with cotton or rayon. An initial drawback to durable press polyesters was that stains were difficult to remove. In 1966, however, this problem was alleviated with the development of a new soil-release technique.

In the 1970s, 100 percent polyester doubleknit fabric became popular, particularly in women's sportswear and dresses. The market became saturated with clothes that looked very much alike and were almost indestructable. The fashion principle that "all fashions end in excess" applied, and polyester doubleknits became associated with bad taste. Killed by lack of style and market saturation, polyester doubleknits lost their fashion appeal by the late 1970s.

During the 1980s polyester fibers were refined and greatly diversified. Polyester became the dominant man-made fiber, a position it still maintains. In 1987 polyester fiber comprised nearly two-fifths of U.S. man-made fiber output. It is used extensively in blends with natural fibers such as wool and cotton, providing the ease of care that consumers demand.

Man-made fibers have changed both the fashion industry and the living habits of consumers. Fibers are constantly modified to meet changing consumer demand. Such developments as "wash-and-wear," "durable-press," wrinkle-resistance, and heat-set pleats have been widely accepted by consumers. These developments make the care of garments much easier and save time for the consumer. Other improvements by the textile industry, such as stain-repellent finishes, help in the upkeep of draperies, upholstery, and carpets. The use of man-made fibers in blends has also increased the popularity of these fibers. A blend is obtained when two or more types of staple fibers are joined in the textile operation producing spun yarns.

Man-made fibers have added new dimensions to the fashion industry and have assumed a dominant role in use for apparel. The use of these fibers in the United States has increased tremendously since the 1950s. In 1950 man-made fibers accounted for 22 percent of fibers used by American mills; by 1984 they provided almost 75 percent of the 11 billion pounds of fibers used annually. As natural fibers became more popular, cotton increased in use and manufactured fibers slipped to approximately 70 percent of the total American mill consumption of 12.8 billion pounds in 1987 (*Textile Organon* 1988).

Generic Names and Trademarks

When a new fiber is created, it is assigned a **generic name** by the U.S. Federal Trade Commission. Twenty-three generic names have been developed; however, not all of these fibers are used in the production of apparel and home furnishings in the United States. The twenty-three generic fiber names are:

Acetate	Lastrile*
Acrylic	Metallic
Anidex*	Modacrylic
Aramid	Novoloid*
Azlon*	Nylon
Glass	Nytril*

Olefin	Spandex
PBI	Sulfar
Polyester	Triacetate*
Rayon	Vinal*
Rubber	Vinyon
Saran	

(An * indicates that the fiber is not currently produced in the United States.)

When a fiber manufacturer produces a generic fiber, it is often given a **brand name** or **trademark.** The trademark is registered with the U.S. Patent Office, and the producer has ownership of the name. Thus only the producer, or a firm licensed by the producer, is allowed to use this name. Some generic fibers have many different manufacturers and, therefore, many different trademarks. Polyester trademarks, for example, include Dacron, Fortrel, and Kodel.

The Textile Fiber Products Identification Act of 1960 requires that all products made of textile fibers carry labels specifying the fiber content by generic name and the percentage of each kind of fiber used. Although not required by law, the brand name or trademark may also be listed on the label. Each company often uses its brand name or trademark to build recognition and acceptance for its particular product. Because of extensive advertising and promotion by fiber producers, consumers are often more familiar with the brand names of fibers than with their generic names.

Today the growth of manufactured fibers is concentrated in the innovation and improvement of already existing fibers rather than in creating new generic fibers. Fiber producers can alter a man-made fiber both chemically and physically to produce a wide variety of modifications called variants. Such fibers are engineered to fit a specific need and can be developed to produce fabrics that are flame-resistant, antistatic, colorfast, soil-resistant, or possess a variety of other characteristics. Fiber producers are turning more attention to designing fibers for specific end-uses. Celanese, for example, has developed a chemically treated fiber that has the comfort qualities of cotton while retaining the performance properties of man-made fibers. Also, a cottonlike staple polyester fiber has been developed by du Pont and is expected to replace Dacron polyester.

End-Use for Man-Made Fibers

The end-uses for man-made fibers are many and varied. Polyester, nylon, and rayon are widely used in the production of clothing. Other fibers used in clothing production are acrylic, acetate, and modacrylic. Man-made fibers are also used extensively in the home-furnishings industry. Acrylic, nylon, olefin, polyester, and rayon are important in upholstery fabrics; nylon, acrylic, and polyester are used in carpeting.

Polyester is the dominant synthetic fiber in use today, comprising, in 1985, 49 percent of world synthetic fiber production. It is widely used in men's and women's outerwear, appearing both in fabrics of 100 percent polyester and in blends with cotton, wool, or rayon. Polyester/wool blends are popular in dress fabrics and men's suits and trousers. Polyester/cotton blends dominate the men's shirt business and have extensive use in sportswear for both men and women. Home-furnishings uses of polyester are also extensive. Polyester is often blended with cotton for use as upholstery and drapery fabrics as well as in sheets, bedspreads, and comforters. Fabrics of 100 percent polyester are used in curtains.

Nylon consumed 26 percent of the world's synthetic fiber production in 1985. It is extremely important in women's hosiery and intimate apparel. Lightweight tights and sheer stockings are a virtual monopoly for nylon because of its strength, easy stretch, and nearly perfect elastic recovery. Nylon is also important in heavier stockings and socks, where it is often used as a reinforcement to improve durability. It also dominates the lingerie industry because of its excellent softness and ease-of-care. In home furnishings, nylon is important in upholstery, curtains, and carpeting. In fact, nylon dominates the carpet industry, where over 80 percent of the face fiber in carpets is nylon.

Acrylic fibers constitute about 15 percent of world man-made fiber production and are most often used in 100 percent construction rather than in blends. Since acrylics closely resemble wool in hand and warmth, they are used in many of the same apparel items, including sweaters, dresses, and skirts. Acrylic fibers are also used to simulate fur and for velvet fabrics used in loungewear and robes as well as in upholstery. Home-furnishings end-uses include carpets, upholstery, curtains, draperies, and blankets.

The cellulosic fibers, rayon and acetate, are used in women's apparel for dresses, blouses, and sportswear. These fibers are also used extensively for linings in women's wear and menswear. Home-furnishings uses include upholstery and curtain fabrics.

Marketing Man-Made Fibers

Man-made fibers are marketed as commodities or as brand-name fibers. A fiber that is marketed as a commodity is not identified with any specific brand name or trademark. The consumer who buys a product made of commodity fiber does not know the name of the company that produced it. The source of a brand-name fiber may be identified through the use of the brand name. The fiber producer may or may not have control over the use of a brand name after the fiber is sold. In some instances the fiber producer maintains quality control by insuring that only products that have satisfactorily passed certain performance tests are allowed to use the fiber brand name.

Fiber producers control the quality of textile products made from their fibers through licensed brand-name or trademark programs and product warranty programs. Under a licensed brand-name or trademark program, a textile mill pays the fiber

This tag says QUALITY
for the American consumer...

ALL-AMERICAN

WEAR-DATED®
apparel

- Tough tested for the things American consumers **want** —but cannot see. Seam strength. Color fastness. Shrink and abrasion resistance. And more.

- For durability. For style. For value. Wear-Dated tags say "Made in America."

WEAR-DATED®
Made in America.

Wear-Dated® is a registered trademark of Monsanto company.

MFIC-5-238

Monsanto's Wear-Dated warranty is a product warranty program offering consumers a guarantee that the textile product will perform as claimed within a stated time period.
Source: Reprinted with permission of the Monsanto Company.

producer for the use of the trade name. Fiber hangtags may then be attached to the garments or other manufactured products identifying the fiber's trade name. Extensive advertising is often done by fiber producers to acquaint consumers with the quality standards of their fiber brand names. In some instances a licensed brand-name or trademark program is controlled by the fiber producer, meaning that the product meets a certain prescribed level of quality.

Product warranty programs offer a guarantee that the textile product will perform as claimed within a stated time period. If a product does not perform as claimed, the customer is compensated for the loss. An example of this type of program is Monsanto's "Wear-Dated" warranty, which assures either replacement or cash refund if the garment containing Monsanto fibers fails to give normal wear for one full year from the date of purchase. Many fiber companies find these types of programs to be important marketing tools. Such programs give fiber companies control over the quality of the final product in addition to control over the fiber.

In addition to licensed brand-name and product warranty programs, man-made fibers are marketed by fiber producers in much the same way as natural fibers are marketed. Several of the large fiber producers, such as du Pont, Hoechst Celanese, and Monsanto, maintain marketing staffs who promote the use of their fibers to textile manufacturers and retailers. Fiber companies often maintain fabric libraries and offer cooperative advertising programs to encourage the use and promotion of their fibers.

American Fiber Manufacturers Association, Inc. The American Fiber Manufacturers Association (formerly called the Man-Made Fiber Producers Association), based in Washington, D.C., promotes the use of man-made fibers. Members of the association include the primary producers of these fibers. Promotional activities include films, visual aids, publications, and other educational literature. Such promotional aids are made available to manufacturers, retailers, and consumers. Among the publications of the association are the *Manufactured Fiber Fact Book, Quick Guide to Manufactured Fibers,* and *Manufactured Fiber Guide.*

The members of the American Fiber Manufacturers Association are:

Allied-Signal, Inc.	Fiber Industries, Inc.
American Cyanamid Company	Hercules Incorporated
Amoco Fabrics & Fibers Company	Hoechst Celanese Corporation
Avtex Fibers Inc.	Monsanto Chemical Company
BASF Corporation	North American Rayon Corporation
Courtaulds Fibers, Inc.	Phillips Fibers Corporation (subsidiary of Phillips 66 Company)
E.I. du Pont de Nemours & Company, Inc.	Tolaram Fibers, Inc.
Eastman Chemical Products, Inc.	

Textile Producers

The major role of the textile industry is to make fibers into yarn and convert yarn into fabrics. Yarns are made from either staple or filament fibers. Staple fibers are short in length, varying from an inch to several inches, whereas filament fibers are of indefinite length. A mass of fiber is converted into yarn by a process called spinning, which consists of the drawing, twisting, and winding of the newly spun yarn onto a device such as a bobbin, spindle, or tube.

A **textile mill** owns textile machinery and produces fabric. Although fabrics may be constructed by a variety of methods, weaving and knitting are the most common methods of production for fabrics used in the apparel and home-furnishings industries. Most fabrics, especially in woven goods, are produced as unfinished fabrics called **gray goods.** Such unfinished goods are sent to converters or finishers for the final steps in fabric production.

The textile industry includes thousands of plants or mills that perform one or more of the processes involved in the production of fabric. Some mills may perform only one phase of a process. For example, a mill may do only one type of finishing, such as bleaching, dyeing, or printing. There are also firms that limit themselves to one narrow product line, such as corduroy or velvet, whereas some mills make only knits, brocades, or novelty fabrics.

The textile industry also includes companies that perform all processes of production such as spinning, weaving, dyeing, and finishing. This type of operation is referred to as a vertically integrated company. Many of today's large textile mills are vertically integrated. They not only make fabric, but they also produce their own yarn and perform the finishing processes required after the fabric is manufactured as gray goods. Such integrated mills do not, however, produce their own fibers. Listed in Table 4.2 are the twelve largest textile companies in the United States and their sales for 1987.

Converters

Textile mills sell their fabrics to **converters,** manufacturers, and/or jobbers. Mills may also sell to retailers who provide fabrics for home sewers. A converter is an individual or a firm that buys gray goods from a mill and has these goods dyed, printed, or finished by other companies before selling the finished fabric to manufacturers or retailers. A true converter serves as a middleman, buying gray goods from mills and contracting with a finisher to perform the needed processes to prepare the fabric to be marketed.

In the 1960s many large textile mills became vertically integrated and moved into the converting business. Thus an integrated converter is part of a large vertical mill that finishes fabrics in its own plants or itself seeks outside finishers to complete the gray goods. The trend in verticalization has continued but today remains concentrated in basic goods rather than fashion goods.

Converters sell their finished fabrics to manufacturers, jobbers, and retail stores.

Table 4.2. Sales of Top Twelve U.S. Textile Mills

Name	Annual sales 1987 (millions of dollars)
Burlington Holdings	3,279
Armstrong World Industries	2,367
West Point-Pepperell	2,067
Springs Industries	1,661
J. P. Stevens[a]	1,615
Fieldcrest Cannon	1,400
DWG	1,214
United Merchants and Manufacturers	762
Shaw Industries	694
Dixie Yarns	581
Guilford Mills	539
Russell	480

Source: *Fortune Magazine*, April 25, 1988, p. 54.
[a] *Purchased by West Point-Pepperell in 1988.*

Sometimes a converter will buy fabric from another converter if the firm is not able to buy enough gray goods from mills to cover an order. The majority of fabric used by converters is American-made. Only about 15 percent of the goods used by converters in the United States is imported (Klapper 1988).

The system of converters within the textile industry offers considerable flexibility and provides for more consistent use of specialized machinery. Converting is a very creative industry. Small converters respond better and differently to fashion change than do big mills. Smaller companies can make available small yardages of fashion goods and are able to respond faster to the demands of manufacturers and retailers.

Jobbers

Jobbers buy fabrics from various sources, including mills, converters, and apparel manufacturers. They often buy fabrics that have been discontinued or are mill overruns. If a mill produces more fabrics than it has orders for, an overrun exists, and jobbers provide a means for the mills to sell this fabric. Jobbers provide a source of fabric for firms wanting to buy small quantities and promotionally priced goods. Jobbers often are able to buy fabrics at a low price because they help mills dispose of surplus fabric or discontinued colors, styles, or prints.

Jobbers are located in cities where fabrics are marketed to the industry and where apparel manufacturing occurs. Many fabric jobbers are found in New York City, concentrated in the lower Broadway–Canal Street area and in the Seventh Avenue–37th Street area, where many apparel manufacturers and their showrooms are located.

THE PRODUCTION OF FASHION

Purchasing of Fabrics

Fabrics are often purchased from samples provided by the mills, or they may be purchased through specification buying. When buying by specification, the fabric buyer spells out every detail of the fabric, including such information as yarns per inch, width, weight, thickness, breaking strength, and color. The fabric mill then follows these stated specifications in producing the fabric.

When buying from samples, the fabric buyer or designer makes a selection, often with the advice of the textile mill's sales representative. Sample cuts of a few yards are then ordered for the designer to make up sample garments to illustrate his or her design ideas. After final decisions are made about what new designs will be shown to customers, more fabric is ordered so that duplicate sample garments can be made to show to retail buyers at markets and to be used by road salespeople. After orders are placed on the sample garments, the manufacturer determines production needs and orders the needed fabric for mass production. Sometimes fabric is reordered if an item proves to be a hot seller.

A manufacturer may request that a particular color, design, or fabric be confined to his or her company. The mill or converter is likely to agree to this, provided that an order is very large. Usually the confinement is limited to one end-use segment of the industry. Thus if the confinement is for women's dresses, the same fabric could be sold to companies making items for other end-uses.

Marketing of Fabrics

Many large textile firms, like the fiber companies, promote the use of their fabrics by providing information on new fashion trends to designers, apparel manufacturers, and retailers. Services offered by the textile industry include fabric libraries, color charts, fashion projections, and textile directories. Textile trade associations also develop directories that list textile firms alphabetically and by category. These directories also include sources for trims, linings, and other findings.

Textile Trade Shows

Textiles are marketed to the trade by means of trade shows and fairs where producers exhibit their latest products. American fiber and fabric producers participate in textile trade shows both in the United States and in other countries. Trade shows not only stimulate sales for the textile producer, but they inform all segments of the fashion industry about new developments and trends. They are a convenient way for designers and manufacturers to view a variety of merchandise in one location.

Fiber producers schedule their presentations up to two years ahead of a season, presenting to textile mills and converters early so that they have sufficient time to plan their color and fabric lines. Fabric producers plan presentations one year in advance of a season to show their products to designers and manufacturers of ready-to-wear and accessories as well as to retail piece goods buyers and the fashion press.

The **Bobbin Show,** the world's largest annual exposition for the sewn products industry, has been held each year since 1960 and includes exhibitors who supply everything from fabric to new machinery and technology. The 1986 Bobbin Show in Atlanta, Georgia, presented expanded exhibits by textile firms and emphasized the importance of buying domestic fabrics over imports. A fabric resourcing room was set up to enable textile manufacturers and designers to meet and view fabrics not selected to appear in the market for several seasons.

The Annual Knitting Yarn Fair is held each year in September in New York City. The three-day fair is the world's largest yarn show. The fair is sponsored by the National Knitwear and Sportswear Association and features natural and man-made yarns and blends. New dyeing and knitting techniques are also presented at the fair. Designers and manufacturers of knitwear, sportswear, general apparel, and home furnishings attend the fair.

The Trimmings, Accessories and Fabrics Expo (TAFE) is held in New York City for the purpose of presenting new trimmings and fabrics from domestic and international suppliers. Fashion trends and developments in trimmings, accessories, and fabrics are shown at this fair. The TAFE is sponsored by the National Knitwear and Sportswear Association. The fair is important to designers and manufacturers, especially since it saves them time in seeking new offerings.

Foreign textile shows and fairs are important for forecasting fashion trends and for manufacturers of higher-priced designer apparel. Many buyers attend several shows to stay on top of the market and abreast of the fashion trends. At such shows fabric producers show new designs and fabric textures for use in the following year's fashion apparel and accessories. Premiere Vision in Paris launches the fabric season twice a year. It is followed in May and November by **Interstoff,** one of the most comprehensive international textile trade shows, held in Frankfort, West Germany. There were 1,070 exhibitors from 39 countries at the November 1985 Interstoff fabric fair. About 12,000 people, 180 from the United States, attended the fair. *Women's Wear Daily* reported that many U.S. buyers use Interstoff to place orders on samples collected at Premiere Vision or to confirm trends (Cochran 1985). Italian fabric producers exhibit their new fabrics at the well-known trade show **Ideacomo,** held in Como, Italy. Other foreign textile fairs include Texitalia, in Milan, Italy, and the Canton Trade Fair, in Canton, China.

Predicting Fashion Trends

Fabric production takes place approximately twelve to eighteen months before garments made of these fabrics are available in retail stores. Since the textile industry must work several seasons ahead of consumer demand, recognizing fashion trends and consumer preferences is important. In order to develop early fashion projections, many textile producers maintain fashion staffs to analyze consumers' preferences and to predict fashion trends. The members of these fashion staffs work closely with designers and manufacturers to determine what styles consumers will accept. Fashion trends are also projected by analyzing the fashion press, by visiting the world's fashion centers, and by observing fashion leaders. Some textile companies conduct

i n t e r s t o f f

Frankfurt, 11.4. – 13.4.1989

Those seeking an adventure need only wait until the summer of 1990. The call of the wild will beckon from Arizona to the Amazonas and full of yearning, we'll answer. Whether strolling through tropical gardens, or wandering through Navaho country where we'll once again note with surprise: The desert lives. We're certain that the „Blues" will jump in common time from the clubs of the 30's to the fashion of the 90's. The lords of creation will finally rediscover the Silk Route and those in love with nature will let themselves be enveloped by its softness. Without a doubt, the summer will be colorful and exciting. Because Monsieur Hulot is inviting us all to a picnic. And once again in Frankfurt you'll be inspired by the right idea for every imaginable topic. The competition will be fierce but fair, and everyone will somehow come out a winner. Because Frankfurt has enough for everyone. interstoff, TrendSet for fashion.

GGK

i n t e r s t o f f

For information, travel reservations, tickets:
German-American Chamber of Commerce, Inc.
666 Fifth Avenue
New York, N.Y. 10103
Tel.: (212) 974-8830
Telex: RCA 234209 GACC UR
Telefax: (212) 974-8867

Please send, free of charge, Preliminary List of Exhibitors to:

_____
Name

_____
Company

_____
Street

_____
Postbox

_____
City/State + Zip Code

_____ DNR

Messe Frankfurt

Interstoff Fabric Fair is one of the most comprehensive international textile trade shows.
Source: _Reprinted with permission of the German-American Chamber of Commerce._

research to analyze and predict trends. Once ideas and recommendations are determined, textile companies produce fibers and fabrics accordingly.

Color Standards

Color is an important element in any fabric. Color is often the first factor the customer considers in selecting or rejecting a garment or a home-furnishings product. An unappealing color may make a fabric unmarketable no matter what other outstanding qualities it possesses. Textile products are dyed or printed with the end-use in mind so that the color and/or print will be suitable and in line with fashion trends.

The textile designer or colorist selects colors based on end-use requirements and predicted consumer preferences. The dyer uses skillful blending of dyes to match colors. Color formulas are first developed in the laboratory. Sometimes computers are used to develop color formulas.

Color standards are used to provide a common color understanding among the fashion industries. American color standards are available from two places: the National Bureau of Standards in Washington, D.C., and the Color Association of the United States (CAUS), based in New York.

The **Color Association of the United States** (CAUS) has been establishing color standards since its formation in 1915. The development of color standards became a necessity because World War I cut off the U.S. supply of German dyestuffs. Thus the American textile industry, manufacturers, and retailers no longer had standards that could provide a common color understanding. To solve this problem a group of presidents of American textile companies met in New York City to establish and issue America's first national color standards.

The first edition of *The Standard American Color Reference* in 1915 presented 106 color shades illustrated by silk ribbon samples. Included among these colors were college colors such as Yale blue, gem colors (garnet, topaz), colors based on foodstuffs (apricot, chestnut, eggplant, lemon, olive, prune), on wines and liquors (burgundy, champagne, claret, chartreuse), on animals (beaver, fawn, seal), on birds (cardinal, peacock), on flowers (geranium, lavender, lilac, pansy, violet, wisteria, wild rose), on plants and shrubs (goldenrod, maize, sage), on military colors, and on precious metals (gold, old gold, silver) (Walch 1984).

The increased importance of color in fashion is illustrated by the tenth edition of *The Standard American Color Reference,* published in 1981, which contains almost double the number of standard colors included in the first edition. Many of the colors in the 1981 edition are the same as those that appeared in the original edition.

Color Prediction

One function of the Color Association of the United States (CAUS) is to recommend colors for use in yarns and fabrics. Forecasts are made twice annually for the women's wear, menswear, and children's wear industries. Color forecasts are published once a year for the interior design industry. CAUS brings together experts in the field of color styling, color research, marketing, and merchandising. Separate committees of eight to twelve experts from women's wear, menswear, and the interior design industries meet two years in advance of a selling season and project the shades they expect to be popular. These experts also make recommendations regarding the types of fabrics to be used. Apparel shades evolve in twenty-four-month cycles, whereas palettes in interior design and home furnishings enjoy acceptances of approximately seven to ten years.

Color charts are assembled by CAUS and made available to fashion firms twice a year. The textiles and yarns for the charts are donated by the textiles industry and are custom-dyed to the specifications of the Color Association. All sections of the fashion industry use these charts as a guide to follow in determining their offerings; thus it is no accident that many firms follow the same color direction each season. Such color direction provides coordination within the industry so that various products will match; thus the consumer can buy shoes, scarves, and other accessories in colors that will coordinate with ready-to-wear. In the home-furnishings industry, it means that colors are available in upholstered furniture, draperies, carpeting, and home accessories that will work together.

Two international color groups meet to project colors on a worldwide basis: the International Color Authority (ICA) and Inter-Color. Both of these groups meet twice a year and include fashion representatives from throughout the world.

The **International Color Authority** (ICA) promotes itself as "the world's number 1 fashions color forecast for menswear, women's wear and home/interiors." The ICA describes its function as "to assist dyers, spinners, weavers and clothing manufacturers to make soundly based long term decisions." Colors are predicted twenty months in advance of the selling season and forecasts are available in March and September. Color cards are designed to be used as a book or wall chart. Key colors are sampled in twists of yarn, and extra detachable samples of all the shades are provided. Separate forecasts for women's wear, menswear, and home furnishings are also offered fourteen months in advance of the selling season in August and February. Another edition of ICA color forecasts designed for the retailer is published eight months ahead of the selling season. Interested parties in the fashion industry subscribe to the services of the ICA to receive these color charts.

Development of the Textile Industry

Spinning fiber into yarn is an ancient craft. Its recorded history dates back to evidence of spindles uncovered in archaeological digs studying Stone Age man in Switzerland. Spinning remained an incredibly slow and tedious task until the sixteenth century, when the spinning wheel was invented.

The production of textiles by factory methods began in England during the eighteenth century when, as part of the Industrial Revolution, a series of inventions converted the art of spinning and weaving into an industry. The invention of the flying shuttle by John Kay in 1733 led the way to mechanically powered weaving.

The invention of James Hargreaves' spinning jenny in 1764, of Richard Arkwright's waterframe in 1768, and of Samuel Crompton's mule in 1779 provided the means of producing yarn that stimulated loom development. The faster methods for spinning fibers into yarns created a surplus of yarns, more than the hand looms of the times could weave into cloth. Thus mechanization of the loom became a necessity if the textile industry were to move forward. Edmund Cartwright made this possible in 1787 with his first practical power loom, and two years later he set up a steam-driven weaving mill with 400 looms. By the beginning of the nineteenth century, the textile industry in England was well under way.

In the early days of the American colonies, production of yarn and fabric was primarily a household industry. Women performed all the processes necessary to transform flax into linen and fleece into woolen fabric. For those who did not weave their own fabrics, itinerant weavers traveled from village to village setting up their looms and weaving into cloth all the woolen or linen yarn that the women had spun since the weaver last visited. One fabric thus produced was called linsey-woolsey, functional but not of high quality.

The first commercial textile enterprise in the colonies was established in 1643 when twenty families of Yorkshire clothmakers migrated to Rowley, Massachusetts, where they established a fulling mill in which greasy matter was removed from new woolens and the cloth was soaked to shrink and thicken it. Families from other European cloth-making towns soon followed, bringing with them their knowledge of spinning and weaving, and establishing textile enterprises in other New England villages.

As early as 1646, the colony of Virginia had two spinning houses in operation where poor children were taught to spin fibers into yarn. Similar establishments were organized elsewhere. Further steps in the development of the textile industry were taken by the United Company of Philadelphia, which during the Revolutionary War employed as many as 500 workers at one time in the production of cotton fabric. Most of them worked in their own homes, but others performed their chores in a central building. The United Company used horsepower for some of its processes and owned a few spinning jennies.

In 1789 the factory method was brought to the United States by Samuel Slater, a twenty-two-year-old English mechanic who had learned the textiles business while serving as an apprentice to Richard Arkwright, inventor of the spinning frame. The British government tried to secure a monopoly on the new technology of the textile industry by prohibiting both the exportation of machinery and the emigration of artisans. Slater left England, however, disguised as a farmer to avoid the British ban on emigration. He was able to reproduce the Arkwright machinery by memory, and in 1790 he established, in Pawtucket, Rhode Island, the first American spinning mill to employ water power. By 1800 four such mills were operating in Rhode Island, three in Connecticut, and one in Massachusetts.

Another important invention for the American textile industry was introduced in 1793 when Eli Whitney developed the cotton gin, a machine that separated cotton fibers from the seeds of the cotton boll. Whitney's gin could separate fifty pounds of cotton lint in a day; removing the seed from a single pound of cotton had previously required ten hours of labor. The gin helped pave the way for the leadership role played by cotton in the expansion of the textile industry.

American textile manufacturing enjoyed its first great boom during the War of 1812, which caused textile imports from Great Britain to cease. Furthermore, the war created a demand for fabric for uniforms and blankets. By the end of the war the investment in cotton manufacture was estimated to be $40 million, with 100,000 workers engaged in the industry. Woolen manufacture was also expanded. The War of 1812 marked many changes in the American way of life, from the replacement of knee breeches with the new fashion of trousers to the beginning shift of industry from homes to factories. By the end of the war there were 170 mills; however, only 5 percent of the textile manufacture came from factories. Gradually factories began to flourish, and fabric making became an industry.

In 1814 Francis Cabot Lowell, a Boston merchant, returned from a visit to English mills to build the first factory that incorporated under one roof all processes to convert raw cotton to woven fabric. Lowell built power looms that were superior to most others and applied his managerial skill to an important experiment in textile manufacturing. At the Boston Manufacturing Company, which he opened in Waltham, Massachusetts, all operations of cloth making were performed by power at a central point. Lowell's Waltham model was soon widely copied.

By 1828 the United States was the second largest consumer of cotton after England, and by 1840 three-fourths of all cotton goods used in America were produced by New England mills. By 1850 there were 1,240 cotton mills located in New England. As for the woolen industry, some 1,600 plants in 32 states were registered in the Census of 1850, employing 50,000 workers and producing finished goods worth $40 million. More Americans worked in textile mills than in any other industry at the time.

The Civil War contributed to the growth of the textile industry in New England. The urgent need for military uniforms caused the sheep and wool industries to flourish. It was estimated that each federal soldier needed fifty pounds of grease wool (newly sheared unwashed fleece) a year. By the end of the war in 1865, methods for mass production of American fabrics had made significant progress. By 1870 the manufacture of cotton fabric was one of the leading U.S. industries. With the expansion of domestic output, the market center for American textile mills was established in downtown Manhattan on and near Worth Street. This area remained the market center for textiles until after World War II, when textile mills began moving their showrooms uptown to be closer to the apparel industry.

Throughout the nineteenth century, most textile mills were located in New England. Gradually, however, cotton textile mills began to shift to the South, where advantages included abundance of water power, proximity to raw materials, available labor supply, and lower wages. By 1920 more than half of the spinning and weaving operations of cotton textiles were located in the South. During the 1920s the textile factories of Virginia, North and South Carolina, and Georgia expanded their operations.

By the 1940s the textile industry was experiencing a trend toward integration and diversification. Some firms began to expand by means of mergers and acquisitions. For example, Burlington Industries, which had originally specialized in woven rayon fabrics, acquired hosiery mills in 1939 and by the mid-1940s produced nylon parachute cloth. Today, Burlington produces fabrics, hosiery, carpets, household linens, and many other products. Independent selling agents such as J. P. Stevens began to integrate by acquiring their own textile mills and finishing plants.

Characteristics of Today's Textile Industry

The textile industry plays a vital role in the economy of the United States, with textile mill products contributing an estimated $57.5 billion to the U.S. Gross National Product in 1987 (U.S. Industrial Outlook 1988, p. 44). More than 5,000 companies operate approximately 6,600 mills engaged in the preparation of fiber and manufacture of yarn, and the manufacture of fabrics, rugs and carpets, and fabric finishing. These mills are concentrated in the eastern United States with ten states accounting for 85 percent of the total value of shipments. North Carolina is the leader, accounting for more than one-fourth of textile production, followed by Georgia with 19 percent, and South Carolina with 14 percent. The remaining states among the top ten textile producers include Virginia, Pennsylvania, Alabama, New York, Tennessee, Massachusetts, and New Jersey.

Employment in the textile industry in 1987 consisted of 689,600 workers, with women accounting for about 47 percent of total industry employment. Wages in the industry are well below the average for all manufacturing; average earnings in 1987 were $7.40 an hour. Future textile jobs are expected to include fewer low-paid, entry-level positions and more positions for highly trained operators and technicians. The nature of textile firms and the jobs involved are expected to change dramatically as the industry becomes more automated.

The textile industry has historically been highly fragmented into various segments, including fiber producers, yarn and fabric manufacturers, and finishers. Today, companies performing the tasks of production vary greatly by size and specialization. Large companies both supply fabrics to apparel manufacturers and sell finished products such as sheets and towels to retailers. Although such large companies as Burlington Industries, West Point–Pepperell, Springs Industries, Fieldcrest Cannon, and Guilford Mills have become increasingly important, many smaller companies still exist. Some still specialize in a specific activity of the industry, producing yarns or providing specialized finishing techniques. A number of small companies today have identified special product niches and have become leading suppliers of these products.

The system of converters and jobbers is still important within the industry in producing and distributing textile products. Because the industry involves many complex processes necessary to convert fiber into consumer goods, contractors make this system more efficient.

Textile production is highly dependent upon consumer demand for clothing and home-furnishings products and is greatly impacted by changing fashion. Although textile mill production and shipments tend to follow store sales, deviations from the trend often occur because retailers sometimes overbuy and cut back on purchases in order to adjust their inventories.

In 1985 about 38 percent of all textile fibers consumed in the United States went to home furnishings, approximately 37 percent were used in apparel, and 22 percent were used for other consumer-type fabrics and industrial uses. Of the 37 percent of total textile fiber used for apparel, approximately 43 percent went into bottomweight fabrics, which are used to make pants, sportswear, tailored clothing, and career apparel. More than 19 percent of apparel fiber used in 1985 was for the manufacture of topweight fabrics, which include shirts, blouses, and lightweight dresses. The retail piece goods market, which produces fabrics used for home sewing, used about 5.4 percent of all apparel fabrics. About 16 percent of apparel fibers went into the various fabrics used for underwear, nightwear, linings, loungewear and robes, and high-pile fabrics for outerwear.

Recent Developments in the Textile Industry

Many changes have occurred in the U.S. textile industry since its inception in the late eighteenth century. The pace of change in the industry has accelerated throughout the twentieth century as advanced technology and automation have moved it from labor-intensive to capital-intensive. Reaction to imports of foreign-produced textiles has changed the industry's structure in recent years. It has responded to imports by restructuring, consolidating, and modernizing. Many outmoded, inefficient plants have been closed. In remaining plants, productivity has been boosted by investing in advanced technology and automation and by focusing on import-resistant areas that are more service-oriented.

Competition from Imports

Although the U.S. textile and apparel industries have extensive capacity for production, considerable amounts of textiles and apparel goods are imported from other countries. Textile and apparel imports doubled between 1980 and 1985, claiming more than 50 percent of the clothing market in the United States. The U.S. textile and apparel trade deficit was $21.2 billion for 1986; total exports of $2.57 billion were dwarfed by $24.7 billion of imports. During the last several years, Japan has been the primary supplier of textile goods to the United States as measured in dollar value, whereas Italy has been the second largest supplier, followed by South Korea, China, and Taiwan (U.S. Industrial Outlook 1988).

As textile imports have increased, the textile industry in the United States has experienced a downward trend in employment. According to the Fiber, Fabric, and Apparel Coalition for Trade, approximately 300,000 jobs were lost between 1980 and 1985. This decline was attributed primarily to imports, but other contributing factors were industry automation and cost-cutting measures. In 1987 employment in the textile industry increased slightly for the first time in the 1980s, as about 20,000 new workers were hired.

It has been predicted that the rate of growth of textile imports will level off in the 1990s because restructuring has made the industry more competitive in the world marketplace. The leading market for U.S. textile exports is Canada. Other important markets are in Western Europe, especially Italy and the United Kingdom.

''Crafted with Pride''

The **Crafted with Pride in the U.S.A.** campaign was developed as a response to the growing threat of imports to American jobs and to the survival of the textile and apparel industries. Sponsored by the American Fiber, Textile, and Apparel Coalition, which includes fiber growers and processors, textile manufacturers, trade unions, and trade associations, this campaign was the first industrywide effort to challenge the problem of imports by promoting the purchase of American-made products. The campaign included "buy American" national television commercials featuring such celebrities as Bob Hope, O. J. Simpson, and Carol Channing. The

The Crafted with Pride in U.S.A. logo was developed in an effort to challenge the problem of imports by promoting the purchase of American-made products.
Source: Reprinted with permission of Crafted with Pride in U.S.A. Council, Inc.

campaign also developed a symbol and slogan to use in advertising and on labels attached to textile products. The logo is a red-white-and-blue star circled by the slogan "Crafted with Pride in U.S.A."

"Crafted with Pride" stands for pride in quality textile and apparel products and in the people who produce them. It reinforces the message that buying American-made merchandise is not only an investment in the communities where textile and apparel employees live, but also means a healthy economy for all Americans. The response of the American public to these efforts is somewhat uncertain. Public opinion surveys taken by national polling organizations found that approximately 70 percent of those surveyed preferred American-made apparel. However, a nationwide telephone survey conducted by the *Wall Street Journal* and NBC News found that when consumers were asked to name the two most important factors when shopping for clothes, only 18 percent responded "national origin." This placed fourth after "fit" (64 percent), "price" (32 percent), and "style" (25 percent). Although responses to surveys suggest that consumers are sympathetic to the workers employed in industries endangered by imports, they continue to purchase textile products that fit, look good, and are priced right.

"Quick Response"

Quick Response was born out of the Crafted with Pride campaign as another industry strategy for fighting imports. The program aids companies in developing programs to increase efficiency and thereby improve profitability and sales. Quick Response aims to make the industry more responsive to customers' changing needs. It seeks to shorten the time needed to get merchandise from the textile supplier to the apparel producer and into the retail store. For textile mills, Quick Response means adopting the technology to produce short runs of fabric, using computerized designing equipment to speed production, and faster handling of shipping. To be successful, Quick Response requires close communications among all segments of the fashion industry. Programs have been developed for exchanging data electronically, and computerized bar coding is being used to improve the speed with which suppliers can respond to fabric producers' demands. New Quick Response information technologies have the potential to unite the entire fiber-yarn-fabric-apparel-retail network in ways that will result in greater responsiveness to changing consumer preferences.

The textile industry is benefiting in several ways from Quick Response programs. Sales are increased because of quicker response time to consumer needs. Less investment is needed in raw materials and inventories. Quality of goods is improved by an increased emphasis on preventing defects, and greater profit occurs because less surplus goods are produced; therefore, there is less need to discount excess inventory to encourage its sale.

Restructuring and Consolidation

As sharply rising imports intensified competition within the textile industry throughout the 1980s, a number of major textile manufacturers responded with restructuring and consolidations. Mergers and acquisitions within the industry have increased horizontal integration and have reduced the number of textile companies. Both plant closings and openings have been numerous. Many older, outdated plants, especially those producing apparel fabrics, have closed, about 350 between 1981 and 1987. In some cases manufacturers have de-emphasized merchandise classifications in which import competition is strong.

Other examples of restructuring in the textile industry include acquisitions in specialized areas or elimination of unprofitable and peripheral businesses. Burlington Industries, for example, purchased C. H. Masland, a carpet manufacturer, while remaining in the apparel fabrics business. Burlington's restructuring also involved the disposition of businesses with sales totaling $600 million and the closing of seventy-four plants. Companies are also emphasizing research and development to find new products or new applications for existing products.

Advanced Technology and Automation

Modernization efforts and the introduction of advanced technology have greatly improved textile production methods during the 1980s. Numerous techniques and processes have improved yarn spinning and fabric weaving, leading to greater capacity with fewer employees. Use of shuttleless looms has increased the speed and efficiency of woven fabric production four times over. In addition, these looms require less floor space. Textile mill productivity increased 5.6 percent annually between 1975 and 1985. This trend is expected to continue with the likelihood of wider use of robots and electronics in the future.

Increasing productivity has required costly capital outlays. Many mills that have not been able to afford this have gone out of business. Plants that lack the resources to improve manufacturing productivity, asset management, marketing, and distribution systems face extinction over the long term.

Product Diversification

Some textile mills have stopped serving markets that offer little or no growth potential and have turned to markets offering less competition from imports. A number have de-emphasized finished apparel fabrics and reoriented their production toward industrial fabrics and the growing home-furnishings markets. Although homes are smaller in size and the rental proportion of homes has increased, the home has become a focus of status and individual style. Virtually all home-furnishings fabric applications expanded in the 1980s because home-fashion trends emphasized more abundant use of fabric and more luxurious fabrics. This raised sales volume for the textile industry led to the development of some new fabric applications, especially in the bedroom.

The trend to textile luxury and abundance is evident in bed and bath linens. Popular interior design trends call for coordinated sheets, comforters, dust ruffles, pillows, blankets, window coverings, tablecovers, and even upholstered headboards and wall fabrics. The trend to luxury is illustrated by the fact that the dominant blend in sheeting is now a 180-thread count, 50/50 cotton polyester blend, and luxurious all-cotton in 200-thread count sheets are growing in popularity. Many of these are sold under a designer name.

New products have been developed, increasing opportunities for the textile industry. Slumber bags and especially designed prints in bed and bath linens for children, throws for use in bedroom and living room, and high-priced fleece mattress pads are examples of new textile products in the home-furnishings market.

The Leather Industry

Leather is an important raw material used by the fashion industry. It is animal hides and skins that have been preserved by tanning. Leather, one of the oldest raw materials used for clothing, was worn as garments long before fabrics were produced. As early as 20,000 B.C., primitive people wore skins of animals. In some early cultures, leather goods were considered to have magical powers and were worn or carried for protection against evil spirits. Years before humans learned to plant cotton and spin yarn, the processes for preserving hides were developed. Decorated leather sandals were discovered in Egyptian tombs, and leather items were uncovered in excavations of ancient Crete.

The process of preserving animal skins and making leather is referred to as **tanning.** Processing leather goods is time consuming and highly specialized. Because of the detailed steps involved, fashion trends for leather goods have to be identified well in advance of most other fashion items. Leather producers make production decisions from eight to sixteen months ahead of the need for leather goods by apparel and accessory manufacturers.

The methods used in tanning leather have improved since 1900. The development of specialized machinery has made it possible to provide consumers with a wide assortment of leather products. New finishes, types of grains, patterns, textures, and properties have been incorporated into the production of leather goods. New chemical treatments have reduced the time required to transform hides and skins into leather. The solutions for tanning can be easily controlled to assure uniformity of leather products.

Most leather hides and skins produced in the United States are a by-product of the meat-packing industry; therefore, their supply depends on the demand for meat rather than for leather. The most dominant leather is cattlehide, which accounts for 88 percent of the shipments by the U.S. tanning and finishing industry. Other leathers are obtained from the hides and skins of calves, goats, sheep, horses, and pigs. Reptile skins from animals such as lizards, snakes, and alligators are also used. Leather is priced by the square foot and is available in a variety of thicknesses and weights. Animal skins weighing under twenty-five pounds are called **kips,** and skins weighing over twenty-five pounds are called hides. Hides are obtained from cattle, ox, buffalo, and horse skins.

Today, durable leather can be produced with deep colors and rich textures. Leather is particularly important in fashion accessories for the production of shoes, handbags, belts, gloves, various small leather goods such as wallets and billfolds, and cases for eyeglasses, cigarettes, and keys. Leather is used in the production of apparel, including jackets, coats, vests, dresses, pants, and skirts. In the home-furnishings industry, leather is used for upholstery.

Organization and Operation of the Leather Industry

Leather and leather products include seven industries: (1) leather tanning and finishing, (2) nonrubber footwear, (3) gloves and mittens, (4) luggage, (5) handbags, (6) small leather goods, and (7) wearing apparel. In 1987 these industries employed an estimated 122,500 people and shipped leather and leather products valued at $8.2 billion. Footwear, the largest of these industries, had shipments of $4.1 billion. The value of leather tanning and finishing industry shipments was $2.04 billion, and the remaining five of the leather industries had shipments valued at $1.82 billion. Table 4.3 shows the distribution of shipments by the seven U.S. leather industries (U.S. Industrial Outlook 1988).

Tanning and Finishing

The leather tanning and finishing industry consists of establishments primarily engaged in transforming raw or cured hides and skins into leather. The industry also includes leather converters and dealers who buy hides and skins and contract with processors to have them tanned and finished. The processing of leather includes tanning, currying, and finishing. Tanning preserves the skin and improves its natural physical properties by applying various substances such as vegetable materials, oils,

Table 4.3. Value of Leather Industry Shipments in 1987

Industry	Shipments (million $)	Percent of leather industry total
Nonrubber footwear	4150	50
Leather tanning and finishing	2040	25
Luggage	732	9
Handbags	500	7
Small leather goods	390	5
Gloves and mittens	180	2
Leather wearing apparel	172	2

Source: U.S. Industrial Outlook 1988.

THE PRODUCTION OF FASHION

or chemicals. Most commonly used in the United States is chrome. Hides or skins that have been chrome-tanned but not yet finished are referred to as "in the blue." After leather is tanned, it must be dyed and finished before it is ready to be sold to manufacturers. Currying is a process used to treat tanned leather by incorporating oil or grease. Finishing involves proceses such as embossing, napping, and glazing. Embossing presses a pattern onto leather, often to give it the appearance of a more expensive skin such as alligator or lizard. Napping changes the texture by raising the surface. Glazing creates a shiny surface, and another finish uses aniline to produce finished leather with a highly polished surface.

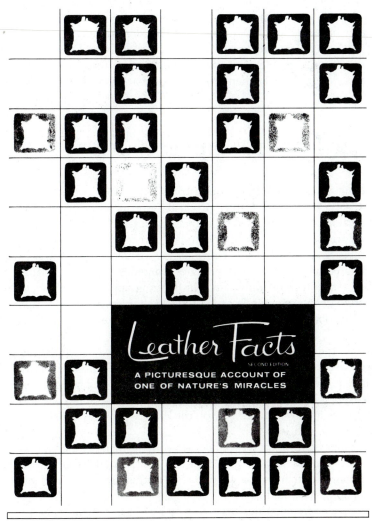

The trade association *The New England Tanners Club publishes* Leather Facts *to promote the leather industry.*

In recent years the U.S. leather industry has experienced considerable contraction and consolidation. For example, in 1982 the tanning and finishing industries consisted of 342 companies operating 384 plants. By 1987 only an estimated 136 establishments were directly tanning raw hides and skins into leather. Employment within the industry has also been reduced from 15,800 workers in 1984 to 13,100 in 1987 (U.S. Industrial Outlook 1988).

Most of the tanning and finishing plants are located in the northeastern and north-central states. Tanneries are concentrated in Wisconsin, Maine, Massachusetts, New York, and Pennsylvania. Also located in these states are the leather tanners' and finishers' major customers, the manufacturers of shoes, apparel, and accessories. The largest market for the tanning industry is the footwear industry, which consumes approximately 60 percent of leather shipments. Marketing and sales offices for the major leather firms are located in New York City. Unlike fiber and textile producers, names of leather tanners and finishers are not well known. These producers do not promote their names to the consuming public. Advertising is done by the manufacturers and designers of leather products but not by the leather producers themselves.

Leather Imports and Exports

Like the textile industry, the leather industry is facing stiff competition from imports. Imports of both leather and leather products have increased dramatically in recent years. The value of U.S. imports of leather and leather products in 1987 was $9.91 billion compared to exports of $669 million, creating a negative balance of $9.2 billion. Footwear and other leather products accounted for 95 percent of the value of total imports, whereas leather tanning accounted for 64 percent of total exports. The highest percentage of imports was in wearing apparel where about 80 percent were imported. Among other leather products, imports were also high—footwear, 64 percent; handbags, 62 percent; and luggage, 59 percent (U.S. Industrial Outlook 1988).

Although the United States is a major exporter of leather, especially cattlehides, imports still exceed exports. In 1987 the United States imported leather valued at $478 million and exported leather valued at $430 million. The primary markets for U.S. cattlehides are in the Far East: South Korea, Japan, and Taiwan. Canada and Mexico are also important markets for cattlehides, whereas calfskins are exported primarily to Japan and Italy.

The United States imports leathers from more than sixty countries. Argentina was the largest leather supplier to the United States in 1987 with almost a third of the total imports. Other major suppliers of leather to the United States are the United Kingdom, Italy, and India.

Many developing countries that are major producers of hides and skins restrict exports of these raw materials to encourage the growth of their own tanning and leather products industries. In contrast, the United States freely trades cattlehides in world markets. Export restrictions depress prices of hides within the controlling countries, thus lowering the cost of raw materials used in leather production. This price control enables some countries to produce leather goods at highly competitive prices. The U.S. tanning and finishing industry, however, is expected to remain competitive in the world marketplace. In recent years, industry investment in new equipment and technology has greatly increased productivity and has assisted the U.S. tanning industry in remaining cost-competitive.

Marketing Leather

Although many advances have been made in processing leather skins and hides, time required is still a major factor. Many of the steps in the process take several weeks to complete. Also, additional time is needed to transport hides and skins from their place of origin to the tanning and finishing factories. It is because of the time involved in purchasing and processing skins and hides that fashion trends for leather goods have to be identified well in advance of most other types of fashion goods. The identification of colors, textures, and finishes must be predicted two years or more before consumers will be ready to buy the goods.

To project consumer preferences, leather tanners work closely with trade associations. Some trade associations promote specific types of leather goods, such as the Sole Leather Council and the Auto Leather Guild. The primary leather trade association is the Leather Industries of America (LIA), previously known as the Tanners Council of America. Located in New York City, it promotes all types of leathers. The LIA disseminates technical and fashion information to producers, retailers, consumers, and the press. A Hide Tanning School for persons involved in the buying and selling of hides or leathers is offered by the LIA. Color seminars are held semiannually for members of the association.

Approximately eighteen months to two years prior to the time that leather products reach retail stores, tanners exhibit their tannages at leather shows. One major leather show, the Semaine de Cuir, is held each year in Paris. The Hong Kong International Fair also attracts buyers and sellers from many countries. In the United States, leather shows take place in New York, Boston, and St. Louis. One of the largest U.S. leather trade shows is the Tanners' Apparel and Garment (TAG) Show held in New York City each October. It is attended by garment manufacturers, suppliers, and retailers.

Market research is conducted by the leather tanners and trade associations to develop innovative uses for leathers. Improved methods of tanning have provided consumers with a greater variety of products. Today leather materials are softer and more pliable, which makes them more desirable for apparel. Because of modern technology, leathers can also be dyed in a wide variety of colors. Leather has become very popular in men's and women's sportswear, including jackets, skirts, and pants. It is even being used for shirts and dresses.

The Fur Industry

The fur industry is another important primary supplier of raw materials for fashion. It is made up of small firms with highly skilled workers. Although concentrated in New York City, fur production is found in many other locations, making the United States the largest consumer and producer of furs in the world.

Fur has been worn for many years because of its beauty and warmth. It has also served as a symbol of prestige and status. Today many different furs are popular. For years only expensive furs such as mink and sable were considered prestigious and desirable. Over the last several decades many of the less expensive furs—raccoon, beaver, rabbit, and muskrat—have grown in fashion acceptance. At one time the predominant fur customer was a middle-aged woman, but today the target customer for furs may be a woman or a man of any age.

Organization and Operation of the Fur Industry

The U.S. fur industry has more than 800 establishments employing almost 5,000 workers. Most of these firms are small, employing fewer than five persons each. Many provide services such as storing, repairing, and restyling of fur garments in addition to processing and manufacturing new garments.

The industry is divided into three phases: (1) the trappers and breeders who produce the pelts, (2) the processors of fur, and (3) the manufacturers of fur garments. The first phase begins with trappers who hunt animals in the wild and breeders who raise animals under controlled conditions at fur ranches. Approximately 80 percent of the fur pelts used in the United States are ranch-produced.

Fur trappers and breeders usually sell their skins to collecting agents, who in turn sell them at auctions or to wholesale merchants. The Hudson Bay Company of Canada is the world's dominant fur-marketing agent. Major international fur auctions are held in London, Leningrad, and Montreal. Fur auctions in the United States take place in New York City, St. Louis, and Seattle, where fur buyers and manufacturers bid for the pelts, which are sold in bundles.

After manufacturers purchase pelts, they contract with dressing and dyeing firms to have the furs processed. Some manufacturers buy furs that have already been processed. Fur dressers prepare the skins to make them soft and pliable and to preserve their natural luster. This process first involves soaking the skins in salt-water solutions to tan the skin side of the pelt. Next, flesh, grease, and dirt are removed before the pelt is dried to raise the pile. Some furs are subject to additional steps, depending upon the type of fur and the condition of the skin. New dyeing techniques have been developed for furs, providing a variety of shades. Although not all furs are dyed, some are given a dye bath to change the color entirely, whereas others are tip-dyed or brush-dyed. Some furs are bleached to lighten the color.

During the production of fur garments, the skins are cut individually and sewn together in sections.
Source: *Reprinted with permission of Szor-Diener Company, Inc.*

The production of fur garments involves several steps. Skins are separated and bundled according to quality and color to achieve a more uniform look in the finished garment. The skins are cut individually and sewn together in sections. Then they are wetted, stretched, and stapled onto the garment pattern on a wooden board, and dried into shape. After drying, the sections are sewn together to complete the garment.

For some types of furs, such as sable or mink, a process called letting-out is applied to the pelts prior to sewing the garments. Letting-out is a hand operation in which the pelts are cut into diagonal strips approximately one-eighth to three-sixteenths of an inch wide. Each strip is then resewn at an angle, creating a slimmer, longer pelt.

Marketing Furs

Because the fur industry contains many small firms, it relies mostly on group efforts for promotional activities. At times traders, dressers, and producers work together to promote their products. Trade associations also assist in many promotional activ-

Letting-out involves sewing diagonal strips of fur at angles, creating a slimmer, longer pelt.
Source: *Reprinted with permission of Szor-Diener Company, Inc.*

ities. The American Fur Industry Inc., (AFI) is a nonprofit promotional organization supported by fur manufacturers and other segments of the fur industry such as the dressers, dyers, and retailers. Its major purpose is to publicize and promote fur products. Promotional activities include distribution of literature on the selection, use, and care of fur garments. The AFI also works with wildlife and sports associations to encourage conservation of wildlife. Individual types of furs are promoted by such specialized trade associations as the Eastern Mink Breeders Association (EMBA), the Great Lakes Mink Association (GLAMA), and the Empress Chinchilla Breeders Cooperative.

Anti-fur activism has become an increasing concern of the fur industry. Animal-rights groups have attracted media attention by protesting at trade shows, demonstrating in front of stores, and confronting consumers wearing fur on city streets. Their goal is to make wearing fur unfashionable. Although furriers have stated that demonstrations by such activists have had little effect on sales, the fur industry has taken action, and several fur trade associations have joined together to combat anti-fur activity. The Fur Retailers Information Council (FRIC) was formed in 1987 to implement pro-fur programs. Two other trade associations, the Fur Retailers Information Council and the Fur Farm Animal Welfare Coalition, have joined the FRIC to develop an effort to project a positive image for the fur industry. The American and Canadian fur industries have also joined to finance an extensive North American consumer informational and educational campaign.

In the United States the primary fur production and market area is located in New York City on or near Seventh Avenue between 23rd and 30th Streets. Men carrying bundles of fur pelts or fur coats are a common sight in New York's fur district. Because of high rents, many firms have moved out of this area in recent years. Some have relocated to nearby Carlstadt, New Jersey, near the headquarters of the Hudson Bay Auction Company.

The first American fur trade show, the American International Fur Fair, was held in New York in 1979. Today, this trade show, scheduled in March each year, is held in different locations throughout the United States. Furs from many countries are on exhibit. Other American fur trade shows include the Master Furriers Guild Fur Expo in New York City and the Fur and Leather Apparel Show in Los Angeles. The largest fur trade show in the world is the Frankfurt Fur Fair held in Frankfurt, Germany, annually in April. Over 30 countries and 550 wholesalers participate in this fair.

Retail sales of fur garments have increased significantly since the early 1970s. In 1972 fur sales were $361,500,000, whereas in 1988 fur sales reached nearly $2 billion. Fur garments are generally sold either through leased departments within stores or through consignment selling. A leased department is an area located within a retail store operated by an outside operation. The store supplies the space and needed services, but the merchandise is selected, owned, and sold by the leasing organization. Under consignment selling, the retailer takes possession of the fur garments but title remains with the producer. Garments not sold by a specified date are returned to the producer for possible sale elsewhere.

Consumers frequently purchase furs directly from the manufacturer. Furriers often have small showrooms that are open to the public, and some even operate their own specialty stores. In addition, weekend fur sales held in hotels, arenas, or convention centers have become a common means of selling to consumers in many cities. Consumers can also buy furs through catalog sales.

Approximately 85 percent of retail fur sales are of fur garments that sell for less than $5,000. The sales are attributed to imports and the younger career customer. A new target customer group for furs is men, whose purchases now account for 15 percent of fur sales. Since the late 1970s, well-known designer names have become associated with the fur industry.

The United States is known for producing fine quality furs. American fur garments are in demand in foreign markets, especially Japan. Despite the desire for American furs, the United States imports a considerable number of fur garments. In 1987 the fur industry estimated that about 50 percent of the dollar volume of furs sold at retail in the United States was imported. Much of this increase was due to the marketing of more affordably priced fur garments produced in foreign countries, mainly the Far East, where production costs are lower.

It is difficult to identify where fur garments have been manufactured when they are imported. The Fur Products Labeling Act of 1952 requires that labels give information concerning the origin of fur pelts, but it does not require that country of manufacture be listed on the label. Other labeling requirements include the English name of the animal and the type of processing, including dyeing, whether paws or tails have been used, or whether parts of used garments have been reused.

Summary of Key Points

1. The primary markets of the fashion industry produce the raw materials of fashion including fibers, fabrics, leathers, and furs.

2. The textile industry is the largest segment of the primary markets and includes fiber producers, yarn producers, textile mills, and finishers.

3. Trade associations for both natural and man-made fibers play an important role in the marketing of fibers.

4. Textile mills sell their fabrics to converters, manufacturers, and/or jobbers.

5. Services offered by textile trade associations and textile producers include fabric libraries, color charts, fashion projections, and textile directories.

6. Color standards are used to provide a common color understanding among all segments of the fashion industry.

7. Because leather production is a slow process, fashion trends for leather goods have to be identified well in advance of most other fashion materials.

8. Leather and leather products include seven industries: leather tanning and finishing, nonrubber footwear, gloves and mittens, luggage, handbags, small leather goods, and wearing apparel.

9. The fur industry includes trappers and breeders, processors, and manufacturers.

10. Competition from imports is the major problem facing the textile, fur, and leather industries.

Key Words and Concepts

Define, identify, or explain each of the following:

Bobbin Show	fabric libraries
brand name	fiber
Color Association of the United States (CAUS)	fiber trade associations
	finisher
color standards	generic name
converter	gray (greige) goods
Crafted with Pride in the U.S.A.	Ideacomo

International Color Authority (ICA)

Interstoff

jobber

kips

leather

man-made fibers

natural fibers

primary markets

Quick Response

secondary markets

synthetic

tanning

textile industry

textile mill

trademark

Discussion Questions and Topics

1. What are the differences between natural and man-made fibers?
2. Explain the importance of the textile industry to the economy of the United States.
3. What role do trade associations play in the marketing of fibers and fabrics?
4. Describe a vertically integrated textile company.
5. What is the function of a textile converter?
6. Why does the textile industry research and anticipate fashion trends earlier than the apparel industry?
7. How have the textile, leather, and fur industries been affected by imports?
8. What is the "Crafted with Pride" campaign, and how has it benefited the U.S. textile industry?
9. What are fiber brand names and trademarks?
10. What trends are taking place in the textile, leather, and fur industries?
11. What measures are being taken by the primary markets to combat imports?

Notes

Leslie Cochran, "U.S. Traffic at Interstoff Slack," *Women's Wear Daily*, November 1, 1985, p. 16.

Martha DeLlosa, "The Story of Polyester," *American Fabrics and Fashions*, no. 132 (1985), p. 12.

I. T. Hamilton, "Linen," *Textiles*, 15(2), 1986, p. 30.

Marvin Klapper, "Converters Forte: Honing the Cutting Edge of Fashion," *Women's Wear Daily*, Sec. II, May 24, 1988, pp. 8–9.

M. I. Piercy, "Wool in Today's Textile Markets," *Textiles*, 16(2), 1987, p. 30.

Standard and Poor's *Industry Surveys,* 1988.

Textile Organon, 59(3), 1988.

Textiles, 15(2), 1986, p. 30.

U.S. Industrial Outlook—Leather, 1988, p. 46–1; Textiles, 1988.

Margaret Walch, "Color Standards in the United States," *American Fabrics and Fashions,* no. 131 (1984), p. 81.

_____

CHAPTER 5

AMERICAN FASHION CREATORS

THE PRODUCTION of fashion apparel is a major industry in the United States. Whereas creating apparel is only one segment of the fashion industry, its styling and design are vital elements in the success of any manufacturing firm. This chapter is a discussion of the designer's role in the production of apparel, including brief profiles of selected American fashion designers.

The role of the American designer has increased in importance during the last several decades, and wearing garments with an American **designer label** has become a status symbol not only in the United States but in many countries throughout the world. Today there are many American designers well known to the public. Their names appear extensively on labels, in advertising, and in the media. Most apparel, however, is designed by those whose names the American public does not know. These designers work behind the scenes, designing thousands of garments and accessories produced under a manufacturer's trade name. In fact, mass-produced ready-to-wear seldom carries the designer's name on the label.

Recognition of American Fashion

For more than 300 years Americans relied on Europe for fashion luxuries. In colonial days beautiful damasks and velvets are brought to America from Italy; woolens,

calicos, and fine leathers from England; perfumes, embroideries, and fine linens from Paris; and laces from northern Europe. During the eighteenth century, American dressmakers imported dolls, called fashion babies, dressed in the latest French fashions to use as models for their clients. In the nineteenth century **dressmakers** copied clothing pictured in European fashion magazines.

By the end of the nineteenth century, several retail stores, such as Lord & Taylor and B. Altman in New York and Marshall Field in Chicago, offered **custom-made apparel** to their customers. These and other retailers sent their buyers abroad to purchase models of designs as well as fabrics and trims from well-known French design houses. Custom-made copies of these designs were then reproduced in the store's own workrooms.

Although Americans still looked to Paris for design inspiration in the early twentieth century, several American fashion publications tried to strengthen an awareness of American designers. In 1914 *Vogue* magazine sponsored a Fashion Fete to encourage American design, and in 1916 *Women's Wear Daily* held the first contest for American textile designers.

During the 1920s and 1930s, designers such as Hattie Carnegie went to Paris to buy from the custom salons. The designs were then imported and copied or adapted for the American market. Carnegie had an outstanding fashion sense for what was right for her clientele. She produced clothes with an American sense of fashion, but Paris inspired her designs. She put dresses together using pieces from the French imports—a collar from one dress, a sleeve from another, a skirt from a third.

During the years of the Depression in the 1930s, fashionable American women began breaking the rule that "all clothes must be French." Dorothy Shaver, vice president of Lord & Taylor, was instrumental in advertising American-designed clothing. For the first time in retailing history, she advertised apparel designed by American designers, such as Claire McCardell, Clare Potter, Tom Brigance, Vera Maxwell, and Elizabeth Hawes. These designers, who showed no interest in Paris high fashion, had their own unique American style.

American fashion creativity grew and prospered during the 1940s when World War II cut America off from imported Paris originals. A truly indigenous American fashion began to emerge under the direction of such designers as Charles James, Mainbocher, and Norman Norell. Gradually these names became recognized as equals to Paris couturiers as they developed their own elegant, sophisticated designs. Following is a list of important American fashion designers of the past (see the end of the chapter for some of their brief biographies):

Gilbert Adrian (1903–1959)

Travis Banton (1894–1958)

Bonnie Cashin (1915–   )

Hattie Carnegie (1889–1956)

Perry Ellis (1940–1986)

Anne Fogarty (1919–1981)

Rudi Gernreich (1922–1985)

Howard Greer (1886–1964)

Edith Head (1907–1981)

Irene (Irene Gibbons) (1907–1962)

Charles James (1906–1978)

Anne Klein (1923–1974)

John Kloss (1937–1987)

Jean Louis (1907–   )

Claire McCardell (1905–1958)

Mainbocher (1890–1976)

Vera Maxwell (1904–   )

Norman Norell (1900–1972)

Giorgio Sant'Angelo (1936–1989)

Willie Smith (1948–1987)

Gustave Tassell (1926–   )

Jacques Tiffeau (1927–1988)

Valentina (1907–   )

Chester Weinberg (1930–   )

Sydney Wragge (1908–   )

Also coming out of the 1930s and 1940s was the **American Look** epitomized in the sportswear designs of Claire McCardell, Clare Potter, Bonnie Cashin, and Vera Maxwell. These designers, recognizing that American women were moving to casual, recreation-derived styles, created casual, comfortable, functional clothes that suited the busy lifestyles of American women. Their simple yet sophisticated look was based on outdoor work clothes and clothes evolved for country living. Claire McCardell in her book *What Shall I Wear?* described the American Look as "a clean-line look, just the opposite of too much dress. It is a comfortable look, neither threatening to burst at the seams nor to smother the wearer" (McCardell 1956). Designers created these clothes, inspired by menswear and the American West as well as work clothes, for the new lifestyles of women like themselves who worked, kept house, managed families, and traveled. Such women led active, fast-paced lives, and they needed clothes suited to this lifestyle.

Claire McCardell, who is often credited with originating the American Look, produced sporty, casual, and comfortable clothing in functional designs. In 1934 she designed a travel wardrobe consisting of a group of jersey separates that could be combined in different ways and worn for almost any activity. She introduced many details into women's clothing from men's apparel: large pockets, trouser pleats, Levi top-stitching, and rivets. She also made denim a fashion fabric.

Vera Maxwell followed a classic approach to go-together separates. Her famous weekend wardrobe created in 1935 included five interchangeable pieces of tweed and gray flannel. Bonnie Cashin initiated the concept of layering in her comfortable country and travel clothes. These designers and others established sportswear as the one characteristically American style of dress to develop in the twentieth century.

Many American designers have since achieved international design authority on the basis of sportswear styles, among them Anne Klein, Calvin Klein, Perry Ellis, Ralph Lauren, Norma Kamali, and John Weitz. These designers recognized in the 1970s the need for the middle class to find clothing that would endure for more than one season, and they made clothes with longevity.

Indicative of the status obtained by American designers in Europe is the fact that five of them were invited to show along with five French designers at a special benefit of the Chateau de Versailles in November 1973. Bill Blass, Stephen Burrows, Oscar de la Renta, Halston, and Anne Klein showed their designs along with those of French designers Marc Bohan, Pierre Cardin, Givenchy, Yves Saint Laurent, and Ungaro.

American designers today are admired by people all over the world for their talent and innovations. Their names have become as prestigious and as widely known as the names of French designers, and American fashion is sold in many countries.

Awards for Fashion Design

Growing interest in American fashion design has been evidenced by several awards given to fashion designers beginning in the 1930s. Among them are the Neiman-Marcus Award, the Coty American Fashion Critics Award, and the Council of Fashion Designers Award. Many other awards have been given by organizations and firms interested in encouraging and promoting American fashion.

Neiman-Marcus Award

In 1938 Neiman-Marcus, the Dallas specialty store, established the **Neiman-Marcus Awards** for Distinguished Service in the Field of Fashion. These awards were designed to recognize the talents of designers as well as others who had contributed "to fashion either in designing, publicizing, or wearing in a way that influenced the public" (Marcus 1974). The first Neiman-Marcus Awards in 1938 went to dress designers Germaine Monteil and Nettie Rosenstein, millinery designer Mr. John, and textile designer Dorothy Liebes. The following year Neiman-Marcus honored designers Hattie Carnegie, Clare Potter, and Elizabeth Arden. In 1940 awards went to Edna Woolman Chase, editor-in-chief of *Vogue,* and European designer Elsa Schiaparelli. Neiman-Marcus has also acknowledged fashion consumers for important contributions to the wearing of clothes. For example, the first fashion consumer

This casual outfit was part of Claire's McCardell's sporty, comfortable collection in the early 1940s.

awardee was Mrs. Howard Hawkes, who was recognized in 1946 for epitomizing the "typical American look."

Coty American Fashion Critics Award

The development of the **Coty American Fashion Critics Award** in 1942 further enhanced the image of American designers. This award, which was discontinued in 1985, recognized American designers who made outstanding contributions to the fashion industry and who gained admiration from their peers. The recipient was selected by a national jury of fashion editors from magazines, newspapers, and news services.

Several Coty awards were developed. The original Coty Fashion Critics Award was called the **Winnie.** The recipient was an American designer of women's wear who had made significant contributions to fashion during the preceding year, and the original award went to Norman Norell. The Coty Special Award was given to an American designer who excelled in a special area of the fashion industry, such as jewelry, headwear, lingerie, or loungewear. The Coty Menswear Fashion Award, developed in 1968, went to an American designer who made outstanding contributions in designing menswear. Designers who received any of these awards more than once were given the Coty Repeat Award. After a designer won three awards, he or she was placed in the Coty Hall of Fame and was not eligible for future award consideration. Several noted designers inducted into the Coty Hall of Fame are Norman Norell, Bill Blass, Calvin Klein, Ralph Lauren, and Mary McFadden.

Until its demise in 1985, the Coty award was considered the most prestigious award given in the fashion industry. However, Coty, the cosmetic company that founded the award, was accused of commercialism by designers when it came out with a line of beauty products called the Coty Awards Collection of Cosmetics, in 1979. Another reason for its demise was that designers expressed boredom with the format of the award presentation and were concerned that it had been given to so many of the same people so often that it had lost its meaning.

Council of Fashion Designers Award

The **Council of Fashion Designers Awards** (CFDA) were first presented in 1981 and have now taken the place of the Coty Awards as the most prestigious in the American fashion industry. These awards are controlled by the designers themselves, who are members of the Council of Fashion Designers. Only one designer is nominated for each category; therefore, there are no winners and losers.

Use of Designers' Names

As previously noted, the majority of American manufacturers do not use the designer's name on the garment label. Especially in firms that produce moderate or budget-priced apparel, the designer's name is usually unknown to the public. A manufacturer hires a designer to develop designs that will be produced under the manufacturer's brand name. Many manufacturing firms have several designers and/or assistant designers. Manufacturers choose not to promote the designer's name partly because designers may change jobs and move to other manufacturing firms, and because they fear giving a designer too much exposure on the label and opening the way for them to start their own businesses. Many small firms do not even employ a permanent designer but rely instead on **freelance designers** to provide fashion design services, and some manufacturers simply copy designs from other firms.

Whereas many manufacturers still do not display designers' names, the designer label has become increasingly important in the manufacturing of apparel, accessories, and even home furnishings. Originally the designer label was restricted to high-priced products, and the target market for them was fashion innovators who represented a small segment of the total group of fashion consumers. Today, however, designer labels have increased greatly in number and appear on moderate-price lines and sometimes even at the budget level. Among today's well-known designer names are Calvin Klein, Bill Blass, Oscar de la Renta, Norma Kamali, and Ralph Lauren. Following is a list of many of today's prominent American fashion designers. Some designers own their own firms; others form partnerships with manufacturers.

Current American Designers

Adolfo	Steve Fabrikant
John Anthony	James Galanos
Jhane Barnes	Halston
Geoffrey Beene	Cathy Hardwick
Bill Blass	Holly Harp
Eleanor P. Brenner	David Hayes
Donald Brooks	Carolina Herrera
Stephen Burrows	Carol Horn
David Cameron	Betsy Johnson
Albert Capraro	Andrea Jovine
Zack Carr	Alexander Julian
Oleg Cassini	Norma Kamali
Arthur Chapnik	Donna Karan
Victor Costa	Herbert Kasper
Oscar de la Renta	Anne Klein (Louis Dell'Olio)
Perry Ellis (Marc Jacobs)	Calvin Klein

Michael Kors

Ralph Lauren

Mary McFadden

Bob Mackie

Isaac Mizrahi

Rebecca Moses

Morton Myles

Leo Narducci

Molly Parnis

Mary Ann Restivo

Carolyne Roehm

Gloria Sachs

Don Sayers

Arnold Scaasi

Ronaldus Shamask

Adele Simpson (Wayne Kastning)

Stephen Sprouse

Pauline Trigere

Joan Vass

Adrienne Vittadini

Michael Vollbracht

(Names in parentheses indicate designers who currently design for the firm founded by the original designer.)

Licensing Agreements by Designers

Designers may participate in licensing agreements that allow manufacturers to use their names on various products. These agreements usually provide the designer with a percentage of the wholesale sales. The licensing of designer names has been a successful practice of European designers for years. Encouraged by their success, many American designers now make licensing arrangements. One of the first American designers to license her name was Claire McCardell, who in the late 1940s had other manufacturers produce and sell the accessories necessary for completing McCardell's "total look."

In the mid-1960s Pierre Cardin, John Weitz, and Ralph Lauren started the trend of **designer licensing** in menswear. Today these designers and many others license apparel for both men and women. During the 1970s and 1980s, the trend of using designer names on products other than clothing increased dramatically, and designer names appeared on everything from chocolates to automobiles.

Many new designer licensing agreements were established in the 1980s, and licensing became both a national and an international venture. American designers no longer make licensing agreements exclusively with American manufacturers. Many successful licensing agreements have been made by American designers in Europe and Japan. Designers from other countries have also found it profitable to license in the United States. Among the most active licensors in the mid-1980s were Guy Laroche, Liz Claiborne, Perry Ellis, Bill Blass, Ralph Lauren, Calvin Klein, Geoffrey Beene, Valentino, and Christian Dior.

The practice of licensing has become popular with both couture and ready-to-wear designers worldwide. It provides designers with a method of promoting their names with little risk involved. However, the licensing value of any designer will usually depend upon the continued success of the designer's apparel lines, especially those that first made him or her popular. The success of licensed products also depends on the maintenance of design quality. In some instances designers have little influence over the design of the licensed products. Because a designer's name appears on a product, it does not mean that the designer had anything to do with designing it.

Style Piracy

Style piracy is a common practice in the American fashion industry. It involves the copying of apparel designs without the permission of the design originator. This practice is especially common when a style shows signs of popular acceptance by consumers. Designers do not have protection from style pirating in the United States because apparel designs cannot be copyrighted. The practice of style piracy is done openly, and designs are often copied or adapted by firms that are known as **knock-off** houses. The copied design is called a knock-off and usually is produced at a lower price than the original design that it imitates.

There are several reasons for the existence of style piracy. First, the copying of a fast-selling design gives the producer a way to make great profit for a modest investment. Price line specialization by fashion manufacturers also contributes to the practice of style piracy. Because a firm that produces a style at a high price caters to a limited clientele, it would not want to produce the style in an inexpensive version. Therefore, piracy allows a producer of lower-priced garments to make the style available to its customers by using less expensive **fabrications** and cutting corners in production. A style may be copied at several price levels, thus satisfying several different consumer market segments.

The Designer's Role

The designer's role in the fashion industry is to create, adapt, or interpret styles. Designers today design everything—apparel, accessories, home furnishings, appliances, automobiles, and homes. The designs they create must reflect the wants and needs of the consumer if they are to be successful. This is especially true in fashion apparel because, above all, fashion is a business, and companies must remain prof-

Designer licensing has become popular with both couture and ready-to-wear designers worldwide.
Source: *Reprinted with permission of Christian Dior, Adrienne Vittadini, Albert Nipon, Calvin Klein, and Carlos Falchi.*

itable if they are to stay in business. Designers must develop products that sell. To do this they must be attuned to consumer lifestyles and must be able to predict fashion trends.

Types of Designers

Different types of designers are found in the American fashion industry. They are: (1) custom designers, (2) couture designers, (3) mass production designers, (4) stylists, and (5) freelance designers. Each designer designs for a specific price range, design level, and target customer.

Custom Designing

Custom-made clothing is apparel made to order for an individual customer. It is cut and fitted to individual measurements. Before the growth and development of the American ready-to-wear industry, custom designing was very important. Many wealthy Americans had clothing custom made at French couture houses or by American retailers who bought the sketches or original French designs and European fabrics. Custom-made clothing remained important for many years. By 1970, however, all major U.S. fashion retailers had discontinued their custom-made operations. Such departments were no longer profitable for large stores to operate.

Today few custom design shops operate in the United States and most of these produce men's tailored clothing. Custom designing is still done by small entrepreneurs who design clothing for special customers who want truly unique and different clothing. Clients for custom designers are often entertainers or wealthy individuals who want something for a special occasion. Custom-made apparel is expensive because of the labor involved in the time-consuming processes of design, fitting, and construction.

There is a difference between a designer of custom-made clothing and a dressmaker. The custom designer designs and produces apparel for an individual customer. The garment pattern is made according to individual measurements, and the garment is fitted to the individual customer. Designs may be one of a kind. A dressmaker works with commercial patterns and does not design the styles to be sewn.

Couture Designing

Couture comes from the French term for dressmaking. As a fashion term, it is widely used to describe apparel that is expensive and produced in limited quantities by designers whose names appear on the labels. Such designers are usually well known even though they may dress only a small number of customers.

A true couture designer produces seasonal collections of clothes that are shown to clients who place orders for apparel that is then custom-made to fit the measurements of the individual client. This type of apparel design is the way French couture designers operate, but it has been limited in its application in the United States.

In the United States the term **couture designer** is often used to describe the name designer who produces high-priced collections that are mass produced and sold to department and specialty stores and often through their own designer boutiques. Such designer apparel is often high fashion, emphasizes quality, and represents distinctive styling associated with the designer. Examples of designers in this category are Bill Blass, Oscar de la Renta, and Mary McFadden.

Designing for Mass Production

Most American designers work in the popular to moderate-price markets where apparel is mass produced to reach a volume market. The apparel produced by these **mass production designers** is called ready-to-wear **(RTW)**. It is made in standard sizes and bought off-the-rack by customers. The RTW designer often works for a manufacturer and is unknown to the public. In some instances the manufacturer places a name on the label that sounds like a designer name but is not. For example, there are no such designers as Evan-Picone or Forenza, although both are often perceived by customers as designer names.

In New York City these designers are associated with Seventh Avenue because many of the firms have their design and marketing offices located in that part of the city. Thus these designers who work for manufacturers may be referred to as **Seventh Avenue designers.**

Knock-off Designing

Many firms that produce popular-priced apparel base their collections on styles that have met with success during the previous season. These manufacturers copy popular styles designed by other firms rather than designing their own originals. The styles they produce, as noted earlier, are called knock-offs, and the firms hire knock-off artists or **stylists** to select the garments to be copied. The stylist also selects the fabrics, **findings,** and trims to be used and may adapt or change the style to make the garment less expensive to produce. The stylist looks for runners or fords that will catch on immediately with the customer and sell in great quantities, and incorporates new versions of these styles into the manufacturer's line.

Freelance Designing

A freelance designer sells sketches of designs to manufacturers. The designs may represent original ideas of the designer or may be adaptations made to the manufacturer's specifications. Manufacturers often contract with a freelance designer to do a specific job. It may be less expensive to hire designers in this way than to maintain a full-time design staff. Once a freelance designer sells a sketch to a manufacturer, the designer's responsibility for that particular design is complete.

Apparel Manufacturing

The organizational structure of a typical apparel manufacturer includes three major divisions: (1) design, (2) production, and (3) sales. The functions of these divisions are interrelated, and the divisions are dependent upon each other. The head of each division reports to the president or head of the firm who directs the general operations necessary to run the company. The designer relates to all three divisions since all are directly concerned with the design function of apparel.

The Design Division

The designer is in charge of the creative process in the design division. The designer may supervise assistant designers, **patternmakers,** and **sample makers.** This division is responsible for creating the firm's new seasonal line or the seasonal collection. The terms *line* and *collection* are frequently used synonymously. American manufacturers usually use the term *line* to refer to moderate and popular-priced garments, while *collection* is reserved for high-priced lines.

The design division is responsible for producing several seasonal lines each year. Typical **production seasons** in women's ready-to-wear include summer, early fall or transitional, fall, holiday or resort, and spring. Some manufacturers do not adhere to a set group of seasons but will work with a loose seasonal feeling by constantly adding and subtracting garments from the lines. Most manufacturers conform to a structured number of lines per year, often filling in lines with new items called **sweeteners.** Shipments to retail stores are often made monthly in order to respond quickly to changing customer needs and demands.

The design process usually begins six to twelve months before the selling season, depending on the type of apparel being made and the availability of materials. Because of the detailed steps in constructing a suit or coat, more time is needed to produce tailored clothing. As previously discussed, producers of garments made of leather must also start planning lines early because of the additional time needed to obtain the leather.

The designer's greatest challenge is the search for fresh, creative ideas. He or she is continually thinking of ways to make the next collection look new. In creating new designs or updating popular styles, the designer draws ideas from many sources. The successful designer watches for the earliest hints of coming trends as well as reviews fashions from the past. Other sources of inspiration include the entertainment world, international fashion leaders, technological developments, and world events. The designer also researches fashion and consumer trends based on the economy, cultural events, and politics.

Designers must also investigate color trends and select colors for the line. The selection of colors for a collection is an important step in the design process. Consumers relate personally to the colors of garments, and many times because of emotional responses, color dominates the selection or rejection of apparel and accessories. Customers also associate certain colors with holidays and seasons of the year. As described in Chapter 4, several fiber companies and trade associations provide information on color trends for the coming seasons. Professional color services are also available to assist designers with color predictions. At times, the designer may select only a few of the predicted colors and then add other color choices for balance. Using color predictions as guides provides designers with an assurance that lines will be in the mainstream of fashion.

Once colors have been selected, the designer works with the fabric buyer in shopping the markets for fabrics, findings, trimmings, and other materials used to construct fashion products. The fabrication used in making the garment may include textile fabrics, leathers, furs, vinyls, or other material. Findings are the functional parts of the garment and include linings, zippers, hooks, snaps, thread, and tapes. Trimmings add decoration to a garment and include items such as buttons, laces, belts, and braids. Sometimes a buyer is responsible only for the purchase of findings and trimmings.

In developing a design and selecting the materials for the line, the designer must consider production costs and stay within the price limits predetermined by the manufacturer. The cost of fabrics, trims, and findings must balance the labor costs. The designer may save money by using a less expensive fabrication or by simplifying the design. The money saved on some materials or details can allow the designer to put more money into labor costs. Ultimately, a garment's success or failure depends to a great extent on cost. In order for a company to make a profit, cost must always be controlled. If a garment has to be priced too high in order to make a profit, consumers may refuse to buy it.

Apparel producers generally specialize in one price range. The most common price ranges used in the apparel industry include budget, moderate, and better. The terms *bridge, designer,* and *couture* also suggest certain price ranges. Bridge merchandise is priced between better and designer, and couture is the highest priced merchandise. Each price range has a different level of customer expectation. Once an apparel manufacturer has established a name for producing certain products in specific price ranges, it is difficult for the firm to build customer acceptance for other price ranges.

Computers are used by apparel manufacturers with both designing and pattternmaking procedures.
Source: *Reprinted with permission of Microdynamics, Inc.*

There are no set rules or methods on how to develop a line. The creation of a line varies with the manufacturing firm and the designer. Some designers sketch the individual items and have assistant designers make the patterns and samples. Other designers create and drape designs on dress forms and then transfer the designs to flat patterns. Some designers prefer to work "on the flat," also called flat pattern-making. In some firms the designer is personally responsible for creating the designs and making the first pattern. In large firms the designer is more likely to have an assistant or a patternmaker who makes the patterns. Computers are now being used to assist with both designing and patternmaking.

Designers may work on two or more lines at once. While the designer is developing a new line, he or she is also working on problems from the current selling line. For example, a certain type of pocket on a skirt may have prevented a style from selling as successfully as another similar style, so the designer may alter the style by designing a new pocket.

Many times styles are carried over from one season to the next. Styles that are hot sellers or winners are identified by high sales volume and reorders by retailers. Such winners may be continued in the line for several seasons. Once these hot sellers are determined, designers **refabricate** the styles to make them suitable for the next season. Sometimes the style remains the same, only the fabric changes. Other times adjustments are made in detail or trim to make the style slightly different from the previous season. To refabricate refers to the practice of placing the most acceptable parts of the style into a new version.

The Production Process

A major decision for manufacturers is to determine what styles are to be mass produced and in what volume. Many of the new styles developed by the designer will never even be shown as part of the line or collection. For example, a manufacturer may begin with 125 styles, discard 40 to 60 in the process of determining what should be offered in the line, show 40 or 50 as a line, establish 15 as possible winners, and end up with 5 or 6 that are strong retail sellers.

A manufacturer edits the line at several points. The first editing comes when the line is initially shown in-house and decisions are made as to which items are to be shown to retail buyers. The line is edited again after retail buyers view the line and submit initial orders. Certain styles will never be mass produced because retail stores do not place sufficient orders to support production. Such styles are dropped from the line.

Once a style is approved for production, it becomes part of the line and is mass produced. The firm determines the minimum number of pieces to be produced according to projected orders. The number of pieces to be considered for a production order will vary with each firm. Some manufacturers may require from 100 to 500 pieces to be ordered before production begins; other firms will place the minimum order in the thousands.

Once a firm decides to mass produce a style, the sample patterns must be made in different sizes. This technique of increasing and decreasing the sample pattern to make a complete size range of patterns is called **grading.** For years, grading was performed by skilled patternmakers and graders. Today, however, some companies are using computers to mechanically grade patterns.

After the patterns have been graded, a master **marker** is made. The marker is made out of a sheet of paper the width of the fabric and is used to help eliminate waste when the fabric is cut. The marker places pattern pieces as close together as possible and serves as a guide in cutting the appropriate number of pattern pieces. Markers may be made by arranging full-size pattern pieces on marker paper or may be designed on a computer screen.

The fabric is laid out in multiple layers, and the marker is placed on top of the layers. Following the patterns outlined on the marker, cutters use electronically powered knives or blades to cut through the multiple layers of fabric. The number of pieces cut at one time varies with the type of fabric, the number of orders, and the price of the garment. More advanced techniques of cutting, such as the laser beam and water jet, are being used by some apparel producers. The laser method, which uses a concentrated light beam, and water jet cutting, which is a thin stream of water fired under high pressure, can both be directed by computers.

Once the fabric is cut, the garment pieces are sorted and tied together in bundles. This assembling process is called bundling. The bundled work is distributed to sewing machine operators or sent to contractors for the sewing process. After the pieces are sewn and the final construction details are completed, the garments are pressed, inspected, and prepared for shipping. The completed garments are transferred to the shipping point where orders are filled. As the season progresses, the manufacturer may recut the best-selling numbers (winners). Manufacturers usually drop items that have only a few reorders. Some winners will become runners and will be continued for more than one season.

The Sales Division

The sales division is responsible for marketing to retailers the lines created by the design division. Various selling methods are used to market the merchandise. The major function of the sales division is to market merchandise profitably.

Manufacturers follow various distribution policies to promote and sell their merchandise. The prices and quality of the merchandise are important factors in attracting certain types of retail stores as potential buyers. Better lines of apparel, those made of expensive fabrics and detailed constructions, are distributed to selected specialty and department stores that sell higher-priced goods to more discriminating customers. Manufacturers that produce moderate-priced lines sell to a wider variety of stores that sell to a mass consumer market. The producers of popular- or budget-priced goods attract buyers from discount and promotionally priced stores. Manufacturers determine policies that influence the distribution of merchandise. Some producers use an open distribution policy of selling goods to anyone who can pay for the merchandise; other manufacturers decide to follow a selected distribution policy, which limits the number of stores in an area that may buy the merchandise. One means by which manufacturers restrict the distribution of their goods is by setting a high minimum order requirement for the retail buyer.

Many manufacturers of fashion apparel market their merchandise through showrooms in the major apparel markets and at temporary markets held in many different cities. Some manufacturers also use road or territorial sales personnel to sell their merchandise by calling on buyers at retail stores. More information on market centers and buying merchandise is provided in other chapters of this book.

Jobs in Apparel Design

Many people are involved in the teamwork of apparel design and manufacturing. Some of the different occupations that constitute the work performed in these processes are those of designer, assistant designer, sample cutter, sample maker, patternmaker, and sketcher.

Designer

As discussed earlier, the activities and direct responsibilities of a designer will vary depending upon the size and nature of the company. In one firm, a designer may be responsible for designing and for supervising the designer workroom. In another, the designer may be creating few-of-a-kind originals for an exclusive boutique, in which case he or she may be involved in every step of creating a line, from the original idea to the completed garment.

Assistant Designer

The assistant designer interprets the ideas of the designer by making the first muslin pattern of the design and then cutting out the original fabric sample. Assistant designers must know how to make patterns. An accurate pattern that translates the designer's working sketch into an actual garment is needed. The assistant designer is often a "gofer," performing whatever duty the designer requests.

Sample Cutter

A sample cutter cuts samples and assists the designer and assistant designer in other ways. A position as sample cutter is often a beginning position leading to an assistant designer position.

Sample Maker

The sample maker is the top dressmaker in a firm. The sample maker constructs the first sample garment of a design. A sample is the model or trial garment. Sample makers sometimes construct the samples that are shown at market or carried by road salespeople. In some apparel firms the samples are made in the factory, but most are made by sample makers rather than produced by factory methods. In either case the samples viewed by a buyer at market may not always be the same quality as the mass-produced garments received at the store. In some instances samples are better constructed than the ready-to-wear products; sometimes the reverse is true.

The sample maker works with the designer and the assistant designer to fit the sample perfectly to a fitting model whose figure corresponds to the sample size used, usually a 7 in juniors and an 8 in misses apparel. The sample maker constructs the entire garment, unlike the sewers in factory production who perform only one operation. Usually the sample maker has had experience in factory sewing methods and can spot potential difficulties in mass production. The success of a designer's styles depends on a good sample maker. For this reason, the sample maker is generally paid a salary rather than by the piece. A well-made sample is more important than the speed of making samples.

Patternmaker

A patternmaker makes the sample and production patterns. The production patternmaker cuts an accurate or perfect pattern for each sample chosen for the line. The patternmaker also tries to simplify the pattern for a couple of reasons. A simple pattern is needed because factory sewers will be constructing the garments rather than a skilled sample maker and because the simpler the design is to construct, the more cost-efficient it becomes. Once the pattern is developed in the standard size used by the manufacturer, a stock sample is cut and made in the factory to test the new pattern. The production sample is fitted on a fitting model whose measurements are identical to the commercial measurements for the stock size. The stock sample is compared with the original designer sample to see that the duplicate fits properly and that it is as desirable as the original.

Sketcher

A sketcher makes working sketches for the designer and illustrations to be used in promoting the line. Working sketches are pencil drawings made from the designer's rough idea of the garment. The sketches are used in the sample room. The sketcher must interpret precisely the silhouette, shape, and outline of the garment and draw all seamlines, details, and trims. Illustrations are used in the showroom catalog or for advertisements. Most of these sketches are color renderings, emphasizing the texture and/or print of the fabrication. Sometimes the designer or assistant designer will do the working sketches, and artists are hired to draw illustrations.

Brief Biographies of American Designers

Many American designers have been recognized for their creative talents and have proved to be world fashion leaders, as the following biographical sketches illustrate. Many of these designers or the firms they founded are still active in the fashion business. Others have been included because of their historical importance.

Adolfo

Adolfo Sardina was born in Havana, Cuba, in 1929, where his early fashion interest was nurtured by his aunt, Mme. Marie Lopez, whose name appeared on several international "best-dressed" lists. She took her nephew to Paris to witness designer showings and introduced him to Chanel and also to Balenciaga, with whom Adolfo began his fashion career as an apprentice. He moved to New York where he designed millinery for Braagaard, and in 1953 went to work for the milliner Emme, and became known as Adolfo of Emme. Adolfo opened his own millinery salon in 1962, and soon thereafter began designing clothing. This endeavor began with the addition of capes, sleeveless shift dresses, and wrap skirts. Adolfo is best known for his Chanel-type suits, and he has a reputation for turning current trends into flattering and wearable styles. Nancy Reagan's selection of Adolfo's clothes has made his name well known. Adolfo sells only to private clientele in his Madison Avenue boutique. He also designs and sells wholesale to a few specialty stores.

Adolfo's millinery designs that began attracting particular attention in the 1960s were the Panama planter's hat, the shaggy Cossack hat, large fur berets, packable jersey snoods, and little-girl straw rollers. He won two Coty special awards for his hats, the first in 1955 and another in 1969. He is noted for his magnificent use of fabrics and for his luxurious evening wear. In 1978 Adolfo perfume was introduced. Since then he has developed an interest in active sportswear, menswear, and accessories.

Geoffrey Beene

Geoffrey Beene, born in 1927 in Haynesville, Louisiana, attended Tulane University in New Orleans as a premed and medical student before moving to Los Angeles, where he worked in display at I. Magnin. Beene next went to New York to study at the Traphagen School of Fashion and completed his education in Paris, where he worked briefly at Molyneux, the noted master of tailoring and the bias cut. In 1949 he returned to New York and worked for several designers before he joined Teal Traina, who put his name on the label. He opened his own business in 1962, offering relaxed, easy-to-wear, feminine clothes in the mood of Chanel, Cardin, and Norell. His taste in combining textures, designs, and colors in fabrics gives them his unmistakable signature. He often produces the unexpected and humorous in his designs and enjoys being somewhat shocking. Today, his business includes Beene Couture for higher-priced lines; Beene Bag, his boutique line; menswear, furs, jewelry, and bathing suits.

Beene has received numerous awards for his creativity, including several Coty awards, two National Cotton awards, and the Neiman-Marcus Award. In 1975 he was elected to the Coty Hall of Fame. Beene gained national attention when he designed Lynda Johnson Robb's bridal gown and bridesmaids' gowns for her White House wedding in 1967. He also created dresses for First Lady Pat Nixon.

Bill Blass

Born in 1922 in Fort Wayne, Indiana, Bill Blass began his career in 1940 as a sketcher for the sportswear firm of David Crystal. After serving in the army during World War II, he returned to New York to work as a designer for Anna Miller and Company in 1946. In 1959 the company merged with Maurice Rentner, and in 1961 Blass became vice president and a full partner. He bought the business in 1970, changing the name of the firm to Bill Blass Ltd.

Blass is known for designing luxury ready-to-wear clothes for wealthy ladies who live active social lives. He designs classic sportswear, elegant dresses and tailored suits, and glamorous feminine evening wear. Blass also does a less expensive line of women's clothing, called Blassport. Under licensing agreements, the Bill Blass name appears on many products, including furs, bed linens, towels, fragrances, watches, scarves, rainwear, women's sportswear, menswear, and even chocolates. He has also designed automobile interiors for Lincoln Continental and uniforms for American Airlines' flight attendants.

During his career, Blass has received many awards. He is a member of the Coty Hall of Fame and holds special Coty awards for fur design and menswear, and a special citation for his overall excellence in many fields. He was one of the top five American designers invited to Paris to show designs at a special **Versailles fashion show of 1973.** He is a member and former vice president of the Council of Fashion Designers of America.

Donald Brooks

Donald Brooks was born in 1929 in New Haven, Connecticut, and educated at Syracuse University and Parsons School of Design. He established himself as a talented freelance designer early in his career, especially in his costume designs for theater and films. His costumes for the Broadway musical *No Strings* won him the New York Drama Critics Award. Among his film credits are costumes for *Star* and *Darling Lili.*

Brooks opened a company under his own name in 1965 with the support of fashion entrepreneur Ben Shaw. When their partnership ended in 1973, Brooks founded his own couture business. He is known for simple, uncluttered lines, superb tailoring, and unusual colors. He designs his own fabrics, and distinctive prints are part of every collection. Brooks presents a full collection of sportswear, dresses, suits, coats, and evening wear. He is involved in all areas of design, including household linens, intimate apparel, menswear, costume jewelry, and shoes.

His many awards include the American Fashion Critics Award for sportswear, the National Cotton Award, the Coty Award, and the American Printed Fabrics Council Award. In 1974 he became the fourth person to receive the Parsons Medal for Design, joining previous recipients Norman Norell, Adrian, and Claire McCardell.

Stephen Burrows

Born in 1943 in Newark, New Jersey, Stephen Burrows was encouraged to sew by his grandmother and began making clothes at the age of eight. He studied at the Philadelphia Museum College of Art and the Fashion Institute of Technology (FIT) in New York. Burrows began his fashion career designing boutique fashions. After several design jobs, he joined the retail store Henri Bendel in 1969 as house designer. In 1973 Burrows and Roz Rubenstein, a former FIT classmate and accessory buyer for Bendel's, formed a partnership and opened their own firm on Seventh Avenue.

Burrows established his reputation with sexy dresses made of soft clingy fabrics like matte jersey and chiffon. His trademark is unhemmed skirts with stitched edges that create his fluttering "lettuce" look. He is known as a fashion leader, not a follower. He has won three Coty Awards including a Special Award for lingerie. Burrows was one of the five American designers invited to show their collections at Versailles in 1973.

Hattie Carnegie

Hattie Kanengeiser (1889–1956) emigrated to America with her family from Vienna when she was eleven. She changed her name to Carnegie in admiration of Andrew Carnegie, and in 1909, with a seamstress friend, Rose Roy, she opened a hat and dress shop on East 10th Street in New York City. Although Hattie Carnegie could not sew, she designed hats and waited on customers. The business flourished, and in 1919 she bought out her partner. Carnegie had outstanding fashion sense and was soon head of a million-dollar business that included a custom operation, a retail store, and a wholesale enterprise that distributed her merchandise to stores throughout the country.

Carnegie went to Paris twice a year and bought originals from all of the custom salons from which she made her own adaptations. She had an uncanny ability to take the best styles from Paris and give them her own special American feel. Although not an innovator, she was a taste maker who had considerable influence on American fashion. She was a perfectionist, and her clothes were the finest made in America during the 1920s and 1930s.

Carnegie had the ability to recognize fashion talent as well as good fashion design. She is credited by some for discovering and encouraging the design talents of Madeleine Vionnet. Several noted American designers worked for her, including Norman Norell, Jean Louis, and Claire McCardell. Norell, in fact, credited Carnegie with teaching him everything he knew. Carnegie's importance as a fashion power was evidenced by her receipt of a Neiman-Marcus Award in 1939 and a Coty American Fashion Critics Award in 1948.

Bonnie Cashin

Bonnie Cashin grew up in California, where she was born in Oakland in 1915. Her mother was a dressmaker. She studied art in New York and Paris, returning to her native state where she became a costume designer for Twentieth Century–Fox. After designing both period and modern clothes for sixty major films, she moved back to New York in 1949 to design sportswear. She is known for uniquely American fashions that are natural and timeless. She pioneered layered dressing and functional clothing. Associated with the "Cashin look" are comfortable country clothes in wool jersey, knits, tweeds, canvas, and leather. She is particularly remembered for her hooded coats trimmed in leather.

In 1950 Cashin received both the Coty and the Neiman-Marcus awards. She received a Coty Special Award for leather in 1961, a Return Award in 1968, and was elected to the Hall of Fame in 1972. She has also been honored with retrospective exhibitions in New York and London.

Oleg Cassini

Although born in Paris in 1913, Oleg Cassini spent the majority of his childhood in Florence, Italy, where his mother managed an exclusive dress shop. He studied design in Florence and began his career as a sketcher for the House of Patou in Paris. By the age of twenty he had his own private couture customers for a small salon in Rome. Moving to the United States in 1938, he worked first in New York as a Seventh Avenue designer before opening his own salon on Madison Avenue. In 1939 he moved to Hollywood, where he designed costumes first for Paramount and then for Twentieth Century–Fox. In 1950 Cassini moved back to New York where he opened a wholesale dress firm. He became the "official" White House dressmaker to Jacqueline Kennedy. In 1963 he returned to Italy and established a ready-to-wear business with his brother in Milan, where he designs both men's and women's apparel.

Liz Claiborne

Although born in Brussels, Belgium (1929), Liz Claiborne spent her early childhood in New Orleans. She began her fashion career in 1949 when she won the *Harper's Bazaar*–Jacques Heim National Design Contest. The prize was a trip to Europe to study design. She worked in New York as an assistant to several designers before she became chief designer at Youth Guild, Inc., where she remained for fifteen years. At Youth Guild she was among the first to merchandise the total clothing concept, which overcame the rigid classification of clothing into either dresses or sportswear. Youth Guild was one of the first volume manufacturers to encourage stores to merchandise total wardrobes aimed for the contemporary customer. In 1976, with her husband Arthur Ortenberg, she formed Liz Claiborne, Inc. Her simple, sporty, moderately priced designs have been highly successful. She is known for a sensitive use of color and for simple, uncomplicated lines.

Oscar de la Renta

Born of Spanish parents in Santo Domingo in 1932, Oscar de la Renta was educated both in the Dominican Republic and in Madrid where he studied art. He had planned to become an abstract painter, but his career plans took a new direction when some of his fashion sketches were seen by Mrs. John Lodge, wife of the American ambassador to Spain. She commissioned him to design her daughter's debut gown. When Miss Lodge was photographed for the cover of *Life* Magazine wearing the white tulle gown designed by de la Renta, his fashion career began.

De la Renta's first professional position was as an apprentice at Eisa, Balenciaga's couture house in Madrid. In 1961 he became Antonio Castillo's assistant at Lanvin-Castillo in Paris. Two years later he moved to New York as designer at Elizabeth Arden, a position Castillo had held in the 1940s. In 1965 de la Renta and Jane Darby signed an agreement leading to the formation of Oscar de la Renta, Inc. Since 1966 he has produced boutique-priced ready-to-wear as well as couture clothes. He is now designing menswear, jewelry, accessories, household linens, and perfume.

In 1967 de la Renta was recognized as a fashion leader when he presented his Russian and gypsy fashion themes, which influenced the fashion trend for ethnic styles. He is best known for his imaginative use of transparent fabrics and for his opulent evening wear. His clothes are popular at both couture and boutique prices for their glamour and elegance. Besides winning the Coty American Fashion Critics

Award three times, he has been honored by his native Dominican Republic for being one of its most distinguished citizens.

Perry Ellis

After receiving a degree in retailing from New York University, Perry Ellis returned to Virginia, where he was born in 1940, and worked for the department store Miller and Rhoads, becoming a sportswear buyer. Ellis became interested in design when he realized he could design better clothes than those he saw being offered by manufacturers. He made a career change in 1968, joining John Meyer. When the company closed following Meyer's death in 1974, Ellis joined Vera Sportswear as vice president. Two years later he was designing sportswear for Vera under the label "Portfolio." This line was so successful that Manhattan Industries, the owner of Vera, established a new division under the Perry Ellis label. His designs were immediately successful. Bloomingdale's became the first store to open a Perry Ellis boutique. In 1979 he received both the Coty American Fashion Critics Award and the Neiman-Marcus Award.

Ellis was known for designing casual, easy-to-wear clothes that were young but also appealed to older women. His designs had a European sense of scale and color. He was not afraid to exaggerate, but his clothes were always wearable. He produced sportswear in the Anne Klein tradition, using natural textures in cottons, linens, and wool, combined with hand-knit sweaters. His approach to fashion was practical and informal. He liked to design clothes that were different from what other designers were doing and he felt that clothes should exhibit the wearer's personality. Since his death in 1986, the Perry Ellis label has been continued by the company.

James Galanos

James Galanos, born in 1925 in Philadelphia, studied fashion at the Traphagen School in New York and began his career by selling sketches to New York manufacturers, including Hattie Carnegie. He went to California, where he worked for Jean Louis, and in 1947 he left for Paris. After a few months working for Robert Piguet, he returned to New York, where he became a designer for Davidow. The structure of Seventh Avenue was not to his liking, and he left for California, starting his own business there in 1951.

Galanos is considered among the top American designers, equal to the great Paris couturiers. His clients include Nancy Reagan and many other prominent, wealthy women. His clothes are very expensive, and his collections show a dedication to quality and perfection. He is known for luxurious day and evening clothes constructed in superb fabrics.

The Fashion Institute of Technology honored him with a retrospective show in

1976. His numerous awards include the Neiman-Marcus Award in 1954, the Coty American Fashion Critics Award in 1954 and 1956, the Coty Hall of Fame in 1959, Filene's Young Talent Design Award, 1958, and the Cotton Fashion Award in 1958.

Halston

Born in Des Moines, Iowa, in 1932, Roy Halston Forwick grew up in Evansville, Indiana, and attended Indiana University and the Chicago Art Institue. While still a student in Chicago, he began designing and making hats, which he sold at small shops at the Ambassador Hotel. In 1957 Halston moved to New York, where he worked for Lilly Dache as a millinery designer. In 1959 he became millinery designer at Berdgorf Goodman, designing the pillbox hat that Jacqueline Kennedy wore at her husband's inauguration in 1961. Halston was so successful as milliner that he began to design apparel for Berdgorf Goodman, and in 1966 the store opened a boutique selling his hats and ready-to-wear. In 1968 he opened his own couture house for custom apparel, adding in 1970 a ready-to-wear line called Halston International. He opened Halston Originals in 1972, which made ready-to-wear available to store buyers throughout the country. In 1973 the business was bought by Norton Simon, Inc., and renamed Halston Enterprises. It expanded in 1975, adding menswear and perfume.

The Halston look is based on minimal and conceptual art principles. His simple, understated clothes have a sense of sophistication and elegance that appeals to the elite fashion leaders. His evening wear is always glamorous and sexy, and his simple, clean-cut day clothes include cashmere sweaters, shirtwaist dresses, wrap-around skirts, and turtlenecks. His classic ultrasuede dress became a status symbol.

Halston has had a wide influence on other American designers and has received numerous awards. He won a Coty Special Award in 1962 and in 1969, a Winnie in 1971, a Return Award in 1972, and was elected to the Coty Hall of Fame in 1974. He participated in the Versailles show of five American designers in 1973.

Charles James

Charles James was the son of a British army officer and an American mother. Born in Sandhurst, England, in 1906, he moved to Chicago, his mother's hometown, at the age of nineteen and opened a hat shop. His hat business was successful, and he moved to New York in 1928, where he made hats and dresses for private customers. In 1929 he went to London to open a dress house. Over the next ten years he moved back and forth between New York and London, and in 1934 he established a salon in Paris. During the 1920s and 1930s James dressed some of the world's most fashionable women from his couture salons in London and Paris. In 1939 he returned to New York to operate his own custom order business.

James was acknowledged as an equal by top Paris couturiers. Balenciaga called him the "world's best and only dressmaker," and Dior claimed that James had inspired his New Look. James was an innovative genius who was unpredictable, complex, and eccentric. He saw his clothes as works of art that belonged in a museum, and he believed he was the greatest couturier of the century. He made clothes in the classic couture tradition but did not believe in fashion seasons. He continued working on his designs and kept them on the market for years. He developed approximately 200 designs that were the basis of all of his work. He is best remembered for his stiff, sculptural ball gowns, many of which are now in museum costume collections.

James was one of the first couture designers to apply his ideas to mass production. In 1949 he established Charles James Services to produce his ready-to-wear. Although this venture met with failure, it was the forerunner of today's designer-label industry.

James retired in 1958 and spent the 1960s lecturing and conducting seminars at the Rhode Island School of Design and the Pratt Institute. He died in New York in 1978.

Norma Kamali

Born in 1945 in New York City, Norma Kamali studied fashion illustration at the Fashion Institute of Technology. After graduating in 1964, she worked for an airline; this enabled her to travel to London, where she spent many weekends and was influenced by London fashion designers. In 1968 she opened a shop with her husband to sell English and French clothes in New York. She soon began designing her own line, and Kamali Ltd. became known for its originality. In 1978 she divorced and established OMO Norma Kamali, the OMO standing for "On My Own."

Kamali's clothes are considered young and modern but never too extreme. They are very up-to-the-minute because she constantly adds new things to her collection. She has introduced several influential looks, such as padded jumpsuits, lycra outfits, quilted sleeping bag coats, and the Ra-Ra skirt. Her use of parachute fabric and cotton sweatshirting has turned sportswear into streetwear. Her ideas have been widely copied, and in 1983 the Council of Fashion Designers of America voted her the outstanding designer of the year.

Donna Karan

Donna Karan was born in Forest Hills, New York, in 1948, and she was raised on Long Island. Karan was influenced by fashion from an early age; her mother was a model and sales manager of a dress firm and her father a well-known haberdasher. She attended Parsons School of Design, quiting to continue a summer job as a sketcher with Anne Klein, where she remained for nine months. After working for Patti Cappalli at Addenda for eighteen months, she returned to Anne Klein as a designer in 1968. Following Klein's death in 1974, Donna Karan became codesigner with Louis Dell'Olio. Together they won Coty awards in 1977, 1982, and 1984. She left Anne Klein in 1985 to produce under her own name. She was an immediate success with her capsule wardrobe approach to dressing based on separate pieces. She has also gained recognition for her elegant accessories.

Anne Klein

Anne Klein (1923–1974) was born Hannah Golofski in New York, where she got her start in the fashion industry at the age of fifteen as a freelance sketcher. In 1948 she and her first husband, Ben Klein, formed their own company, Junior Sophisticates. In 1968 she and her second husband founded Anne Klein and Company and Anne Klein Studio, both purchased by Takiho Company of Japan in 1973.

Anne Klein was well known for designing classic sportswear and for transforming junior-size clothing from little-girl cuteness to adult sophistication. She is considered the designer who epitomized the American sportswear look. She designed clothes to fit the lifestyles of active career women and understood clearly a woman's need for classic blazers, pants, and skirts. She received many awards, including the Neiman-Marcus Award in 1959 and 1969, and several Coty awards, leading to election to the Hall of Fame in 1971. She was one of the five designers invited to show at Versailles in 1973.

Calvin Klein

Calvin Klein was born (1942) and spent his childhood in the Bronx, New York. He attended the New York High School of Art and Design and graduated from the Fashion Institute of Technology in 1962. After five years with three Seventh Avenue firms, Klein joined forces with his childhood friend, Barry Schwartz, and opened Calvin Klein, Ltd., in 1968. His first collection of three dresses and six coats was bought by Bonwit Teller and sold rapidly. The business was an immediate success, shipping a million dollars in orders the first year.

Klein's first coats were classic styles inspired by Yves Saint Laurent. Klein soon found his own distinctive style but one that remains more European than that of many New York designers. He designs simple, classic, understated clothes that age well, becoming more beautiful as they are worn. He prefers natural fibers, using mohair, cashmere, wool, silk, and suede. His subtle use of color emphasizes earth tones and neutrals, and brown is his signature color.

In addition to ready-to-wear, Calvin Klein's name appears on shoes, handbags, menswear, hosiery, and perfume. His best-known product is his designer jeans. His approach to fashion based on jeans may prove to be his most lasting contribution to fashion. He makes clothes that are wearable, and he understands his customers well. Klein was the first designer to win the Coty American Fashion Critics Award for three consecutive years: 1973, 1974, and 1975.

Ralph Lauren

Ralph Lauren, born in New York in 1939, studied business at night school at the College of the City of New York while he sold ties at Brooks Brothers. He later became an assistant buyer for Allied Stores. In 1967 Beau Brummel Neckwear hired Lauren to design ties under the name Polo. The name was chosen to suggest classic clothes with an understated, gentlemanly look reminiscent of the elegance of the 1930s. In 1968 Lauren established Polo as a separate business and broadened the concept to a total look, including clothing, shirts, sportswear, knitwear, shoes, and luggage. In 1971 he introduced a line of man-tailored women's shirts. His first complete women's collection under the Ralph Lauren label was introduced in 1972. Later he added boy's wear under the Polo name, fragrances for men and women, Polo Western Wear, and Chaps, a less-expensive menswear line. His more recent contributions include designing furniture, and linens for bed and bath. All of Lauren's designs bear his hallmarks of fine quality, exact detailing, and expensive natural fibers. His inspirations are all-American, and his style has been widely copied. Particularly popular are his Wild West and prairie styles.

In 1973 Lauren gained recognition for designing the men's costumes for *The Great Gatsby*. His costumes for this film and for *Annie Hall* in 1977 greatly influenced fashions for both men and women. Lauren received the Neiman-Marcus Award in 1973 and has received six Coty American Fashion Critics awards.

Mainbocher

Main Rousseau Bocher (1890–1976) was the first American to design couture apparel in Paris and had a noted career as a fashion journalist before becoming a designer. Born in Chicago, he wanted to be an opera singer and was also interested in art. In 1917 he went to Paris with an American ambulance unit. After World War I, he remained in Paris, where he first worked for *Harper's Bazaar* and later became the editor of *French Vogue*. He left his successful career in 1929 to open his own couture house under the name of Mainbocher. His clothes had classic elegance and often incorporated the bias cut, which made them drape with ease. World War II forced him to close his successful establishment, and in 1940 he moved to New York, where he opened a salon, producing very expensive, elegant clothes in the tradition of French haute couture. His clothes were custom-made for private customers only; none were sold for copying or were mass produced. His name appeared only on his own clothes; he never licensed it to use on accessories.

Some of Mainbocher's fashion firsts were the strapless dress (1934), short evening dress (1941), decorated evening sweaters (1941), waist cinch (1930), and theater-dinner suits (1934). He also designed the uniforms for the Waves (women's navy corps), the Women's Marine Corps, and the Girl Scouts. He was most famous for designing the wedding gown for Mrs. Wallis Simpson for her marriage to the Duke of Windsor. Simpson's pale blue gown was perhaps the most photographed and widely copied dress ever designed.

Mainbocher was the first couturier to impose a caution fee or guarantee of purchase on those who came to view his collection. He did this to bar copiers and tourists from his shows. Clients were required to sign for the purchase of a dress in advance or deposit a fee equal to the price of the cheapest dress in the collection.

Vera Maxwell

Vera Maxwell, born in New York City in 1904, studied tailoring in London where she was influenced by traditional menswear. After working as a model and a designer on Seventh Avenue in New York, she opened her own firm, Vera Maxwell Originals, in 1946. She designed timeless clothes and is considered one of the original group of designers, which included Bonnie Cashin and Claire McCardell, who designed in the American style. She designed simple, timeless, sporty clothes that were easy to wear. Following a classic approach to coordinated separates, she is famous for her weekend wardrobe of 1935, riding habit suits, and war worker's clothing designed during World War II. She won a Coty Special Award in 1951 and was given the Neiman-Marcus Award in 1955. In 1970 the Smithsonian Institution in Washington, D.C., honored her with a retrospective show.

Claire McCardell

Claire McCardell (1905–1958) attended Hood College in Frederick, Maryland, where she was born, for two years before transferring to Parsons School of Design in New York to major in fashion design. She began her fashion career in 1929 as assistant to dress designer Robert Turk. In 1931 Turk's company closed, and he moved to Townley Frocks, taking McCardell with him as assistant designer. Following Turk's death a year later, McCardell took over as designer. In 1938 she created her first innovative fashion, the Monastic dress, so named because of its robelike appearance before it was belted. It was cut on the bias without a waistline seam and formed a tent silhouette until it was belted. The simplicity of this style made it easy to copy, and it was soon available at bargain prices. The enormous success of this dress led the way to a more casual, easy style of dressing for the American woman. Soon after the success of the Monastic dress, Townley Frocks closed, and McCardell went to work for Hattie Carnegie, one of the most prestigious designers of the time. She worked with Carnegie for two years, designing a line called Workshop Originals. In 1940 Townley reopened, and McCardell was brought back as the designer. Soon the company's label was changed to "Claire McCardell Clothes by Townley." McCardell remained with the company until her death.

Considered one of the most innovative and independent American designers, McCardell is credited with founding the American Look in clothes. She designed practical clothes that were functional, relaxed, casual, and comfortable, designed to suit the lifestyle of the American woman. The philosophy of the McCardell look was that clothing should fit the individual as well as the occasion, be comfortable as well as attractive, and flow naturally with the body. Claire McCardell clothes included dresses, coats, suits, separates, raincoats, ski wear, bathing suits, and even wedding dresses. Her favorite fabrics were cotton denim, ticking, gingham, calico, and wool jersey. She introduced to women's wear practical details from men's clothing, such as pockets, deep armholes, trouser pleats, and top-stitching. Her trademarks were functional metal fastenings, double stitching (sometimes called blue-jean stitching), brass hooks and other hardware closings, and spaghetti or shoestring ties.

McCardell's most productive period was during the 1940s, when she clearly established her unique look and introduced several clothing classics still wearable today. Some of her firsts, in addition to the Monastic dress, were the diaper bathing suit (1942), the popover, which was a surplice-wrapped housedress (1942), leotards (1943), and flat Capezio ballet shoes (1944). In 1946 McCardell designed a group of spring dresses with full circle skirts ten to twelve inches below the knee. Her thinking was clearly in line with Dior's New Look, which appeared at the same time. *Time* magazine cited her design talents as an "artist's sense of color and a sculptor's feeling for form," in 1955 when the magazine pictured her on its cover. Only two designers, Elsa Schiaparelli and Sophie Gimbel, had previously appeared on the cover of *Time*.

McCardell received the Coty American Fashions Critics Award in 1944, and was posthumously elected to the Hall of Fame in 1958. Her other awards were the Neiman-Marcus Award in 1948 and the Parsons Medal for Distinguished Achievement in 1956. Her book, *What Shall I Wear?*, was published in 1956. In 1972, fourteen years after her death, two major retrospective shows devoted entirely to McCardell designs were presented, one at the Fashion Institute of Technology in New York and the second at the Los Angeles County Museum. McCardell left a strong legacy to fashion, and her influence continues to be felt today.

Mary McFadden

Born in 1936 in New York City, Mary McFadden lived on a cotton plantation near Memphis, Tennessee, where her father was a cotton broker, until she was ten. Following her father's death, her mother moved the family to Long Island. After graduating from a Virginia military school, McFadden spent a year studying in Paris. In 1957 she returned to New York, where she studied at the Traphagen School of Design for one year and then earned a degree in sociology from Columbia University. Upon graduating, she was hired as public relations director for Christian Dior New York. In 1964 she moved to South Africa after marrying a DeBeers executive. She became merchandising editor for South African *Vogue*. After her marriage broke up, she remarried and moved to Rhodesia, where she founded a sculpture workshop for African artists. In 1970 she returned to New York to work as a special projects editor for *Vogue*.

McFadden's entry into fashion design came in 1973 when she designed three silk tunics that were featured in *Vogue*. Henri Bendel, a New York specialty store, bought the garments, and McFadden's career as a fashion designer was under way. She designs very expensive, elegant, highly individualistic clothing. Her trademarks are slim tunics and dresses with tiny knife pleats, silk pajamas, and quilted jackets and coats. Recognition of her talent has included the Coty American Fashion Critics Award in 1976 and the Return Award in 1978. She was elected to the Coty Hall of Fame and received the Neiman-Marcus Award in 1979.

Norman Norell

Norman Norell (1900–1972) was born in Noblesville, Indiana, as Norman Levinson. He was raised in Indianapolis, where his father owned a haberdashery store. From an early age he wanted to be an artist. In 1919 he went to New York to study illustration at the Parsons School of Design, but he switched to Pratt Institute where he majored in figure drawing and costume design. After graduating in 1921, he became a costume designer at the Astoria studio of Paramount Pictures; he designed clothes for Rudolph Valentino in *The Sainted Devil* and Gloria Swanson in *Zaza*. When the studio closed, he joined the staff of the Brooks Costume Company, designing for vaudeville and nightclub reviews. In 1924 he moved from costume to fashion design by accepting a position as designer for dress manufacturer Charles Armour. Four years later he joined the prestigious firm of Hattie Carnegie, where he remained until 1941.

Norell learned much about taste, style, and fashion from Carnegie. Accompanying her on trips to Paris, he was able to assimilate the European approach to fashion. He examined clothes that were purchased in Paris twice a year, pulling them apart to see how they were made. By doing this he learned to recognize and appreciate quality. Norell remained with Carnegie as a designer for twelve years until 1941 when he joined manufacturer Anthony Traina to form Traina-Norell. In 1960 Norell took over the business when Traina became ill, and with the help of some silent backers he purchased the firm.

Norell was a trendsetter who made many contributions to fashion. Among the trends associated with Norell are the sequined cocktail dress, the cloth coat lined with fur, the sweater-topped evening skirt, and the revival of the chemise dress. The backbone of his collections was the simple wool jersey dress. One of his trademarks was the simple, high round neckline. He believed that the function of fashion was to enhance a woman's beauty. He encouraged simplicity in dress during the day and elegance at night. His perfume, introduced in 1968, was the first successful American designer perfume.

Called the Dean of American fashion, Norell built a reputation equal to those of the top French designers. He provided the bridge between the tradition of couture design and ready-to-wear. He freed American fashion from dependence on foreign sources of inspiration and showed it was possible to create artistically in ready-to-wear. His elegant sophisticated clothes were impeccably tailored and the equal of any produced in Europe.

Norell was the first to receive the Coty American Fashion Critics Award in 1943. He again won a Coty in 1951, and in 1958 he became the first designer elected to the Hall of Fame. Other awards he received include the Neiman-Marcus Award in 1942 and the Parsons Medal for Distinguished Achievement in 1956. Pratt Institute awarded him an honorary degree, Doctor of Fine Arts, in 1962. The final honor of his career was a retrospective showing of his work at the Metropolitan Museum of Art on October 16, 1972. On the eve of the show, Norell suffered a stroke and never regained consciousness.

John Weitz

Born in 1923 in Berlin, Germany, John Weitz studied at St. Paul's and Oxford in England and came to the United States in 1940. He worked as a designer for several firms, and in 1954 started to design his own collection, producing practical, young, and sporty menswear. Soon afterward he began designing women's clothing with the same masculine, casual, easy-to-wear look. In the 1960s he devised a system for ready-to-wear couture whereby clients chose the style and fabric from a series of sketches and fabric swatches. Since 1970 he has concentrated on menswear and has opened a chain of boutiques. He received a Coty American Fashion Critics Award in 1974. In addition to being a designer, he has written three books. The first, *The Value of Nothing,* is a novel based on the fashion world. *Man in Charge* and *Sports Clothes for Your Sports* are guides to dress.

Summary of Key Points

1. Today, many American designers are fashion leaders, and their labels have become status symbols throughout the world.

2. Important American fashion design awards include: the Neiman-Marcus Award, the Coty American Fashion Critics Award, and the Council of Fashion Designers Award.

3. Many American designers participate in licensing agreements with manufacturers to use their name on various products for a share of the profits.

4. There are five types of designers: custom designers, couture designers, mass production designers, freelance designers, and stylists.

5. The three major divisions of an apparel manufacturer include: design, production, and sales.

6. Various occupations involving the processes of apparel design include: designer, assistant designer, sample cutter, sample maker, patternmaker, and sketcher.

Laura Ashley, Inc.

The Laura Ashley business, famous for its dainty Victorian prints and English country clothes, was founded in 1953 by Laura and Bernard Ashley. Laura provided the designs for both the fabrics and the products while Bernard, her husband, was the strategist who handled the production. The Ashleys' first products were tablemats and scarves that they printed on an old kitchen table in the living room of their London apartment and sold to small shops and department stores throughout the city.

The kitchen-table process that they used limited them to printing only squares of fabric. Bernard moved the business forward when he designed the textile printing machines Laura needed to produce her patterns. Bernard's system moved the fabric in a roll from a feed roller to a batch roller across a short printing bed where each repeat of the design was printed using hand screens. A curing oven located at the end of the printer fixed the dyes to the fabric. This new machinery enabled the Ashleys to greatly increase their production and widen their market. Home-furnishing fabrics and dress fabrics were added to their merchandise offerings.

The Ashley family by this time included two children, and the decision was made to move the family to the country. In an idyllic country setting—a cottage set in an orchard and facing open farmlands—Laura Ashley developed her design philosophy. The family's lifestyle of quiet country living became the inspiration for Laura Ashley's romantic Victorian floral prints.

Bernard soon moved the factory from London to a location a few miles from the cottage. He built a bigger printing machine, and the business was expanded to international markets, with fabrics exported to customers in Paris, Amsterdam, the United States, and Australia.

In 1957 the company opened a showroom on Burlington Street, London, and this led to greatly increased sales of Laura Ashley fabrics. More employees were added to the factory. By the end of the 1950s the Ashleys' business was growing, but they could not expand the factory because southeastern England did not want factories built. The family decided to return to Laura's home, Wales. Bernard continued to run the factory and London showroom while Laura moved the family to Wales, where a second small factory was soon opened, and Laura added dresses to her product line. Laura's original dresses were not intended to be fashionable but simply dresses to wear at home. The dresses were an immediate success, and a new factory was added to meet production needs.

The Laura Ashley firm entered the retail business in the 1960s with the opening of a small (500-square-foot) store in South Kensington. At first the shop had so little business that it was used as a wholesale showroom. Following the advertising of a dress on London subway posters, sales increased, and the successful Laura Ashley retail business was under way. Since the late 1960s, the firm has continued to move into retailing. By 1985 the company operated 220 stores worldwide plus factories in Wales, Holland, Ireland, and Kentucky.

By 1980 Laura Ashley was very much a family business, including as it did the participation of the four Ashley children. Son Nick became head of the design department in 1982, and David directed retail development in the United States. The two daughters, Jane and Emma, have been involved through photography and design. In 1985 the company went public, but the family orientation of the business continued.

Laura Ashley died in 1985 at the age of 60 after suffering a fall at her daughter's home. Since her death, the business has continued to expand, and Laura's prints have been becoming increasingly popular. In addition to selling fabrics Laura Ashley stores now offer a wide variety of coordinated home furnishings and apparel. Among the home-furnishing products are bed and bath linens, cushion covers, lampshades, vinyl wallcoverings, wallpaper borders, ceramic tile, china dinnerware, and collectibles such as vases, cups and saucers, pitchers, and picture frames. Paint that coordinates with the fabrics and wallcoverings is also sold. Several books illustrating how to furnish a home in the Laura Ashley style are available.

Included in the apparel offerings are dresses and jumpers with the classic Laura Ashley styling of long, soft skirts, floral prints, and romantic trimmings. The romantic and innocent Laura Ashley look is also available in sportswear separates and coordinated fashion accessories such as scarves, hats, and shoes. Dressing-room accessories provide a coordinated look for the customer's closet. Laura Ashley prints decorate picture frames, padded hangers, jewelry and hat boxes, and dressing-table accessories. Other miscellaneous products include luggage and small travel bags covered in cotton chintz, stationery, fragrances, and personal toiletries. All Laura Ashley products are distinguished by the same English country look featuring floral prints.

Recently the firm has added specialty stores under the names Laura Ashley Mother & Child and Laura Ashley Home. Mother & Child shops feature classic Laura Ashley clothing for maternity wear and children's wear. The Laura Ashley Home stores sell home furnishings and offer custom decorating and interior design services. In-shop consultants advise customers in their selection of products to create the Laura Ashley look in their homes, and on-site consultations with interior designers are also available. Custom-made window treatments, bedcoverings, and furniture are offered.

Laura Ashley stores offer a nationwide gift registry service for the bride-to-be. Mother & Child also provides a gift registry for newborns through which the mother can select her preferences in fabric colors and prints, wallcoverings, bed linens, decorative accessories, and baby garments. Gift selections are monitored nationally to help eliminate duplications.

Laura Ashley shops are generally small in size and do not carry a full range of products. Any Laura Ashley product may be mail ordered, however, either direct or through one of the stores. Catalogs are produced seasonally, and customers may place orders by using a toll-free number.

Key Words and Concepts

Define, identify, or explain each of the following:

American Look	line
collection	marker
Coty American Fashion Critics Award	mass production designer
Council of Fashion Designers Award	Neiman-Marcus Award
couture	patternmaker
couture designer	production seasons
custom-made apparel	refabricate
designer label	RTW
designer licensing	sample maker
dressmaker	Seventh Avenue designer
fabrication	style piracy
findings	stylist
freelance designer	sweetener
grading	Versailles fashion show of 1973
knock-off	Winnie

Discussion Questions and Topics

1. What are some of the ways in which the talents of American designers were strengthened and enhanced during the first half of the twentieth century?

2. Why are the names of many American designers unknown to the buying public?·

3. Name the five types of designers, and explain the responsibilities of each.

4. Describe the steps in designing a line for a manufacturer.

5. Describe the steps involved in production of fashion apparel.

6. Why is it that all of the styles by a designer are not mass produced by the manufacturer?

7. Why do designers make licensing agreements with manufacturers?

8. Describe the responsibilities of the workers who assist the designer with the design process.
9. Name the American designers who were invited to show in the Versailles fashion show in 1973. What Parisienne designers also participated in this show?

Notes

Claire McCardell, *What Shall I Wear?* New York: Simon and Schuster, 1956, p. 107.

Stanley Marcus, *Minding the Store*. Boston: Little, Brown, 1974, p. 101.

CHAPTER 6 _____

MANUFACTURERS OF APPAREL

THE PRODUCTION of ready-made apparel and accessories in the United States is a large, many-faceted industry that includes firms manufacturing products for men, women, children, and infants. These firms produce a wide range of products, including outerwear, undergarments, fur goods, millinery, gloves, belts, shoes, handbags, and small leather goods. The largest segment of the industry is ready-made apparel. According to the latest U.S. Census of Manufacturing, 19,000 companies produce apparel in more than 21,000 plants (U.S. Department of Commerce 1982).

The apparel industry is made up of firms ranging in size from small entrepreneurial operations to large industrial **conglomerates** located in almost every state. It is a highly volatile industry in which a manufacturer's performance is subject to the demands of an often fickle consumer, and cyclical consumer trends have a strong effect on profitability. The company with the hottest selling merchandise today may be out of business next year or even next season because of its failure to recognize changing fashion trends and to make appropriate adjustments in production.

The American apparel industry is known by several names: the needle trade, the cutting-up trade, the rag business, the garment business. The women's segment of the industry is also referred to as the **ready-to-wear** (RTW) business. The ready-made apparel industry, which began in the early nineteenth century with a few small entrepreneurs, today serves as a major part of the U.S. economy and impacts many businesses. In 1988 U.S. apparel production (Figure 6.1) totaled $71 billion in retail value (*Focus* 1988, p. 4).

This chapter presents the history and development of ready-made clothing. Also discussed are the locations, operations, and economics of the American apparel industry, including apparel for men, women, and children. The businesses that produce fashion accessories are discussed in Chapter 7.

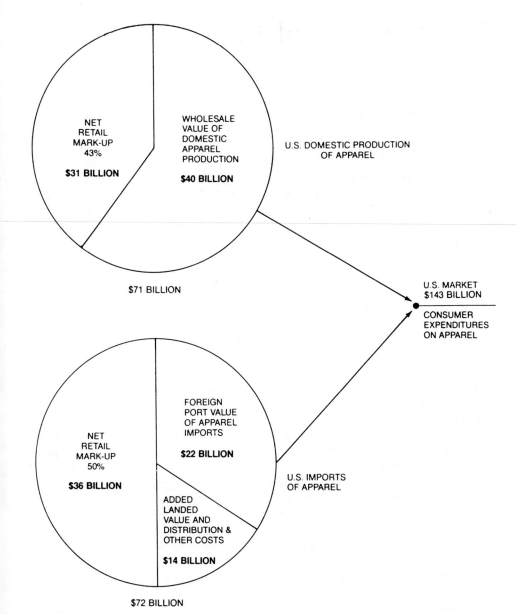

FIGURE 6.1
1988 Consumer expenditures in apparel. (Source: *American Apparel Manufacturers Association.*)

Development of Ready-Made Apparel

The first ready-made clothing was produced for men and sold in London in the early seventeenth century. For the next 200 years the manufacture of ready-made clothes was opposed by traditional tailors, who were afraid that such clothing would put them out of business. Despite their attempts to stop the production of ready-to-wear, it continued. By 1770 ready-made men's suits were sold in Paris, and between 1804 and 1806 several shops selling ready-made coats opened there.

Slop Shops

In the United States all clothing was made on an individual basis either at home or custom-made by professional dressmakers and tailors until about 1790. Ready-made clothing stores began to appear in New York before 1800 and in Boston and Baltimore by 1820. These stores cut the garments and contracted out to tailors who sewed at home.

The first American ready-made clothing was produced in the port cities of New York, Boston, Philadelphia, and Baltimore. It consisted of simple shirts, trousers, and jackets sold in stores called **slop shops,** so named because their primary customer was the sailor who stowed his gear on board ship in a slop chest. The term *slop* also described the quality and fit of this merchandise. Even though slop shops sold poorly constructed garments made of low-quality fabrics, sailors patronized them because they could be outfitted quickly and inexpensively during their brief visits onshore. They often did not remain in port long enough to have clothing custom-made. These shops also provided ready-made clothing for slaves and laborers.

Shortly after 1800 the slop shops began to "trade up" by offering higher priced, better quality ready-made clothing. Men who did not have a wife or other family member to sew for them were attracted to these shops as were those who wanted less expensive clothing or did not want to wait for apparel to be custom-made. As cities grew and more white-collar jobs became available, the demand for better ready-made clothing increased.

Brooks Brothers is an example of one of these early slop shops. Established in New York City in 1818 by Henry Sands Brooks, today Brooks Brothers is a large chain of stores specializing in traditional tailored apparel for the businessman. Brooks Brothers remains a vertically integrated company producing much of the merchandise it sells. Such **dual distribution** was a characteristic of early slop shops and is a practice still found in menswear today.

At the same time the slop shops were developing, other merchants did a large business selling secondhand clothes or clothes that had been made-to-order by traditional tailors and dressmakers but had been refused by the clients who had

Brooks Brothers is a vertically integrated company producing much of the merchandise it sells.
Source: Reprinted with permission of Brooks Brothers, Inc.

ordered them. Prior to the Civil War the trade in secondhand clothing was more important than that in ready-to-wear. Much of this apparel was shipped to the West and the South where it was worn by laborers and slaves. Such secondhand stores remained important even into the early twentieth century in New York, providing clothing for immigrants and transients.

Expansion of the Apparel Industry

By 1840 ready-made garments were accepted by many consumers. Stylish clothing was available in retail stores in many cities. The manufacture of ready-to-wear was on the threshold of tremendous growth, and many new firms were entering the business. By 1835 New York City was already established as the nation's center for ready-made clothing. Boston, Philadelphia, Newark, and Baltimore had also become important production areas. In the 1850s Cincinnati and St. Louis became manufacturing centers as well.

Two historical events in the middle of the nineteenth century encouraged the development of the apparel industry in the United States: the California Gold Rush in 1849 and the Civil War, which began in 1861. Both of these events created a need for faster production of men's clothing to meet increased demand.

The Gold Rush and Levi Strauss

The Gold Rush led to the development of the first and probably the most American of all garments—blue jeans. Levi Strauss went west hoping to strike it rich in the gold rush, carrying with him a roll of sailcloth with which to make tents. When he arrived, he found prospectors in desperate need of durable work clothes. Using his sailcloth to make work pants, he created the first "Levi's," which he double-topstitched for extra strength. Later, Strauss changed to a cotton fabric imported from France called *serge de Nimes*. The name of the fabric was shortened to de Nimes and later became known as denim. Levi Strauss set up his manufacturing business in San Francisco, where the company headquarters remains today.

The Civil War

The great demand for uniforms created by the Civil War encouraged further growth of the apparel industry. The Civil War also helped to develop the first system for the standardization of sizes. A study of the height and chest measurements of army recruits by the U.S. government provided the first data on the form and build of American men. This data was later used by apparel manufacturers to establish standards for sizes in men's clothing. Sizing standards for women's ready-to-wear did not develop until the early 1900s.

Technological Developments

Until the mid–nineteenth century, all ready-made clothing was cut and constructed by hand. Several important technological developments were necessary to make mass production of ready-made clothing possible. The first of these developments involved the manufacture of textiles. As discussed in Chapter 4, several inventions enabled the textile industry to grow during the first half of the nineteenth century so that by 1850 the industry could produce sufficient raw material to support mass production of apparel. Other technological developments needed to fully develop the apparel industry were the sewing machine and graded patterns.

The Sewing Machine

Probably the most important invention needed for the development of the apparel industry was the sewing machine. In fact, the perfection of the sewing machine was a necessity if clothing were to be mass produced. During the eighteenth century, several inventors in Germany, England, and Austria tried without success to develop a satisfactory sewing machine. In 1830 a French tailor, Barthelemy Thimonnier, patented a chain-stitch, one-thread sewing machine. By 1841 eighty of his machines were installed in a Paris factory producing army uniforms. Tailors, who were afraid that the machines would put them out of business, stormed the factory and destroyed all of the machines. Thimonnier produced additional machines in 1848, but they, too, were destroyed by a mob of tailors.

In America beginning in 1832, there were literally dozens of men working on the invention of the sewing machine. The four considered the most important contributors to the sewing machine in America were Walter Hunt, Elias Howe, Isaac Singer, and Allen Wilson. Between 1832 and 1834 Walter Hunt developed a two-thread machine that made a lockstitch. Elias Howe made improvements on this machine and was the first to take out a patent in 1846. During the next few years, several Americans, including Isaac Singer and Allen Wilson, continued making improvements in the sewing machine. Singer began manufacturing his machines in 1850, and by 1860 manufacturers began to use sewing machines for the mass production of clothing.

The sewing machine was seen as a great benefit to women who made the family's clothing. Louis Godey, publisher of *Godey's Lady's Book,* wrote in 1856 that "next to the plow the sewing machine is perhaps humanity's most blessed instrument." Undoubtedly, it released women from hours of sewing drudgery. In addition to benefiting the person who sews at home, the sewing machine opened the way for the apparel industry.

The original sewing machines were cumbersome and difficult to operate. They were also expensive, selling from $100 to $150 in the 1850s. By 1858, however, prices had dropped dramatically because of mass production, and by 1860 the sewing machine led to a revolution in the apparel industry. It made faster production possible at the same time that the Civil War created a considerable demand for **men's clothing.** The mass-market ready-to-wear industry was founded on the factories that made uniforms for Union soldiers in the Civil War. Following the war, production in some of the factories was converted to women's and children's wear.

Graded Paper Patterns

The third invention that helped to develop the ready-to-wear industry was the sized or graded pattern. In 1863 Ebenezer Butterick and his wife introduced the first graded paper patterns, for boys' shirts. By 1871 the Buttericks produced six million patterns a year, mostly for women's clothing. The patterns were marketed through the Buttericks' own magazine, the *Metropolitan*, which later became *The Delineator*. Another line of paper patterns was introduced by Madame Demorest, who also sold her patterns through a magazine, *Mirror of Fashion*. Although these patterns were meant to be used by dressmakers and those who sewed at home, the concept was adopted by apparel manufacturers.

Women's Ready-to-Wear

The women's ready-to-wear industry developed at a much slower pace than did the menswear industry. The elaborate styles of women's clothing in the nineteenth century made mass production difficult. As early as 1820 a few stores sold imported ready-made dresses. Examples of retail advertisements for ready-made suits and dresses can be found dating from the 1830s and 1840s, but it was not until after the invention of the sewing machine that the women's ready-to-wear business really began. The first mention of women's apparel production was in the U.S. Census of 1860, which listed ninety-six manufacturers of cloaks (coats), **mantillas** (short capes), and hoop skirts. The industry grew rapidly after this time, increasing to 562 firms in 1880 and 2,700 by 1900.

Between 1870 and 1880 most of the clothes being made were still for men and children. Cloaks and mantillas continued to be the primary garments made for women. Few, if any, dresses were ready-made because of their complex style.

In 1884 women's wear **manufacturers** were located in New York, Philadelphia, Boston, Chicago, Cleveland, and Tennessee. Whereas the ready-to-wear industry continued to grow, the clothes produced were considered to be for those of the lower classes who could not afford to hire a seamstress or to have them custom-made at the large stores. This was to change as the end of the century neared.

The Shirtwaist Craze

The garment most responsible for making women's ready-made clothing more acceptable was the blouse, called a **shirtwaist** or waist, which was worn with suits. During the 1890s the suit with a shirtwaist became the standard daytime dress of the middle-class woman, especially the secretary or typist. The shirtwaist provided versatility in women's wardrobes and could be worn alone with a skirt during hot summer weather. Because of its simple design and easy fit, manufacturers were able to mass produce the shirtwaist in a variety of styles, fabrics, and prices. The first shirtwaist manufacturer opened in 1891, and soon every store was featuring waists. They ranged in price from 50 cents to as high as $150 for one handmade of silk.

The shirtwaist became even more popular when it was featured in the illustrations of the Gibson girl by Charles Dana Gibson near the turn of the century. The Gibson girl made the shirtwaist worn with a skirt a national symbol, and the shirtwaist became the first national fashion craze. The 1900 Census listed shirtwaist manufacturers as a separate branch of the apparel industry and reported 472 such manufacturers in New York alone.

At the beginning of the twentieth century, the source of most women's clothing was still fabric departments or dressmakers. An illustration of the importance of dressmakers and home sewing in the first decade of the twentieth century was the size of the fabric department at B. Altman in New York. The first floor fabric department had 250 salespeople selling yard goods to retail customers, and on the third floor fourteen salespeople sold wholesale fabrics to dressmakers. B. Altman also sent its buyers to Paris to buy models and fabrics from the French couture to be copied by American dressmakers.

Dress Production

About 1900 someone originated the ready-to-wear street dress by joining a shirtwaist to a skirt. Dress firms gradually evolved from shirtwaist makers and some from makers of wrappers. The **wrapper** was a robelike dress that women wore at home. It was floorlength with a pinched waist and leg-of-mutton sleeves. By 1905 the wrapper had become a housedress. At this time dress manufacturers were classified as either housedress or **silk dress firms,** the latter being any firm that did not produce housedresses, regardless of the fabric used in production. In 1909 there were 1,600 waist and dress factories in the United States, and by 1920 the Census listed 2,655 factories making waists and dresses.

Both the automobile and World War I greatly influenced women's lifestyles and the way that they dressed. Automobile registration grew from 8,000 in 1900 to 8 million in 1920 and 28 million in 1926. Automobiles made it easier for people to go to the city to shop in the large stores where they were exposed to the latest fashions. The automobile greatly increased mobility and broadened people's activities, creating a need for more and different types of clothes. In 1900 the average woman had a few housedresses and one or two "Sunday" dresses for church and special occasions. By 1920 she needed a far greater variety of dresses for her different activities. Women now bought different dresses for business, travel, sports, and formal activities.

World War I also changed women's lifestyles. Many women went to work outside the home for the first time, and clothing became more practical to suit the requirements of the workplace. The end of World War I was followed by many political and social changes. Some middle-class women who had worked outside the home during the war continued to do so, receiving economic independence for the first time. After a long struggle, women were given the right to vote in 1920. More women were going to college and some even attended coeducational schools. Whether they were housewives or followed careers, American women felt the beginnings of emancipation.

During the 1920s dresses reflected the changes in women's lifestyles and became much simpler and easier to produce. Dresses also gained in popularity over the suit. By 1925 the cloak and suit segment of the industry had slipped from 50 percent to 35 percent of industry production. Many middle-class women turned to ready-to-wear as an easier way to obtain fashionable clothes rather than sewing clothes for themselves. Wealthy women still had clothes custom-made, but middle-class women preferred ready-to-wear, and the industry expanded to meet the demand. As the demand for ready-made clothing grew, manufacturers improved their skills in patternmaking and sewing and produced better fitting ready-to-wear.

During the Depression decade of the 1930s, dresses continued to grow in popularity. Women's first reaction to the hard economic times brought about by the Depression was not to buy fewer but to buy cheaper clothes. Housedress manufacturers, many located in Chicago, began to produce **daywear** dresses at lower prices. They were able to do this by replacing silk with less expensive rayon and by encouraging the wearing of cotton and its acceptance for wear outside the home as well as for housedresses. By 1935 the dress branch of the industry accounted for 41 percent of total production, more than any other industry segment.

Dresses remained the primary garment in women's wardrobes until the 1970s. The decline of the dress began in the 1960s when pants and separates became a practical, more creative way of dressing. In the 1970s many women began wearing pantsuits to work as well as for casual wear. In the 1980s many working women returned to wearing dresses, but dresses are not expected to regain the dominance they once held.

Sportswear

In the 1930s sportswear became a separate segment of the women's apparel industry, and California developed as a leader in sportswear production. College shops featuring more casual clothes began to appear in many of the department stores during the 1930s and 1940s, helping to foster this industry. Sportswear continued to be refined into the early 1950s and developed into a uniquely American style of dress. Sportswear has continued to grow in importance until today sportswear separates have replaced dresses for many women to wear to work as well as for casual activities. The housedress has been almost entirely replaced by pants.

Systems of Production and the Work Force

The apparel industry has always been a labor-intensive industry requiring many workers to produce its products. Early manufacturing of ready-made clothes was

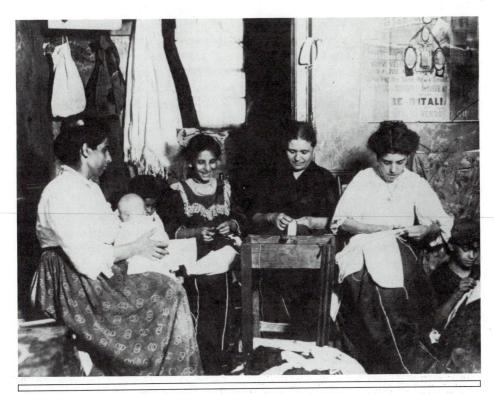

Early manufacturing of ready-made clothes was done by workers who took sewing home.
Source: *Records of the International Ladies' Garment Workers' Union, Labor-Management Documentation Center, Cornell University.*

done by workers who collected the work to be done at the factory and took it home to do the sewing. Most of these homeworkers were women, although in many instances the whole family worked at home to make the clothing. Homeworkers had to pay their own rent, heating, and lighting and were often expected to purchase their own thread, needles, and even trimmings used on the garments. After 1850 homeworkers provided their own sewing machines or rented them from their employers. The **homework system** prevailed until about 1880. Most of these workers made the entire garment; some did only finishing. The hours for these workers were exceedingly long and their earnings meager. They often worked fifteen to eighteen hours a day, seven days a week, in crowded unsanitary conditions in tenement buildings.

The Factory System

During the 1880s the clothing industry began to change over to the factory method of production with all workers located under one roof. Centralizing all of the operations in making garments in one building is also called an **inside shop.** Prior to this time one worker usually made an entire garment, which was a time-consuming process. With the **factory system** the garment was divided into sections and each worker constructed one section of it. Clothes were passed in bundles from one worker to another. This system decreased the time needed to construct a garment. Workers were paid a set rate for each piece completed. **Piecework,** as this is called, is still the method of payment commonly used in the industry today.

Immigrant Labor

In the earliest years of the apparel industry, much of the sewing was done by Native American, English, and Irish women. As the sewing machine was introduced to the industry, many women were employed to work in the factories. In 1860, 4,850 out of a total women's wear industry employment of 5,739 were women. Women were employed both to sew and to cut the fabric until the introduction of the cutting knife about 1875, when men replaced women as cutters. With the immigration of many Jewish tailors from Austria, Germany, and Hungary about 1880, men also started to fill positions as sewing operators. Even so, 22,253 workers out of the total work force of 25,192 were women.

About 1850 the number of Irish workers in the apparel industry increased, and many immigrant German tailors and their families performed much of the sewing labor. Many immigrants who came to American during the late 1880s and early 1900s provided workers for the growing clothing industry. From 1880 to 1900 the vast majority of immigrants entering the industry were German and Austrian Jews, many of whom had been in the new and secondhand clothing business in their homelands; so entering the clothing business in America was a logical step. Many Jewish immigrants from Eastern Europe continued to come to the United States throughout the 1890s. Coming from Austria, Poland, Rumania, and Russia, many entered the apparel business either as employer or employee. Also about 1890, Italian immigrants began to enter the industry. These immigrants, who were willing to work long hours in order to survive in a new country, provided plentiful and cheap labor for the industry from the 1880s into the early twentieth century. In port cities such as New York, Baltimore, and Philadelphia, clothing manufacturers literally met the boats to get workers. This influx of immigrants ended in the 1920s, and today the apparel industry employs many women and minorities. The new immigrants who enter apparel manufacturing today are most often Oriental or Hispanic.

The Contracting System

During the 1880s **contracting** became a common practice in the apparel industry. Some large manufacturers operated inside shops where all of the processes of clothing manufacture were performed, but many preferred to use contractors who operated

outside shops that constructed the garments cut by the manufacturer. Obviously, to make a profit contractors had to pay workers less per garment than they received from the manufacturer.

The contracting system was encouraged by the plentiful supply of labor and the simple organization of the early clothing industry. All a contractor needed to go into business was space, a few machines, and workers. As already noted, some employers required their workers to supply their own machines, thread, and needles, and a plentiful supply of cheap labor was available because of the influx of many immigrants. Thus the contracting business was easy to enter and offered opportunity for many abuses. As more and more contractors entered the business, manufacturers took advantage of the situation, and contractors could make a profit only by taking greater advantage of the workers. The contracting system, at least in part, led to the condition in the industry known as *sweating*.

The Sweatshop

It is often said that the garment industry grew out of one of the most sordid chapters in American business. By the 1880s cloaks were made almost entirely by **sweatshop** workers. The terms *sweating* or *sweatshop* relate to the deplorable working conditions that prevailed in the clothing industry. Sweating was characterized by poverty-level wages, a low standard of living, irregular employment, excessive hours of labor, unsanitary conditions, and exploitation of workers. Under the homework system of clothing manufacture, entire families often worked, cooked, ate, and slept in the same small, poorly ventilated tenement room without running water or plumbing. They existed in poverty, hunger, and dirt, often sleeping on bundles of clothing. Ready-made clothing was thus produced in surroundings characterized by dinginess, squalor, and filth. Although this situation is often blamed on the practices of contracting and homework, many of the manufacturers' inside shops provided no better environment for the worker. Inside shops were typically located on the upper floors of tenement buildings that were breeding grounds for disease. Conditions were dirty, crowded, and dangerous.

Although labor unions did much to eradicate the conditions of the sweatshops in the early years of the twentieth century, the term still applies to some apparel factories today. By definition, a sweatshop is a business that regularly violates both safety or health and wage or child labor laws. Because of increased competition from imports, sweatshops are again operating with workers who are paid low wages and work in unsafe, unsanitary conditions. The workers in such sweatshops are often illegal aliens or recent immigrants who are eager to have any job and are willing to work for less than union wages. Workers who cannot speak English feel more comfortable with others who speak their language. The sweatshops offer these immigrant workers a familial atmosphere where several members of a family can work in the same illegal factory, and sometimes the employer even allows children

In the late 1800s ready-made clothing was often produced in small, dirty, crowded areas.
Source: *Records of the International Ladies' Garment Workers' Union, Labor-Management Documentation Center, Cornell University.*

to be brought to work. Undocumented workers are also attracted to the sweatshops because of the anonymity they offer. Such illegal aliens are unlikely to complain to the authorities about working conditions or substandard pay.

Labor Unions

The appalling conditions in the garment industry late in the nineteenth century encouraged the organization and establishment of labor unions. In 1900 the **International Ladies Garment Workers Union** (ILGWU) was chartered as a national organization by the American Federation of Labor. Started with approximately 2,000 workers, the union made little progress until 1909 when it conducted a successful strike among 20,000 shirtwaist makers, called **The Big Strike.** Although the strike ended with few results, it paved the way for a much larger strike of 60,000 cloak-makers in 1910. **The Great Revolt,** as this strike was called, lasted from July to September, ending in a settlement known as the **Protocol of Peace.**

Grievances of the apparel workers included the spoils system, which charged employees for use of electricity and materials. Workers also objected to tenement work, overtime and night work, and holiday and Sunday labor. In addition, they protested low wages, irregular payment of wages, the system of contracting and even subcontracting, and unsanitary working conditions.

The Protocol of Peace granted the workers a fifty-hour week, double pay for overtime, and higher wages. In addition, special joint committees including representatives of labor and management were set up to determine piece rates and working conditions. The settlement also established a **closed shop,** meaning that employers could hire only union members. Most importantly, the Protocol of Peace established a means for collective bargaining within the industry. Sanitation and safety improved as a result of the Protocol, and the union attracted many new members.

Not all areas of the industry, however, saw improvement in working conditions as a result of the Great Revolt and the Protocol of Peace. Public concern about the conditions under which many in the industry worked was awakened by the horrible **Triangle Shirtwaist Fire** in lower Manhattan on March 25, 1911. The fire broke

Results of the fire at the Triangle Shirtwaist Company led to improving working conditions in the apparel industry.
Source: *Records of the International Ladies' Garment Workers' Union, Labor-Management Documentation Center, Cornell University.*

out on the eighth floor of a supposedly "fireproof" building, spreading quickly to the three upper floors where the Triangle Shirtwaist Company was located. Locks had been put on the doors two years earlier when the 700 women who worked at the factory took part in the Big Strike of 20,000 waistmakers. The fire lasted less than thirty minutes. Trapped in the building, 146 young women died either in the flames or by jumping to the street below.

The tragic Triangle fire rallied public support for improving conditions within the apparel industry and finally led to a series of new laws for the safety of all workers. The ILGWU also grew in membership and public recognition. Unionization spread to other branches of the industry and to other cities where clothing was produced. By 1920 the ILGWU boasted a membership of 105,400 out of 165,649 workers in the women's clothing industry.

Although several local unions were organized in the menswear industry during the 1800s, the first large-scale attempt to unionize the men's clothing industry was the United Garment Workers of America, founded in 1891. The impetus for this union came primarily from Jewish workers in New York who were concerned about the industry's low wages, long hours, and unsanitary working conditions. Workers' dissatisfaction with the union led to the formation of the Amalgamated Clothing Workers Union (ACWU) in 1914, which followed a growth pattern almost identical to the ILGWU. The union worked for arbitration and better working conditions for its members. The ACWU remained the primary union in the menswear industry until the 1970s when it merged with the Textile Workers of America and the United Shoe Workers of America to form the **Amalgamated Clothing and Textile Workers Union** (ACTWU).

Labor unions in the clothing industry have gained considerable importance in the twentieth century. In addition to bargaining for higher wages, shorter hours, and better working conditions, these unions have taken an active part in establishing and operating a number of social welfare programs. The ILGWU, for example, operates health centers, a retirement fund, cooperative housing, and a nonprofit vacation retreat for its members. Unions have been particularly important in the North where most factories are unionized. In the South unions have had less impact on the industry and fewer factories are unionized. More than half of today's apparel industry's production workers are union members. The two major unions are still the ILGWU and the ACTWU.

Types of Employers

The apparel industry involves the three functions of design, production, and sales. Within the industry, production is often separated from the other two functions; not all apparel firms actually cut and sew garments. Because of the separation of functions in the industry, three types of employers or establishments operate in the apparel industry: (1) regular manufacturers, (2) jobbers, and (3) contractors.

Manufacturers

Regular manufacturers design, produce, and market garments. They operate an inside shop and perform the full range of operations necessary to produce and distribute apparel. Manufacturers may own several sewing plants in different locations and in some instances may hire outside shops to assist with the production of their merchandise. Manufacturers produce goods that carry the company's own labels or brand names. They usually operate their own showrooms located in fashion markets such as New York, Los Angeles, or Dallas. Some manufacturers are dual distributors, selling their own products through company-owned retail outlets. Regular manufacturers dominate the men's and boys' segments of the industry and are less frequently found in the women's and children's segments. Hartmarx and Levi Strauss are examples of regular manufacturers.

Jobbers

Jobbers are independent entrepreneurs who buy the raw materials, design and market the finished product but do not do the sewing. They are middlemen who contract for the production of apparel that they market to a variety of retail outlets. In some instances jobbers contract out the pattern and sample making in addition to the cutting and sewing. Other jobbers make their own patterns and samples as well as cut the fabric before sending it to an outside shop to be sewn. In the knit outerwear business, the term *converter* is used rather than jobber. Apparel jobbers are responsible for a major proportion of women's and children's apparel.

Contractors

Contractors run outside shops. They hire workers and operate factories where fabric is sewn into garments. Contractors are paid for the work completed. They are hired by jobbers, retailers, or sometimes by regular manufacturers who have oversold their own capacity to produce garments to meet orders placed by retailers. Contractors produce garments to specification. The fabrics and designs produced by contract factories are supplied by the firm that contracts to have the work completed. They never take title to the goods and are not involved in marketing the finished product. Sometimes contractors work for retailers producing **private label** merchandise to be sold by one store or a group of jointly owned stores. Such contractors are referred to by retailers as a **source.** When a retailer, manufacturer, or jobber is looking for a contractor, this is called **sourcing.**

Contractors specialize in the sewing phase of garment production. Some contractors will also cut the garments. Most manufacturers, however, prefer to do their own cutting, knowing that they will make the most economical use of their goods.

Contractors, used by apparel firms of all sizes, play an important role in the American apparel industry. The practice of using contractors makes it possible for new apparel firms with limited capital to produce garments in large quantities. Apparel firms also use contractors when they need extra production during busy periods, when they do not want to invest in specialized machinery and new equipment, and when they want to diversify their product mix. For example, a manufacturer might want to add sweaters to match dresses or skirts in the company's line. Rather than making the investment in the necessary knitting machines to produce the sweaters, the manufacturer would contract with an outside firm. Sometimes manufacturers even help finance contractors to assure that they will be available for production when needed.

The system of jobber-contractor in the apparel industry offers two primary advantages: specialization and flexibility. Each type of employer concentrates on an area of operations; the contractor is the production expert, and the jobber specializes in merchandising. Flexibility helps combat the uncertainty and seasonality of the apparel industry. Demand for fashion goods is especially unpredictable, and since a firm cannot know exactly what its sales volume will be for each season, contracting relieves the need to maintain factories large enough to fill maximum orders. The jobber or the manufacturer can find contractors to fill orders as they are placed. Contracting is particularly prevalent in the women's and children's industries because of the greater emphasis on fashion. Contracting is used most in women's outerwear.

Contractors' factories do not have to be located in market centers. They are spread all across the United States and are also located abroad. Many are found in small towns where labor is less expensive than in large cities. Because price competition is strong in the apparel industry, an increasing number of manufacturers and jobbers are contracting to have work performed in areas outside the United States where production and labor costs are lower.

Jobbers and contractors have become increasingly important in recent years because of the flexibility they have to increase and decrease production. This has led to the growth of "underground" apparel operations paying substandard wages and providing working conditions reminiscent of the sweatshops discussed earlier. Some sources estimate that such firms are now producing one-third of all garments manufactured in the United States.

Characteristics of Today's Apparel Industry

Traditionally, the U.S. apparel industry has been highly fragmented, including many small privately owned firms, each producing a narrow range of products. Because of the highly competitive nature of the industry and increased imports, many changes have occurred in recent years. Much apparel manufacturing is now done outside of the United States, and the number of apparel firms has decreased due to business failures and acquisitions.

Industry Size and Structure

The American Apparel Manufacturers Association (AAMA) estimates that about 12,000 firms, which employ 1.1 million people, produce apparel in the United States. Half of these firms employ twenty or more workers and account for 80 percent of U.S. apparel employment. The apparel industry, in contrast to the textile industry, is still primarily an industry of small firms. According to the AAMA, the average apparel firm employs fifty-two people. Most are small operations that produce under contract for a larger apparel firm or a retailer. In 1988 U.S. apparel production approximated $39.5 billion at wholesale. Retailers obtained a net markup of 43 percent on these goods, giving a retail value of $71 billion (*Focus* 1988).

The apparel industry includes both privately and publicly owned firms. Until the middle of the twentieth century, most apparel firms were privately owned businesses. By the 1960s large **public ownership** apparel firms had emerged, and by 1968 one hundred firms had become public corporations. Firms decide to go public and sell shares usually for financial reasons. Becoming a public corporation provides additional capital that may be used to expand the business and to hire specialists to ensure quality production.

During the 1970s apparel firms were acquired by publicly owned conglomerates. The expansion of conglomerates took place by two methods, horizontal and vertical integration. **Horizontal integration** occurs when a company purchases firms that produce and market the same type or similar types of merchandise. Conglomerates expand vertically by acquiring firms that are engaged in a variety of operations, marketing different types of merchandise, including apparel and nonapparel.

Vertical integration operations are more common in the textile industry than in the apparel industry. They are most common among knitwear producers where firms perform all of the operations from spinning the yarn to completing the knitted garments. Such firms are more common outside the United States. Benetton, for example, is a fully integrated firm that produces and sells knitwear for men, women, and children. Vertically integrated apparel firms that produce products made from woven fabrics are seldom found in the United States. One example with a well-known brand name is Pendleton Woolen Mills.

The VF Corporation became the world's largest publicly held apparel company in 1986 when it purchased Blue Bell, producer of Wrangler jeans. The company now has annual sales of $2.6 billion produced by twelve divisions making jeans, sportswear, **intimate apparel,** and work apparel. In 1986 other large publicly owned apparel firms included Interco, Hartmarx, Liz Claiborne, Oxford Industries, and Kellwood. See Table 6.1 for a list of the top ten publicly owned apparel companies.

Interco, Inc., is an example of a large diversified company involved in retailing, footwear manufacturing, furniture and home-furnishings manufacturing, and apparel manufacturing. Among the nine companies in Interco's apparel group are Abe Schrader Corp., a dress firm; Londontown Corp., a men's and women's outerwear manufacturer based in Eldersburg, Maryland, which produces London Fog rainwear; and the Biltwell Co., Inc., a St. Louis men's apparel group. The company announced in July 1988 that it was restructuring and planned to sell its apparel manufacturing

Table 6.1. Ten Largest Public Apparel Firms

Firm	1987 Sales
VF Corporation	$2,573,762,000
Sara Lee	1,630,622,000
Liz Claiborne	1,053,324,000
Fruit of the Loom	870,300,000
Interco	817,660,000
The Leslie Fay Co.	582,023,000
Kellwood	571,861,000
Oxford Industries	553,380,000
Phillips-Van Heusen	514,387,000
Hartmarx	492,400,000

Source: *Apparel Industry Magazine*, July 1988.

group because of declining sales and earnings. Although the apparel group represented almost one-fourth of Interco's total sales, it made up only 6.7 percent of the company's operating earnings.

Although the trend has been for apparel firms to grow and become publicly owned, many privately owned businesses still exist in the apparel industry. Some of these private firms are large giants while most are very small. Levi Strauss, for example, is privately owned and with $2.5 billion in sales remains the largest producer of jeans worldwide.

Product Specialization

Traditionally, apparel manufacturers have specialized in the production of one type of garment usually at one price line. Today, many firms are developing diversified lines at a variety of price ranges. For example, Haggar Apparel Company, once known only for the production of men's pants, now produces men's jackets and tailored business suits as well as several lines of boys' wear and women's wear.

Apparel firms often expand and diversify their lines by developing new divisions. Others expand by purchasing businesses that are already producing goods that they plan to offer. Multiproduct businesses have found it more advantageous for each business to operate on its own. Each firm has its own production and marketing procedures, but relies on the parent firm for financial support and guidance.

Location

The availability of labor is the most important determinant of the location of manufacturing facilities. Because the apparel business is a labor-intensive industry, it must locate where a plentiful supply of affordable labor exists. New York became the center of the apparel industry before the end of the nineteenth century because of the steady supply of immigrant labor. Today, New York is still the largest producer of apparel, but apparel production is found in forty-five additional states as well. The apparel industry is less concentrated on a state basis than is the textile industry; however, ten states lead in the production of apparel, accounting for 70 percent of total production (see Table 6.2). New York produced 19 percent of total shipments in 1986, followed by California with nearly 11 percent. Georgia, North Carolina, and Pennsylvania each contributed about 6 percent of the apparel shipments. Other states included among the top ten in order of the value of their shipments were Texas, Michigan, New Jersey, Alabama, and Tennessee (U.S. Bureau of the Census 1986).

Most high-fashion and tailored clothing producers are located in the metropolitan areas of the Middle Atlantic states and in California. Factories making such products as jeans and casual slacks are concentrated in the South and Southwest.

Work Force

The apparel industry employs approximately 1.1 million people as compared to about 700,000 for the textile industry. As a labor-intensive industry, production workers constitute 85 percent of the apparel work force as compared to 68 percent for all

Table 6.2. Top Ten States in Production of Apparel and Other Textile Products (1986)

State	Number of Employees (in thousands)	$ Value of Shipments (in millions)	Percent of Total
New York	120.6	10,749.6	18.6
California	93.6	6,147.4	10.6
Georgia	69.5	3,689.9	6.4
North Carolina	74.2	3,673.5	6.3
Pennsylvania	96.4	3,628.0	6.3
Texas	41.7	2,646.0	4.6
Michigan	20.0	2,580.5	4.5
New Jersey	42.3	2,517.4	4.3
Alabama	56.3	2,418.2	4.2
Tennessee	55.9	2,224.4	3.8
Ten-State Total	671.5	40,274.9	69.6
Industry Total	1,016.5	57,918.6	

Source: U.S. Bureau of the Census, 1986 Annual Survey of Manufacturers, *Geographic Area Statistics* (M86[AS]-3).

U.S. manufacturing. The industry is also an important employer of women and minorities. Women make up nearly 80 percent of industry employment, and almost a third of the employees are minorities. Many are Hispanic, Vietnamese, Laotian, Korean, or Haitian.

Apparel production involves tasks that can be performed by unskilled or semi-skilled labor. Consequently, wages are about 40 percent lower in the apparel industry than in other U.S. manufacturing industries. Production workers averaged about $6 an hour in 1988. Apparel wages in some parts of the country are lower, averaging little more than the minimum wage. In spite of the low wages, labor is the single largest cost component of apparel production, accounting for about 35 percent of the industry's total costs. Foreign producers therefore have a competitive advantage because of the availability of cheap labor in developing countries. Although wages in the U.S. apparel industry are low compared to other U.S. industries, they are high in comparison to the wages paid workers in Asia, which range from 20 cents an hour to a little more than $2. To take advantage of this cost difference, some U.S. manufacturers have opened their own factories abroad.

Ease of Entry

The apparel industry has always been relatively easy to enter because it requires less capital than most forms of manufacturing. A sewing plant, for example, requires a few sewing machines, a cutting table, and workers, who can be trained relatively easily. Elaborate facilities are not needed; a sewing factory can be set up in almost any building that has electricity. The contracting system also contributes to the ease of entering the business. Someone with a design idea can produce samples and hire an outside contractor to produce the goods, if the necessary financial backing is found.

Factoring

Apparel manufacturers must have money in advance in order to purchase fabrics and materials for production as well as to pay workers and cover overhead expenses. Since retailers usually buy from manufacturers on credit allowances, their payments are not due for at least a month and sometimes several months after an order is placed. Most manufacturers rely on **factors** for financial assistance. A factor is a financial institution that assists manufacturers as a credit and collection department. The unpaid orders are given to the **factoring** firm, which supplies the manufacturer with cash advances and assumes the responsibility for collecting payments from the manufacturer's customers. The factor assumes the risk of collection and becomes responsible for credit losses. Manufacturers pay factoring firms a fee for servicing their accounts.

Licensing

During the last two decades, **licensing** has become an important trend in the apparel industry. Licensing involves the purchase of the right to use someone's name on various products and/or garment labels and usually involves famous designers or other well-known personalities. The definition of licensing has been modified to include corporations such as Coca-Cola, Pepsi, and Walt Disney.

Celebrity licensing has also become popular in the apparel industry. Nolan Miller, costume designer for the television program "Dynasty," launched the Dynasty Collection in the fall of 1984 in connection with Twentieth Century–Fox Licensing and Merchandising Corporation. Other celebrities who have made licensing agreements are Richard Simmons, who put his name on a line of casual sportswear for large-size women, and Jaclyn Smith, whose name was licensed for a line of sportswear available through K mart stores.

Another type of licensing is character licensing of consumer products for children. Character licensing is found in all categories of children's apparel from T-shirts to underwear and sportswear. It was estimated that 30 percent of the 1984 children's apparel retail sales of $10 billion was derived from licensed characters. It is possible for a single character to generate sales volumes of $30 to $35 million.

One of the first characters to be licensed was Buster Brown, a comic strip character popular in the early 1900s. In 1904 Brown Shoe Company purchased the right to use the name Buster Brown as a promotional tool for its children's shoes.

Walt Disney characters have been licensed since the 1930s. One of the most popular is Mickey Mouse, whose image has appeared on many items including toys, watches, storybooks, and apparel. In November 1984 the Mickey and Co. line by J. G. Hook was introduced and for the first time Mickey Mouse appeared on better-priced apparel manufactured by a company recognized in large department stores.

Hanes Knitwear Inc. has obtained licenses for many cartoon characters who appear on the ShowToons line of underwear for little boys and girls. Prior to its first licensing agreements in 1981, the company conducted market research to look for characters that were both popular and had proven sales success in other types of children's products. Characters used by Hanes include Scooby Doo, the Smurfs, Mickey Mouse, Minnie Mouse, Bambi, Thumper, and Raggedy Ann and Andy. Character licensing is very popular in children's apparel and has also become fashionable in junior apparel. Today, many adults wear sportswear featuring cartoon figures, and those who wore the first Mickey Mouse watches in the 1940s can now purchase an adult version.

Corporate licenses were the fastest-growing segment of the licensing market in the mid-1980s. In 1984 corporate licenses accounted for 12 to 15 percent of the total licensing market, that percentage increasing in 1986 when Coca-Cola clothing became a major fashion item. Coca-Cola clothes were followed by Pepsi and Dr Pepper apparel, which did not prove as successful. Such clothing tends to be a fad, lasting for only a season or two, but during the time it is in fashion, sales flourish.

There are several reasons for the growing interest in corporate licensing. It helps to protect a company's trademark because the license controls the use of the licenser's name, logo, and package design. Manufacturers seek to become licensees because of the popularity and high recognition of the licenser's trademark. Advertising of one product reinforces the sales of the other product. Licensed merchandise can be used to drive sales of the principal product, or vice versa.

Character licensing, such as Mickey Mouse, is found in many categories of fashion apparel and accessories.
Source: Reprinted with permission of J. G. Hook, Inc., Mickey and Co. by J. G. Hook © 1989 Walt Disney Company.

Sasson, Jordache, Gitano, and Bon Jour are all companies that became recognized for their jeans in the 1970s. These companies have successfully used their licensed corporate names to branch out into other apparel categories, which include swimwear, children's wear, hosiery, underwear, and large-size sportswear.

Trends in the Apparel Industry

Apparel imports, economic declines, and the cyclical nature of consumer trends have made survival in the apparel industry especially difficult in recent years. As in the textile industry, imports have offered the greatest threat and have provided the primary catalyst for change within the apparel industry. Apparel companies have adopted a number of strategies to combat the effects of imports, including technological improvements, increased emphasis on marketing, expanded sourcing options, and the Quick Response program.

Apparel Imports

Since 1980 U.S. imports of apparel have increased at an annual rate of 13 percent. In 1986, 44 percent of the dollar value of apparel sold in the United States was imported, but in terms of the number of garments, 50 percent was imported. According to the American Apparel Manufacturers Association, 2.38 billion outerwear garments were imported in 1986, enough to provide each person in the United States with ten garments (*Focus* 1987, p. 4).

The production of American-made apparel totaled $39.5 billion at wholesale in 1986. Retailers obtain an average markup on this apparel of 44 percent, making the retail value of domestic apparel approximately $71 billion. Imported apparel in 1986 had a port value of $17.3 billion. Since the port value does not include duty, it must be increased by 60 percent to equate the foreign port value with an equivalent wholesale price. The wholesale value of this merchandise, therefore, would be $28 billion. Since retailers obtain a net 50 percent markup on imported apparel, the retail value of this imported merchandise would be $56 billion.

Imports have been increasing in part because of the labor cost savings they provide. The labor-intensive apparel industry is particularly vulnerable to foreign competition. Labor costs, as previously stated, are about 35 percent of the U.S. apparel industry's total costs. Because labor is the single largest cost component of apparel products, many foreign producers have a decided advantage due to the low wages that they pay. The primary countries from which the United States now imports apparel are Taiwan, China, Hong Kong, and South Korea. Wages in these countries range from as low as 20 cents an hour to a little over $2.

Low prices for merchandise are not the only reason much apparel is imported, according to importers. Other advantages that foreign-made apparel and accessories offer are better quality, reliability, and quick delivery. Foreign producers are also more willing to produce in small amounts than are many U.S. manufacturers and contractors.

Emphasis on Marketing

A major trend in apparel production today is a change of emphasis from manufacturing to marketing. Until the 1960s almost all U.S. apparel companies emphasized manufacturing rather than marketing. Their strategy was to identify what they could produce in their factories and sell what they could best make. Their marketing strategies reflected the capacity, product, and cost structures of their manufacturing facilities and not necessarily what consumers and retailers wanted to buy. In the 1970s apparel firms began to turn away from an emphasis on manufacturing and sought new apparel products designed to fit new consumer lifestyles and targeted for specific consumer groups such as working women. Companies now made or obtained products that the market demanded. For some companies this meant turning to production facilities outside their own firms to produce their merchandise.

Today, many companies are de-emphasizing manufacturing while stressing marketing and services as a means of fighting imports and maintaining profitability. Such companies are making fewer garments in their own factories. Some are selling operating divisions and acquiring domestic apparel companies that do not have a manufacturing base. Products are being manufactured to the company's specifications by independent contractors in the United States and abroad. Thus companies have de-emphasized or eliminated sewing operations and are applying their efforts to design and marketing.

Another way that marketing is being emphasized is by combining the apparel manufacturer and retailer in the same conglomerate. For example, in 1988 Liz Claiborne opened retail stores carrying a new line of clothing different from what the company sells to other retailers. A number of apparel firms and designers have opened their own retail stores selling the same apparel that they also sell to traditional department and specialty stores. Examples include Esprit, Ralph Lauren, and Calvin Klein.

Manufacturers have focused on marketing to maintain market share and continue sales growth. They are targeting specific market segments and seek brand-name recognition, especially in upscale markets. Apparel companies are doing more national advertising to increase consumer awareness of their products.

Apparel Sourcing Strategies

Once an apparel company knows what products it wants to market, it has to select an appropriate sourcing strategy. This involves determining where and how to obtain products. Four major sourcing options are available to apparel producers: (1) company-owned domestic manufacturing facilities, (2) domestic contractors, (3) company-owned foreign factories, and (4) foreign contractors.

Apparel firms are taking a global perspective in seeking the best sources for their products. Sourcing for apparel has expanded to include several options in addition to domestic manufacturing. Many apparel companies now contract with independent producers located outside the United States, and some even own their own factories located abroad. Fewer American apparel firms now own their own factories. According to the Commerce Department's census on manufacturing, the number of companies engaged in all aspects of the apparel business declined 16 percent between 1977 and 1982. Companies such as Liz Claiborne and Bernard Chaus, for example, design and market women's apparel but now manufacture almost all of their clothing in the Far East. Many retailers are also having apparel made to their specifications outside the United States. Such private-label merchandise has become 20 percent or more of the merchandise mix in many department stores, whereas in some specialty stores all of the merchandise is private label.

Some apparel companies are, however, trying to emphasize domestic sourcing. The Limited, for example, has held sourcing fairs at its Columbus, Ohio, headquarters. Manufacturers from throughout the United States were invited to these fairs to discuss The Limited's problems in finding domestic suppliers of apparel to meet the company's specific needs. Sourcing fairs have also been held by trade associations. Such fairs have made manufacturers more aware of the opportunities to work with American retailers to the mutual benefit of both parties. Domestic manufacturers do have one significant advantage over foreign contractors—closer proximity to their customers. This proximity offers the opportunity for quick response.

Quick Response

Retail success often depends on having fresh apparel merchandise in the right quantities, color, and style at the right time. Because of this, retailers have pressured manufacturers to shorten the time cycle between placement of orders and delivery of the goods to the store. Manufacturers have responded by accelerating the manufacturing and delivery process through the Quick Response program.

As noted, the one advantage the domestic apparel manufacturing industry has over foreign producers is proximity to U.S. markets. Quick Response capitalizes on this by applying technology to speed communications along the **apparel pipeline** from fiber producer to textile mill to apparel company to retailer. Quick Response is designed to shorten this long product pipeline from raw materials to garment to the selling floor. *Pipeline* is the term used in the textile and apparel industries to describe the process through which fiber evolves to completed garments in the retail store.

Quick Response, as presented in the discussion of the textile industry in Chapter 4, developed as an industry strategy for fighting imports. It is estimated that Quick Response can reduce the apparel pipeline from sixty-six weeks to forty or less by using new technology and providing greater cooperation between retailer and manufacturer. For example, with Quick Response point-of-sale data are transmitted directly to the manufacturer by a computer. This enables the manufacturer to plan production directly based on consumer demand. Stock can be replenished quickly at the retail level, the order process time can be reduced, and goods can be shipped to the retailer more quickly. All of this can lead to improved profits because of fewer markdowns and fewer lost sales due to out-of-stock situations.

Computer systems are necessary to allow the company to know just where everything is in the production pipeline. Direct computer linkups between retailer and manufacturer reduce delivery time. Quick Response can improve retail sales, reduce inventory levels throughout the pipeline, lessen the degree and frequency of price discounting, and improve profitability. As the price of manufacturing in the Far East is escalating, manufacturers are beginning to reexamine the advantages of domestic sourcing, and Quick Response offers a special advantage to using U.S. producers.

Improved Technology

The apparel industry is being revolutionized by new technology. The industry is in the middle of a new industrial revolution, which is being driven by the new computer technology commonly called **CAD/CAM,** or computer-aided design/computer-aided manufacturing. Such advances in technology have enabled the industry to speed up the manufacturing process and shorten the distribution pipeline as well as to reduce labor time per garment. At present, larger manufacturers are most able to utilize technological innovations because of the high cost of equipment needed to initiate such technologies. The capital costs of many new technologies are often prohibitive for small firms. Another factor holding back many firms in the apparel industry has been their tendency to hold onto traditional methods and resist change.

Since the 1970s the computer has been used for business management, and larger apparel companies have utilized computerized production tools for cutting, marking, ticketing, and patternmaking. More recently computer-aided design (CAD) has gained acceptance and is changing the way the industry views technology. It is now possible for the designer to design garments, produce and grade patterns, lay out the pieces to fit the material, and cut the clothes all by pushing keys on an electronic keyboard. Today about a third of the garment makers in the United States use some part of computer-aided design or cutting. Computer-aided garment design is expected to continue to be advanced and refined through better software and faster computers. Computer softwear is becoming less expensive and easier to use, making it more appealing to manufacturers. Automated marker-making systems are widely used, and further advances in this area are expected. Computer inspection of fabrics, scanning, measurement of fabric-width variance, and recognition of shading are expected to become integral parts of a fully automated operation.

Water-jet and laser methods have been used successfully for fabric cutting. For a long time the preferred way of cutting multiple layers of fabric has been with a manually operated cutting knife, which is being replaced by a computerized system. Cutters connected to computerized marker-making systems are widely used. New cutting systems permit efficient cutting of more tightly spaced pattern layouts that reduce material waste. The sewing room is still labor-intensive, with the majority of employee time spent handling and positioning piece goods. New programmable sewing units utilizing microprocessors are faster and more flexible, further reducing labor content. Other technological advances are taking place in the areas of robotics and automated warehouse facilities. The future is expected to bring many more exciting technological changes and increased automation to the apparel industry. If the U.S. apparel industry is to compete with cheaper foreign labor, these technological advancements are necessary for the industry's survival.

The Men's Apparel Industry

As we have seen, the American ready-made apparel industry began with the production of clothing for men. For many years men's apparel was conservative and traditional, consisting primarily of structured tailored clothing. Men's coats and suits, made of the same fabric with little style variation from year to year, were almost timeless. Design changes usually involved only a slight modification of details, and for many years the men's apparel industry was a placid, classic business that provided firms with much longevity. During the 1960s, however, significant changes began to occur. Men's fashions were stimulated by changing lifestyles and influenced by younger men who had an increased interest in casual apparel. Men began to demand a greater variety in styles with emphasis placed on color, fabric, design, and comfort. Men's sportswear has since become an important part of the men's apparel industry as manufacturers have adapted to the changing demands of their customers.

Categories of Menswear

In the men's apparel industry the term *clothing* refers to one category of apparel rather than to the entire industry. In the menswear industry garments are classified in the following categories:

1. *CLOTHING:* tailored suits, overcoats, topcoats, sport coats, and separate trousers.

2. *MEN'S FURNISHINGS:* shirts, ties, underwear, socks, sleepwear, and robes.

3. *HEAVY OUTERWEAR:* windbreakers, snowsuits, ski wear, and similar items of sportswear.

4. *WORK CLOTHES:* workshirts and pants, overalls, jeans.

5. *MISCELLANEOUS WEARING APPAREL:* raincoats, uniforms, hats.

Some menswear firms produce only one specialized category of apparel; others are greatly diversified. Many men's apparel manufacturers produce both menswear and boys' wear. With the growing popularity of tailored apparel for executive women in the late 1970s, a number of menswear firms entered the women's manufacturing business as well.

Size Specialization

Menswear sizing is much more standardized than is sizing in women's wear. Men's suits, for example, are sized according to chest measurements, 38 to 46, but also in short, average, and long lengths to fit various heights. Trousers are sized by waist measurement and length of the inside leg seam. Long-sleeved dress shirts are sized by neck measurements, 14 to 17½, and sleeve length, 32 to 35. Shirts are also described by whether they are tapered or regular cut.

Sizing in menswear runs much truer to specification than it does in women's apparel where each manufacturer's size may vary somewhat from the standard. With the increased production of men's sportswear, sizing for many of these items has become less specific and is often identified as small (S), medium (M), large (L), and extra-large (XL). Such sizing is also appearing in tailored clothing designed for the young contemporary market. The movement toward an easier, more comfortable tailored silhouette made this sizing possible. The catalyst for this fuller silhouette with wide shoulders was the television show "Miami Vice." Fewer sizes also make production less expensive and thus save money for the industry.

Size and Structure

Today, the men's apparel industry contributes significantly to the economy of the United States. It consists of 3,000 firms that support over 4,100 plants and employ more than 300,000 workers with a payroll of over $3 billion (U.S. Department of Commerce 1987). The menswear industry includes many small firms, more than 80 percent employing fewer than fifty workers. However, the menswear industry has several large firms that account for a significant share of the total output. These firms generate a greater percentage of the total output than the large firms in other clothing manufacturing businesses. More than 25 percent of the total value of output is generated by four large firms that produce menswear.

Dual distribution is still found in the menswear industry where large manufacturers sell their goods directly to the consumer through their own retail stores. Such firms also sell their merchandise to other retail stores, becoming both supplier and competitor to retailers. Some of the dual distributors are Botany Industries, Eagle Clothes, Phillips-Van Heusen, and Cluett Peabody. One of the giants in dual distribution is Hartmarx, a billion-dollar-a-year company based in Chicago that owns more than 250 stores located throughout the United States. These stores sell merchandise produced by other manufacturers as well as that produced by Hartmarx. About 80 percent of the apparel produced by Hartmarx is wholesaled to other department and specialty stores. The company's best-known tailored clothing brand is Hart Schaffner & Marx. Among the approximately forty brands produced by Hartmarx are Hickey-Freeman, Jaymar, Sansabelt, and Austin Reed. Hartmarx also has a licensing agreement with Christian Dior to manufacture and market the line of designer clothing for men in the United States. Hartmarx also manufactures women's apparel under the Country Miss label.

Location

Menswear manufacturers are located in all sections of the country, but the majority of the firms are concentrated in the Middle Atlantic states. More than 60 percent of the total dollar volume of men's coats and suits is produced in New York, New Jersey, and Pennsylvania. Many plants producing pants, work clothes, and furnishings are located in the South and Southwest. California has become a production center for men's sportswear. Almost all menswear manufacturers have sales and marketing offices in New York City, and many also maintain showrooms or have sales representatives in key regional market centers.

Fashion Seasons

Menswear has always been less seasonal than women's wear. Traditionally, the menswear business has been limited to two seasons a year: fall-winter and spring-summer, with the former considered the most important. In tailored clothing the primary difference between seasons is fabric weight and fiber content, although many suits are constructed of lightweight wools or wool blends that are considered all-season fabrics. As menswear has become more fashion-oriented and as sportswear has increased in importance, some manufacturers have shifted to four seasons a year, corresponding to those in women's apparel.

The Women's Apparel Industry

Although the U.S. apparel industry originated with menswear, it built its worldwide reputation on women's ready-to-wear. The United States assumed the leadership role in the development of mass production of apparel and early on gained a reputation for quality production. Mass production has made fashionable apparel readily available in a wide range of prices enabling American women to be among the best dressed in the world.

The production of women's apparel is similar in many ways to that of men's apparel. The differences between the industries have become less significant as menswear has become more fashion-oriented, and both industries face similar problems today.

The sales of women's apparel account for about 60 percent of all apparel sales. The women's divisions of the apparel industry comprise more than 50 percent of the employment within the total industry. Approximately 8,000 establishments produce outerwear for women, including dresses, blouses, suits, coats, and skirts. These firms employ more than 83,000 workers. Small firms still dominate the industry and in comparison to the menswear industry, contractors and jobbers are of greater importance.

Product Specialization and Sizing

The women's industry has been typified by a high degree of specialization according to product, price range, and size category. Specialization is less apparent today as companies have expanded by diversifying their product mix and their price lines. Large firms have added separate product divisions to oversee each new category added to their production. Such firms may have separate divisions for misses' and juniors' sportswear and dresses, children's wear, menswear, and accessories.

Specialization by Classification

Whereas firms are less likely today to limit production to only one merchandise classification or category, most firms do still limit their production to one or a few related types of goods. The following are typical product classifications of women's wear:

1. *OUTERWEAR:* coats, suits, rainwear, jackets.

2. *DRESSES:* one- or two-piece styles and ensembles with a coat or jacket.

3. *SPORTSWEAR AND SEPARATES:* activewear, pants, tops, jackets, sweaters.

4. *AFTER-FIVE AND EVENING CLOTHES:* dressy apparel, cocktail dresses, and formal attire.

5. *BRIDAL AND BRIDESMAID ATTIRE.*

6. *UNIFORMS AND APRONS:* housedresses, career apparel.

7. *MATERNITY.*

8. *SWIMWEAR AND BEACHWEAR.*

9. *BLOUSES.*

10. *INTIMATE APPAREL:* lingerie, **foundation garments,** sleepwear, and **loungewear.**

Size Specialization

Some manufacturers produce apparel in several of the size ranges listed below; others specialize in only one size category. Most apparel is produced in misses and juniors sizes.

1. *MISSES:* even sizes 8 to 14, may extend from as small as 2 and large as 20.

2. *JUNIORS:* uneven sizes 5 to 15; sometimes sizes 1 and 3 are also cut.

3. *PETITES:* may be cut in either misses or junior sizes.

4. *HALF-SIZES:* 14 1/2 to 16 1/2.

5. *WOMEN'S SIZES:* large sizes 38 to 52; some firms are using a size designation of 1, 2, 3, 4 for large sizes to avoid the negative connotation associated with these sizes.

Some manufacturers double-ticket their sizes, marking them with both junior and misses sizes. In reality no such size categories exist as indicated by such sizing as 7/8, 9/10, 11/12. When manufacturers do this, they are usually trying to sell in both the misses and junior markets.

The size categories for petite and large-size women, ignored to a great extent until recently, have been growing. Department stores emphasize traditional junior and misses sizes and usually devote limited space to such fringe sizes. Petite and large sizes are more often sold in speciality stores that limit their offerings to one size category.

Standardization in sizing in women's apparel is not found throughout the industry as it is in menswear. A specific size made by one manufacturer may vary in dimensions from one made by another manufacturer. This variation allows consumers who do not conform to the ideal body form to find a manufacturer's line that is sized for different body proportions. For example, some manufacturers will cut the waist length of their dresses long, whereas others are cut shorter than average. Generally speaking, more expensive apparel lines are sized larger than are less expensive lines. Thus a woman may find that one manufacturer's size 8 fits her, but she needs a 12 in another's apparel.

Price Specialization

Women's ready-to-wear is produced and marketed in several price ranges. Price is determined by several factors, including quality of workmanship and fabric, the amount and type of labor involved in production, the newness and uniqueness of the styling, and the reputation of the designer or manufacturer. The women's apparel industry is divided into the following price categories: designer, bridge, better, moderate, and budget or popular.

1. *DESIGNER:* the high-priced prestige market, which includes the lines of name designers. Examples are Bill Blass, Oscar de la Renta, Donna Karan, Calvin Klein, and Ralph Lauren.

2. *BRIDGE:* priced lower than designer but has the look of designer apparel and usually is associated with a designer name. **Bridge merchandise** examples include the brands Anne Klein II, DKNY, Ellen Tracy, Tahari, and Adrienne Vittadini.

3. *BETTER:* medium- to higher-priced merchandise that includes many well-known brand names such as Evan-Picone, J. H. Collectibles, Jones New York, Prophecy, Liz Claiborne, and Carol Little.

4. *MODERATE:* medium-priced merchandise that includes many nationally advertised manufacturers' brands. Examples include Jantzen, Villager, White Stag, Catalina, Koret of California, and Levi Strauss.

5. *BUDGET:* lower-priced merchandise. **Budget** or **popular-price** examples are in-house brands of discount stores such as K mart and Target.

Location

Manufacturers of women's apparel have historically been concentrated in the New York City Seventh Avenue garment district. Although New York remains the primary market for women's apparel and leads the industry in apparel production, it has lost ground in recent years to production in other areas of the country, in particular Los Angeles, Dallas, and Atlanta. New York still has nearly 5,000 apparel firms employing more than 61,000 workers in the Seventh Avenue center. In addition, nearly 20,000 garment workers are located in New York's Chinatown and over 40,000 in other boroughs of New York City (Fairchild Fact File 1987).

Various apparel production centers are known for producing different types of women's apparel. New York, for example, is noted for production of apparel in the higher price lines. California is noted for innovative styling in sportswear in particular. Dallas is known for dresses and moderately priced lines.

The Children's Apparel Industry

Historically, children have been dressed as miniature adults. To a great extent this is still true today. A visit to the children's department will reveal the same fashion trends as those displayed in apparel for juniors, misses, or men. This characteristic is particularly apparent in casual apparel styles but is also seen in dress-up apparel for children. A little boy will be dressed for church or a special occasion in a suit, shirt, and tie just like a man.

Even clothing for infants and toddlers incorporates some of the same fashion trends found in clothing for teenagers or adults. Calvin Klein denim diaper covers were introduced, for example, in the late 1970s when Calvin Klein designer jeans were a strong fashion item. Fleece jogging suits for infants and toddlers that look just like the ones worn by the child's parents are another example.

Fashion has been a dominant factor in the growth of the children's wear industry since the mid-1940s. Although children's fashions are usually adapted from apparel worn by teenagers or adults, occasionally a new trend appears first in children's wear and then becomes an adult fashion. T-shirts, for example, were first introduced for children and later were adopted by adults.

Development of Children's Apparel

Before 1910 there was no real children's apparel. Manufacturers of adult apparel merely adapted styles from men's and women's clothing and cut them smaller to fit children. Design did not consider children's special activities or the changing proportions of their growing bodies. Even in infants' apparel, there was little proportioning for fit or designing for needs. All babies, regardless of gender, were dressed the same way in a straight, narrow, ankle-length dress.

During the 1920s more functional clothing began to be designed for children at the same time that women's clothing styles began to reflect more liberated female lifestyles. Manufacturers began to produce children's clothing that suited children's unique physiques and was more comfortable for their active play. By the 1930s consumer demand for more functional children's apparel led to development of self-help garments with drop seats, snaps, and zippers. For the first time, sizing for children's clothing was developed to suit their body structure.

The end of World War II brought the baby boom, a period that lasted from 1946 to 1960. During this time, the number of births each year averaged four million. With the growth in the number of children came an interest in producing apparel for this obviously increasing market. New items for children grew out of a better understanding of their needs, new technology, and changing lifestyles. Clothing for children stressed comfort for the child and easy care for the mother.

Structure of the Children's Wear Industry

The children's wear industry is made up of approximately 1,000 firms with a total value of production over $3 billion. Most children's wear producers are small with the exception of a few large firms such as Carter and Healthtex. Manufacturers usually produce for three seasons a year—spring/summer, fall, and holiday. Fall is the most important season because of its back-to-school emphasis. Children's wear manufacturers are concentrated in New York, but they are also found in many other locations. In recent years the Miami fashion industry has developed a number of children's apparel manufacturers.

Boy's wear has long been produced by firms that also produce menswear, but women's wear firms have been less likely to enter the children's apparel business.

Modular Clothing

Modular clothing is a generic system of dressing based on interchangeable basic bodies that remain constant. The styles are drawn from the centuries-old simple designs of the kimono, tunic, sarong, and pant. Clothing pieces are constructed of easy-care lightweight knit fabrics usually of cotton/polyester blends or 100 percent cotton. Solid colors dominate the offerings, but stripes and prints are also available in some modular lines. No buttons or zippers are used, and styles are loose-fitting so that few sizes are needed to fit most consumers. In fact, some modular clothing is designed as one-size-fits-all. Garments are made to be mixed and matched and layered to create different looks. Many combinations are possible depending on the creativity of the wearer.

The concept of modular clothing was developed by apparel designer Sandra Garratt as a class project in 1974 while she was a student at the Fashion Institute of Design and Merchandising in Los Angeles. Her idea was ahead of its time but was to become a fashion success story in the 1980s. Garratt began production of her modular designs in New York but was forced to close her business when her investors backed out. In 1977 she moved to Dallas where she began sewing colorful modular pieces from her apartment, and in 1982 she opened a store called Units from which she sold her knit apparel. Three years later, with the support of investors, Garratt began to expand her business. Disagreements with her investors led to the sale of Units, and a year later the designer developed another modular line, Multiples. By 1989 the Multiples line was sold at more than 600 department stores.

Units modular clothing is sold at over 160 franchise and company-owned Units specialty stores located throughout the United States primarily in malls. The company producing Units is named Stinu, which was derived by spelling Units backwards. Located in Garland, Texas, Stinu is owned by the J. C. Penny Co.

Multiples and Units, the two leading modular lines, had combined sales in 1988 of nearly $200 million. Both firms projected sales to double in 1989. Units added one hundred new store locations in 1988 and planned to add fifty to seventy in 1989 in the United States and four stores in Great Britain. Multiples is also continuing to add shops in more department stores.

Although Multiples and Units dominate the market, modular lines are being marketed by a number of other companies, and in addition some department and specialty stores are producing their own private-label modular lines. Most lines are inexpensive, but a Chicago firm, Sasha Designs, sells modular apparel that includes coats made of wool selling for $200. Furthermore, modular clothing has attracted the interest of noted fashion designers such as Donna Karan, who is producing higher-priced modular-style clothing.

Stores and departments selling this apparel are also based on the modular concept. In Units stores crisp, rectangular, white shelving displays the apparel

Units stores sell modular clothing, which is produced by Stinu, located in Garland, Texas.
Source: *Reprinted with permission of Units.*

components, which are folded in packages. Graphics on the packages illustrate the varied pieces, and a video screen shows the customer how the units may be coordinated. Stores are staffed by salespeople called "fashion coordinators," who wear the modular apparel that they sell and help each customer create her own unique look. After customers try on the merchandise, they come out of the fitting rooms to view themselves in mirrors located on the sales floor. Here they are assisted by a fashion coordinator in using the accessory pieces and layering techniques. Dressing the customer in this way in view of other store customers and passersby in the mall attracts attention and encourages additional sales.

Among the reasons for the success of modular clothing are its flexibility, easy care, and packability. It suits the lifestyles of many different women who have little time to spend shopping or caring for clothing, and it is easy to wear and comfortable. A few pieces combined in different ways can give a woman a total wardrobe with varied looks. The clothing takes little storage space and can be folded and kept in a drawer. The fabric wrinkles little and is washable. Reasonable price is another reason for the popularity of modular clothing. Most of the clothing sells for $5 to $50 a piece; thus three pieces including top, skirt or pants, and jacket can cost less than $100.

Retailers have found that modular clothing eliminates some of the problems associated with merchandising sportswear. Many folded garments can be stocked in a small amount of space and few sizes are needed to fit all customers. Also, modular clothing appeals to many different customer types and ages.

Some fashion experts have questioned whether the modular concept will be just another trendy fad. It appears, however, that modular clothing is becoming a basic. It has been so successful in women's wear that it is now produced for children and is also appearing in menswear.

Beginning in the 1970s, a number of large apparel companies with well-known brand names entered the children's wear business. Among them were Liz Claiborne, Jordache, Levi Strauss, and Esprit. The Gap entered the children's business in 1987 by opening a chain of stores called the Gap Kids. These stores carry Gap clothing with the same fashion look as the Gap stores selling to adults. Two foreign dual distributors that opened children's wear stores in the United States during the 1980s were Benetton and Laura Ashley.

Product Specialization and Sizing

Children's wear manufacturers usually specialize by price range, size, and type of merchandise. Price ranges, as in women's wear, include budget, moderate, and better. Designer apparel is also found in children's wear with very high prices, but it covers only a small percentage of the total market. The U.S. industry today emphasizes the moderate price range. Much of the budget-priced merchandise is now produced offshore by low-wage foreign manufacturers. Some U.S. producers have closed their children's wear divisions because children's apparel has become too expensive to source profitably.

Sizing in the children's apparel industry includes six categories that are geared to figure proportions and somewhat to children's ages. The size categories in children's wear include the following:

1. *INFANTS:* sizing geared to age and ranges from 3 to 24 months in increments of 3 months. Some infant apparel is sized newborn, small, medium, large, and extra large.

2. *TODDLERS:* children who are learning to walk. Sizes range from T2 to T4.

3. **CHILDREN'S:** worn by children usually ages 3 to 6. In girls apparel the sizes are 3 to 6X; in boy's sizes 3 to 7.

4. **GIRLS:** sizes range from 7 to 14.

5. **PRETEEN:** sizes are 6 to 14. Preteens provide more sophisticated styling similar to the junior size range in women's apparel.

6. **BOYS:** includes sizes 8 to 20. Boys' sizes 14 to 20 are usually produced in the menswear industry. The terms *young men, student,* or *teen* sizes have been developed to suggest more sophisticated styling for boys as they become teenagers.

Some children's wear manufacturers are highly specialized as to type of product. For example, one manufacturer may produce only children's sleepwear, dresses, coats, or sportswear. Frequently, however, a manufacturer produces a single type of product in several size ranges. A firm might specialize in sleepwear and produce sizes for infants, toddlers, and children.

Marketing Activities and Trends

Children's apparel is marketed in much the same way as apparel in the women's and men's apparel industries. The National Kids Fashion Show is held three times a year in New York. This market features more than 350 lines of children's wear. Merchandise is also presented at regional apparel marts often in conjunction with scheduled women's wear markets. Advertising and sales promotion have been less extensive; however, we are seeing more national advertising by manufacturers as more large firms have entered the children's wear business. Most advertising is still done by retailers, however, and manufacturers encourage this with cooperative advertising programs. Advertising directed to the industry appears in trade publications such as *Earnshaw's Girls and Boys Wear Review, Women's Wear Daily,* and the *Daily News Record.*

Designer labels in higher priced children's apparel and accessories have become highly visible in stores throughout the United States. Children can now express status with such domestic and foreign designer names as Dior, Pierre Cardin, Yves Saint Laurent, Calvin Klein, Ralph Lauren, and Laura Ashley.

Licensing has made a strong impact on the children's wear business. Licensed characters have become exceedingly popular and are often reinforced by the popular television shows for children. Some of the licensed characters have long-lasting qualities; others have a short-lived popularity. Many of the Disney characters, such as Mickey Mouse and Donald Duck, have now decorated the apparel of three generations of children. Some of the characters made popular by television programs include the Smurfs, Yogi Bear, Hello Kitty, the Muppets, Sesame Street characters, and, more recently, Alf. Many characters that originated in the comics now are featured on television—Peanuts characters and Garfield, for example. Many T-shirts, sweatshirts, and sleepwear display the image of a licensed character. The list of characters is endless and new ones appear as they are popularized by the media.

The Intimate Apparel Industry

The intimate apparel industry is a special segment of the women's and children's apparel industry. This segment produces loungewear, sleepwear, women's and children's undergarments, and foundation garments. Intimate apparel and its use varies with changing fashions in outerwear. After suffering a decline in the 1960s and early 1970s, when many women gave up slips, girdles, and bras, the intimate apparel business is now enjoying a renewal.

Intimate apparel involves three categories of merchandise, including:

1. *FOUNDATION GARMENTS:* bras, girdles, garter belts, and body shapers.

2. *LINGERIE:* two general divisions of merchandise: daywear and sleepwear. *Daywear* is slips, petticoats, camisoles, and panties. *Sleepwear* includes nightgowns, pajamas, and night shirts.

3. *LOUNGEWEAR:* robes, housecoats, negligees, bed jackets, and other casual apparel for at-home wear.

Sometimes the distinction between loungewear and sportswear is unclear. Although loungewear is meant to be worn at home, the styles are sometimes identical to active sportswear apparel worn in public. Jogging suits, for example, are often produced by sportswear manufacturers and by producers of loungewear.

Intimate apparel is a major industry in the United States. Total production for women's and children's intimate apparel in 1984 was over $3.9 billion. The largest segment of the industry is in sleepwear and robes. The lingerie segment includes 604 companies, which employ over 67,000 workers. About half of these employees work in North Carolina, Pennsylvania, Alabama, and New York. Located primarily in New York, California, Pennsylvania, and Georgia, 151 companies produce foundation garments and employ 13,800 workers. The smallest segment of the intimate apparel industry is loungewear, with 135 companies.

Fashion trends are important in intimate apparel. As noted, lingerie and foundations must be geared to what is happening in outerwear. A good example is changing skirt lengths. Miniskirts tend to lead women to dispense with wearing a slip at all, whereas long skirts are good for the slip business, and a variety of skirt lengths, causing women to need several different slips, is even better. The popularity of the poof skirt in 1987 brought back the crinoline to fashion, if only for a brief time. Emphasis on the waistline brings waist-cinchers back, and body-conforming skirts lead to increased interest in girdles or body shapers, as today's softer molding garments are called. Sports bras for jogging and athletic activities are an example of the industry responding to current interest in physical fitness.

Summary of Key Points

1. The apparel industry, which is known as the needle trade, the cutting-up trade, the rag business, and the garment business, plays an important role in the economy of the United States.

2. The first ready-made clothing to be produced in the United States was sold in early nineteenth-century slop shops located in port cities. The poor-quality clothing sold in these shops met the needs of sailors, laborers, and slaves.

3. Two major historical events that spurred the development of the American apparel industry in the mid–nineteenth century were the California Gold Rush and the Civil War. Both of these events created a demand for men's apparel.

4. The production of ready-made clothing was made possible by several technological developments, including mass production of textiles, the sewing machine, and graded patterns.

5. Ready-to-wear for women developed after the Civil War, but cloaks and mantillas continued to be the primary garments made until the shirtwaist craze of the 1890s. Changing women's lifestyles after World War I assisted the growing apparel industry by encouraging a simpler style of dressing, which was easier to mass produce.

6. Several systems of apparel production are used to mass produce apparel. Still used today, these systems include (1) the homework system, (2) the factory system, and (3) the contracting system.

7. The influx of many European immigrants from the 1880s to 1920 provided the apparel industry with a plentiful supply of cheap labor that contributed to the acceleration of the industry.

8. Labor unions such as the International Ladies Garment Workers Union helped to correct the appalling conditions of the early twentieth-century sweatshops. Strikes such as the Big Strike and the Great Revolt led to more sanitary working conditions, higher wages, and shorter hours for workers in the apparel industry.

9. The three types of employers or establishments that operate in the apparel industry are regular manufacturers, jobbers, and contractors.

10. Contractors play an important role in the apparel industry by allowing firms to enter the apparel business with relatively limited capital and by providing for specialization and flexibility within the industry.

11. Strategies used by the apparel industry to combat apparel imports include technological developments, increased emphasis on marketing, expanded sourcing options, and the Quick Response program.

12. Fashion has been a dominant factor in the growth of the children's wear industry since the mid-1940s. Both designer labels and licensing have become important in children's apparel.

13. The intimate apparel industry includes women's and children's apparel in three categories: (1) foundation garments, (2) lingerie, and (3) loungewear.

Key Words and Concepts

Define, identify, or explain each of the following:

Amalgamated Clothing and Textile Workers Union (ACTWU)

apparel pipeline

The Big Strike

bridge merchandise

budget or popular price

CAD/CAM

closed shop

conglomerates

contracting (contractors)

daywear

dual distribution

factoring (factors)

factory system

foundation garments

The Great Revolt

homework system

horizontal integration

International Ladies Garment Workers Union (ILGWU)

inside shop

intimate apparel

licensing (celebrity, character, corporate)

loungewear

mantillas

manufacturers

men's clothing

outside shop

piecework

private label

Protocol of Peace

public ownership

ready-to-wear (RTW)

shirtwaist

silk dress firms

slop shops

sourcing (source)

sweatshop

Triangle Shirtwaist Fire

vertical integration

wrapper

Discussion Questions and Topics

1. What factors have contributed to the development and expansion of the American apparel industry from the early 1800s to today?

2. Describe the conditions in the apparel industry that led to the development of labor unions. Trace the development of the labor unions.

3. What two historical events accelerated the development of ready-made apparel during the mid-1800s? Describe the specific contributions of these two events.

4. Discuss the technological developments that made mass production of apparel possible.

5. Explain the differences between the factory system and the contracting system of apparel production. What are the advantages of each system?

6. Why are outside shops and jobbers used in the apparel industry?

7. Discuss the development of licensing arrangements in the apparel industry. Explain the different types of licensing.

8. What differences and similarities are found between the men's and the women's apparel industries?

9. How are the fashion industries being affected by the growth in imports? What are the various segments of the industry doing to combat imports?

10. Explain the four major sourcing options available to apparel producers.

11. Discuss the economic significance of the fashion industries to the United States.

12. Name and describe the five major garment categories in the menswear industry.

13. Explain how women's apparel is categorized by price.

14. Describe the children's wear industry and discuss current industry trends.

15. Fully define intimate apparel, explaining each of the categories within this apparel classification.

Notes

Fairchild Fact File, *The Textile/Apparel Industries*. New York: Fairchild Publications, 1987, p. 18.

Focus: Economic Profile of the Apparel Industry. Arlington, Va.: American Apparel Manufacturers Association, 1988.

U.S. Department of Commerce, Bureau of the Census, *1982 Census of Manufacturers; 1986 Annual Survey of Manufacturers Geographic Area Statistics*.

U.S. Department of Commerce, *U.S. Industrial Outlook*, 1987.

CHAPTER 7 _____

MANUFACTURERS OF FASHION ACCESSORIES, COSMETICS, AND HOME FURNISHINGS

WHEREAS apparel manufacturers make up a major part of the fashion industry, manufacturers of other products are also industry components. Accessories are necessary to complete a total fashion look and must be designed to coordinate with and accentuate apparel fashions. Cosmetics are also considered by many to be a necessary part of a total fashion look and must be produced in the right colors and textures to accompany the new season's fashion apparel. Another integral part of the fashion industry concerns the furnishings used in our environments.

This chapter presents a discussion of the operations of the industries that produce fashion accessories, cosmetics, and home furnishings. Each of these industries is an important part of the fashion business.

The Fashion Accessories Industries

Whenever a fashion change occurs in apparel, the fashion accessories industries must react to produce accessories appropriate for the new apparel styles. Accessories manufacturers must constantly forecast trends in ready-to-wear so that their accessories will coordinate with the new apparel. For example, shoes change shape, and heel heights vary with changing skirt length and silhouette. Hosiery becomes more important with short skirts and less important with pants. Jewelry must be coordinated with changing necklines, collars, and lapel widths. Every aspect of apparel design impacts accessories in some way. If accessories manufacturers are to sell their products, they must produce goods that coordinate with the fashion looks of the season. Makers of footwear, handbags, hosiery, gloves, hats, jewelry, belts, scarves, and other various small accessories must closely watch the development of fashion trends because their success depends to a great extent on their ability to coordinate with products of the ready-to-wear industry.

Accessories are often purchased by consumers as impulse items with little thought or planning. Because of this, retailers usually place accessories in convenient locations. For example, a specialty retailer often arranges costume jewelry and belts near the store's cash register and wrap desk so that the customer will see these items while waiting for a purchase to be completed. Department stores concentrate accessory items on the first floor of the store or near a main entrance so that customers can find them easily and will have to walk past them on their way to other departments. Department stores have also learned the value of carrying appropriate accessories in various ready-to-wear departments throughout the store, thus making it easier for the customer to coordinate accessory and apparel purchases.

Some stores also feature designer departments or boutiques that offer both a designer's apparel and accessories lines. This concept of a specialty store within a department store allows the customer one-stop shopping where the total fashion look can be purchased. This saves the busy customer time, providing she finds a department that has the total look she desires.

Fashion accessories have not always enjoyed the importance they had in the 1980s. In fact, because accessories are always subject to the influence of changing outer fashions, accessories industries may experience dramatic ups and downs. For example, belts suffered a major decline in sales when dresses did not emphasize the waistline, and the pantsuits of the 1970s led to a reduction in hosiery sales. Although new fashions in ready-to-wear lead to changing consumer preferences in accessories, these new fashions may also encourage the development of new products. The miniskirt, for example, hurt the sales of stockings but led to the development of pantyhose. During the 1980s, accessories became a strong growth area in the fashion industry, and retailers increased the amount of floor space allotted to many accessory classifications. Consumers bought accessories because of the popular fashion looks and because many accessory items were more affordable than apparel and offered a less expensive way to update their wardrobes.

The accessories industries include several businesses. Each accessories category is produced in a separate industry with its own distinctive characteristics. Some accessories industries are large and dominated by big producers; others remain the realm of small firms. Some categories have become highly mechanized in their production methods; others use hand operations that have changed little in recent years. Although concentrated in or near New York City, accessories manufacturers are found in many different locations throughout the United States.

Traditionally, the accessories industries have been divided into separate businesses, but some companies are now designing and sourcing several categories of accessories. Liz Claiborne Accessories is an example of a company that has become a multiproduct business. As a division of Liz Claiborne, Inc., the company produces handbags, small leather goods, scarves, belts, hats, and sunglasses.

The accessories industries have certain elements in common. Among these common elements are:

1. All are responsive to fashion trends because their success depends on their ability to coordinate their products with ready-to-wear.

2. All present at least two new seasonal lines a year: fall/winter and spring/summer.

3. Competition from imports is becoming an increasing problem for all segments of the accessories industry.

4. Designer names have become increasingly important in accessories. Many producers have licensing agreements with apparel designers.

5. Few mergers and consolidations have taken place among accessories manufacturers.

Footwear

The U.S. footwear industry has changed dramatically since 1968 when domestic production of nonrubber footwear reached its highest level of 642 million pairs. Since 1968 U.S. footwear production has declined steadily, falling to an estimated 226 million pairs in 1987. Industry experts predict that footwear production will stabilize because many of the weaker firms have closed. Between 1982 and 1987, 377 plants closed, and employment declined from 121,000 to 75,400 (U.S. Department of Commerce 1988).

Since the 1960s footwear imports have gained an increasing share of the U.S. market. In 1968 imports totaled 175 million pairs and comprised 21.5 percent of the market. By 1975 imports had risen to 288 million pairs, or 41 percent of the market. The increase expanded to 77 percent in 1985, and 81 percent in 1987.

The greatest number of imports is in women's footwear; about 85 percent of women's footwear is imported as compared to 66 percent of men's footwear. The United States imports footwear from more than ninety countries. In 1987, 50 percent of imports were from Taiwan. Other major countries from which the United States imports footwear are Korea, Brazil, Italy, China, Hong Kong, and Spain. The primary suppliers of women's footwear are Brazil, Italy, and Taiwan; men's leather footwear is imported mainly from South Korea and Taiwan. Children's and infants' footwear imports come primarily from Taiwan and Brazil. For several years most athletic shoes have been imported from South Korea. Better-quality leather shoes have long been imported from Italy, whereas budget-priced shoes are produced in the Far East.

Large U.S. producers of footwear have responded to the increase in imports in several ways. Many have closed domestic plants and have switched to importing

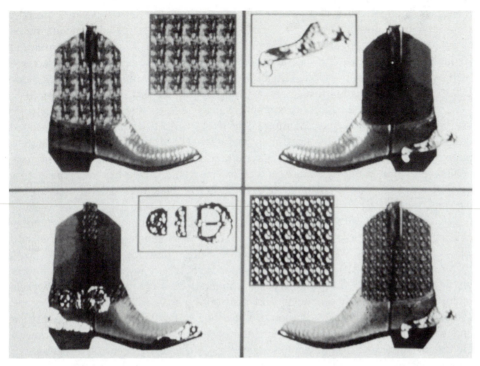

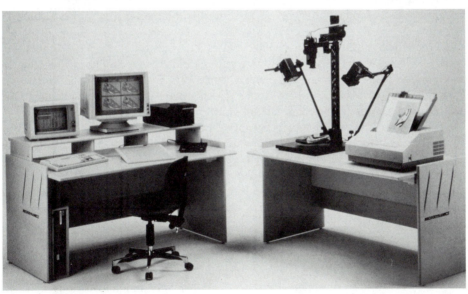

The use of computers in the production of footwear has improved efficiency and quality.
Source: *Reprinted with permission of Microdynamics, Inc.*

their own branded lines of footwear. Others have moved into shoe and specialty store retailing. Another means of combating imports has been for U.S. manufacturers to export cut footwear parts to developing countries, such as Mexico, the Dominican Republic, Brazil, India, Taiwan, and South Korea, where they are assembled and then exported back to the United States as finished or partly finished products. Some U.S. firms are performing final manufacturing operations that require less labor.

Another response to import competition has been for the footwear industry to use technology as a means to improve its cost competitiveness. Computer-aided design (CAD) and computer-aided manufacturing (CAM) systems are being used to improve efficiency and quality. CAD systems provide three-dimensional design capability in which patterns, texture, and colors may be changed instantaneously on a computer screen. These systems then computerize data that can be used to cut patterns, make lasts, cost the product, and operate CAM systems.

Companies are also adopting modular production techniques, which combine four or more operations under fewer operators. This reduces handling time and allows for closer quality inspection between manufacturing operations.

Approximately 210 companies with ten or more employees produce footwear in the United States. The industry is dominated by large firms that often have multiple divisions, each producing and distributing footwear under its own brand name. For example, Joyce, a division of U.S. Shoe Company, also produces footwear under the brands of Pappagalo and Red Cross shoes. In 1987 twenty producers with multiplant operations accounted for slightly more than 50 percent of the industry's production in 30 percent of the industry's plants. The largest firm produced 9.5 percent of U.S. production, whereas the twentieth-largest firm produced only 1 percent.

Production of shoes in the United States is concentrated in the northeastern states of Maine, Massachusetts, New Hampshire, and New York. Shoe production is also found in Missouri, Tennessee, Pennsylvania, Wisconsin, and Illinois. Most shoe firms maintain showrooms in New York City, the major shoe marketing center. The two primary seasons in shoes are fall and spring/summer.

The production of footwear is complex and requires skilled labor. The making of a shoe involves more than 200 operations with the use of a wide variety of equipment. Small footwear firms usually lease equipment or contract out some of the production processes. Some firms own facilities outside the United States.

Consumers spent $26.6 billion on footwear in 1987 and purchased 1.19 billion pairs. Per capita consumption was five pairs. For several years demand has been particularly high for athletic footwear, such as aerobic, running, fitness, and tennis shoes. This segment of the industry has experienced unprecedented growth over the past decade and shows no signs of slowing down. Many consumers have multiple pairs of athletic shoes. Gone is the time when one pair of white sneakers would meet every athletic need. Consumers have also become very brand conscious in their selection of athletic footwear, and brands such as Adidas, Reebok, Keds, Converse, Nike, and Puma have become highly visible. Athletic footwear is very much a fashion item and is available in a wide variety of styles and color combinations. Its popularity illustrates the importance that today's consumers place on comfort as well as fashion.

It is not unusual in big cities to see women going to and from work dressed in suits and wearing athletic shoes.

Manufacturers of footwear must be as aware of fashion as apparel firms. Changes in shoe styles correlate with changes in fashion apparel. New colors, styles, heel heights, and materials are needed for each season. Fashion has made the manufacturing, marketing, and retailing of shoes much more complicated than it used to be when a women purchased a pair of black leather dress shoes in the winter and a pair of white or black patent leather for summer. Now she needs a pair designed for many different activities and coordinated with each outfit. The production and retailing of footwear are further complicated by the many intricate sizes for men's, women's, and children's shoes.

Handbags and Small Leather Goods

The handbag industry includes manufacturers that produce women's handbags and purses made of leather and other materials with the exception of precious metals. Approximately 360 factories located primarily in New York and New England employed nearly 14,000 workers and produced shipments valued at $579 million in 1987. More than 60 percent of the handbags and purses sold in the United States are imported. In 1987 the value of handbag imports reached $757.6 million. The principal suppliers for lower-priced nonleather products were Taiwan, Korea, and China. Italy was the primary source for higher-quality leather products (U.S. Department of Commerce 1988).

Small leather goods include such items as wallets, billfolds, and coin purses, and cases for cosmetics, credit cards, glasses, cigarettes, keys, and business cards. The range of products manufactured by this industry has increased as women have entered the business world. Popular small leather goods today include cases for calculators, pocket appointment calendars, business organizers, notebooks, and various briefcase accessories. Because these items are usually carried in a briefcase, a woman's handbag, or a man's pockets, they are sometimes called **flatgoods.** More than 60 percent of the value of the materials used in these items is leather. Other materials often used are vinyl and textile goods.

The value of shipments of small leather goods in 1987 was $408.2 million. Imports have supplied an increasing percentage of sales in recent years. In 1987 alone the value of imports increased by 26 percent to $344.9 million. Taiwan and Korea provided approximately 50 percent of these imported products, which were made mostly from nonleather materials. Italy was the third largest supplier, providing slightly more than 12 percent of the total. Italy furnishes the United States with higher-priced quality leather goods (U.S. Department of Commerce 1988).

Fashion trends are important in handbags and small leather goods. Most women have a wardrobe of handbags designed to coordinate with their apparel. Handbags are made in a variety of materials, including leather, fabric, and vinyl. They come in many different styles, such as clutch, envelope, pouch, box, duffle, and tote. Some are meant to be carried by hand; others are designed to be worn over the shoulder. They range in size from small to large enough to be used as a weekend suitcase.

The trend to designer licensing is apparent in handbags and small leather goods as it is in other accessories. Well-known designer names in the handbag business are Liz Claiborne, Christian Dior, Anne Klein, and Donna Karan. Handbags are available in a wide range of prices from budget to designer. Two noted designers of handbags made from expensive materials such as exotic skins and leathers are Carlos Falchi and Judith Leiber.

Hosiery

The hosiery industry is the second largest accessory industry, after footwear, and is dominated by large firms. Examples of large hosiery firms are Hanes, Round-the-Clock, Bonnie Doon, and Kayser-Roth. Some large hosiery firms such as Adams-Mills Corporation make private-label hosiery for men, women, and children. Other hosiery firms are owned by large multiproduct conglomerates such as Hanes, which is owned by Sara Lee Corporation. Brands produced by Hanes include Underalls, Slenderalls, Fitting Pretty, Hanes Too!, Hanes Alive, Just My Size, Silk Reflections, Bill Blass, Showtoons, Today's Girl, L'Eggs, Sheer Energy, and Sheer Elegance. Other apparel divisions owned by Sara Lee are Hanes Knitwear, which manufactures men's and boy's underwear; Bali Foundations; Sirene, Inc., a women's swimwear firm; and Aris Isotoner, manufacturer of gloves, hosiery, and slippers. Additional Sara Lee subsidiaries include food and beverage companies, and the consumer direct sales companies Electrolux and Fuller Brush.

Most hosiery plants are located near southern textile mills. About 60 percent of hosiery is manufactured in North Carolina. Most hosiery manufacturers perform all of the steps necessary to make hosiery. In 1988, 331,682 dozens of pairs of hosiery were produced for men, women, and children. The industry employed 68,500 workers in 414 plants, most located in North Carolina, Alabama, and Tennessee (National Association of Hosiery Manufacturers 1988).

Women's hosiery producers have long emphasized brand names, and consumers have tended to purchase hosiery by brand because of consistency of fit and durability. Some of the major national brands such as Hanes, Evan-Picone, and Round-the-Clock are sold to department and specialty stores. Other brands such as L'Eggs and No Nonsense are mass-merchandised through self-service discount, grocery, and drug stores. Private brands are available at many chain stores. A store will often use the name of the store to identify its private store brand. The big three chains, Sears Roebuck, Montgomery Ward, and J. C. Penney, all have their own hosiery brands, as do many department stores.

Hosiery has become more fashion-oriented leading to a greater variety of style and colors. Few women wear only skin-colored hose today, and even men's and children's socks have become more colorful. Wearing socks has also returned to women's wear, brought back by the interest in physical fitness and the wearing of athletic shoes. Designer names, both European and American, now appear in hosiery; some of the designer names on the market are Dior, Givenchy, Ralph Lauren, Calvin Klein, and Liz Claiborne.

As hosiery has become a fashion accessory, it is being promoted more aggressively, and the number of markets has been increased from two to three a year. Market weeks are now held in March to present fall merchandise, in August to introduce holiday and early spring merchandise, and in November for spring merchandise. Emphasis is placed on decorative legwear, and the products offered have been expanded to include leg warmers and bodywear, which were introduced to be worn for exercising but are now promoted for wearing with other ready-to-wear apparel.

Jewelry

Jewelry is defined as articles of personal adornment including necklaces, rings, earrings, pins, chains, and bracelets. The jewelry industry is divided into two categories: fine and costume jewelry. Jewelry continues to draw a strong share of the consumer dollar because of the large number of women in the work force who buy jewelry for themselves. Approximately 40 percent of these women buy jewelry for themselves annually, twice the rate for nonworking women (U.S. Department of Commerce 1988).

Fine Jewelry

Fine jewelry is made of precious metals such as gold, silver, or platinum, and is often set with precious or semiprecious stones. In the 1970s the fine jewelry industry was impacted by the escalated costs of gold and silver. A drop in the cost of precious metals in 1980 led to an increase in the production of fine jewelry. Product shipments of precious metal jewelry in 1987 were estimated at $3.2 billion. The industry employed some 35,000 workers who worked in 2,193 firms, 68 percent of which were located in New York, Rhode Island, California, and Massachusetts (U.S. Census of Manufacturers 1988).

Gold is the preferred precious metal in fine jewelry. Because gold is too soft to be used in its solid twenty-four karat (24K) state, it must be combined with base metals. The most commonly used alloys are rated 18K, 14K, or 12K. Pure 24K gold is mixed with copper, silver, palladium, or nickel to produce an acceptable alloy. An alloy must be at least 10K to be called karat gold. Silver is the least expensive of the precious metals, which has helped it to become a fashion favorite.

Another trend that has led to less expensive fine jewelry is the use of synthetic gemstones set in 14K gold. Synthetic diamonds, emeralds, rubys, and sapphires, among others, can be made to look so much like real precious gemstone that only a jeweler can tell the difference.

Bridge jewelry has also developed as an answer to the high cost of fine jewelry. Such jewelry provides a fine jewelry look but with less expensive stones, such as onyx, ivory, coral, or freshwater pearls. Bridge jewelry sometimes uses gold-plated metals rather than karat gold.

Costume Jewelry

Costume jewelry, sometimes called fashion jewelry, is made from relatively inexpensive materials such as glass, base metals, wood, ceramics, plastics, and sometimes imitation gems. The costume jewelry industry is heavily concentrated in Rhode Island and New York, which together account for 65 percent of industry employment. Approximately 800 companies, which employ 21,000 people, mass produce costume jewelry. In 1987 the wholesale value of shipments for the industry was $1.4 billion (U.S. Department of Commerce 1988). Many of the factories producing costume jewelry are small, often employing fewer than twenty workers.

Brand names in costume jewelry are well known. Among the mass producers of jewelry at moderate prices are Monet, Trifari, Napier, Marvella, and the 1928 Jewelry Company. More expensive names are Miriam Haskell, Kenneth J. Lane, and Carolee. Designers have licensed their names for jewelry as well. Among the more widely distributed designer lines are Christian Dior, Anne Klein, Donna Karan, and Yves Saint Laurent.

Jewelry Imports and Exports

Imports are beginning to have a greater impact on both fine and costume jewelry. U.S. imports of precious metal jewelry increased 12 percent in 1987 to $2.2 billion. Imports also rose in costume jewelry an estimated 19 percent to $680 million. The previous year imports increased 15 percent in fine jewelry and 6 percent in costume jewelry. Fine jewelry is imported most often from Italy, which accounts for about one-half the U.S. total. Imports from Hong Kong, Israel, and Thailand are increasing. Costume jewelry is imported primarily from Taiwan, Hong Kong, and South Korea. Japan is the fourth largest supplier of costume jewelry (U.S. Department of Commerce 1988).

The United States has increased its exports of costume jewelry in recent years. In 1988 costume jewelry exports totaled $97.8 million, a 29 percent increase from $75.8 million exported the previous year. Industry efforts are under way to continue increasing jewelry exports. The International Jewelry Trade Association was founded in 1988 for the purpose of marketing the U.S. jewelry industry worldwide. This association hosts four annual trade shows and has participated in foreign trade shows to Japan. It plans to build a national jewelry trade center in Rhode Island, which will showcase U.S. jewelry manufacturers and will offer facilities to foreign jewelry manufacturers who want to increase U.S. imports of costume jewelry.

Gloves

Prior to the 1960s gloves were a necessary part of the total fashion look. Gloves of fabric or leather were worn whenever a women dressed up to go out. They were an important fashion accessory. Most women owned several pair of white fabric gloves in various lengths, and leather gloves were considered classic. During the 1960s, when the style of dressing became much more casual, gloves were no longer considered a necessary part of a "ladies' wardrobe." The glove industry has never fully recovered from this fashion change, and today gloves are worn primarily for protection and warmth.

The glove industry started in Gloversville, New York, where the first U.S. glove factory originated in 1760. Gloversville remains a center for the production of leather gloves today and is the site of the headquarters for the National Glove Manufacturers Association. Plants that manufacture leather gloves are located primarily in the Northeast. Fabric glove manufacture takes place throughout the country, with the greatest number of plants found in North Carolina, Mississippi, Alabama, and Tennessee.

Today's glove industry employs approximately 6,800 production workers who produce $208 million worth of gloves at wholesale value. In 1987 shipments of leather gloves and mittens reached an estimated $156 million (U.S. Department of Commerce 1988). Imports of leather gloves have been a problem for the already threatened industry. The principal foreign suppliers of gloves are the Philippines, China, and Mexico. Fine quality leather gloves are imported from Italy and France.

Millinery and Hats

The hat business has suffered from the same fashion malaise as the glove business. Until the late 1950s both men and women wore hats when they dressed to go out. Hats were a necessary fashion item for women when attending many social events such as weddings, luncheons, or teas. As the movement to the suburbs began following World War II, lifestyles began to change. With more informal ways of entertaining came casual dressing, and the suburban style of dress spread to the city. Hats began to fade as a fashion accessory during the 1950s, and by the early 1960s both men and women ceased to consider hats a necessary accessory for everyday wear or for more formal occasions as well.

Millinery is the term used for the women's hat industry. Today's millinery industry is small, consisting of approximately one hundred firms with about 2,500 employees located primarily in New York City. The men's hat and cap business includes approximately 300 establishments, 70 percent of which are located in Missouri, New York, Texas, Virginia, and Pennsylvania. The *1982 Census of Manufacturers* reported the value of shipments for millinery at almost $90 million, whereas the value of hats and caps was $432.4 million. Although hats are still used by fashion designers to complete a fashion look, more consumers consider them a relatively unimportant accessory, and hats are most often worn for protection from the elements.

Miscellaneous Accessories

A number of other accessories are used to complete the fashion look. The importance of items such as belts, scarves, lace collars, artificial flowers, umbrellas, handkerchiefs, hair accessories, and eyewear varies with fashion trends. Belts, for example, become important when waistlines are in fashion. They enjoyed a tremendous revival in popularity in the 1980s, whereas in the late 1960s and early 1970s they were an unnecessary item with shift dresses and pantsuits.

Accessories such as neckwear, hair ornaments, and artificial flowers enjoy periodic fashion success. Such items provide a relatively inexpensive way for women to achieve a new fashion look; consequently, such accessories often become very popular during times of economic downtown. Accessory sales may also increase when consumers are dissatisfied with styles in apparel. Accessories offer them a way to update existing wardrobes or to give the right fashion look to new clothing styles. In either case, accessories are important fashion items.

The Cosmetics Industry

For many women cosmetics are as important as any accessory in completing the total fashion look, and men, too, are using cosmetics in increasing numbers. Growth in the cosmetics industry has been stimulated in recent years by a strong interest in self-image by men and women of all ages. Product shipments by the cosmetics industry exceeded $14 billion in 1987 (U.S. Department of Commerce 1988). The complex of suppliers and product developers involved in the output of products in the cosmetics and personal products industries includes 800 to 1,0000 manufacturers. About 500 of these firms focus on end-use products (Fairchild Fact File 1986).

Cosmetics are defined by the Federal Trade Commission as articles other than soap that are intended to be "rubbed, poured, sprinkled or sprayed on, introduced into, or otherwise applied to the human body for cleansing, beautifying, promoting attractiveness or altering the appearance without affecting the body's structure or functions." The cosmetics industry produced three categories of merchandise: (1) cosmetics, (2) toiletries, and (3) fragrances. **Cosmetics** products are designed to be applied to the face, skin, or hair for improving the user's appearance. These products include such items as skin care creams and lotions, makeup bases, rouge, mascara, eye shadows, lipsticks, and nail products. Toiletries include personal-care products such as antiperspirants, toothpaste, shaving creams, shampoos, and hair-care products. **Fragrances** are applied to the body for the purpose of adding a pleasant scent and include items such as toilet water, cologne, perfume, and scented bath products.

According to *Product Marketing,* a trade magazine pertaining to the cosmetics, fragrance, and beauty markets, retail sales of cosmetics and toiletries are proportioned as follows: cosmetics 28 percent, women's fragrances 18 percent, women's hair products 18 percent, men's toiletries 6 percent, skin preparations 16 percent, and personal cleanliness items 14 percent.

Imports and Exports

Imports are becoming a problem in the cosmetics industry just as they are in many other fashion industries. The first trade deficit in cosmetics appeared in 1985 when imports were $20 million more than exports. In 1987 the deficit approximated $71.5 million, and France and Germany were the primary exporters of cosmetics to the United States (U.S. Department of Commerce 1988).

The importation of **diverted goods** is becoming an increasing problem in the cosmetics industry. Diverted or gray market goods are genuine trademarked products that are made abroad by legitimate manufacturers but imported into the United States and sold by distributors other than those authorized by the firms holding the trademarks. These products are intended for sale in markets other than the United States but are shipped by independent American importers and often sold in discount retail stores. Fragrances are among the products most often sold in this manner.

Gray market goods are in many cases barred from this country by U.S. trade laws. But the U.S. Customs Service grants an exception when the American and foreign trademarks are owned by the same or related companies, or when the American trademark owner has authorized a foreign entity to use the trademark.

Counterfeit goods are another import problem facing the U.S. cosmetics industry. These are unauthorized copies of products. They are becoming a greater problem because they can easily be intermingled with diverted goods. Prestige fragrances are among the cosmetics items most often counterfeited. Unauthorized copying is also a problem with many designer accessories, especially those carrying a designer logo.

U.S. exports of cosmetics, toiletries, and fragrances have been increasing according to figures compiled by the Commerce Department. Total exports of cosmetics, including toiletries and fragrances, were $454,851,000 in 1988, compared to $348,694,000 in 1987 and $291,387,000 in 1986. The largest export market for the United States is Canada, followed by Great Britain and Japan.

The potential exists for increasing exports of cosmetics and toiletries. Countries with a high level of disposable income, such as Mideast oil-producing nations, offer good potential markets. New markets are opening in China where prior to 1980 laws banned the wearing of cosmetics. Some countries with developing economics have demonstrated great demand for American products. For example, ethnic hair products are in strong demand in some West African nations where there is no local industry to compete with U.S. companies. Identifying and developing such markets could lead to substantial increases in exports of U.S.-produced cosmetics.

The Cosmetic, Toiletry, and Fragrance Association

The major trade association in the cosmetics industry is the **Cosmetic, Toiletry, and Fragrance Association** (CTFA), headquartered in Washington, D.C. Members include manufacturers and distributors of finished cosmetics, fragrances, and toilet preparations. The CTFA conducts safety research and testing, supports quality standards, and provides a means for information exchange about scientific developments among members, government regulating agencies, and consumers. The CTFA also keeps members informed on government regulations and offers advice on interpretation and compliance.

The CTFA is leading an effort to sell more U.S. products abroad. Although efforts have concentrated on promoting exports to Western Europe and Japan, the association maintains files on more than one hundred countries, detailing conditions and regulations for exporting and other information needed by U.S. firms interested in targeting a certain country.

Another activity of the CTFA is the Look Good, Feel Better Program. Organized in conjunction with the American Cancer Society and the National Cosmetology Association, this program is designed to help women cope with the appearance changes that often accompany chemotherapy and radiation treatments. The program includes a package of training information for hospitals and other health facilities that may want to implement their own Look Good, Feel Better Program. A training manual includes information on how to structure the program, a patient handbook showing basic grooming techniques, a cosmetologist's handbook with facts about cancer and the effects of treatment, and a video featuring women who tell how cosmetics helped them through their cancer treatments.

Government Regulation of Cosmetics

Legislation passed by both federal and state governments concerns the content and labeling of cosmetics products. Some states have passed their own laws, which are more restrictive than federal statutes. At the federal level the Food and Drug Administration (FDA) is responsible for regulating the cosmetics industry concerning the safety of its products. FDA regulations prevent cosmetics manufacturers from using potentially harmful ingredients and from making exaggerated claims regarding the effectiveness of their products.

The Federal Food, Drug, and Cosmetic Act was the first federal law controlling cosmetics in the United States. It became effective in 1938 and prohibited adulteration and misbranding of cosmetics. In 1960 it was amended to require government review and approval of the safety of color additives used in cosmetics.

The Fair Packaging and Labeling Act of 1966 prevented unfair or deceptive methods of packaging and labeling in the cosmetics as well as other industries. Since 1977 all cosmetics must be labeled with their ingredients listed in descending order by weight. This does not apply to fragrances.

As a response to growing pressure from Congress to disclose ingredients in all cosmetics products, the industry instituted a voluntary program in 1988 to disclose ingredients in products used in salons by professionals. The cosmetics industry has become increasingly concerned about efforts on the part of both federal and state governments to regulate the industry. New laws are likely to be considered regarding the safety of products, the disclosure of ingredients in fragrances, and protection of the environment from atmospheric pollutants used in spray products.

Structure of the Industry

Mergers and acquisitions are changing the structure of the firms in the cosmetics industry. As in other segments of the fashion industry, it has become increasingly difficult to keep up with changes in company ownership. In any case, the number of firms is becoming fewer, and most are part of large corporations. Some national brand cosmetics companies are owned by large drug conglomerates. Recently, cosmetics firms have been diversifying, and some noncosmetics firms have sold off their cosmetics divisions. In 1986 Chesebrough-Ponds was purchased by Unilever, an Anglo-Dutch firm. Revlon was acquired by Pantry Pride in 1985, and the company's name was changed to Revlon Group, Inc. In 1987 Revlon purchased Max Factor and Germaine Monteil. Also in 1987 Yves Saint Laurent of France bought the Charles of the Ritz Group, Ltd., from Squibb, a large drug company, and another drug company, Eli Lilly, sold its Elizabeth Arden prestige cosmetics business to Faberge, Inc.

Two of the largest companies that manufacture cosmetics and fragrances are Avon and the Revlon Group. Other large companies are Cosmir, which is the U.S. licensee for L'Oreal and Lancome; Chesebrough-Ponds, producer of Cutex, Prince Matchabelli, and Ponds; Noxell Corp., producer of Cover Girl and Noxzema; and Maybelline, owned by Schering-Plough.

Avon Products, Inc. is one of the largest volume U.S. producers of cosmetics and sells its products by direct sales from door-to-door rather than through retail stores. Avon's sales in recent years have been declining because the increased number of women in the work force has meant that fewer women were at home for Avon sales representatives to service. Avon now trains its representatives to sell to women at the workplace. Avon is also using direct-mail catalogs to reach customers. It is a diversified company that includes separate divisions for beauty products, health care, and direct-response sales. The company manufactures and sells cosmetics, fragrances, toiletries, fashion jewelry, and accessories. Sales in 1988 were $3,364.5 million (*The Fortune 500* 1989).

Revlon is another large firm engaged in the beauty products and health-care business. Its beauty products business consists primarily of the manufacture and distribution of cosmetics and fragrances, including face and eye makeup, lipsticks, hair color and nail products, fragrances, and beauty care and treatment products, including shampoos, conditioners, cleaning and moisturing creams and lotions, and antiperspirants. The company also manufactures beauty implements and professional beauty products and equipment. Revlon's health-care business consists of vision care products, and the company operates clinical diagnostic laboratories in the United States.

Revlon manufactures and sells cosmetics in more than one hundred countries through Revlon subsidiaries in nineteen countries. The company's products are designed to reach many different segments of the consumer market with varying tastes, lifestyles, ages, and spending patterns. Each consumer segment is served by a specific brand designed to meet the characteristics of the demographic group. Popular-priced cosmetics and skin treatment lines sold in drug and mass volume retailers include Revlon, Moon Drops, and Natural Wonder. Revlon's popular-priced fragrances are Charlie, Jontue, and Scoundrel. Prestige or higher-priced lines include Ultima II and Princess Marcella Borghese. Prestige fragrances, sold primarily to department and specialty stores, include Ciara, Bill Blass for women, Norell, and Di Borghese. Revlon also owns Max Factor, which sells cosmetics under the Max Factor and Maxi labels; the Almay line of hypo-allergenic cosmetics; and the Halston fragrance lines for women and Halston Limited fragrances for men. In addition, Revlon sells toiletries and beauty care products under the labels Flex, Milk Plus 6, Colorsilk, Clean and Clear, Mitchum, and Hi and Dri. Sales for the Revlon Group in 1988 were $2,477 million (*The Fortune 500* 1989).

Not all cosmetics firms manufacture name-brand products. Some specialize in producing private-label merchandise to be sold by retail stores and beauty salons. Many department and chain stores carry their own brand of cosmetics and skin care products. Private-label products cost the retailer less because their packaging is kept to a minimum and the manufacturer does not have the expense of promoting and advertising the product.

Growing Market Segments

Growth in the cosmetics industry is being affected by the changing demographics of the population. The age group eighteen to twenty-four years has been declining since 1981 and is not expected to begin to increase until 1997. This eighteen- to twenty-four-year-old age group is the population segment that uses the most makeup and the one most likely to experiment with new products. Although the industry has felt the loss from the decline in the younger market of those in their teens and twenties, it is being stimulated by the larger number of older consumers. Two of the fastest growing segments of the U.S. population are the forty-five to fifty-five and the over sixty-five age groups. These demographic groups open opportunities for selling new skin care products, such as moisturizers, skin lotions, wrinkle removers, and cell renewal enhancers. Research on aging skin is increasing, and anti-aging or antiwrinkle creams are expected to become major products in the near future.

Another prime market for cosmetics is the ethnic market, with about 50 million people. Black Americans spend four times more per capita than whites on health and beauty aids. This market is estimated at between $2.5 and 3 billion. (U.S. Department of Commerce 1988 and Standard and Poor's 1987). Blacks are a promising target market for cosmetics because this market is growing and is younger than the white market. A few cosmetics producers are working on developing cosmetics that will be suitable for a wide variety of skin shades for ethnic groups.

In recent years men have become more interested in the use of cosmetics. Many cosmetics firms now make men's products in addition to products for women. The male consumer is purchasing products such as cologne, moisturizers, hair colorings, wrinkle-removing eye creams, and hair conditioners. Men's cosmetics and fragrances are a small market; however, it is a growing market that offers tremendous potential for expansion because few men presently use these products. The industry is emphasizing educational advertising, explaining to men the benefits of cleansing and protecting their skin.

Because consumers have become more aware of the hazards of sun exposure, the cosmetics industry has developed a variety of suntan and sunscreen products. It is emphasizing sunscreens, tanning accelerators, and tanning sustaining products. Sunscreens are being used in shampoos, skin creams, makeup, and aftershave lotions. Also, new products are combining skin care benefits such as moisturizers with color.

Marketing Cosmetics

The cosmetics business is characterized by strong competition. Therefore, marketing of products is very important. It is estimated that marketing accounts for one-third of manufacturers' cost (U.S. Department of Commerce Industrial Outlook 1988). Marketing of cosmetics is also very important because cosmetics are essentially discretionary items and are often bought on impulse. In fact, impulse buying is estimated to account for more than half of retail sales (Standard and Poor's 1987). Although product quality, performance, and price influence consumers' product choices, advertising, promotion, merchandising, and packaging all have a marked influence on consumers' decisions to buy cosmetics products.

Companies are using increasingly elaborate packaging for cosmetics. A cosmetics package projects a company's image and says something about both the customer who buys it and the product beneath the wrapping. With higher-priced prestige cosmetics, sometimes as much as 60 to 80 percent of the retail price comes from the packaging. For example, Elizabeth Arden repackaged its lipsticks, as well as other makeup products, in an effort to upgrade the company's image and to attract a higher-income customer. Plastic lipstick cases were replaced with metal cases having a fluted column and a wavy base. Although the price was raised by 29 percent, sales increased by 40 percent. The company attributed this increase entirely to the packaging (Wells 1988).

Cosmetics are distributed to retail outlets in a manner different than most other fashion products. They are distributed by either franchise or mass distribution. With

franchise distribution, manufacturers or their designated exclusive distributors sell directly to retailers. No middlepeople are involved with franchise distribution, and the cosmetic manufacturer knows who is selling the product. In contrast, with **mass distribution,** a third party such as a wholesaler or rack jobber is involved. A **rack jobber** is a type of wholesaler who provides, sets up, and maintains the merchandise as it is displayed in the store. These third parties may sell to a number of different types of retailers; therefore, manufacturers may not know what retail outlets are selling their products. Examples of mass-distributed cosmetic lines are Almay, Aziza, Coty, Lip Quencher, Maxi, Maybelline, Cover Girl, Revlon, and Max Factor. These cosmetic lines are usually sold in drug stores, discount stores, and mass-oriented department stores.

Prestige lines are usually limited in sales by manufacturers to those retail stores that they feel will provide the proper prestige setting for the product. Each store that sells the prestige cosmetics line is referred to as a **door.** The number of doors is the number of stores in which a company's products are offered for sale. Especially when a new cosmetic or fragrance is introduced, the number of doors making the introduction may be limited to well-known upscale department and specialty stores that carry higher-priced merchandise. Examples of prestige lines are Estee Lauder, Clinique, Elizabeth Arden, Princess Marcella Borghese, Charles of the Ritz, Germaine Monteil, and Ultima II.

Because of the intensely competitive nature of the cosmetics industry, some prestige products are now being sold in stores traditionally reserved for mass distribution products. This is particularly true with fragrances that are sold in drug stores.

Cosmetics companies take an active part in training salespeople to sell their products. It is common for salespeople in large specialty stores to be **line representatives** of a cosmetics company. Such salespeople may receive their salaries directly from the company and often receive a commission on all cosmetics sold in the line they represent. These salespeople are trained by the cosmetics company and are responsible for stock inventory.

Cosmetics manufacturers do extensive national advertising in magazines and on television to gain consumer recognition of their products. A common promotional device is the "gift-with-purchase" or a "purchase-with-purchase" offer. The gift is usually an assortment of trial-size cosmetics. Such gifts attract customers to make a purchase in order to receive the bonus gift and provide customers an opportunity to try a product that they might not otherwise purchase.

The introduction of new fragrance lines has become an expensive proposition requiring extensive promotions. Calvin Klein Cosmetics reportedly spent $15 million to introduce Obsession, and Parlux Fragrances spent $3.5 to 4 million on TV and radio commercials as well as print ads with scented strips to launch Spectacular by Joan Collins. In-store sampling and designer/celebrity endorsements and appearances are often part of introducing new fragrances. In addition to designers introducing their own fragrances, a major 'trend has been for cosmetics and fragrance firms to introduce a fragrance carrying a celebrity name. Examples include Cher's Uninhibited, Elizabeth Taylor's Passion, and Linda Evans' Crystal.

Unlike other fashion products, prestige cosmetics are rarely lowered in price for special sales or merchandise clearances. When products are replaced or become outdated, they are usually returned to the manufacturer. This system is called **rubber-banding,** which means that unsold cosmetics products are returned by the retailer to the manufacturer who replaces them with current products. Thus markdowns of such products are rare in prestige lines. Cosmetics are one product that the consumer does not expect to find on sale in a department store at a reduced price.

The Home-Furnishing Industries

The selling of home-furnishings products such as home textiles and furniture has increasingly become a fashion business. Various styles and colors periodically become more or less fashionable, and home-furnishings merchandisers must be aware of the trends if they are to provide what customers want to buy. Often trends in the apparel industry are duplicated in the home-furnishings industry; however, changes do occur more slowly because home-furnishings products are more durable than clothing. Designer names, for example, have become important in home furnishings just as they are important in fashion apparel and accessories. Designers are licensing their names to appear on bed and bath linens as well as on furniture lines.

Household Furniture

Furniture includes two basic categories: upholstered furniture and case goods. Upholstered furniture is the category most concerned with fashion because it is covered with fabrics that vary in color, design, and texture. Upholstered furniture includes chairs, sofas, loveseats, sectionals, and sofa beds. **Case goods** are pieces of furniture used for storage or as a receptacle. They include boxlike structures such as dressers, chests of drawers, china cabinets, or buffets. Also considered case goods are tables, bookcases, desks, and beds. These pieces are most often found in bedrooms and dining rooms. Case goods, however, are becoming increasingly more important in the living room or den. In fact, case goods and modular units designed to house home entertainment systems are among the fastest-growing furniture categories. Case goods are most frequently constructed of wood or simulated wood materials. Other materials such as wicker, rattan, and metals are also used.

The U.S. household furniture business is an $18 billion industry, consisting of nearly 4,000 manufacturers that employ 278,000 workers (U.S. Department of Commerce 1988). Most are small shops doing custom work. The largest firms are clustered at the lower price points. Traditionally, the furniture industry has been highly fragmented because of its numerous product lines and lack of import penetration. Because of growing imports in the 1980s, however, U.S. furniture producers have incorporated more advanced technology and become more marketing-oriented. Large firms are better able to compete, and according to the trade publication *Furniture Today*, the top ten furniture manufacturers now control almost 30 percent of the market. As in many other fashion industries, a trend toward industry consolidation has been occurring, and large firms are becoming increasingly important. The trend toward mergers and consolidations started about 1970 and initially involved the acquisition of furniture operations by companies not in the furniture industry. Now the trend is for these companies to divest themselves of their furniture holdings. More recently consolidation has taken place by furniture companies buying other furniture companies. Volume leaders in furniture manufacturing are Interco, which owns the brands Broyhill, Ethan Allen, and Lane; Bassett Furniture Industries; Mohasco; La'z'Boy; and Thomasville.

Interco became the first furniture firm to exceed $1 billion in annual sales in 1987 when it purchased the Lane Company. Large holding companies with several name-brand furniture lines as well as other home-furnishings and accessory lines are expected to become increasingly important in the industry. Such firms will use national advertising to create strong company images and brand-name identification.

Furniture production is concentrated in North Carolina with other leading states including California and New York. North Carolina is the leading state in the number of upholstered furniture plants. California leads in the production of wood household furniture. Low- and mid-priced furniture manufacturing is concentrated near the furniture market in High Point, North Carolina. Several high-end furniture manufacturers are located in Grand Rapids, Michigan, which until the 1920s was the major furniture production center in the United States.

Styling competition in furniture creates product lines with many items and is likely a reason why many small producers still flourish in high-priced, top-of-the-line furniture. Some of these high-quality manufacturers include Baker, Knapp & Tubbs, John Widdicomb Co., and Kindel Furniture Co., all located in Grand Rapids, and Karges Furniture Co. of Evansville, Indiana. Private ownership still prevails among these companies where fashion and craftsmanship are very important. Small manufacturers such as these can set themselves apart with unique styling that caters to people's desire to have something different. Production of high-quality furniture is a slow process involving craftsmanship that has changed little from the nineteenth century.

Imports and Exports

Nearly 20 percent of the furniture sold in the United States is imported. Much is lower-priced goods, although some consists of higher-quality goods in unique styling not produced in the United States. In 1987 furniture imports totaled more than $3.7 billion. Taiwan is the number-one foreign furniture supplier, accounting for one-third of total U.S. furniture imports. Other important furniture suppliers to the United States are Italy, West Germany, Denmark, and Japan. Imports are expected to continue to increase because low-wage countries like Taiwan have a significant advantage in the labor-intensive furniture industry. To an increasing extent imports consist of knock-down furniture, which is easy to ship and relatively inexpensive to produce.

U.S. exports of furniture have generally been small, relative to total industry shipments. High transportation costs and different style preferences abroad have kept U.S. exports low. After reaching a peak of $260 million in 1981, U.S. furniture exports in 1987 were valued at $183 million. Canada provides the primary market for U.S. furniture production, accounting for more than one-fourth of total U.S. exports.

Imports have not been a major problem in home textiles as compared to apparel. The primary difference is that home textiles production is not labor-intensive. Curtains, draperies, sheets, bedspreads, and towels require less cutting and sewing. Also, the shipping of comforters, bedspreads, or pillows is expensive due to the bulk and density of these items. However, imports are increasing in sheets, pillowcases, bed coverings, and pillows.

Marketing Home Furnishings

Residential furniture sales are more than a $30-billion business at retail. The majority of furniture is sold through independently owned furniture stores, and only at the lower price points are chains important. Some of the large chain furniture stores are Levitz, Breuner's, Haverty's, Rhodes, and Wickes. Many department stores have discontinued furniture sales, although some large stores such as Macy's, Marshall Field, and Bloomingdale's still emphasize their furniture departments. High-end home furnishings are often sold through interior designers who work independently or who are employed by prestige department and furniture stores.

A major trend in retailing home furnishings is **gallery programs,** which are exclusive displays of a particular company's line of furniture with promotional support from the manufacturer. Gallery programs often include exclusive accessories as well and may provide complete home decorating services. Galleries are either independent manufacturer-direct outlets, such as those pioneered by Ethan Allen, or stand-alone displays in furniture or department stores. A survey by *Furniture Today* found 2,400 installed galleries at the end of 1986, and the number was predicted to more than double by 1991.

Furniture manufacturers are providing more sales support to retailers, including merchandising, advertising, sales training, and inventory management. On-line computer systems for gallery stores are allowing the retailer and manufacturer to quickly analyze sales, leading to better control of inventories and deliveries. The U.S. furniture industry is expected to continue to change from an industry made up of dominantly small operations to one dominated by large companies.

Several noted interior designers and furniture marketers have entered licensing agreements with high-quality manufacturers to design their own lines of furniture. These lines are aimed at upper-middle income customers who want well-made, good-looking furniture that is affordable. An example is Pierre LeVec and Pierre Moulin of Pierre Deux, a chain of designer shops that feature country French home furnishings. The two owners are working with Henredon Furniture Industries to produce a line of French provincial furniture.

Licensing agreements have also become important with home textiles. Several

Tiffany & Co.

Tiffany & Co., the New York–based jewelry firm, was founded in 1837 by Charles Lewis Tiffany and John B. Young. Since its establishment more than 150 years ago, Tiffany & Co. has grown from one small store into a multimillion-dollar legend in the jewelry business. Tiffany initially sold Chinese goods, Japanese papier-mâché, umbrellas, walking sticks, pottery, and stationery. Gradually the company added gold, silver, and diamond jewelry. Today the firm designs, manufactures, retails, and distributes fine jewelry, timepieces, sterling silver, china, crystal, and stationery. The company's newest product is a women's fragrance named simply Tiffany. These products are sold through nine U.S. and four foreign Tiffany & Co. stores. Tiffany products are also sold through the company's own direct marketing catalog, known as the Blue Book, and selected independent retailers.

The first Tiffany store in 1837, located at 259 Broadway, was named Tiffany & Young after its two founders. A third partner, J. L. Ellis, joined the firm in 1841, and the store, operating under the name of Tiffany, Young & Ellis, was moved to 271 Broadway in 1847. Following the retirement of Young and Ellis, the name of the firm was changed to Tiffany & Co., and the store moved to a four-story building at 555 Broadway. Tiffany & Co. merged with John C. Moore's Silverware company, which had been supplying the company's American-made silverware, in 1868, and the company was incorporated with Charles Tiffany as the company's first president. Union Square was the next location in 1870, followed by Fifth Avenue at 37th Street in 1905; in 1940 Tiffany moved to its present location, Fifth Avenue at 57th Street.

The present store is a seven-story building constructed of pinkish granite and limestone. It was the first completely air-conditioned building in New York. It is noted for the old Tiffany clock over the front door, supported by a nine-foot-tall carved wood figure of Atlas. The clock dates from 1853 and was moved from the earlier store location at 555 Broadway. According to legend, the only time the clock has ever stopped was at the exact hour of President Abraham Lincoln's death at 7:22 A.M. on April 15, 1865.

Through the years Tiffany & Co. has been more than a retail store. It is part showplace and part museum. Charles Tiffany's business sense and flair for sensation helped mold the company's reputation for quality and integrity. One of Tiffany's unique ideas was to use leftover sections of the first transatlantic cable (laid in 1858) to fashion paper weights and cane and umbrella handles. Over the years Tiffany's has had a talent for acquiring unusual items. In 1877 the company acquired the world's largest and finest canary diamond, a 128.5 carat gem as big as a bird's egg. Appropriately named "The Tiffany Diamond," it cemented the store's reputation as America's most discriminating jeweler. Before Charles Tiffany's death in 1902, Tiffany & Co. had been appointed gold and silversmith to virtually every crowned head in the world, including Queen Victoria, the Shah of Persia, and the Czar of Russia.

Charles Tiffany was the only Tiffany to run Tiffany & Co. Neither of his two sons was interested in the business, although one did have an more important influence on public taste than even his father. Louis Comfort Tiffany was an artist who became world famous for his stained-glass windows and the objects he designed from the iridescent glass Favrile. As an artist and interior decorator, he became a leader in the Art Nouveau movement that swept Europe and America at the turn of the century.

Tiffany has made many unique products for special customers. A jeweled inkstand was designed for President Lincoln and a sword encrusted with precious stones for General Ulysses S. Grant. Presidents from Abraham Lincoln on have ordered from Tiffany's many gifts chosen for heads of state and other foreign dignitaries. President Lyndon B. Johnson, for example, gave Pope Paul VI a small silver globe from Tiffany's. Tiffany artisans have designed a number of trophies such as the Vince Lombardi Super Bowl Trophy, a simple silver football on a pedestal. A replica of the ornate Woodlawn Vase, made by Tiffany in 1860, is presented annually to the owners of the horse winning the Preakness Stakes in Baltimore.

Two important contributions made by Tiffany's to the jewelry trade are the Tiffany catch and the Tiffany setting. The Tiffany catch is a device for the safe locking of a brooch. The Tiffany setting is the widely used six-prong setting for engagement rings that holds and protects a stone and makes it appear a little larger.

Tiffany has long been known for its artistically beautiful and eye-catching window displays. Gene Moore, who is considered a legend in display, has been designing Tiffany's windows since 1955. One of his famous displays was created during a New York City water shortage and consisted of a fountain gushing with gin. A small sign stated: "No! This is not precious city water. It's just some unprecious old gin."

Many of Moore's displays have created controversy. An example was a display that contrasted the intense poverty of New York City with its extreme wealth. The display pictured a bag lady and a derelict with a $50,000 gold-and-diamond necklace. Following objections by the *New York Daily News* and the Coalition for the Homeless, Moore removed the bag lady from the window.

Moore sees displays as pictures, and Tiffany windows frequently feature art by noted artists. Andy Warhol, Jasper Johns, and James Rosenquist have all contributed art works to be used in the windows, as have more than 800 other artists over the years. Moore wants people to look at the windows and feels that the merchandise is of little importance. Often each window features a single item of merchandise while the background and the props used in the display draw the viewer's attention. Among the many unusual props Moore has used in his creative displays are artificial cobwebs, chunks of coal, real grass, stuffed animals and birds, eggs, and gumdrops.

Today Tiffany & Co. operates nine stores in the United States and fifteen stores in other countries. In addition to the New York flagship store on Fifth apparel designers, such as Bill Blass, Ralph Lauren, and Laura Ashley, have become involved in designing coordinated bed and bath linens. These designers and others were influential in developing the decorating trend in the 1980s emphasizing abundant use of fabrics. The popularity of coordinated sheets, comforters, dust ruffles, pillows, and window treatments helped home textiles grow to a more than $12-billion market.

Summary of Key Points

1. The production and marketing of fashion accessories vary with each accessory category, and all accessory manufactures must be responsive to trends in fashion apparel. The success of accessories manufacturers often depends on their ability to coordinate their products with fashions in ready-to-wear.

2. Competition from imports is becoming an increasing problem for most segments of the accessories industry. The U.S. shoe industry in particular has suffered a serious decline because of imports.

3. Designer names have become increasingly important in fashion accessories as well as in home furnishings.

4. Few mergers and consolidations have occurred among accessories manufacturers. Consolidations, however, are a major trend in the furniture industry.

5. The cosmetics industry produces three categories of merchandise: (1) cosmetics, (2) toiletries, and (3) fragrances. Because the cosmetics business is highly competitive, the marketing of cosmetic products is very important. Marketing is estimated to include one-third of manufacturers' costs.

6. Major growth areas predicted for the cosmetics industry are antiaging creams, ethnic products, men's cosmetics, and sunscreen products.

7. Both accessories and cosmetics are often purchased by consumers as impulse items with little thought or planning.

8. The selling of home-furnishings products has increasingly become a fashion business. Trends in the apparel industry are often duplicated in home furnishings.

9. Traditionally, the furniture industry has been highly fragmented because of its numerous product lines and limited import penetration. Today, many large firms that specialized in low-end home furnishings are consolidating, where as many small manufacturers that produce high-quality, high-priced furniture still flourish.

10. Gallery programs are a major trend in retailing home furnishings. Some programs may present coordinated merchandise either through manufacturer's own outlets or stand-alone display areas in furniture or department stores.

Key Words and Concepts

Define, identify, or explain each of the following:

case goods

Cosmetic, Toiletry, and Fragrance Association (CTFA)

cosmetics

counterfeit goods

diverted goods

door

flatgoods

fragrances

franchise distribution

gallery programs

line representatives

mass distribution

prestige lines

rack jobber

rubber-banding

small leather goods

toiletries

Discussion Questions and Topics

1. Why do accessories often increase in popularity during times of economic downturn?

2. What are the common characteristics of the fashion accessories industries?

3. Why do department stores usually locate accessories departments on the main floor near the main entrance to the store?

4. What are the geographic locations for the production of shoes, hosiery, gloves, and costume jewelry?

5. Discuss the current fashion importance of accessories. What categories are most important today? Why?

6. Describe the various marketing activities currently used by the cosmetics industry.

7. How are cosmetic products distributed to retail outlets, and how does the marketing of cosmetics differ from the marketing of other fashion products?

8. Discuss the growing market areas for cosmetics.

9. Why are the prices for prestige cosmetics seldom lowered for special sales or for merchandise clearances?

10. Discuss the effect of imports on the accessories industries, the cosmetic industry, and the home-furnishings industries.

11. Describe the household furniture industry.

12. Why are many small producers still found in high-end furniture manufacturing?

Notes

Fairchild Fact File, *Toiletries, Cosmetics, Fragrances, and Beauty Aids.* New York: Fairchild Publications, 1986.

The Fortune 500, April 24, 1989.

National Association of Hosiery Manufacturers, *1988 Hosiery Statistics,* Charlotte, N.C., 1988.

Standard and Poor's, *Industry Surveys,* 1987.

U.S. Census of Manufacturers, 1982.

U.S. Department of Commerce, *U.S. Industrial Outlook, 1988.*

Linda Wells, "Leaders of the Pack," *New York Times Magazine,* August 28, 1988, p. 70.

PART III _____

FASHION MARKETING CENTERS

AFTER fashion products are designed and manufactured they must be presented and sold to retailers who distribute the goods to the ultimate consumer. Part III describes the domestic and foreign fashion markets that bring together producers and distributors of fashion.

Buying direct from manufacturers or their representatives who show at markets is the most common way for retailers to view fashion merchandise. Visiting markets is considered the best way to see the latest fashions and obtain the lowest prices. Markets throughout the world provide a wide array of products and give retailers an opportunity to comparison shop. Retail buyers attend markets for a number of reasons, which are detailed in Chapter 8. The primary market centers for fashion goods in the United States are also described and compared in this chapter.

Fashion goods today enjoy a worldwide market. Foreign markets are increasingly competing with American markets for the retailer's business. Producers of fashion merchandise have proliferated in almost every country of the world, and the importation of these goods has grown steadily in recent years. Chapters 9 and 10 explore primary foreign fashion centers, emphasizing the global market for fashion goods. Discussed are the growing penetration of foreign-made fashion merchandise into the United States, the methods of importing merchandise, and the attempts by governments and industry to control fashion imports.

CHAPTER 8 —————————————————————

DOMESTIC FASHION MARKETS

BUYING direct from manufacturers has become the accepted way for fashion retailers to acquire merchandise. For most retail buyers, this means going to market rather than waiting for sales representatives to visit their stores. Visiting the market is considered the best way to get the latest fashions and the lowest prices. Markets provide the widest selections of merchandise and give retailers the best opportunity to comparison shop. Markets also offer the best way for buyers to make contacts with new resources for merchandise.

Fashion markets are held in numerous cities throughout the United States and bring together manufacturers and retailers. A market is a place where sellers display sample goods and buyers place orders for the purchase of goods to be delivered at a later date. In some cities the market is dispersed among many buildings covering a wide area. In other cities the market is held in permanent facilities, called **marts,** built exclusively for this function. In some cities the market is set up on a temporary basis in an exhibition space.

Market centers and manufacturing areas are not always found in the same location. Although the major market centers are all located in areas that are also manufacturing sites, many smaller markets are held in cities that have little or no fashion production.

In the United States several cities serve as major market centers. Great numbers of retail buyers come to these centers to seek sources for merchandise. Here lines are presented by manufacturers or their representatives, and retail buyers select what will be offered to consumers throughout their stores. Some market centers operate five days a week year round; others are open only during scheduled market weeks.

Why Retail Buyers Attend Markets

Although going to market is expensive and time-consuming, most retailers find that shopping at markets is the best way to buy merchandise. To get the most out of a market the buyer must make adequate preparation. The well-organized buyer completes a written **buying plan** before going to market. It describes the types and quantities of merchandise that a buyer expects to purchase for delivery within a specific period of time. The plan also sets a limit on the amount of money to be spent so that purchases will be kept in line with planned sales and planned inventory levels.

Obviously, a key reason the buyer goes to market is to buy merchandise, but this is not the only reason a buyer visits a market. Among other reasons are the opportunities to:

1. See actual merchandise and view the entire line offered by manufacturers.

2. Seek new sources of supply.

3. Compare a wide variety of merchandise.

4. Study market conditions.

5. Observe fashion trends.

6. Observe and confer with other buyers.

7. Observe showroom display techniques.

8. Obtain promotion and advertising ideas or assistance.

9. Seek special terms and purchases.

10. Meet and consult with firm principals.

11. Attend seminars and meetings.

12. Observe market-area stores.

See Actual Merchandise and View the Line

A buyer can usually make a better buying decision by seeing the actual merchandise rather than basing a decision on viewing a photograph or a sketch with an accompanying fabric swatch. It is important to see the actual goods to judge how the merchandise will look in the store. By going to market the retailer is able to see the entire line and purchase what is best for his or her store. It is important for the buyer to see the breadth and depth of product offerings to make the best selection for the store. Sales representatives who visit stores do not always have the entire line with them; therefore, the buyer may not be shown the merchandise that is best for the store to carry.

It should be noted that buyers usually do not write orders while first viewing a line. Buyers will make notes and wait until all vendors have been viewed before placing orders or, as is said in the market, "leave **paper.**" Often, larger stores will require that an order by cosigned by the buyer's boss, the merchandise manager, before being left with a vendor. This means that the buyer may need to return to the store and confer with his or her merchandise manager before writing orders.

Seek New Supply Sources

Buyers are constantly looking for fresh new merchandise. In today's highly competitive retail environment, it is desirable for a store to be the first to have a new look. In order to do so, the buyer must always be alert to new resources for merchandise. The buyer goes to market to see new items and new sources of supply. The fashion industry is constantly changing, and the buyer who continues to carry the same merchandise from the same manufacturers may fall behind the store's competitors. The successful buyer must always be looking for new sources of supply.

Compare a Variety of Merchandise

Attending the market enables the buyer to see a great deal of merchandise within a brief period of time. Thus the buyer is able to readily compare one vendor's merchandise with another's and decide which is best for his or her store's customers. The buyer may see a line that is stronger than what the store is presently carrying and adjust purchases accordingly.

Study Market Conditions

By going to market the buyer is able to observe and study current market conditions. Information concerning availability of merchandise, pricing, and delivery schedules is important in making intelligent buying decisions. While at the market, the buyer can easily learn of current conditions and compare not only merchandise offerings but also terms of sale and delivery schedules of various vendors.

Observe Fashion Trends

Because of the ever-changing nature of fashion, the retail buyer must constantly be studying fashion trends. Each season brings changes in colors, fabrications, and styles that influence consumer preferences. By attending fashion shows at market and viewing lines in showrooms, buyers keep aware of changing fashion trends. Each buyer must evaluate the trends observed in terms of the store's customer.

Observe Other Buyers

Meeting and sharing experiences with buyers from other geographical areas are advantages to many retailers. A great deal can be learned by observing other buyers' activities in the market and by sharing secrets of success with noncompeting retailers. Sometimes buyers will meet as a group at the market to share ideas and discuss what they have seen.

Observe Showroom Display Ideas

Buyers are always looking for ways to display their merchandise in a more appealing fashion. By observing how showrooms display merchandise, the buyer gains ideas for in-store merchandise presentation. Showroom managers often pay considerable attention to displaying their merchandise in new and exciting ways to attract the customer. They may also show the merchandise accessorized as it should be shown to the ultimate consumer.

Obtain Promotion and Advertising Ideas

Many manufacturers offer assistance to retailers in advertising or promoting the goods purchased. Buyers learn about these promotional aids by going to market.

Manufacturers often plan advertising layouts that may be used by retailers to advertise their products. Manufacturers may provide sample advertisements clipped from newspapers throughout the country, which may be viewed for ideas. Cooperative advertising programs are offered through which manufacturers share the cost of advertising with the retailer. This saves money or enables the retailer to do more advertising than he or she could afford to do alone.

A variety of **point-of-purchase** (POP) selling aids may be offered by the manufacturer. Examples include promotional signs, brochures, display fixtures, and counter displays. POP aids encourage impulse buying and are especially valuable in self-service stores.

Manufacturers also offer sales training aids such as brochures, slide shows, and videotapes showing product benefits and features. Vendors may actually visit the store to train salespeople and assist with selling to the customer. Designers or other representatives from the manufacturer may provide trunk shows for retailers where they take all or part of the line to the store and accept orders directly from the store's customers.

Seek Special Terms and Purchases

The buyer who wants to make special purchases must go to market to do this effectively. **Special purchases goods** are bought at lower-than-usual prices. Such merchandise may include broken sizes, end-of-season goods, or goods that are less than first quality. Sometimes the retailer buys in great enough quantity to qualify for a lower price. The retailer may also negotiate with the **vendor** for special terms leading to a more favorable arrangement for payment of the invoice.

Meet and Consult with Principals

It is very important for the buyer to meet and become better acquainted with the top people in a firm, referred to as the firm's **principals.** Getting to know these people is often advantageous to the retailer in acquiring better service in dealings with the company. Problems can be discussed and solved more effectively face to face, and personal knowledge of the firm's principals may assist the retailer in building a better working relationship with the vendor.

Attend Seminars and Meetings

Educational seminars and meetings that are of interest to retailers are often held at markets. These meetings are sponsored by groups that include the management of the mart, trade associations, colleges and universities, and various suppliers. Typical topics include visual merchandising, advertising and promotion, management techniques, and financial management. Retailers attend such seminars to gain assistance in improving their stores' profit picture.

Observe Market-Area Stores

While in the market area retailers plan their schedules to allow time to visit local retail stores. Stores located in the market area are often the first to carry new or unique merchandise manufactured in the area. Also, retailers get ideas by observing how other retailers are displaying and merchandising their goods.

Why Manufacturers Show at Markets

Showing merchandise at market is advantageous for both manufacturer and retailer. Obviously, manufacturers present merchandise at markets for the purpose of making sales, but there are other reasons, too. Manufacturers display merchandise at markets to:

1. Determine which items will be mass produced and to acquire ideas for new products.

2. Show merchandise in the most effective and efficient manner.

3. Meet principal retail customers.

4. Make a fashion statement and gain media exposure.

5. Train sales representatives.

Determine Items to be Mass Produced

The majority of merchandise shown at apparel markets consists of sample lines that have not yet been mass produced. Manufacturers determine the items that will remain in the line and be produced in volume after buyers place their initial orders. Some items will be dropped from the line because not enough orders are placed to warrant production.

Changes may be made in merchandise based on orders received and comments from buyers. A fabrication may be dropped, a skirt made fuller or longer, or other design detail changed, based on input received at market. Sometimes manufacturers get ideas for new products when talking with their market customers. These new products, as suggested by retailers, may appear at a subsequent market.

Show Merchandise Efficiently and Effectively

Manufacturers have found that it is more efficient for buyers to come to market than for **sales representatives** to carry the merchandise to buyers in the stores. Buyers' offices are often small and do not offer the best atmosphere in which to show merchandise.

Merchandise may be shown properly accessorized and in an appealing manner at market. Models are often used to show the clothes in action. An attractive showroom backs up the merchandise and presents it in the best possible light.

Meet Principals with Retail Firms

Markets provide a convenient meeting place for both key retail executives and key manufacturers' executives. Customer relationships between vendor and retail store executives are enhanced by direct personal contact. Both manufacturer and retailer benefit by getting to know each other.

Make a Fashion Statement and Gain Media Exposure

Markets assist fashion designers and manufacturers with projecting their image to the retailer and to the public. To be successful manufacturers must identify the market segment they want to fill and develop a marketing plan that will create for them an image as a reliable resource for their type of merchandise. Some firms design for the fashion-forward customer; others design for the contemporary, classic, or traditional customer.

Exposure at the market helps companies enhance the fashion image of their merchandise. This exposure is assisted by inviting the fashion press to cover the market. Press kits may be provided describing the company and the new line to encourage the press to publicize the manufacturer and his or her products. High-fashion designers often go to the great extremes to attract the attention of the press.

Train Sales Representatives

Markets offer an opportunity to gather together all of the company's sales representatives and review the selling features of the new merchandise. Meetings can be held to discuss product benefits, pricing, delivery dates, and other pertinent matters. Sales representatives have the opportunity to share ideas with one another and to ask questions.

Geographic Locations of Market Centers

Market centers for fashion goods are found in several locations throughout the United States. Some of these centers pull retail buyers from the entire country and from outside the United States as well. Other market centers are regional and attract buyers from a limited geographical area.

Apparel Market Centers

The five major fashion apparel distribution areas in the United States are New York City, Los Angeles, Dallas, Chicago, and Atlanta. The first fashion market center to be established in the United States and the primary center today for men's, women's, and children's apparel and fashion accessories is New York City. Particularly for better-priced apparel, New York City is considered the fashion capital of the United States. It is the only truly national fashion market in the country and also serves as a **regional market** for the northeastern area of the country.

The most important regional apparel markets are Los Angeles, Dallas, Chicago, and Atlanta. These markets serve primarily the geographic region in which they are located, although the major regional markets may pull some buyers from almost every state. Dallas dominates the Southwest, Atlanta the Southeast, Chicago the Midwest, and Los Angeles and San Francisco share the Western United States. Smaller markets are located in a number of other cities, including Boston; Charlotte, North Carolina; Denver; Kansas City, Missouri; Miami; Minneapolis; Pittsburgh; San Francisco; and Seattle. All of these cities have marts that provide space for permanent showrooms as well as temporary display areas.

Not all markets are held in facilities built especially for them. Numerous temporary markets are set up in hotels and exhibit centers in major cities throughout the United States. These markets are designed to serve buyers in local areas where they are held.

Home-Furnishings Market Centers

For furniture and home furnishings, the major markets are located in High Point, North Carolina; Dallas; Chicago; New York; Los Angeles; San Francisco; and Seattle. Temporary home-furnishings exhibits, set up for a market only, are held in Atlantic City, Boston, Columbus, Denver, Miami, Minneapolis, New Orleans, Pittsburgh, and St. Louis.

Seasonality of Apparel Markets

Markets are held corresponding with the seasons in which manufacturers produce fashion goods. In the women's and children's apparel industries, four or five new lines are produced each year. Typical seasons for a dress or sportswear firm are summer, early fall or transitional, fall, holiday or resort, and spring. Summer markets are held mid- to late-January; early fall or transitional markets are scheduled for March or April; fall and winter markets are held in May or June; holiday and resort fashions are shown in August or early September; and spring-summer fashions appear in October or November. Figure 8.1 shows a typical schedule of **market weeks** for women's and children's wear in New York and various regional markets as published annually by *Women's Wear Daily*.

Fashion accessory markets are held less frequently than ready-to-wear markets.

1989 market weeks

Below is the schedule of 1989 market weeks for women's apparel in the various regional markets and in New York. Unless a separate children's wear show is listed, the regional markets include women's and children's wear. Dates are subject to revision. Readers are advised to check with the marts prior to the scheduled show.

	SUMMER	FALL I	FALL II	RESORT	SPRING
ATLANTA					
Atlanta Apparel Mart	Feb. 2-8	April 6-12	June 1-7	Aug. 10-16	Oct. 26-Nov. 1
BIRMINGHAM, Ala.					
Civic Center	Jan. 21-23	March 18-20	May 29-31	Aug. 5-7	Oct. 21-23
BOSTON					
Bayside Expo Center	Jan. 15-18	April 2-5	June 4-7	Aug. 20-23	Oct. 22-25
Children's Market (Bayside Merchandise Mart)	Jan. 9-12	March 12-15	April 9-12	Sept. 24-27	Oct. 29-Nov. 1
			July 30-Aug. 2		
CHARLOTTE					
Charlotte Apparel Center	Jan. 27-Feb. 1	March 31-April 5	May 26-31	Aug. 18-23	Oct. 20-25
Children's Market (Charlotte Merchandise Mart)	Jan. 31-Feb. 1	April 1-5		Aug. 19-22	Oct. 21-25
CHICAGO					
Apparel Expo Center	Jan. 21-25	April 8-12	June 3-7	Aug. 26-30	Oct. 28-Nov. 1
DALLAS					
Dallas Apparel Mart	Jan. 27-Feb. 1	March 31-April 5	May 26-31	Aug. 18-23	Oct. 20-25
DENVER					
Denver Merchandise Mart	Jan. 20-23	April 7-10	June 2-5	Aug. 4-7	Oct. 13-16
KANSAS CITY					
Kansas City Market Center	Jan. 7-10	April 7-11	June 3-6	Aug. 5-8	Oct. 27-31
LOS ANGELES					
California Mart Pacific-Coast Travelers	Jan. 13-17	April 7-11	June 9-13	Aug. 25-29	Oct. 27-31
California Kids Show		March 13-15			Oct. 16-18
MIAMI					
Miami International Merchandise Mart					
Southern Apparel Exhibitors, Inc.	Jan. 14-17	April 1-4	June 10-13	Aug. 5-8	Oct. 28-31
MINNEAPOLIS					
Hyatt Merchandise Mart	Jan. 15-18	March 5-8	June 11-14	Aug. 6-9	Oct. 22-26
		April 2-6			
NEW YORK	Jan. 23-Feb. 3	Feb. 21-March 3	April 3-10	July 31-Aug. 11	Oct. 23-Nov. 3
PITTSBURGH					
Pittsburgh Expo Mart, Monroeville	Jan. 22-24	April 9-11	June 11-13	Sept. 10-12	Nov. 5-7
Children's Market	Feb. 1-2	March 11-14		July 30-Aug. 1	Nov. 18-21
PORTLAND					
Montgomery Park	Jan. 13-16	April 21-24	June 9-12	Aug. 11-14	Oct. 20-23
SAN FRANCISCO					
San Francisco Concourse	Jan. 7-10	April 1-4	June 3-6	Aug. 20-23	Oct. 21-24
San Francisco Children's Wear Association, 833 Market St.	Jan. 8-11	April 1-5		Aug. 5-9	Nov. 11-15
SEATTLE					
Seattle Trade Center	Jan. 21-24	April 15-18	June 17-20	Aug. 19-22	Oct. 28-31
VIRGINIA					
Old Dominion Fashion Exhibitors, Marriott Hotel, McLean, Va.	Feb. 26-27	April 30-May 1		Sept. 10-11	Oct. 29-30
Radisson Hotel, Virginia Beach	Feb. 22-23	April 26-27	June 21-22	Sept. 6-7	Nov. 1-2

FIGURE 8.1

Most accessory market weeks are held twice a year for spring and fall. In the regional marts retailers usually buy accessories at the same time they purchase outerwear.

Menswear traditionally has been shown twice a year, for fall and spring. Tailored suit and coat market week in New York is scheduled for late January or February to show fall fashions and late August or September for spring apparel. The National Association of Men's Sportswear Buyers shows fall lines in March or April and spring lines in October.

As menswear has become more fashion-oriented, the number of markets held has increased. Sportswear manufacturers have added a third or fourth line and increased market weeks accordingly. The Dallas Menswear Mart, for example, schedules four men's and boys' apparel markets a year. Early fall is shown in February; fall and back-to-school in April; holiday/spring market is in July; with the spring/summer market in September.

The New York Market

New York City is the dominant wholesale fashion market in the United States. New York is both the fashion apparel production center of the country and the sales headquarters for manufacturers whose design and production facilities may be located elsewhere. New York City is the major wholesale market for men's, women's, and children's apparel at all price ranges and is by far the leader in "better" apparel. The fashion industry is the third-largest employer in the city and the wholesale trade is the number-two employer. The largest employer is business services, which include advertising, marketing, and management consulting firms.

Why New York Is the Dominant Market

Historically, New York developed as the center for apparel production in the United States. Following the invention of the sewing machine, mass production of apparel was not limited to any one city or area, but as New York City became the major port of entry for immigrants during the late 1800s, the garment industry grew. Immigrants eager to find jobs were often met by manufacturers and contractors who immediately hired whole families to work in their factories. New York quickly became the leader in apparel production in the United States.

Today, New York retains its position as the number-one wholesale market in the U.S. fashion industry. There are several reasons for this dominant position. First, New York is number one because of its location. The American textile industry originated in New England, and it was logical for New York City to become the center for wholesale trade as the apparel industry grew and developed in the city.

New York was and is the main port in the United States and the number-one business center.

New York offers many advantages to the apparel industry. Located in the city are the central offices for the trade associations, consumer and fashion periodicals, and leading fashion retailers. Also found in Manhattan are the leading advertising agencies. New York brings together a great number of executives in retailing, manufacturing, and textile and fiber production, thereby creating an interaction of ideas important to the ever-changing fashion industry. Furthermore, New York City is the business and cultural hub of the country. It is the central clearinghouse for all communications, including the three major television networks and many publications. Because of its size and wealth, New York City dominates the nation in terms of ideas and issues. New York provides a stimulating atmosphere for business and fashion. It is the design center for apparel and textiles, and as the wholesale center of the United States, more buyers go to New York than anywhere else.

Seventh Avenue

The **New York garment district** consists of many buildings in a thirty-two-square-block area of midtown Manhattan. The garment district extends between Ninth Avenue on the west and Avenue of the Americas (Sixth Avenue) on the east, 35th Street on the south, and 41st Street on the north. **Seventh Avenue,** often abbreviated SA, is the central focus of the garment district, and the term *Seventh Avenue* has become synonymous with the fashion industry and market in New York. In the early 1970s the garment industry sponsored a campaign known as the "Fashion Capital of the World." The purpose of this publicity campaign was to draw attention to the New York fashion business and attract more retail buyers to the market. In 1972 as a part of this campaign, Seventh Avenue was renamed Fashion Avenue in the area known as the garment district. In this area of the city, street signs actually display both names.

Various showrooms are scattered throughout the garment district. Showrooms are generally housed in buildings according to merchandise classification and price range. Certain types of apparel are concentrated in some areas, and some buildings are noted for a particular type of merchandise. For example, better and designer apparel is found at 512, 530, and 550 Seventh Avenue. Located on Broadway are showrooms for moderately priced women's wear. Major showrooms are concentrated at 1407, 1410, and 1411 Broadway. Medium-priced missy and junior dresses are found at 1400 Broadway.

Various accessories showrooms are located near the Seventh Avenue garment district. Intimate apparel is found south and east on Fifth and Madison Avenues between 29th and 43rd Streets. Accessories such as handbags, gloves, headwear, and costume jewelry are located on Fifth Avenue and on 31st to 35th Streets. Figure 8.2 shows the locations of major market areas in New York.

In New York some manufacturer's showrooms are located in the same buildings

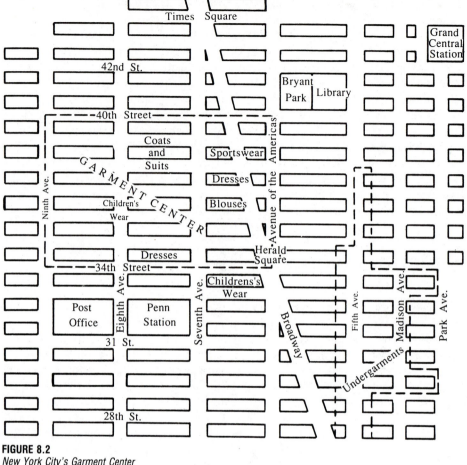

FIGURE 8.2
New York City's Garment Center

with their design workrooms. Although in recent years many firms have relocated their production facilities to areas outside of Manhattan because of escalating rents, some firms still manufacture in the area. The streets in the garment district are filled with trucks loading and unloading apparel and fabrics. Crowding the streets are men pushing carts of fabrics and rolling racks hanging with clothing. The area is congested with people and traffic. No other market area in the country has the same feeling of activity and excitement as New York.

New York showrooms are open year-round, five days a week. Buyers from New York stores and resident buyers use this market every day. During scheduled seasonal markets, New York draws buyers from stores throughout the United States, making the city the one truly nationwide market. Stores of every type, size, and price range send buyers to New York. Buyers from major stores find it particularly important to shop the New York market because it offers more merchandise than any other.

FASHION MARKETING CENTERS

Why Buyers Shop the New York Market

Buyers shop the New York market for a number of reasons. New York has more resources offering a greater variety and selection of fashion merchandise than any other market. New York presents the widest offering of merchandise at all price ranges and all fashion levels. Buyers can discover small, new resources. Merchandise is available in New York that is not available elsewhere. New small resources may not be able to afford to show their lines at the major regional markets. These resources can be found only by visiting New York City. Buyers also visit New York to seek promotional purchases to offer their customers reduced prices on merchandise.

In addition, buyers in New York can meet the principals of the manufacturing firms to develop better working relationships. Large retail stores particularly want to work directly with the major executives of the manufacturing firms and find it necessary to be in New York to do this because the principals are most likely to be available at this market. Knowing the key executives in a firm enables the retailer to negotiate more favorable terms of sale and to seek merchandise exclusives. In addition, the retailer may receive better service when a firm's principal executives are known.

Buyers also visit New York because it is a stimulating city, the hub of the American fashion industry and the hub of the country. Buyers seek this stimulation and to look for ideas to help them in promoting the sale of their merchandise and planning their buys. In summary, buyers choose the New York market because it is the most comprehensive fashion market in the United States.

Drawbacks of the New York Market

Although the New York market offers many advantages, it presents certain drawbacks as well. New York is an expensive city to visit. Hotel rates are among the highest in the United States. Transportation costs may be high for stores located some distance away. Higher freight charges on delivery of goods manufactured in the New York area are another drawback if the retailer is located far from the city.

New York is a crowded, noisy, bustling city that is confusing and overwhelming to some. Some people view it as dingy, dirty, cold, and unfriendly. The city and the garment district have a reputation for crime, and this discourages some retailers, especially if they are unfamiliar with the area.

Shopping the New York market involves going from building to building. It means walking the streets in all kinds of weather, hailing cabs, or taking crowded public transportation. To many American retail buyers, especially those from small towns, New York presents an environment very different from what they are used to at home.

Regional Market Centers

In recent years the development and expansion of regional apparel marts have changed the pattern of wholesale fashion merchandising in the United States for the first time since the industry was established in New York City almost a century ago. Regional marts offer convenience to both the seller and buyer of wholesale goods. Such marts lease space to manufacturers and sales representatives who carry lines of more than one manufacturer. Marts provide the convenience and comfort of many showrooms located under one roof.

Besides the major regional apparel marts of Los Angeles, Dallas, Chicago, and Atlanta, other regional marts include the Denver Merchandise Mart, the Carolina Trade Mart (Charlotte, N.C.), the Miami International Merchandise Mart, the Northeast Trade Center (Woburn, Mass.), the San Francisco Mart, Radisson Center in Minneapolis, and the Trade Center in Kansas City (Mo.).

Although buyers from major fashion stores shop the New York market regularly, many smaller department or specialty stores have found that trips to New York can be reduced or eliminated by using the regional markets. These markets have expanded business by catering to the specific needs of smaller stores located within their geographic areas. Many small store owners have found that regional markets better understand their needs and offer merchandise attuned to their market areas. For many retailers, buying at a regional mart is less expensive, takes less time, and is a more enjoyable experience than shopping the New York market. Regional marts have succeeded to a great extent because they have met the needs of mom-and-pop stores.

Major department stores have not been appreciably affected by regional marts. They still do most of their buying in New York and use the regionals for fill-in buying.

Origin of Regional Markets

The concept of regional fashion markets began in the 1930s as important fashion markets developed in cities other than New York City. Manufacturers' sales representatives in other cities first set up showrooms in hotels or factories where exhibit space was available. Buyers came to the exhibits to view the merchandise and make selections. The development of such markets was undoubtedly aided by the difficulties buyers faced in traveling to New York and to the slowness in obtaining goods from the East. Manufacturers' sales representatives soon discovered that they could sell to many more retail buyers in a brief period than they could by traveling on the road and visiting retailers. Buyers also found that markets saved them time and money.

Different regions of the country were known for the production of specialized types of apparel, and market centers were developed to facilitate distribution of merchandise. By 1950 major market centers existed in several cities. Chicago, known as the misses dress market, was the second largest market in the country. Los Angeles, the third largest market, was known for "California" sportswear, bathing suits, and the Hollywood glamour look. Boston and Philadelphia were known for coats, suits, skirts, blouses, and dresses. St. Louis was noted for menswear, junior clothing, and dresses. Cleveland was known for coats and suits; Kansas City for house dresses; Dallas and Miami for sportswear; and Denver for western wear.

Reasons for the Success of Regional Markets

Several factors have contributed to the success of regional markets and marts. They include (1) savings in dollars and time, (2) convenience, (3) merchandise offerings, (4) service, and (5) atmosphere.

Savings

One of the primary motivations for retailers to use regional marts is the savings in time and money. The cost of transportation, lodging, and meals is frequently lower when a buyer travels to a closer regional market. Shipping costs for merchandise are also less if goods are manufactured closer to the retail store. The buyer saves time as well as money in traveling to a regional market located closer to home and is kept away from the store for a shorter period of time.

Convenience

Marts offer retailers convenience in shopping much like a shopping mall offers the consumer one-stop shopping. Buyers are able to shop and compare many lines offered under one roof in a climate-controlled environment. Many marts are self-contained, offering everything that the buyer needs while attending market. Restaurants, lounges, and sometimes even hotel facilities are found within the mart. On-site parking is often provided for the convenience of buyers.

Merchandise Offerings

Regional markets have manufacturers showing products better suited to an area's climate and lifestyles. Items unique to an area may also be found at regional markets. With the continued growth in popularity of regional markets, more and more manufacturers from outside the area are opening showrooms and showing their lines. Thus regional marts now offer a wide variety of merchandise and are no longer identified with having only regional merchandise.

Services

A small retailer often obtains better service from manufacturers at regional markets since these markets are designed to cater to the smaller retailer. Reordering becomes easier for these stores, and they are made to feel more important to their resources.

Marts offer nearby retailers an opportunity to build personal relationships with vendors. Retailers in the area may see some vendors as often as once or twice a month. These local sales representatives know what is selling in the geographical area better than showroom people located in New York.

Marts have developed many services to make shopping easier for the retailer. It is common for marts to schedule entertainment and educational programs for buyers. Buyers are attracted to marts by seminars and workshops that provide them with current information helpful in improving the profitability of their businesses.

Atmosphere

The atmosphere of regional markets and marts is perceived by buyers as relaxed, comfortable, and friendly. Marts are located in cities where buyers, particularly those from small towns, feel more at home than they do in New York City.

Reasons Larger Stores Use Regional Markets

Although regional marts have been designed primarily to serve small department and specialty stores, they are used by larger stores to a limited extent. Larger stores find that regionals offer them a feel for the market. Larger stores may visit regional markets to enrich their knowledge of another market area and to keep abreast of local market trends. Larger stores located near a regional mart often use that mart to give assistant buyers and department managers experience in the market.

Disadvantages of Regional Markets

Regional markets offer many advantages to retailers, but shopping the regionals offers some drawbacks as well. The fashion retailer should consider the following problems regarding regional marts:

1. *TIMING.* The regional markets may be held before the manufacturer has determined the direction of the line. In fact, manufacturers often use regionals as "indicators" to see which items in the line are preferred by retail buyers. This means that the store places many orders for numbers that are never cut and never delivered. This ties up buyers' open-to-buy dollars. It is not uncommon for as much as 40 percent of the orders placed in some regional markets never to be shipped. Because of this, buyers have to overbuy to be assured of receiving enough merchandise to meet their sales goals.

2. *NONPROFESSIONAL SELLING.* Nonprofessional sales personnel are often hired to work market weeks. Such inexperienced part-time help can give little guidance to store buyers regarding purchases. They are likely to have limited knowledge about the merchandise and may not be working at the next market. The practice of hiring such sales personnel makes it more difficult for the retailer to build a relationship with the vendor.

3. *LACK OF SMALL RESOURCES.* Many new, small manufacturers can be seen only in New York City. They may not be able to afford to show at the regional markets. Finding such manufacturers is important to stores that desire to be first with new and unusual fashion merchandise. Although some new small resources may be found in regional markets, they are few in number when compared to New York. This is especially true in designer and higher-priced apparel lines.

4. *LACK OF PROMOTIONAL GOODS.* New York offers the best selection of promotional or special purchase goods. The local sales representatives may not be aware of such goods or may not be interested in selling promotional goods because of reduced commission.

5. *FEW RESIDENT BUYING OFFICES.* Except for Los Angeles, regional markets have few resident buying offices. New York has many resident buying offices staffed with professional buyers and merchandisers who can offer many services to retail stores.

Dallas Market Center

The Dallas Market Center has eight buildings that make up the largest wholesale merchandise complex in the world. It is located five minutes north of downtown Dallas along a major freeway. The eight Market Center buildings include (1) the Dallas Apparel Mart, (2) the Menswear, Mart, (3) the Trade Mart, (4) the Home-furnishings Mart, (5) Market Hall, (6) World Trade Center, (7) the Infomart, and (8) the Decorative Center.

The total market center complex contains 8.7 million square feet. The Trade Mart, Homefurnishings Mart, Decorative Center, and World Trade Center contain approximately 12,000 lines of furniture, floor coverings, gifts, and decorative accessories for the home, housewares, consumer electronics, toys, lighting fixtures, bed and bath linens, and contract furnishings. The Apparel Mart and Menswear Mart, located in interconnecting buildings, present approximately 16,000 lines of wearing apparel and fashion accessories for women, children, men, and boys. The Infomart opened in 1985 as the first computer hardware and software mart in the world.

The Dallas Market Center conducts more than thirty-six major markets annually attended by more than 600,000 professional buyers. Although buyers come from almost every state and a number of foreign countries, the greatest concentration of buyers is from the mid-South and Southwest.

Decorative Center

The first building in the Dallas Market Center Complex was the Decorative Center, built in 1955. The showrooms face latticed terraces in a complex of one-level buildings that circle an open tree-shaded square and parking area. Originally containing 71,336 square feet, the Decorative Center district now totals almost 750,000 square feet. The Decorative Center is designed primarily to service interior designers and features high-priced lines of home furnishings and antiques. Home-furnishings retailers, interior designers, and architects may bring their clients to the showrooms of the Decorative Center to select furniture, fabrics, and decorative accessories.

Homefurnishings Mart

The Homefurnishings Mart was built in 1957 to serve retail buyers, and it displays furniture in a 437,000-square-foot area. More than 300 manufacturers are represented in the two-story building, which now connects to both the Trade Mart and the World Trade Center, making it convenient for retail buyers to view furniture, decorative accessories, and floor coverings all under one roof.

The Trade Mart

The Trade Mart opened in 1958 and was last expanded in 1976 to contain approximately one million square feet of display space. Located in this building today are furniture, gifts, decorative accessories, housewares, floor coverings, hardware, window treatments, lamps, and toys. The five-story building surrounds a grand courtyard containing a fountain, a gazebo, plants, and even colorful birds that fly freely within the open area. Four floors are devoted to showrooms, and the fifth floor contains the offices of the Dallas Market Center Company.

World Trade Center

When opened in 1974, the World Trade Center had seven floors. In 1979 an additional eight floors were added for a total of fifteen floors with 3.1 million square feet. The ground floor has as its focal point the Hall of Nations. This fifteen-story, glass-topped courtyard or atrium features plants, twenty-five-foot trees, a fountain, and glass-capsule elevators. Natural light filters through the glass ceiling, from which cylindrical flag sculptures of international code flags are suspended. Flags of nations represented in the center are mounted around the fourth-floor balcony. Two restaurants on the ground floor are open to the public. Also located on the first floor are consular offices, trade commissions, foreign buying offices, customs brokers, and other services relating to international consumers.

The upper floors of the World Trade Center are open only to professional buyers. These fourteen floors contain showrooms for furniture, floor coverings, gifts, decorative accessories, toys, hobbies and crafts, bed and bath linens, fabrics, gourmet items, housewares, and jewelry. Some of the showrooms provide **contract furniture** designed and purchased for use in nonresidential interiors.

Market Hall

Market Hall was opened in 1960 and expanded to 214,000 square feet in 1963. This exhibit hall can be used as one continuous showplace or divided into four separate display halls. Market Hall can accommodate more than 16,000 persons seated or up to 1,400 display booths for temporary markets. The building is used for transient exhibits for home furnishings or gift markets, conventions, private meetings, and parties. Among the events held there are automobile and boat shows and artist and craft shows.

The Apparel Mart

The Dallas Apparel Mart opened in 1964 and was expanded in 1968, 1973, and 1981. More than 14,000 lines of women's and children's wearing apparel, shoes, and fashion accessories are presented in the building's six floors and 1.8 million square feet. The Dallas Apparel Mart covers four city blocks on a twenty-acre site and is advertised as the world's largest wholesale building.

Distinctive features of the Apparel Mart include two large atria, the Great Hall, and the West Atrium. The Great Hall forms the central cores of the Mart. The walls are fifty-seven feet high and balconies open onto the Great Hall from four floor levels. The floor of the hall accommodates 4,000 persons auditorium-style and 2,400 banquet-style. The hall is used to present fashion shows and other fashion extravaganzas during market and is often rented for other activities when markets are not

The Dallas Apparel Mart.
Source: *Reprinted by permission of The Dallas Market Center Company.*

being held. Located at one end is a stage and at the other a cafeteria. A sculpture and art collection enhances the architectural design.

Also located within the Apparel Mart is a completely equipped fashion theater, and several restaurants and buyer lounges. Escalators and elevators move traffic between floors where sculptures and paintings accent the architecture.

Each year more than 100,000 buyers shop the five women's and children's apparel markets in Dallas. They choose from resources showing couture, better ready-to-wear, juniors, missy, lingerie, bridal, fashion accessories, shoes, active sportswear, western wear, furs, outerwear, and large sizes in more than 1,700 permanent and 300 temporary showrooms housed under one roof.

Each level of the Apparel Mart has been departmentalized concentrating merchandise into areas, making it easier for buyers to locate specific lines and to comparison shop. The first and second floor showrooms feature junior, missy, maternity, and large-size apparel. Located on the third and fourth floors is Group III, which includes couture and better apparel, and children's wear. Floor five features shoes, leather goods, and active sportswear, and the sixth floor includes accessories and lingerie.

Although the Dallas Apparel Mart attracts buyers from across the United States to its markets, most who purchase goods there for later retail sale are from small stores in the mid-South and the Southwest. Large department stores located in the Dallas area, such as Neiman-Marcus, Mervyn's, Foley's, and J. C. Penney do the bulk of their apparel purchasing in New York. They do, however, say that they find the Dallas Apparel Mart useful for gathering information, for review of lines, as a teaching ground for assistant buyers, and for fill-in purchases between New York trips.

Buyers with major retail stores usually deal with the owners of a company rather than with their sales representatives. Few manufacturers and designers are based in Dallas as compared with New York.

Menswear Mart

The Menswear Mart opened in 1982 and, according to facts released by the Dallas Market Center, houses the greatest permanent concentration of menswear companies in the world. This six-level, 400,000-square-foot building was built as an addition to the northwest end of the Apparel Mart. An atrium connects the Menswear Mart on each floor to the Dallas Apparel Mart. The building was constructed to allow for expansion upward, with floors seven through twenty to be added in the future.

Infomart

The Infomart opened in 1985 as the first information-processing market center in America. This 1.5-million-square foot, six-floor building houses the showrooms of computer hardware and software firms. Its design is based on the Crystal Palace, the famed 1851 London exhibition hall, which was one of history's most successful marketing expositions.

Infomart offers permanent exhibition facilities for more than 200 information-processing hardware and software companies and related service organizations. A Resource Center is located on the first floor to help customers identify automation requirements. The Resource Center features a research and reference library that focuses on the computer and its applications. Also available is a computer program, The Simplified Needs Assessment Profile, designed to help first-time purchasers identify their business computing needs. By asking a series of questions, the system helps the user define and identify product requirements. The developer of the Infomart hopes to open additional computer marts in other major cities.

California Apparel Mart

The primary regional market for the western United States is the California Apparel Mart in downtown Los Angeles. The California Mart vies with Dallas as the leading regional apparel market in the country.

The California Mart, Los Angeles.
Source: *Reprinted with permission of California Mart.*

The California Mart building opened in 1964 and has been expanded four times. The twenty-floor building now contains over 2,000 showrooms with approximately 10,000 lines represented in one million square feet.

The California Mart is noted for its support of the California apparel industry known for sportswear and swimwear designed for the California lifestyle. California is also known for the production of formal wear and after-five wear associated with the Hollywood look. Buyers from the Midwest and Northeast have long visited California to seek out its unique fashion looks. Buyers from the South and Southwest travel to California to buy garments made of lightweight fabrics, which are more appropriate for their warmer climate than are many of the clothes produced in New York. Today, many California manufacturers maintain showrooms in New York City as well as other regional marts so that buyers can purchase from California manufacturers without traveling to the West Coast.

The California Mart offers broad ranges of apparel and accessories at moderate to higher price levels. Manufacturers of men's, women's, and children's apparel and accessories from throughout the United States are now represented at the California Mart. Because of its location, the Mart also has built a reputation for presenting fashions from the Orient.

The California Mart, in contrast to many other regional marts, remains open fifty-two weeks a year and maintains a more continuous flow of buyers than is found in other regional marts. Market weeks are scheduled, however, as they are in all other markets.

Comparison of Dallas and Los Angeles

The marts in Dallas and Los Angeles both claim to be the number-two apparel market following New York. They both opened in 1964 and have a number of other similarities. Both are owned by family companies and both offer thousands of apparel and accessory lines in one conveniently located building.

Differences between the two markets include the following:

1. California Mart showrooms are open year-round, whereas most Dallas Mart showrooms are open only during markets.

2. The California Mart has a much larger manufacturing base than does Dallas. The California apparel industry consists of an estimated 4,000 firms with 112,500 employees; approximately 85 percent of these firms are in Los Angeles (Drizen 1987). The Texas Apparel industry employs approximately 41,700. U.S. Bureau of Census estimated value of apparel shipments in 1986 at $2,646,000 for Texas and $6,147,000 for California.

3. The California Mart is described as a vertical mart; the Texas Apparel Mart is basically horizontal. The twenty-story California Mart is in a downtown location and looks like an office building with a businesslike interior that is somewhat cramped. The six-floor Dallas Mart is located in a landscaped parking lot situated along a freeway north of the downtown area. It is very spread out with many large open spaces decorated with tapestries, artifacts, and sculpture. The showrooms are sometimes spacious and have individually designed and decorated fronts.

4. Access to the California Mart mezzanine and patio area is open to the public. Entrance to the Dallas Mart is restricted to registered buyers.

5. Both marts offer a wide selection of apparel lines, and there is little difference between merchandise available in both. Dallas, California, and New York manufacturers show in both marts. California is noted for junior apparel, swimwear, and sportswear. The Dallas Mart is noted for missy dresses and better ready-to-wear. Both markets are known for apparel that is suited for warmer climates.

6. California is noted as an innovative, sophisticated fashion market where trends develop. Dallas is considered less trend-setting but representative of mid-American tastes. Both markets are used by manufacturers as test markets in order to evaluate what items are likely to sell well throughout the country.

7. The Dallas Mart draws buyers largely from the middle section of the United States. Whereas the California Mart draws primarily from states west of the Rockies, it is the one regional mart that pulls buyers from New York and from major department stores. Few buyers shop both markets.

Chicago Market Center

The Chicago Market Center consists of two buildings, the Merchandise Mart and the Apparel Center. Both offer retailers a comprehensive center for wholesale buying of apparel, furniture, and home furnishings. The Market Center buildings are located in downtown Chicago on the bank of the Chicago River. Within close proximity are the corporate offices for Sears Roebuck and Montgomery Ward. Also nearby are the downtown State Street department stores and the North Michigan Avenue shopping area, which includes such major retailers as Marshall Field, Lord & Taylor, Saks Fifth Avenue, Bonwit Teller, I. Magnin, Neiman-Marcus, and Bloomingdale's.

The Market Center has its own ZIP code, U.S. Post Office, boat landing, and railroad tracks running beneath the Merchandise Mart. Some of the many services available at the Market Center include accounting firms, addressing, direct mail, printing and employment offices, clothing and shoe stores, attorney offices, banks, barbershop, hair salon, brokerage firm, currency exchange, dry cleaner, drugstores, florists, medical and dental services, newspaper and magazine stands, photographers, travel agency, buying office, inventory control specialists, and trade promotion service. Restaurants located within the Market Center range from casual to elegant, from McDonald's to health food. The M & M Club, a private dining facility in the Merchandise Mart, offers a variety of dining and meeting facilities.

The Chicago Market Center is easily accessible for retailers. Chicago is the hub of the air transportation system of the United States, with O'Hare Airport serving more than 100,000 arrivals per day. Parking garages are located on-site at both the Apparel Mart and the Merchandise Mart. In addition, Chicago has a public transportation system with shuttle buses, elevated trains, city buses, and airport limousine service stopping at the Market Center.

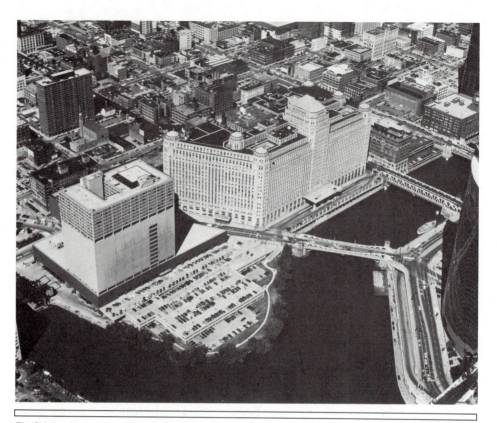

The Chicago Market Center: The Apparel Center and the Merchandise Mart
Source: Reprinted with permission of The Chicago Market Center.

The Merchandise Mart

The Chicago Merchandise Mart was conceived and built by Marshall Field in 1930. The massive twenty-five-story building occupies two city blocks and was the world's largest building until the Pentagon was constructed in Washington, D.C. (1941–43).

The Merchandise Mart is a unique regional market center that serves the public as well as the wholesale industry and retail buyer. It occupies 4,200,000 square feet of floor space. Rentable area accounts for over three million square feet with the remaining square footage devoted to public areas. Located on the first two floors of the building are retail stores, restaurants, drugstores, medical and dental offices, a newspaper and magazine stand, a post office, and a bank. A station of the elevated train public transportation system connects with the building.

Housed in the Merchandise Mart are wholesale showrooms of furniture, home-furnishings accessories, giftware, housewares, curtains and draperies, floor coverings, fabrics, and contract furnishings. Prior to the opening of the Chicago Apparel Center, women's, children's, and men's apparel and accessories were also located in this building.

Chicago Apparel Center

The Chicago Apparel Center, located across the street from the Merchandise Mart, opened in 1976 with more than 850 permanent showrooms and a 140,000-square-foot Expocenter exhibit hall providing temporary exhibit space. Some 6,000 lines, manufactured both in the United States and abroad, are shown in the Apparel Center, covering every men's, women's, and children's classification.

The Apparel Center's one million square feet of space on eleven floors of permanent showrooms are segmented by classification to facilitate shopping by retail buyers. The eleven floors of apparel and accessory display showrooms include all categories of men's, women's, and children's ready-to-wear and accessories.

The second floor of the Apparel Center houses the Expocenter. This 140,000-square-foot exhibit hall holds more than thirty trade shows each year. The main lobby of the building has four restaurants, a florist, a newsstand, a drugstore, a dry cleaning and tailor shop, a travel agency, full medical and dental offices, and a college-accredited school of merchandising and design. Located on top of the Apparel Center is a 527-room hotel featuring an atrium lobby, two restaurants, and meeting rooms.

Educational seminars are held during and between markets dealing with all phases of maximizing the profit potential of retail stores. Special events accompanying markets include fashion shows, visits from guest designers, and social events.

The Apparel Center offers five seasonal women's and children's apparel markets. A variety of specialized shows are also offered by the Mart, including the National Bridal Mart, the National Large-Size Market, Mid-America Footwear and Accessories Market, and four men's markets. The Apparel Center is open fifty-two weeks a year to service retailers. The Apparel Center primarily services the Midwest, an area of twenty states. However, it draws forty to forty-five states at any given market.

Atlanta Market Center

The three components of the Atlanta Market Center include the Atlanta Apparel Mart, the Atlanta Merchandise Mart, and the Atlanta Decorative Arts Center. Encompassing more than 3.5 million square feet of display space, these three facilities are the home of major markets in the home-furnishings, floor covering, apparel, and giftware industries.

The concept of the Atlanta Market Center originated in 1960 when the Atlanta Decorative Center opened as a wholesale display facility for designer-oriented fabrics, furniture, floor coverings, and decorative accessories. The Atlanta Decorative Arts Center has been expanded three times since it opened with only twenty showrooms. With one hundred showrooms totaling 450,000 square feet, this center is now the largest design facility east of the Mississippi River.

The first phase of the Merchandise Mart was completed in 1962 to house home furnishings, gift and decorative accessories, and apparel. Following expansions in 1978 and 1986, the Mart's twenty-two floors totaled 2,600,000 square feet.

In 1975 a feasibility study was conducted that surveyed tenants of the Mer-

The Atlanta Market Center.
Source: *Reprinted with permission of the Atlanta Market Center.*

chandise Mart on future space needs and completed demographic profiles of buyers. The study concluded that a tremendous demand existed for an apparel mart. High energy costs made it uneconomical for southeastern retailers to travel to distant markets to view apparel lines. A need existed to make more lines available in Atlanta to serve the southeastern United States.

The Atlanta Apparel Mart opened on November 3, 1979, during the spring women's and children's market. The grand opening was promoted as the "World's Greatest Premiere Since *Gone with the Wind.*" On hand for the opening were apparel designers, industry and government leaders, southeastern trade officials, members of the press, and members of the southeastern foreign consulate group.

The old Merchandise Mart housed 300 showrooms with 300,000 square feet devoted to apparel. The new Atlanta Apparel Mart opened in 1979 with more than

5,000 apparel lines on six floors. Apparel categories represented included apparel and accessories for men, women, and children. In 1989 the Apparel Mart doubled its size to 14 floors with 2.2 million square feet. The Atlanta Mart is noted for its better apparel and sportswear lines but is recognized as a market offering a well-balanced selection of merchandise for buyers.

The Atlanta Apparel Mart has developed services designed to make the trip convenient, economical, and enjoyable for buyers. Fashion shows and concerts during markets entertain and inform buyers. Seminars on topics of importance to apparel retailers are planned for every market. Topics include advertising and promotion, inventory control, and sales.

The Apparel Mart is located in the downtown center close to stores, hotels, and restaurants. The Atlanta subway system connects the Apparel Mart to the Lenox-Buckhead area where many shops, hotels, and restaurants are located, including Atlanta's two major prestige shopping centers, Lenox Square and Phipps Plaza.

The Atlanta Apparel Mart has its strongest draw of buyers from the southeastern United States. The most important states for the market include Georgia, Alabama, northern Florida, Kentucky, North and South Carolina, Mississippi, Virginia, and Tennessee.

Other Domestic Fashion Market Centers

A number of smaller regional merchandise marts serve limited geographical areas. Like the larger market centers, these marts house permanent showrooms of fashion goods produced by local, national, and foreign manufacturers. Regularly scheduled market weeks, often sponsored by various sales representatives' associations, are held at these marts. Examples are the Carolina Trade Mart, Miami International Merchandise Mart, and the Seattle Trade Center.

The Carolina Trade Mart

The Carolina Trade Mart, in Charlotte, North Carolina, serves buyers primarily from the Carolinas, Virginia, and Tennessee. Five times each year the Charlotte Market Week is sponsored by Carolina Virginia Fashion Exhibitors, a regional association of sales representatives in the women's and children's apparel and accessories industry. The market presents more than 2,500 lines of merchandise under one roof. The markets include fashion shows, entertainment, workshops, and seminars planned to inform buyers about fashion trends, color coordination, new products, industry regulations, and other important subjects.

Each market runs five days, Saturday through Wednesday, and is held in the Carolina Trade Mart located in uptown Charlotte. This mart houses more than 500 permanent showrooms. Exhibit floors are connected by elevators as well as pedestrian ramps. Eating facilities are located in the building and parking space is available beneath the building.

The Charlotte market dates from 1944 when salesmen in the area gathered

IN CHARLESTON

"When I was on the elevator at the Charlotte market, I thought of you."

"Because of how much time we spend riding those elevators in Atlanta?"

"Yeah. Charlotte's move fast. Zip, zip and you're there.

"So what all did you see?"

"Everything. Must have been 4,000 lines, and I saw a lot of new stuff."

"Nice?"

"Very nice. And the Charlotte market's easy to work. Everything's grouped by category and price point."

"So you liked Charlotte?"

"Yeah. It's a beautiful place. And I felt perfectly safe."

"Expensive?"

"Not at all. My hotel—you know where I stayed—cost $50 a night."

"Unbelievable. That same hotel cost me $89 in Atlanta."

"So it sounds like I'll see you in Charlotte."

Fall Market March 31-April 4.
Pre-registration number, **1-800-228-5063.**

An advertisement for the Charlotte Apparel Center.
Source: *Reprinted with permission of the Charlotte Apparel Center.*

together to show their goods because of the gasoline shortage that resulted from World War II. The efforts of approximately ninety women's and children's apparel and accessories salesmen resulted in the formation of the Carolina Virginia Fashion Exhibitors, Inc. In 1972 the group moved into the Carolina Trade Mart. The organization is now composed of 600 salespeople who represent more than 2,500 women's and children's apparel and accessories lines.

Miami International Merchandise Mart

The Miami International Merchandise Mart is Florida's wholesale market for the apparel and giftware industries. Developed in 1969, the Mart serves as a market for retail stores in Florida and the southeastern United States, the Caribbean, and Central and South America. The three-story Mart contains 520,000 square feet with more than 525 permanent showrooms displaying men's and ladies' apparel, gift and decorative accessories, fashion accessories, infants' and children's apparel, shoes, packaging, and furniture. Regularly scheduled trade shows with temporary exhibitors are held throughout the year. More than 125,000 retailers visit each year, of which more than 20,000 are from Central and South America and the Caribbean.

Like other regional marts, the Miami International Merchandise Mart offers conveniences for buyers including on-site parking. It adjoins the Miami Expo/Center, an exhibition hall that contains 65,000 square feet on two floors, is adjacent to 20,000 square feet of retail shops, and connects to a hotel.

Seattle Trade Center

The Seattle Trade and Exposition Center is principally an apparel mart hosting markets for men's and women's apparel and accessories. Shows are regularly hosted by the Pacific Northwest Apparel Association, the Pacific Northwest Men's Apparel Club, and the Pacific Northwest Shoe Travelers. Occasional home-furnishings shows are held there.

The Seattle Trade Center has 350 permanent apparel showrooms and more than 50,000 square feet of exhibition space on two floors available for trade shows. The Trade Center is conveniently located on the waterfront near downtown Seattle. Covered parking is available at a garage located across the street.

The Southern Furniture Market

The largest wholesale furniture market in the world, the Southern Furniture Market, is centered in High Point, North Carolina. Held twice a year in April and October, each market lasts nine days. During these two markets, nearly 50,000 people come to the furniture market. Visitors include buyers from all fifty states and sixty countries, furniture manufacturing executives, manufacturer's sales representatives, interior designers, and members of the press. The Southern Furniture Market is sponsored by

The International Home Furnishings Center, High Point, North Carolina.
Source: *Reprinted with permission of the International Home Furnishings Center.*

the Furniture Factories Marketing Association, which has offices in High Point and Hickory, North Carolina.

The Southern Furniture Market covers a 150-mile area in North Carolina, ranging from Burlington in the east to Lenoir in the west, and encompassing more than 1,300 furniture manufacturers displaying their goods in five million square feet of permanent exhibit space. More than ninety buildings are devoted exclusively to the display of home furnishings. Concentrations of showroom facilities are found in High Point, Lexington, Thomasville, Statesville, Newton, Conover, Hickory, and Lenoir. Showrooms are located in these cities in lease-space buildings, at manufacturers' factories, and in free-standing showrooms found throughout the market area.

The focal point of the Southern Furniture Market is High Point, where the greatest concentration of furniture showrooms are found. The International Home

Merchandising Mart Hall of Fame

The Chicago Merchandise Mart extends 577 feet along the north bank of the Chicago River. Located in front of it along the riverfront area is the Hall of Fame, which was established in 1953 to honor American merchants whose contributions to merchandising have had an impact on the economy of the nation. Bronze busts of the honored merchants are mounted on pillars in the plaza facing the Merchandise Mart. Those merchants elected to the Merchandise Mart Hall of Fame include the following:

- *Marshall Field:* founder of Marshall Field & Co. and builder of the Merchandise Mart in Chicago.

- *George Huntington Hartford:* founder of the A & P grocery store chain.

- *John R. Wanamaker:* founder of Wanamaker's in Philadelphia.

- *Frank W. Woolworth:* founder of F. W. Woolworth Co., variety store chain.

- *Edward A. Filene:* son of William Filene, who founded Filene's in Boston; noted as a merchandising genius who originated Filene's automatic markdown basement.

- *Julius Rosenwald:* former Sears, Roebuck and Co. president and chairman of the board.

- *General Robert E. Wood:* former president of Sears, Roebuck and Co.; the first living person elected to the Retailing Hall of Fame.

- *Aaron Montgomery Ward:* founder of Montgomery Ward and Co., the first mail-order retailer.

Furnishings Center in High Point is a 2.5-million-square-foot complex of five buildings containing more than 700 manufacturers' exhibits. It is the world's largest concentration of home-furnishings showrooms. The buildings are connected by enclosed bridges allowing buyers to shop the market under one roof. Furniture and accessory manufacturers represent more than 160 product categories, ranging from case goods, upholstery, and rattan and metal furniture to antique reproductions and playground equipment. Also displayed are decorative accessories such as lamps, statuary, planters, and decorative mantels.

In addition to the International Home Furnishings Center, other showrooms are located throughout the city of High Point. For example, a high-end showroom complex, Market Square, is found down the street from the Home Furnishings Center. This complex includes the Southern Market Design Center offering top lines in furniture, accessories, lighting, rugs, and wall and floor coverings. Both the Design Center and Market Square are open year-round to the trade.

The North Carolina market is the primary national furniture market in the United States. The Southern Furniture Market is attended by nearly all manufacturers and top furniture executives. It is the principal introductory market for almost all new goods. High Point is strategically located within a 200-mile radius of many major furniture manufacturers. Sixty percent of all wood bedroom furniture, 52 percent of all wood dining room furniture, and 28 percent of all upholstered furniture in the United States are made in the area. Buyers attending the Southern Furniture Market spend 85 percent of the total purchasing dollars in the home-furnishings industry. Many buyers do not place orders while at market but wait and place them at a later date. Orders flow in to manufacturers a week to six weeks after buyers attend market.

Summary of Key Points

1. Buying at market is considered the best way for retailers to purchase the latest fashion merchandise at the best prices. Markets enable retailers to comparison shop and see the greatest number of lines in the shortest period of time.

2. Buyers go to market for a number of reasons other than to see lines and place orders for merchandise. Some of these reasons are to seek new resources, to study market conditions, to observe fashion trends, and to get ideas for merchandising and promoting goods.

3. Markets offer advantages to manufacturers as well as to retailers. Markets provide manufacturers with an efficient way to reach many retailers and help them gain direction concerning the products retailers want to buy.

4. The primary market for apparel and accessories for men, women, and children is New York City. The dominant regional markets are located in Los Angeles, Dallas, Chicago, and Atlanta.

5. The largest wholesale furniture market is the Southern Furniture Market centered in High Point, North Carolina. This market is not limited to one building or one city but covers a 150-mile area.

6. New York City remains the dominant wholesale fashion market for a number of reasons. New York brings together all of the related segments of the fashion industry in one location, providing the stimulas needed for new ideas. Seventh Avenue remains the "Fashion Capital of the World."

7. Regional market centers have been successful because they have met the needs of smaller mom-and-pop stores. They offer savings in time and money, convenient shopping, service, and a pleasant, comfortable atmosphere.

Key Words and Concepts

Define, identify, or explain each of the following:

buying plan	point-of-purchase (POP)
contract furniture	principals of a firm
market centers	regional market
market weeks	sales representatives
marts	Seventh Avenue (SA)
New York garment district	special purchase goods
paper (signed orders)	vendor

Discussion Questions and Topics

1. What are the reasons why retail buyers attend fashion markets?
2. What are the reasons why manufacturers display their merchandise at markets?
3. Name and describe the characteristics of the five major fashion apparel distribution areas (markets) in the United States.
4. Where was the first fashion market center in the United States located? What factors led to the development of this location as the dominant market center in the United States?
5. Discuss the advantages and drawbacks of New York City as a fashion market.
6. Discuss the advantages and disadvantages of regional fashion markets.
7. In what ways do major retail stores use regional markets?

Note

Ruth Drizen, "California Dreamin'," *Apparel Industry Magazine,* January 1987, pp. 36–44.

CHAPTER 9 _____

FOREIGN FASHION CENTERS

IN TODAY'S highly competitive retail environment, buyers are constantly seeking creative and innovative fashion merchandise to offer their customers. Because of the rapidly changing fashion industry, successful retailers are always looking for new sources of supply. Many American buyers travel to markets all over the world to observe new trends, to buy samples to copy, and to purchase merchandise for resale to their customers. Foreign markets also attract textile producers, apparel manufacturers, designers, and fashion forecasters who are seeking both merchandise and ideas.

For years Americans, along with much of the world, have looked to France for fashion innovations and trends. During the early 1900s French designers had a particularly strong influence on what fashions were produced and sold in the United States. American retailers and producers of better-priced merchandise expressed their admiration of the haute couture houses by purchasing the right to copy model garments and producing exact **line-for-line copies** of these garments. The prestige of the Paris couture diminished during the 1960s, and French couturiers, as well as designers from other countries, began to enter the ready-to-wear industry. As ready-made clothing was offered to a wider audience and provided a greater financial return, designers from many countries began to acquire international reputations. The exchange of technological, economic, and social ideas today among foreign countries has made fashion a worldwide force.

Today, fashion centers are located in numerous cities all over the world. Some fashion centers have been established for many years, whereas others have only recently become important to the fashion industry. Many fashion retailers and manufacturers now travel to the primary foreign fashion centers of Paris, Milan,

Florence, and London to view merchandise and access new fashion trends. In addition to the primary fashion centers in France, Italy, and England, many other countries attract buyers from the United States and all over the world. Japan, South Korea, Hong Kong, and China are among other locations increasingly receiving attention from the fashion industry. Some countries offer only one or two specialized fashion products that entice buyers, whereas others provide many fashion products. Markets are often planned to allow buyers to schedule visits to several countries during one buying trip. Discussed in this chapter are the development and operations of French haute couture design, other European couture designers, and the growing importance of foreign ready-to-wear markets.

The Role of French Fashion

Since the eighteenth century, Paris has been a center of fashion creativity, dominating the world with talented dressmakers, tailors, and fashion designers. In fact, Paris set fashion trends as early as medieval times when small **mannequins** or dolls attired in the latest fashions were sent to other European courts. Paris became the undisputed fashion capital of the world in the late nineteenth century with the establishment of the first top fashion design houses. Today, Paris remains one of the primary fashion leaders in the world, but that leadership is now shared with other cities. Milan, London, and New York have joined Paris in importance, and growing in stature are Florence, Rome, and Tokyo.

Paris became the fashion capital of the world and has maintained its fashion leadership position for a number of reasons. Certainly one of those reasons is tradition. Paris has a long history of dressmaking as well as other forms of artistic creation. As an established center for the arts, Paris has recognized fashion design as an art form. The city has long been a meeting place for talented artists and has provided an atmosphere conducive to artistic creation. In Paris are concentrated many creative stimuli such as art museums and theatres. There has always been less division between the decorative and the fine arts in Paris than in other European countries. Parisian artists have always taken *couture fashion* seriously, and many apparel designers have had close relationships with prominent artists. Only in Paris has the creation of one-of-a-kind garments been considered an art form.

Paris also has had the craftsmen and raw materials necessary to produce couture apparel. Skilled cutters, dressmakers, and tailors in the city perform work to meet the highest standards of demanding designers and private clientele. French textile firms furnish designers with the finest fabrics and trims, and accessory manufacturers are available to produce the necessary items to complete a total fashion look. In addition, French women have provided a clientele for apparel who cared about fashion and were willing to take the time for fittings and did not mind waiting for the delivery of custom-made garments. French women dress in a different manner than do American women. They prefer to buy one outstanding outfit for a season and wear it extensively rather than have a whole closet full of clothes. Thus they are more willing to spend a great deal of money on one outfit.

Other factors have contributed to making Paris a world fashion center. Along with the concentration of resources, materials, skilled labor, and artistic surroundings, the additional support of the French government has aided fashion designers. The government, for example, provides couture designers with free television exposure through the government-owned television system.

The fashion press has traveled to Paris from throughout the world since early in the twentieth century to cover the openings of the couture designers and report the trends presented in their showings. Until the late 1960s several U.S. stores sent representatives to the Paris couture collections twice a year to buy original models to be copied line-for-line in original or similar fabrics. This was a means of providing American women with Parisian styles at a lower price. Although line-for-line copies are no longer made in the United States, fashion personnel from manufacturers, retailers, and the press still go to Paris in their search for new fashion ideas.

Until recently the world looked exclusively to Paris for fashion direction. The best-known, most creative fashion designers operated houses there. Not all of the designers were French, however. Worth and Molyneux were British, Mainbocher was American, Schiaparelli was Italian, and Balenciaga was Spanish. Today, included among the couture designers is Hanae Mori, who is Japanese. All of these designers went to Paris because they found the best environment there for producing quality fashion apparel and because the world's clientele for **haute couture** design went to Paris to buy. Had these designers remained in their native countries, they probably would never have become as well known as in Paris.

Interest in couture fashion began to fade during the 1960s and emphasis switched to ready-to-wear. As this happened, some began to predict the demise of Paris as the fashion capital of the world. In the 1980s, however, the city's reputation as a fashion center regained strength. In 1986 Christian Lacroix, like Dior forty years earlier, was credited with reviving a failing institution. Paris remains one of the leading fashion centers in the world, especially in regards to high fashion. Wealthy women still go to Paris to purchase expensive custom-made outfits, and the fashion world still looks to Paris for trend direction.

The Development of French Haute Couture

Before the establishment of French couture houses and the development of the French apparel industry, the clothing of the wealthy aristocracy was designed and constructed in shops owned by dressmakers or tailors who were known as **couturiers.**

Until the late seventeenth century the professional business of making clothes was controlled by male tailors. In Paris in 1675 a law was passed that allowed women to become **couturieres.** Although most of the couturieres received little recognition, several became well known because of the famous people they dressed.

Rose Bertin was the first great dressmaker to become celebrated for her innovative fashion creations. Bertin sold bonnets, fans, and lace as well as making garments. Her customers included royalty in Paris, London, Madrid, and St. Petersburg. She communicated with these customers by dressing fashion dolls in her designs and sending them to her clients for approval. As dressmaker to Marie Antoinette, Bertin was largely responsible for many of the styles of formal costumes during the 1770s. She also influenced the elaborate hairstyles and wigs of her time. Rose Bertin did not create fashions as a haute couture designer does today; rather her clothes were the result of discussions between the queen and the ladies of the court and were then constructed under the direction of Bertin. In recognition of her contribution to dress, Bertin was given the official title of Minister of Fashion by the French government.

After the French Revolution and the execution of Marie Antoinette and Louis XVI in the late 1700s, the new regime in France chose **Leroy** to make clothing with a new look, one not as ostentatious as earlier fashions. Leroy's clothes reflected the new political philosophy of France and consisted of adaptations of ancient Greek styles. Leroy made clothes for the Emperor Napoleon and both of his wives, the Empress Josephine and the Empress Marie-Louise. The clothes and ceremonial court wear were actually designed by artists such as David, Isabey, and Garnerey and then made up by the tailor Leroy.

Although Rose Bertin and Leroy were successful dressmakers, they were not really designers and their operations were not true couture houses. The term *couture* refers to fine sewing and is used to refer to French dressmaking houses. A couture house is an apparel firm headed by a designer called a couturier if male, and a couturiere if female, who creates original designs that are duplicated for individual customers on a made-to-order basis. The business is referred to as a house since it is often located in a residential building instead of a commercial area. The workrooms are called **ateliers,** and the showrooms are called **salons.** The term *haute couture* is used to describe the top houses that produce high-fashion clothes. Haute couture houses are usually established by a designer and named for the founder. In the event the founder dies, the house may continue to function under the original designer's name with a successor hired to fulfill the responsibilities of designer. The following list (Picken and Miller 1956) defines terms important in the operation of a French couture house.

ADAPTION: a copy of a garment having features like that of an original.

ATELIER: a workroom where the models are made and duplicated.

BOUTIQUE: a shop where accessories and apparel are sold.

COLLECTION: the group of models shown by a couturier.

COMMISSIONNAIRE: a firm that handles purchases for both manufacturers and retailers.

COPY: reproduction of a model made outside the house that originated it by a copyist.

COUTURE: a collective term used for French dressmaking houses.

COUTURIER: a male dressmaker.

COUTURIERE: a female dressmaker.

CROQUIS: fashion sketches.

HAUTE COUTURE: top houses, regarded as creators.

HOUSE: abbreviation used for a dressmaking house.

LANDED COST: cost of model, plus duty, plus transportation.

MAISON DE COUTURE: a dressmaking house.

MANNEQUIN: a young woman who wears models in a collection.

MIDINETTE: literally, "a work girl who comes out at twelve to have her lunch and a walk." Midinettes are classified as first hands, second hands, and apprentices.

MODEL: a garment shown in a collection.

MODELLISTE: one who designs in a house, but whose designs are shown under the name of the house.

NUMBER: a number given a model in a couture house for identification.

OPENINGS: the first showings of the new collection.

ORIGINAL: a design created for showing in a collection. A duplication is made to order of the original model shown in the collection.

PREMIER: male head of a workroom.

PREMIERE: female head of a workroom.

PREMIERE MODELLISTE: assistant to the head of an atelier.

SALON: a spacious room where the collections are shown.

TOILE: muslin that duplicates the original in line.

VENDEUSE: a saleswoman.

After the downfall of Napoleon, the female dressmaker again became the principal creator of women's clothing. The dominant Parisian dressmaker in the 1830s was Mme. Delatour, and in the 1850s dressmakers to the Empress Eugenie were Mmes. Vignon, Palmyre, and Roger. The nature of dressmaking was changed, however, in the 1860s by an Englishman who was to become the founder of French haute couture.

The First True Couturier

The designer credited with beginning French haute couture was **Charles Frederick Worth,** an Englishman, born in 1825. At the age of thirteen Worth was apprenticed to the owner of a London fabric shop; there he gained an appreciation of fine quality fabrics and apparel. He moved to Paris when he was twenty, and in 1847 became a sales assistant at Maison Gagelin, a shop that sold fabrics, shawls, and mantles. He remained with Gagelin for twelve years, eventually designing dresses for the firm. While working at Gagelin, Worth fell in love with co-worker Marie Vernet. He began designing simple dresses for her that would display the shawls they were selling to the best advantage. The shop's customers admired Marie's dresses and asked Worth to make such apparel for them. Worth finally succeeded in convincing his employer to let him open a dressmaking department in the store, and his design career was launched.

The House of Worth opened in Paris in 1858. One of Worth's early clients was the Empress Eugenie, wife of Louis Napoleon III. Her endorsement and patronage helped to make his business a success. Many other ladies of social position and wealth in Europe and the United States numbered among his clients, and the reputation of designs from the House of Worth lasted for decades, longer than for any other couture firm. Worth was best known for the use of beautiful fabrics in the design of his gowns and cloaks. The size of his dressmaking establishment was astonishing: by 1871 he had a staff of 1,200. (de Marly 1980). Worth made dressmaking big business and gave the role of the couturier power and status.

At Worth's death in 1895, his sons, Jean Philippe and Gaston, took over the firm with Jean Philippe as the designer and Gaston the administrator. When Jean Philippe retired in 1910, his son, Jean Charles, became the house designer. The House of Worth remained an important name in fashion throughout the 1920s. It continued to operate under the control of the Worth family until 1954 when it was

This look of layers of fabrics and crinoline was typical of Charles Worth's creations.

taken over by Paquin. A London branch of Worth continued to operate under nonfamily management until the early 1970s.

Other Early Couturiers

After the House of Worth was established, other couture houses were opened in Paris, such as one by another British designer, John Redfern, in 1881. Several other couturiers opened houses before the end of the nineteenth century, including Jacques Doucet (1870), Mme. Paquin (1891), and the House of Callot Soeurs (1895). After the turn of the century came houses such as Doeuillet (1900), Drecoll (1905), and Cheruit (1907), and many others followed. Here are names of some of the noted French couturiers of the past and their dates of influence:

Cristobal Balenciaga: 1937–1968

Pierre Balmain: 1945–1982

Beer: 1905–World War I

Marie-Louise Buyere: 1929–1950

Callot Soeurs: 1895–1953

Carven: 1944–1970

Gabrielle Chanel: 1914–1940; 1954–1971

Mme. Cheruit: 1905–1923

Jules François Crahay: 1950–1984

Madeleine de Rauche: 1932–1973

Jean Desses: 1937–1965

Christian Dior: 1947–1957

Jacques Doucet: 1870–1928

Georges Doueuillet: 1900–1928

Drecoll: 1900–1925

Jacques Fath: 1937–1957

Michel Goma: 1958–1973

Jacques Griffe: 1946–1970

Jacques Heim: 1923–1963

Mme. Jenny Sacerdote: 1911–1920s

Jeanne Lanvin: 1890–1946

Guy Laroche: 1957–1988

Lucien Lelong: 1919–1947

Louiseboulanger: 1923–early 1930s

Edward Molyneux: 1919–1950

Paquin: 1891–1956

Jean Patou: 1919–1936

Robert Piguet: 1933–1951

Paul Poiret: 1904–1925

Nina Rici: 1932–1959

Marcel Rochas: 1930–1955

Maggy Rouff: 1929–1940

Elsa Schiaparelli: 1929–1954

Madeleine Vionnet: 1912–1939

Charles Frederick Worth: 1858–1895

Although only a few grand houses remain in the couture today, for the first sixty years of this century, a considerable number of houses, both large and small, produced custom-made apparel. Following are the names of today's major Paris couture houses (names in parentheses indicate house designer).

Pierre Balmain

Pierre Cardin

Carven

Chanel (Karl Lagerfeld)

André Courreges

Dior (Gianfranco Ferre)

Louis Feraud

Hubert de Givenchy

Christian Lacroix

Lanvin (Claude Montana)

Ted Lapidus (Oliver Lapidus)

Guy Laroche (Angelo Tarlazzi)

Lecoanet/Hemant (Didier Lecoanet)

Serge Lepage

Hanae Mori

Jean Patou

Per Spook

Paco Rabanne

Nina Ricci (Gerard Pipart)

Yves Saint Laurent

Jean-Louis Scherrer

Torrente

Emanuel Ungaro

Phillippe Venet

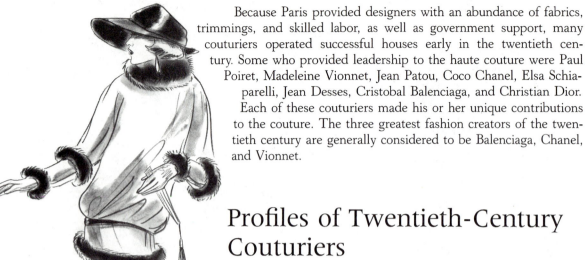

Because Paris provided designers with an abundance of fabrics, trimmings, and skilled labor, as well as government support, many couturiers operated successful houses early in the twentieth century. Some who provided leadership to the haute couture were Paul Poiret, Madeleine Vionnet, Jean Patou, Coco Chanel, Elsa Schiaparelli, Jean Desses, Cristobal Balenciaga, and Christian Dior. Each of these couturiers made his or her unique contributions to the couture. The three greatest fashion creators of the twentieth century are generally considered to be Balenciaga, Chanel, and Vionnet.

Profiles of Twentieth-Century Couturiers

Paul Poiret (1879–1944). After selling his designs to most of the top houses in Paris, Paul Poiret agreed to work for Doucet in 1896 where he remained until 1900 when he joined the House of Worth. Opening his own house in 1904, he quickly displayed a new spirit of fashion. By 1906 he had loosened the shape of women's clothes and was producing soft, amorphous shapes. He is best known for banning the corset and for creating hobble skirts so narrow at the bottom that women could hardly walk. Poiret dominated fashion for almost two decades. He changed the shape of the female figure by banishing the tightly corseted curves of the previous generation and creating the slender modern women. He became the first couturier to launch a perfume with his "Rosine." He traveled to numerous foreign countries to promote his clothes, taking along his own mannequins to model the clothes. Although Poiret dominated fashion from 1910 to 1914, after World War I he never regained the great success he had enjoyed before the war. He closed his house and by 1929 was bankrupt. He died in Paris in 1944 of Parkinson's disease after years of poverty.

This evening ensemble trimmed with fur was part of Poiret's collection for 1922.

Madeleine Vionnet (1876–1975). Madeleine Vionnet began her fashion training at the age of twelve by working with a well-known Paris dressmaker named Vincent. She married at eighteen and was divorced at nineteen. The next year she went to London where she worked in a tailor's workroom for five years. Upon returning to Paris she worked for Callot Soeurs and then Doucet. She opened her own house in 1912 but was soon forced to close because of World War I. She did not reopen her business until 1922; after that she became legendary in French fashion. She is viewed today as one of fashion's true immortals. She was known for inspiring other designers and for creating a totally new way of manipulating fabric with her introduction of the bias cut, a way of cutting fabric diagonally across the grain, resulting in a garment that clings to the body. Other innovations attributed to Vionnet include the asymmetrical neckline, the halter neckline, the cowl neckline, and the handkerchief hem, all developed from the principle of the bias cut. Her design philosophy was that "one should dress a body in a fabric, not construct a dress."

Jean Patou (1887–1936). Jean Patou was an important couturier in the 1920s and the 1930s. He was working on his first collection in 1914 when World War I interrupted his debut. After serving in the army, he presented his first collection in 1919. Like Chanel his fashions were designed for the sporty, emancipated woman. His clothes suited active women such as the actress Mary Pickford, and sportswear became his specialty. Patou designed simple elegant lines that were easy to wear. In 1929 he became the first designer to lengthen skirts and put the waistline back in its natural position. He introduced his perfume "Joy" in 1924. Patou admired Americans, and in 1925 he attracted attention by using six American models to show his clothes. The House of Patou has continued since his death in 1936 with a series of prominent designers including Marc Bohan, Karl Lagerfeld, Michel Goma, Angelo Tarlazzi, and Christian Lacroix.

Gabrielle (Coco) Chanel (1876–1971). Coco Chanel entered fashion in 1912 when she rented a small shop in Deauville where she designed hats and dresses. In 1914 she moved to Paris and opened a dress shop, which was soon forced to close by World War I. She reopened in 1919 and quickly achieved success. In 1939 war again forced her to close. She did not reopen her business until 1954 but continued designing until her death in 1971 at the age of ninety-five.

Chanel was one of the best-known couturiers of the twentieth century, a trend-setter who based her designs on her personal liking for simple, comfortable, sensible clothes that became the basis of modern dressing. She simplified the shape of women's clothes to a square cardigan and rectangular skirt. Her look in the 1920s and 1930s consisted of cardigans, wool jersey dresses, pea-jackets, bell-bottomed trousers, demure white collars and bows, hair ribbons, and chunky fake jewelry. Her designs were widely copied, and her look became a classic. She produced clothes of longer-lasting acceptability and influence than any other designer. In fact, a Chanel suit dating from the 1950s could be worn anywhere today without looking out-of-date. The classic Chanel suit in jersey or soft tweed is usually collarless and trimmed in braid. Included in the classic Chanel look are beige shoes with black toes, a chain-handled quilted handbag, and multiple strands of pearls and gold chain necklaces. She is also remembered for her famous scent "Chanel No. 5," introduced in 1921. Her house has continued since her death, and the Chanel name remains among the best known in the couture. Karl Lagerfeld is the current designer for the House of Chanel.

Elsa Schiaparelli (1890–1973). Born in Rome, Elsa Schiaparelli moved to New York after her marriage. After her husband left her in 1920, she and her

Vionnet designed clothing of intricate bias cuts and believed in retaining the natural lines of the body.

Schiaparelli is responsible for introducing the padded shoulder look during the 1940s.

daughter went to Paris. She designed a black sweater with a white collar, which was purchased by a buyer, and she was on her way in the fashion business. In 1928 she started her own couture shop, and in 1935 she moved to the Place Vendome where she opened one of the first couture boutiques, selling sweaters, blouses, scarves, and jewelry. Schiaparelli had the courage to be outrageous, and she was noted for her ability to take something ordinary and transform it into something amusing and new. She made hats in the shape of a shoe, a lamb, or whatever amused her. She is best remembered for introducing the color shocking pink, and she even named her perfume "Shocking." She was responsible for the wide padded-shoulder look, which dominated fashion until Dior's New Look was introduced after World War II. She spent the war years in the United States, returning to Paris to reopen in 1945. Her house remained active until 1954, but she never again dominated couture fashion. The 1930s was her period to epitomize fashion.

Jean Desses (1904–1970). Born of Greek parents in Alexandria, Egypt, Jean Desses went to Paris to study law and entered fashion instead. After designing for Mme. Jane from 1925 to 1937, he opened his own couture house where he dressed many wealthy discerning clients. His clothes were admired for their soft feminine draped lines. As a result of a trip to the United States in 1949, he signed agreements with two firms to manufacture a less expensive line of clothes. In 1950 he initiated his ready-to-wear line called Jean Desses Diffusion. This has been considered by many as the real beginning of the involvement of the French couture in mass production. Desses closed his house in 1960, but he continued to produce freelance designs until his death in 1970.

Cristobal Balenciaga (1895–1972). Generally regarded as the greatest designer of the twentieth century, Cristobal Balenciaga was born in a Spanish fishing village and began his career by opening a small shop in San Sebastian. He later established himself as a couturier in Madrid and Barcelona under the name of Elsa. When civil war curtailed the Spanish fashion business, Balenciaga opened a couture house in Paris in 1937. He closed his house during World War II and returned to Madrid, but reopened in Paris after the war and soon became the world's leading designer. His work followed the tradition of the couture and each collection made a clear fashion statement with clothes that had progressed logically from his previous collections. He was a perfectionist and was often referred to as the master. His elegant clothes had a dignified, structural quality. He created many new silhouettes and changed the shape of garments by such inventions as the stand-away collar and the three-quarter length sleeve. In the early 1950s he moved away from the close fit of the New Look and created softly unshaped jackets for his suits. He also introduced the straight chemise or "sack dress" in 1957. Another of his innovations was the small pillbox hat.

Balenciaga was strongly independent and loathed publicity. He moved the time of his press showings and presented his clothes weeks after the other designers, and he never joined the Chambre Syndicale, the trade association for the couture. Except for his perfumes, he refused commercial exploitation. When the wave of kooky mod fashions started in 1960, he refused to compromise. Although Balenciaga closed his house in 1968, his legacy is continued by Givenchy, Ungaro, and Courreges, all of whom worked with the master.

Christian Dior (1905–1957). Christian Dior's family encouraged him to study political science and to enter the diplomatic service, but he was not interested in such a career. After completing his studies in 1928, he ran an art gallery with a friend in Paris, and in the mid-1930s he began to sell sketches to the couture houses and magazines. In 1937 Robert Piguet bought some of Dior's sketches and later hired him as a design assistant. He joined Lucien Lelong in 1941 where he remained until 1946. With the financial backing of Marcel Boussac, a textile millionaire, Dior opened his own house. In February 1947 his first collection presented the revolutionary New Look. His ultra-feminine look was a bold change from the styles of the war years. Its long full skirt, nipped-in waist, and tight bodice re-established Paris as the world's fashion center. The influence of Dior's New Look was so great that all couturiers had to follow its shape and proportions in their subsequent collections. Dior remained the preeminent couturier for the next ten years, dominating the 1950s. In 1954 he presented his "H" line; in 1955 he introduced the "A" and "Y" lines. His last collection was presented in 1957. Since Dior's death, the House of Dior has continued, first under the leadership of Yves Saint Laurent and then under designer Marc Bohan. In 1989 Gianfranco Ferre became house designer. The Dior organization has remained highly successful, producing haute couture, ready-to-wear, jewelry, accessories, and perfumes. The name of Dior has been licensed for many women's and men's products, and Dior has become the most widely recognized designer name in the world.

In the 1950s Balenciaga created softly unshaped jackets and suits.

The Chambre Syndicale de la Couture Parisienne

The **Chambre Syndicale de la Couture Parisienne** was established in 1868 to coordinate the activities of the French fashion industry, a service it still provides. To be officially known as a "grand couturier," a designer must meet certain specifications developed by the Chambre Syndicale, the trade organization of the Paris couture. Although Chambre acceptance of a designer is prestigious, not all well-known and qualified couture houses are members. Christobal Balenciaga and Coco Chanel, for example, never joined the Chambre Syndicale.

Requirements for Membership

Membership in the Chambre Syndicale was, and still is, limited to couturiers who meet certain requirements. Today, an establishment must agree to abide by the following rules to qualify as an haute couture house:

1. A formal written request by the couture house must be presented and voted on by the Chambre Syndicale. A firm requesting membership must be sponsored by two current members.

2. Workrooms must be established in Paris providing quality workmanship.

3. Collections must be designed by the designer or a staff member and must be custom-made to fit clients' measurements.

4. Collections must be presented twice a year on the dates in January and July as established by the Chambre Syndicale.

5. A collection must include at least seventy-five designs.

6. Three models must be employed by the house throughout the year.

7. A minimum of twenty sewing workers must be employed in the firm's couture workrooms.

Few haute couture houses have been accepted by the Chambre Syndicale since Ungaro opened his house in 1965. The firms admitted since then are Paco Rabanne (1973), Hanae Mori (1977), Lecoanet Hemant (1982), and Christian Lacroix (1987).

Services Offered

The original objective of the French Chambre Syndicale was to deal collectively for its members in problems concerning taxes, wages, and other administrative matters. Today's Chambre Syndicale offers members a number of services, including the following:

1. Represents its members in their relations with the French government and arbitrates disputes.

2. Regulates uniform wage arrangements and working hours.

3. Sponsors a school for the education of students in the business of creating couture.

4. Registers and copyrights new designs of its members. Since 1920 couture designs have been accorded by French law the same protection from plagiarism as literary works, films, and patent inventions.

5. Coordinates the opening dates of the twice-yearly collections.

6. Organizes press and buyer accreditation and issues admission cards for the openings.

Recognition of Ready-to-Wear

In 1975 the importance of French ready-to-wear, called **prêt-à-porter,** was recognized by the Chambre Syndicale with the formation of the **Chambre Syndicale du Prêt-à-Porter des Couturiers et des Createurs de Mode.** Organized by Pierre Berge, business administrator for Yves Saint Laurent, this trade association represents both couture designers who also produce ready-to-wear lines and those who design only ready-to-wear. The Chambre represents France's most prestigious designers. Of fourty-four members, twenty-four produce only ready-to-wear. Those who produce couture collections are called couturiers, whereas those who produce only ready-to-wear are called **createurs.** Among the createurs are Karl Lagerfeld (who also designs the couture collection for Chanel), Angelo Tarlazzi, Sonia Rykiel, Claude Montana, Thierry Mugler, Jean-Charles de Castelbajac, and Enrico Coveri ("Chambre Goal," 1987). In 1988 the first American designer was admitted to the group: Patrick Kelly, a native of Mississippi.

Operations of the Paris Couture

Each couture house is headed by a designer called a couturier. In some cases a house is owned by someone who is not skilled as a designer, and therefore a designer must be employed. Such is the case in the houses of Chanel, Dior, Patou, and Ricci. The designer often hires a **modelliste** who helps with the creation of designs and may even create designs of his or her own. The designer and the modelliste select fabrics and trims from those offered by a manufacturer or they may design such fabrications themselves and have them manufactured. French textile manufacturers are willing to produce fine quality fabrics in small runs to meet the needs of the couture.

Designers may work from sketches or may prefer to drape in muslin on a live model or a dress form. Such muslin is called a **toile.** It is carefully fitted to the mannequin who will wear the final garment during the showings. In France the person who models the dress is called a mannequin and the original design is called a *model.* The toile is given to the head of the workroom who is responsible for cutting the fashion fabric and making the sample model.

A couture house has one or more workrooms called ateliers. Each house has two divisions of work. Workrooms that do the soft delicate work of dresses are called *flou,* whereas coats and suits are made by the *tailleur* division. In large houses an assistant designer serves as a liaison with the ateliers. The garments are sewn in the ateliers by **midinettes,** who are classified as apprentices, second hands, and first hands. Only first hands are allowed to work on a new model. The midinettes are supervised by a **premier** who is the head of the workroom. The premier interprets the designer's drawings or muslins into real, three-dimensional forms. They may also do private fittings with couture clients, and are aided by their own assistants and the **vendeuse,** who is the client's salesperson.

EUROPEAN COUTURE SCHEDULE

PARIS — The schedules for the couture collections showings in Europe this month are as follows:

ROME

Monday, Jan. 16
8 p.m. .... Rocco Barocco

Tuesday, Jan. 17
Noon .... Raniero Gattinoni
3:30 p.m. .... Clara Centinaro
5 p.m. .... Irene Galitzine
7 p.m. .... Litrico

Wednesday, Jan. 18
10 a.m. .... Andre Laug
Noon .... Fausto Sarli
6 p.m. .... Renato Balestra
7:45 p.m. .... Gianfranco Ferre

9:15 p.m. .... Lancetti

Thursday, Jan. 19
Noon .... Mila Schon
4 p.m. .... Raffaella Curiel
8:30 p.m. .... Valentino

PARIS
Sunday, Jan. 22
12:30 p.m. .... Torrente
2 p.m. .... Christian Lacroix
5:30 p.m. .... Hanae Mori

Monday, Jan. 23
9:30 a.m. .... Pierre Balmain
10:45 a.m. .... Pierre Cardin
12:15 p.m. .... Jean-Louis Scherrer
2:30 p.m. .... Nina Ricci
4 p.m. .... Christian Dior

7 p.m. .... Carven

Tuesday, Jan. 24
9:15 a.m. .... Philippe Venetl
10:30 a.m. .... Emanuel Ungaro
Noon .... Ted Lapidus
2 p.m. .... Louis Feraud
3:30 p.m. .... Chanel
5:30 p.m. .... Lanvin

Wednesday, Jan. 25
11 a.m. .... Yves Saint Laurent
2:30 p.m. .... Lecoanet Hemant
3:30 p.m. .... Guy Laroche
5 p.m. .... Paco Rabanne

Thursday, Jan. 26
9:30 a.m. .... Givenchy
11:15 a.m. .... Per Spook

Schedules of couture collections showings in Rome and Paris.
Source: *Reprinted with permission of WWD, Fairchild Publications.*

The selling organization of the house is composed of women who are called vendeuses. A vendeuse sees that the customer is completely satisfied. She processes the order and checks fabrics, colors, and trimmings to make certain that all agree with the client's order. She supervises fittings and checks on the progress of the garment to see that the promised delivery date is met. She is then responsible for the delivery of the garment to the customer. Assistants to a vendeuse are called *secondes*.

The cost of presenting a couture opening show every six months is about $100,000. The audience for couture openings is made up of about 1,000 members of the press, 50 private customers, and a few retailers. American retailers no longer buy haute couture, but a few attend the shows as guests of the individual houses. These retailers include fashion executives from I. Magnin, Bergdorf Goodman, Bloomingdale's, Saks Fifth Avenue, Neiman-Marcus, and Martha's, a specialty store located in New York and Palm Beach, Florida ("Fall 1988" 1988). Private couture customers are estimated at between 500 and 2,000 worldwide, but only 50 to 90 attend the openings at the top houses. The remaining customers view the collections in person at a later time or order the clothes from videos sent to their homes by the couture houses. Most of these customers go to Paris for the two or three fittings required to complete their clothes. Sometimes fittings are done on a dressform that conforms to a client's measurements.

Couture Business Activities

Although the haute couture openings receive worldwide attention, most haute couture firms operate at a loss. The rising cost of producing the showings and the custom-made garments has caused haute couturiers to seek profits in other ways. The association of a designer's name with other activities has provided many houses with more lucrative and profitable businesses. Some of the activities couture houses use to increase revenues include developing ready-to-wear lines, opening boutiques, and making licensing agreements to manufacture fashion accessories, apparel, fragrances, and other products.

Development of Ready-to-Wear Lines

One of the most profitable activities for couture houses is the production of ready-to-wear lines; therefore, many couture designers have added prêt-à-porter to their operations. The collection openings for prêt-à-porter are scheduled earlier than the couture showings because the production of ready-made clothing requires more time. Although ready-to-wear lines are designed by the couturier, the production is performed by ready-to-wear manufacturers who may not be located in the same city or even the same country as the couture house.

The Establishment of Boutiques

Another profitable business activity for couture houses is the establishment of small shops called **boutiques.** Accessories such as jewelry, scarves, and handbags, as well as clothing, are sold in the boutiques. The products are designed by the couturier or a member of his or her staff, yet they are manufactured by outside producers. The boutiques may be owned and operated by the couture firm, or they may be run by independently owned retail stores under a **franchising arrangement.** Under such an agreement, the franchisee or the independent retailer is given permission by the franchising parent company to sell certain merchandise in a store that bears the name of the parent company. Some of these boutiques are free-standing stores; others are small shops located within large department or specialty stores.

Many of the couturiers have boutiques located outside of France. For example, Yves Saint Laurent has more than 180 franchised boutiques selling his ready-to-wear and accessories that operate under the name **Rive Gauche.**

Licensing Agreements by Couturiers

Many haute couture designers receive lucrative royalties from licensing agreements with manufacturers. As discussed in an earlier chapter, licensing agreements give manufacturers permission to produce and market products carrying a couturier's name. A wide variety of products such as luggage, perfumes, linens, eyeglasses, jewelry, and home furnishings are sold through licensing agreements. Yves Saint Laurent has even licensed the use of his name on designer cigarettes. Licensed products are usually, but not always, designed by the couturier or a member of his or her staff.

Eighty-five percent of the business of couturier Pierre Cardin comes from 800 licensees produced by manufacturers in ninety-three countries selling over $1 billion a year wholesale in Cardin-labeled products. These products include men's and women's apparel and home fashions such as sheets and clocks. Cardin receives between 5 and 12 percent of the sales depending on the agreement. Cardin's great success with licensing has earned him the title of the Napoleon of Licensors (Meyers 1987).

Licensing provides the couturier with a method of promoting his or her name. Many couture firms have become widely known by the general public because of the widespread distribution of their licensed products. Licensing also gives the couturier a business activity involving limited financial risk.

Current Status of the Paris Couture

The French haute couture houses no longer hold the dominance and fascination they once did. By the 1970s the rising cost of custom-made garments, the shift in women's lifestyles to more casual living, and changing women's roles all contributed to declining interest in haute couture. The buying habits and wardrobe needs of couture customers also changed. Even women who could afford couture apparel were no longer willing to spend the time having fittings and waiting for clothes to be delivered. Women's active lifestyles have made ready-to-wear more desirable, and fine quality ready-to-wear is now available that meets the demand of discriminating clientele. The social life of the wealthy has also become more informal, and there are fewer occasions to wear extravagant custom-made outfits.

Prices of haute couture garments have also become prohibitive for many customers. With the price of a haute couture outfit ranging from $4,000 to as much as $100,000, few women can afford to be dressed in such apparel. Today's couture houses are losing sales because of astronomical prices, which begin at $2,000 for a blouse, $4,000 to $6,000 for a dress, $9,000 to $12,000 for a suit, and range from $25,000 to $100,000 for an elaborate ballgown.

Since the 1950s when couture sales were at their peak, there has been a sharp decline in the number of customers for such apparel. At that time the haute couture had more than 12,000 private customers. Today, couture customers are estimated at between 500 and 2,000 worldwide. According to the Chambre Syndicale, about 60 percent are American, 20 percent are from the Middle East, and 20 percent from other countries. Only about 2 percent are French.

With the decline in customers and the growing competition from ready-to-wear lines, custom-made apparel provided by the couture houses has ceased to be profitable, and, in fact, most couture houses lose money on their couture apparel. Jacques Mouclier, secretary general of the Chambre Syndicale, has estimated that each couture house loses more than $1 million a year. Until 1981 the French textile industry helped support haute couture with subsidies. Today, the couturiers must depend on their business partners in the world of high finance, their private customers, and their licensing of products such as perfumes, ready-to-wear, and accessories.

The sales figures for most haute couture houses are not publicly reported. Annual couture sales for twenty-two houses are estimated at $50 million by the Chambre Syndicale de la Couture Parisienne. The Chambre also reported that licensing of ready-to-wear and accessories is a $500 million business for the couture, whereas perfume is a $1.16 billion industry.

Although the couture's influence on international fashion declined in the 1960s and 1970s with the infusion of younger, trendier ready-to-wear designers, the couture has enjoyed a rebirth in the 1980s. This has been largely attributed to the presentation of new ideas by the designers Karl Lagerfeld for the House of Chanel and Christian Lacroix. These designers have received extensive coverage from the fashion press and are attracting younger private customers to the couture.

Function of Today's Haute Couture

The function of the couture is not to make money, at least not directly. Although the sales of custom-made garments are usually unprofitable, the couture generates priceless publicity and builds fashion image for the couturiers and for France. The presentations of couture collections stimulate sales of other fashion goods. The fame gained from the made-to-order collection means prestige and leads to marketability for a name or a label. The designer can create lines of ready-to-wear clothing and license them to be manufactured and mass-marketed. The label can be licensed for all sorts of accessories—cosmetics, fragrances, shoes, handbags, home fashions. In addition, the haute couture serves as a laboratory for fashion ideas where cost is no object and designers have free reign to express their ideas. Fashion trends still originate in the Paris couture that are copied or adapted and influence the apparel worn by the general population all over the world.

Changing Meaning of the Word *Couture*

As the role of the French haute couture has diminshed, the word *couture* has slipped into the public domain. Today, the use of the word without the term *haute* has come to mean simply "the top of the line." Many American and European designers have named their highest priced collections "couture" because of the quality and price of the garments, even though these clothes are not custom-fitted. Many stores have given the title to their department presenting expensive ready-to-wear by designers such as Valentino, Ungaro, and Chanel. Advertising copywriters also use the word to create an aura of high class around expensive quality merchandise.

Other European Couturiers

Although the greatest number of couture designers are found in Paris, other European couturiers also make important contributions to fashion with their custom-design collections. Operating in a manner similar to the couture industry in France, couturiers are also located in Milan, Rome, Florence, London, and Madrid. Like the Parisian couturiers, they operate a variety of business activities in addition to couture showings, and for most, ready-to-wear has become more important than their custom-apparel. Much of their publicity, however, is derived from the showings of their custom designs.

Italian Couture

The Italian couture, established in the mid-1940s soon after the end of World War II, has received strong government support. The governing body of the Italian fashion industry is the **Camera Nazionale della Alta Moda Italia,** which provides designers with a collective voice. The Camera's more than one hundred members include couture designers, ready-to-wear manufacturers, and shoe and accessory people. The Camera serves mainly to organize group events involving Italian designers, including the couture shows in Rome and the ready-to-wear shows in Milan.

Although Rome is the couture center for Italy, houses are also found in Milan and Florence. Well-known Italian couture designers are Emilio Pucci, Irene Galitzine, and Valentino. The following designers show at the couture shows in Rome.

Renato Balestra

Rocco Barocco

Clara Centinaro

Barocco Circolo

Raffaella Curiel

Trinita dei Monti

Mirella di Lazzaro

Gianfranco Ferre

Irene Galitzine

Raniero Gattinoni

Fendi (furs only)

Lancetti

Andre Laug

Angelo Litrico

De Carlis Pelicceria

Fausto Sarli

Mila Schon

Valentino

The collections of the Italian couturiers are shown a week prior to the French showings to allow buyers to cover a variety of European collections. The Italian couture today has diminished in importance, and most of Italy's fashion trends emerge from the ready-to-wear industry. Although Milan has become Italy's most important fashion center, Rome remains the center for alta moda, or high-fashion, houses.

British Couture

Several British couture houses were established in the early to mid-1900s, and England continued to have a prestigious couture until ready-to-wear and escalating costs forced many houses to close in the 1960s. A formal association of couturiers called the Incorporated Society of London Fashion Designers was formed in 1942. This organization had the backing of the British government during World War II, and its purpose was to promote the export of British clothing. Founding members included Hardy Amies, Norman Hartnell, Edward Molyneux, Digby Morton, Victor Stiebel, Bianca Mosca, Peter Russell, and the London branch of the House of Worth. Other designers who joined later included John Cavanagh, Charles Creed, Michael Donellan, Guiseppi Mattli, Ronald Patterson, Michael Sherard, and Elspethy Champcommunal, who designed for Worth.

During the war, the Society of London Fashion Designers cooperated with the British government to promote what was called the Utility Scheme, which restricted the amount of material to be used in garments to conserve fabric needed for the war effort. After the war, the Society coordinated dates for the showings by London couture houses. A London fashion week was held immediately prior to the Paris showings to encourage buyers from other countries to attend. The Society was dissolved in the mid-1970s after the number of British couture firms had dwindled.

Two of the best-known names in British couture design are Norman Hartnell and Hardy Amies. Hartnell opened a London couture house in 1928 and successfully showed his designs in Paris. He had a long association with the royal family that began with Queen Mary and continued until his death in 1979. He designed the wedding dress and coronation robe for Queen Elizabeth II in addition to many of the wardrobes for her foreign tours. He was knighted in 1977 and is best remembered for his sumptuous evening gowns.

Hardy Amies is also known for dressing the royal family. He has become one of Great Britain's most famous designers and has an international reputation. Opening his house in 1945, he began making clothes for Princess Elizabeth and after her coronation was awarded a warrant as dressmaker to the Queen. Amies entered the ready-to-wear business in 1950 and in 1961 began designing menswear. British couture designers and houses, with dates of influence, are listed below.

Hardy Amies: 1945–today

John Cavanagh: 1952–1974

Elspethy Champcommunal (designed for Worth): 1940s

Charles Creed: 1946–1966

Norman Hartnell: 1923–1979

House of Lachasse: 1929–today*

Lucile (Kennedy): pre-World War I

Guiseppi Mattli: 1934–1955

Michael (Donellan): 1953–1971

Edward Molyneux: 1919–1950

Digby Morton: 1934–1958

Ronald Patterson: 1947–1968

Peter Russell: 1930–1953

Michael Sherard: 1946–1964

Victor Stiebel: 1932–1963

* Note that the House of Lachasse was a made-up name. Designers have included Digby Morton (1929–1933), Hardy Amies (1934–1941), Michael (1941–1952), Charles Owen (1953–1974), and Peter Crown (1974).

Few British haute couture firms remain today. Hardy Amies and the house of Hartnell still function and dress members of the royal family. Other couturiers include Murray Arbeid and Victor Edelstein. Today, London fashion is noted most for ready-to-wear.

Spanish Couture

The association of haute couture designers in Spain is the Alta Costura, headquartered in Madrid. Showings of the designs of Spanish couturiers are held twice a year. Some of the most renowned members of the Spanish couture include Balenciaga, Pertegaz, Carmen Mir, and Pedro Rovira.

Foreign Ready-to-Wear Market Centers

Many fashion innovations and trends in the ready-to-wear industry have emerged from foreign countries, especially from France, Italy, and England. The production of ready-to-wear by foreign fashion producers did not receive much recognition in the United States until the 1960s. Now, twice a year, buyers and members of the press go to London, Milan, and Paris where designers present their ready-to-wear collections. The fashion images and traditions established by the couture houses in some countries, particularly France and Italy, have helped to enhance the appeal of ready-made clothing. Other countries, such as West Germany, South Korea, and Japan, that have not had such historically renowned fashion images have emerged as productive fashion centers. As exports in fashion apparel have expanded, many countries have gained recognition as fashion centers.

France

Because of their pride in the institutions of haute couture, the French initially resisted the acceptance of ready-made clothing. It did not take long, however, for them to see the need to develop the ready-to-wear industry.

During the 1960s the French couturiers began to enter into ready-made clothing. Yves Saint Laurent was one of the first couturiers to successfully design ready-to-wear. He was soon followed by Cardin, Givenchy, Ungaro, and many others in the design of ready-made clothing. When couture designers joined in the production of ready-to-wear, women throughout the world discovered that they could purchase a prestigious French designer label from a local retailer. The entrance of French couture designers into the mass production of apparel increased the prestige of ready-made clothing. During the late 1960s French exports of fashion goods began to expand, and by 1971 France was exporting over $550 million worth of fashion merchandise.

As much of the excitement and glamour diminished in the custom-made salons in the 1960s and 1970s, the designers of French prêt-à-porter became innovators in the fashion industry. Prêt-à-porter designers began to set the fashion trends and attract increased publicity. Today, France remains an important source in the world for new, innovative fashions, and attending both the couture and the prêt-à-porter showings is necessary to keep abreast of major fashion trends. Prominent French ready-to-wear firms and designers are listed below (names in parentheses indicate firm designer).

Marc Audibet	Emanuelle Khanh
Anne-Marie Beretta	Karl Lagerfeld
Dorothee Bis	Claude Montana
Nino Cerruti	Popy Moreni
Chloe (Martine Sitbon)	Thierry Mugler
Comme Des Garcons (Rei Kawakubo)	Guy Paulin
Jean-Charles de Castelbajac	Bernard Perris
Jean-Claude de Luca	Sonia Rykiel
Jean-Paul Gaultier	Angelo Tarlazzi
Phillippe Guibourge	Chantal Thomass
Hermes (Eric Bergere)	Kansai Yamamoto
Patrick Kelly	Yohju Yamamoto
Kenzo	

In the early 1970s, because of the growth of the ready-to-wear industry, French apparel manufacturers formed a trade association, **Federation Française de Prêt-à-Porter Feminin.** This organization represents ready-to-wear producers who do not belong to the Chambre Syndicale. Along with promoting French ready-to-wear, the trade organization helps members to find selling agents for their products and assists in planning retail store promotions featuring French apparel.

Many prêt-à-porter collections are shown twice a year, usually April and October, in the Porte de Versailles, a suburb of Paris. Exhibitors from other countries also feature fashion merchandise in the Porte de Versailles shows.

The couture houses present their ready-to-wear collections during the same weeks as the prêt-à-porter; however, the couture showings are not held in conjunction with the pret shows or in the same place. The ready-to-wear collections of the couturiers and createurs, sponsored by the Chambre Syndicale, are shown in tents set up in the Cour Carree of the Louvre.

The men's ready-to-wear showings, Salon de l'Habillement Masculin, are also held at the Porte de Versailles in France twice a year in February and September. This showing represents major designers from all over the world. The shows cover every aspect of men's clothing, such as suits, shirts, ties, and accessories. Exhibitors of children's wear and knitwear are also included at the same time.

France is also an important market for fabrics. One of the largest fabric fairs, **Premiere Vision,** is held in Paris. Designers, manufacturers, and retailers view new fabrics at Premiere Vision each fall and spring.

Italy

In recent years Italian fashion has made a strong impact on international fashion, and Milan has become Europe's second major fashion center after Paris. Italy has more than 100,000 registered dressmaking firms, ranging from the haute couture to the neighborhood seamstress. A number of prestigious manufacturers have developed whose merchandise has enjoyed success around the world. These firms rarely acknowledge the name of their designer, but they employ top designers to create their lines. Many of the designers are French or English as well as Italian. Some famous designers work for these firms in addition to the one using the designer's own name. This practice has made Italian sportswear among the best in the world. Included are the Italian firms of Cadette, Genny, Girardi, Halyett, Maxmara, Pims, San Lorenzo, Timmi, and Touche.

Much of the success of the Italian ready-to-wear industry is due to the influence of Italian sportswear, knitwear, and leather goods. Products such as Gucci shoes,

MILAN RTW SHOW DATES ANNOUNCED

MILAN — The Camera Della Moda, organizer of the Milan collections, has announced the following schedule for the spring-summer designer ready-to-wear showings in October.

Sunday, Oct. 2		
12:15 p.m.	Romeo Gigli	
2:30 p.m.	Max Mara	
6 p.m.	Gianni Versace	

Monday, Oct. 3	
9:30 a.m.	Emporio Armani
11 a.m.	Byblos
12:15 p.m.	Moschino
2 p.m.	Mario Valentino
3:30 p.m.	Rocco Barocco
4:30 p.m.	Enrica Massei
5:30 p.m.	Erreuno
6:30 p.m.	Blumarine

Tuesday, Oct. 4	
10 a.m.	Krizia
11:30 a.m.	Fendi
12:30 p.m.	Laura Biagiotti
2:30 p.m.	Gianfranco Ferre
4 p.m.	Mila Schon
5 p.m.	Luciano Soprani

6 p.m.	Chiara Boni

Wednesday, Oct. 5	
9:30 a.m.	Complice
11 a.m.	Basile
12:30 p.m.	Missoni
2:30 p.m.	Salvatore Ferragamo
3:30 p.m.	Alberta Ferretti
4:30 p.m.	Gianmarco Venturi
5:30 p.m.	Gianna Cassoli
6:30 p.m.	Andre Laug
7:30 p.m.	Giorgio Armani

Thursday, Oct. 6	
9:30 a.m.	Genny
10:30 a.m.	Callaghan
11:30 a.m.	Sanlorenzo
12:30 p.m.	Trussardi
2:30 p.m.	Sportmax
3:30 p.m.	Gherardini
4:30 p.m.	Mariella Burani

Schedules for designer ready-to-wear showings in Milan.
Source: *Reprinted with permission of* WWD, *Fairchild Publications.*

Fendi furs, Missoni knits, and Benetton sweaters are well-known fashion exports of Italy. Prominent Italian ready-to-wear firms and designers are listed below (names in parentheses indicate designer name different from that of firm).

Giorgio Armani

Rocco Barocco

Basile (Luciano Soprani)

Laura Biagiotti

Blumarine

Byblos (Keith Varty and Alan Cleaver)

Complice (Muriel Grateau)

Dolce e Gabbana (Domenico Dolce and Stefano Gabbana)

Fendi (Karl Lagerfeld)

Salvatore Ferragamo

Genny (Donatella Girombelli)

Gianfranco Ferre

Romeo Gigli

Krizia (Mariuccia Mandelli)

Andre Laug

Mariuccia Mandelli

Max Mara

Missoni (Rosita and Tai Missoni)

Franco Moschino

Jil Sander

Luciano Soprani

Pour Toi (Sam Rey and Luca Coelli)

Mario Valentino

Gianmarco Venturi

Gianni Versace

Zuccoli (Cesare Fabbri)

Fashion has become big business in Italy today. Milan is now the international center for high-quality ready-to-wear, and Florence is the market for cheaper ready-to-wear, menswear, children's wear, and knitwear. Italy does not have one fashion trade show but rather several showings held on a scheduled basis. The major ready-to-wear presentations are held in Milan in late March or early April for the fall/winter collections and in late September or early October for the spring/summer showings. The Milan ready-to-wear shows are fast-paced and efficient. The most famous designers show their collections at the Fiera, a pavilionlike three-story convention center on the outskirts of Milan. Exceptions are Giorgio Armani and Krizia, who show in theatres located in their own facilities.

Shows for the Italian menswear industry are held in Florence in February and September. The largest shoe collections are shown in Bologna each March. Italy has been long known for producing fine quality shoes; some of the major brand names are Salvatore Ferragamo, Bruno Magli, Gucci, and Amalfi. In the fall and spring in Como, Italian fabric producers present the large fabric fair, Ideacomo.

Great Britain

Prior to the development of the ready-to-wear industry, the British were known for their tailoring abilities, and England became the world's fashion center for menswear.

Efforts of the British couture houses, however, have had limited impact on the development of fashion trends. The few designers of the British couture houses today cater to the British royal family and have limited influence on world fashion.

During the 1960s the British ready-to-wear industry made a major impact on worldwide fashion by setting the trend for miniskirts and the "Mod look" among the youth of the period. The English designer Mary Quant is credited with introducing the miniskirt and for recognizing the importance of the young in setting trends for all age groups. Other young designers followed her lead and began to sell their interpretations of the London Mod look. About the same time, several boutiques on London's Carnaby Street attracted considerable attention by influencing new, colorful styles for men. The trend for the new look from London quickly spread throughout Europe and to the United States, helped by the popularity of British entertainers such as the Beatles and the Rolling Stones.

In the 1970s the ready-to-wear industry in England changed. British influence on young fashions disappeared and much of the fashion leadership held by London diminished. In trying to attract the attention of fashion buyers, British apparel firms began to present their merchandise at one large event in London rather than in individual showings. These showings are held in April and October to coincide with other European markets. The British Fashion Council coordinates the dates for the showings. The following is a list of firms exhibiting at the British Design Show.

Ally Capellino	Jean Muir
Anthony Price	John Flett
Betty Jackson	John Galliano
Caroline Charles	Katharine Hamnett
David Fielden	Michiko Koshino
Eight Names	Murray Arbeid
Emanuel	Ozbek
Ghost	Sara Sturgeon
Hyper Hyper	Vivienne Westwood
Janice Wainwright	Workers for Freedom
Jasper Conran	Zandra Rhodes

London is the major fashion center for the British fashion industry. Most of the apparel producers maintain permanent showrooms in London, and the headquarters for the major trade associations are located there, as are trade fairs and permanent showrooms for many accessory firms.

The London Designer Collections, a cooperative association of London ready-to-wear designers, was formed in 1975. Members who are elected to this group work at the top end of ready-to-wear apparel. The London Designer Collections has included many of the younger British fashion designers who have emerged since its founding. Among its members are Bellville Sasson, Benny Ong, Bruce Oldfield, Christopher Trill, Gina Fratini, Hardy Amies, Thea Porter, Wendy Dagworthy, Zandra Rhodes, Jean Muir, Maxfield Parrish, Roland Klein, Jacques Azaguary, and Edina Ronay of Edina and Lena.

London fashion is based on two foundations. First and most important is the classic, high-quality clothing that has long symbolized British excellence. This type of clothing comes from Britain's long tradition of fine men's tailoring from **Savile Row,** a street in London's West End, long known for custom-made apparel. The best natural fabrications such as cashmere, lambswool, and tweed are used to produce traditional clothing that never goes out of style. Two of the most famous British producers of such classic clothing are Burberry and Aquascutum.

The second major contribution of British fashion is the **punk look,** which is in direct opposition to the classic traditional look. Punk fashion was introduced by working-class London teenagers in the late 1970s as a demand for attention and a protest against the establishment. The look included pasty white makeup, blackened eyes, and heavy lipstick. Hairstyles were short and dyed or painted startling colors such as yellow, orange, green, or purple. Clothing included black leather jackets, stud-decorated jeans, and T-shirts printed with vulgar messages. This way-out look broke all the rules of fashion and good taste. The American version was an exag-

---

RTW SLATE FOR LONDON, PARIS

NEW YORK — The schedule for the designer ready-to-wear collections to be held in London and Paris next month is as follows:

LONDON		4:15 p.m.	Bruce Oldfield	7 p.m.	Jean Paul Gaultier	11:30 a.m.	Emanuel Ungaro
Friday, March 10		**PARIS**		**Saturday, March 18**		1:30 p.m.	Jean Marc Sinan
5 p.m.	Rifat Ozbek	**Wednesday, March 15**		9:30 a.m.	Jean Charles De	2:30 p.m.	Hermes
		9:30 a.m.	Barabara Bui		Castelbajac	4 p.m.	Lecoanet Hemant
Saturday, March 11		10:30 a.m.	Doby Broda	10:30 a.m.	Guy Paulin	6 p.m.	Claude Petin
9:30 a.m.	Janice Wainwright	11 a.m.	Hiroko Koshino	Noon	Claude Montana		
10:45 a.m.	Workers for	12:30 p.m.	Lolita Lempicka	2 p.m.	Agnes B.	**Wednesday, March 22**	
	Freedom	2:30 p.m.	Junko Shimada	3:30 p.m.	Balenciaga	11 a.m.	Yves Saint Laurent
Noon	Sara Sturgeon	4 p.m.	Patrick Kelly	5 p.m.	Issey Miyake	1 p.m.	Michel Klein
1:30 p.m.	Zandra Rhodes	5:30 p.m.	Christian Dior	6:30 p.m.	Dorothee Bis	3 p.m.	Myrene De Premonville
2:30 p.m.	Ally Capellino	6:30 p.m.	Chantal Thomass				
3:30 p.m.	Vivienne Westwood			**Sunday, March 19**			
6:30 p.m.	Katharine Hamnett	**Thursday, March 16**		10:15 a.m.	Woolmark/I.W.S.	**BY INVITATION**	
7:45 p.m.	Jasper Conran	9:30 a.m.	Daniel Hechter	11:15 a.m.	Enrico Coveri	Emanuelle Khanh	
		10:30 a.m.	Commes Des	12:30 p.m.	Martine Sitbon	Kenzo	
Sunday, March 12			Garcons	2 p.m.	Hanae Mori		
9:45 a.m.	Paul Costelloe	11:30 a.m.	Junko Koshino	3:30 p.m.	Lanvin	**BY APPOINTMENT**	
10:45 a.m.	Betty Jackson	12:30 p.m.	Helmut Lang	4:30 p.m.	Kansai Yamamoto	Carven	
12:15 p.m.	Jean Muir	2:30 p.m.	Yohji Yamamoto	6 p.m.	Sonia Rykiel	Courreges	
1:45 p.m.	Joe Casely-Hayford	3:30 p.m.	Jean Louis	7:30 p.m.	Givenchy Life	Jacques Esterel	
3 p.m.	John Galliano		Scherrer			Louis Feraud	
4:15 p.m.	Antony Price	4:30 p.m.	Christian Lacroix	**Monday, March 20**		Nina Ricci	
5:15 p.m.	Alistair Blair	6:30 p.m.	Thierry Mugler	9:15 a.m.	Odile Lancon	Pierre Cardin	
6:30 p.m.	Michiko Koshino			10:30 a.m.	Chanel	Philippe Venet	
7:30 p.m.	Joseph	**Friday, March 17**		Noon	Jin Abe	Ted Lapidus	
		9 a.m.	Givenchy	2:30 p.m.	Jacqueline De	Torrente	
Monday, March 13		10 a.m.	Bernard Perris		Ribes		
9:30 a.m.	British Couture	11:15 a.m.	Karl Lagerfeld	4 p.m.	Pierre Balmain	The schedule for the designer	
	Collections	12:30 p.m.	Popy Moreni	5:30 p.m.	Valentino	ready-to-wear shows in Milan,	
11 a.m.	Caroline Charles	2 p.m.	Anne Marie Beretta			which run March 4 through	
1:45 p.m.	Murray Arbeid	3 p.m.	Chloe	**Tuesday, March 21**		March 9, was printed on page	
2:45 p.m.	Hyper Hyper	4:30 p.m.	Angelo Tarlazzi	10:30 a.m.	Guy Laroche	2, Feb. 10.	

Schedules for designer ready-to-wear collections held in London and Paris.
Source: *Reprinted with permission of WWD, Fairchild Publications.*

gerated theatrical look not associated with the working class. It was worn primarily by rock entertainers and their followers. The look included ripped shirts, leather clothing, and extreme hairstyles often featuring bright colors.

West Germany

West Germany is one of Europe's largest producers of fashion apparel. Several German cities have impressive trade fairs where producers of fashion merchandise from other countries can exhibit their products. In April and October the largest international trade fair in Germany is held in Dusseldorf for exhibitors of ready-to-wear and related products. A fashion fair is also held in Munich in April and October, and a men's fashion fair takes place in Cologne in February and August. A major leather goods fair is held in Offenbach. The German fashion fairs have developed into important markets because they represent international manufacturers, presenting a cross section of European and even worldwide fashion merchandise. These exhibits of fashion goods are visited by buyers from all over the world.

One of the most noted textile trade shows, Interstoff, is held twice a year in Frankfort. Major textile producers from all over the world, including American companies, exhibit new fabrics. Many apparel manufacturers and fashion designers attend this show for ideas and to purchase fabrics. Frankfort also holds one of the largest fur auctions in the world. The fur fair is held each year in April.

West German manufacturers are increasingly gaining the attention of the U.S. sportswear market. Leading firms are Escada and Mondi, but many smaller manufacturers are also selling in the United States. Escada is known for elegantly tailored sportswear, which is carried by many leading department and specialty stores. Mondi has opened its own stores in addition to selling to independent retailers.

Scandinavia

The Scandinavian countries of Denmark, Norway, Sweden, and Finland hold a semiannual Scandinavian Fashion Week in Copenhagen, Denmark, during March and September. Producers from other countries are invited to exhibit women's ready-to-wear at these international showings. Trade fairs are also held twice a year for menswear. These shows are coordinated by the Scandinavian Clothing Council, headquartered in Copenhagen.

The Scandinavian countries are known for their work with wool, fur, and leather. Their fashion industry is best known for the production of jacquard sweaters and ski wear. Although the term *Scandinavian fashion* suggests a traditional sportswear look, each country has its own specialties. Finland produces exciting original fashions, and its best-known name is Marimekko, a firm that produces unique fabric designs and home-furnishings products. Sweden has a reputation for young fashions and claims to have introduced the string bikini. Wool sweaters and knitted sportswear are other popular Swedish products. Norway produces a wide range of moderately priced clothing and exports a great deal of outerwear. Denmark produces more highly styled, expensive clothes and is known for avant-garde jewelry, silverware, and housewares.

Spain

Madrid and Barcelona are among the several ready-to-wear production centers in Spain. Currently Madrid leads as Spain's primary fashion center. The Madrid showings attract designers from throughout Spain and receive promotional and financial backing from the government. Barcelona has a number of locally based young designers who show just before the more formally structured Salon Cibeles collections premiere in Madrid. Barcelona is also home to the biannual men's collections.

Most of the fashion goods that Spain exports to the United States are leather and suede products such as shoes, handbags, small leather goods, jackets, and coats. **Camara de la Moda Espanola** is the formal association for the Spanish ready-to-wear industry. It serves women's and children's wear manufacturers and organizes trade shows. Many ready-to-wear firms show merchandise at European fashion fairs as well as in Spanish cities.

Eastern Europe

Most of the countries in Eastern Europe—Poland, Hungary, Yugoslavia, and Romania—are producers of apparel through contract agreements with manufacturers in other countries such as France, Germany, and England. Yugoslavia is the only country in Eastern Europe that has made major efforts to promote its fashion products internationally.

The Soviet Union

Because the apparel industry in the Soviet Union is highly structured and directed by a central bureau, few fashion selections and choices are available. Recently, however, the Soviets have made efforts to improve their fashion industry. As part of his program of reform, Soviet leader Mikhail S. Gorbachev is encouraging the production of consumer goods, including clothing, and his wife has made it acceptable for Soviet women to take a keen interest in fashion. Raisa Gorbachev has established a more fashionable image for Soviet women with her wardrobe of clothes made from European fabrics as well as the designs of Russian couturiers. In 1987 she met with fashion representatives to discuss the future of their industry. Efforts to expand the Soviet apparel industry have been hampered by shortages of raw materials and machinery. Moreover, the Russians are unfamiliar with Western marketing techniques. Still they want to learn and would like to export fashions to the West.

To advance their apparel industry, the Soviets have sought foreign partners to provide equipment and technical expertise for the production of Russian designs. Two of the largest French manufacturers, Boussac Saint Freres and Bidermann, have negotiated to upgrade several Soviet textile mills and apparel factories. French designer Pierre Cardin was one of the first European fashion leaders to work with the Russians, beginning in 1986. Ten factories in the Soviet Union now produce men's and women's apparel with the Cardin label, and more are planned. The New York–based firm of Owen & Breslin has also negotiated to license a line of clothing created by a twenty-member Soviet-American design team to be manufactured in the United States.

The Soviet Union has about thirty fashion houses creating designs that are mass produced in factories. Fashion houses are located in Leningrad, Moscow, Tbilisi, and Kiev. Houses in the Balkin republics have traditionally produced more stylish fashions because of their proximity to the fashion firms of Finland and other Scandinavian countries. Moscow, however, remains the primary Russian fashion center. One of Moscow's premier fashion houses is the Dom Modi where the designer Viyacheslav (Slava) Zaitsev has been called the "Saint Laurent of the Steppes." Zaitsev was the first Soviet couturier permitted by the government to put a label in his clothing. Other Soviet fashion designers include Alexander Igmand, Irina Krutikova, Elena Khudikova, Garic (whose real name is Oleg Kolomeichuk), Irene Buourmistrova, and Katya Filippova.

The Far East

For many years the Far East has been a major producer of ready-to-wear. Japan, Hong Kong, Indonesia, South Korea, Taiwan, India, and the Philippines have been important sources of low-priced, moderate-quality, and high-volume fashion apparel. More recently the People's Republic of China has begun to emphasize apparel production for export and has become the world's largest textile producer. Most ready-to-wear produced in the Far East is exported, and much of this apparel is contracted by Western retailers and manufacturers and made to meet their prescribed specifications.

Because the price of labor is one of the major cost components in the manufacturer of apparel, low wages in the Far East provide manufacturers in those countries a comparative advantage in labor cost. Many American manufacturers own factories in the Far East, and some manufacturers send personnel there to supervise production and ensure that quality standards and production schedules are met.

Some Far Eastern countries have upgraded their fashion images by producing more high-fashion, high-priced apparel. Several well-known Far Eastern fashion designers, especially from Japan, have emerged in recent years and have helped to enhance the fashion images of their countries' fashion industries. A number of

Japanese designers now work and show their lines in Paris. Japanese designers such as Kenzo, Hanae Mori, Issey Miyake, Yohji Yamamoto, and Rei Kawakubo of Comme des Garcons are now known worldwide, and their clothing is sold in the finest U.S. and European fashion stores. See the list of Japanese designers below.

Yiekiko Hanai	Issey Miyake
Yoshie Inaba	Hanae Mori
Isao Kaneko	Kei Mori
Rei Kawakubo	Kansai Yamamoto
Kenzo	Yohji Yamamoto
Junko Koshimo	

In addition to designs now originating in the Far East, some of the ready-to-wear lines of prestigious American and French designers, such as Pierre Cardin, Oscar de la Renta, Givenchy, and Calvin Klein, are produced there.

Latin America

In recent years many of the Latin American nations have developed fashion industries and are exporting goods to the United States. Brazil now has a major leather goods industry and has become a primary producer of shoes as well as handbags and belts. Argentina, Colombia, and Uruguay are also producing leather goods.

Textile production, especially wool, is increasing in Latin America. Sportswear production is also becoming important in Brazil and Colombia. Latin American countries have the potential to become more important fashion production centers in the future.

Canada

The Canadian fashion industry plays an important role in the nation's economy and is the country's fourth-largest employer. Montreal, where approximately 65 percent of the Canadian garment industry is located, is the country's major fashion center, and Toronto is number two. Major trade shows are held in both cities.

The apparel industry in Canada is diversified, encompassing the production of a variety of fashion merchandise, ranging from inexpensive mass-produced garments to better-priced designer apparel. Major fashion exports include outerwear, furs, leather goods, and children's wear.

Much of the success of the apparel industry in Canada is attributed to several trade organizations that promote Canadian fashion products and designers. Both

Fashion Canada, a private corporation, and the Fashion Designers Association (FDAC) were established to assist with the development of Canadian fashion and to increase its international fashion image.

Canada has long been known for the production of outerwear. One of the largest showings of outerwear in North America is the Canadian Outerwear Fashion Fair held each year in Winnipeg, Manitoba. Exhibited at this fair are furs, leathers, ski wear, heavy knitted goods, and coats.

Profiles of Selected Foreign Designers

Hubert de Givenchy (French). Hubert de Givenchy was born in Beauvais, France, in 1927. He is the last of the aristocrats of couture and is respected in Paris as a totally dedicated designer. Givenchy began his fashion career in 1945 with Lucien Lelong, moved to Robert Piguet the following year, and then worked with Jacques Fath for two years. From 1949 to 1951 he designed for Elsa Schiaparelli. With the encouragement of Balenciaga, he opened his own house in 1952. Givenchy was strongly influenced by Balenciaga and his collections reflect much of the same refined elegance. Balenciaga considered Givenchy his heir, and when the Balenciaga firm closed, many of the employees joined Givenchy's atelier. Givenchy designs clothes of lasting quality in the grand tradition of the couture. His daywear is understated and his evening wear richly glamorous. The basis of his success has been his perfection of cut. Givenchy's couture business has remained profitable, and he has also enjoyed success with his Nouvelle Boutique ready-to-wear, which is distributed worldwide. He has a vast number of licenses and he heads an empire that includes fragrances, furs, sportswear, and home furnishings.

Karl Lagerfeld (French). Karl Lagerfeld was born in 1939 in Hamburg, Germany, of Swedish and German parents. At the age of fourteen Lagerfeld moved to Paris after his parents sold their prosperous German dairy business. Even at this young age he knew he wanted to be a fashion designer. Lagerfeld received his first fashion award at the age of sixteen when he won second place for a coat design in an International Wool Secretariat competition. First place in the same contest was won by Yves Saint Laurent. After four years as an assistant on the design staff at Pierre Balmain, Lagerfeld became bored with the atmosphere of haute couture and left to study art and become a freelance designer. Among the firms buying his designs were Krizia in Italy, various shoe manufacturers, and textile firms. He joined the House of Chloe in the early 1960s and made it a leader in prêt-à-porter. In 1965 he began designing furs for the Italian Fendi sisters. His freelance activities have included knits for Ballantyne, shoes for Mario Valentino, men's clothes for Club Roman Fashion, and designs for Chanel couture.

Lagerfeld's clothes for Chloe were noted for handwork and extravagant beading and were at the top of the deluxe ready-to-wear market. He has never been afraid to make a fashion statement. He takes new direction with confidence, and his collections show a total concept. He introduced his last collection for Chloe in 1983 and took over complete responsibility for Chanel ready-to-wear in addition to the couture. In March 1984 he presented his first collection under his own name.

Tai and Rosita Missoni (Italian). Tai Missoni was born in Yugoslavia in 1921, the son of an Italian sea captain and a Serbian countess. He met Rosita in London in 1948 where she was studying English and he was competing in the Olympics as a member of the Italian track team. Tai had started a business in 1946 producing track suits, which were the Italian Olympic team's official uniform. Tai and Rosita were married in 1953, after which they started their own small knitting business with five workers and four knitting machines. Their first designs appeared in stores under the names of other firms. They hired Parisian designers Emmanuelle Khanh and Christiane Bailly before Rosita decided to assume the design responsibility. The Missonis were responsible for moving the design of knitwear from "basic but boring" into the high glamour and sophisticated fashion world. They have been pioneers in the development of fashionable knitwear, and their designs have become international status symbols. Tai produces the inventive geometric patterns of their knitwear, and Rosita creates the shapes and the line. She works by draping the knitted lengths on a model. Production of Missoni knits is limited and the prices are very high. The Missonis received the Neiman-Marcus Award for design in 1973 and their knitwear designs were hung like works of art in a 1978 exhibition at the Whitney Museum in New York.

Sonia Rykiel (French). Sonia Rykiel was born Sonia Flis on May 25, 1930, in Paris. She began her fashion career in 1962 when she was pregnant and became frustrated at the maternity clothes available in shops. She first designed maternity clothes for herself and continued to design for her special friends after her son was born. Her husband owned a chain of shops named Laura, and she began to design on a small scale for them. In 1968 she opened her own Sonia Rykiel boutique located in the Paris department store Galeries Lafayette. Later she opened her boutique on the Paris Left Bank. Today she has boutiques in several locations throughout the world. Rykiel has developed a strong personal fashion look. Her feminine wearable clothes have been very successful. Her look is based on soft jersey, crepe, and city knits. Her colors are beige, gray, and black, and her line is glamorously sophisticated.

Yves Saint Laurent (French). Yves Saint Laurent was born to French colonial parents in Oran, Algeria, in 1936. At the age of eighteen he went to Paris to study art where his instructors recognized his ability to design clothing. In 1953 he entered a design competition sponsored by the International Wool Secretariat, winning third place. The next year he placed first with a design for a cocktail dress. In 1954 he enrolled at the Chambre Syndicale school and in 1955 he was hired by Dior as an assistant. Following Dior's death in 1957, Saint Laurent took over as designer for the House of Dior at the age of twenty-one.

Saint Laurent's first collection for Dior was a great success, but subsequent collections were not well received. In 1960 he was drafted for military service, and the House of Dior replaced him with Marc Bohan. Three months later he was released from the army following a nervous breakdown, and in 1962 he opened his own house. Saint Laurent has been highly successful and is considered the most influential modern designer. John Fairchild, publisher of *Women's Wear Daily*, has called him "the complete innovator." As the fashion genius of the second half of the twentieth century, Saint Laurent has been influenced by Chanel, Balenciaga, and Dior. He produces beautiful clothes that can be worn by anyone. He is known for his trapeze line, pea-jacket, blazers, chemises divided into Mondrain-like blocks of bold colors, sportive leather, city pants, and military jackets. He was the first couturier to realize that the basis of modern fashion was casualness. He popularized a masculine-appearing day wardrobe consisting of blazers, trousers, and shirts. In contrast his evening wear is romantically feminine.

Saint Laurent entered the ready-to-wear business in 1966 with his Rive Gauche boutiques. His menswear division was begun in 1974, and a children's line made in the United States was introduced in 1978. His YSL initials appear on many licensed products such as sunglasses, scarves, bed linens, and even cigarettes. His name also appears on cosmetics and fragrances. His perfumes include "Y" (1964), "Rive Gauche" (1970), "Opium" (1977), and "Paris" (1983).

Considered the greatest designer since Balenciaga, Saint Laurent was the first living designer to be recognized by a retrospective of his work at the Costume Institute of the Metropolitan Museum of Art in New York in 1983. Balenciaga was the only designer previously honored by the Metropolitan.

Christian Lacroix (French). One of the newest names among the Parisian couturiers is Christian Lacroix. His creative designs are full of surprises and have brought youth, excitement, and fun back to the couture. He is being heralded as the first designer since Saint Laurent to give the fashion business uncompromising direction and has been credited with bringing life back to a fading, staid couture. He designs clothes that are fun to wear and appeal to a younger, more daring woman than the typical couture customer. In 1986 he attracted the attention of the fashion world when he introduced his "pouf" or "bubble" cocktail dresses. This style was quickly copied and gained wide acceptance.

Lacroix was born in 1951 in Arles in southeastern France to a family involved in designing oil drilling equipment. He studied in Paris at the Ecole du Louvre, hoping someday to be in charge of a provincial costume museum. In 1973 he met Francoise Rosensthiel, who is now his wife. She worked in the office of Jean-Jacques Picart, a public relations man and marketing consultant specializing in the fashion business. Picart was impressed with Lacroix's ideas and his sketches. In 1981 Picart's firm was hired by the couture house of Jean Patou to help give the house a more youthful image, and Picart persuaded the company to engage Lacroix as designer. At Patou, Picart and Lacroix worked closely together. Lacroix designed the collection and Picart advised him from the sketch stage through the final accessorizing of each outfit.

In 1986 Lacroix and Picart formed a company called Lacroix and Picart Associates and sought financial backing to open a couture firm. An agreement was arranged with Financiere Agache, a French conglomerate that also owns the House of Dior. Under their agreement Lacroix will design or have approval of all products, including licensed products that carry his name. Supported by an $8 million initial investment from Agache, Lacroix showed his first collection in July 1987. He was declared a "new star" by *Women's Wear Daily*, and like Christian Dior forty years previously he was credited with reviving the failing institution of haute couture. American fashion stores were eager to be the first to present Lacroix's clothes. Bloomingdale's became the first to offer a garment bearing the Lacroix label on September 16, 1987, displaying one dress selling for $15,000. Bergdorf Goodman followed by showing a selection of his couture clothes at a gala charity benefit on October 28 and introduced thirty more affordable evening dresses averaging $3,000.

In 1987 Lacroix signed a licensing agreement with an Italian firm, Genny Moda, to produce, distribute, and market his first ready-to-wear collection. Shown in March 1988, this collection received rave reviews from the fashion press. Lacroix announced plans to develop a fragrance and is expected to expand his licensed products. Such activities are necessary to compensate for the lack of profit received from his couture business. In 1987 Lacroix reportedly had a first-year loss of $4 million on sales of under $1 million.

Summary of Key Points

1. The three major European fashion centers are France, Italy, and England. Other important centers are found in Europe, the Far East, Latin America, and Canada. The most important fashion cities are Paris, Milan, and London.

2. The French haute couture includes designers who produce custom-made clothes. The couture is regulated by the Chambre Syndicale de la Couture Parisienne, but not all haute couture designers are members of this trade association.

3. The designer credited with founding French haute couture is Charles Frederick Worth, an Englishman. The House of Worth opened in Paris in 1858 and continued to be an important influence on fashion through the 1920s.

4. The couture business itself is not profitable, but it is supported by the profits of a couturier's other fashion products such as prêt-à-porter, fragrances, and fashion accessories. Licensing of products often provides a lucrative business for couture designers and has led to high recognition of designer names by the public. In addition, licensing has made designer products more affordable for many consumers.

5. Today, designer ready-to-wear is very important in projecting and establishing fashion trends. The most important foreign ready-to-wear showings are held in Paris, Milan, and London.

6. The word *couture* is often used today by both fashion producers and retailers to refer to the highest-priced apparel ready-to-wear designer collections.

Key Words and Concepts

Define, identify, or explain each of the following:

atelier	Leroy
Rose Bertin	line-for-line copies
boutique	mannequins
Camara de la Moda Espanola	midinette
Camera Nazionale della Alta Moda Italia	modelliste
	premier
Chambre Syndicale de la Couture Parisienne	Premiere Vision
Chambre Syndicale du Prêt-à-Porter des Couturiers et des Createurs de Mode	prêt-à-porter
	punk look
couture house	Rive Gauche
couturiers (couturieres)	salon
createur	Savile Row
Federation Française de Prêt-à-Porter Feminin	toile
	vendeuse
franchising arrangement	Charles Frederick Worth
haute couture	

Discussion Questions and Topics

1. What factors have contributed to making Paris a world fashion center?
2. What is the Chambre Syndicale de la Couture Parisienne and what services does it provide to its members?
3. How does a designer qualify to be a couturier, and what are the requirements to be a member of the Chambre Syndicale de la Couture Parisienne?
4. Explain the difference between a couturier and a createur.
5. Name the three primary foreign fashion centers and discuss the contributions each makes to international fashion.
6. Discuss the business activities a couture house uses in order to maintain a profitable business.

7. Why is haute couture fashion important today even though it had ceased to be profitable?

8. Why are there fewer private customers for haute couture clothing today than there were in the 1950s?

9. Explain the different definitions of the word *couture*.

10. For what type of apparel is each of the following Italian cities noted: Florence, Milan, and Rome?

11. What countries are important producers of leather goods?

12. Discuss the importance of the Far East to international fashion.

13. How is fashion changing in the Soviet Union? What are the Soviets doing to update their fashion industry?

14. Discuss the major contributions to fashion by Vionnet, Balenciaga, and Chanel. Why are these couturiers considered the most influential of the twentieth-century designers?

15. Who are the designers most important in establishing today's fashion trends? Discuss their specific contributions.

Notes

"Chambre Goal: Raise RTW Image," *Women's Wear Daily,* December 18, 1987, p. 11.

Diane de Marly, The History of Haute Couture 1850–1950. New York: Holmes & Meier, 1980.

"Fall 1988 European Haute Couture Collections," *Fashion Flash,* Fashion Group, August 10, 1988.

William H. Meyers, "Maxim's Name Is the Game," *New York Times Magazine,* May 3, 1987, p. 33.

Mary Brooks Picken and Dora Loues Miller, *Dressmakers of France.* New York: Harper, 1956.

CHAPTER 10 _____

FASHION IMPORTS AND EXPORTS

THE U.S. apparel and textile industries are facing the problem of steadily rising import competition. Since the 1960s the dollar volume and percentage of foreign-made goods have increased significantly. The increasing degree of foreign penetration into the fashion market has created economic problems for American apparel and textile producers. Although government regulations designed to reduce the flow of **exports** do exist, the flow continues, and **imports** have not been offset by increases in exports.

A global market exists today for fashion goods. Most fashion stores carry foreign-made goods, and many send their own fashion buyers on trips to foreign markets to provide their customers with new and unique merchandise. Buyers need to understand the reasons for having foreign-made goods in their stores and must be able to identify the best methods for obtaining such goods. Buyers also should recognize the problems inherent in purchasing foreign-made fashion merchandise.

Presented in this chapter is a discussion of the growing penetration of foreign-made fashion merchandise into the United States, the methods of importing merchandise, and the attempts by government and industry to control imports. Also discussed are the reasons that retailers buy foreign-made goods and the problems involved in purchasing and selling imported merchandise.

Definition of Imports

Fashion merchandise has been imported by the United States since before it became a nation. Early fashion retailers offered their customers fine fabrics and trimmings imported from Europe and the Orient. Beginning in the nineteenth century, American retailers bought models from French couturiers to copy in their workrooms. With the development of American ready-to-wear in the early twentieth century, most American women wore mass-produced clothing made in the United States. Today, however, this has changed, and much of the clothing worn by American men, women, and children is manufactured abroad. As pointed out in previous chapters, imports have made an increasing impact on textile, apparel, and accessories industries in recent years. More than 50 percent of the apparel sold in the United States today is imported, and the ILGWU has projected that import penetration may soon account for 56 percent of men's, women's, and children's wear. Imports may be defined in two ways.

1. *IMPORTATION OF FASHION GOODS AT MARKETS.* Fashion merchandise may be selected and purchased at international fashion fairs or exhibits. These goods are designed and produced totally by foreign manufacturers.

2. *IMPORTATION OF FASHION GOODS WITH SUPERVISED OFFSHORE PRODUCTION.* Domestic apparel producers may import goods either from their own plants operating outside the United States or through supply arrangements made with foreign producers. Both American manufacturing firms and retailers often contract for such offshore production of fashion merchandise. The goods may be constructed totally in the foreign country, or they may be only partially made, with offshore production limited to certain processes, such as sewing. The American firms involved in the production set detailed specifications for the construction of the goods.

Methods of Producing Goods Offshore

Today many American manufacturers are producing fashion goods in foreign countries. A primary advantage of producing merchandise abroad is that production costs are lower than in the United States largely because of low-wage labor. Even with the addition of shipping costs and import **duties,** total production costs are often less than for comparable goods made domestically. The following three methods are used for **offshore production:**

1. *PRODUCTION PACKAGE.* The American manufacturer makes a **production package** agreement through a production agent located in the country where merchandise is to be produced. The package agreement allows the foreign manufacturing plant to perform all the steps involved in production, including acquiring raw materials, cutting, sewing, finishing, labeling, packaging, and shipping the completed goods. Although the American manufacturer may send a personal representative to

work with the offshore producer, the foreign agent is responsible for production, quality control, and delivery time schedule. This method is one of the most expensive ways for an American manufacturer to produce goods abroad.

2. *SEGMENTS OF PRODUCTION PERFORMED BY DIFFERENT COUNTRIES.* An American manufacturer may include more than one country in the production of merchandise. The fabric and findings may be purchased from one country, whereas another country cuts and sews the goods. Finishing and final packaging may be completed in the United States.

3. *SEWING PERFORMED OFFSHORE.* Some manufacturers choose to cut their own fabrics in the United States and send the pieces to a low-wage country to be sewn. This method is often used when the goods require detailed labor. When manufacturers use this method, the garments are usually made of lightweight fabric because of the expense involved in shipping the cut garments.

Middlemen Involved in Offshore Production

American apparel firms producing merchandise in foreign countries must closely supervise production and shipping processes to assure a quality product. The details of production, such as patterns, samples, construction detail, and quality control, must be clearly specified, and the merchandise must be carefully routed back to the United States by one or a combination of means.

To accomplish the production of offshore merchandise, certain middlemen may be involved. Some American firms may hire an agent to represent them in the country where production is performed. Other manufacturers may use a **freight-forwarding** agent to assist with the shipping details. Sometimes the manufacturer hires a **customs broker** to seek permission from the American government to bring the goods back into the United States.

Regulation of Imports

Countries may use a variety of means, such as **quotas** and **tariffs,** to regulate imports. The United States has generally followed a policy that excessive restrictions on foreign trade will produce a lowered standard of living for its citizens. Trade barriers are seen as leading to higher retail prices for consumers, and concern exists that nations affected by restrictive import regulations will retaliate by restricting their own importation of American-made goods; thus other industries may suffer if an attempt is made to protect one industry by use of import restrictions. Domestic producers are largely expected to meet foreign competition by producing goods that are more desirable to American consumers than imported items.

Quota Allocations

One means by which the U.S. government regulates imports is by quotas that set limits on the number of units of specific items that may be shipped from a particular exporting country to the United States over a period of time. Quotas are established relating to fiber content, total yardage (expressed in square-yard equivalents), and quantities of apparel items. In most instances a foreign producer must have a quota allowance to ship goods into the United States.

Governments may charge for the use of the quota, or they may try to regulate the amount of capital investiture made in their country in exchange for the quota allocation. Quota allotments and the classification for quota allocations differ from country to country. Classifications are influenced by politics and by the need to balance trade with other countries.

The United States takes domestic production of the goods into account before allocating quotas. Quotas are assigned to a foreign government, which in turn assigns a quota to manufacturers requesting it. Quotas are usually assigned to individual manufacturers based on the amount shipped in previous years. Thus a manufacturing firm that goes out of business or reduces production can make money by selling its quota allowance to another manufacturer who needs additional quota.

The United States negotiates separate *bilateral treaties* with each exporting nation in order to establish quotas. Quotas, or annual maximums, are established on hundreds of textile and apparel categories. Bilateral agreements are established by the office of the U.S. Trade Representative, and the Customs Service is responsible for monitoring import and quota levels. Not all countries that export goods to the United States have quota restrictions. For example, the European Economic Community (EEC) is exempt from quotas because these high-wage countries produce products that are not price-competitive with American-made goods and do not cause domestic market disruption. Exemptions may also be given when U.S. exports to a country balance imports.

In some instances more than one country is involved with the manufacturing and export of an apparel item. For example, the fabric may come from one country, assembly of a garment may take place in another, with finishing and exporting done elsewhere. Some countries have attempted to circumvent quota regulations through incorrect labeling of the country-of-origin. New country-of-origin rules established in January 1985 state that the first manufacturing steps determine a product's origin. A garment must be labeled with that country's name, and the garment is subject to that country's quota limitations.

When importing goods, U.S. buyers must be aware of the availability of quotas. If a country has used up its quota, a merchandise order cannot be delivered to a store. The merchandise will be denied entry to the United States and will be stored at the port of entry, at the importer's expense.

Import Tariffs or Duties

In addition to regulating fashion imports by means of quotas, most fashion merchandise is subject to an import tax known as a duty or tariff. The amount of duty varies depending on the type of merchandise and is usually a percentage of the invoice cost. The purpose of an import duty is to protect domestic industry by making prices of textile or apparel goods made abroad comparable to those produced domestically. Duties are established and regulated by the U.S. government and collected by the U.S. Customs Service. Duties are highest on items that have competing domestic industries. For example, a duty is charged on imported products that cost more to produce in the United States than abroad so that the American product will remain competitive. Even with added tariffs and shipping costs, the **landed cost** of fashion merchandise is often less than the cost to produce comparable American-made apparel. Landed cost is the total cost of imported merchandise, including the cost of loading, transporting, and unloading at destination.

Section 807

American manufacturers who use overseas production for partial completion of apparel goods have a special tariff advantage provided by the Tariff Classification Act of 1962, **Section 807,** which allows an American apparel manufacturer to design and cut garments in the United States and ship the materials out of the country for sewing. The goods are then sent back to the United States for finishing and packaging. This procedure allows the manufacturer the advantages of cheap labor and a minimum duty paid only on the value added to the garment by the work done outside the United States. Many American apparel companies are increasing their use of Section 807 since labor-intensive operations are much less costly in certain low-wage countries. Much 807 business is conducted in the Caribbean, with Mexico and the Dominican Republic as primary sources. (*Standard & Poor's* 1987). To facilitate their production of goods under Section 807, some U.S. manufacturers have established **maquiladoras,** twin plants located on each side of the U.S.-Mexican border.

U.S. Penetration of Foreign Markets

The higher cost to produce American goods, combined with restrictive trade barriers imposed by other governments, often makes them economically unsuitable for export. A number of foreign countries impose additional excise taxes, value-added taxes, and restrictive quotas on American goods. After shipping costs are added to the cost of other trade barriers, the price of American-produced apparel may be extremely high. American-made goods become even less attractive for export when the value of the dollar is high compared to other world currencies.

American manufacturers have found ways to penetrate foreign markets in spite of the problems related to the export of their products. To avoid the additional expenses and high tariffs imposed by foreign governments, American apparel producers have used several means to develop markets abroad. Among these methods are (1) licensing agreements, (2) joint ownership ventures with foreign producers, and (3) direct ownership of foreign production plants.

One method of circumventing the cost penalties is to license foreign producers in return for a percentage of sales. With licensing agreements the American firm gives a foreign producer the right to use its manufacturing process and its trademark name. Another method is for an American firm to make a joint agreement or form a partnership with a producer in a foreign country. In both the licensing agreement and the joint-ownership agreement, the American firm is in charge of the design, patterns, and technical expertise, whereas the foreign licensee or partner provides the labor for production and markets the merchandise abroad. A third alternative is for U.S. firms to establish their own manufacturing plants in foreign countries. This method allows the American firm to use workers and materials from the country of location.

Balance of Trade

Trade among nations goes back to the beginning of civilization. Ideally, a country tries to establish a **balance of trade** in which its amount of exports equals or exceeds the amount of imports. To trade profitably, a country should export products it has in abundance or can produce with some advantage and import those products that it makes least efficiently.

For many years the United States exported more goods than it imported. In the 1970s, however, the export-import balance changed and the United States began to incur annual **trade deficits.** In 1974 the U.S. trade deficit was $4.5 billion, and by 1980 the trade deficit had increased to $24.2 billion. This unfavorable balance of trade has continued to increase significantly. In 1985 the U.S. trade deficit was more than $132 billion, and by 1987 it had reached $158.3 billion. In 1988 the deficit decreased for the first time since 1980 to $137.3 billion. Table 10.1 shows the changing U.S. balance of trade dating from 1960. Trade with Canada, Mexico, Brazil, Taiwan, South Korea, Singapore, and Hong Kong account for a large percentage of the U.S. trade deficit.

The balance of trade in textile and apparel products has been unfavorable for several years (see Figure 10.1). In 1987 U.S. apparel trade resulted in a $20.7 billion

**Table 10.1. Merchandise Trade Balance
for the United States 1960 to 1988**

Year	Trade Balance in Billions of Dollars (minus indicates debit)
1960	4.6
1965	5.3
1966	3.8
1967	4.1
1968	0.8
1969	1.3
1970	2.7
1971	− 2.0
1972	− 6.4
1973	1.3
1974	− 4.5
1975	9.1
1976	− 8.3
1977	− 29.2
1978	− 31.1
1979	− 27.6
1980	− 24.2
1981	− 27.3
1982	− 31.8
1983	− 67.5
1984	− 107.9
1985	− 132.1
1986	− 152.7
1987	− 158.3
1988	− 137.3

Source: Statistical Abstract of the U.S.

deficit. Apparel imports were $22.1 billion, whereas exports totaled only $1.4 billion. The trade imbalance was also extensive in the textile industry where imports were $4.6 billion as compared to $1.9 billion for exports (U.S. Industrial Outlook 1988, p. T44).

Expansion of Fashion Imports

America has imported textiles since colonial days. For many years expensive imported fashions have been status symbols. The U.S. government remained complacent about the importation of high fashion products, and both the textile and apparel industries were unconcerned because the importation of small amounts of high-style fashions

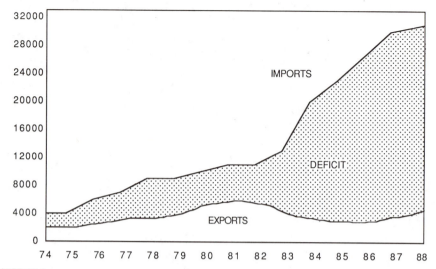

FIGURE 10.1
U.S. Textile and Apparel Trade C.I.F. Import Values F.A.S. Export Values (millions of dollars). (Source: U.S. Department of Commerce, FT-135, FT-140, SITC Classification 65 & 84 and American Textile Manufacturers Institute. Data are in millions of dollars.)

did not present a threat to American production, which concentrated on volume fashion. As we have seen, some American apparel manufacturers even imported expensive couture fashions, which they copied and sold at moderate prices. Such line-for-line copies were produced by U.S. manufacturers until the late 1960s.

The import situation changed following the end of World War II as more retailers began to send buyers to European fashion markets, and the amount of imported apparel began to increase. Whereas some retailers had carried a wide selection of imports, especially high-priced fashions, for many years, by the mid-1960s many U.S. department stores were importing fashion merchandise. Especially popular in the late 1950s and early 1960s were Italian wool double-knit dresses and suits, hand-knit sweaters, and leather goods. Retailers wanting to be fashion leaders found it increasingly important to send buyers abroad to seek out unusual merchandise for their stores that was not carried by other stores. U.S. manufacturers soon recognized the advantages of European products and began to establish plants or enter partnerships with manufacturers located in other countries.

Although Europe remained an important market for U.S. retailers, buyers began to seek products from other parts of the world. Hong Kong and Japan were among the first areas explored by American buyers and manufacturers. Soon buyers began to purchase fashion merchandise from countries such as Korea, Taiwan, Malaysia, and the Philippines. More recent markets have opened in Mexico and South America.

Today U.S. apparel manufacturers and retail stores of all sizes and price offerings are involved with fashion imports. American fashion merchandisers have become veterans of foreign travel and constantly seek new markets offering unique merchandise and better values.

Apparel and Textile Imports

Importing foreign goods is a major activity of U.S. textile, apparel, and retailing businesses. In 1960 apparel and textile imports totaled $866 million, and by 1987 the dollar volume of these products had reached $20.7 billion.

The number of countries supplying the United States with apparel products has increased considerably in recent years. The top five suppliers of apparel in 1985, on a volume basis, were Taiwan, Hong Kong, Korea, the People's Republic of China, and the Philippines.

For the last several years Japan has been the largest supplier of textile mill products, accounting for 17 percent of total U.S. textile imports in 1985. Japan was also the fifth-largest foreign customer for U.S. textiles, purchasing 6 percent of total American textile exports. One-fourth of the U.S. $2.3 billion textile trade deficit in 1985 was with Japan. The second-largest supplier of textile goods to the U.S. market was Italy, followed by South Korea, China, and Taiwan. Canada consumed the largest share of U.S. textile exports in 1985, purchasing 12 percent. The second-largest market in 1985 was Saudi Arabia, followed by Mexico, the United Kingdom, and Japan (U.S. Industrial Outlook 1986).

The penetration of apparel imports measured as a percentage of domestic production has also increased rapidly. As shown in Table 10.2, in 1974 the categories with low import penetration included skirts (2.5 million units), suits/blazers (6.3 million units), and dresses (9.9 million units). By 1984 a considerably higher import penetration was evident. For the category of skirts, import penetration increased to 24.7 million units, suits/blazers to 21.2 million units, and dresses to 43 million units. Blouses and sweaters have the highest penetration of imports (U.S. Bureau of the Census 1986).

Table 10.2. Apparel Imports—Women's and Girls' Garments (in millions of units)

Category	1974	1981	1982	1983	1984
Coats	12.8	23.8	33.5	39.3	40.7
Suits/blazers	6.3	11.3	34.9	17.6	21.1
Dresses	9.9	19.5	26.6	36.9	43.0
Skirts	2.5	18.9	16.1	19.5	24.7
Shorts	12.6	13.3	30.6	37.0	40.4
Slacks	20.1	18.9	35.9	45.4	57.0
Blouses/shirts	124.8	215.2	293.9	322.7	337.3
Sweaters	61.4	121:6	137.6	157.9	174.9
Underwear	41.2	88.5	96.0	114.6	133.9
Nightwear	8.1	10.0	23.9	24.2	27.2
Hosiery	26.7	23.3	47.5	54.2	76.5

Improved Quality of Foreign-Made Apparel

At one time apparel produced in low-wage areas such as Taiwan, South Korea, and Hong Kong was of inferior quality. Now, however, the quality of production from these countries has improved greatly, and many are producing high-quality apparel. As noted earlier, many U.S. retailers have established buying offices in low-wage countries to purchase foreign goods, and many well-known designer firms are producing goods in foreign countries with cheap labor.

The quality of foreign apparel has improved for several reasons. Much of the goods produced by low-wage countries are now made according to specifications established by American manufacturers or retailers who import the goods. Another important reason is that foreign countries have acquired better, more modern machinery, and, in addition, worker skills have improved.

Reasons Retailers Buy Foreign Merchandise

The retail buyer is constantly looking for new merchandise and new sources of supply. The highly competitive nature of fashion retailing keeps the buyer in search of creative and innovative merchandise. Buyers frequently turn to sources outside of the United States in their attempt to find new and unusual merchandise. Retailers are increasingly attracted to foreign-made merchandise for several reasons, including uniqueness and individuality, prestige and fashion leadership, quality, and lower prices. Retailers' growing interest in private-label merchandise has also attracted many to send buyers abroad to seek fashion goods.

Uniqueness and Individuality

Merchandise produced in foreign countries is often unique and different from that produced in the United States. Sometimes foreign merchandise is handmade and produced from native materials not found in other locations. Designs may be indicative of the country of origin and may be difficult, if not impossible, to copy or to mass produce. Such products offer special appeal to discriminating customers who want something unusual. Intense competition among retailers leads them to seek out merchandise not found in other stores. This exclusivity offers the retailer a competitive advantage provided the merchandise is in demand by consumers.

Prestige and Fashion Leadership

Many countries have reputations for providing fashion leadership, and, in fact, new styles in both men's and women's apparel often originate abroad, especially in Europe. Stores enhance their fashion images by carrying goods produced in countries known for providing fashion leadership. For example, for many consumers a label stating "made in France" suggests high fashion, and "made in Scotland" on a cashmere sweater denotes prestige and quality.

Quality

Many foreign producers are known for producing quality goods. For example, Swiss watches are considered the best in the world; Italy is known for quality leather goods; England for bone china; and Japan for outstanding home electronics. Many foreign-made goods today are considered superior in quality to those made in America. Carrying such products is important when a store wants to be known for selling quality merchandise.

Low Prices

Retailers are often attracted to foreign-made goods because they are available at a lower price than comparable American-made goods. Many developing countries are using labor-intensive products such as apparel and footwear as a means of building their economies. Low labor costs enable these goods to be produced at highly competitive prices. When low prices are coupled with high quality, foreign-made goods become particularly attractive to retail buyers. When the merchandise is exclusive and thus free from competition, the retailer is able to place a higher markup, and the store is provided with a greater profit.

Private-Label Merchandise

Retailers are also attracted to foreign-made products because of their growing interest in carrying merchandise with the store's own private label. Retailers have found that many foreign manufacturers, particularly in the Far East, are willing and eager to produce private-label merchandise to meet the retailer's specifications. With **specification buying** the retail buyer provides specific directions for manufacture of goods from the styling and fabrications to be used to the final production and packaging. Foreign producers are often willing to produce such goods in a short time period.

The strong work ethic, particularly among Far Eastern nations, leads these manufacturers to work hard to solve production problems to produce the desired goods in a short period of time. Thus foreign-made goods are sometimes manufactured and shipped more quickly than are American-made goods. Foreign manufacturers are also more willing than many American manufacturers to produce small manufacturing runs for and to restrict the sale of a particular product or fabrication to one buyer.

Sources of Foreign Merchandise

Retailers may acquire foreign-made merchandise by several different methods. The retailer chooses a method on the basis of such factors as the size of the store, the categories of goods being purchased, the degree of exclusivity desired, and the cost of buying the merchandise. Both domestic and foreign sources are available for purchasing foreign-made goods. Some retailers send buyers abroad to make direct contacts with foreign resources. Others cannot afford the time or money to make foreign buying trips. These retailers may use domestic sources for purchasing foreign-made goods.

Buying Foreign Goods from Foreign Sources

To buy directly from a foreign resource usually involves foreign travel on the part of store buyers. Such travel is expensive and often requires more time than buying from domestic markets. Foreign sources used by American buyers include buying from (1) the manufacturers themselves, (2) foreign **export merchants** who are wholesalers specializing in exporting goods and who provide faster delivery than buying direct from manufacturers, and (3) **export sales representatives** who represent selected manufacturers and do not maintain a wholesale inventory. Making contact with any of these resources often requires the assistance of a resident buying office. These buying offices may be foreign-operated branches of U.S. resident buying offices or may be independent foreign buying offices, called **commissionaires.** The commissionaire usually charges a commission for its services, whereas American buying offices charge a monthly fee.

Buying Direct

Large retail institutions are most likely to send their buyers abroad to purchase merchandise and to negotiate with manufacturers for the production of private label goods. Buyers from department and specialty store chains travel to foreign markets on a regular basis to select goods to sell in their stores. Such stores often send groups of merchandising executives including buyers, merchandise managers, and fashion directors on foreign buying trips. These merchandising teams make decisions about the purchasing of foreign merchandise to be carried throughout the store. Team efforts are also used by stores that are jointly owned. Representatives from stores with common ownership may meet with representatives of their resident buying office, forming buying committees to make decisions about foreign merchandise, which will then be made available to all stores in the ownership group.

Advantages of Buying Direct

Buying direct from foreign resources offers several advantages. Among them are:

1. Prices are often lower than those offered by intermediate sources.

2. Buyers can establish specifications with manufacturers to assure quality, style, and fit suitable for the American consumer.

3. The buyer may acquire exclusive merchandise that will not be carried by competing stores and can be sold at a higher markup offering the store an opportunity for greater profit.

4. Fashion trends often originate in foreign markets. Buyers who visit such markets can spot these trends more quickly and incorporate them into their merchandise offerings. Spotting fashion trends is especially important for fashion-forward stores that want to be the first to offer new merchandise.

5. Foreign visits with manufacturers and their representatives offer the buyer an opportunity to develop rapport, which leads to better working relationships between retailer and producer.

Disadvantages of Buying Direct

Making foreign buying trips has certain disadvantages. Some of the drawbacks to buying directly from a foreign resource are:

1. The cost of foreign travel is high in terms of dollars and the time that the buyer must be away from the store. Cost must be taken into account when determining the cost of the merchandise purchased.

2. There is danger of overbuying or buying merchandise that is not suitable for a store's customers because it may look more appealing in a foreign setting.

3. Foreign buying sometimes requires placing orders far in advance of the time the goods will be received in the store. Payment is usually required at the time of shipment and slow delivery time ties up store funds that could otherwise be used to purchase stock that would produce immediate sales.

4. Reorders of fast-selling merchandise are usually impossible to obtain.

5. Returning damaged or defective merchandise for refund or replacement is likely to be impossible.

6. With direct buying the retailer usually assumes all of the costs of importing that would otherwise be assumed by the importer or U.S. selling agent.

Buying Foreign Goods from Domestic Sources

It is possible for buyers to purchase foreign-made goods without making foreign buying trips. Several domestic sources offer foreign goods for sale to those retailers who want the flavor of imported merchandise in their stores but do not have the time or the resources to buy these goods directly. The primary domestic sources for foreign goods are wholesale importers and import trade fairs. Although merchandise bought from these sources usually costs more than goods purchased abroad, the sources assume many of the problems and disadvantages of direct buying.

Wholesale Importers

The import wholesaler serves as a middleman who purchases foreign merchandise and in turn offers the goods to retailers. Although goods purchased through an import wholesaler cost more than they would if a direct foreign contact were used, the private import wholesaler is usually highly experienced in the merchandise lines carried and has excellent foreign connections. Although buyers can purchase a variety of foreign-made products through importers, exclusive merchandise or merchandise made expressly to the retailer's specifications cannot be purchased.

Three types of wholesale importers who sell foreign-made goods in the domestic markets are (1) import merchants, (2) resident sales agents, and (3) import commission houses. The **import merchant** may offer a single classification or category of goods and sometimes carries domestic as well as foreign-produced goods. The **resident sales agent** represents a group of foreign manufacturers and may or may not carry stocks. The agent is knowledgeable in the paperwork involved in importing merchandise and handles all of the importing procedures. An **import commission house** represents foreign manufacturers and collects a commission from the buyer as well as the manufacturer.

Import Trade Fairs

Buyers often attend foreign import shows held in the United States in major market cities. Some of the import fairs feature fashion merchandise from only one country; others display merchandise from a number of countries. Manufacturers and sales representatives rent space at these fairs and exhibit sample merchandise to visiting buyers. One of the largest fashion import fairs in the United States is the New York Pret held in the Jacob K. Javits Convention Center in Manhattan. The

COLORES DE MODA

NEW YORK PRET

MOD COLORS IS WHAT YOU'LL SEE.
Dazzling custom-made jewelry, daytime lines, cocktail evening wear,
linen and tailor coordinates, separates, linen statements and evening bustiers.
All this and much, much more.

MODA DE PUERTO RICO INC . and the DESIGN COUNSIL FOR PUERTO RICO
Invite you to the NEW YORK PRET SHOW. March 5-7.
JACOB K. JAVITS CONVENTION CENTER.
Booth 410. Show hours: **Sunday** 10 am to 6 pm **Monday** 9:30 am to 6 pm. **Tuesday** 9:30 am to 5:30 pm.

Illustration: Carlos Aponte

An advertisement for fashion apparel and accessories from Puerto Rico that were shown at the New York Pret.
Source: *Moda De Puerto Rico, Inc. and The Design Council for Puerto Rico.*

New York Pret presents manufacturers from all parts of the world and enables buyers to view many lines of foreign merchandise in one location. Included in the more than 13,000 lines are ready-to-wear, casual sportswear, and a complete range of accessories.

Problems in Buying Foreign Merchandise

Depending on the type of method used, several problems may complicate the purchase of foreign-made goods. The problems involved in buying foreign merchandise must be carefully evaluated by the buyer before a purchasing decision is made. When making direct purchases from foreign countries, communication problems often occur because of failure to understand the language. Cultural differences in relation to social or business practices may also make negotiating purchases difficult. It is not always easy for the American buyer to make needs clearly understood and for the foreign vendor or manufacturer to explain the features of the merchandise and the conditions of the sale.

It is difficult to determine the total cost of the goods when making foreign purchases. The retailer must consider the cost of acquiring the goods as well as the price when evaluating foreign purchases. Also included in the cost of the goods is the transportation, which may be considerable, and in addition, most foreign merchandise is subject to an import duty when it arrives in the United States. Another factor that may change the cost of the merchandise is the fluctuating value of the U.S. dollar in relation to foreign currencies. When the value of the dollar falls, foreign goods become more expensive.

Other problems with buying foreign-made goods relate to unpredictable delays in delivery. Particularly when purchasing goods from developing nations or from areas where modern communications and transportation systems do not exist, delivery can be delayed by adverse weather conditions or communication failures. Delivery of items shipped by sea can be delayed by an unexpected longshoreman's strike. The store expecting merchandise for a planned import festival promotion can have advertising and sales plans disrupted by the failure to receive the goods as scheduled.

Reorders of foreign-made goods are seldom assured. If the buyer does not place a large enough initial order to cover demand, chances are that not enough lead time exists to guarantee delivery of reorders while demand still exists. With seasonal and fashion merchandise, reorders are virtually impossible. The selling season will be over before the goods arrive.

There are problems in relation to quality standards and size variations with imported merchandise. Quality standards and sizing measurements vary among countries. Imported merchandise may not be produced to the standards expected in the United States. What is considered to be a high quality standard in one country may be considered low quality elsewhere. Sizing and body proportions also vary among different countries. Often it is not possible for the buyer to inspect imported merchandise before it is shipped, and return for replacement or adjustment is likely to be impossible. Today there are fewer problems with imported merchandise in relation to quality and size than in the past. Foreign producers have learned how to produce goods that are acceptable to the U.S. market and have worked out many of the old problems. Yet these problems are more common with foreign merchandise than with American-made goods.

Concerns about Fashion Imports

In recent years much controversy has existed regarding imports. Each segment of the fashion industry, from producers to retailers to consumers, has responded to the issue in a different way. Whereas retailers want free trade, many producers want **protectionism,** which means protecting American production by reducing, limiting, or excluding foreign goods. **Free trade** means allowing goods to flow freely among countries without the restraint of protectionism.

Trade unions, workers, and many manufacturers favor federal legislation to curb imports and raise tariffs. These groups contend that cheaper foreign merchandise eliminates jobs in U.S. textile and apparel production and makes for unfair competition. Unions note that when Americans buy foreign-made goods, they subsidize foreign producers who are not required to pay taxes, unemployment insurance, and other levies that are part of the cost of producing goods in the United States.

Retailers argue that workers in foreign countries can produce quality merchandise at lower prices, enabling them to offer consumers lower prices. Retailers want the opportunity to shop foreign markets so that they can provide their customers with the widest variety of merchandise at the lowest prices. Shopping foreign markets allows retailers to purchase quality goods that often cannot be produced by American firms. Unique and exclusive imported goods can generate storewide excitement and at the same time enable the store to obtain a higher markup because the merchandise is free from competition. Imported goods, especially those made in low-wage countries, allow retailers to express creativity in fashion, with the added incentive of stimulating sales with lower prices for comparable quality.

Although not as concerned about imports as producers and retailers, consumers have varying viewpoints about imported fashion products. They often voice a preference for American-made goods when asked their opinion, but they tend to purchase to obtain the fashion look they want and for value. Consumers enjoy imported goods that are unique, offer prestige, and many times are a better value for their dollar. Some consumers, however, want to buy American-made goods to support U.S. workers and the economy.

Government Efforts to Control Imports

Since the early 1960s, the dollar volume and percentage of fashion imports have increased significantly, rising to a degree of foreign penetration into the fashion market that has created an economic problem for U.S. textile and apparel producers. By regulating the flow of fashion imports, the federal government has tried to respond to the needs of the textile and apparel industries. Governmental regulations are limited, however, by foreign policy considerations and the potential effect of retaliation against exported American goods by some foreign countries. To provide additional support to American producers, the government has offered incentives such as tax breaks, deferral of taxes, and low-interest credit rates.

The federal government has been reluctant to establish import regulations pertaining to any one industry. The larger consideration is the total import/export picture and the development of regulations that will help the United States achieve a favorable balance of trade. The government does not want to jeopardize the total American export position and has been reluctant to provide the textile and apparel industries with the protection they have requested against imports.

GATT and MFA

Since 1948 the United States has been a member of the **General Agreement on Tariffs and Trade** (GATT). This international organization, headquartered in Geneva, gives meaning and perspective to all aspects of international trade among its ninety-five contracting members. Originally organized to reduce tariffs and other trade barriers, much of GATT's work consists of consultations and negotiations on specific trade problems affecting individual commodities or member countries. At times, major multilateral trade negotiations also take place under the auspices of GATT.

As an advisory organization, GATT has no real power; however, the opinions of the organization do have considerable influence because so many trading nations are members and agree to abide by GATT's decisions. The emphasis of GATT is on world relations, and its decisions are generally unbiased.

One of the major efforts to keep international trading efforts fair and to control the flow of imports is the **Multi-Fiber Textile Arrangement** (MFA), which became effective under GATT auspices in 1974. It is an international trade agreement governing trade in textiles and apparel. Its purpose is to allow foreign textiles and apparel to be exported to the United States and other developed countries at a growth rate that does not disrupt domestic industries. Under the provisions of the MFA, disruptive imports can be controlled by negotiating individually with exporting countries and entering into bilateral agreements that establish import quotas.

Although the MFA does provide some relief to a country suffering from disruptive imports, its provisions have several shortcomings, including the following:

1. Imports by the United States are allowed to remain high because the MFA assumes levels of domestic growth beyond what is actually occurring.

2. The quantity and number of units rather than the value of the merchandise brought into the country are limited.

3. The agreement encourages foreign producers to produce higher-priced goods, a situation that makes a deeper cut into the dollar value of the domestic market.

Footwear Industry Revitalization Program

By 1977 the shoe industry had experienced a serious decline in sales because of foreign competition. In an effort to combat the problem, President Carter developed the Footwear Industry Revitalization Program, administered by the Department of Commerce, to:

1. Identify and develop new technologies that could significantly improve the competitive position of the entire domestic shoe industry.

2. Work with the industry to establish a footwear center that would provide continuing educational and technical assistance to shoe manufacturing companies.

3. Recruit domestic shoe retailers to help manufacturing firms with their revitalization efforts.

4. Organize teams of specialists from consulting firms with expertise in shoe manufacturing to help certified companies deal with problems in operations, marketing, technology, and management.

5. Revamp the adjustment assistance program to speed the department's certifications procedures and to make loans and loan guarantees more attractive to certified firms.

The Footwear Industry Revitalization Program did little to impede the rise of imports and the continuing decline of the American shoe industry. Unable to compete with imported shoes, which are often available at lower prices, many American shoe manufacturers have closed their operations. In 1968 approximately 600 shoe firms were in operation in the United States; by 1985 only 250 American companies were producing shoes. The largest number of closings occurred in 1984 when ninety-four companies discontinued operation (U.S. Industrial Outlook 1986).

Multilateral Trade Agreement of 1979

In July 1979 President Carter signed a trade liberalization pact intended to aid the import-weakened textile and apparel industries. The agreement was the culmination of multilateral trading negotiations that had extended over more than five years. Although ninety-eight nations participated in the talks, only forty-one countries agreed to the final terms. The provisions allowed tariff cuts on specific items during the next decade. The agreements helped to constrain the imports that threatened the American fashion industry.

The Textile and Apparel Export Expansion Program

As a result of government efforts to fight fashion imports, the Department of Commerce established the Textile and Apparel Export Expansion Program in 1979 to increase U.S. exports. At the same time, the fashion industry organized the United States Apparel Council to work with the Commerce Department program.

A major objective of the Department of Commerce program is to educate domestic producers about the exporting of goods to foreign markets. In addition, the program offers American firms assistance with export financing, participation in domestic and foreign trade shows, and assistance through seminars designed to meet the needs of the fashion industry.

Other Governmental Efforts

The Department of Commerce has given research grants to several universities and private research organizations to study ways to fight foreign imports through technological applications. Other government grants have been provided to the Amalgamated Clothing and Textiles Workers Union to coordinate efforts by labor and management in the men's tailored clothing industry.

One interesting project supported by the federal government in 1979 was Boatique America, cosponsored with the American Apparel Industry. The project's goal was to establish ongoing relationships with Japanese retail buyers. Boatique America was a floating department store that carried a variety of American products ranging from menswear to meat, to entice Japanese buyers and develop new Japanese markets. The project, however, was largely a failure. Sales of only $3 million were achieved, although original projections had been for sales of $7 million.

Look for the union label.

Think of it as a little American flag in your clothes.

Union Label Department, International Ladies' Garment Workers' Union,
1710 Broadway, New York, New York 10019

The song "Look for the Union Label" has been used by the International Ladies' Garment Workers' Union to make the public aware that goods made by union members in America enhance the job security of fashion industry workers.
Source: *The International Ladies' Garment Workers Union, Label Department.*

Liz Claiborne, Inc.

One of today's most widely recognized labels in women's apparel and accessories is Liz Claiborne. The company was founded in 1976 by Elisabeth Claiborne Ortenberg and her husband, Arthur Ortenberg. Established with $50,000 in savings and $200,000 raised from investors, the company grossed $2.6 million its first year and has since become one of America's fastest-growing firms. By 1981 when the company went public, sales were $117 million, and in 1985 with sales of $560 million, Liz Claiborne was listed for the first time in the Fortune 500 directory of the largest U.S. industrial corporations, ranking as number 437. In 1989 with sales of $1.2 billion, the company ranked number 299 in the Fortune 500. In addition, *Fortune* magazine identified Liz Claiborne as the top company in a listing of stars of the Fortune 500 based on a special study of sustained profitability.

One reason for Claiborne's success is that the company identified a niche in the market whose needs were not being adequately met by other clothing lines—the updated, professional woman. The first Liz Claiborne line offered businesslike, moderately priced clothes that were more casual and more imaginative than other competing lines. The company has continued to target this same working woman who shops primarily in department stores. The continued success of the Liz

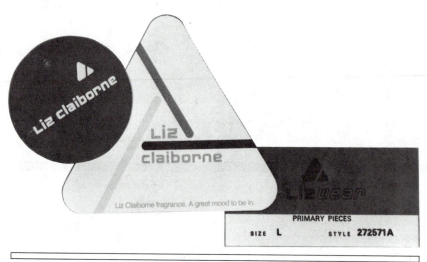

Liz Claiborne fragrance. A great mood to be in.

PRIMARY PIECES	
SIZE **L**	STYLE **272571A**

Liz Claiborne labels are widely recognized with fashion apparel and accessories in the United States and foreign countries.
Source: *Reprinted with permission of Liz Claiborne, Inc.*

Claiborne label has proven that the firm knows its customers well and produces quality clothing that they want to buy and at the price they are willing to pay. Today the company is the largest women's apparel manufacturer supplying better sportswear to major department and specialty stores. It controls an estimated one-third of the $2 billion market for better women's sportswear, and is the number-one or -two selling line at most department stores it supplies. Liz Claiborne women's apparel produces annual sales averaging over $400 per square foot, which is twice the department store average ("Ms. Fashion," *Business Week*, January 16, 1989, p. 64).

Other reasons for its success are that the company does not have its own manufacturing plants or a traveling sales force. Lack of factories has given it more production flexibility than its competitors. Not having a road sales force has enabled the company to focus on building orders from large department stores, whose buyers are accustomed to traveling to the New York market. Both of these factors mean that Liz Claiborne has less overhead than many of its competitors, which has assisted in the rapid growth of the company.

Since its establishment in 1976 with only one sportswear line, the company has added several divisions. In 1981 it added the Petite Sportswear Division; in 1982 the Dress Division; in 1984 Girls' Sportswear. In 1985 three divisions were added: Lizwear, a more casual sportswear line, the Menswear Division, and the Petite Dress Division. In 1986 the company purchased its Accessories Division, which has been licensed to Kayser-Roth. Also added in 1986 was a fragrance called Liz Claiborne. In 1989 plans were formulated to enter the large-size market under the brand name Elisabeth.

Liz Claiborne products are conceived and marketed as designer apparel. Clothing is updated and fashion-forward without being trendy. Although clothing is considered upscale, it is priced in the upper moderate or better range. Liz Claiborne successfully combines traditional or classic design with contemporary fashion influences such as blazer jackets in bright fashion colors. Each sportswear collection includes an extensive selection of blouses, skirts, jackets, and pants as well as jeans, knit tops, and shirts. Although all items are sold as separates, they are coordinated through the use of related styles, colors, and fabrics so that the customer can assemble outfits. Color schemes are offered over an extended period so that the Liz Claiborne customer can coordinate her wardrobe with items from past seasons.

Offices and showrooms for Liz Claiborne, Inc. are located on seven floors of 1441 Broadway in the center of the New York garment district, and the company has warehouse facilities in Secaucus, New Jersey. Because it does not own any manufacturing facilities, it contracts with independent manufacturers in the United States and abroad with much of the apparel produced by firms located in the Far East. A full-time overseas staff of 300 coordinates and ensures the quality of the production of six collections a year.

Many of the fabrics used by Liz Claiborne are also sourced abroad. In an interview conducted by *Women's Wear Daily*, Arthur Ortenberg explained the reasons why Liz Claiborne shops world markets for its fabrics and production (Marvin Klapper, "Ortenberg Tells Why Claiborne Shops Abroad," *Women's Wear Daily*, February 4, 1978, pp. 1, 18). Lower price was cited as one reason, but

Ortenberg described an interconnecting set of circumstances involving both textiles and apparel production. These circumstances included lack of availability of certain types of fabrics in the United States, lack of sewing facilities in the United States capable of handling Claiborne's requirements for as many as 120,000 units at once, and the outstanding quality of some overseas producers.

The company works closely with retailers selling its products. It has a reputation for prompt delivery and high sell-through rates, meaning that few markdowns are needed to sell the merchandise. In fact, an estimated 75 percent of Liz Claiborne merchandise sells at full price compared to less than 50 percent for many competing lines. To better serve both retailers and consumers, Liz Claiborne developed a computerized system that tells what styles, sizes, and colors have sold in a cross section of stores each week. This enables the company to quickly identify customers' preferences.

A desire to serve the consumer also encouraged Liz Claiborne to produce more seasonal lines a year and to provide stores with clothing that the customer can purchase and wear immediately. This has led to the production of new lines every two months.

To assist with marketing its products, Liz Claiborne has developed the shop-within-a-store concept where Claiborne apparel, shoes, and other accessories are sold together. The first of these shops was opened in the flagship stores of Jordan Marsh in Boston and Marshall Field in Chicago.

Liz Claiborne has followed the apparel industry trend toward vertical integration by opening its own retail stores called First Issue. Thirteen stores were opened in 1988 with plans for twenty by 1990. First Issue apparel is casual, inexpensive women's sportswear designed to compete with clothing chains such as the Gap and the Limited. The merchandise is designed by a separate Liz Claiborne division and is not available in stores other than First Issue.

In February 1989 Elisabeth Claiborne Ortenberg, chairman and chief executive officer, and her husband, vice chairman, announced their retirement. The new chairman is Jerome A. Chazen, who joined Liz Claiborne in 1977 and played an active part in the development of the company.

The American Fashion Industry's Fight Against Imports

The competition of increasing imports is changing the way the U.S. textile and apparel industries operate. Domestic firms increasingly devise innovative operational and marketing techniques and work to increase consumer awareness of the origin of products. Both producers and trade unions have sought increased consumer awareness and support.

An early effort to fight against imports by the ILGWU was the use of the union's theme song, "Look for the Union Label," in a multimedia advertising campaign involving newspapers, radio, and television. The song was used to make the public aware that goods made by union members in America enhance the job security of fashion industry workers.

As discussed in Chapter 4, the American Textiles Fiber Apparel Coalition, a group composed of apparel and textile industry and labor associations, launched an advertising campaign in 1983 to make consumers and retailers aware of the quality and value of American-made products. The name of this campaign was "Crafted with Pride in the U.S.A." In April 1984 the Crafted with Pride Council was incorporated to unite the traditionally fragmented apparel and textile industries around the common cause of promoting merchandise made in the United States.

Another fashion industry strategy for fighting imports is Quick Response, also discussed in Chapter 4. The program was developed to shorten the time needed to get merchandise through the textile-apparel pipeline from producers to the retailer. Quick Response is beginning to change the way that large companies operate and when in operation has led to more efficient production and distribution of products.

Summary of Key Points

1. One of the major problems facing the apparel and textile industries is the rising competition from imported merchandise. The United States is now importing more than 50 percent of its apparel needs.

2. American manufacturers produce fashion goods in foreign countries by agreeing to production packages, having garments sewn offshore, and involving more than one country in the segments of production.

3. The U.S. government regulates fashion imports by means of quotas and import duties.

4. The Tariff Classification Act of 1962, Section 807, provides for special duty treatment of garments that have been cut in the United States, shipped outside the country for further processing, and then brought back.

5. American textile and apparel producers are concerned with unfavorable trade deficits. In 1987 the trade deficit for the textile and apparel industries was $20.7 billion.

6. Major suppliers of textile goods to the United States are Japan, Italy, South Korea, China, and Taiwan.

7. Key reasons why U.S. retailers purchase foreign-made fashion goods are exclusivity, prestige, quality, and lower prices.

8. Emphasis on private-label merchandise has encouraged many retailers to work with foreign suppliers. Foreign producers are often willing to work with retailers to produce goods to meet the retailers' specifications.

9. Both foreign and domestic sources for purchasing foreign-made goods are available to retailers. Methods of buying goods without making foreign buying trips include buying from domestic import trade fairs and from wholesale importers, which include import merchants, resident sales agents, and import commission houses.

10. Whereas many American producers want to restrict imports, retailers favor free trade.

11. Examples of government efforts to control the growth of imports include the Multi-Fiber Textile Arrangement (MFA), the Footwear Industry Revitalization Program, the Multilateral Trade Agreement, and the Textile and Apparel Export Expansion Program.

12. The American fashion industry has developed programs such as Crafted with Pride in the U.S.A. and Quick Response to combat the growth of imports.

13. A multilateral agreement, the General Agreement on Tariffs and Trade (GATT), was established in 1948 to liberalize and govern world trade.

Key Words and Concepts

Define, identify, or explain each of the following:

balance of trade

bilateral treaties

commissionaires

customs broker

duties

exports

export merchant

export sales representative

free trade

freight forwarding agent

General Agreement on Tariffs and Trade (GATT)

import commission house

import merchant

imports

landed cost

maquiladoras

Multi-Fiber Textile Arrangement (MFA)

offshore production

production package

protectionism

quotas

resident sales agent

Section 807

specification buying

tariffs

trade deficits

Discussion Questions and Topics

1. What methods are used by American manufacturers to produce goods abroad?

2. What advantages does offshore production offer to U.S. apparel manufacturers?

3. Why has the United States generally followed a policy avoiding excessive restrictions on foreign trade?

4. How do countries attempt to regulate imports?

5. Why does the United States exempt some countries from quota allowances?

6. How is country-of-origin determined for imported products?

7. Discuss the Tariff Classification Act of 1962, Section 807. What advantages does it offer U.S. manufacturers?

8. Why has U.S. penetration of foreign markets been limited? What are manufacturers doing to increase the sale of American-made apparel abroad?

9. Explain balance of trade. Why does the United States have such large trade deficits for textiles and apparel?

10. Why has apparel produced by many low-wage countries increased in quality?

11. What countries are the primary suppliers of textiles and apparel to the United States?

12. What are the reasons retailers buy foreign-made fashion goods?

13. Discuss the advantages and disadvantages of buying foreign-made goods by direct means.

14. Discuss the special problems inherent in buying foreign-made fashion merchandise.

15. Discuss the foreign and domestic sources used by retail buyers to purchase foreign-made merchandise.

16. What steps has the U.S. government taken to respond to the needs of the textile and apparel industries?

17. What has the fashion industry done to fight increasing imports of fashion merchandise?

Notes

Standard and Poor's Industry Surveys, August 27, 1987, p. T83.

U.S. Bureau of the Census, 1986.

U.S. Industrial Outlook, 1986, 1988.

PART IV

RETAIL DISTRIBUTION OF FASHION

FASHION products are distributed to the ultimate consumer by retailers who purchase goods from manufacturers or wholesalers with the intent of reselling the goods at a profit. In the process of buying and selling goods, retailers often provide a medium for disseminating information and stimulating demand for fashion products. Today's retailers must listen to consumers and respond to their concerns to remain profitable. Successful retailers know that they must identify consumer preferences even before consumers themselves know what they desire. Because of their close association with the customer, retailers are often the first to recognize changing consumer demand and have a responsibility to share this information with fashion producers.

Part IV provides information about the retail firms that distribute fashion goods; the merchandising activities involved in retailing fashion goods; the methods used to create a fashion image and promote fashion goods; and trends in retail merchandising. Key topics covered by the seven chapters include the following:

The historical development of retailing and the many types of retail businesses and shopping centers that distribute fashion merchandise.

The organizational structure of retail stores, the key functional areas of retailing, and a description of store ownership.

The kinds of retail buyers, a description of the buyer's job responsibilities, and how the buyer's performance is evaluated.

The role of resident buying offices, including the different types of offices, how they are organized, and the services they provide to retail store buyers.

How the buyer determines consumer demand and the process for planning to buy.

The process of buying the merchandise, including making buying contacts, identifying and selecting resources, planning and making the market trip, selecting the merchandise, and negotiating the purchase.

Creating a fashion image and how the activities of sales promotion are used to project a store's image to the public.

Trends in retail merchandising emphasizing retailers' responses to increasing competition, dealing with an identity crisis in retailing, new forms of retail distribution, increasing globalization of retailing, and changing consumer buying patterns.

CHAPTER 11 —————————————

FASHION RETAILING

THE BRIDGE between the producer and the ultimate consumer of fashion goods is the retailer. Ultimately everyone in the fashion industry relates to the retailer in some way. **Retailing** simply defined is the distribution of goods and services to the ultimate consumer; therefore, retailing is the center around which the marketing of consumer goods revolves. The retailer acquires goods from the manufacturer or wholesaler and presents them to the consumer in as convenient and attractive a manner as possible. The end goal of the retailer is a satisfied customer, and in today's highly competitive retail market the retailer is constantly striving to give the customer a reason for choosing his or her store. The first rule that the retailer should remember in merchandising is to make the store as easy and as pleasant a place for the customer to shop as possible. With many stores carrying similar or identical merchandise, the customer selects the store that offers desired services or provides the atmosphere preferred by the customer.

This chapter discusses the historical development of retailing in the United States and defines the various types of retail businesses that sell fashion goods. Types of stores include department stores, chain stores, discount and off-price stores, variety stores, specialty stores, and boutiques. Nonstore retailing, including direct selling and catalog retailing, is presented. Also discussed are shopping centers and malls.

Types of Retail Businesses

Today several kinds of retail businesses in the United States sell apparel and accessories for men, women, and children as well as home fashions. Although specialty stores and department stores are most important in selling fashion apparel, accessories, and home furnishings, such fashion merchandise is also sold by supermarkets and drug, discount, and variety stores. All of these stores sell goods to the consumer "over the counter." Goods are also sold to consumers through other means, including catalog sales (mail order), door-to-door sales, and vending machines. All of these methods are also considered retailing. Retailing, remember, is defined as the distribution of goods and services to the ultimate consumer. It includes both over-the-counter and direct-sales methods of selling.

Stores are often classified by the type of merchandise they sell and how they sell it. Some stores sell a wide variety of goods; others specialize in limited lines or in only one type of product. Some stores offer few customer services and emphasize discount prices; others offer many services designed to assist the customer in purchasing merchandise.

A store that offers a wide variety of merchandise lines representing a broad product mix is classed as a **general merchandise store**. These stores have in common a wide range of merchandise lines, often including food, apparel, accessories, hardware, and home furnishings. General merchandise stores all attempt to provide consumers with the convenience of one-stop shopping. They range in size from the large urban department store to the rural general store. Also considered general merchandise stores are junior department stores, discount stores, and variety stores.

Department Stores

The **department store** is well known by the consumer. If you ask a consumer to name a department store, chances are that he or she can name stores located in many cities even though that person has never visited these stores. The names of large stores are recognized because they are widely advertised and promoted. Consumers who read fashion magazines such as *Vogue* and *Harper's Bazaar* become familiar with the names of the major fashion stores that advertise in these magazines. A mystique often accompanies the names of stores such as Bloomingdale's, Macy's, Marshall Field, and Neiman-Marcus. Many people have definite impressions of these stores without ever having entered their doors.

Movies, novels, and plays have popularized certain stores. Names such as Neiman-Marcus, Bloomingdale's, and Tiffany's are used to suggest style and fashion. Sometimes consumers' perceptions of stores are incorrect because of what has been projected by books and movies. For example, some people think that meals are served at Tiffany's on Fifth Avenue in New York because of the Truman Capote novel and movie made from it, *Breakfast at Tiffany's*.

Prestigious stores are often included in itineraries of visiting dignitaries. Queen Elizabeth II of Great Britain went to Bloomingdale's when she visited the United States in 1976. Prince Charles visited Marshall Field's State Street flagship store in Chicago in 1986 in support of a special event featuring British merchandise that was taking place at the store. Tourists often include a visit to local retailers when vacationing in a city. As Macy's New York advertises, "If you haven't seen Macy's, you haven't seen New York."

A department store is a large-scale retailing institution that sells a wide variety of goods. The department store's name comes from the fact that merchandise is offered for sale in separate units or departments. Related kinds of merchandise are grouped into departments for purposes of promotion, service, and control. The U.S. Department of Commerce defines department stores as "establishments normally employing 25 people or more, having sales of apparel and soft goods combined amounting to 20 percent or more of total sales, and selling each of the following lines of merchandise: (1) furniture, home furnishings, appliances, and radio and TV sets; (2) a general line of apparel for the family; and (3) household linens and dry goods." An establishment with total sales of less than $5 million in which sales of any one of these three lines is greater than 80 percent of total sales is not classified as a department store.

Conventional Department Stores

The Department of Commerce also differentiates the **conventional department store** from discount and national chain department stores by specifying that conventional department stores are establishments that satisfy the criteria of a department store and usually provide checkout service and customer assistance within each department. Conventional stores may also have a catalog order desk but are not affiliated with a company that operates similar establishments on a national basis.

Because the conventional or traditional department store emphasizes fashion and service, it targets customers in the middle to upper-middle income brackets with fairly large discretionary incomes. It gives these customers a place to shop for the entire family's personal and household needs. The conventional department store is the most widely recognized form of department store. Examples of this type of store are New York–based Bloomingdale's, Marshall Field in Chicago, Woodward & Lothrop in Washington, D.C., Atlanta–based Rich's, Houston–based Foley's, and Emporium-Capwell in San Francisco.

Today many department stores are no longer independently owned but are owned by large corporate ownership groups. These groups are retail organizations in which member stores are centrally owned and controlled in terms of broad policymaking but are operated and merchandised autonomously. The individual stores usually retain their own names when purchased by an ownership group, and the general public is often unaware of the store's affiliation with the group. These ownership groups are discussed in Chapter 12.

Branch Stores

A retail trend among department stores that accelerated in the 1950s was the addition of the **branch store**. Initially branch stores were smaller stores located in the suburbs. These smaller retail units were satellites of a larger **parent store,** which was usually located downtown in the central business district. Today, frequently, the downtown store has grown smaller in terms of square footage and sales volume than any of the branch stores. This has occurred because shopping patterns have shifted to suburban store locations. Some department stores have even closed their older downtown stores and moved the store's administrative offices elsewhere.

A type of branch store is the **twig**. This is a relatively small store that carries a selection of its parent store's merchandise, generally targeting a specific customer. For example, a large store may open a twig near a university campus carrying merchandise that appeals to college students. Another example would be a twig opened in a hotel or airport carrying gift items or a limited selection of apparel targeted toward the tourist or conventioneer. Twigs are classified as department stores only because they are owned and operated by department stores.

Flagship Store

When a store has branches, the store in which the operating executives are found is called the **flagship store**. Often this store is the original downtown store, and it houses the executive, merchandising, and promotional personnel responsible for the centralized operation of the entire retail company. A flagship store is also called a parent store.

Basement Store (Budget Store)

Another term sometimes used in relation to the department store is the **basement** or **budget store**. The basement store is a division of the store that is organized separately from the main store departments. It handles merchandise in lower price lines, features frequent bargain sales, may purchase less-than-first quality merchandise, and usually offers a much more limited range of services and breadth of assortment than the main store departments. The name *basement store* comes from the fact that most such low-price divisions of the traditional department store in the northern part of the United States are actually located in the store's basement. Sometimes the name *budget store* is used rather than basement store.

In recent years many department stores have discontinued carrying basement merchandise and no longer operate a budget store. Competition from discount and off-price stores has caused conventional department stores to emphasize moderate and better-priced merchandise.

Special Types of Department Stores

Other types of stores that may be classified as department stores include the junior department store, chain department store, and specialty department store. Each of these stores operates with separate departments but does not carry the full merchandise lines of a conventional department store.

A **junior department store** is not as large in size as the usual conventional department store and does not carry as full a range of merchandise. It carries soft goods (family apparel), housewares, gifts, and home textiles. The merchandise is presented in a departmentalized form of organization. Major appliances and furniture are not included in the offerings. Price lines are usually in the moderate range. Examples of these stores include Anthony's, Bealls, and Belk Stores. Small locally owned department stores often fit the definition of a junior department store.

The **chain department store** category includes the general merchandise stores of Sears Roebuck, Montgomery Ward, and J. C. Penney, sometimes referred to as "The Big Three." In recent years these stores have assumed many of the characteristics of the traditional department store. Another type of chain department store is the **discount store,** including such stores as K mart, Wal-Mart, Target, and Zayre. Although characterized by low margins and self-service, these stores sell general merchandise in great varieties. Today many conventional department stores have also become chains as they have added many branch stores, and some now have stores located in several states.

The **specialty department store** carries a narrower assortment of merchandise than does the conventional department store. Goods are often concentrated at the high end in terms of price and fashion. These stores usually carry apparel and accessories for men, women, and children, as well as soft goods for the home, and gifts. Examples of specialty department stores are Bergdorf Goodman, Bonwit Teller, Saks Fifth Avenue, Neiman-Marcus, Nordstrom, and I. Magnin. Today many of these stores have locations in more than one city. Saks Fifth Avenue and Neiman-Marcus, for example, have become national chains. Many large specialty stores have broadened their merchandise assortment to appeal to a more moderate income-level customer. Still, they target a more specific customer than does the conventional department store and often have a strong fashion image. The stores given as examples all target a high-income customer. Some specialty department stores such as Mervyn's target a moderate-income customer and carry less fashion-forward merchandise. Specialty department stores are also referred to as **departmentalized specialty stores.**

Top One Hundred Department Stores

Annually in July *Stores* magazine publishes a list of the top one hundred department store divisions and companies. The list includes both traditional and specialty department stores (see Table 11.1 for a listing). Excluded from the listing are general merchandise chains, catalog chains, discount stores, mass merchandisers, and specialty stores.

In compiling the top one hundred department store list, *Stores* borrows from the U.S. Department of Commerce definition of a conventional department store. To be eligible, a store must have checkout service and salespeople within each department; may have a catalog order desk; and must not be a national general merchandise chain. *Stores* does not, however, define the merchandise lines as the government does. According to *Stores'* definition, the ranking includes "traditional department stores and multi-department soft goods stores (specialized department stores) with a fashion orientation, full markup policy and operating in stores large enough to be shopping center anchors."

Several large departmentalized specialty stores are now included in *Stores'* ranking of the top 100 department store divisions. Among such stores for 1987 were Nordstrom, Saks Fifth Avenue, Neiman-Marcus, I. Magnin, Jacobson's, and Bergdorf

Table 11.1 Top 100 U.S. Department Store Divisions for Fiscal 1987

Rank	Company/Division (headquarters)	Affiliation	Units	Volume (000,000)
1.	Dillard's (Little Rock)	(Ind)	135	$2,206.3
2.	Nordstrom (Seattle)	(Ind)	56	1,920.2
3.	Macy's (New York)	(RHM)	23	1,780
4.	Macy's (New Jersey)	(RHM)	26	1,635
5.	Dayton Hudson (Minneapolis)	(DH)	37	1,552.3
6.	Macy's (California)	(RHM)	25	1,450
7.	Foley's (Houston)	(Fed)	38	1,170
8.	Bloomingdale's (New York)	(Fed)	16	1,120
9.	Saks Fifth Avenue	(Bat)	44	1,110
10.	The Broadway (Southern California)	(CHH)	43	1,090
11.	Marshall Field (Chicago)	(Bat)	25	988
12.	Lazarus (Cincinnati)	(Fed)	44	945
13.	Lord & Taylor (New York)	(May)	46	938
14.	Neiman-Marcus (Dallas)	(NMG)	22	890
15.	May Co. (California)	(May)	34	853
16.	Burdines (Miami)	(Fed)	29	850
17.	Abraham & Straus (Brooklyn)	(Fed)	14	805
18.	Bullock's (California)	(Fed)	29	775
19.	Emporium-Capwell (San Francisco)	(CHH)	22	710
20.	Rich's (Atlanta)	(Fed)	20	710
21.	Hecht's (Washington)	(May)	23	700
22.	Jordan Marsh (New England)	(All)	25	690
23.	Maas Brothers/Jordan Marsh Florida	(All)	38	615
24.	Robinson's (Los Angeles)	(May)	24	576
25.	Macy's Atlanta	(RHM)	16	575
26.	Hess's (Allentown, Pa.)	(CAC)	71	516.6
27.	The Bon (Seattle)	(All)	40	515
28.	Sterns (New Jersey)	(All)	27	506
29.	Carson Pirie Scott (Chicago)	(CPS)	19	505
30.	Woodward & Lothrop (Washington, DC)	(WL)	16	500.1
31.	Famous-Barr (St. Louis)	(May)	17	496
32.	Kaufmann's (Pittsburgh)	(May)	14	480
33.	Strawbridge & Clothier (Philadelphia)	(Ind)	13	450
34.	John Wanamaker (Philadelphia)	(WL)	15	411.1
35.	P.A. Bergner (Milwaukee)	(Ind)	31	410
36.	Filene's (Boston)	(Fed)	18	410
37.	Gayfer's (Mobile, Ala.)	(MS)	12	375
38.	L.S. Ayres (Indianapolis)	(May)	18	374
39.	Thalhimer's (Richmond)	(CHH)	24	365
40.	Maison Blanche (Baton Rouge, La.)	(Ind)	17	360
41.	McAlpin (Cincinnati)	(MS)	9	360
42.	McRae's (Jackson, Miss.)	(Ind)	28	344
43.	Boscov's (Reading, Pa.)	(Ind)	14	337
44.	G. Fox (Hartford)	(May)	10	330
45.	Jacobson's (Jackson, Mich.)	(Ind)	21	327
46.	I. Magnin (San Francisco)	(Fed)	25	325
47.	Higbee's (Cleveland)	(IEPL)	12	312
48.	Elder-Beerman (Dayton)	(Ind)	24	302
49.	Younkers (Des Moines)	(Eofl)	37	291.7
50.	Liberty House (Honolulu)	(Amf)	9	283.5
51.	Ivey's (Charlotte)	(Bat)	24	280
52.	D. H. Holmes (New Orleans)	(Ind)	19	274.9
53.	Joseph Horne (Pittsburgh)	(Ind)	16	265

Rank	Company/Division (headquarters)	Affiliation	Units	Volume (000,000)
54.	Castner-Knott (Nashville)	(MS)	11	253
55.	May (Denver)	(May)	14	246
56.	Parisian (Birmingham)	(Hook)	16	243.1
57.	Jones Store (Kansas City)	(MS)	8	240
58.	Weinstock's (Sacramento)	(CHH)	12	240
59.	Meier & Frank (Portland)	(May)	8	238
60.	May Co. (Cleveland)	(May)	9	236
61.	Joslin's (Denver)	(MS)	11	232
62.	Frederick & Nelson (Seattle)	(Ind)	15	230
63.	B. Altman (New York)	(Hook)	6	215
64.	The Broadway Southwest (Phoenix)	(CHH)	11	210
65.	Steinbach's (White Plains, NY)	(Amc)	29	195
66.	Gayfer's (Montgomery)	(MS)	6	185
67.	Goldsmith's (Memphis)	(Fed)	6	180
68.	H. C. Prange (Sheboygan)	(Ind)	21	178
69.	ZCMI (Salt Lake)	(Ind)	10	177.6
70.	O'Neil's (Akron)	(May)	8	177
71.	Donaldson's (Minneapolis)	(CPS)	15	175
72.	Sibley's (Rochester)	(May)	11	171
73.	Goldwaters (Phoenix)	(May)	9	161
74.	Bacon's/Roots (Louisville)	(MS)	7	160
75.	Bonwit Teller (New York)	(Hook)	12	160
76.	Gottschalk's (Fresno)	(Ind)	14	156.6
77.	J.B. White (Augusta)	(MS)	7	155
78.	Hahne's (Newark)	(May)	8	148
79.	Miller & Rhoads (Richmond)	(Ind)	16	145
80.	Bergdorf Goodman (New York)	(NMG)	1	130
81.	Adam Meldrum Anderson (Buffalo)	(Ind)	10	120.6
82.	Pomeroy's (Pennsylvania)	(Ind)	11	120
83.	Garfinckel's (Washington)	(Ral)	10	120
84.	Lion (Toledo)	(MS)	3	115
85.	Crowley-Milner (Detroit)	(Ind)	11	113.7
86.	Beall's Florida (Bradenton)	(Ind)	37	112.3
87.	Stone & Thomas (Wheeling)	(Ind)	19	110
88.	Buffum's (Long Beach)	(Ind)	16	110
89.	Hutzler's (Baltimore)	(Ind)	9	92
90.	Sage-Allen (Hartford)	(Ind)	13	84.7
91.	Harris' (San Bernardino)	(Ind)	6	82.5
92.	May—Florida (Jacksonville)	(May)	5	80
93.	Hennessey's (Billings)	(MS)	5	70
94.	McCurdy & Co. (Rochester, NY)	(Ind)	7	68
95.	Uhlman's (Bowling Green, Ohio)	(Ind)	33	47.7
96.	Proffitt's (Alcoa, Tenn.)	(Ind)	5	45.9
97.	Carlisle's (Ashtabula, Ohio)	(Ind)	10	43
98.	Dey's (Syracuse)	(Ind)	4	36.5
99.	Swezey's (Patchogue, NY)	(Ind)	3	35
100.	Loveman's (Chattanooga)	(Ind)	5	35
101.	Watt & Shand (Lancaster)	(Ind)	2	33.3

Affiliation code: *All,* Allied Stores; *Amc,* Amcena Corp; *Amf,* Amfac Corp; *Bat,* Batus Retail Group; *CAC,* Crown American Corp; *CHH,* Carter Hawley Hale; *DH,* Dayton Hudson Corp; *Eofl,* Equitable of Iowa; *Fed,* Federated Department Stores; *Hook,* Hooker Development; *IEPL,* IEPL Holding Co; *Ind,* Independent; *May,* May Department Stores; *MS,* Mercantile Stores; *NMG,* Neiman Marcus Group; *RHM,* R. H. Macy & Co Inc; *Ral,* Raleigh's; *WL,* Woodward & Lothrop.

Reprinted from *Stores* magazine © National Retail Merchants Association, 1988.

Goodman. Prior to 1986 these stores appeared on *Stores'* Top 100 Specialty store list rather than the department store list.

The reason cited by *Stores'* for making this change was that specialty department stores have more in common with traditional department stores than with chain specialty stores. It is important in retailing to compare what a store is doing with its competitors, and it is more valid for such stores as Saks Fifth Avenue and Neiman-Marcus to compare themselves with traditional department stores than with specialty chains such as The Limited or Casual Corner. According to Joan Bergmann, editor of *Stores* magazine, "store size, expense structure, merchandise lines, departmental structure, ways of operating are much more similar in the departmentalized specialty stores than in the narrowly focused specialty stores" (*Stores* 1987).

Discount Stores

Discount stores are retail establishments that offer merchandise at prices below the recognized market level. Discount retailers are not easily defined because of the diversity of their operations. Generally the term **discounter** is used in the trade to identify a store that undersells other retail stores by emphasizing self-service and using other devices to control expenses. Discounters are typically volume-oriented and are distinguished primarily by an emphasis on price. Expense-saving techniques employed by these stores include no or limited services, such as alterations, delivery, mail or telephone orders; low-rent locations; and limited return privileges. By eliminating customer services and reducing various operational expenses, discounters can operate profitably on lower margins than other types of retail stores.

Discount stores borrowed many of their merchandising techniques from supermarkets. During the 1930s supermarkets began offering lower food prices by utilizing self-service selling displays, low-rent locations, inexpensive fixtures, and selling on a cash-and-carry basis. The early discounters offered large and small appliances at below manufacturers' list prices. Because of fair trade laws in existence at that time, such a practice was illegal. Customers, however, were drawn to the often out-of-the way locations of the stores because they could easily compare products and recognize the value received.

During the 1950s many of the early hard-goods discounters began adding limited lines of soft goods and apparel to their assortments. Discounters followed their customers to the suburbs and began to trade-up apparel offerings and stress fashion as well as price.

Along with efforts to trade-up, discounters began to use the term **mass merchandiser** to describe themselves. A mass merchandiser has come to mean retailing on a large scale with staple goods at prices lower than those found in conventional department and specialty stores. Mass merchandising is characterized by emphasis on (1) products whose market is not highly segmented, (2) customers who are willing to sacrifice sales assistance and store service in return for lower prices, (3) high volume and rapid stock turnover, and (4) a highly competitive marketplace. Examples of mass merchandisers or department store discounters include K mart, Wal-Mart, and Target. Sometimes the large general merchandise chains of Sears Roebuck and Montgomery Ward are also considered mass merchandisers because they merchandise to mid-America or the mass market. *The Buyers' Manual* refers to Sears, Ward's, and Penney's as mass merchandise chains (Cash 1979).

Off-Price Retailers

Mass merchandisers or discounters are not the only form of of discount stores. The specialty discount apparel store or the **off-price store,** has been in existence since the 1920s. Alexander's and Loehmann's are two New York–based stores known for discounting apparel. Early discount retailers believed that success could be found in either of two directions: one in providing customers with every imaginable service and charging them accordingly; the other in cutting services to bare essentials and sharing the savings with the customers. **Off-price retailers** followed the second direction.

One of the oldest and best-known off-price fashion stores is Loehmann's. The original Loehmann's opened in Brooklyn, New York, in 1920. Today Loehmann's is one of the largest retail discount chains in the country specializing in women's apparel. Frieda Loehmann, the store's founder, sought out the best buys on Seventh Avenue, purchasing overcuts, odd lots, and samples. She paid cash on the spot to get the best price—a practice still followed by Loehmann's buyers.

A number of the stores listed in the National Retail Merchants Association's annual listing of the top one hundred specialty chains are off-price apparel specialty stores. Examples include Marshall's, T. J. Maxx, Ross Stores, Burlington Coat, Pic n' Save, Loehmann's, Hit or Miss, Syms, and Clothestime.

During the late 1970s and early 1980s, off-price retailing became the fastest growing segment of retailing. Conventional department and specialty stores became concerned with the competition as these stores often carried brand-name merchandise at lower prices.

Both discount and off-price retailing are the selling of merchandise, often brand names, at less-than-regular prices. There is a slight difference, however, between off-price and discount retailing in terms of how the merchandise is acquired. In discount retailing the discounter pays the same price for merchandise as everyone else and sells it for less than traditional retailers, whereas with off-price retailing, merchandise is purchased at cut-rate prices and the savings are passed on to customers. Off-price retailers specialize in making special purchases, including manufacturers' surplus stock, overcuts, distress merchandise, closeouts, and job lots. Although technically there is a slight difference in meaning between discount and off-price retailing, the terms are often used interchangeably. Most off-price retailers stress branded merchandise in their assortments, which are a mix of current and out-of-season goods. Some also sell merchandise that they have developed themselves and have had produced to sell under their own private brand names.

One special type of off-price retailer is the **factory outlet store.** Originally the term meant a manufacturer-owned store often located at the factory site or nearby. The factory outlet was just that, a place where unwanted inventory could be sold.

These stores sold production overruns, merchandise returned from retailers, irregular, and second-quality goods. Today the term *factory outlet* is being used by a variety of off-price or discount stores that may sell in-season, first-quality merchandise from more than one manufacturer. Factory outlet stores are often located in factory outlet malls competing directly with traditional retailers.

Wholesale Warehouse Clubs

One of the newer formats in discount retailing is the **wholesale warehouse club,** which combines the concepts of wholesaling and retailing. The first wholesale warehouse club in the United States was the Price Company founded in San Diego in 1976 by father and son, Sol and Robert Price. The Price Company, also known as the Price Club, began as a cut-rate wholesaler to small retailers and businesses, which paid a $25 annual fee. Later, membership was broadened to include consumers who were government employees or members of certain credit unions and banks. Consumers pay no membership fee but are charged 5 percent over the marked wholesale price of merchandise.

Since 1982 other retailers have followed the direction of the Price Company and have opened warehouse clubs. Some of these stores have been founded by discount department store firms, such as Sam's Wholesale Clubs founded by Wal-Mart Stores and BJ's Wholesale Clubs established by Zayre Corporation. In 1987 sales of 328 wholesale warehouse clubs totaled $12 billion, advancing rapidly from 1983 sales of approximately $1 billion.

These stores sell a limited selection of brand-name goods on a cash-and-carry basis. Stores are typically located in warehouse buildings with concrete floors and high ceilings allowing for high steel warehouse shelving. Merchandise is offered in bulk quantity and is displayed stacked in packing cartons or on pipe racks. The decor is "no frill" as are the services. Credit or delivery services are not offered nor are there the usual store amenities of restrooms and paper bags. Little advertising or promotion is done. Price is the primary appeal to the customers.

Warehouse clubs are basically in the commodity business, not the fashion business. They combine the selling of commodity products such as groceries with hardware and soft goods. Typical merchandise includes food, liquor, sundries, housewares, appliances, electronics, hardware, and automotive products. Some warehouse clubs carry furniture and plants. Although certainly not fashion stores, warehouse clubs do sell some basic apparel items and footwear as well as home textiles such as sheets and towels. All merchandise carried by warehouse clubs is brand name because these stores do not carry private-label merchandise.

Wholesale clubs are expected to have their biggest impact on supermarkets, small wholesalers, and appliance stores. Yet these stores are representing a new competitive force for traditional department stores and discounters. Warehouse clubs are providing a new form of competition for consumers' disposable dollars, and traditional retailers are concerned that their market share will be reduced because of the expansion of these stores.

Hypermarkets

The latest entry into the discount market is the **hypermarket,** which is basically a wholesale club for consumers. It combines the conventional discount store with a supermarket into one super-size store ranging from 225,000 to 300,000 square feet on one level. Like warehouse clubs, hypermarkets feature a broad assortment of commodity goods, general merchandise, and food in a simple, self-service atmosphere. The stores, however, are less warehouselike than wholesale clubs are. Shopping in hypermarkets is like shopping in a gigantic discount department store.

Hypermarkets were pioneered in France in the late 1960s. The first to open in the United States was Bigg's in Cincinnati. Wal-Mart and K mart both joined forces with grocery stores to open hypermarkets beginning in 1987. Approximately 60 percent of the volume of these stores is in groceries. Like wholesale warehouse clubs, hypermarkets compete with traditional department and specialty stores for the consumer's dollar. The stores sell basic items of brand-name apparel.

Variety Stores

The **variety store** carries a variety of merchandise in the low and popular price range, such as stationery, gift items, women's accessories, toilet articles, light hardware, toys, housewares, and confectionery. Originally called "five and ten" or "dime stores," variety stores now stock a wide range of product classifications but in a limited number of assortments. Fashion merchandise is found in their assortments primarily in basic utilitarian articles such as underwear, T-shirts, scarves, and simple hair and dress ornaments.

Most variety stores are chains. Examples include F. W. Woolworth, T. G. & Y., Ben Franklin, and M. E. Moses. At one time every downtown had at least one of these stores. Today much of the variety store business has been taken over by discount houses, drug stores, and grocery stores.

Specialty Stores

The **specialty store** is defined as a store that concentrates on specific classifications of merchandise. These stores carry limited lines of apparel, accessories, and/or home fashions. Examples are a shoe store, accessories store, hosiery store, or a store carrying apparel and accessories for men, women, and/or children. A specialty store has a merchandise assortment narrower than a department store and a more clearly defined market segment as its target. Merchandise is selected to meet the demands of the store's target customer. Although the term *specialty store* tends to suggest high fashion and high price, the target customer may be the budget or moderate-price customer as well. A specialty store usually seeks to have broad and shallow assortments within the merchandise classifications carried. A broad and shallow assortment means that the store offers the customer a wide variety of styles from which to choose, but only stocks a few of each item.

The term *specialty store* covers a wide variety of different stores, such as mom-and-pop stores, chain specialty stores, boutiques, and departmentalized specialty stores. These different types vary widely in size, price emphasis, and merchandise carried.

Mom-and-Pop Stores

The **mom-and-pop store** is a small specialty store run by the proprietor and possibly a few employees. Often these stores are operated by a husband and wife, which explains the derivation of the name. These stores are found in every community, large and small. They usually have no branches and do not belong to a chain. According to the U. S. Census, there are more stores of this type than of any other kind. The sales of mom-and-pop stores, however, total less than 50 percent of the total sales volume of all specialty stores.

Chain Specialty Stores

Although the majority of specialty stores are individually owned, such stores may belong to a chain and consist of tens or even hundreds of stores spread throughout the country. Examples of chain specialty stores found in many shopping centers from coast to coast are those owned by The Limited, including The Limited, Limited Express, Lerner's, and Lane Bryant. Other widely distributed chain specialty stores are Casual Corner, Ups 'N' Downs, Gap stores, County Seat, Chess King, Foxmoor, Paul Harris, and the Children's Place.

Boutiques

A boutique is a type of specialty store that sells fashion apparel and accessories selected for a very specific customer. In French the term means "little shop," but in American retailing the term may be applied to a small specialty store or to an area within a larger store where the emphasis is on merchandise selected for a specific customer type. Boutiques present merchandise in an attractive and unified manner often with an atmosphere of individualized attention from the sales personnel. The term *boutique* is especially associated with small shops that carry few-of-a-kind merchandise, generally in fashion-forward or extreme styling, and presented in a creative manner. Boutiques may be described as having a distinct personality and appealing to a customer who also is distinctive.

The original boutiques were found in France where couture designers offered a select group of accessories designed to accompany the designer's apparel creations. Although few categories of merchandise were offered, the merchandise was highly coordinated to complete the total fashion look for the designer's customer.

Boutiques became popular in the United States and England during the early 1960s as an outgrowth of the antiestablishment "do your own thing" attitude of the times. Boutiques carried the off-beat clothing popularized by the avant-garde youth of the population. They provided one-stop shopping where a specialized customer could find outerwear and accessories that expressed both the store's and the customer's personality.

Department stores and large specialty stores adopted the boutique concept of merchandising. These stores added boutiques each designed to meet the needs of a specific customer type. Some of the boutiques carried unusual merchandise appealing to the avant-garde customer; others pulled together the total look for the high-fashion customer. Department stores even carried the boutique concept into home fashions, housewares, gourmet food, and menswear.

The boutique concept continued to be popular as European couture designers entered ready-to-wear production and selected stores to carry their lines in the United States. Yves Saint Laurent's licensing of boutiques for his Rive Gauche collection is an example.

Many department and specialty stores today present each designer's line in a separate department or boutique. In addition, it has become popular for both American and European designers to open their own boutiques. Yves Saint Laurent opened his Rive Gauche boutique on Madison Avenue in New York in 1968, beginning the change from mom-and-pop stores along Madison Avenue to European designer boutiques. By the mid-1980s numerous European designer boutiques had appeared along Madison Avenue between 65th and 75th Streets, including such names as Givenchy, Gianni Versace, Giorgio Armani, Emanuel Ungaro, Sonia Rykiel, Valentino, and Daniel Hechter.

Located in the downtown SoHo area of New York are many independently owned fashion boutiques. SoHo extends south from Houston Street five blocks to Canal Street and west from Mercer Street five blocks to Sullivan Street. Owners of the SoHo boutiques often design and produce all or part of their merchandise. Some also operate their own workrooms for custom production. These boutiques offer unusual merchandise too limited in appeal for mass production. Store decor and fixturing are often creative, innovative, and expressive of the store's personality.

The first clothing stores to open in SoHo beginning in the mid-1970s were run by designer-craftspeople. As rents increased many of the original designers moved away, but other fashion boutiques moved in. One such shop is Parachute, opened in 1980 by architect Harry Parnass and British designer Nicola Pelly to sell their own line of clothing. Located in the store's basement is a showroom that sells to buyers from stores such as Bergdorf Goodman and Neiman-Marcus. One of the oldest shops in the area is Le Grand Hotel/Tales of Hoffman. Conceived as a showcase for new American talent, it specializes in women's party clothes ranging in price from $225 to $5,000 for beaded and sequined gowns. The shop also sells shoes and handmade jewelry.

Many cities have an area where boutique stores are concentrated. Often the area also includes art galleries and restaurants. Some boutiques are found in city areas where rents are lower, whereas high-fashion designer boutiques may be concentrated in more expensive areas. One of the most exclusive shopping streets with numerous designer name boutiques is Rodeo Drive in Beverly Hills, California.

Today the term *boutique* is often misused by being applied to a small specialty store that does not truly carry unique merchandise or accessories. Thus it is often incorrectly used to describe a small specialty store that carries women's apparel.

Top One Hundred Specialty Stores

Each August *Stores* magazine publishes a list of the top one hundred specialty retailers (see Table 11.2). *Stores'* list no longer includes the large departmentalized specialty stores. As discussed earlier, these stores are now included in *Stores'* list of the top one hundred department stores. Included in the specialty list are companies specializing in a variety of fashion products such as apparel, jewelry, shoes, and textiles. Other stores on the list carry home fashions such as domestics and furniture. Stores carrying nonfashion hard lines, such as books, consumer electronics, appliances, and toys, are also part of the specialty store list.

All of the apparel stores listed among *Stores'* top one hundred specialty stores are units of a chain. Stores include companies with a discount pricing policy as well as regular-price stores. The two largest volume specialty stores are The Limited and Mervyn's. The Limited listing includes all eight divisions owned by the company, not just the stores with The Limited name.

Chain Stores

A chain store consists of a group of stores, usually a dozen or more, that are commonly owned and centrally merchandised and managed. Each store in the chain carries similar if not identical merchandise lines, and stores are very similar in appearance. Chains may be national, regional, or local. There are department store chains, specialty store chains, variety store chains, and discount store chains. Some specialty chains carry exclusive fashion-forward merchandise at high prices; others focus on fashion for the masses at popular prices. Specialty chains focus on a certain size, age, or income group.

Characteristics of chain stores include:

1. Decisions regarding store operations and merchandising are made from a central headquarters office.

2. Buying is done from a central headquarters office.

3. If stores are divided into regions, they report to the central office.

4. Store units are similar in appearance and merchandise lines carried.

5. Ownership, management, control, and policymaking are centralized.

6. Chain stores do not have a flagship or parent store as do multiunit specialty or department stores.

National chain specialty stores selling apparel are often located in shopping centers or malls. These stores tend to do little advertising and rely on their key shopping center locations to draw traffic. They appeal to a specific target market. During the late 1960s and early 1970s, stores of this type often sought the eighteen-to-twenty-five-year-old customer or the teenager. Today their market has grown older, and many are carrying apparel targeted for the working woman. Some of the largest multiunit chain specialty stores in women's apparel are The Limited, Casual Corner, and Lane Bryant.

As noted earlier, the big three general merchandise or department store chains are Sears Roebuck, Montgomery Ward, and J. C. Penney. These stores are literally merchants to millions of people, selling a wide variety of hard and soft goods. A unique characteristic of these stores is that they mass produce and market much of their own merchandise.

The advantage of the chain store system comes from volume. Because these stores buy tremendous dollar amounts of merchandise, they wield considerable power in the marketplace. Their buyers are said to write with a "big pencil," meaning that they place orders in very large dollar figures.

Franchise Stores

In a franchising agreement, a manufacturer sells the rights to retail a product within an area. With a **franchise store,** an agreement is made between a franchiser (market supplier) and a franchisee (retail owner/operator) giving the franchisee the right to operate a specific business, using an established store name and merchandise within a trading area. The franchiser agrees to provide the retailer with assistance in organizing, training, store operations, and merchandising. The uniform appearance of most franchise stores gives the customer the impression that the stores are members of a chain. However, each store is run by an individual owner/operator.

The Singer Sewing Machine Company introduced the franchise store in 1863. Another of the early franchisers was General Motors, and the automobile industry remains one of the strongest users of franchising. The major growth in the franchise industry began in the 1950s with the introduction of many food franchisers such as McDonalds and Kentucky Fried Chicken. Many service agencies were also franchised, including auto repair services, motels, and car rental agencies.

Beginning in the 1960s franchise stores in apparel retailing were slow to develop but became more popular during the 1980s. Some examples of franchise stores include Lady Madonna and Mothercare, both maternity specialists, and Benetton, an Italian knitwear specialist. Examples of high-fashion designer franchise stores or departments within department stores include Yves Saint Laurent's Rive Gauche boutiques, Ralph Lauren's Polo Shops, and Charles Jourdan shoe stores.

Leased Departments

The **leased department** is a common practice among department stores, large specialty stores, discount department stores, and chain stores. Under a lease arrangement, the store rents space to an outside firm, which runs the designated department.

Table 11.2 Top 100 U.S. Specialty Stores for Fiscal 1987

Rank	Company/Chain (Headquarters)	Parent	Type	Sales (000,000)	Units
1.	The Limited (Columbus, Ohio)	(Ind)	Apparel	$3,528	3,095
2.	Mervyn's (Hayward, Cal.)	(DH)	Apparel	3,183	199
3.	Toys "R" Us (Rochelle Park, N.J.)	(Ind)	Toys	3,137	350
4.	Radio Shack (Fort Worth)	(Tan)	ConsEl	2,950	4,820
5.	Kinney Shoe (New York)	(FWW)	Shoe	2,055	2,450
6.	Marshall's (Woburn, Mass.)	(Mel)	Apparel	1,603	256
7.	Circuit City (Richmond, Va.)	(Ind)	ConsEl	1,350	105
8.	Petrie Stores (Secaucus, N.J.)	(Ind)	Apparel	1,242	1,601
9.	T.J. Maxx (Framingham, Mass.)	(TJX)	Apparel	1,200	265
10.	Volume Shoe (Topeka, Kan.)	(May)	Shoe	1,065	2,436
11.	Gap Inc. (San Bruno, Cal.)	(Ind)	Apparel	1,062	815
12.	Zale (Dallas)	(People)	Jewelry	909	1,262
13.	Levitz (Miami)	(Ind)	Furn	879	105
14.	Waldenbooks (Stamford, Conn.)	(Kmt)	Books	760	1,260
15.	Highland Superstores (Plymouth, Mich.)	(Ind)	ConsEl	753	72
16.	Child World (Avon, Mass.)	(Ind)	Toys	749	152
17.	Brown Shoe (St. Louis)	(BrGr)	Shoe	665	1,369
18.	Herman's (Carteret, N.J.)	(Ind)	SptGds	650	241
19.	Charming Shoppes (Bensalem, Pa.)	(Ind)	Apparel	639	840
20.	Lechmere (Woburn, Mass.)	(DH)	HrdGds	636	24
21.	Kay Bee (Lee, Mass.)	(Mel)	Toys	610	676
22.	Casual Corner (Enfield, Conn.)	(USS)	Apparel	586	737
23.	Silo Electronics (Philadelphia)	(Dix)	ConsEl	578	162
24.	Ross Stores (Newark, Cal.)	(Ind)	Apparel	576	131
25.	Musicland (Minneapolis)	(Ind)	Records	510	623
26.	Thom McAn (Worcester, Mass.)	(Mel)	Shoe	499	1,007
27.	Burlington Coat (Burlington, N.J.)	(Ind)	Apparel	491	20
28.	Edison Bros. Shoe (St. Louis)	(EB)	Shoe	445	1,150
29.	Brooks Fashion (New York)	(Dyl)	Apparel	445	866
30.	B. Dalton (Minneapolis)	(BD)	Books	445	575
31.	Best Buy (Minneapolis)	(Ind)	ConsEl	439	40
32.	Federated Group (City of Commerce, Cal.)	(Atar)	ConsEl	435	60
33.	Hartmarx Specialty (Chicago)	(Hmx)	Apparel	420	233
34.	C.R. Anthony (Oklahoma City)	(Ind)	Apparel	416	247
35.	Edison Apparel (St. Louis)	(EB)	Apparel	399	1,085
36.	Pier One (Fort Worth, Tex.)	(Ind)	Home-Furn	372	396
37.	Kay Jewelers (Alexandria, Va.)	(Ind)	Jewelry	366	385
38.	Pic n' Save (Carson, Cal.)	(Ind)	Apparel	362	126
39.	Ups 'N' Downs (Cincinnati)	(USS)	Apparel	356	834
40.	Lionel (Philadelphia)	(Ind)	Toys	341	78
41.	The Talbots (Hingham, Mass.)	(GM)	Apparel	338	126
42.	Tandy Brand Names (Fort Worth)	(Tan)	ConsEl	335	293
43.	Loehmann's (New York)	(May)	Apparel	334	80
44.	Oshman's (Houston)	(Ind)	SpGds	333	213
45.	Hit or Miss (Staughton, Mass.)	(TJX)	Apparel	330	485
46.	Bealls (Jacksonville, Tex.)	(Ind)	Apparel	323	149
47.	House of Fabrics (Sherman Oaks, Cal.)	(Ind)	Textiles	322	672
48.	Spencer Gifts (Atlantic City, N.J.)	(MCA)	Giftware	320	435
49.	Crazy Eddie (Edison, N.J.)	(Ind)	ConsEl	316	42
50.	Barnes & Noble (New York)	(BD)	Books	306	44
51.	LensCrafters (Cincinnati)	(USS)	Eyewear	305	241
52.	Heilig-Meyers (Richmond, Va.)	(Ind)	Furn	304	258
53.	Hancock (Tupelo, Miss.)	(Ind)	Textiles	298	346

Rank	Company/Chain (Headquarters)	Parent	Type	Sales (000,000)	Units
54.	Top Appliances (Edison, N.J.)	(Ind)	ConsEl	280	2
55.	Wherehouse Entertainment (Torrance, Cal.)	(Ind)	ConsEl	275	212
56.	Rhodes (Atlanta)	(Ind)	Furn	274	89
57.	Fabri-Centers (Cleveland)	(Ind)	Textiles	267	636
58.	County Seat (Dallas)	(CPS)	Apparel	265	338
59.	Weiner's Stores (Houston)	(Ind)	Apparel	265	120
60.	Richman Brothers (Cleveland)	(FWW)	Apparel	263	299
61.	Brooks Brothers (New York)	(All)	Apparel	260	65
62.	Filene's Basement (Boston)	(Fed)	Apparel	260	22
63.	Syms (New York)	(Ind)	Apparel	257	22
64.	Chess King (Worcester, Mass.)	(Mel)	Apparel	255	553
65.	Merry-Go-Round (Towson, Md.)	(Ind)	Apparel	255	432
66.	Seaman's (Carle Place, N.Y.)	(Ind)	Furn	254	30
67.	Fretters (Livonia, Mich.)	(Ind)	ConsEl	250	47
68.	Foxmoor (New York)	(Dyl)	Apparel	250	607
69.	Florsheim (Chicago)	(Int)	Shoe	250	525
70.	Ann Taylor (New York)	(All)	Apparel	249	99
71.	Gordon Contemporary (Houston)	(GJC)	Jewelry	247	433
72.	W.S. Badcock (Mulberry, Fla.)	(Ind)	Furn	247	251
73.	Newmark & Lewis (Hicksville, N.Y.)	(Ind)	Appl	242	46
74.	Fayva (Newton, Mass.)	(Morse)	Shoe	242	489
75.	J. Byrons (Miami)	(Amc)	Apparel	235	55
76.	Hahn/Banister (Cincinnati)	(USS)	Shoe	228	383
77.	The Wiz (New York)	(Ind)	ConsEl	220	24
78.	Haverty (Atlanta)	(Ind)	Furn	218	80
79.	Cloth World (St. Louis)	(BrGr)	Textiles	215	306
80.	Audio/Video Affiliates (Dayton, Ohio)	(Ind)	ConsEl	212	117
81.	American TV (Madison, Wis.)	(Ind)	ConsEl	210	6
82.	Lamonts (Seattle)	(Ind)	Apparel	200	33
83.	Brueners (San Ramon, Cal.)	(Bat)	Furn	200	17
84.	Deb Shops (Philadelphia)	(Ind)	Apparel	189	273
85.	Pic 'n Pay (Charlotte, N.C.)	(Bata)	Shoe	193	731
86.	Reliable Stores (Columbia, Md.)	(Ind)	Furn	190	148
87.	Paul Harris (Indianapolis)	(Ind)	Apparel	190	368
88.	Dress Barn (Stamford, Conn.)	(Ind)	Apparel	188	302
89.	Art Van (Warren, Mich.)	(Ind)	Furn	180	15
90.	Clothestime (Anaheim, Cal.)	(Ind)	Apparel	179	347
91.	Linens 'n Things (Roseland, N.J.)	(Mel)	Domestics	176	144
92.	Wickes Furniture (Wheeling, Ill.)	(Wic)	Furn	175	18
93.	Crown Books (Landover, Md.)	(Ind)	Books	169	205
94.	Kuppenheimer (Atlanta)	(Hmx)	Apparel	168	207
95.	The Children's Place (Pine Brook, N.J.)	(Fed)	Apparel	165	190
96.	Sound Warehouse (Dallas)	(Ind)	ConsEl	162	107
97.	Tiffany (New York)	(Ind)	Jewelry	155	8
98.	Sussex Group (Secaucus, N.J.)	(Ind)	Furn	154	20
99.	Value City (Columbus, Ohio)	(Ind)	Furn	150	32
100.	Roberds (Dayton, Ohio)	(Ind)	Furn	150	9

Affiliation code: All, Allied Stores; Amc, Amcena; Atar, Atari; Bat, Batus Retail Group; BD, B. Dalton & Co; BrGr, Brown Group; CPS, Carson Pirie Scott; DH, Dayton Hudson; Dix, Dixon PLC; Dyl, Dylex; EB, Edison Brothers; Fed, Federated Department Stores; FWW, F. W. Woolworth; GJC, Gordon Jewelry Corp; GM, General Mills; HMX, Hartmarx; Ind, Independent; Kmt, K mart Corp; May, May Department Stores; Mel, Melville; People, People Jewellers; Tan, Tandy; TJX, TJX Cos; USS, U.S. Shoe.

Reprinted from *Stores* magazine © National Retail Merchants Association, 1988.

FASHION RETAILING _____

The leasing company has full responsibility for merchandising and operating the department. The store provides the space and necessary support services. In most cases the customer is not aware that a department is leased because it follows basic store policies and conforms to the store's overall image.

Departments requiring specialized knowledge to operate or are expensive to stock are most often leased. Among fashion stores certain merchandise and service departments are often leased. Services commonly leased include the beauty salon, shoe or jewelry repair, the photography department, and restaurants. Fashion merchandise departments that are most often leased include shoes, fine jewelry, and furs. Some budget women's ready-to-wear departments located in discount department stores are also leased.

When a store leases a department, its investment is minimal because the inventory is owned by the lessee. This often enables a store to offer merchandise to the customer that the store could not afford to purchase on its own. The primary disadvantage of leasing, from the store's perspective, is the difficulty that may be encountered in maintaining the store's fashion image with an outside organization managing the department.

Nonstore Retailing

Not all fashion merchandise is sold through retail stores. **Nonstore retailing** means that goods and services are sold to consumers by such methods as direct selling, electronic retailing, and catalog or mail-order retailing. Such methods offer the retailer the advantage of avoiding the overhead expenses of a store building, fixtures, equipment, display space, or retail stock space.

Direct Selling

Direct selling firms sell their products directly to the consumer without an intervening middleman. Direct selling uses the door-to-door approach or in-home party plan to sell merchandise that is not available through retail stores. Products commonly sold by this method include cosmetics, encyclopedias, and cookware. Fashion fabrics, apparel, accessories, lingerie, and gifts are also sold by direct sales.

In the fashion business two well-known direct sales firms are Avon and Mary Kay. Both sell cosmetics, but Avon has broadened its merchandise lines to include jewelry and apparel. The two companies use different approaches to sell their products. Avon sells primarily door-to-door; Mary Kay uses the party plan.

The party plan enables a salesperson to demonstrate products to several people at a time. The party may be held in the home of the salesperson or more often is held in a customer's home. Friends of the customer are invited to attend a party where products are demonstrated, and customers place orders for merchandise. The party hostess usually receives a gift for holding the party or may receive a discount on purchases placed. Sometimes the hostess gift varies depending on the dollar value of orders placed at the party.

Some retail stores also engage in direct selling by sending salespersons to call on customers in their homes. Interior designers from stores often go into homes to assist customers with their selection of floor coverings, window treatments, or home furnishings. Suggestions of additional furniture or accessories may result in added sales for stores. Wardrobe consulting is a service that retail stores have developed more recently to increase sales of apparel and accessories and provide service to customers. The consultant may visit the customer's home to assist with organizing her closet. The consultant makes recommendations concerning clothing to be discarded and additions needed to complete the customer's wardrobe.

Another form of direct selling is *street selling*. Street salespeople range from the driver of the Good Humor truck to vendors who set up booths on busy corners or simply spread their wares on the sidewalk. In some cities such selling is illegal; in others it is licensed. In New York City, for example, one finds a wide range of fashion items sold on the street, ranging from accessory items such as leather goods and jewelry to sportswear items such as T-shirts and jeans. Frequently, merchandise sold on the street consists of illegal counterfeit goods of inferior quality.

The vending machine is another form of direct selling. Although vending machines are currently used to distribute a wide variety of general merchandise and food items, they are not important in selling fashion apparel or accessories. However, vending machines have been used to sell blue jeans and T-shirts.

Electronic Retailing

A new type of direct retailing has emerged in the 1980s—**electronic retailing,** which uses computer, television, and telephone technologies in marketing and merchandising. A study conducted by the accounting firm Touche Ross, released May 26, 1987, predicted that electronic shopping could be a $5 billion to $8 billion business by 1990. Although still in its infancy stage, electronic retailing offers tremendous possibilities for the future.

Television shopping has already become popular with some home viewers. Several home shopping television networks have emerged on cable TV or on the public networks. Most popular products sold through television catalog programs are jewelry, gifts, and home electronics. A limited selection of apparel is being sold. Much television shopping at this time uses a price-cutting approach to selling the goods. When viewers see an item they wish to purchase, they telephone in the order, which is then shipped to them. Some cable TV systems are interactive, allowing viewers to place the order directly through their television sets.

Another form of electronic retailing takes place through interactive computers. Shoppers view merchandise descriptions and visuals on their personal computer screen and place an order directly with the computer shopping service. CompuServe Information Service based in Columbus, Ohio, has developed a successful computer shopping service called the Electronic Mall. Shoppers enter the Electronic Mall using a personal computer and a telephone modem. Once connected, they can browse through a comprehensive product index or a directory of all Mall merchants. They can scan a complete listing of merchandise categories or go directly into specific stores. Questions are answered by the Mall Manager, CompuServe's online representative. Shoppers can make requests by pressing a computer key and can purchase items using their credit cards. A bimonthly publication is mailed to all subscribers to the shopping service. Mall retailers can attract shoppers' attention by advertising in this magazine. CompuServe offers items from several leading retailers including Bloomingdale's, Neiman-Marcus, and Sears. CompuServe subscribers pay a fee for the use of the service.

As computer graphics improve in quality, computer shopping is expected to become a more popular means of shopping. Electronic shopping from the home is anticipated by some to replace both in-store and catalog shopping. This seems unlikely for fashion merchandise because consumers like to see, touch, and try on apparel and many accessories before buying. Also, shopping is often a social activity and is even a form of entertainment for many. For computer shopping to work, shoppers must have some preconceived ideas of what they want to buy. Window shopping just is not the same with electronic systems.

Computers are also being used in stores or in shopping malls to allow customers to place orders directly for merchandise. Such computers can offer the customer all available sizes and styles. The customer can view the merchandise and written specifications on a video screen and place an order through the computer to be delivered to the consumer's home or office; thus avoiding the need to deal with a salesperson or to return to a store to pick up the ordered merchandise.

Catalog Retailing

Catalog retailing is a form of selling in which the retailer provides the consumer with a catalog that illustrates and describes the merchandise offered. The consumer submits an order by mail, telephone, or in person at a facility maintained by the mail-order firm for that purpose. A mail-order firm by definition is a retail firm that sells to its customers through catalogs and makes most of its deliveries by mail or other common carrier.

Some mail-order firms sell exclusively through catalogs. Others may operate a retail store but do the majority of their business through the mail. Catalog retailing has been so successful that many conventional department and specialty stores have added catalog sales divisions to their companies. Catalogs have provided a way for these stores to expand their market area and increase company sales. Stores such as Bloomingdale's and Neiman-Marcus through their catalogs have many customers who never enter any of the company's stores.

A catalog may provide as wide a variety of merchandise as that offered by general merchandisers such as Sears and Penney's, or may be highly specialized, presenting only apparel or gift items. For example, L. L. Bean features sporting goods; Horchow, gift items; and Talbots, women's wear.

Today mail-order catalogs offer the customer the convenience of shopping at home at leisure. Many catalog firms provide toll-free telephone numbers and receive orders twenty-four hours a day, seven days a week. The use of credit through MasterCard, VISA, and American Express has made mail order even easier for the customer. One of the secrets of success of mail-order firms has been service, and

Catalog retailing has become a popular form of selling fashion apparel, accessories, and home furnishings.
Source: *Reprinted with permission of* Lands' End, L. L. Bean, Trifles, Honeybee, *and* Victoria's Secret.

most operate under a policy of customer satisfaction guaranteed with full refunds for returned merchandise.

By shopping at home the customer saves time and avoids the expense of driving to the store. Customers who are housebound, dislike driving in traffic, or have limited time for shopping find that anything can be ordered from a catalog firm. There are specialty catalogs today for almost anything the customer can imagine, from apparel to home furnishings, hardware, food items, and gardening supplies.

Classifying retail firms as to type is not always easy. Many of the store types overlap, and it may be possible to classify a store as more than one type. As retailing changes, the characteristics of the various store types change as well. A store may begin as one type of store but may gradually grow and mature into another type. A fact about retailing is that no store can remain stagnant and remain in business. As customers change, so must retail stores.

Shopping Centers

As automobiles clogged downtown streets and encouraged the growth of suburban communities, retailing changed with the times. Downtown stores began to establish outlying branches with free parking, and shopping centers developed. Specialty stores led the way and were the first to open branches in the suburbs. I. Magnin, San Francisco, provided leadership by opening its first branch in Santa Barbara, California, in 1912, following with a second branch in Pasadena the next year.

In Chicago, Marshall Field was one of the first department stores to move to the suburbs when it opened a free-standing branch in Lake Forest, Illinois, in 1928, quickly followed by two other branches. On the West Coast, Bullock's and The Broadway were the leaders, opening branches in 1929 and 1930, respectively. In the East, stores leading the movement to the suburbs in the 1930s were Strawbridge and Clothier in Philadelphia and B. Altman in New York.

One of the earliest planned shopping centers in the United States was Country Club Plaza in Kansas City, Missouri, opened in 1923. This was the first integrated suburban shopping center of any size in the United States. Under a single landlord, it had a wide variety of tenants and provided off-street parking. Starting with small, locally owned stores, the center expanded to include regional and national apparel, department, and variety store chains.

Another of the early shopping centers was Highland Park Village, built in 1931 in suburban Dallas, Texas. This center was the second in the nation to use a single style of architecture for all of its stores. The Spanish-style store fronts turned inward and were grouped about a court with parking available in front of the stores.

Although shopping centers originated in the early 1930s, it was not until after World War II that major expansion took place. During the 1950s it was recognized that large, planned, controlled centers rather than free-standing stores were the key to meeting American shopping needs. Among the first planned regional shopping centers were Town and Country, which opened in Columbus, Ohio, in 1949, and

Northgate, built in Seattle by Allied Stores and opened in 1950. The first big shopping center in the East was Shoppers World in Framingham, Massachusetts, opened in 1951. Many additional regional shopping centers were built during the 1950s, including Northland located north of downtown Detroit, Evergreen Plaza in Chicago, and Lakewood Center in Los Angeles.

Suburban shopping center development in the 1950s was encouraged by a number of factors.

1. The post–World War II baby boom brought an expanding population whose needs could not be met adequately by downtown and neighborhood stores.

2. Middle-class families moved out from the cities to the suburbs.

3. Average incomes of consumers increased.

4. Tremendous growth occurred in the number of automobiles coupled with an increase in multicar families.

5. Mass transportation failed to meet the needs of cities with spreading suburbs.

6. Improved roads and freeway systems made it faster and easier for consumers to reach the shopping malls.

7. The five-day work week allowed increased leisure time for consumers.

8. Business facilities grew in the suburbs due to cheaper office space and greater convenience for workers.

9. Competition among stores increased the desire among department stores to be bigger, better, and newer than competitors.

10. Suburbs lacked community identity.

During the 1950s and 1960s shopping center developers built on the fringes of populated areas, and markets grew around them. This was the period of the postwar baby boom when many families were moving into new homes in the suburbs. Downtown areas were becoming congested and families wanted to shop in more convenient locations near where they lived.

In the 1960s the enclosed mall became the dominant trend in shopping centers. As new centers were enclosed, older open centers were often remodeled and enclosed and air conditioned, providing customers with a comfortable controlled shopping environment. It has been said that such shopping centers have changed the American way of life. Today the air-conditioned enclosed mall has become not only a place to shop but is also a community center. People go to the malls to be entertained, to eat, and to socialize. Because of the increasing popularity of such shopping malls, many downtown shopping areas ceased to exist during the 1960s and 1970s. Movie houses, restaurants, and stores moved to the suburban malls. Consumers found it much easier to go to the mall where ample free parking was available and where everything was under one roof. In addition to department stores and specialty stores, today's malls contain movie theaters, restaurants, video arcades, ice rinks, and community meeting rooms. Shopping centers attract shoppers by featuring special events such as plays, movies, concerts, mini-amusement parks, flea markets, fashion shows, seminars, and petting zoos. Also held in malls are numerous special exhibits such as art shows, antique shows, handicraft shows, and flower shows. All of the traditional promotions and special events held by department stores are now offered by shopping malls to attract customer traffic.

Although primarily a post-World War II phenomenon, today's shopping centers have roots that date back to ancient Greece and Persia. Among the forerunners of these centers are the bazaars of Persia, the agoras of ancient Greece, the forums of Rome, and the fairs and marketplaces of medieval Europe. Out of such ancient marketplaces grew small shops of merchants and craftspeople. The fairs of Europe, dating back to the tenth or eleventh centuries, brought together merchants from far-off exotic lands such as Arabia, Egypt, and Byzantium. Like some of today's shopping centers, such markets attracted artists, actors, singers, poets, and storytellers as well as merchants.

Even enclosed shopping malls are not a new idea. The Pardis des Femmes in Paris dates back to 1300, and London's Royal Exchange was built in 1566. One of the most famous and widely copied is the Galleria Vittorio Emmanuele constructed in 1867 in Milan, Italy, to revive the center of the city. The Galleria was designed with a large glass dome that covered two city streets lined by buildings containing shops and restaurants. The Galleria concept has been widely imitated throughout the United States with a number of shopping centers carrying the Galleria name.

Shopping Center Types

Today's planned shopping centers consist of three basic types: (1) neighborhood, (2) community, and (3) regional shopping centers. The **neighborhood shopping center** consists of a small strip of stores typically covering about three acres and ranging in size from 30,000 to 100,000 square feet. The anchor store is often a supermarket or drug store. Small independently owned specialty stores—the mom-and-pop stores— may be located in such neighborhood centers. These centers offer consumers who live in the area surrounding them convenient shopping by providing frequently needed convenience goods and services.

The **community shopping center** is of an intermediate size. In addition to convenience stores, it contains a variety, discount, or junior department store. Community centers range in size from 100,000 to 300,000 square feet and have a trading area of 40,000 to 150,000 people.

The **regional shopping center** serves a trading area of 150,000 or more people. This type is anchored by one or more large full-line department stores. Occupying 30 to 50 acres, the regional center includes from 300,000 to 750,000 square feet. Some regional centers today are super-regionals or mega-malls, having as many as six or eight large anchor department stores and consisting of 2,300,000 or even more square feet of gross leasable space.

In 1985 West Edmonton Mall in Edmonton, Alberta, Canada, became the

RETAIL DISTRIBUTION OF FASHION

largest shopping center in the world. This amazing mall has been described as "part shopping center, part amusement center, part zoo, part tropical garden." West Edmonton Mall has 3.8 million square feet of retail space and 5.2 million square feet overall. It includes 800 stores, an ice rink, Fantasyland indoor amusement park, movie houses, animal and bird exhibits, a ten-acre indoor water park, an indoor lake with four submarines, a miniature golf course, and Bourbon Street, an entertainment area with a New Orleans atmosphere. The mall is promoted as a place "where all your fantasies come true." This center is truly a community center where people can shop, relax, and be entertained. It attracts local residents as well as tourists who come to shop.

Another such mega-mall is Del Amo Fashion Center in Torrance, California, with 2.6 million square feet of retail space. Del Amo has eight anchor stores, including The Broadway, J. W. Robinson, Bullock's, Sears Roebuck, J. C. Penney, Montgomery Ward, I. Magnin, and Ohrbach's. Other huge regional centers are Lakewood Center Mall, Lakewood, California, 2,400,000 square feet; Roosevelt Field Mall in Garden City, Nassau County, New York, with 2,400,000 square feet; and Woodfield in Schaumberg, Illinois, near Chicago's O'Hare Airport with 1,900,000 square feet.

Shopping Center Layout Patterns

Shopping centers follow three basic layout patterns: (1) the strip, (2) the cluster, and (3) the mall. The strip center parallels the street with parking provided in front of the stores. This is the most common pattern and is widely used for neighborhood and community types of centers.

In the cluster arrangement, stores are grouped around a large central department store. The cluster is appropriate only where a single store dominates the center; it is the least-used layout for shopping centers.

The mall is the most popular layout for regional shopping centers. The mall groups retail stores near the center of the plot with parking surrounding the stores. Usually the stores face the center of the mall or pedestrian walkway. Such centers may be open-air, but today most are enclosed and air conditioned. Malls may be one level or multilevel.

Often found within a shopping mall are kiosks. A **kiosk** is an open gazebo or pavilion used for retail sales. Sometimes push carts are also used to gain additional selling space in a mall. Small items, seasonal merchandise, or food are often sold from push carts.

Downtown Shopping Centers

Although movement to suburban shopping malls during the 1960s and 1970s brought the demise of some downtown shopping areas, during the late 1970s and 1980s attention to downtown shopping areas returned in some cities with the construction of downtown shopping malls. A number of cities succeeded in revitalizing their downtowns by constructing enclosed malls and attracting people back to the center city to shop. Such shopping malls serve three groups of customers: (1) those who live downtown, (2) downtown workers, and (3) tourists or convention and business visitors.

America's first inner-city enclosed shopping mall was the Gallery, which opened in 1977 in downtown Philadelphia. It included more than 200 shops and restaurants on four levels linked by three major department stores, Strawbridge and Clothier, Gimbels, and J. C. Penney. The J. C. Penney store, built in 1983, was the first Penney downtown store to be built since World War II.

Another example of a major downtown shopping mall is Horton Plaza in San Diego, which was planned as a key element in the renaissance of the downtown area. Downtown San Diego had been without a major department store for some time prior to the opening of this 900,000-square-foot center in 1985. The center has four anchor stores, J. W. Robinson, Nordstom, Mervyn's, and The Broadway. Also included in the center are two legitimate theatres, movie houses, an art museum, a nightclub, several restaurants, and a farmer's market.

St. Louis sought to rejuvenate its fading downtown with the St. Louis Center, opening in 1985. This two-block enclosed shopping mall is anchored by Famous-Barr and Dillard's department stores.

In New Orleans the Fashion Mall at Canal Place brings upscale shopping to both tourists and residents. Anchored by Saks Fifth Avenue, the mall also includes Brooks Brothers and a variety of specialty stores such as Crabtree and Evelyn, Laura Ashley, Gucci, Ann Taylor, and Charles Jourdan. A second mall, anchored by Macy's and Lord & Taylor, opened in downtown New Orleans in 1988.

In Minneapolis a different approach has been used to make downtown shopping more attractive to people. Stores in Minneapolis are connected by what is called Nicollet Mall, a futuristic maze of twenty-five enclosed, temperature-controlled skyways. Among stores connected by the skyway system are Dayton's, Saks Fifth Avenue, and Brooks Brothers.

The success of downtown shopping centers has varied greatly. Although some have succeeded in bringing about a return to downtown shopping, others have attracted fewer customers.

The Vertical Center

Another approach to the urban shopping center is the vertical mall, consisting of multiple shopping levels much like large central city department stores. Examples of this type include Water Tower Place in Chicago and New York's Trump Tower and Herald Center.

Water Tower Place in Chicago is the largest vertical shopping center in the United States. It features eight levels of shopping and restaurants anchored by Marshall Field and Lord & Taylor. Above the stores are a luxury hotel and forty floors of condominium residences. Four levels of underground parking are available

Trump Tower is a well-known vertical urban shopping center located on Fifth Avenue in New York City.
Source: *Reprinted with permission of the Trump Corporation.*

for the convenience of shoppers. Water Tower Place is located on North Michigan Avenue, which is known as "the magnificent mile." Nearby stores on Michigan Avenue include Bonwit Teller, Bloomingdale's, Neiman-Marcus, Saks Fifth Avenue, and I. Magnin, making this area one of the strongest concentrations of prestige fashion stores in the United States.

New York City has two vertical urban shopping centers, Trump Tower and Herald Center. Trump Tower, located on Fifth Avenue next to Tiffany's, is anchored by Bonwit Teller. A six-tiered atrium with Italian marble walls, a waterfall, and greenery create a luxurious setting for exclusive and expensive merchandise. Doormen usher customers into a world of luxury and elegance. Also part of the Tower are sixty-eight stories of condominium residences.

Herald Center, which opened in 1985, is located in Herald Square at 34th Street, across from Macy's. This vertical center has nine levels, each designed to reflect a famous New York locale. Included are the Village, Herald Square, Fifth Avenue, Broadway, Madison Avenue, Central Park, Columbus Avenue, and SoHo. The top floor is named the United Nations Food Fair and presents foods from around the world.

Festival Marketplaces

Festival marketplaces, also called entertainment or theme shopping centers, are used to attract people to central city areas. Examples of these centers include St. Louis Union Station, Pier 17 in New York City, Ghiradelli Square and Pier 39 in San Francisco, Jax Brewery and the Riverwalk in New Orleans, Harbourplace in Baltimore, and Faneuil Hall in Boston.

Many of these shopping centers have involved use of historic buildings that might have otherwise been destroyed. Others are new construction built to look old. Such centers emphasize leisurely shopping, eating, and entertainment. The centers are designed to appeal to both tourists and city residents.

In St. Louis, what was once one of the busiest train stations in the United States has been turned into a 160,000-square-foot shopping center with about one hundred specialty shops and restaurants. Built in the late nineteenth century, Union Station provides an historical feeling for shopping and entertainment. On a smaller scale in Washington, D.C., the Old Post Office has been turned into 60,000 square feet of sixty shops and restaurants in an historic setting. In New Orleans the old Jax Brewery on Jackson Square is now a place to shop, eat, and view the Mississippi River.

The South Street Seaport and Pier 17 in lower Manhattan have revitalized New York's Fulton Fish Market area. South Street Seaport is an eleven-block area encompassing both new construction and renovation. Included are clothing and gift shops, restaurants, museums, and a multimedia show, "The Seaport Experience." Stores include Abercrombie and Fitch, Ann Taylor, Benetton, and Laura Ashley. In the area also are performers ranging from puppeteers, balladeers, and mimes to storytellers, dancers, and jugglers, all in the spirit of the ancient medieval marketplace.

Pier 17, part of the South Street area, is a 132,000-square-foot, three-story glass

Riverwalk in New Orleans is a festival marketplace that appeals to both tourists and city residents.
Source: *Reprinted with permission of Riverwalk, Inc.*

and steel structure built to look like an old pier. The eighty stores and restaurants draw local traffic as well as tourists to shop, be entertained, and enjoy the view of the Brooklyn Bridge, the East River, and the old shops that make up the South Street Seaport Museum.

In San Francisco, Pier 39 offers a similar environment for tourists and city residents. It houses two levels of restaurants, shops, a carousel, and a multimedia show, "The San Francisco Experience," which traces the history of the city. Also included as part of the forty-five-acre complex are a marina and a cruise fleet providing daily scenic cruises on San Francisco Bay. Located near Fisherman's Wharf, another popular tourist area, Pier 39 presents a turn-of-the-century theme that provides a relaxing atmosphere.

International Council of Shopping Centers

The **International Council of Shopping Centers** (ICSC), founded in 1957, is a trade association representing shopping centers. According to this organization, there were fewer than 3,000 shopping centers in the United States in 1957, and most were strip centers. By 1976 there were 18,000 shopping centers in the United States and Canada, and by 1985 there were 27,000.

Membership in the ICSC has grown steadily. In 1957 only thirty-six people attended the first convention in Chicago. When the second annual convention was held in New York in 1958, the ICSC had 118 members. By June 1963 the Council had more than 1,000 members. In 1985 Council membership numbered 13,150 with 12,000 in the United States, 900 in Canada, and 250 from other countries.

The ICSC has developed courses, institutes, and schools to prepare shopping center managers and marketing directors. The group's University of Shopping Centers grants Certified Shopping Center Manager and Certified Marketing Director diplomas. The ICSC also publishes books and periodicals dealing with shopping center information.

Historical Development of Retailing

The actual beginnings of retailing date back to when primitive peoples first began to produce or acquire goods for trade with others. As civilization developed, people found it easier to exchange goods through merchants, and modern retail stores evolved from the shops of early craftspeople and the stalls of itinerant merchants at fairs and bazaars. Today's version of the ancient outdoor bazaar is the shopping center, which provides customers the convenience of shopping for a wide variety of goods offered by different stores in one location. Sometimes the stores are located under a single roof, offering the customer the comfort of a controlled environment. Such shopping malls have become community centers providing a gathering place for customers where they can be entertained as well as shop.

Early American Retailing

America's early merchants and store founders included craftspeople of various kinds, importers, tailors, druggists, and peddlers (Mahoney and Sloane 1974, p. 5). The first retail selling in much of America was done by peddlers. A peddler led a strenuous, lonely, and even hazardous life as he traveled from place to place. Many peddlers grew tired of traveling, and as towns grew, they settled in a community and became shopkeepers. Many of the stores they established grew into noted specialty and department stores. Examples of stores still in operation today that were founded by peddlers included Rich's, L. S. Ayres, and Saks Fifth Avenue.

Andrew Saks became a peddler before saving enough money to open a men's clothing store in Washington, D.C. After founding additional stores in Richmond and Indianapolis, he moved to New York where he established Saks and Company on 34th Street near Herald Square. Gimbels acquired the Saks Company in 1924, and a year later Saks was relocated to Fifth Avenue and the name changed to Saks Fifth Avenue. Today Gimbels is no longer in business, but Saks Fifth Avenue has stores throughout the United States and is one of the nation's largest volume specialty department stores. Saks is now owned by Batus, a major store ownership group that also owns the Chicago-based Marshall Field and Company and the Charlotte, North Carolina–based Ivey's.

Many of the early retail stores were general merchandise or **dry goods** stores, which were very unlike today's elaborate department and specialty stores that sell fashion apparel and home furnishings. Dry goods stores took their names from shops run by New England merchants, many of whom in colonial times were ship owners and direct importers. Their two chief imports were rum and bolts of fabric, which were traditionally carried on opposite sides of the store. The fabric was referred to as *dry goods* and the rum as *wet goods* (Hendrickson 1979, p. 30). Dry goods became a broad term applied to merchandise made from textile fabrics. Included are piece goods, textile items of women's accessories and men's furnishings, and household textiles such as towels and sheets. Dry goods are also referred to as *soft goods*.

Early dry goods stores sold mainly staple and utilitarian products. In these general stores women could buy fabric and findings to sew apparel for family members. Little ready-to-wear was available. Fashionable apparel was produced primarily by Paris couture houses. In America tailors and dressmakers brought the sketches or the original Paris models and made reproductions for individual wealthy customers. Toward the end of the nineteenth century a few stores such as Marshall Field in Chicago, B. Altman and Bergdorf Goodman in New York, and I. Magnin in San Francisco did custom dressmaking. A number of stores established fashion reputations through their custom salons where expensive, fine-quality fashionable clothing was produced. Ready-to-wear was slow to develop and had to wait until the textile and apparel industries were advanced sufficiently to mass produce goods.

Custom-made clothing continued to be important for a few fashion retailers until the mid-twentieth century. By the mid-1970s, however, all major American fashion stores had discontinued their custom operations. Bergdorf Goodman in New York produced custom apparel for seventy years from 1888 to 1969. When the store closed its custom department in 1969, Andrew Goodman cited several reasons. Among them were (1) the rising cost of fabrics, (2) the shortage of skilled seamstresses, (3) dwindling customer demand for custom service, and (4) the fact that custom-made apparel had become so out of step with the times that to offer this service did nothing to enhance a store's fashion image. As *Women's Wear Daily* quoted Goodman at the time of the closing of Bergdorf Goodman's custom design department, "Custom-made clothes are of another era, another world, and have no relevance to today's times. They are anachronistic where opulence and self-indulgence are giving way to greater social awareness and consciousness" (*Women's Wear Daily* 1969).

The last major American store to discontinue custom design for women's apparel was I. Magnin in California, which closed its exclusive made-to-order salon in the Los Angeles Wilshire Boulevard store in 1976. This marked the passing of an era and brought an end to haute couture design operations in American high-fashion department stores.

Women were no longer willing to spend time having fittings. Why should they wait for a garment to be constructed when they could select from quality ready-to-wear and wear it immediately? As retailers found their customer base for custom apparel dwindling, the most important factor in their decision to discontinue offering it was the fact that the sale of this type of apparel was no longer profitable.

Development of Department Stores

American general stores reached their peak between 1820 and 1860 during a period when personal income was rising and population was growing rapidly. Department stores often grew out of general stores or specialty shops, which provided ladies with fabrics and findings for making apparel and accessories. By the middle of the nineteenth century, economic conditions and technological developments made the existence of the department store possible. Historians do not agree on which store was actually the first to become a department store. Advancement toward becoming a department store appears to have occurred more or less simultaneously in Paris, London, and New York. Credited with being among the first stores to reach department store status were the Ville de Paris and the Bon Marché in Paris, and William Whiteley in London. In the United States the earliest department stores included R. H. Macy and A. T. Stewart in New York, Wanamaker's in Philadelphia, and Marshall Field in Chicago. Joseph Nathan Kane in *Famous First Facts* claims that the first department store in America was Zions Cooperative Mercantile Institution (ZCMI) founded in 1867 in Salt Lake City, Utah. Each of these stores, undoubtedly, developed and popularized the department store during the 1870s.

One of the early merchants who helped develop the principles upon which the early department stores were developed was Aristide Boucicaut, founder of the Bon Marché in Paris. Boucicaut's first shop, which opened in 1838, sold piece goods and carried merchandise similar to that in other shops of the time. He soon added dresses, ladies' coats, underwear, millinery, and shoes—each sold in separate departments. By the 1850s the Bon Marché had begun to assume the proportions of a department store. In fact, it may have been the first store to qualify for the title of department store.

What was different about Boucicaut's store were his operating principles, which were opposed to the current practices of the dry goods trade of the period. Boucicaut followed four innovations, considered revolutionary for retail stores of the time:

1. He sold his merchandise at a small markup with the idea of compensating for the smaller gross margin by increasing his sales volume and causing a more rapid stock turn. The retail practice of the time was to sell merchandise at a high markup, providing a slow turnover.

2. He offered only merchandise with fixed marked prices assuring that all customers paid the same price for identical goods. The retail practice of the times was to bargain over prices. Boucicaut permitted no haggling between customer and clerk.

3. He ran his shop on the principle of free entrance. Potential customers could enter the shop and look at the merchandise without feeling obligated to buy. In other shops of the time the customer was expected to make a purchase upon entering the store.

4. He also introduced the practice of returns, allowing customers to exchange purchases or to have their money refunded upon return of the merchandise. The practice in other stores was all sales are final and "let the customer beware" (Pasdermadjian 1954, pp. 3–4).

American retailers were quick to follow the example set by Aristide Boucicaut in the Bon Marché. A. T. Stewart, John Wanamaker, R. H. Macy, Marshall Field, and other American retailers credited Boucicaut's advanced trading practices as the source of many of their ideas as their stores progressed from dry goods or specialty stores to department stores. These American retailers added another principle to those established by Boucicaut. They sold for cash and did not extend credit as was the custom among general merchandise stores and specialty stores of the time. This enabled them to operate more efficiently and maintain their lower markups.

During the 1870s a number of American stores expanded merchandise assortments and grew into department stores. American department stores continued to offer merchandise at a lower markup than other competing stores. They carried a far greater variety of merchandise lines than other stores and segregated their merchandise in separate selling departments. Department stores offered the customer convenience by permitting him or her to shop for many needs under one roof. These early department stores succeeded primarily because of two reasons: (1) they sold merchandise at a lower price, and (2) they offered shopping convenience.

The American department store was largely a product of the years between 1860 and 1914. During this time, economic conditions were favorable for the department store to develop. Availability of capital, low taxes, and cheap labor to build and staff stores contributed to their growth. Americans enjoyed an improved standard of living, which created a demand for more and better quality of goods and encouraged many merchants to expand their businesses during the years following the Civil War. The early department store customer was a member of the middle class. The increase in disposable income of the middle class during the nineteenth century was undoubtedly one of the factors contributing to the development of the department store.

Following the example set by the Bon Marché, many American stores grew and prospered. Several factors were necessary for these stores to succeed. Among these factors were (1) population growth and concentration of people in cities, (2) mass transportation systems to transport customers to city centers where stores were located, (3) more and better advertising, and (4) technical innovations in construction of buildings.

Population growth and concentration in cities was necessary to support larger stores. By 1860 American cities had increased greatly in size and many new cities were established that grew rapidly. Cities provided customers for the developing department stores located at their centers, and mass transportation systems made it possible for customers to reach the stores. Horse-drawn streetcars brought people from every section of town to shop in the stores. After 1880 electric streetcars and suburban railroad lines brought more people downtown to shop and got them there faster. By 1914 subways and motorized buses were being used in major cities.

More and better advertising helped merchants attract customers to their stores. The lowering of the price of paper in about 1830 made it possible for retailers to use larger advertisements and to add illustrations. Advertisements began to give specific information about merchandise carried by stores and made it possible for the customer to compare store offerings.

Technical innovations in building, including the use of iron, steel, and reinforced concrete, allowed construction of buildings with increased column spacings and with lightwells suited to the needs of larger stores. Building innovations provided a more open view of the store and impressed customers with the feeling of the size and unity of department stores. Larger, well-lighted space displayed the merchandise to greater advantage.

The coming of the electrical age in the 1870s contributed considerably to the rise of department stores. Stores began to install elevators and add electric lighting in the 1880s. Wanamaker's and Macy's both installed electric lights in 1878. John Wanamaker contacted Thomas Edison shortly after the inventor's first public demonstration of electric lighting concerning installation of lights in his Philadelphia store. The first day the lights were turned on, a crowd outside the store waited for it to explode. Several weeks passed before some customers felt safe to venture inside the store. In the early 1880s electric elevators permitted large stores to make more efficient use of space by using upper floors for selling. Wanamaker's became the first store in the country to use a ventilation fan system in 1882, which was the ultimate in cooling until Rich's in Atlanta became the first store to be completely air conditioned in 1937.

Other technical innovations that helped the department store grow in size and customer popularity included the telephone, the pneumatic tube system, and the cash register. All made the operation of large stores more effective and efficient.

Many stores built new buildings about the turn of the century, adding large display windows. Specialty stores also adopted some of the features of department stores, such as no bargaining over price, attractive displays, and increased stock turn. Department stores gained a stronghold on the middle-class shopper, whereas specialty stores catered to higher-income shoppers.

During the late 1880s new lines of merchandise were introduced and merchandise was grouped on the basis of related needs. Some stores even opened their own production and manufacturing units. Ready-to-wear became increasingly important at the cost of piece goods. Display techniques were advanced and advertising became increasingly important. Due to increasing competition, stores began to add services such as restaurants, restrooms, delivery, and personal shopping departments. Stores also began to send buyers to Europe to purchase the latest fashions and some opened permanent European offices. Macy's, for example, opened its first foreign office in Belfast, Ireland, in 1885 to take care of the Irish linens and laces that the store imported. In 1893 Macy's opened an office in Paris.

Founders of American Department Stores

The story of the development of the American department store is also the story of the great men who founded and built them. Pasdermadjian, in writing about the history of the department store, says:

> . . . that new form of distribution represented by the department store has been possible only on account of the economic and technical development of the 19th century. But these development have offered but the frame, the background of the stage. The department store as such has been the result of the energy and imagination of some men of exceptional ability, who had a strong sense of the needs of their time. It was their driving power, their grasp of essentials, and their willingness to take necessary risks which engendered the first large-scale retail establishments. (Pasdermadjian 1954, p. 8)

The founders of the large stores in the United States generally fall within three groups—those who came over from Great Britain during the period of great poverty to find opportunities in a new country, Jewish immigrants from oppression in Germany and eastern Europe, and descendants of Quaker families who settled in New England in the seventeenth century. The individual records of department stores prove this. Many businesses of a century or more ago were founded by young men often in their late teens or early twenties. Many of them started with nothing and built great institutions. Some of the men who laid the foundations for great stores were Alexander Turney Stewart, John Wanamaker, R. H. Macy, and Marshall Field.

Alexander Turney Stewart (1801–1876)

America's leading merchant in the middle of the nineteenth century was Alexander Turney Stewart, who founded one of America's first department stores. Born near Belfast, Ireland, he emigrated at age twenty to New York, and two years later, in 1823, he acquired a small dry goods store in New York City. His store expanded and in 1848 he built the fabulous Marble Dry Goods Palace located at Broadway and Chambers Street, the first example in America of so large a building devoted to retail trade. His store continued to expand until it extended for a whole city block on Broadway. Nothing like this huge store had been seen before, and people came from great distances to view it. In 1862 Stewart moved his store up Broadway between Ninth and Tenth streets. This was the first modern department store building in America. Consisting of eight floors and employing more than 2,000 persons, Stewart's Cast Iron Palace remained the largest store in the world for more than ten years (Hendrickson 1979, p. 36). At his death in 1876 Stewart left an estate of over $50 million. The great A. T. Stewart Company was eventually purchased by John Wanamaker, who operated it until 1922.

Stewart was a pioneer of the one-price system, assuring that all of his customers paid the same price for the same goods. He also hired handsome and courteous clerks to charm his women customers, and he sold quality merchandise, much of it imported from Europe. "I got it at Stewart's" was a phrase denoting value and satisfaction. Mary Todd Lincoln, President Lincoln's wife, purchased many of her clothes at Stewart's and redecorated the White House with goods from the store (Mahoney and Sloane 1974, p. 10).

John Wanamaker (1838–1924)

John Wanamaker probably brought the most important and original contributions to the development of the department store (Pasdermadjian 1954, p. 6). A son of a bricklayer, he became a partner in 1861 with his brother-in-law in the Oak Hall, a Philadelphia men's clothing store. Wanamaker expanded the business into a great department store by adding an endless series of new departments. He was also the first merchant to buy a full-page newspaper advertisement and personally wrote much of his own copy. He advertised in national magazines as well as in Philadelphia and New York newspapers. He earned the title "The Father of Modern Advertising."

Wanamaker revolutionized the storekeeping of his age by helping to establish in America the one-price system; originating the money-back custom by freely offering the public the privilege of returning goods that were unsatisfactory or unwanted; substituting hospitality for hostility in retailing; offering the freedom to shop without obligation to buy; making buying safe by guaranteeing the quality and the marking of merchandise and the accuracy of representation both by spoken and printed word.

Wanamaker was a merchant who believed that the Golden Rule of the New Testament was the Golden Rule of business as well. He was a religious man active in the Presbyterian Church, its Sunday school and foreign missions, and an active participant in the Y.M.C.A. Appointed postmaster general by President Benjamin Harrison, he abolished the mail privilege of lotteries, pioneered rural free delivery, parcel post, and postal savings, and fought for government ownership of telegraph and telephone.

As early as the Civil War, his famous money-back guarantee appeared in print. Wanamaker ran the following advertisement in 1865:

> Any article that does not fit well, is not the proper color or quality, does not please the folks at home, or for any reason is not perfectly satisfactory, should be brought back at once, and if it is returned as purchased within ten days, we will refund the money. It is our intention always to give value for value in every sale we make, and those who are not pleased with what they buy do us a positive favor to return the goods and get the money back (Mahoney and Sloane 1974, p. 11).

In 1878 Wanamaker moved his store to a vast Philadelphia freight depot and advertised his ground floor of nearly three acres as "the largest space in the world devoted to retail selling." His was the first store completely lighted by electricity. This store sold nearly everything. For a time Wanamaker's even sold airplanes and Ford automobiles.

Wanamaker's two sons, Thomas and Rodman, followed in their father's footsteps and became great retailers in their own rights. John Wanamaker continued to be an alert merchant as long as he lived. In 1920 when nearly eighty-two years old, he foresaw a postwar downturn in business. Though prices were at a peak, he ordered storewide 30 percent discount sales. On Saturday, May 8, 1920, more than $1 million worth of merchandise was sold—a world record up to that time.

John Wanamaker was a pioneer in employee training and the relations of a store to its customers. One of the last lines that he wrote before his death in 1922 was "You have got to run a store that people will feel at home in." This is certainly good advice for any modern-day retailer to remember. Wanamaker was one of the first four merchants elected to the Merchandising Hall of Fame in the Chicago Merchandise Mart.

R. H. Macy (1822–1877)

After failing in six previous retail businesses, Rowland Hussey Macy founded his famous store in New York City in 1858. Feeling that the retailing opportunity was greater in New York, he moved his family there from Boston and opened a small fancy dry goods store on Sixth Avenue near Fourteenth Street.

Macy, like both Stewart and Wanamaker, was a pioneer in the fixed-price system. He also adopted the policy of pricing merchandise at uneven amounts, such as $1.98. This was done not to make the selling price of goods seem a little less than it was but rather to keep the sales personnel honest. Macy felt that in most transactions the customer would pay in even amounts. In order to give back the change from an

Macy's flagship store is located at Herald Square in New York City.
Source: *Reprinted with permission of R. H. Macy and Company.*

odd selling price, the salesperson would have to go to the cashier for change where a full record of the transaction would be made. With the prices in even dollars, the salesperson might be tempted to pocket the entire amount and never record the sale.

Macy, like Wanamaker, was a leader in advertising. Writing his own advertisements, he spent an unheard-of 3 percent of sales on advertising. He was the first to use plain white space to attract attention to his advertisements. The accepted advertisements of his time were crowded little items that packed as many words as possible into the smallest space. He was also among the first to quote prices in advertisements.

Professor M. Hower of the Harvard Business School spent several years studying the archives of Macy's. He concluded that the secret of Macy's success was the continuity with which the store maintained four basic policies for over a century: (1) selling at definite prices, (2) selling for less, (3) buying and selling for cash, and (4) advertising vigorously. Macy did not invent any of these policies, but he stuck to them and passed them on to his successors. Selling for cash only was continued until 1939 when the store began to extend credit to customers.

Macy was the first great merchant to employ a woman in a prominent position of high authority when in 1860 he hired Margaret Getschell as a cashier. She rose to bookkeeper and in 1866 became the store's first general superintendent with full responsibility for almost 200 employees.

Macy died in 1877, but he laid the foundation for one of the largest department stores in the country. Today Macy's operates department stores through three regional divisions, and a sign on the flagship store located at Herald Square in New York City proclaims it to be the "world's largest store."

Marshall Field (1834–1906)

Another outstanding leader in American retailing was Marshall Field. Through his famous Chicago store he helped to develop the American department store concept. He built up a fortune of over $150 million during his lifetime.

Growing up on a farm in Massachusetts, he began his retailing career as a clerk in a Pittsfield dry goods store. In 1856 he was offered a partnership in the store, but he decided to go west. Upon leaving Massachusetts he predicted that some day he would have a store and the doors would be worth more than the whole Pittsfield store.

In Chicago he worked until he was able to buy an interest in the store in which he worked. In time he was able to buy his own store, which he built into the leading department store in the Midwest.

Field operated on the principle of cash buying only, always money in the bank, get the best goods, tell the truth, and be a little better than the demand. The statement "The customer is always right" is attributed to him. He probably said, "Assume the customer is right until it is plain beyond all question that he is not" (Tebbel 1947).

Field was the first to use the basement for selling, the first to offer a personal shopping service, and among the first to exchange goods and offer a delivery service. "Give the lady what she wants" became the store's motto, reflecting Marshall Field's emphasis on customer service (Wendt and Kogan 1952).

Store Employees

The story of the department store also includes many employees who made up the backbone of the institution. Some idea of conditions that prevailed during the formative years of the department store may be seen in the rules set by a Chicago store in 1860:

The store must be open 6 a.m. to 9 p.m. the year round. The store must be swept; counters, shelves, and showcases dusted; lamps trimmed, filled and chimneys cleaned; pens made; doors and windows opened; a pail of water, also a bucket of coal brought in before breakfast (if there is time to do so); and attend to customers who call. The store must not be opened on the Sabbath unless necessary, and then only for a few minutes. The employee who is in the habit of smoking Spanish cigars, being shaved at the barber's, going to dances and other places of amusement, will surely give his employer reason to be suspicious of his integrity and honesty. Each employee must pay not less than $5.00 each year to the church, and must attend Sunday school regularly. Men employees are given one evening a week for courting and two if they go to prayer meeting. After fourteen hours of work in the store, the leisure time should be spent in reading (Ferry 1960).

Early stores were staffed almost entirely by men. There has been a complete reversal of this today with women now forming the majority of the labor force, particularly in retail sales positions. Immensely improved working conditions since 1920 have been an important factor in attracting women to retailing, but another attraction for young women to work in a department or specialty store is the close contact with the world of fashion. The pleasant atmosphere created for the customer

PROFILE

R.H. Macy & Co.

Mention Macy's and many people think of the Thanksgiving Day Parade in New York City that is sponsored by the store. But the company is not just a New York store. Today, R.H. Macy & Co. operates from coast to coast from three divisions, which include Macy's Northeast, Macy's South, and Macy's California.

Since its founding in 1858 by Rowland H. Macy, the company has focused on serving the needs of family-oriented customers. In recent years changes have been made to attract affluent, upscale customers, but Macy's has maintained its family orientation. It has strived to maintain full department-store status by carrying a balanced mix of both hard and soft goods. Whereas many department stores have dropped furniture and home electronics, Macy's continues to sell these items.

During the 1960s the company experienced problems relating to its older downtown locations, as did many other department store retailers. In a move that proved to weaken the company, a competitive pricing policy was adopted, detracting from the store's fashion image. Macy's was trading down while competitive stores were trading up; thus the company lost many of its long-standing customers.

The revival of R. H. Macy & Co. was started in the late 1960s by Edward S. Finkelstein, at that time executive vice president of the New Jersey–based Bamberger's division. Finkelstein turned the marginally profitable Bamberger's stores into Macy's largest and most productive division by opening branch stores in suburban areas and building them into highly profitable centers to support the downtown Newark store.

Finkelstein was moved to Macy's California division where he employed the has benefited the employee as well. However, in recent years department stores have become troubled with high turnover of sales employees because of low pay and low prestige of retail sales jobs. Sales employees often begin at minimum wage with only slight increases occurring in their hourly wages.

The Birth of Mail-Order Retailing

In the late 1800s the mail-order business developed to meet the needs of the many Americans who lived in rural areas and did not have convenient access to retail stores. Mail order was made possible by the introduction of rural free delivery of

same techniques he had used in New Jersey to revitalize the company. He was next transferred to New York where he undertook the transformation of the dowdy Herald Square store into a dynamic retailing showcase displaying the most advanced methods in visual merchandising, including colorful displays, high-tech lighting, and video presentations. He started by renovating the bargain basement, which he turned into "The Cellar," a spectacular presentation of housewares, gift items, and gourmet foods. This was a continuation of a concept he had initiated at the San Francisco Macy's.

Macy's turnaround was more than just a renovation effort. Finkelstein ushered in a new philosophy, first at Bamberger's, then Macy's California, and last at Macy's New York. The old philosophy of selling for less and attracting customers with bargains was discarded and replaced with the idea of improving profits by increasing sales per square foot. This philosophy comes from Finkelstein's view of departments as specialty stores within the store, each addressing the specific needs of its clientele. This view is evidenced in Macy's new store designs and renovations of existing stores.

Macy's merchandising policy is based on high style, properly positioned promotional activities, and ample stocks of trendy merchandise that are attractively displayed and moderately priced. The store also features merchandise from leading designers. The Macy's tradition of taking markdowns rapidly and keeping stocks current increases customers' chances of finding what they came after.

In 1986 R.H. Macy & Co. returned to private ownership through a leveraged buyout led by chairman Edward Finkelstein and his executive staff. Under private ownership, 346 Macy employees own 20 percent of the company compared with only about 2 percent when the firm was public. Finkelstein explained that he took the company private to give the management team an incentive to stay with the company and to perform better than before (Pete Born, "Macy's Tops Post-LBO Projections," *Women's Wear Daily*, December 29, 1986, pp. 1, 4–5).

mail and of parcel post, which allowed packages of goods to be delivered by mail to isolated areas throughout the United States.

Montgomery Ward founded the mail order industry in 1872. Sears Roebuck followed in 1886. These two firms met the needs of millions of rural Americans. The first Montgomery Ward catalog was a one-page list of thirty items. Today the Sears catalog lists an overwhelming variety of merchandise, more than any single store can carry.

By the late 1920s the automobile changed the pattern of American life. As rural families acquired greater mobility, retail stores became more accessible to them. During the 1920s Sears Roebuck and Montgomery Ward both opened chains of retail stores while continuing their mail-order catalogs. In the 1930s they opened catalog sales stores where customers could place orders. Today Sears is the largest retailer in the world with central headquarters located in Chicago in the Sears Tower, one of the world's tallest structures.

The leading fashion specialty catalog retailer today is Spiegel's, Inc., and the two largest catalog department stores are Sears Roebuck and J. C. Penney. Penney's is a latecomer to the catalog business. J. C. Penney started first as a retail store and did not enter the catalog sales business until the 1960s. Montgomery Ward, long number two in catalog sales, discontinued mail-order sales at the end of 1985 because catalog sales were no longer profitable.

The Chain Store Age

The chain store concept was introduced in the mid-1800s by the Great Atlantic and Pacific Tea Company, better known today as the A & P Grocery Store. By the late 1800s chain store retailing was important in groceries, drugs, variety goods, shoes, and clothing. F. W. Woolworth and the J. C. Penney Company were two of the early chain stores that offered apparel. The retailing innovation of the chain store was the centralizing of the buying operations. These stores established power in the market-place because of the large volume provided by multiple stores.

In tracing the history of retailing, the period of the 1920s is called "the chain store era." During this decade, chain stores grew substantially in numbers and importance in the market. Sears added its first retail store in its Chicago mail-order plant in 1925, and by 1929 Sears had 324 stores. Montgomery Ward followed by adding stores in 1926 and had 244 stores in 1928 including its first full-line department store in Birmingham, Alabama.

During the period from 1920 to 1940, department and specialty stores became more alike, and competition increased. Chain stores continued to expand while mail order declined. Characteristics of large stores during this period include increased advertising, more varied merchandise assortments, growing emphasis on fashion, and trading-up to better-quality merchandise. The department store dominated as the most important form of retailing through the 1960s.

Discount Retailing

Discount stores first appeared during the Great Depression of the 1930s when times were hard and price was of utmost importance to many consumers. The discount house as we know it today got its start following World War II, and discounters became increasingly important in the 1950s and 1960s. Although stores that cut prices and sold for less had been around for some time, it was not until the 1960s that discounters began to impact other forms of retailing.

Initially the emphasis of discount merchandising was on hard goods like appliances and luggage. These stores had little to offer but low prices and convenient hours, including being open at night and on Sunday. Gradually discounters expanded their merchandise assortments to include soft goods.

Discount stores were most successful in the suburbs. The growth of suburbs following World War II created a new type of family-oriented market where the car was necessary for shopping. Customers could easily take their purchases with them. Although department stores moved to the suburbs, too, many did not take their traditional bargain basement with them. Discounters moved to fill this void and provided merchandise for families at reasonable prices.

Discounters brought a revolution to merchandising in the 1950s and 1960s. Discount stores helped to force retail prices down in conventional department stores. They also led the way to offering the convenience of Sunday shopping and longer store hours in the evening. Increased competition from discounters has led conventional department stores to discontinue certain merchandise classifications that competed with discounters.

Today the largest discount retailer in America is K mart. The first K mart opened in a Detroit suburb in 1962, and by 1988 K mart operated 2,145 stores in the United States and 118 in Canada. With sales of $25.6 billion in 1987, K mart was the second-largest volume retailer in the United States following Sears Roebuck.

Specialty Store Chains

Although specialty store chains date from the decade of the 1920s, it was not until the 1970s that apparel specialty chains began to take market share away from large department stores. Beginning in the 1970s specialized apparel chains became regional or national in scope, operating stores appealing to a specific customer. Often the target customer was young and liked shopping in a store designed just for him or her. The growth of shopping malls beginning in the 1960s and accelerating in the 1970s encouraged the expansion of chain specialty stores. Each mall typically included two or three anchor stores, which were usually department stores or one of the big three mass merchandisers. These stores were separated by specialty stores. Chain specialty stores found it easy to expand by moving into these malls.

Specialty stores are expected to continue to increase their share of the retail market. Their success has encouraged department stores to adopt a specialty store approach within their larger store environments. Some department stores have also entered the specialty store business by opening their own chain of specialty stores. J. C. Penney, for example, has invested in a number of specialty businesses and has started its own specialty chain, Mixit, featuring moderate-price merchandise for juniors. Mixits were originally launched in the San Francisco, Southern California, Arizona, and Texas areas. The merchandise offered by these stores is private label, coordinated career apparel, and sportswear. Mixit was designed to compete against The Limited, Petrie Stores, and Clothestime.

The Future of Retailing

Over the years retailing has been forced to change in order to satisfy ever-changing consumer preferences. New forms of retailing have emerged, whereas older forms have evolved to suit consumer demand. Those stores that do not change with changing consumer demand eventually find themselves out of business; those stores that do adjust will survive. As social, political, and economic changes occur in the United States and the world, challenges emerge for retailers.

During the 1970s and 1980s, uncertain economic times, inflation, energy shortages, and escalating operating expenses forced retailers to adjust their ways of doing business. Shifting populations and changing consumer values have had a strong impact on strategies followed by retailers. Retailing today has become more complex, requiring retailers to engage in strategic planning and to fight for market share in order to increase sales.

In the 1950s and 1960s opportunities for growth seemed limitless. Today retailing has become highly competitive as many stores have expanded, building stores within overlapping trading areas. As retailers have sought increased business through expansion, many geographical areas have become overstored. Stores have adjusted by reducing the size of their stores, closing unproductive locations, and dropping unprofitable merchandise categories.

New retail formats will undoubtedly appear to supply consumers with the merchandise they desire. Innovative retailers will continue to recognize voids in the marketplace and will devise store formats to fill those voids. Department and specialty stores will seek consumer groups that are not having their needs met and will merchandise to these groups. Successful retailers know that finding out what consumers need and want, and how and where they want to buy this merchandise are important secrets to success in retailing.

Summary of Key Points

1. The retailer is the distributor who provides the bridge between the producer and the ultimate consumer. This is accomplished through several kinds of retail businesses including different kinds of department and specialty stores as well as various forms of nonstore retail firms.

2. A department store is a large-scale retailing institution that sells a wide variety of goods, including home furnishings, household linens and dry goods, and apparel and accessories for the whole family. The department store takes its name from the units in which related kinds of merchandise are grouped for purposes of promotion, service, and control. Several different kinds of department stores include the conventional, junior, chain, discount, and specialty department stores.

3. Discount stores and off-price retailers are retail establishments that offer merchandise at prices below the recognized market level. These stores differ in the way in which their merchandise is purchased. The discount store pays the same price for goods as other types of stores, whereas the off-price store obtains merchandise at lower prices by purchasing special purchase goods.

4. Specialty stores concentrate on specific classification of merchandise. They carry a narrower merchandise assortment than department stores and target a more clearly defined market segment. Different types of specialty stores include the mom-and-pop store, the boutique, and the chain specialty store.

5. Nonstore retailing includes catalog or mail-order retailing, direct sales, vending machines, and electronic shopping.

6. Suburban shopping centers developed in the 1950s as a result of demographic and lifestyle changes.

7. The modern department store was based on four innovative principles that were considered revolutionary when they were introduced in the mid-1800s. These principles included selling merchandise at a small markup, offering merchandise with fixed marked prices, allowing free entrance, and allowing customers to exchange purchases or have their money refunded.

Key Words and Concepts

Define, identify, or explain each of the following:

basement (budget) store	discount retailing
branch store	discount store
catalog retailing	discounter
chain store	dry goods
community shopping center	electronic retailing
conventional department store	factory outlet store
department store	flagship store
departmentalized specialty store	franchise store
direct selling	general merchandise store

hypermarket

International Council of Shopping Centers (ICSC)

junior department store

kiosk

leased department

mass merchandiser

mom-and-pop store

neighborhood shopping center

nonstore retailing

off-price retailing

off-price store

over the counter

parent store

regional shopping center

retailing

soft goods

specialty department store

specialty store

twig

variety store

wholesale warehouse club

Discussion Questions

1. Define and describe the characteristics of each of the following store types: (a) department store, (b) specialty store, (c) discount store, (d) chain store, (e) boutique, (f) mom-and-pop store.

2. Explain the difference between a discounter and an off-price retailer.

3. Discuss the different methods of nonstore retailing.

4. What factors encouraged shopping center development in the 1950s?

5. Describe the three basic shopping center types.

6. What three basic layout patterns are used for shopping centers?

7. What were Aristide Boucicaut's four revolutionary innovations that contributed to the birth of the department store? What additional innovation was added by American retailers?

8. Why did early department stores succeed in the United States? Discuss the factors necessary for their success.

9. Discuss the technical innovations that helped the department store develop and expand.

10. Name the first American stores to become department stores.

Notes

R. Patrick Cash, ed., *The Buyer's Manual.* New York: NRMA, 1979, p. 11.

John William Ferry, *A History of the Department Store.* New York: Macmillan, 1960, p. 25.

Robert Hendrickson, *The Grand Emporiums*. New York: Stein and Day, 1979.

Tom Mahoney and Leonard Sloane, *The Great Merchants*. New York: Harper, 1974.

Hrant Pasdermadjian, *The Department Store: Its Origins, Evolution and Economics*. London: Newman, 1954.

Stores, July 1987, p. 81.

John Tebbel, *The Marshall Fields—A Study in Wealth*. New York: Dutton, 1947, p. 60.

Lloyd Wendt and Herman Kogan, *Give the Lady What She Wants*. New York: Rand McNally, 1952.

Women's Wear Daily, May 13, 1969, p. 31.

_____

CHAPTER 12

STRUCTURE OF RETAIL FIRMS

A CLEARLY defined organizational structure is necessary for every business to perform at an optimum level, and retailing is no exception. The organizational structure of retail stores varies widely; however, all stores regardless of size must perform the same basic functions. Merchandise must be purchased, received into stock, priced, and made available for purchase by customers. Merchandise must be displayed, advertised, and promoted in some manner so that customers know where it can be purchased. The store must keep records of merchandise received and sold. Employees have to be hired, trained, and supervised. Bills must be paid and reports prepared for state and federal agencies. Stores and fixtures must be maintained and provision made for store security. All of these functions must be performed by someone, and store employees need to know who is responsible for carrying out each function.

Discussed in this chapter are various organizational structures for retail stores ranging from small single-unit shops to large departmentalized stores and chain stores. The key functional areas of retailing are described, including merchandising, financial control, store operations, personnel, and sales promotion. Also presented are the primary store ownership groups.

Store Organizational Structure

An organizational chart presents a visual picture of the structure of a firm. It shows how responsibility and authority are delegated and specifies who has the responsibility

_____

and authority for each function that must be performed in the achievement of the goal of selling goods to satisfy customer wants and needs. **Responsibility** is the obligation to perform certain tasks and to be accountable for that performance. **Authority** is the power needed to use the available resources and people necessary to perform those tasks. All employees within an organization should know both their responsibility and the extent of their authority. Employees should also know to whom they are accountable or, in other words, who is responsible for their actions and who has authority to tell them what to do. All workers in any organization should be made aware of their functions within the total structure of that organization.

Small Store Organization

Retail store organization varies depending upon the size of the store, the number of stores, geographical locations, type of merchandise sold, and services offered. In the small single-unit or mom-and-pop store, the owner/manager is a jack-of-all-trades, personally performing all of the functions of retailing. The owner is a stockperson, buyer, salesperson, janitor, financial officer, and promotion director rolled into one. This owner/manager holds total responsibility and authority for the store.

As a store grows, the owner/manager may no longer be able to perform all of the functions necessary to operate the business. Other employees must be hired and responsibilities divided among them. The larger a company becomes, the more employees are needed to carry out the functions of the business, and a more complicated organizational structure evolves.

Two-Function Organization

The first employee hired by the owner/manager would probably be a salesperson. As a store grows in size and sales volume, employees are added to perform more specific duties such as bookkeeper or stockperson. As long as the store has only a few employees, they all report directly to the owner/manager. As more people are added, the job of supervising all employees becomes too much for one person to handle. At this point the store might be divided into a **two-function organization** with merchandising and operations separated and the person responsible for each reporting to the owner/manager. Figure 12.1 illustrates a simple two-function organizational chart.

The small store owner may use outside sources for advice concerning buying, promotion, and financial management. Resident buying offices, for example, may assist independent stores with buying merchandise as well as offering advice and assistance in the general operation of the store. The services of resident buying offices are discussed in detail in Chapter 13. Advertising agencies may work with stores in planning and preparing advertising for various media.

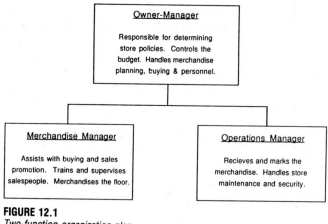

FIGURE 12.1
Two-function organization plan.

The Mazur Plan

As a company continues to expand, a three- or four-function plan may become necessary. A **three-function organization** adds a controller or financial manager, and a **four-function organization** adds a division to handle sales promotion and advertising. The organizational structure of most mid-size department stores is based on

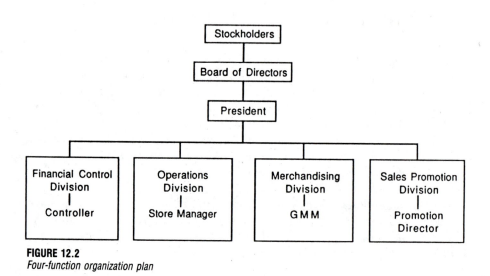

FIGURE 12.2
Four-function organization plan

a four-function plan as developed by Paul M. Mazur and published in 1927 (see Fig. 12.2). The **Mazur Plan** established four divisions:

1. *MERCHANDISING DIVISION:* responsible for buying and selling of the goods and merchandise planning and control.

2. *FINANCIAL CONTROL DIVISION:* responsible for supervising the budget; supervises the credit department, accounts payable, and inventory control.

3. *OPERATIONS DIVISION:* responsible for store maintenance and housekeeping, security, customer services, receiving and marking of merchandise, and personnel.

4. *SALES PROMOTION DIVISION:* responsible for advertising, display, and public relations.

As stores continue to expand, it becomes necessary to add separate divisions for personnel and branch store operations. With large multiunit stores, the trend has been toward increased executive specialization. Figure 12.3 shows an expanded **organizational chart** based on the Mazur Plan.

Chain Store Organization

The organization of chain stores is characterized by central management with most or all major decisions made at central headquarters. As conventional department stores have expanded by adding numerous branches, their organizational structure has become more like that of the chain store; however, differences still exist.

In national chains authority and responsibility are centralized at headquarters, and the management of each store is controlled by central headquarters. Major decisions are made centrally with lesser decisions delegated to the stores. In general the functions of buying, sales promotion, accounting and control, store design and construction, executive training, traffic and warehousing, and quality control are handled centrally.

Chain stores vary as to the extent of central control. In a highly centralized chain store operation, individual store managers carry out the policies of central management with little autonomy. The manager is responsible for selling merchandise, supervising store operations, and reporting trends to central headquarters. Considerable paperwork is usually needed to keep central management informed of each store's activities.

As some chains have become giants with hundreds of store units, corporate authority has been divided among regional management with the central headquarters determining policy decisions and handling financial control.

Characteristics of chain store organization include the following:

1. Strict hierarchy of superordinate and subordinate relationships.

2. Separation of buying and selling functions with all or most of the buying concentrated in central headquarters from which store managers may requisition merchandise.

3. Many functional specialists housed in the central headquarters. Among these are specialists dealing with real estate and location analysis, store maintenance and operations, warehouse and traffic control, merchandise control, and sales promotion.

Key Functional Areas
of Retail Stores

According to *The Buyer's Manual*, "the key to understanding the question of a

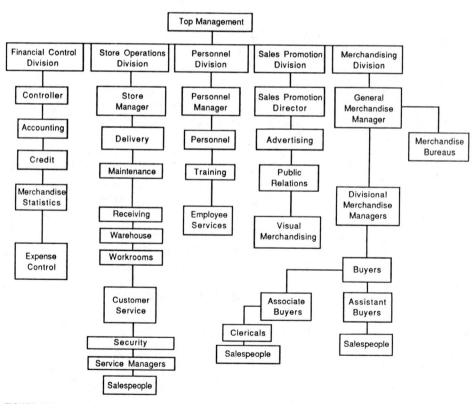

FIGURE 12.3
Organization chart for a large department or specialty store based on the Mazur Plan.

department store's organization is to familiarize oneself with the function and responsibilities of executives in each of the functional areas" (Cash 1979). Although stores vary considerably in their organizational structures, all stores, large and small, must perform the same basic functions. The five key functional areas of retailing are (1) merchandising, (2) store operations, (3) sales promotion, (4) financial control, and (5) personnel. All stores must see that each of these functional areas is provided for in the company's organizational structure. A smaller store may combine several areas under one division, whereas a larger store will operate with a separate specialized division for each function.

Merchandising

The central structure of a departmentalized department store is the **merchandising division** (see Fig. 12.4). Its functions center around buying, selling, and stock planning. The merchandising division is headed by the **general merchandise manager** (GMM) who often carries the additional title of vice president. This person's job is to guide the merchandising division in achieving a satisfactory profit for the store. The GMM reports to the store president and is responsible for establishing and interpreting the store's merchandising policies. As a member of top management, the GMM takes an active part in the formulation of store policies. Policies are a plan or a method of doing business. In retailing, a policy helps to define procedures and

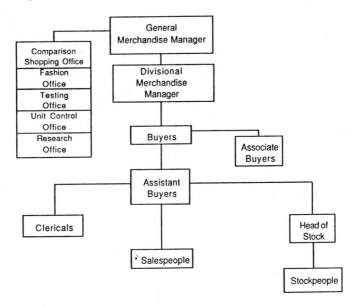

*In Multi-unit organizations salespeople may report to a department manager who is in the operations division rather than in the merchandising division.

FIGURE 12.4
Merchandising division.

objectives for the store's employees and promotes consistency. Merchandising policies as established help to develop the image of the store and guide it in the selection of merchandise by defining merchandise classifications, price lines, brand names, and fashion orientation.

In large department stores having many divisions, groups of departments report to a **divisional merchandise manager** (DMM) who reports directly to the general merchandise manager. The DMMs are the middle-management representatives of the merchandising division and serve as the liaison between upper management and the buyers in presenting and interpreting store merchandising policies. The divisional merchandise managers function as advisors to and coordinators of the various buyers in their divisions.

The **buyer** reports directly to the DMM and is responsible for implementing company policies, plans, and procedures within his or her department. Under the supervision of the DMM, the buyer is responsible for planning purchases and buying the merchandise for a department. The buyer is also actively involved in planning promotional activities. Usual responsibilities of the buyer include determining buying plans, selecting merchandise, establishing retail prices, placing orders and reorders, maintaining proper vendor relations, maintaining merchandise assortments, and co-ordinating advertising and promotional plans. The specific responsibilities vary considerably depending on the structure and size of the store. In a single-unit store the buyer may also be the department manager directly responsible for merchandise training and supervision of salespeople, for arrangement of merchandise in the department, and for maintaining stock records. In retail firms with multiple branches the buyer's job has become more specialized. Such buyers no longer perform the duties of a department manager and are able to concentrate specifically on merchandise planning, buying, and promotion. The chain store buyer specializes to an even greater extent in the buying functions of retailing.

The successful operation of a retail store or a department depends largely on the buyer. It is the view of Sanford Zimmerman, former chairman of the board and chief executive officer of Abraham and Straus, that all functional activities of the store facilitate and assist the buyer. All divisions facilitate the buying and selling of merchandise to the store's customers (*Stores* 1975).

Reporting to the buyer may be an associate buyer, assistant buyer and/or clerical assistant. The **associate buyer** is found only in large stores. Associate buyers serve as understudies for the buyer's position and are often given the responsibility of buying one or more classifications within a department; they are the buyer's substitute when the buyer is out of the store.

The **assistant buyer** is also a buyer in training. The degree of responsibility given to the assistant buyer depends upon his or her level of experience. The job of assistant buyer usually involves considerable detail work. Duties are likely to include analyzing unit control records, initiating transfers between store units, writing reorders for staple goods, and checking on merchandise.

A clerical assistant may be assigned to the buyer for the purpose of handling much of the detail work. If there is no clerical assistant, the assistant buyer is responsible for this work.

When the buyer is also the department manager, salespeople and heads of stock are directly responsible to the buyer. Large stores or departments may have a **head of stock** who maintains reserve merchandise in the stockroom, keeps stock on the selling floor in good order, and monitors inventory levels. The head of stock may also handle merchandise transfers between stores or departments. He or she works closely with the buyer and assistant buyer to maintain the proper flow of merchandise to the stores.

In recent years as stores have added multiple branches, sometimes with wide geographical dispersion, store organization has changed to reflect the increasing importance of branches. It has become necessary for buyers to maintain close contact with department managers/merchandisers and area sales managers in all stores to provide information important to the promotion and selling of the department's merchandise. Duties that at one time were carried out by the buyer are now often the responsibility of other store personnel. The buyer's job has become more specialized, emphasizing merchandise planning and procurement.

Merchandising Staff Bureaus

Staff bureaus that provide specialized information of importance to the buying and merchandising of goods may be part of the merchandising division. Examples of such bureaus include comparison shopping, the fashion bureau, quality assurance, merchandise research, unit control, and the store's own resident buying office. Many of these bureaus are found only in larger stores.

Comparison Shopping Bureau

The basic function of a comparison shopping bureau is to check competing stores and provide the buyer and merchandise manager with information concerning competitors' stock assortments, prices, and services. Comparison shoppers will sometimes shop departments within their own store to check the selling service given by store employees.

The Fashion Bureau

Large fashion-oriented stores often have a fashion bureau headed by the store's fashion director or fashion coordinator. The fashion director serves as a consultant to fashion buyers and merchandisers assisting in their assortment planning and merchandise selection. The director or coordinator is primarily concerned with forecasting fashion rather than working with budgeting and inventory control. An important function of the fashion bureau is to see that merchandise selected by fashion buyers is coordinated to project the desired fashion image for the stores. In addition, the fashion bureau often plans and directs fashion shows to be presented to customers or to show store employees current fashion trends.

Quality Assurance

This bureau serves the buyer by testing and evaluating merchandise to determine if quality standards are met as established by the retail firm. Only a few large companies maintain their own standards and testing bureau. Examples include J. C. Penney, Sears Roebuck, R. H. Macy and Company, and the Army Air Force Exchange Service. Stores may use an outside testing service to evaluate merchandise for them.

Unit Control Bureau

In some firms the analysis of sales and stock is handled by each buyer, or this function may be centralized in a unit control bureau. With computerization the unit control bureau designs and manages the control systems used by the store.

Unit control is a system of record keeping of individual units of merchandise on hand. Under a unit control system a record is kept of the physical inventory on hand, amount of stock on order, and amount sold. This information assists the buyer in planning proper inventory levels and balancing assortments.

Resident Buying Office

Some stores maintain their own private resident buying offices in important market centers. These offices provide assistance to store buyers when they visit the markets and serve as the stores' market representatives at all times. Because such offices are very expensive to maintain, few stores operate their own private office. Most subscribe to the services of an independent office or use an office that is owned and operated by the organization that also owns the stores.

Functions of the Merchandising Division

Although the functions of the merchandising division vary, they typically include the following activities:

1. Determining future customer demand in terms of styles, quantity, colors, prices, and fashion emphasis.

2. Planning to meet future customer demand and assure a profit.

3. Selecting resources and buying merchandise.

4. Coordinating advertising and sales promotion to assist in bringing the customers into the store to buy the merchandise.

5. Projecting store image.

6. Establishing sound merchandising policies to ensure the success and growth of the business and to assist in meeting competition.

The merchandising division with the buyer at its center is often viewed as the hub of the retail store. Without it, the other divisions would have no reason to exist. Although the central function of retailing is carried out by the merchandising division, the success of this division is dependent upon the efficiency of the other store divisions. If the merchandising division is to achieve its sales goals and the store is to make a profit, close cooperation must be maintained with the other store divisions.

Financial Control

The **financial control division** supervises the budget. This division is headed by the **controller** or chief financial officer who is concerned with controlling the spending activities of all divisions. Typically the controller supervises the activities of the credit department, accounts payable, and the statistical department.

The control division works with the merchandise division in preparing and maintaining all merchandising plans and expense budgets. The controller has the responsibility for preparing statistical reports that are used in guiding the buying and selling activities of the merchandising division and seeing that budgets are maintained.

A large store may have assistant controllers who work with the controller in carrying out the functions of the division. In a large firm the controller may report to the company treasurer.

Operations

The store **operations division** is headed by the store manager or superintendent. This division is responsible for a wide variety of activities including store maintenance and housekeeping, delivery, receiving and marking, warehousing, workrooms, customer services including sales supervision, store security, and purchasing of supplies. Under the original four-function Mazur Plan, this division also supervised the functions of personnel and training. As stores have expanded in size and number of branches, personnel has become a separate division in most stores.

Personnel

The **personnel** (or human resources) **division** is responsible for hiring and training new employees. It is also concerned with providing services to store employees and evaluating them for raises and promotions. The relationship of this division to all divisions is obvious, as capable, well-trained employees are necessary for the profitable operation of any business. In some companies the personnel division is also responsible for supervising salespeople; in other firms this responsibility rests with the operations division.

Sales Promotion

The **sales promotion division,** headed by the promotion director, is concerned with any activity that a store uses to influence the sale of merchandise or services. The usual activities of retail sales promotion include advertising, display, publicity, special events, and fashion shows. The basic function of retail sales promotion is to communicate information about the store and its merchandise and present to potential customers and to bring those customers into the store with a desire to buy.

The sales promotion division is often divided into three departments: (1) advertising, (2) public relations, and (3) visual merchandising. The advertising department is responsible for planning, preparing, and placing advertisements in the media. Most stores handle their own print advertising but may use an outside advertising agency to prepare ads for more specialized media such as television or video.

The public relations department includes special events and publicity. Public relations is concerned with broad-range policies and programs to create favorable public opinion about a firm. Public relations covers everything a store does to influence public opinion about the store. Publicity is a tool used to create favorable public opinion.

Visual merchandising is the visual presentation of the store and its merchandise. Visual merchandising includes window and interior display, signs and posters, and the fixturing or arrangement of merchandise within the store. The visual merchandising department may include separate areas of window display, interior display, and the sign shop. In addition, store planning and design may be part of this division.

Competition has made sales promotion very important. Many stores carry the same merchandise and offer the same services. Sales promotion is the key to building store image and bringing in the customer. It disseminates information about the store and its merchandise, generates interest among present and potential store customers, and builds customer loyalty.

Department Store Ownership Groups

Store **ownership groups** are corporations that own a number of autonomous retail stores. Many of the stores owned by an ownership group are multiunit retailers such as department or specialty stores with branches. Often, department stores owned by ownership groups were once independently owned. When the individual stores retain their own names, the general public is seldom aware of their group affiliation. For example, few customers may realize that New York–based Bloomingdale's, Lazarus in Cincinnati, and Rich's in Atlanta are all owned by Federated Stores, or that May Department Stores owns Manhattan-based Lord & Taylor, Houston-based Foley's, and Robinson's in Los Angeles.

Stores owned by an ownership group should not be confused with chain retailers. Chain stores are highly controlled from the central office, and usually all of the stores operate under the same name. Chain stores are likely to be almost identical in appearance and merchandise assortment. Stores owned by an ownership group, although centrally owned and controlled in terms of broad policymaking, retain their individual personalities. They are operated and merchandised autonomously. Each retail division continues to be merchandised and operated primarily as an individual organization with central guidance from the ownership group rather than central management or direction. Ownership groups have provided stores with the capital necessary for expansion and have given them the volume buying power necessary to meet the competition of chain stores.

Among the major department store ownership groups today are Federated Department Stores and Allied Department Stores, both owned by Canadian-based Campeau Corporation, Dayton-Hudson Corporation, May Department Stores Company, Carter Hawley Hale Stores, R. H. Macy & Company, Batus Retail Group, and Mercantile Stores Company. Table 12.1 shows the sales of these eight department store ownership groups.

Table 12.1 Sales of Top 8 Department Store Ownership Groups for Fiscal 1987

Group (Headquarters) (Total Sq. Ft.)	Store Total by Type		Sales (millions)	
Federated Department Stores Cincinnati, OH 61,600,000	578	Total	$11,118	Total
	238	Dept. stores	7,298	Dept. stores
	233	Specialty stores	550	Specialty stores
	76	Mass merchandise	970	Mass merchandise
	129	Supermarkets	2,300	Supermarkets
Dayton-Hudson Corp. Minneapolis, MN 57,453,000	577	Total	$10,677	Total
	37	Dept. stores	1,552	Dept. stores
	317	Target	5,306	Target
	199	Mervyn	3,183	Mervyn
	24	Lechmere	636	Lechmere
May Department Stores Co. St. Louis, MO 72,606,000	2,960	Total	$10,314	Total
	258	Dept. stores	6,205	Dept. stores
	116	Caldor	1,502	Caldor
	70	Venture	1,208	Venture
	80	Loehmann	334	Loehmann
	2,436	Volume	1,065	Volume
R. H. Macy & Co. New York, NY 24,381,000	93	Total	$5,451	Total
	90	Dept. stores		
	3	Specialty stores		
Allied Stores Corp. New York, NY not available	292	Total	$3,263	Total
	128	Dept. stores		
	164	Specialty stores		
Carter Hawley Hale Stores Los Angeles, CA 19,044,000	112	Total	$2,617	Total
	112	Dept. stores		
Batus Retail Group New York, NY 6,439,000	168	Total	$2,569	Total
	49	Dept. stores		
	119	Specialty stores		
Mercantile Stores Co. New York, NY 11,124,000	79	Total	$2,156	Total
	79	Dept. stores		

Source: *Stores*, July 1988, p. 33.

In recent years several corporate ownership groups have expanded, acquiring more large multiunit stores. The pattern of expansion has continued so that today few large multiunit department or specialty stores remain independently owned. Examples of some of the large independents include Dillard's, Nordstrom, and Maison Blanche. During the 1960s and 1970s, many ownership groups diversified and added other forms of retailing, such as specialty stores, discount stores, and even grocery stores. In the 1980s the trend has been for large ownership groups to divest themselves of store groups and become more specialized. For example, in 1987 and 1988 Allied and Federated sold most of their nondepartment store divisions, and Carter Hawley Hale split off its specialty stores into a separate group named the Neiman-Marcus Group.

Federated Department Stores

Federated Department Stores, headquartered in Cincinnati, Ohio, is one of the oldest and largest department store ownership groups. The idea for Federated originated in 1929 aboard the yacht of the president of the Brooklyn department store Abraham and Straus. Also on board the yacht were Louis Kirstein, general manager of Filene's of Boston; Fred Lazarus, Jr., of F & R Lazarus and Co., Columbus, Ohio, and owner of Shillito's of Cincinnati; and Samuel Bloomingdale, head of Bloomingdale's of New York. An agreement was reached that they share the risks of their businesses by forming a holding company to be established by an exchange of stock. Federated Department Stores was incorporated in November 1929, including Filene's of Boston, Lazarus of Columbus, Shillito's of Cincinnati, and Abraham and Straus of Brooklyn. The next year Bloomingdale's became the fifth store in the group.

Federated continued to be a holding company without central offices or any formal activity until 1945 when the individual corporations were dissolved and each company became an operating division of Federated Department Stores. This new corporation was formed to diversify capital investments and to offer wider opportunities for promotion and assignment of promising store personnel. The offices for the headquarters were established in Cincinnati across the street from Shillito's. The original office included two secretaries, a telephone operator, and two researchers who studied ways in which the stores could share their successful merchandising and operating techniques. An early idea developed by Federated in the late 1940s was the use of revolving credit, which allowed customers to pay a portion of their credit balance each month rather than paying the bill in full (Mahoney and Sloane 1974).

Through the years, Federated assembled a team of experts in Cincinnati to assist the stores in the group in improving operations, store planning, and acquiring stores sites. The goal was to make the maximum profit by dominating the center of the middle-class trade. Federated stores sought to have the largest selections and competitive prices in every merchandising area in which Federated chose to compete. Under the leadership of Fred Lazarus, Federated assembled a national network of department stores. According to Leon Harris, Federated attempted to buy the dominant store in a community, and where this was not possible Federated bought stores that had the potential to become the dominant store (Harris 1979).

Federated's first acquisition came in 1945 with the purchase of Foley's of Houston and was followed in 1948 by the acquisition of the Boston Store in Milwaukee. The Boston Store was held by Federated until 1984 when it was sold to another group. During the 1950s Federated purchased Sanger's (Dallas), Burdine's (Miami), Goldsmith's (Memphis), and Rike-Kumler Company (Dayton, Ohio). In 1961 A. Harris Co. (Dallas) was bought and merged with Sanger's to become Sanger-Harris. In 1964 Federated purchased two California stores, Bullock's and I. Magnin, and in 1976 it bought Rich's, the largest department store in Atlanta. In 1986 Federated combined its previously merged department store divisions of Shillito/Rikes with Lazarus, based in Columbus. Thus all of Federated's department stores located in Ohio and Indiana now operated under the name Lazarus. This merger made Lazarus the largest Federated department store division in number of units. In terms of volume, however, Bloomingdale's remained the leading Federated store. The merger in 1987 of Federated's two Texas-based stores, Sanger-Harris and Foley's, made Foley's the highest volume Federated store.

In 1987 Federated operated nine department store divisions, including Foley's, Bloomingdale's, Lazarus, Burdine's, Abraham & Straus, Bullock's, Rich's, Filene's, and Goldsmith's. In addition, it operated one discount division consisting of Gold Circle Stores, Richway, and Ralph's Supermarkets in Southern California, and four specialty store divisions, including I. Magnin, Filene's Basement, Bullocks Wilshire, and the Children's Place. Federated also operated a value-oriented store division called MainStreet, which was established in 1985 and centered in Chicago. In addition, shopping centers were owned and operated by a subsidiary, Federated Stores Realty, Inc.

In May 1988 Federated Department Stores was purchased by Campeau Corporation, a real estate firm based in Toronto, Canada, which had previously entered retail ownership with the purchase of Allied Stores Corporation in 1986. The Federated purchase followed a difficult battle between Campeau and R.H. Macy to take over the store group. As part of the transaction, Campeau agreed to sell Federated's California stores, Bullock's, Bullocks Wilshire, and I. Magnin, to Macy's. In addition Filene's and Foley's were to be sold to May Department Stores Company.

At the time of the purchase Robert Campeau, chairman and chief executive officer of Campeau Corporation, announced plans to sell Federated's nondepartment store operations to raise funds for servicing and reducing debt stemming from Campeau's $6.6 billion offer for Federated. Before the end of 1988 Ralph's Supermarkets were spun off as a separate subsidiary of Campeau, and the Gold Circle discount division was sold with plans to dismantle it. Filene's Basement was sold to an investor group. MainStreet and the Children's Place were sold as well. Department stores remaining in the Federated group include the following five divisions: Brooklyn-based Abraham and Straus, New York-based Bloomingdale's, Miami-based Burdine's, Cincinnati-based Lazarus, and Atlanta-based Rich's, which was combined with Goldsmith's of Memphis. Future plans for the company announced by Robert

Campeau include expansion of Bloomingdale's with possible locations in Boston, Canada, and on the West Coast.

Allied Stores Corporation

Allied Stores Corporation was acquired by Campeau Corporation in December 1986 for $3.6 billion. As one of the oldest department store ownership groups, Allied was formed in 1935, and at the time of its purchase by Campeau operated both department and specialty store divisions located throughout the United States. Since Campeau's takeover, eighteen Allied store divisions have been sold. By 1989 Allied consisted of four department store divisions: the Bon Marché (Seattle), Jordan Marsh—New England (Boston), Maas Brothers/Jordan Marsh (Tampa, Florida), and Stern's (Paramus, New Jersey).

In 1988 Allied's headquarters was moved from Manhattan to Cincinnati, and some operational functions were combined with Federated. What the future holds for Allied and Federated store divisions is uncertain. Consolidation of various Allied and Federated divisions located in the same geographical areas is likely to occur. In any case the purchase of these two major store ownership groups has led to fewer department store divisions.

Dayton-Hudson Corporation

The executive offices for the Dayton-Hudson Corporation are located in Minneapolis, Minnesota. As the second-largest ownership group, Dayton-Hudson draws its name from its two founding stores, Dayton's of Minneapolis and Hudson's of Detroit. These two stores operated as separate divisions until 1983 when Dayton-Hudson Corporation combined the divisions into one entity known as Dayton-Hudson Department Stores. The combining of these two stores made them the largest single volume department store division in the United States at that time. They have since been surpassed by Dillard's, Nordstrom, and the New York and New Jersey divisions of Macy's (Table 11.1).

Today the Dayton-Hudson Corporation operates retail stores in forty-eight states, including department, discount, and specialty stores. The fastest growing divisions for Dayton-Hudson in recent years have been Target Stores and Mervyn's. Target Stores offer a wide assortment of merchandise at discount prices on a self-service basis. Mervyn's operations, located in the West and Southwest, feature popular-priced merchandise lines of apparel, accessories, and household soft goods. Mervyn's describes its target customer as the value-conscious family.

Dayton-Hudson's one specialty division, Lechmere, operates stores in Massachusetts and New Hampshire and specializes in national brands of consumer durables, including major appliances, televisions and stereos, photographic equipment, and sporting goods.

May Department Stores Company

May Department Stores Company, headquartered in St. Louis, Missouri, merged with Associated Dry Goods Corporation in October 1986, nearly doubling the size of the ownership group. The retail businesses owned by the May Department Stores Company include full-line department stores, discount stores, and self-service family shoe stores. The corporation is also a national developer and operator of shopping centers in the United States.

Department store divisions operated by May Department Stores include the following:

Store Division	Headquarters Location
L.S. Ayres	Indianapolis, Indiana
Famous Barr	St. Louis, Missouri
Filene's	Boston, Massachusetts
Foley's	Houston, Texas
G. Fox	Hartford, Connecticut
The Hecht Company	Washington, D.C.
Kaufmann's	Pittsburgh, Pennsylvania
Lord & Taylor	New York, New York
The May Company	North Hollywood, California
The May Company	Cleveland, Ohio
May D & F	Denver, Colorado
Meier & Frank	Portland, Oregon
The M. O'Neil Company	Akron, Ohio
J.W. Robinson	Los Angeles, California
Sibley's	Rochester, New York

Discount divisions operated by May Department Stores Company include Caldor in the Northeast and Venture in the Midwest. However, plans to sell Caldor and

Vendor were announced in 1989. May also owns and operates Volume Shoe, the largest chain of self-service family shoe stores in the country. Volume Shoe features a complete line of footwear for men, women, and children. Most of these stores operate under the name of Payless Shoe Source. May's largest department store division is Lord & Taylor, closely followed by the May Company, California.

R. H. Macy and Company, Inc.

R. H. Macy and Company is a privately held firm with headquarters in New York City. Macy's full-line department stores sell a wide assortment of merchandise primarily in the medium-to-higher price lines. Stores are operated through three regional store divisions: (1) Macy's-Northeast, based in Manhattan; (2) Macy's-California, based in San Francisco; and (3) Macy's-South, based in Atlanta, which includes stores in Georgia, Alabama, Florida, Louisiana, and Texas. In 1988 Macy acquired San Francisco-based I. Magnin and Los Angeles-based Bullock's from Federated Department Stores. Macy's has reorganized Bullock's under the supervision of the Atlanta division and I. Magnin under Macy's-California. Since 1985 R. H. Macy has combined several operating divisions and changed the names of stores in two of its major divisions, Bamberger's of New Jersey and Davison's of Atlanta, to Macy's.

Breaking with Macy's tradition of operating only department stores, the company entered specialty retailing in 1988 with the opening of three stores carrying private label merchandise. The first of these, Aeropostale, carries unisex apparel, Charter Club offers women's sportswear, and Fantasies by Morgan Taylor carries intimate apparel.

To assist buyers from the various divisions, the R. H. Macy corporation has a domestic buying office in New York and foreign buying offices in twenty-nine countries in Europe, the Near East, the Far East, and Asia. Among the cities represented are Copenhagen, Dublin, Florence, Frankfort, Hong Kong, London, Madrid, Manila, New Delhi, Paris, Osaka, Peking, Seoul, Singapore, and Tel Aviv.

Carter Hawley Hale Stores, Inc.

Headquarters for Carter Hawley Hale are located in Los Angeles. The company operates full-line department stores including the Broadway in Southern California; the Broadway Southwest based in Phoenix; San Francisco–based Emporium-Capwell; Weinstock's in Sacramento, California; and Thalhimer's based in Richmond, Virginia.

Prior to August 1987 Carter Hawley Hale also operated specialty stores, but they were split off, forming the Neiman-Marcus Group in which General Cinema Corporation owns a controlling interest. The Neiman-Marcus Group includes the high-fashion specialty stores of Neiman-Marcus and Bergdorf Goodman. Bergdorf

Goodman operates only one store located on New York's Fifth Avenue; Neiman-Marcus, based in Dallas, has stores spread from coast to coast and is still building new ones. These two divisions sell apparel for men, women, and children, and accessories and gifts. Also part of the Neiman-Marcus Group are Contempo Casuals, a women's sportswear chain, and Horchow Mail Order, a Dallas-based firm specializing in home furnishings, gifts, and apparel.

Batus Retail Group

Batus Retail Group is owned by B. A. T. Industries, a publicly held British company that also owns department stores in Germany, England, and Wales. The U. S. Batus Retail Group, headquartered in New York City, owns both department and specialty stores. Specialty store divisions include New York-based Saks Fifth Avenue and the John Breuner Company, a furniture retailer. Batus's two department store divisions are Marshall Field in Chicago and Ivey's in Charlotte, North Carolina. Since 1985 Batus has sold a number of department stores under its ownership, including Frederick and Nelson of Seattle and separate divisions of Gimbels in New York, Milwaukee, and Pittsburgh. Batus also sold the Thimbles specialty store chain.

Mercantile Stores Company, Inc.

Mercantile Stores Company with headquarters in New York City consists exclusively of department stores. It is one of the few major department store firms that has not diversified into specialty retailing. Forty percent of the company is owned by the Milliken family, which makes it less vulnerable to takeover than the other major department store groups. Although the company has maintained one of the best profit records of any retailer, Mercantile is less well known than other store groups. According to *Women's Wear Daily*, Mercantile has never made a major acquisition, never pursued an aggressive store-opening strategy, and never sought publicity outside normal advertising (Moin 1988).

Stores operated by Mercantile include both full-line and junior department stores, featuring women's, men's, and children's ready-to-wear and general dry goods. Over the years Mercantile has dropped home electronics from its merchandise assortment and has de-emphasized home furnishings. Total apparel, including accessories, shoes, and cosmetics, represents 82 percent of the merchandise offerings, which is higher than most department stores. The company emphasizes moderate to upper moderate-price apparel with 15 to 20 percent in private label goods. Although the company's image is a volume department store with moderate prices, many of the stores carry both bridge and designer lines of apparel.

Mercantile has eleven traditional department store divisions with no stores operating under the Mercantile name. In most cases each store is the number-one volume retailer in its market. The largest division is Gayfer's based in Mobile, Alabama. Stores owned by Mercantile include the following:

Store Division	Headquarters Location
Bacons/Roots	Louisville, Kentucky
DeLendrecie's	Fargo, North Dakota
Gayfer's/Montgomery Fair	Montgomery, Alabama
Gafer's	Mobile, Alabama
Glass Block	Duluth, Minnesota
Hennessey's	Billings, Montana
The Jones Store Co.	Kansas City, Missouri
Joslin's	Denver, Colorado
Lion	Toledo, Ohio
McAlpin's	Cincinnati, Ohio
J.B. White	Augusta, Georgia

Specialty Store Ownership

Although specialty stores are owned by several of the large department store groups, in recent years the number of specialty stores has expanded with several owned by large parent corporations. Among the major chains and multiple format companies operating fashion soft goods are The Limited, the Gap, U.S. Shoe, F. W. Woolworth, Melville, and Hartmarx.

The Limited, Inc.

The largest specialty retailer in the United States is The Limited, which is based in Columbus, Ohio. Its retail divisions comprise The Limited, Limited Express, Lerner, Lerner Woman,* Lane Bryant, Victoria's Secret, Limited Express for Men, and Henri Bendel. Combined volume for these stores in 1987 was over $3,500,000,000. The Limited also owns the upscale sportswear and sporting goods

---

*Lerner Woman was sold in April, 1989. It was the first divestiture for The Limited, which historically has bought businesses.

chain Abercrombie & Fitch. The Limited has expanded in recent years by purchasing existing fashion retailers and by adding new branches. It has plans to open additional branches of Henri Bendel, a single-unit, fashion-oriented women's store based in New York.

The Gap, Inc.

Another chain that has enjoyed considerable success with stores located in shopping centers throughout the United States is the Gap. Its divisions are the Gap, GapKids, Banana Republic, and Hemisphere. The Gap started as a store featuring Levi's jeans for "guys and gals." As the market for jeans declined, it shifted its emphasis to colorful sportswear. The GapKids carries this same colorful merchandising concept to children's wear. Banana Republic stores initially featured the safari look exclusively, but their merchandising mix is changing because the safari look has lost some of its popularity. Hemisphere is Gap's upscale, European-style sportswear store for women and men. In addition to operating stores throughout the United States, the Gap has stores in England.

United States Shoe Corporation

U.S. Shoe Corporation, a manufacturer-retailer of apparel, shoes, and accessories, owns and operates women's specialty stores, including Casual Corner, August Max, Ups N' Downs, Caren Charles, Petite Sophisticate, and T. H. Mandy. U.S. Shoe also operates Lenscrafters, an eyewear chain. In 1989 the company sold its footwear division to an investment group.

F. W. Woolworth Co.

F. W. Woolworth Co. is best known for its variety store chain by the same name; however, much of Woolworth's business today comes from its specialty stores. In recent years Woolworth has changed many of its units from variety stores to 1,000-square-foot operations featuring one of thirty specialties, including apparel, shoes, handbags, costume jewelry, cosmetics, drugs, stationery, or home fashions. Specialty companies owned by F. W. Woolworth include the Kinney shoe chain, the Richman Bros. apparel chain for men, and the Little Folks/Kids Mart chain. Other Woolworth divisions are Athletic X-Press, Sportelle women's casual apparel stores, Frugal Franks promotional footwear, Frame Scene, and Herald Square stationery. In 1986 Woolworth's specialty stores produced 35 percent of the company's sales. Woolworth plans to increase this to nearly 50 percent by 1991 (Feinberg 1988).

The Limited, Inc.

The Limited, Inc. is a group of more than 3,000 apparel stores, including seven fashion retail and two catalogue businesses, which now make up the leading specialty retailer in the country. In fact, the company sells more women's clothing and accessories than any other merchant in the world. In spite of setbacks along the way, The Limited has shown remarkable growth, reporting a sales volume of nearly $4.1 billion for fiscal 1988. According to *Stores* magazine, six of The Limited's seven divisions would have made the NRMA list of Top 100 Specialty Stores except that the company chooses to combine its divisional sales. The company's seven store divisions include The Limited, Express, Lerner, Lane Bryant, Victoria's Secret, Henri Bendel, and Abercrombie & Fitch.

Leslie H. Wexner, founder and chairman of The Limited, Inc., opened his first store in Columbus in 1963 with $5,000 borrowed from his aunt. Wexner's new store offered a limited selection of clothing consisting of moderately priced sports-

The three units, The Limited, Limited Express, and Victoria's Secret, are located in a multilevel store on Madison Avenue at 62nd Street.
Source: *Reprinted with permission of The Limited, Inc.*

wear such as skirts, sweaters, and shirts, and so came the name The Limited. Wexner soon built a thriving business that included six stores with which he went public in 1969. During the 1970s he expanded his company by opening stores in prime shopping center locations. By 1976 he was operating 100 stores.

Wexner adopted a merchandising strategy that was different than what other fashion retailers were following in the 1970s. Rather than selling designer labels or national brands, Wexner had his merchandise manufactured by low-cost, non-union shops in the Orient. This enabled him to charge what the market would bear. In 1978 he bought Mast Industries, a contract manufacturer, to source apparel for The Limited. Mast, located in Andover, Massachusetts, contracts with some 200 factories in thirty countries. Mast does 90 percent of its business with The Limited, Inc. and the remainder with other retailers and manufacturers.

In the 1980s Wexner had to adapt to his changing customer. The baby boomers he had catered to as teenagers with his stores were now adult working women with elevated tastes and incomes. He began to upgrade the quality of his merchandise and although the majority of it remained private label, he sought well-known designers, such as Kenzo, Mariuccia Mandelli of Krizia, and Carol Horn, to create exclusive collections for The Limited. He also established a new store division, originally called Limited Express, offering popularly-priced sportswear and accessories that appealed to younger women. The division, now called Express, presently offers the latest European fashions.

Throughout the 1980s Wexner expanded his company by continuing to open additional stores and by an aggressive campaign to acquire chains of stores selling to other consumer markets. His acquisitions included the following: Lerner, the now-upgraded, popularly-priced apparel chain; Victoria's Secret, designer lingerie boutiques; Lane Bryant, large-size women's apparel retail chain; and Brylane, the largest catalogue retailer of women's special sizes. In 1985 he purchased Henri Bendel, a single-unit store located on Manhattan's 57th Street specializing in international fashion for the sophisticated fashion-forward customer. In 1988 the twenty-five-store Abercrombie & Fitch upscale sportswear and sporting goods chain was acquired; it now emphasizes its men's collection and exclusive gifts. In 1987 the company entered the men's business with Express for Men sections in some of its stores, and Limited Stores also entered the children's and intimate apparel businesses with Limited Too and Lingerie Cacique, respectively.

The company heightened its presence in Manhattan in 1985 by opening an impressive store on Madison Avenue at 62nd Street in an area dominated by designer boutiques. Included are The Limited, Express, and Victoria's Secret—units catering to potentially different customers—under one roof. What resulted was a multilevel store that allows each of the three units to express its own personality yet offer transitional displays between the shops, on ledges and stairways, designed to draw customers into the other units. The end product is a store striking in layout, design, and visual display.

Wexner is considered a retailing genius in the degree of flexibility he has been able to achieve in his empire through vertical integration and standardization of merchandising procedures. The ownership of Mast Industries allows the company to control both manufacturing and retailing operations. The Limited does not design but rather bases its retail business on private label production of fashion ideas taken from the international fashion market. According to Wexner, the success of The Limited's businesses is that the companies are customer-driven. Merchants determine customer demand by testing items in their stores before having them reproduced in volume and distributed to the stores. Private labels, such as Forenza, Hunter's Run, Venezia, and Outback Red, have become some of the best-selling brands in the country. This approach has enabled The Limited to abandon the traditional selling seasons and move new merchandise into the stores in six to nine weeks—in contrast to other retailers, who take six to nine months. Wexner believes that customers will come more often if they expect to see new merchandise.

Although very dynamic and highly copied, visual displays and methods of presenting the merchandise are standardized for all of The Limited stores to ensure the best merchandise presentation possible. Props and furniture are sent to the stores with photographs and blueprints of how the visual displays must be set up. The look is the same for every store, and Wexner depends on store display and mall traffic to secure business.

Wexner is known for his aggressive acquisition style. After The Limited buys a company, changes are made quickly. The newly acquired company is connected to The Limited's computer operation in Columbus, giving Wexner and company executives the information needed to make quick decisions. After purchasing Lerner, for example, Wexner canceled approximately $100 million worth of orders for new merchandise—a move that did not win him friends among apparel manufacturers.

In 1984 Wexner attempted an unfriendly takeover of Carter Hawley Hale Stores, which at that time owned the prestigious specialty stores Bergdorf Goodman and Neiman-Marcus as well as a number of department stores. The attempt failed, but The Limited was able to move into upscale fashion retailing with its purchase of Henri Bendel. Wexner has announced plans to open additional units of Henri Bendel and has forecast that the volume of The Limited, Inc. will triple to $10 billion by the early 1990s (Pete Born, "Limited Expects $10B in Volume by Early 1990s," *Women's Wear Daily*, May 24, 1988, pp. 1, 15).

Melville Corp.

Melville has been an industry leader in buying out small specialty operations and expanding them. Its largest division is the off-price specialty store Marshall's. Other Melville specialty stores are Kay-Bee toy operation, Thom McAn shoe stores, Linens 'n Things, which sells domestics and home textiles, Wilson's House of Leather, and menswear retailer Chess King. Smaller divisions of Melville's include This End Up and the Fan Club/Open Country. This End Up stores sell popular-priced casual furniture. The Fan Club sells brand-name athletic footwear and activewear, and Open Country specializes in upscale, branded footwear.

Hartmarx

Hartmarx operates a number of store formats. The Hartmarx Specialty Stores division operates upscale men's stores under a number of names, and women's apparel stores under the name Corporate Woman. Hartmarx also operates apparel discount stores under the names of Kuppenheimer and Country Miss/Old Mill. As discussed previously, Hartmarx is a vertical company that manufactures much of the apparel it sells through its retail stores.

Trends in Store Ownership

Most conventional retail department and specialty stores were originally single-unit, independently owned and operated stores. Today few large stores remain that are independently owned. Most are multiunit divisions of an ownership group. Most of the ownership groups are publicly owned corporations, but a few, such as R. H. Macy, are privately owned. Many old names in retailing disappeared as mergers of divisions within ownership groups accelerated during the 1980s. Ownership groups combined divisions in order to increase buying power and save operating expenses. Both the merging of store divisions and the sale of divisions by ownership groups make it difficult to keep up with what companies own what stores.

Although ownership groups have historically been organized on a decentralized basis, many are becoming more centralized. The consolidation of functions is making stores owned by ownership groups more efficient in their operations and making their divisions more like chain stores. Often buying is done at the divisional level in conjunction with the central office. Buyers for each division meet with personnel from the central office and shop the market by committee.

An increasing number of U.S. fashion stores are owned by foreign corporations. Three of the top eight department store ownership groups now have foreign owners: Canadian Campeau Corporation owns both Federated Department Stores and Allied Stores Corporation, and Britain's B. A. T. Industries is owner of Marshall Field, Saks Fifth Avenue, and Ivey's.

Another example of foreign ownership of American department store and specialty stores is Australia's Hooker Corporation, which owns Bonwit Teller and B. Altman, both based in New York, the Parisian based in Birmingham, Alabama, and Sakowitz in Houston. In addition, Brooks Brothers is owned by the British retail firm of Marks and Spencer, and Talbots, a women's apparel retailer and mail-order firm, is owned by Jusco, a Japanese consortium. C. R. Dressman from Holland has a minority interest in Dillard Department Stores.

An increasing number of stores are owned by manufacturer-retailers. U.S. manufacturers and designers are opening or franchising stores of their own. Liz Claiborne has stores named First Issue carrying merchandise designed specifically for these stores. Claiborne has other shops in the planning stage that will feature the same apparel and accessories that the company sells to other retail stores. Ralph Lauren has more than sixty shops in the United States, and Calvin Klein opened his first franchise store in Dallas in 1988. Some additional American design firms that have opened their own stores include Adrienne Vittadini, Betsey Johnson, Alexander Julian, WillieWear/Willi Smith, and Anne Klein.

Many foreign companies are also operating stores or franchises in the United States. Examples include Benetton of Italy, Mothercare and Laura Ashley of England, and many European designer boutiques such as Gucci, Krizia, Ungaro, Lagerfeld, and Saint Laurent.

The ownership of retailing changed greatly in the 1980s, and changes are expected to continue in the 1990s. Two retail strategies are emerging for selling fashion merchandise. One is the upscale department store and the other is the even more upscale specialty store group. These stores feature merchandise to attract the upscale customer who is well educated, is sophisticated in fashion taste, and has a high disposable income. In between are a few local mom-and-pop specialty stores and some nationally distributed specialty stores.

Summary of Key Points

1. The organizational chart for a retail firm presents a visual picture of the firm's structure and shows how responsibility and authority are delegated within the company. It shows employees to whom they are accountable and who has the authority to direct them in carrying out their responsibilities.

2. All stores, regardless of size, must provide for performing the same five basic functions in their organizational structure. The five key functional areas of retailing are merchandising, store operations, sales promotion, financial control, and personnel.

3. The merchandising function is concerned with buying, selling, and stock planning. Merchandising is the central focus of the store.

4. The financial control function is concerned with controlling the spending activities of the store. This involves the activities of the credit department, the accounting department, which pays the bills, and the statistical department, which provides important information to the buyer.

5. The operations function is concerned with store management, protection, service, maintenance, delivery, and receiving merchandise.

6. The personnel function is concerned with interviewing, hiring, training, terminating, and record keeping for all store employees.

7. The sales promotion function is concerned with advertising, visual merchandising, publicity, and special events.

8. The general merchandise manager is the chief merchandising officer and top management's link to the divisional merchandise managers and the buyers. The primary duty of the GMM is to guide the merchandising division in achieving a satisfactory profit for the store. The GMM is responsible for establishing and interpreting the store's merchandising policies. In a large company the GMM is assisted by divisional merchandise managers who oversee groups of related departments headed by buyers.

9. Merchandising staff bureaus provide assistance and advice to buyers. These include comparison shopping, the fashion bureau, quality assurance, unit control, and resident buying office.

10. Mergers and acquisitions in retailing have led to fewer stores in the United States. Major trends in store ownership include greater centralization of operations, foreign ownership, and designer/manufacturer-operated stores.

Key Words and Concepts

Define, identify, or explain each of the following:

assistant buyer

associate buyer

authority

buyer

controller

divisional merchandise manager (DMM)

financial control division/function

four-function organization

general merchandise manager (GMM)

heads of stock

Mazur Plan

merchandise staff bureau

merchandising division/function

operations division/function

organizational chart

ownership groups

personnel division/function

responsibility

sales promotion division/function

store ownership group

three-function organization

two-function organization

visual merchandising

Discussion Questions

1. Name the five key functional areas of retailing, and describe the primary responsibilities of each area.

2. Discuss the relationship of the merchandising division to the other divisions within the organizational structure of a large store.

3. How does chain store organization differ from the organizational structure of conventional department stores?

4. Discuss the responsibilities of the GMM, DMM, buyer, and assistant buyer.

5. Explain the various staff bureaus that may be found in a merchandising division, and discuss how each assists the buyer.

6. How do store ownership groups differ from chain stores?

7. Name the major store ownership groups, and identify the ownership of the major department and specialty stores located in your community.

8. Discuss the trends in store ownership, and give current examples.

Notes

R. Patrick Cash, ed., *The Buyer's Manual*. New York: NRMA, 1979, p. 38.

Samuel Feinberg, "Stores Finding Nordstrom Gains Hard to Repeat," *Women's Wear Daily*, August 26, 1988, p. 8.

Leon Harris, *Merchant Princes*. New York: Harper, 1979, p. 345.

Tom Mahoney and Leonard Sloane, *The Great Merchants*. New York: Harper, 1974, p. 11.

David Moin, "A Passive Power at Mercantile," *Women's Wear Daily*, March 30, 1988, pp. 1, 15.

Stores, June 1975, p. 2.

CHAPTER 13 _____

THE ROLE OF THE RETAIL BUYER AND RESIDENT BUYING OFFICES

THE BASIC function of retail merchandising is to buy and sell goods to the ultimate consumer. The buyer is the retail specialist who is responsible for performing this function. Although the duties of the buyer vary in different types of buying positions, all retail buyers have one function in common—to select merchandise for resale to the ultimate consumer. The other functions performed by the buyer will vary depending upon the type of buying position held. This chapter is a discussion of the different kinds of retail buyers and their job responsibilities. Included are buyers employed by different types of stores and buyers who work for resident buying offices.

Kinds of Retail Buyers

There are four kinds of retail buyers: (1) the entrepreneurial buyer, (2) the specialized store buyer, (3) the central buyer, and (4) the resident buyer. Their job responsibilities vary but all are concerned with estimating the customer's demands and buying the merchandise to meet these demands. Most buyers are also involved with promoting the goods in order to motivate customers to buy. These three activities comprise what is called the **buying-selling cycle.**

The three activities of the buying-selling cycle, estimating consumer demand, buying merchandise, and selling merchandise, form a continuing circle. The buyer controls the first two activities, estimating demand and purchasing merchandise, but in the third activity of the cycle the consumer assumes control. By accepting or rejecting the merchandise offered for sale, the consumer sends a message to the buyer concerning consumer demand. The buyer then uses this information in forecasting consumer demand. Future buying decisions are based in part on the customer's decision to buy or not to buy the merchandise provided by the retail buyer. Thus the buying-selling cycle continues in a never-ending circle.

The Entrepreneurial Buyer

The **entrepreneurial buyer** is a small store executive who is responsible for the total operation of a store. In most instances this person also owns or is part owner of the store. The mom-and-pop store owner/buyer is this kind of retail buyer.

The entrepreneurial buyer has the widest variety of functions to perform of all the kinds of buyers. In addition to buying the merchandise, this buyer is responsible for performing or overseeing all of the functions concerned with store operation, including buying, selling, promoting, and storekeeping. The entrepreneurial buyer is a small store executive who is truly a jack-of-all-trades. In the smallest store setting this small store executive may do everything him- or herself with only the help of one or two salespeople. As a store becomes larger and more personnel are hired, the buyer's job may become more specialized.

The Specialized Store Buyer

The **specialized store buyer** buys goods for a department or a group of departments of a larger store. This buyer's job may be limited to the functions of buying, or the buyer may also be a department manager responsible for the basic duties of supervising salespeople and running a selling department.

In the single-unit department store, this buyer is likely to serve as both buyer and department manager. In this situation the buyer's office is usually located in a stockroom near the selling floor. The buyer, in all likelihood, spends time on the salesfloor actually selling to customers, handling customer complaints, and making merchandise adjustments. This buyer is close to the pulse of his or her customers and should have a clear understanding of customer demand.

As stores grow larger and add multiple branches, the specialized store buyer's job becomes even more specialized. The buyer's office may be moved away from the department, possibly even away from the retail store itself. The buyer is no longer responsible for supervising the sales personnel and is able to concentrate on the buying aspect of the buying-selling cycle. The buyer may no longer have any direct contact with customers and very little contact with salespeople. A separate department manager is responsible for managing the salesfloor.

The Central Buyer

The **central buyer** is a member of the headquarters' staff who buys for a chain or group of stores. This buyer specializes in the market end of the work, leaving the functions of selling and stockkeeping to department managers and other personnel located in the stores. The central buyer usually works out of a company's central headquarters rather than having an office within one of the stores. Often the central buyer's office is situated in a major market center such as New York or Los Angeles, making it easier for this buyer to concentrate on the buying of merchandise.

Although the mass merchandising chains and the apparel specialty chains have this kind of buyer, central buying is not synonymous with chain store buying. Central buying means that the authority and responsibility for merchandise selection and purchase is in the hands of headquarters' staff rather than with individual store units. Any type of store that is part of a group can use central buying, and chain stores do not always use central buying.

The Resident Buyer

A fourth kind of buyer is the **resident buyer,** who is headquartered in a major market center such as New York, Los Angeles, Dallas, or Chicago and assists the entrepreneurial buyer and the specialized buyer in performing the functions of their jobs. The primary function of the resident buyer is to provide assistance and market representation to store buyers. Resident buyers work under less pressure than other kinds of buyers because they are not directly responsible for making a profit. Resident buying offices are discussed in detail later in this chapter.

Basic Responsibilities of the Buyer

In many stores the buyer performs basic merchandising functions including (1) planning, (2) buying, (3) pricing, (4) stockkeeping, and (5) selling. Each of these five functions involves different activities necessary to manage a profitable department. In some stores all of these functions are the responsibility of the buyer. In larger stores a number of people share the responsibilities of these buying-selling activities.

Planning to Buy

The buyer's job begins with planning. A major portion of any buyer's time is spent planning and coordinating the buying and selling operations in order to achieve the basic goal of retailing, which is to profitably sell merchandise to satisfied customers. The buyer works with the merchandise manager in carrying out the planning process.

Planning to buy begins with analyzing consumer demand and determining the merchandise that will meet the needs and demands of the store's customers. The buyer must plan the merchandise assortment and determine what, when, and how to buy. The buyer also prepares the **merchandise plan,** which is the dollar control budget for the department for a six-month period. The merchandise plan looks to the future, projecting the dollar amount of merchandise needed to achieve planned sales.

The most important factor in planning is flexibility. The merchandise plan is based on estimated figures. Since it is a forecast for the future, the buyer must constantly check results against the plan and make adjustments as needed.

Buying

After completing the planning process, the buyer is responsible for buying the merchandise to meet the plan. Planning determines the amount of money to be spent in order to meet planned sales, but fashion buying must be done by classification, price line, size, color, and quantity. The buyer must understand what customers want to buy, when they want it, in what sizes, colors, and fabrics, and what they want to pay for it.

Buying involves determining from whom to buy as well as selecting and purchasing the merchandise. A buyer purchases from vendors who are also referred to as resources or suppliers. A vendor is a person or a firm such as a manufacturer, importer, wholesaler, or jobber from whom a retailer purchases goods.

The buyer must make contact with merchandise sources, select the merchandise, and handle all of the necessary negotiations with the vendor to get the merchandise delivered to the store according to the scheduled plan. The buyer is responsible for writing the order, communicating and negotiating with the vendor concerning prices, credit, and shipping terms, and for following up on orders to assure the timing of deliveries.

Pricing

The buyer, guided by policies established by store management, is responsible for setting markup goals and pricing the merchandise. Pricing may include checking prices of competitive stores if the store follows a competitive pricing policy. This means that the store sets its prices at or below the prices of competing stores. The buyer must establish prices that will achieve markup goals and make a profit for the department. In selecting merchandise the buyer must always consider the retail price the customer would be willing to pay.

Part of pricing is **repricing,** which includes both markdowns and price increases. **Markdowns** are reductions in price from the original or previous retail price. The buyer has to determine markdowns for special sales and to move slow selling goods. Price increases are most important when the replacement cost of merchandise increases, and price on the merchandise already in the store is increased or marked up to cover the higher replacement cost.

Stockkeeping

Stockkeeping is concerned with receiving, protecting, and controlling the merchandise. In some instances buyers are not directly involved with stockkeeping activities, but in any case someone must be responsible for handling stock that has not yet been sold.

Receiving involves checking incoming goods to see that they concur with the buyer's order. Merchandise should be the correct sizes, colors, styles, fabrics, and quantities. **Quality control** is also part of the receiving process. In quality control the merchandise is checked to assure that its condition agrees with what the buyer ordered and that the merchandise is not damaged or flawed.

Markers in the receiving department must be given the necessary information to place on price tickets: price, season letter code, classification, vendor number, style number, and any other information the buyer requires on the ticket. Goods received must be distributed to stores in a multistore operation, and invoices must be authorized for payment.

Protection is another aspect of stockkeeping. The buyer must be concerned with protecting goods after they are received by the warehouse or store. Protection is concerned with safeguarding against shoplifting, internal theft, breakage, or damage. Arranging for proper storage of the merchandise is also part of the buyer's responsibility.

Stock control involves checking to see which items of the merchandise are fast-selling and which are slow-selling. The buyer makes decisions concerning what merchandise classifications need to be controlled and sets up an appropriate system to provide the information needed to analyze sales. Stockkeeping also concerns handling returns and transfers of merchandise.

Stockkeeping concerns handling returns to vendors **(RTV)** and transfers of merchandise between stores. Goods are authorized to be returned to a supplier by a store when errors are made in filling the order, goods are received after a specified delivery date, merchandise is defective, or some other breach of contract is made by the vendor. Usually the buyer is required to request permission from the vendor to make the merchandise return.

Selling

Although the buyer may or may not be directly involved in selling the merchandise within the store, he or she always has a responsibility to the selling function. In order to make a profit for his or her department, a buyer must purchase merchandise that is salable. It is often said in retailing that "goods well bought are half sold." In addition to buying merchandise that will sell, the buyer must communicate to the appropriate employees the information needed to effectively present and sell the merchandise. The buyer may be involved directly in training salespeople or may provide information used to train them. The buyer knows the merchandise and its selling features better than anyone else. The buyer has a responsibility to excite the salespeople who in turn will communicate to the customers about the merchandise.

The buyer also has a responsibility to direct promotional activities to motivate customers to buy. The buyer usually determines when and what merchandise will be advertised and presents ideas for ways to promote, advertise, and display merchandise effectively. Because of the trend toward central buying, promotion has become a vital part of successful buying. Ultimately the buyer is responsible for making a profit, and the merchandise must be sold to do this. The functions of the fashion buyer are summarized in the following list.

Plan to Buy

1. Completes six-month merchandise plan.

2. Develops model stock plan.

3. Makes out buying plan and determines open-to-buy.

Develop Resources for Buying

1. Finds resources whose merchandise will appeal to department's customers.

2. Establishes and maintains good vendor relationships.

3. Evaluates style, workmanship, fabrications, value, and other important merchandise selection factors.

Buy

1. Determines the best buying methods to use.

2. Attends fashion markets.

3. Interviews sales representatives who visit the store.

4. May place small test orders, then reorder good sellers.

5. Writes orders.

Study Consumer Market

1. Knows store's target customer and type, quality, and price level of merchandise sold throughout the store.

2. Studies customers' reactions to merchandise in the department.

Study Fashion Trends

1. Watches for trends in color, silhouette, and fabrics.

2. Shops other stores for ideas and to observe what is selling.

3. Reads fashion magazines and trade publications.

4. Reads fashion bulletins from fashion services and resident buying office.

5. Attends fashion shows and buying clinics when at market.

Work with Other Departments

1. Selects merchandise for promotion or advertising; checks and approves ads.

2. Pushes merchandise for promotion, publicity, and display.

Maintain Stock

1. Sees that adequate stock is on hand to meet planned sales.

2. Prices merchandise and provides information for ticketing stock.

3. Distributes stock to the stores.

Maintain Records

1. Keeps complete records on amount of merchandise bought and sold, stock on hand, style numbers, and price.

2. Checks on delivery dates and cancels orders when appropriate.

Prepare Written Materials

1. Writes market reports.

2. Writes memos and letters.

Organize and Manage Office

1. Selects staff.

2. Trains and supervises assistant buyer, head of stock, and clerical assistants.

3. Sees that salespeople and department managers have necessary product information to sell effectively.

How the Buyer Is Evaluated

The buyer is judged by management largely on the objective results of his or her activities. There are standards to measure the efficiency of every department or buyer. Buyers are expected to plan realistically and to achieve or better their planned figures. The overall objective in retailing is to sell merchandise at a profit. In the end the buyer is evaluated by the bottom line, the profit achieved by the department. Management also evaluates the buyer using the measures of sales and inventory results.

Sales Results

The buyer's performance is easily measured by sales results in terms of total dollars and units of merchandise sold, or sales per square foot of selling space. Management usually looks for increase over last year's figures, and buyers often keep a **beat yesterday book,** which provides a running comparison of daily sales figures with those of the previous year. Buyers are expected to establish realistic sales goals and to achieve or better those figures. The buyer's results can be compared to results in similar departments in other stores. Government agencies and trade associations such as the NRMA provide comparative data.

Inventory Results

Another area of objective measurement used in evaluating the buyer is inventory results revealed by (1) stock turn, (2) prior stock, and (3) merchandise shortages. **Stock turn rate,** also referred to as **stock turnover,** is the number of times the average inventory has been sold and replaced in a given period (usually a year). It is calculated by dividing net sales in dollars by average inventory at selling price in dollars. **Prior stock** is the proportion of old goods versus new goods in the inventory. Usually goods left over from the previous selling season are considered prior stock. Particularly with fashion merchandise, stock needs to be turned over and kept fresh and new. A **stock shortage** occurs when actual stock inventory is less than the written records indicate should be on hand. When merchandise is stolen, broken, or somehow disappears, a shortage occurs. Shortages are expressed as a percentage of sales and are established when a physical count of the merchandise is taken and compared with the book inventory figures.

Profit Results

Profit results are analyzed based on (1) **initial markup,** which is the difference between the cost price of merchandise and its first retail price, (2) **maintained markup,** the difference between net sales and the cost of goods sold, which represents the actual markup achieved for a selling period, (3) **gross margin** or gross profit, which is the amount of profit before selling and other operating expenses have been deducted, and (3) **operating profit,** gross margin less all expenses chargeable to the selling department. The specific criteria used in evaluating the buyer depend on the degree to which management considers the buyer responsible for price changes and expenses. Buyers cannot control the expenses of promotion and selling when they are not directly responsible for these activities. Profit results may be expressed in dollar amounts or as a percent of sales.

Results of the Buyer's Evaluation

The buyer's results are compared to previous figures in his or her department and to goals established by the buyer and store management. Typical figures are also available from trade associations, such as the National Retail Merchants Association, which can be used as a standard of comparison to see how a department is performing.

Buyers are usually reviewed by management on a semiannual or annual basis. When the evaluation is favorable, the buyer may receive a raise in salary or a bonus based on the sales results of the department. Successful performance may result in promotion to a department with a greater sales volume or to the position of divisional merchandise manager. Unsatisfactory performance can lead to transfer to a less challenging department or to dismissal.

Resident Buying Offices

Resident buying offices, briefly discussed in an earlier chapter, are located in major market centers where they are representatives of noncompeting retail client stores in the marketplace and provide these client stores with many market-related services. The primary responsibility of the resident buying office is coverage of the market. Resident buying offices provide their client stores with information about market trends and serve as consultants and advisors to buyers in purchasing goods for retail stores. Resident buyers shop the market daily in order to give their clients or member stores current information and provide services as requested by the store buyers they represent. They act as assistants and advisors to store buyers when they visit the

Schwab-Taylor-Gavender

1G22 APPAREL MART • DALLAS, TEXAS 75258

FROM OFFICE TO GARDEN PARTY

Bonnie Boynton

CITY CIRCUIT
19104 Concrete Jungle Jacket/$44.50
19152 Black Out Shirt/$32.50
19101 Crisp Trouser/$34.50
19193 Heavy Metal Belt/$12.50

Plaid & Stripe: 100% Cotton
Black: 100% Rayon Challis
Sizes: P-S-M-L

COUNTRY GARDENS
19312 Garden Party Blouse/$42.50
19311 Full Bloom Dirndl/$37.50

Florals: 100% Rayon
Sizes: P-S-M-L

TERMS: NET 30
DELIVERY: 2-28-89
SALES REPRESENTATIVES:
Room 4B11
Alvin Jacobs
Gary Hill
Alex Canaan
John Cockrell
BUYER:
Liz Martin
(214) 638-7762

Schwab, Taylor and Gavender provides bulletins for their clients or member stores with current fashion news.
Source: *Reprinted with permission of Schwab, Taylor and Gavender.*

market, and they represent the buyer in the market when they are back at their home stores. Thus resident buying offices are the market representatives for stores and provide headquarters offices for store personnel during their buying trips.

The greatest number of resident buying offices are located in New York City, the primary fashion market for the United States. A limited number are found in the major regional markets such as Los Angeles, Dallas, Chicago, and Atlanta. Some are scattered in a few other market cities, and some major resident buying offices maintain branch offices in foreign market centers.

A listing of buying offices can be found in *Sheldon's Retail Directory of the United States and Canada* and *Phelon's Resident Buyers and Merchandise Brokers*. Published annually, this directory lists buying offices according to location. The 1988 directory devotes seventy-two pages to buying offices located in New York City, eight pages to Los Angeles offices, and five pages to other locations, which include Chicago, Dallas, Miami, and New Jersey and New York states. In addition to giving the name and address for each buying office listed, the directory provides the following information: types of stores serviced, buyers' names and categories of merchandise bought, and an alphabetical listing of the client stores served. Also included is an index of stores, followed by the buying office or offices used by each store.

Resident buying offices are usually specialized in the type of stores they service. Stores are usually similar in size and target customer and are located in different cities and towns so that they are not in competition with one another. Some offices serve large-volume department stores or specialty stores. Some cover all classifications of merchandise ranging from apparel and accessories for men, women, and children to home furnishings. Other offices service only specialty stores carrying a single line of merchandise such as children's wear, furs, or bridal wear.

Buying offices vary greatly in size. Some are one-person operations providing limited buying services to a small number of stores. Other offices are large operations with many resident buyers and other specialists serving hundreds of stores.

Buying offices play an important role in store merchandising and distribution. They provide retail stores with continuous coverage in the marketplace. Most large departmentalized stores and many small stores use the services of at least one resident buying office. Some stores use more than one buying office. For example, a specialty store carrying apparel for men and women may use one buying office that specializes in women's wear and another that specializes in menswear, or a store may be represented by one buying office in the New York market and another in Los Angeles.

Types of Resident Buying Offices

Resident buying offices are classified according to their ownership structure. There are two broad classifications: (1) independent offices and (2) store-owned offices. An independent office services noncompeting client stores, which pay for the office's services. Store-owned offices are owned by the store or stores they service and work only for these stores.

Independent Offices

Paid Office

The most common type of resident buying office is the paid office, which is also called a *fee* or *salaried office*. These offices are independently owned and operated and seek noncompeting stores as paying clients. Stores contract on a yearly basis for the services of the offices and pay a fee based on the store's sales volume. The usual fee varies from 1/2 to 1 percent of the store's past year's sales volume.

Some paid offices specialize in serving department stores and larger specialty stores; others concentrate on small specialty stores. Two larger paid offices that serve department stores are Henry Donegar Associates and Atlas Buying Corporation. Most paid offices concentrate on meeting the needs of apparel specialty stores. Certified Fashion Guild, for example, services specialty stores selling moderate to better price apparel for men and women. A subsidiary, Youth Fashion Guild, covers children's wear. Some buying offices are highly specialized and limit their market coverage to one merchandise category such as large, petite, or tall sizes, bridal wear, maternity wear, girl's wear, juniors, furs, off-price apparel, fabrics, accessories, men's and boy's wear, or home furnishings (see Table 13.1 for some of the major New York resident buying offices).

Some independent offices service a large number of client stores. Henry Donegar Associates has the largest client roster, representing 565 stores doing a total of $12 billion in sales. Other offices have only a few client stores. Betty Cohen, for example, caters to upscale carriage trade stores and has about ninety accounts. Vicki Ross also limits her service to stores carrying high-fashion ready-to-wear in designer labels and services only seven accounts.

Merchandise Broker

Another type of independent buying office, the merchandise broker or commission office, as it is sometimes called, receives its fee directly from the manufacturer

Table 13.1 Representative List of Resident Buying Offices

Salared/Fee/Paid	Associated/Cooperative	Syndicate/Corporate
Anstendig, Blitstein & Gillenson	Associated Merchandising Corp.	Belk Stores Services, Inc.
Atlas Buying Corporation	Frederick Atkins Inc.	
Burns Winkler/Innovators		
Certified Fashion Guild		Federated/Allied Merchandising Services
Henry Doneger Associates		
Jack Braunstein		R. H. Macy Corporate Buying Office
Martin Bayer		May Merchandising Corp.
Van Buren/Carr Associates		Mercantile Stores Co., Inc.

or vendor with whom it places orders. With this type of office the merchandise broker is really a representative of the manufacturer rather than of the store and, therefore, is not a true resident buying office. Fees from vendors range from 3 to 5 percent of purchases. This is an increase from the commission bases a few years ago, which began at 2 percent (Feinberg 1988).

Merchandise brokers or commission buyers survive on personalized service to smaller stores. They are sometimes used by retail stores because stores cannot afford the services of a resident buying office. In some instances, wholesalers or jobbers also use merchandise brokers to purchase merchandise for them. Merchandise brokers are not as prevalent today as in the past. In fact, many of the early firms of this type changed into paid buying offices years ago. Growth in number of manufacturer's road salespeople has made merchandise brokers less essential as has the emergence of regional market centers. In recent years the number of merchandise brokers has decreased due to mergers, acquisitions, and closings of offices. Only about six offices of any size now remain in New York City. Among these are Carly Day, Karl J. Marx Co., Joseph D. Barzilay, Samuel S. Newman Associates, Nurik and Goldberg, and Tankel & Berstein.

Store-Owned Offices

The three types of store-owned offices include (1) private offices, (2) associated or cooperative offices, and (3) corporate or syndicate offices. Each of these offices is owned and operated by the store or stores it services.

Private Office

A private office is owned and operated by a single retail organization and services only that store. Such offices are actually a staff bureau of the store and are an extension of the store in the marketplace. Such private resident buying offices are not common because of the high cost of establishing them. Neiman-Marcus, for example, operates its own private office.

Associated/Cooperative Office

The associated or cooperative buying office is jointly owned and operated by a group of independently owned stores. The expenses of operating such an office are distributed among the member stores. Fees paid vary with the size and sales volume of each store. Membership in an associated office is by invitation only. Member stores are usually very similar as to sales volume, store policies, and target customer. Because few large independently owned stores remain today, the associated or cooperative buying office has declined in numbers and membership in recent years. By 1986 the Associated Merchandising Corporation (AMC) and Frederick Atkins were the only remaining cooperative buying offices in operation.

Corporate/Syndicate Office

The corporate or syndicate office is maintained by a parent organization, which owns a group of stores. Most store ownership groups and chains own and operate their own corporate resident buying office, which performs market services exclusively for those stores owned by the group. Examples of such offices are Federated/Allied Merchandising Services and May Merchandising Corporation.

Organization of Resident Buying Offices

Large resident buying offices are organized in much the same way as are large department or specialty stores. The merchandising division consists of buyers and merchandise managers whose jobs are similar to the same positions in departmentalized stores. Resident buyers are the store buyer's market representatives and are often referred to as "market reps" rather than buyers. They are specialists who cover a segment of the total market and provide information about general market conditions to buyers from client stores. Unlike store buyers, resident buyers are in the market every day. They are authorities on current market conditions and new resources. They visit resources and view lines almost daily. They are always available to troubleshoot for their client stores or look for special items and place orders as requested by a client. Although the resident buyer's job is similar to that of a store buyer, it is more specialized. The market rep is an expert on the market and has no direct responsibility to sales or managing a department.

Usually when a store buyer visits the market center, the first stop is the resident buying office to meet with his/her market representative. A store will often require its buyers to register with the buying office before visiting vendors. When a store pays for the services of a buying office, it wants to assure that store buyers use these services to the fullest extent. A buying office provides store buyers with another viewpoint and additional information to aid in making buying decisions. The buyer who learns to use the resident buying office to its fullest capacity can make market trips more productive and profitable.

Services Offered by Resident Buying Offices

The buying office began about 1900 as an organization devoted solely to placing orders for retail stores. Since then buying offices have expanded their services to provide information and services that individual stores cannot afford. Services offered vary depending upon the size and extent of the buying office. All buying offices provide services related to buying and merchandising. Large full-service offices provide services in three broad areas: merchandising, promotion, and research.

Merchandising Services

Merchandising services relate to (1) providing buying assistance to store buyers both when the buyers are at home and in the market, (2) reporting market information to client stores, (3) facilitating group buying, (4) developing private-label merchandise, and (5) central buying.

Providing Buying Assistance

When buyers are in the stores, the resident buying office is the buyer's representative in the market, providing buyers with information concerning current market conditions, following up on orders and checking on deliveries, handling adjustments and complaints with vendors, and placing orders for buyers when requested to so do by the store buyer. The market representative constantly keeps an eye open to find new vendors and new merchandise that may interest the store buyer and keeps the store informed on what is available in the market.

When store buyers come to market, the resident buying office assists the buyer with the visit. Resident buyers locate the best sources for merchandise in advance of the buyer's visit, make appointments for buyers with showrooms, and may even accompany the buyer on visits to vendors and manufacturers. The resident buying office provides basic office facilities for the buyer while in the market. Resident buying offices may even make hotel reservations for buyers and assist with personal reservations.

Reporting Market Information

Reporting market information is an important part of the job of the resident buying office. Through periodic and special bulletins or reports, the resident buying office keeps client stores informed of such information as (1) fashion trends for each season, (2) hot new items available in the market, (3) **opportunistic buys** that are unexpected opportunities to purchase merchandise at a good price, (4) reorder bulletins noting fast-selling items that the store may want to reorder, and (5) descriptions of what is selling in market-area stores.

Group Buying

Resident buying offices provide a means by which member stores can come together and buy as a group. Group buying is a form of purchasing where a number of noncompeting stores consolidate orders for goods to secure lower prices through volume purchasing. Group buying is also a way for some stores to meet the minimum order requirements set by some manufacturers.

Goods most commonly bought in this way are staple or semistaple items. Group buying is also done, however, with fashion merchandise. With group buying, store buyers meet with the resident buyer and discuss and evaluate the merchandise available. Each store decides individually whether or not to participate in the group buy.

Private Branding

A private brand is developed, owned, and controlled by the retailer or middle-man such as a resident buying office. Private brands are developed to help retailers meet competition and provide store individuality. Private branding has long been an important function of store-owned offices and is also done by independent offices to help their store compete with large companies. A private label gives a store exclusivity and the opportunity for a higher markup.

The resident buyer may work with a committee of store buyers developing specifications for products. The resident buying office seeks out the best resources and has the samples made. Member stores then are free to make their own decisions regarding buying the merchandise.

Central Buying

Sometimes resident buying offices serve as central buyers for a portion of a store's inventory. Under a central buying arrangement, the retail store buyer turns over buying authority to the resident buying office for selecting a portion of the store's merchandise.

In some instances resident buying offices figure monthly for their client stores the dollar amount of merchandise the store needs to buy to meet planned sales. Whereas many stores prefer to make the final decision on merchandise themselves and place their own orders, other stores hand over the buying responsibilities to the buying office allowing it to decide what merchandise to purchase.

Promotional Services

The promotional departments of resident buying offices assist clients with planning and executing promotional campaigns. The resident buying office will suggest or prepare direct mail pieces, catalogs, and advertising layouts. Resident buying offices also conduct clinics to assist stores in planning sales promotions, special events, and displays. Sometimes representatives from buying offices will visit stores to assist with training sales personnel and merchandising the stores.

Research Services

Research is an important function of many resident buying offices. Many engage in carrying out research to aid member stores in performing their business. The resident buying office often provides a means of exchanging operating statistics among stores. Such statistics offer stores a basis of comparison and aid in the development of standards.

Resident buying offices also study economic trends and consumer behavior, making the results of such studies available to their member stores. The buying office thus becomes a clearinghouse of information used to help stores compete effectively in their trading area.

Whereas buying offices began as a buying extension of the store, the present-day office is marketing-oriented providing many services designed to meet the needs of client or member stores. The term *buying office* may have become outdated as research and promotional services have become increasingly important. Buying offices have become consulting firms and research organizations ("Buying Offices" 1981).

Associated and syndicate offices cover all aspects of retailing, including operations, electronic data processing (EDP) systems, management information systems (MIS), sales promotion, financial control, credit, and more.

The Future of Resident Buying Offices

The future of the resident buying office is somewhat uncertain. In recent years many resident buying offices have gone out of business and others have been bought out or merged with other firms. A number of reasons have been projected for their high mortality rate. Samuel Feinberg in his "From Where I Sit" column in *Women's Wear Daily* gave the following reasons for the demise of many buying offices (Feinberg 1988).

1. Many offices have not provided stores with essential advice on market research and strategic planning.

2. Pay for market representatives and office management personnel has been too low to attract and keep strong personnel.

3. Too many offices have not given effective market coverage.

4. Growth of regional marts has cut down on visits of smaller store buyers to New York, and buyers shopping regional marts have felt less need for the services of a buying office.

5. Demise of mom-and-pop stores.

Another reason for the continued decline in the number of resident buying offices today is the trend toward mergers and acquisitions among department stores. There are simply fewer independent stores for resident buying offices to seek as clients.

The trend to mergers and acquisitions of large retail companies has been repeated in resident buying offices. During the 1980s a continuing series of mergers by independent buying offices in the fashion industry took place. Now only about six sizeable firms remain, which is down from more than two dozen in 1980. Larger buying offices have increased buying power, which enables them to offer their clients greater price incentives.

Mid-size firms have been squeezed out as buying offices have combined. The successful buying firms today are either very large or very small. To survive, buying offices must offer their client stores services that lead to improved retail business. Large offices have the advantage of buying power, whereas small buying offices must concentrate on offering specialized services.

Polo/Ralph Lauren, Inc.

Polo/Ralph Lauren, Inc. is a privately owned corporation with franchised and company-owned stores in the United States and Europe. The stores carry only the designs and licensed merchandise of Polo/Ralph Lauren, Inc. and pay no franchise fee or royalties. Lauren makes money by serving as wholesaler for the franchised shops, which range in size from 1,200 to 8,500 square feet. In general, they generate sales of from $400 per square foot to more than $1,000 per square foot. This compares to an industry average of $215 per square foot for specialty stores.

The mix of products offered by individual Polo shops can vary considerably. The offerings of Ralph Lauren's designer business include Polo for Men, owned by Lauren, and a number of domestic licenses for such lines as women's apparel,

The Polo/Ralph Lauren, Inc. store on Madison Avenue is a five-story flagship store with 20,000 square feet of selling space.
Source: *Reprinted with permission of Polo/Ralph Lauren, Inc.*

footwear, boys' wear, girls' wear, eyewear, scarves, hosiery, fragrance, handbags, luggage, and small leather goods. In addition Lauren has licenses for home fashions, which include domestics and furniture. Lauren designs the products for his licensees and maintains total control.

In April 1986 Ralph Lauren opened a five-story flagship store with 20,000 square feet of selling space on New York's Madison Avenue at 72nd Street. This store is one of two Ralph Lauren boutiques directly owned by the designer (the other is in London). Lauren's New York store is in the former Rhinelander mansion, which was renovated and the inside restored at a cost estimated at more than $14 million. The project took over a year, but the results are spectacular. The elegant mansion provides an appropriate setting for Ralph Lauren merchandise. The store is by far the largest and most deeply stocked of the more than one hundred Polo/Ralph Lauren shops worldwide. In its first year of operation the store did over $30 million in retail sales, which averages to more than $1,500 per square foot (Pete Born, "Lauren Store Tops $30M in First Year, *Women's Wear Daily*, July 14, 1987, p. 1).

Lauren sees his New York store as "a way of living," and describes it as "a labor of love" ("Lauren Launches NY Flagship," *Women's Wear Daily*, April 21, 1986, p. 1). He has paid great attention to detail in the design and furnishing. The store projects the total Lauren style in its decor as well as in the merchandise. The elegant atmosphere is both gracious and comfortable. The store has a lived-in feeling reinforced by the expensive antique furnishings and fixtures. Merchandise is displayed in lighted armoires and on tables. Leather sofas and chairs are next to tables covered with books and various decorative items. Pictures and elegant mirrors line the walls. Herringbone-patterned wood floors are covered with Oriental or Aubusson rugs, and the windows are draped in a grand scale. Everywhere one looks are decorative items used to complete each room's decor.

Because of its size, the New York store has the broadest selections and includes merchandise and fabrications not carried in other Ralph Lauren stores. The main floor houses men's furnishings and accessories. A staircase with a hand-carved balustrade leads to the second floor, where Polo menswear is found. The women's collection is on the third floor, and the fourth floor displays home furnishings. Each room in the house reflects the Ralph Lauren lifestyle. The basement level has an alterations shop and credit offices.

Lauren offers a number of reasons for his move into retailing as a manufacturer/designer. The Madison Avenue store gives him a showcase to show other Polo shops how to display the merchandise as he would like it to be shown. The store also serves as a testing ground for special styles. But underneath all of this is the effort to protect Lauren's own interests. Department stores are not relying on designer labels as much as in the past, turning instead to selling private label apparel. Some of his New York retail outlets have voiced objections to Lauren's New York superstore, but retailers are unlikely to stop selling his merchandise as long as it pulls customers into their stores. The impact of Ralph Lauren's mansion has been to bring more prestige to the Polo label.

What is the magic behind the Ralph Lauren stores that makes their upper-class customers come back again and again? The magic is in the merchandise itself and the mood that Lauren has developed to surround it. The Ralph Lauren look has always presented the same updated, nontrendy, quality look. The clothes have a sense of tradition and are designed to last. They are meant to be added to an existing wardrobe rather than to be thrown out after a season. Lauren's customers appreciate the quality workmanship and extra details that go into his designs. They say that they like wearing his clothes because people do not stare at them when they are wearing them.

Intensified competition among retailers offers opportunity for strong resident buying offices. The services of a strong office can help independent retailers better meet the challenge of major retailers moving into their trade areas. Buying offices can help smaller retailers compete by giving them a means to develop private branding and gain better prices through group buying. Promotional and research services provided by resident buying offices can also enable retailers to be more competitive in the marketplace.

Summary of Key Points

1. The one function all buyers have in common is to select merchandise for resale to the ultimate consumer. The buyer's responsibilities vary depending upon the type of buying position held.

2. The three activities of the buying-selling cycle include estimating consumer demand, buying merchandise, and selling merchandise. The first two activities are controlled by the buyer; the third activity is under the customer's control.

3. Basic merchandising functions performed by store buyers include planning, buying, pricing, stockkeeping, and selling.

4. Planning to buy begins with analyzing consumer demand. The buyer plans the merchandise assortment and determines what, when, and how much to buy.

5. Buying involves selection and purchase of merchandise to meet planned sales goals.

6. Merchandise must be priced to meet markup goals and to meet the customer's price demands. Pricing also involves repricing, which includes both markdowns and price increases.

7. Stockkeeping concerns receiving, protecting, and controlling the merchandise.

8. Although the store buyer may not be directly responsible for selling, the buyer is responsible for communicating sales information and for directing promotional activities to motivate customers to buy.

9. Buyers are evaluated by management based primarily on objective measurements, which include sales, inventory, and profit results.

10. Resident buying offices located in major market centers provide client stores with market representation. Buying offices offer important services to their client stores in the areas of merchandising, promotion, and research.

11. The greatest number of resident buying offices are independently owned and operated and represent smaller retailers.

12. Resident buying offices are structured in much the same way as stores. Some are full line; others specialize in one particular line of merchandise.

13. Changes in buying offices have mirrored changes that have occurred in retail stores. Mergers and acquisitions have reduced the number of buying offices in the 1980s.

Key Words and Concepts

Define, identify, or explain each of the following:

beat yesterday book	merchandise plan
buying office	operating profit
buying-selling cycle	opportunistic buys
central buyer	prior stock
commission office	protection
entrepreneurial buyer	quality control
gross margin	repricing
group buying	resident buyer
initial markup	retail buyer
maintained markup	RTV
markdowns	specialized store buyer
market representatives	stock shortage
merchandise broker	stockturn rate, stock turnover

Discussion Questions

1. What one function do all retail buyers have in common?

2. What are the three activities of the buying-selling cycle?

3. Name the four types of buyers and discuss how their job responsibilities differ.

4. Discuss the five basic merchandising functions performed by many store buyers.

5. What is the basic goal of retailing?

6. What objective measurements are used in evaluating the buyer's job performance?

7. What is the major function of a resident buying office?

8. Explain the difference between independently owned resident buying offices and store-owned offices. Name and define the three types of store-owned offices.

8. How are merchandise brokers different from resident buying offices?

9. What services do resident buying offices offer retail stores?

10. Where could a retailer find information about resident buying offices?

11. Discuss the future of the resident buying office.

Notes

"Buying Offices: The New Retail Consultants," *Retail Week*, May 15, 1981, p. 28.

Samuel Feinberg, "Buying Offices, Once Thriving, Now Are Falling by the Wayside," *Women's Wear Daily*, November 20, 1985.

Samuel Feinberg, "Personal Service Vital to Success," *Women's Wear Daily*, September 13, 1988, p. 27.

CHAPTER 14 ─────────────────────

DETERMINING WHAT TO BUY

MUCH OF THE buyer's time is spent planning to buy. Before the planning process can begin, however, the buyer must identify the store's target market and understand what motivates these consumers to buy. The buyers who are most successful in building a profitable business for their stores are the ones who are best informed. In today's highly competitive fashion market, buyers must pay attention to the many sources of information available to assist them in learning about customer preferences. Successful fashion merchandising requires a well-planned stock that is in harmony with what customers want to buy. A buyer uses dollar planning and assortment planning to provide a well-balanced assortment that the store's customers will want to buy.

In this chapter discussion centers on understanding customer demand and planning to buy. Emphasized are consumer buying motives and the sources of information that assist the buyer in determining customer preferences. Also discussed are the tools used by the buyer in planning the merchandise assortment.

Understanding Consumer Demand

Retailing today is highly consumer-oriented. Before buying merchandise the retailer must first define the store's target market and have a thorough understanding of consumer behavior. To succeed the retailer must offer the merchandise the store's customers want to buy. Before purchasing merchandise the retailer must answer the following questions: Who is the store's target customer? What are the target customer's wants, needs, and desires? What motivates these customers to buy? Why should consumers choose my retail store rather than a competitor's store?

Identifying the Target Customer

Stores that are highly successful today are those that have clearly identified their target customer and have positioned their stores to appeal to them. Retailers have learned that no store can be all things to all people. Stores that try to appeal to everyone end up appealing to no one and are likely to go out of business. Retailers are subdividing the population in smaller groups having similar characteristics. These smaller segments exhibit homogeneous responses to various products and services. Such division is called **market segmentation.** The market of potential customers may be segmented according to demographic or psychographic factors.

Demographic and Psychographic Segmentation

Demographic segmentation provides a statistical picture of the target market. Demographic factors include age, sex, marital status, family size, stage in the family life cycle, social class, income, education, occupation, race, and religion. Knowing such facts about a market helps the retailer determine the types of goods to be sold by a store.

Psychographic segmentation refers to the division of a market into subgroups based on subjective or psychological factors such as lifestyle, attitudes, interests, and values. Such psychographics often cut across age groups and are more important in determining consumer buying behavior than are many demographic factors such as income and age.

Describing Customer Groups

Psychographic and demographic segmentation are used together to identify and describe customer groups. Knowing such information about a store's customers, or its potential customers, enables the store's buyers to select merchandise to meet the needs, wants, and desires of these customers. This information is also used to plan sales promotional activities and advertising to attract the target group to the store to buy merchandise. Listed below are some of the important facts a buyer should know about a store's customers (adapted from Wingate and Friedlander 1978).

1. Size of the population in trading area

2. Age

3. Sex

4. Occupation

5. Income

6. Marital status

7. Stage in family life cycle

8. Number and ages of children

9. Type of residence

10. Ethnic background

11. Religion

12. Tastes

13. Habits and customs

14. Interests and hobbies

15. Lifestyle, social activities, and standard of living

16. Attitudes and values

In addition to being able to describe customers according to demographics and psychographics, the retailer needs to be aware of other factors affecting consumer demand. Geographic features, climatic conditions, transportation patterns, and institutions within a community all influence what consumers want to buy. Central buyers who buy for stores located in many different geographical areas need to be aware of variations caused by different lifestyle patterns and climatic conditions. What sells in New York City may be very different from what sells in Chattanooga. Not only is the weather different, but the atmosphere of the cities differs. Every area has different institutions, such as museums, theatres, schools, that influence the activities of residents. People live different lifestyles and engage in different leisure-time activities related to their personal interests and their surrounding environment. The buyer must understand these differences as they affect consumer demand.

Consumer Buying Motives

Consumer motivation explains why people buy what they buy. Melvin T. Copeland, as one of the early marketing authorities to study consumer motivation, divided consumer **buying motives** into two categories: (1) rational buying motives and (2) emotional buying motives (Copeland 1924). He saw rational buying motives as based on appeal to reason and emotional motives based on instinct and emotion.

Rational buying motives involve the consumer's ability to reason and make effective use of resources. The consumer who is being motivated by rational motives considers such factors as durability, comfort, quality, economy of operation, and price in making a purchase.

Emotional buying motives are based on emotions and involve little logical thought. The consumer makes decisions based on feelings. Emotional motives may be based on such factors as imitation, emulation, desire for status and prestige, sex appeal, desire for distinctiveness, ambition, fear, and personal pride.

Another theory explaining consumer motivation is one developed by Jon G. Udell. According to Udell (1964–65), consumer buying motives develop from both conscious and unconscious reasoning. Motives are measured along a bar scale, which runs from operational satisfactions to psychological satisfactions. Operational satisfactions are derived from the physical performance of a product, and psychological satisfactions are derived from the consumer's social and psychological interpretation of a product and its performance.

Midpoint

—————————————— × ——————————————

Operational   Psychological

Satisfactions   Satisfactions

In the selection of fashion apparel and accessories, buying decisions are likely to be a combination of rational and emotional motives. Psychological satisfactions are important to the fashion consumer, but operational satisfactions are also considered. The fashion retailer realizes that the reason a customer states for buying a product may not be the real reason a purchase is made. For example, how many women purchase a mink coat to keep warm? Fur coats are often worn as status symbols to show that the consumer can afford a luxury item. Furs are also worn for their beauty and elegance. If furs were worn only for warmth, few consumers in Southern California or the South would have a reason to buy a fur coat.

Patronage Motives

Retailers know that they must give customers a reason for shopping in their stores. Why do people select one store over another? **Patronage motives** explain why the customer shops and purchases from a particular store. Common patronage motives are (1) merchandise assortment, (2) price, (3) convenience, (4) fashion image, and (5) store services.

Merchandise Assortment

A consumer selects a store that carries the merchandise he or she wants to buy. Fashion merchandise carried must be the correct size category for the customer and at the desired quality, price, and fashion level. Stores often specialize in merchandise in one of three fashion levels: traditional, updated, or advanced. Traditional apparel is what the majority of consumers buy. It consists of styles that have already been widely accepted by most consumers. Updated apparel is more fashion-oriented but has still achieved wide acceptance. Advanced fashions are for the consumer who wants to be first to have a new fashion look and who likes to stand out from the crowd.

Customers also expect a store to offer an assortment that allows them sufficient variety of selection. People may want to be dressed similar to their peers, but they do not want to be dressed exactly like them. Variety in apparel selection is needed to allow for choice.

Price

Price is often a reason consumers state for deciding to shop in a certain store or department. Consumers seek merchandise that they perceive as affordable or the price they desire to pay. Particularly during poor economic periods, the value received for merchandise purchased may be the single most important factor in store patronage (Bohlinger 1983). Stores or departments specialize in a certain price line. They may offer budget, moderate, or better-priced apparel.

Convenience

Today, with time being a major concern of many consumers, convenience often becomes a primary patronage motive. The consumer may choose to shop at the store that is conveniently located. This may be the store passed on the way home from work or the shopping mall offering one-stop convenience where the consumer can shop for many different items under one roof. Grocery stores, for example, have found that convenience prompts many women to buy hosiery when doing their weekly grocery shopping.

Convenience related to shopping within the store is another reason for choosing a store. Merchandise should be easy for customers to find once they are inside the store. Clothing should be arranged conveniently for the customer to view, select, try on, and buy. All retailers should remember a basic principle of retailing—make it easy for the customer to shop in your store.

Fashion Image

Fashion customers may choose a store because of its reputation for understanding fashion and because shopping is an enjoyable, exciting, visual experience in the store. Bloomingdale's and Macy's New York have both established reputations for being first to have fashion. These stores and others have made their stores a visually stimulating environment in which to shop.

Store Services

Another reason for patronizing a store is service, an intangible element offered by the retailer to encourage customer patronage. Services are used by retailers to distinguish their store from competitive stores and may include credit, delivery, gift wrap, alterations, and return policy. Service also involves selling service, which may be self-selection or personal selling. Part of selling service is the way customers are treated by store personnel. The customer may look for salespeople who are knowledgeable about the merchandise, courteous, and helpful.

The reasons customers decide to shop in one store rather than another will vary depending on the item of merchandise being selected as well as other factors. How much time the customer has to shop, means of transportation, and amount of money available to spend all influence patronage motives.

Determining Customer Demand

It is the buyer's job to buy the merchandise that best meets the needs, wants, and desires of the store's customers. To do this the buyer must study the store's customers and interpret their demands. It is often necessary for the buyer to predict what customers want to buy even before customers know what they want to buy. The buyer must have a clear picture of his or her customers and what motivates them to buy. The buyer must also understand how customers evaluate merchandise selection factors when making buying decisions.

Merchandise Selection Factors

Merchandise selection factors are qualities inherent in merchandise that help customers make buying decisons. These factors provide the basis for the customer's acceptance or rejection of specific items of merchandise. Merchandise selection factors that influence customers' choices of fashion goods include the following (adapted from Wingate and Friedlander 1978, p. 107):

1. Silhouette or style

2. Color

3. Fabrication

4. Decoration or trim

5. Workmanship and quality

6. Size or fit

7. Brand or designer name

8. Sensory factors of taste, odor, sound

9. Ease and cost of care

10. Utility

11. Price

12. Fashion level

13. Product packaging

14. Taste

Silhouette or style refers to the general contour or outline of an item. A skirt, for example, may have several silhouettes or styles such as bell-shaped, straight, dirndl. Examples of different styles in men's shirts are the dress shirt, sport shirt, polo shirt, and T-shirt.

Color is the hue, value, and intensity of each color in the item of merchandise. Color is an important selection factor for the fashion consumer. It is likely to be the first factor observed and considered in the selection process. An item will be immediately rejected from consideration if it is the "wrong" color. The consumer often enters the store looking for a specific color or a color that will go with something in his or her wardrobe. Color has also become an important selection factor in housewares, appliances, and even brown goods (television sets and home electronics).

Fabrication refers to the fabric or material used in making the fashion item. In apparel and accessories fabrication may include textile fabric, leather, fur, vinyl, or any other material used to construct the merchandise. Fabrication involves the hand (feel) of a fabric, its weight, texture, and fiber content. Finish and weave are also part of the fabrication.

Decoration or trim includes such items as buttons, piping, rick-rack, ruffles, or anything that adds decoration to the basic style or silhouette of the fashion item. Decoration is particularly important in women's and children's apparel.

Workmanship is concerned with the quality and type of construction used in the merchandise. In apparel items workmanship includes such factors as seam widths and finishings, quality of pressing, neatness of finishing detail, and use of linings, interlinings, and interfacings.

Size or fit is the basic selection factor. If a garment is not the right size or does not fit, the customer will usually reject the item immediately. Size is an important factor in the customer's initial selection of a store or department within a store. A customer will avoid shopping in a store that does not carry his or her size. Size and fit are closely related to comfort as an item that does not fit is likely to be uncomfortable to wear.

Brand and designer names have become status symbols and often are important selection factors for fashion apparel and accessories. Furthermore, the consumer may see brand as an indicator of quality. Sometimes customers limit their selection to certain brands because experience has shown them that the brand is consistent in quality and fit. Fashion stores often organize departments according to brand or designer name, thus making it easy for the customer to use this as the initial selection factor in choosing where to shop within a particular store. Some stores even sell only one manufacturer's or designer's merchandise.

Sensory factors include scent, taste, touch, and sound. Obviously scent is the primary selection factor when buying cologne or perfume and is important in selecting many cosmetic products. The makers of chocolate chip cookies, baked fresh in many shopping centers and department stores, also know the value of scent in selling a product. How difficult it is for customers to resist the aroma of freshly baked cookies when they pass the cookie counter. Potpourri is often used in home-furnishings stores, in gift departments, or even in lingerie departments to create a pleasant aroma.

An unpleasant odor can be a problem with some merchandise. Cheap leathers and vinyls may have an unpleasant odor and may turn off the customer. Certain fabric finishes may also have unappealing odors and may have fumes that cause the eyes to burn.

Touch is of obvious importance in buying many apparel items. The feel of luxury fibers, such as cashmere, angora, and vicuna, are a primary reason for their appeal. Getting the customer to touch and feel the difference is important in selling many fashion products.

Sound can be important in certain items of apparel and accessories. For example, taffeta rustles, cheap leather squeaks, metal jewelry may clank and rattle.

Ease and cost of care are very important to some customers. Customers may look for items that can be laundered at home with limited expense. Ease and cost of care usually rate high as selection factors when the customer purchases children's wear or active sportswear but may not be important when selecting formal wear. The high-income customer may consider apparel that must be dry-cleaned to provide easier care than apparel that must be laundered.

Utility refers to the usefulness of an item. An item may provide versatility in that it has several uses. A versatile dress or suit may meet the needs of several occasions, including office and social functions. Utility can also refer to the degree of warmth of a sweater, coat, or down comforter.

Price is one of the most observable selection factors. Sometimes price determines whether a customer can afford to make a purchase. All factors being equal, the customer will most likely choose the lower-priced item; however, price is not usually the most important selection factor to the customer. The price the customer is willing to pay depends not only on how much money the customer has but how important having a particular item is to him or her, the availability of an item, its versatility, and its quality. A customer may pay more when an item is difficult to find or when he or she has already spent considerable time shopping for it. An item that is well made and highly durable may also rate a higher price. "Investment dressing" has been promoted by retailers as a reason to pay more for a garment because it will give the customer greater value by being longer lasting.

Fashion level, or stage of a fashion item in the fashion cycle, is another factor considered in the selection process. Some customers want to be the first to have a new fashion look. Others prefer to be fashion followers and wait to purchase until the item has become widely accepted by others.

Product packaging is the way the product is presented to the customer. Packaging may encourage a customer to make a purchase or may discourage the customer. Cosmetics manufacturers and merchandisers know the importance of an attractive package in selling merchandise. Where self-selection is the method of selling service, packaging is particularly important.

Taste is difficult to define because not everyone agrees on what is good taste. According to *The Dictionary of Retailing*, "Taste level refers to that subjective level of individual preference which includes a sense of quality, beauty and appropriateness" (Ostrow and Smith 1985). Taste changes with the times. What is accepted by the majority of people, and is therefore in fashion, is generally considered to be in good taste.

A purchase is seldom decided based on one selection factor but rather is based on a combination of factors. Which factor or factors are most important to the customer depends upon a number of considerations. As previously discussed, customers' selection decisions are not always prompted by rational factors but may be based to a great extent on emotions. Also, what the customer states as a reason for accepting or rejecting fashion merchandise may not be the real reason for the decision. The buyer needs to be aware of all the factors influencing customers' purchasing decisions. When the buyer goes to market, he or she must always view the merchandise from the customer's point of view. The buyer must think like a customer and consider the selection factors from the point of view of the store's target customer. Buying decisions should not be made based on the buyer's own personal likes or dislikes. The buyer should always remember that the customer is the one who makes the final purchasing decision.

Sources of Information About Customer Demand and Fashion Trends

Many sources of information are available to help the buyer learn about a store's actual customers or the potential customers who live within a store's trading area. A buyer needs to make use of all available sources of information in learning about customer needs and wants. Sources of information are available both within the retail store and from various sources located outside the store.

Many sources of information are available to help the buyer learn about consumers in general. Basic demographic information concerning a population is available from federal, state, and local government agencies. Numerous private business summaries and trend analyses are also available to assist the retailer. In addition, trade magazines and trade associations publish research reports and comparative data to give the retailer an overview of general consumer and business trends.

Information Sources Outside the Store

Many outside sources of information are available to assist the buyer in learning about consumers. Some of the most important are (1) other retail stores, (2) resident buying offices, (3) vendors and manufacturers, (4) trade and consumer publications, (5) trade associations, and (6) fashion reporting services.

Shopping Other Retail Stores

Both competing and noncompeting stores provide sources of information concerning merchandising trends and consumer purchasing behavior. Stores that are not in competition with one another may share information directly or through a reporting agency or resident buying office. Buyers and other store executives also visit with one another when at market and often share ideas and information.

When a buyer goes to market, he or she should always allow time to visit stores to see the merchandise carried and observe window and interior displays. A buyer may be introduced to new merchandise resources through such observations and may gather ideas for displaying and promoting goods back in the home store. Market center stores are often first to have new merchandise and help establish trends that will later become important at the buyer's home store. In New York important trend-setting stores are Bloomingdale's, Macy's, Saks Fifth Avenue, and Henri Bendel. Many small boutiques in the city also carry innovative merchandise and provide the buyers with unique ideas for merchandise display. Every market city has stores that are trend-setters in their geographic area.

One of the best ways to learn about other stores is by studying their advertisements. A buyer can do this without leaving his or her office. Advertisements provide information about the merchandise carried by a store, pricing policies, and promotional activities such as special events and fashion shows. A buyer needs to learn which stores and cities tend to forecast trends that are likely to be picked up by the buyer's customers and, consequently, should follow the advertising of these stores.

Information can be gathered also from competing stores located in the same community with the buyer's store. Competing stores should be visited regularly. The buyer should observe the stock carried in the stores, visual display techniques used, and services offered. The buyer should also observe actual consumer behavior in competing stores and follow competitors' advertising closely. A buyer has an opportunity to learn by watching both competitors' successes and failures.

Resident Buying Offices

As discussed in Chapter 13, resident buying offices provide a number of services to their client stores. One of their primary services is to provide information on market trends, including new resources and general market conditions. Resident buying offices also forecast fashion trends and large offices may be involved in consumer research.

Vendors and Manufacturers

Vendors are anyone from whom a retailer purchases goods. A vendor may be a manufacturer, a wholesaler, or a sales representative who serves as an agent for several manufacturers. All have close contacts with many retailers and are aware of what is selling or not selling in different areas of the country. Vendors are usually a reliable source of information about those hot-selling items in a line called winners. They often will provide information about what other stores have ordered or reordered. Sometimes vendors do consumer research that they make available to retailers. Both vendors and retailers are concerned about meeting the needs of the ultimate consumer and find it advantageous to share appropriate information with one another.

Trade and Consumer Publications

Newspapers and magazines provide an important source of current information for retailers. Trade publications cover retail and wholesale market news, present industry statistics, fashion and merchandising trends, and carry manufacturers advertising for appropriate products. Publications are available that specialize in each division of the fashion industry. For example, Fairchild Publications in New York publishes *Women's Wear Daily* for the women's and children's apparel and accessories markets, *Daily News Record* for menswear and textile news, and *HFD Retailing Home Furnishings*, covering furniture and accessories for the home. As noted earlier, each of these daily newspapers is considered the "bible" of its division of the industry.

Some trade publications are aimed at the retail manager and provide overviews of business conditions and retail trends. Examples are *Stores*, published monthly by the National Retail Merchants Association, *Chain Store Age Executive*, *Discount Merchandiser*, *Discount Store News*, and *Shopping Center News*.

Some trade publications deal with advertising and sales promotion, including *Advertising Age*, *Madison Avenue*, and *Visual Merchandising and Store Design*. Reading these publications provides retailers with ideas for store advertising, special promotions, and display.

The consumer fashion press is an important source for fashion trends. Major consumer fashion publications include *Vogue*, *Harper's Bazaar*, *Glamour*, *Mademoiselle*, *Seventeen*, and *Gentlemen's Quarterly*. Buyers should read the publications that would appeal to their customers and should also read the high-fashion magazines because they project trends.

It is important for the buyer or retail executive to do general reading of newspapers and magazines to be aware of business and consumer trends. The daily newspaper keeps the buyer on top of happenings in the local community, including the business news and lifestyle interests of consumers. Reading newspapers from different cities keeps the buyer aware of trends developing elsewhere. A weekly news magazine, such as *Time*, *U.S. News & World Report*, and *Newsweek*, provides a summary of events taking place worldwide, which may influence consumer demand. Such basic sources of information help the buyer gather data about demographic trends, economic conditions, changing consumer lifestyles, and interests that affect consumer demand.

Scholarly publications such as the *Journal of Retailing*, *The Journal of Marketing*, and *The Journal of Consumer Research* present information concerning business trends and academic research. Although written primarily for academicians and researchers, they present current research findings of importance to the retailer. Below is a list of selected industry publications of value and interest to the retailer.

General Retailing Trade Publications

> *Chain Store Age Executive*
> *Direct Marketing*
> *Discount Merchandiser*

Discount Store News
Shopping Center World
Stores

Advertising and Sales Promotion Trade Publications
Advertising Age
Madison Avenue
Visual Merchandising and Store Design

Apparel and Accessories Trade Publications

Accessories
Body Fashions/Intimate Apparel
California Apparel News
Daily News Record
Earnshaw's Infants, Girls & Boy's Wear Review
Fashion Jewelry Review
Footwear Focus
Footwear News
Intimate Apparel
Knitwear Fashions
Modern Jeweler
Product Marketing (cosmetics)
Women's Wear Daily

Home Furnishings Trade Publications
Contract Magazine
Decorating Retailer
Furniture Today
Furniture World
Gifts and Decorative Accessories
HFD Retailing Home Furnishings
Housewares Buyer
Southwest Homefurnishings News

Consumer Fashion Publications

Apparel	*Home Furnishings*
Elle	*Architectural Digest*
Gentlemen's Quarterly	*Colonial Homes*
Glamour	*Country Living*
Harper's Bazaar	*HG (House and Garden)*
Mademoiselle	*House Beautiful*
L'Officiel	*Metropolitan Home*
Seventeen	*Southern Accents*
Vogue	
W	

General News and Business Periodicals

Barron's National Business & Financial Weekly
Business Week
Forbes
Fortune
Newsweek
New York Times
Time
U.S. News & World Report
Wall Street Journal

Academic Publications

Clothing and Textiles Research Journal	*Journal of Consumer Affairs*
Harvard Business Review	*Journal of Consumer Research*
Journal of Advertising	*Journal of Marketing*
Journal of Advertising Research	*Journal of Marketing Research*
	Journal of Retailing

Fashion Reporting and Consulting Services

Retailers can subscribe to a number of reporting services that provide current information about fashion trends, market news, and store happenings. For example, *Retail News Bureau*, a fashion reporting service, provides its subscribers with monthly news flashes featuring best-selling style numbers and resources where items may be purchased.

Fashion consulting firms or individuals provide fashion expertise to retailers. A consultant may be hired on a continuing basis or to help with a specific project. Some consultants are highly specialized, whereas others offer a wide range of services. One of the oldest fashion consultant firms still in business today is Tobé Associates, founded in 1927. Its illustrated bulletins, which report and interpret fashion trends and market conditions, specify style numbers with manufacturing names and whole-sale prices. Following is a list of some of the available fashion reporting and consulting services.

Benjamin Dent

Color Projections, Inc.

IM International

Merchandising Motivation, Inc. (MMI)

Nigel French Enterprises

Prism

Promostyl

Tobé Associates

Trade Associations

Trade associations exist for every area of the fashion industry. Many conduct research and report information concerning consumer preferences and market conditions. Trade associations are interested in promoting the division of the fashion industry that they represent; see the representative list of trade associations in fashion manufacturing and retailing below.

American Cloak and Suit Manufacturers Association

American Fur Industry

American Fur Merchants Association

American Home Sewing Association

Associated Corset and Brassiere Manufacturers

Clothing Manufacturers Association of the United States

Cotton Incorporated

Direct Marketing Association

Federation of Apparel Manufacturers

Fur Merchants Employers Council

Fur Wholesalers Association of America

Furriers Joint Council of New York

Headwear Institute of America

Infants, Childrens and Girls Sportswear and Coat Association

Jewelry Industry Council

Ladies Apparel Retailers Guild

Menswear Retailers of America

The Men's Tie Foundation

National Association of Blouse Manufacturers

National Handbag Association

National Knitwear and Sportswear Association

National Outerwear and Sportswear Association

United Better Dress Manufacturers Association

United Infants and Childrens Wear Association

As previously discussed, the major retailing trade association is the National Retail Merchants Association (NRMA). It provides many services to its member stores and is dedicated to research and education in general merchandise retailing. The NRMA publishes many books and periodicals to assist retailers with various aspects of retailing. Educational programs, seminars, and conferences are planned and offered by NRMA for informing retailers.

In-Store Information Sources

Of utmost importance to the store buyer is having detailed knowledge about the store's own customers. A number of sources of information are available within the store for this purpose. Some of these sources may include the following:

1. Sales records, including customer returns

2. Salespeople

3. Want slips

4. Buyer contact with customers

5. Advertising results

6. Observations and counts

7. Customer surveys

8. Focus groups

9. Customer advisory panels

10. In-store merchandising bureaus, such as fashion bureau, comparison shopping, and standards and testing

Sales Records

Readily available and the most valuable information source to all established retailers is the store's sales records. An analysis of merchandise sold, merchandise returned, and markdowns taken will tell the buyer a great deal about customer demand. It is important for the buyer to establish a system for keeping track of sales and stocks. The buyer determines what facts are important to include in the record keeping system. Records need to include the selection factors that are important in analyzing customer demand. With fashion apparel the buyer needs to know style number, size, color, fabrication, brand, and other factors to analyze the stock. The **stockkeeping unit** (SKU) is set up to record this information. The SKU represents the smallest unit for which sales and stock records are kept. Each SKU is identified by a two- to four-digit number, which refers to a single item or a group of items within a merchandise classification. For example, a shirt in one style and color would be one SKU number, and each different style or color would add another SKU.

A weakness of sales records as a source of information about customer preferences is that they show only what sold from the merchandise provided by the store for customers to select from. Sales records do not show what could have been sold if the store had made the merchandise available for purchase.

Salespeople

In stores that use personal selling rather than self-selection, salespeople are the primary representatives with the customer. Salespeople hear customer's positive comments about the store and its merchandise, and they also hear the complaints. Personal selling is an effective way for buyers to get customer feedback. The buyer needs to maintain contact with salespeople as a means of acquiring information about customers. In some stores the buyer is able to have weekly meetings with salespeople, whereas in other stores the feedback must come to the buyer through department or store managers. Some means for communication of information to the buyer from the salespeople should always be established.

Want Slips

One means by which the salespeople communicate customer requests with the buyer is the **want slip,** a form used to note consumer requests for merchandise either out of stock or not carried by the store. The buyer analyzes want slips and determines whether to add the items requested to the merchandise assortment.

A store must have personal contact between salespeople and customers for a want slip system to work. In many stores today the selling system is based on self-selection and customers have little opportunity to voice their wants.

Buyer Contacts with Customers

At one time it was customary for department stores to require their buyers and assistant buyers to spend time on the salesfloor every week. This allowed first-hand interaction with customers. As department stores expanded by adding branches, buyers' jobs became more specialized and they were less likely to have time to spend selling and talking with customers. One advantage the single-unit store buyer has is the opportunity to know the store's customers personally. The single-unit store buyer often goes to market with the needs of specific customers in mind and is able to buy merchandise for these individuals. Buyers from large multiunit stores seldom have the opportunity to know their customers personally.

For many buyers customer information must be second-hand from sales records and other store personnel. Whenever possible, it is valuable for the buyer to have direct contact with customers by spending time on the salesfloor.

Advertising and Promotion Results

Accurate records of advertising and special promotions should be kept by the buyer. Such information assists the buyer with knowing what to buy and promote at different times of the year. The buyer also learns to avoid mistakes. Records should include information such as sales results, weather conditions, advertising media used, publicity received, and evaluation of the reasons for success or failure of the promotion. Sales results alone will not tell the story. The buyer needs to analyze why the sales results were high or low. Factors uncontrollable by the buyer may affect the results of a promotion. Bad weather conditions, a transit strike, or competing store activities may affect a store's sales during a promotion.

Observations and Counts

The buyer can learn much by observing consumers in the store's locale. What the fashion leaders in the community are wearing may indicate what soon will be in demand by the general public. Observing what people are wearing at public events or while shopping may assist the buyer in confirming store sales records or may point out a trend the buyer has failed to purchase.

Observations may be approached on a statistical basis. The buyer should first determine what factors are important to count. Factors must also be observable. For example, it is not possible to observe price; however, readily observable are classification (merchandise type or category), color, silhouette, skirt length, style, and fabrication. Once it is determined what to observe, the count can be taken.

The buyer also needs to observe what people are doing and what their reactions are to merchandise offerings in various retail stores.

Customer Surveys

Formal or informal surveys can be taken to identify customer preferences concerning merchandise or store promotions and services. Many methods of gathering data from the consumer are available. Customers may be contacted personally in the store, by mail, or by telephone. Stores may interview customers or send them questionnaires to be completed and returned to the store. Questionnaires may be enclosed with customers' charge account billings. A technique for encouraging return of questionnaires is to give the customer a merchandise discount for bringing in a completed questionnaire. Retailers often discover that customers love to tell them how better to run the store. Retailers may learn much by asking their customers and listening to their responses.

Surveys offer retailers the advantage of asking questions to find out whatever they want to know. Retailers may survey their actual customers or potential customers. It is possible to identify specific customer segments to survey. A store may want to know more about its active charge customers or it may be interested in seeking information from those customers who are infrequent shoppers at the store. The survey may be set up to meet the retailer's needs. Surveys often deal with consumers' reasons for choosing to shop or not to shop a certain store. Surveys may be as simple as salespeople asking a question when customers make a purchase, or a detailed survey involving lengthy interviews. Customer surveys may be completed by the store's research department or by outside research specialists.

Focus Groups

The **focus group** is another source of information for the retailer. It consists of a representative group of consumers brought together for a single meeting to share their views about a store and its merchandise. Focus groups are led in discussion by someone trained in such direction. The leader may be an outside specialist or a store employee. Stores can learn much about how they are perceived by forming focus groups and listening to the opinions of the participants.

Customer Advisory Panels

The **advisory panel** is put together by retailers to secure opinions of different groups of consumers. A common consumer advisory panel used by department stores is the teen board. High school students who serve on such boards may fill the role of advisors, salespersons, and models. The board usually meets periodically to advise the retailer on the type of merchandise and services desired by teenagers. The teen board members often serve as models in fashion shows directed to their age group and in some instances also work as salespeople, frequently in the store's junior department.

In recent years a number of stores have added advisory boards consisting of career women. These boards advise stores on the wardrobe and service needs of career women in the community.

In-store Merchandising Bureaus

Larger stores have in-store bureaus that provide information to assist the buyer in understanding consumer demand. Examples are the fashion bureau, comparison shopping, and standards and testing. The most common is the fashion bureau headed by the store's fashion director or fashion coordinator. This person is an expert in forecasting fashion trends and works closely with store buyers in providing information about trends and in assisting with coordinating and projecting the store's fashion image.

The comparison shopping bureau assists buyers by checking competitors' merchandise assortments and pricing. The comparison shopper often shops store personnel to see if they are providing appropriate selling service and to check salespeople's knowledge of merchandise and store policies.

Only a few very large stores have their own standards and testing departments. Those that do provide an invaluable assistance to the buyer by checking merchandise performance to see if it meets company standards.

Planning to Buy

Once the buyer has a clear understanding of consumer demand, he or she is ready to begin the planning process, translating needs into quantitative considerations. Included are both financial and merchandise assortment planning. In assortment planning the buyer projects the variety and quantity of merchandise to be carried in a department to meet customer demand. Amounts may be expressed in terms of units or in dollars. Two major tools are used by the buyer in financial planning: (1) the dollar merchandise plan, and (2) the open-to-buy.

The Dollar Merchandise Plan

The **dollar merchandise plan** is prepared to assist the buyer in planning dollar purchases in order to have stock available to meet planned sales goals. The merchandise plan is the dollar control budget for a store or department. It balances planned sales and planned stocks in terms of dollars. The plan is sometimes called the six-month plan because it typically covers a six-month period; thus two plans are developed for the year. One plan is for the period February through July, and a second plan covers August through January. Whether called the merchandise plan, the dollar plan, or the six-month plan, it is one of the most important tools the buyer uses as a guide in achieving a profit for a store or department.

The merchandise plan is a guide for a period not yet begun. It looks to the future and serves as a guide to help plan purchases in terms of dollars. The merchandise plan deals with dollar amounts only and does not describe units, assortments, or quantities of merchandise.

The form used for the merchandise plan and the elements included in the plan are not the same for all stores, but the main objective is to guide the buyer in purchasing the right dollar amount of merchandise to meet consumer demand at a given time. Figure 14.1 is an example of a typical form used for a six-month merchandise plan.

Elements of the Merchandise Plan

A good merchandise plan is developed through the efforts of those who are responsible for the merchandising activities; therefore, cooperation is needed among all levels of management, including the buyer, the merchandise manager, and top level management. The plan is an estimate based on anticipated sales for the period it covers. Because all planning begins with sales, stock needs must be related to planned sales. The essential elements of a dollar merchandise plan include the following:

1. Planned sales: dollar sales estimates for the total plan period broken down for each month of the plan.

2. Planned stock: estimated dollar value of the inventory needed at the beginning of each month of the plan.

3. Planned markdowns: estimated dollar reductions from the retail value of the goods for each month of the plan.

4. Planned purchases: estimated dollars to be spent for purchases for each month of the plan.

The following elements are frequently included in the dollar merchandise plan:

1. Cash discounts: discounts allowed by vendors or manufacturers for payment of invoices prior to a specified due date, stated as a percent of net sales.

2. *Stock turnover*: net sales divided by average inventory at retail.

3. *Shortage*: difference between book inventory in retail dollars and the physical inventory at retail; stated as a percent of net sales.

4. *Average stock*: beginning-of-the-month inventories divided by the number of months in the period.

5. *Initial markup percent*: difference between the cost of merchandise and the original retail price.

6. *Gross margin percent*: difference between net sales and total merchandise costs. The gross margin must be high enough to cover all operating expenses and taxes as well as allow for a profit.

7. *Advertising expenses*: expressed as a percent of net sales.

8. *Alteration or workroom cost*: costs of garment alterations, repairs, or other workroom expenses such as drapery or slipcover construction.

The form used for the merchandise plan provides space to record last year's figure, the planned figure for each element in the plan, and the actual figure obtained. The actual figure is filled in as the plan progresses. When figures do not turn out as estimated, adjustments are made for the remaining period of the plan. A plan is viewed as a guide for a period of time and adjustments are made as needed.

Planning Sales

The first step in planning is forecasting sales for the period and for each month of the period. Sales should be estimated as realistically as possible because all other figures in the merchandise plan are based on planned sales. To estimate sales the buyer needs a clear understanding of trends in consumer demand and purchasing behavior.

In planning sales the buyer begins by analyzing the sales in the department for the previous year and looks at the sales trend over the past several years. The buyer should consider all factors that might affect sales. Sales may be increased or decreased by employment conditions, the state of the economy, population shifts, changing pattern of retail competition, and changing fashion trends. Changes within the store also must be taken into account when projecting sales. The sales potential of a department will be influenced by management decisions concerning space allotted to a department, remodeling, and special events planned for the store. The buyer should make use of all available sources of information to assist in accurately estimating sales. If planning is to be effective, sales must first be forecast realistically.

Planning Stock

The second step in merchandise planning is to plan the amount of stock, in terms of dollars, needed to meet consumer demand and to support planned sales. At the beginning of the month sufficient stock should be available to cover sales and

6-MONTH MERCHANDISE PLAN	Dept Name_____ Dept No. _____	PLAN (this year)	MOR	ACTUAL (last year)
	MARK UP %			
	MARK DOWN %			
	SHORTAGE %			
	CASH DISCOUNT% EARNED			
	WORKROOM			
	TURNOVER			

Spring 19__	Feb	March	April	May	June	July	SEASON
Fall 19__	Aug	Sept	Oct	Nov	Dec	Jan	TOTAL
SALES Last Year							
Plan							
Revised							
Actual							
STOCK (BOM) Last Year							*
Plan							*
Revised							*
Actual							*
MARKDOWNS Last Year							
Plan ($)							
Plan (%)							
Revised							
Actual							
PLANNED PURCHASES Last Year							
Plan							
Revised							
Actual							

Merchandise Manager_____   Buyer_____

Controller _____

* Represents stock at end of period

FIGURE 14.1
Merchandise plan.

to provide customers an adequate merchandise selection. It is not sufficient to have only enough stock on hand to cover sales. There must be enough additional reserve stock to give the customer a selection. The buyer's goal is to balance the inventory in relation to sales. One guideline used to assist the buyer in balancing stock to sales is stock turnover.

Stock turnover, also called stock turn, is the number of times the average stock (inventory) is sold during a given period of time in relation to the sales for the same period. Stock turn is usually based on a period of six months or one year. The formula for determining stock turnover rate for any period of time is:

$$\text{Stock turnover} = \frac{\$ \text{ net sales}}{\$ \text{ average inventory}}$$

Stock turnover, as we have already seen, is one of the measurements used to compare and evaluate the performance of a buyer. The buyer's goal is usually to increase stock turnover rate. A higher stock turn means that less money needs to be invested in inventory at a given time because the merchandise is turned over (sold) within a shorter period of time. The rate at which stock is sold directly affects profit because the store does not receive income until merchandise is sold. Increasing stock turn can maximize profits. Buying merchandise that is in demand and selling it quickly at full price increase turnover and profit. A major advantage to a higher stock turn for fashion merchandise is that stocks remain fresher and more appealing to the customer. Merchandise that is replaced more often is less likely to become shopworn, soiled, or outdated. Fewer markdowns, therefore, need to be taken when the merchandise is turned more quickly.

The buyer should realize, however, that it is possible for stock turn to be too high. Too rapid a stock turn may lead to lost sales because the store is out of merchandise customers want to buy.

The National Retail Merchants Association provides annual comparative data on stock turnover rates for various merchandise classifications in department and specialty stores, which a buyer can check to see how a department's stock turn rate compares to industry averages. Listed in Tables 14.1 and 14.2 are selected merchandising and operating results, including stock turn rates, for department and specialty stores. Stock turnover rates vary depending upon the type of merchandise, price range, and depth and breadth of assortment carried. Overall, the stock turnover rate is higher in women's apparel than in men's clothing, children's wear, or home furnishings. It is also higher in departments selling lower price ranges than in those selling higher price ranges. Departments such as women's shoes that must stock assortments in many different colors and sizes will also have a lower stock turn rate.

Planning Markdowns

After planning sales and beginning-of-the-month stocks, the buyer plans markdowns, which are reductions in the selling price of merchandise. Markdowns reduce the retail value of the inventory and must be realistically estimated in the planning

Table 14.1 Merchandising and Operating Results for 1987, Department Stores over $2 Million in Sales

Department	Stock Turn at Retail	Cumulative Markup %	Markdown %	Sales/Sq. Ft. of Selling Space
Female apparel	3.2x	53.2	29.0	$133.00
Female accessories	2.6x	53.7	13.8	$183.00
Men's & boys' apparel & accessories	2.5x	52.1	20.6	$123.00
Infants' & children's clothing & accessories	2.9x	51.1	22.0	$ 82.00
Shoes	1.9x	50.7	22.7	$205.00
Cosmetics & drugs	2.1x	40.4	2.2	$235.00
Home furnishings	1.7x	47.1	15.3	$ 62.00
All other merchandise	4.8x	39.2	10.4	$113.00

Source: *Stores,* November 1988, p. 60.

process. Markdowns are planned as a percentage of sales for the season and allocated for the months in the season.

Buyers use markdowns as a merchandising tool to sell merchandise. Markdowns encourage sales of slow-moving, damaged, and out-of-season goods. Some markdowns may be taken to meet competitors' prices. Markdowns are usually greater in fashion goods than in staple goods because of the more rapidly changing nature of fashion and the greater difficulty in determining customer preferences. Fashion goods are also highly affected by seasonal change. Markdowns must be taken at the right time when customer demand is still present and set high enough to move the goods. The buyer who fails to take markdowns when customers are still interested in purchasing may find that the merchandise cannot be sold at any price. Markdowns should not be viewed as a loss but as a promotional tool that may be used to encourage sales and increase profits.

Markdowns can be expressed as a dollar amount or a percent. By definition markdowns are the difference between the previous selling price of an item and the reduced selling price. The markdown percent is determined by dividing the dollar

Table 14.2 Merchandising and Operating Results for 1987, Specialty Stores over $2 Million in Sales

Merchandise Category	Stock Turns at Retail	Cumulative Markup %	Markdown %	Sales/Sq. Ft. Selling Space
Female apparel	3.1x	51.4	27.3	$154.00
Female accessories	2.6x	52.8	15.6	$159.50
Men's & boys' apparel & accessories	2.4x	52.4	23.2	$155.00
Infants' & children's clothing & accessories	3.0x	50.3	22.1	$136.00

Source: *Stores,* November 1988, p. 61.

DETERMINING WHAT TO BUY _____ 447

amount of the markdowns taken during a selling period divided by the net sales during the same period. The formula for determining markdown percent is as follows:

$$\text{markdown \%} = \frac{\$ \text{ markdown}}{\$ \text{ net sales}} \qquad \frac{\$5,200}{\$65,000} = 8\%$$

Fashion merchandisers know that in order to give customers sufficient assortment choice, more merchandise needs to be purchased than can be sold at regular price. The buyer purchases fashion goods knowing that some markdowns will be necessary to clear out seasonal goods and to offer customers special sales values. Greater risk, however, is involved with fashion merchandise than with staple goods.

Planning Purchases

After planning sales, beginning-of-the-month stocks, and monthly markdowns, the purchases needed for each month are calculated. Planned purchases indicate the dollar value of merchandise that can be added to the inventory during a given period without exceeding the value of the inventory the buyer plans to have on hand at the end of that period. Purchases are usually planned on a monthly basis, although they may be planned seasonally. The buyer must plan purchases in order to maintain a balance between stock and sales throughout a season.

Monthly purchases are based on planned sales, stock, and markdown figures according to the following formula:

Planned purchases = planned monthly sales + planned end-of-the-month stock + planned monthly markdowns − planned beginning-of-the-month stock.

Open-to-Buy

The dollar merchandise plan balances planned sales and planned stocks in terms of dollars for a store or department. It is one tool used in merchandise planning. The other tool is the **open-to-buy** (OTB).

The open-to-buy is used as a control device to see that purchases are made according to the merchandise plan. Whereas the dollar merchandise plan looks to the future, serving as a guide for a selling period that has not yet begun, the open-to-buy is a control device that deals with the present. The open-to-buy tells the buyer what dollar amount of purchases can be received into stock at a particular time. The open-to-buy is calculated by subtracting the merchandise available for the sale from the merchandise needed to meet the plan. Merchandise needed includes planned sales, planned markdowns, and planned end-of-the-month stock. Merchandise available includes the inventory on hand and merchandise on order. The formula for open-to-buy is as follows:

OTB = planned sales + planned end-of-the-month stock − present inventory − goods on order.

When needs exceed merchandise available, the buyer is said to be "open to buy." When merchandise available is greater than needs, the buyer has no open-to-buy; in fact, the buyer is said to be overbought. To create open-to-buy, the buyer must sell merchandise that is on hand.

Merchandise Assortment Planning

Financial or dollar planning is one aspect of the buyer's job. The buyer is also concerned with quantitative planning of the merchandise assortment. The dollar merchandise plan provides the foundation for this quantitative assortment planning, which is concerned with determining the number of units of merchandise to buy. The merchandise assortment must be in line with planned sales and anticipated customer demand.

The assortment plan is a projection of the variety and quantity of merchandise to be carried in stock to meet customer demand. A fashion assortment lists all items to be carried in stock by size, classification, price line, colors, or whatever factors are important in describing the assortment. A buyer's goal is a balanced assortment that adequately meets consumer demand and allows for a sufficient reserve. Assortment plans are developed by two methods: (1) basic stock list, and (2) model stock plan.

Basic Stock Plan

The **basic stock plan** is composed of staple items that enjoy such consistent demand that they should be in stock at all times. **Basic stock,** also called **staple stock,** has a highly predictable sales history with a stable customer demand over a long period of time. It is relatively easy for the buyer to determine basic stock needs just by studying sales history. The basic stock list details the name of the item, brand, physical description, cost and retail price, and other information that precisely identifies the merchandise. It lists the exact merchandise items to be purchased. Even fashion departments carry basic stock items that remain in fashion for several seasons. Examples would include neutral shades in women's pantyhose, men's dress shirts, jeans, and certain basic styles in both men's and women's sweaters, tops, and slacks.

Model Stock Plan

The **model stock plan** is another method used for developing the **assortment plan** that is used primarily for fashion merchandise. Because sales of fashion merchandise are less predictable than for staple stock, the model stock plan is less specific than the basic stock plan. The model stock plan breaks down merchandise needs according to such factors as classification, price, color, and size, but cannot describe the exact items to be purchased.

Spiegel, Inc.

Spiegel, Inc., founded in Chicago by Joseph Spiegel in 1865, is one of the oldest general merchandise catalog firms in the United States and has a tradition of innovation. The catalog company began as a way to sell products by mail to rural America. Conceived as a department store in print, Spiegel provided easy credit while selling useful merchandise to low-income and rural customers.

During the 1970s Spiegel found it was not competing with the other general merchandise catalog companies, and its customer base was shrinking. Loyal customers were leaving Spiegel for discount stores such as K mart and Wal-Mart. Children of customers were becoming better educated and shopping at more upscale stores.

In 1976 Henry A. Johnson joined Spiegel as president and chief executive officer, starting with greatest turnaround story in the mail-order business. Johnson, formerly president of Family Fashions by Avon, recognized a dramatic shift in the nature of American consumers. The increasingly prosperous middle and upper middle-class customers were clearly becoming the majority. Contributing significantly to this was the fact that nearly 50 percent of all American women were working outside the home, and the number was increasing.

Spiegel focused on this new target customer, generally a working woman between the ages of twenty-five and fifty-four with an above-average household income. She is an upscale, busy person who enjoys fashion, recognizes quality, but is extremely pressed for time and appreciates the convenience of mail-order shopping. The key to addressing this new customer for Spiegel was to upgrade its catalog and merchandise offerings, transforming the company's fashion image.

Johnson cut $40 million worth of mail-order products from the catalog. Many were top sellers, including automobile tires, batteries, and double-knit suits at budget prices. These products were replaced by name-brand apparel, fragrances, cosmetics, and small-space home furnishings that met the needs of the new target customer. Although not for the super rich, Spiegel has changed its products to reflect the tastes of the upper middle class. Since 1984 Spiegel has featured designer apparel and accessories from resources such as Liz Claiborne, Anne Klein, Escada, and Ralph Lauren. Higher price home lines are carried from Bill Blass and Laura Ashley among others. Also, private label has been developed to represent from 50 to 60 percent of the total merchandise offerings.

As part of this repositioning, Spiegel had to remodel its catalog. The full-color catalog was printed on heavier paper with a larger page size for the look of a first-class fashion magazine. Gaudy graphics and exaggerated copy were eliminated. The company began a high-profile, first-class advertising and publicity campaign that includes full-color, one-page ads in status fashion magazines.

The risks that Spiegel took have paid off. Between 1976 and 1982, despite massive reductions in merchandise offerings and initial loss of customers, sales increased more than 40 percent. Since the friendly acquisition of Spiegel by Otto-Versand, a West German retailer second only to Sears in size, the future seems bright.

Today's typical Spiegel customer is a female in her late thirties with an average household income of $45,000. Sixty percent of Spiegel's sales are in women's apparel, 10 percent in menswear, and 30 percent in home furnishings.

In addition to Spiegel's two major seasonal catalogs and its Christmas book, the company has twenty-two specialty catalogs that generate more than 20 percent of total sales. These specialty books require less lead time than the major catalogs and allow buyers to respond more quickly to fashion trends. Among the specialty catalogs are *Together*, which features private label sportswear; *Vibes, Rhythm and Fashion* with moderately priced women's private label sportswear targeted to twenty-five-year-old fashion-forward customers; and *For You*, featuring large-size women's apparel.

Spiegel is using video to augment its catalogs and enhance the customer's shopping experience. The first video cassette, "Just for You Fashion Video Journal," targeted to women size 16 and over, was released in January 1988. The thirty-minute VCR program featured fashions for the office, home, and leisure. It also included interviews with apparel designers and beauty, hair, and makeover experts.

Now as the largest nonstore retailer in the United States, Spiegel boasts virtually total automation in its Oakbrook, Illinois, order-filling operation. When customers call in their orders toll-free, operators can immediately access all customer activity on-line for the last six months, greatly speeding adjustments and other inquiries.

Spiegel strengthened its position in catalog sportswear sales in 1988 by acquiring two established retail store mail-order chains: Honeybee and Eddie Bauer. At the time of the purchase Honeybee did about 50 percent of its volume in catalog sales, and Eddie Bauer about 40 percent. Spiegel hoped to gain 2,200,000 new customers from Eddie Bauer and 600,000 from Honeybee to add to its active customer list of 5 million. Spiegel announced plans to operate both newly acquired businesses as autonomous subsidiaries.

From the rural American of the late 1800s to the working woman of today, Spiegel has found success through catalog sales. Although the customer has changed considerably over the years, Spiegel has changed with her, moving from fourth place to first.

Objectives of Assortment Planning

The overall goal in assortment planning is to have a **balanced assortment** of merchandise with sufficient breadth and depth to meet the demand of the store's target customers. **Assortment breadth** is the number of different classifications or items offered the customer. The quantity of each item available is the **assortment depth.** An assortment containing a few items with each in great quantities is said to be narrow and deep. An assortment is described as broad and shallow when a great variety of different items or styles are available but with only a few of each on hand.

Prestige stores that cater to the fashion-forward customer emphasize broad and shallow assortments in which a large selection of styles, colors, and fabrications are offered in limited depth. Mass merchandisers usually feature narrow and deep assortments of proven styles, offering a limited number of styles but stocking many of each in all sizes and colors carried. Stores catering to the middle group of customers often feature broad and shallow assortments early in the season as a means of testing new styles, but assortments become narrower and deeper later in the season after customer preferences have been identified.

The primary objectives of merchandise and assortment planning are as follows:

1. To provide sufficient inventory consisting of the right styles, sizes, colors, prices, and other important selection factors to satisfy customer demand.

2. To time merchandise deliveries to correlate with customer demand and in line with the store's ability to stock, display, and promote the goods.

3. To plan purchases so that some open-to-buy is available at all times, enabling the buyer to have funds available to purchase new items that appear on the market, place reorders for fast-selling goods, and take advantage of special buying opportunities.

A well-balanced assortment sells because it contains what the store's customers want to buy. A well-planned assortment contains merchandise of the right type, in the right quantities, at the right price, at the right time, and at the right place.

Summary of Key Points

1. Before the buyer is ready to plan, he or she should identify and clearly understand the store's target customer.

2. Because no store can be everything to every customer, stores segment their customers according to demographic and psychographic factors.

3. In addition to being influenced by demographic and psychographic factors, customer demand is affected by geographic features, climatic conditions, transportation facilities, and community institutions.

4. Consumers are motivated to buy by rational and emotional motives. In selecting fashion merchandise, buying decisions are usually based on a combination of these motives.

5. Patronage motives, such as merchandise assortment, price, convenience, fashion image, and store services, explain why customers select one store over another.

6. Selection factors are qualities inherent in merchandise that help customers make buying decisions and provide the basis for the customer's acceptance or rejection of merchandise.

7. A consumer purchase is seldom decided based on one selection factor but rather is based on a combination of factors.

8. When selecting merchandise, the buyer should consider it from the customer's viewpoint because the customer makes the final buying decision.

9. Many in-store and external sources are available to assist the buyer in learning about merchandise preferences of both current and potential store customers.

10. The single most important source of information available to the buyer is the store's past sales. A weakness of sales records is that they only show whether or not what the buyer bought was sold; they do not show what the buyer did not buy but should have bought.

11. Store sales personnel provide a valuable in-store information source because they have direct contact with the customer. Salespeople can provide information concerning customers' comments about the merchandise.

12. Two major tools used by the buyer in financial planning are the dollar merchandise plan and the open-to-buy.

13. Buyers prepare two dollar merchandise plans for the year. Each six-month plan is based on planned sales, stocks, markdowns, and purchases.

14. Assortment plans project the variety and quantity of merchandise to be carried in stock to meet customer demand. The two methods used to develop assortment plans are the basic stock list and model stock plan.

Key Words and Concepts

Define, identify, or explain each of the following:

advisory panel

assortment breadth

assortment depth

assortment plan

balanced assortment

basic stock or staple stock

basic stock plan

buying motives

demographic segmentation

dollar merchandise plan (six-month plan)

emotional buying motives

focus group

market segmentation

merchandise selection factors

model stock plan

open-to-buy (OTB)

patronage motives

psychographic segmentation

rational buying motives

staple stock

stock turnover

stockkeeping unit (SKU)

want slip

Discussion Questions

1. Consider retail stores that have gone out of business and analyze the reasons for these failures.

2. What demographic and psychographic trends are impacting retail stores in your local community?

3. Explain the difference between rational and emotional buying motives. Using each, give examples of factors that the consumer would consider in making a buying decision.

4. Identify the geographic features, climatic conditions, and institutions that influence consumer lifestyles and interests in your community. How do these factors influence what fashion products consumers want to buy?

5. What is your favorite store? What patronage motives attract you to this store? Why does a customer choose to patronize one store over another?

6. Review the selection factors discussed in this chapter. What selection factors can you add to those presented? Discuss the important selection factors for each of the following: (1) children's clothing, (2) men's suits, (3) junior sportswear, (4) women's better and designer dresses.

7. What outside sources of information about customer demand would be of most value for each of the following buyers: better dresses, menswear, children's wear, tabletop (gifts, china, crystal, silver), furniture?

8. Why should a buyer "think like a customer"?

9. What weakness is inherent in using sales records as a source of information about customer preferences?

10. Why is merchandise planning important? Discuss the two tools of financial planning.

11. What is the difference between a basic stock plan and a model stock plan?

12. Describe a balanced assortment.

13. What are the advantages and disadvantages of a higher stock turnover?

Notes

Maryanne Bohlinger, *Merchandise Buying*. Dubuque, Iowa: Wm. C. Brown, 1983, p. 189.

Melvin T. Copeland, *Principles of Merchandising*. New York: A. W. Shaw, 1924, pp. 155, 167.

Rona Ostrow and Sweetman R. Smith, *The Dictionary of Retailing*. New York: Fairchild Publications, 1985, p. 234.

Jon G. Udell, "A New Approach to Consumer Motivation," *Journal of Retailing*, 40 (Winter 1964–65), 6–10.

John W. Wingate and Joseph S. Friedlander, *The Management of Retail Buying*. Englewood Cliffs, N.J.: Prentice-Hall, 1978.

Buying the Merchandise

Buying the merchandise to meet the needs of the store's target customer is the buyer's most important responsibility. Once the planning process is completed, the buyer must identify sources of supply and decide from whom to buy. The buyer has almost a limitless number of vendors from whom to choose. Vendors must be evaluated according to their merchandise offerings, services, and performance. The buyer must also select the specific items of merchandise and negotiate the purchase from the vendor. The selection and buying of merchandise is a never-ending responsibility for the buyer.

This chapter is a discussion of how the buyer makes contacts with suppliers and decides which vendors with whom to do business. Also discussed are planning the market trip, steps in making a market trip, and selecting merchandise at market.

Making Buying Contacts

Merchandise may be viewed and obtained by the buyer in a number of different ways. The primary sources of merchandise for fashion buyers include: (1) markets, (2) visiting sales representatives, (3) catalogs, (4) resident buying offices, (5) wholesalers, and (6) store-owned resources. An additional way in which buyers obtain merchandise is by consignment or memorandum buying.

Markets

Buying through a market is considered the best way for fashion buyers to obtain the lowest prices and to view the widest variety of merchandise in the shortest possible time period. Markets and trade shows provide concentrations of merchandise displayed by manufacturers or their sales representatives. Many lines are shown at market that the buyer cannot see any other way. Small, new resources as well as

Buyers view and compare many lines of merchandise.
Source: *Reprinted with permission of Maison Blanche.*

established ones are found at market. Markets enable buyers to see and compare many lines of merchandise within a relatively brief period of time. (The major fashion markets are discussed in detail in Chapter 8.)

Buying through markets is the most common method for purchasing fashion merchandise. The market trip exposes the buyer to many lines and to fashion trends and new merchandising ideas. The ordering of merchandise, however, is usually done back at the buyer's office away from the pressures of the market and the influence of manufacturers' sales representatives.

Visiting Sales Representatives

Although buying through markets is the most common method, buyers also make purchases from manufacturers' sales representatives who call on them in their offices. In this way the market comes to the buyer. Sales representatives bring samples to show the buyer who is able to see the merchandise and make decisions on his or her own home ground. Most large established manufacturers hire sales personnel who travel and visit stores within a certain geographic area. Some buyers with small stores select a large portion of their merchandise in this way. All buyers see manufacturers' sales representatives and make some purchases in this manner.

Large firms are not the only ones to sell merchandise by calling on buyers. Sometimes new designers or manufacturers make their first contacts with store buyers by calling on stores where they would like to see their merchandise sold. Such new firms may not be able to afford the cost of market or road sales representatives. Through such contacts a buyer may "discover" a new designer and may be the first to present the merchandise to consumers.

Buying from visiting sales representatives offers several advantages. First, the buyer saves the time and expense of going to market and being away from the store or office. Also, the buyer has available in his or her office many resources to assist in making a buying decision. Sales records and plans aid in determining the need for the merchandise. The buyer can also include other store personnel, such as the assistant buyer, merchandise manager, or salespeople, in making a decision. It is easier for the buyer to maintain control when viewing a line in the buyer's own territory rather than in the vendor's showroom. When the buyer is in the store, he or she can see exactly how the merchandise looks in the store in relation to the present merchandise assortment. The buyer is less likely to be influenced by the sales representative's enthusiasm for a product.

Catalogs

Another way in which buyers select merchandise without leaving the store is by using a catalog. Certain categories of merchandise can be viewed easily and selections determined by looking at sample fabrics and/or illustrations featured in catalogs.

Basic items such as hosiery, underwear, men's shirts, women's lingerie, and foundation garments are often purchased through catalogs. Sometimes a sales representative will visit a store to explain catalog offerings and show samples of merchandise. Catalogs offer the buyer the advantage of considering merchandise at leisure without the influence of a manufacturer's sales representative.

Resident Buying Offices

The buyer whose store contracts for the services of a resident buying office has another source available for acquiring merchandise. As discussed in Chapter 13, the resident buying office assists the buyer in purchasing goods both when the buyer is in the market and back at the store. The buyer's market representative in the resident buying office will go into the market and seek out merchandise according to directions provided by the store buyer. Resident buyers also bring sample merchandise to the resident buying office to be viewed when the buyer visits the market.

Wholesalers

True **wholesalers** are middlemen who purchase goods from manufacturers in large quantities and sell goods to retailers in smaller quantities. Wholesalers are used most often when buying **convenience goods**, which are items that must be replaced in small quantities at frequent intervals. The customer expects stores to have convenience goods readily available for purchase at all times. Wholesalers are willing to fill small orders and offer the advantage of quick delivery.

Fashion goods are usually purchased directly from the manufacturer or through a manufacturer's representative. Wholesalers who stock ready-to-wear usually limit offerings to basic classic styles and sell primarily to small, less fashion-oriented stores. Wholesalers are most successful when demand for merchandise is fairly constant. Fashion sales are highly seasonal and fluctuate considerably throughout the year. Also, fashion changes rapidly, and wholesalers are not geared to handling such fluctuations in consumer demand and preferences. Only two categories of fashion goods are commonly bought through wholesalers: furs and millinery.

Store-Owned Resources

Some large retailers own their own manufacturing facilities and produce their own private label merchandise. Such retailers have total control of the goods produced. When the store owns the resources, the buyer may become involved in designing merchandise or suggesting items to be produced. Retailers receive higher markups on this merchandise because the middleman has been deleted.

Consignment and Memorandum Buying

Buyers may also obtain merchandise through consignment or memorandum buying. With **consignment buying** the retailer takes possession of the merchandise, but title (ownership) remains with the vendor until it passes to the store's customers when sold. Merchandise that does not sell within a specified time period may be returned to the vendor. **Memorandum buying** is similar except that the retailer takes title to the goods at the time the goods are received; however, as with consignment purchases, unsold merchandise may be returned to the vendor after a specified time period. The retailer may also have the right to pay for the goods as they are sold. Consignment and memorandum buying are common practices in the jewelry business. The primary advantage for the retailer is that his or her risk is reduced; however, the retailer's markup on the merchandise is also reduced. Because the vendor bears the risk, a higher price is charged for the goods than with other types of purchases. Buying on consignment allows a retailer to test new types of goods without making a financial investment in the goods. When sales are uncertain or merchandise is too expensive for a retailer to afford, consignment buying is a means by which the merchandise may be offered to the customer.

Learning about Resources

The buyer is responsible for identifying merchandise resources and for making contacts with those resources in order to view merchandise lines and place orders. A buyer learns about resources in several ways. The buyer's own past experience is one obvious source of information. The buyer should maintain a reference file summarizing the performance of all resources used in the department. This type of reference file provides an invaluable source of information when a new buyer enters a department. The buyer should keep a record of the name, address, phone number, and purchases made with a resource. Also included should be information about the performance of the resource.

A store may subscribe to several services that provide information concerning merchandise resources. Examples include resident buying offices, fashion reporting services, and fashion consultants, as discussed in Chapter 14. The buyer often learns about new resources by reading the trade press and consumer fashion press. Advertising, feature articles, and news items provide names of possible resources.

When in the market, the buyer may learn of new resources in several ways. Market directories are published, listing resources by name and category. If the buyer is looking for a new resource, he or she can follow up on new listings. Talking with buyers from other stores, resident buyers, and sales representatives at market can lead to information. Attending fashion shows held at market is another means of exposing buyers to new merchandise lines as well as giving them an overview of fashion trends. Sometimes the buyer learns of new resources by observing merchandise offerings in other stores.

Factors in Selecting Resources

A buyer wants to select the resources that will be most profitable for the store. This means that the buyer must select resources offering merchandise that will sell. To do this, the buyer must choose the best resources from the many available. In determining which resources to use, the buyer must give careful consideration to a number of factors. Some of the key factors relate to merchandise offerings, vendor policies and services, and quality and consistency of vendor performance.

Merchandise Offerings

The most important considerations in selecting a resource relate to the merchandise offerings of a vendor. The vendor must provide merchandise that the buyer's customers want to purchase. The merchandise must be the right price, quality, and fashion level for the store's customers. If the merchandise is not right for the store and its customers, the resource should be eliminated from consideration.

Some retailers engage in what is called *specification buying* where manufacturers produce goods to the exact requirements of the retailer. When this is desired by the retailer, the buyer must look for a resource willing to do this kind of production. Sometimes retailers want to design the entire item themselves; other times they only want to change the fabric or certain design details and have the merchandise confined to their store. Specification buying assures that a store will have exclusive merchandise. No other store will carry the particular item purchased through specification buying.

Sometimes a manufacturer will agree to confine a particular style or fabric to one store or to one store within a geographical area. Confining merchandise is another way for a store to have exclusive merchandise. **Confined merchandise** is sold only to a limited number of stores within a trading area, thus limiting a store's competition for a particular item.

Decisions to carry certain brands may be made by key store executives leaving the buyer no choice about selecting from the resource. Consumers may expect the store to carry certain brand or designer names, and the buyer knows that business will be lost if these brands are not made available to the store's consumers.

Vendor Policies

Vendors often establish policies relating to distribution, clearance merchandise, shipping, and inventory control. Such policies must be considered by the buyer in selecting resources from which to buy.

Manufacturers may require a minimum purchase in terms of dollars or units of merchandise. This may prevent some small stores from doing business with the vendor because they cannot afford to place such large orders. Manufacturers also may restrict production as a means of controlling how much of a certain item will be available to sell. The manufacturer thus discourages unwanted retail accounts by not guaranteeing shipments.

Some vendors will sell to any store all items they offer; others will limit the sales of certain items within a trading area. A store seeking exclusives on merchandise looks for a vendor who will limit sales within a trading area or will confine a particular style, number, or fabric to one store.

Vendors have varying policies relating to the selling of promotional or clearance goods. Just like retailers, manufacturers cannot sell all of the goods they produce. Some merchandise will be available late in the season either because of overproduction or because of orders that have been canceled by retailers. Some manufacturers will sell leftover merchandise and merchandise that is not first quality only through their own outlet stores. Others will dispose of such merchandise by selling it to the retailer in job lots at a reduced price. A **job lot** is a promotional grouping of merchandise that consists of an unbalanced assortment, end-of-the-season goods, leftover merchandise, or canceled orders. In some instances a job lot will include irregular or second-quality merchandise. An **irregular** is merchandise that contains a minor flaw or imperfection that does not reduce the serviceability of the goods. Such items may be a good buy for the store and its customers. **Seconds** may have a defect that will affect the serviceability of the goods. Thus a second may or may not be a good buy for the store and its customers.

Some stores specialize in **clearance merchandise** and seek it out in the market. Other stores have policies against carrying clearance merchandise or may restrict it to certain departments within the store. Many fashion-oriented stores do not wish to damage their fashion image by carrying such merchandise in an apparel department but will carry irregulars in household lines such as sheets and towels. Some retailers do not want to do business with a vendor who will sell **closeout goods** to a store in their trading area. When a vendor operates its own outlet stores, these stores are often located in isolated areas and do little if any advertising so as not to offend retail stores carrying the merchandise at regular retail prices.

Vendor Services

Vendors frequently offer retailers various services to assist with selling the goods. Such services include training salespeople, sharing advertising costs, providing point-of-purchase selling aids, or preticketing goods.

Vendors may provide training programs and seminars to teach store salespeople how to sell the merchandise. Vendors may also send their own specialists to the store to assist customers in making purchases. **Trunk shows** are often given by apparel manufacturers or designers who come to the store to show the line through informal fashion modeling and assist customers in selecting and accessorizing garments.

Many manufacturers share the cost of advertising with retailers. This may be in the form of preparing advertisements to be used by the retailer or by paying part of the cost of advertisements produced by the retailer. Such sharing of the cost of an advertisement is called **cooperative advertising**.

Point-of-purchase aids are offered by many vendors to assist with selling merchandise. Examples of such aids are displays, signs, video tapes, and display fixtures. Some vendors even send specialists into the store to take merchandise counts for the retailer and restock display fixtures. In fashion, such services are most often found in accessory items such as sunglasses, costume jewelry, hosiery, and cosmetics.

Preticketing is a service desired by some retailers. It refers to the vendor's placing the retail price tag on the merchandise. Such goods may be placed directly on the selling floor without being price ticketed by the retailer; thus the retailer saves time and money in handling the goods.

Vendor Performance

The retailer seeks vendors who are dependable and consistent in their performance. The buyer expects the vendor to deliver the goods as ordered in agreement with the purchase order. Goods should be shipped on time and the merchandise should be exactly as ordered in terms of quality, fabrication, color, sizes, and quality. The vendor should carry through on all agreements made with the retailer.

The retailer has the right to return merchandise shipped by a vendor that does not comply with specifications on the order form. Vendor acceptance and handling of such returns are other factors that should be considered when selecting resources.

The buyer must constantly analyze and evaluate resources to determine their performance level. The key word in evaluating vendors is profitability. The buyer should continue to buy from those resources that are profitable. The most satisfactory vendors become the buyer's key resources and should continue to be the ones from which the majority of purchases are made. Those resources that are no longer satisfactory should be eliminated from consideration.

Vendors are commonly analyzed according to the selection factors presented in Chapter 14. Most important in evaluating resources are statistical facts such as sales, markups, markdowns, and turnover. Stores frequently give vendors a rating based on quality of merchandise, compliance with the purchase order, and return policy. Figure 15.1 shows a form used by retailers when evaluating resources. Each season the buyer should record information concerning vendors. Before going to the market the buyer should study the resource evaluation forms and use this information in completing the buying plan.

Developing Key Resources

Although it is desirable for the buyer to develop as many market contacts as possible, a large part of the purchases should be concentrated with a few key resources. **Key**

```
┌─────────────────────────────────────────────────────────────┐
│                                                              │
│   Resource_____Date_____      │
│                                                              │
│   Address_____ _____Dept.No._____     │
│                                                              │
│   Telephone_____Classification_____      │
│                                                              │
│   Factory Address_____      │
│                                                              │
│   Buyer contacts                                             │
│                                                              │
│   Dun & Bradstreet rating                                    │
│                                                              │
│   Quality of merchandise                                     │
│                                                              │
│   Ethics of firm (compliance with purchase order)            │
│                                                              │
│   Position in industry                                       │
│                                                              │
│   Vendor importance to store                                 │
│                                                              │
│   Store importance to vendor                                 │
│                                                              │
│   Record of terms (discounts, dating and delivery)           │
│                                                              │
│   Cooperative advertising and promotional aids               │
│                                                              │
│   Return policy                                              │
│                                                              │
│   Markdowns                                                  │
│                                                              │
│   Remarks (any additional information that would assist      │
│   store in dealing with resource)                            │
│                                                              │
│                                                              │
│                                                              │
│   Evaluator's signature_____      │
│                                                              │
└─────────────────────────────────────────────────────────────┘
```

FIGURE 15.1
Resource evaluation form.

resources are those vendors from whom a retailer has consistently bought a substantial portion of the store's merchandise. Such key resources have an established record of excellent past performance and are expected to continue to provide strong sales. Buyers should have key resources for each merchandise category carried.

Concentrating purchases with key resources enables retailers to qualify for the lowest prices and leads to the best service from vendors. Stores also benefit from simplified record keeping when they limit their buying to fewer resources. The object of developing key resources is for the store to make itself important to the resource. Because of the dollar volume of business done by some stores, it is easier for such large companies to develop their importance with key resources than it is for small stores. Buyers who place large orders with vendors are said to write with a "big pencil." These buyers are very important to vendors and often receive preferential treatment by sales representatives.

Retailers have increasingly recognized the importance of developing key resources. Some retailers feel that as much as 50 percent of the total volume in some departments should come from two or three key resources (Osborne 1979).

There are some drawbacks, however, to depending too heavily on key resources. The store should not become so dependent that the buyer forgets to keep aware of changes in the marketplace. Consumer preferences change and so do vendors' merchandise offerings. When a resource no longer produces sales and profits, a buyer must seek other sources of supply. Buyers should not wait until the need arises for a new vendor to be looking for new resources. Buyers should constantly search for new vendors and new merchandise items. Each time a buyer goes to market, he or she should visit two or three resources that the store is not currently using. By doing this, the buyer begins to build relationships with possible future suppliers.

Market Trip Planning

Although buyers go to market primarily to view lines, there are several other reasons for making market trips. The cultivation of good relations with resources is an important reason. Buyers go to market to meet the principal executives with manufacturers and vendors and to develop business relations with these key people. Market trips also enable buyers to broaden their knowledge concerning the particular categories of merchandise they carry, to discover new items and sources of supply, to find out what leading market stores are doing, and to learn about current and probable future conditions in the marketplace.

To make the best possible use of the time spent at market, the trip is usually timed to coincide with a scheduled market. Timing the trip when the most lines are being shown enables the buyer to view more merchandise in a shorter period of time. Planning the trip is also important to make it successful.

Timing the Market Trip

When buyers go to market and the frequency of the trips will vary depending on the type of merchandise being purchased, the size and fashion orientation of the store, and the location of the market. For example, buyers in ready-to-wear departments make more frequent trips to market than do buyers in home-furnishings departments. A dress or sportswear buyer may go to market five times a year or even more. A furniture or housewares buyer may go to market only twice a year. The size, location, and fashion orientation of the store also influence the frequency of buying trips and the markets attended. The small store buyer probably goes to market less often than does the buyer for a large department store. The small store located near a regional market may go to all five seasonal fashion markets but may remain only one or two days. The buyer who must travel farther may go to market less often but will stay for a longer period of time.

In general, buyers follow a cycle in making market trips. The timing of line openings or market weeks as set by market or trade associations will determine when a market will be held. Dates of line openings and market weeks are scheduled to allow for the lead time that manufacturers require for production and delivery of goods. The timing of these openings determines when the buyer goes to market.

Some large manufacturers are bringing out new fashion merchandise as often as every six weeks; consequently, buyers from fashion-oriented stores are making more frequent trips to market to view new offerings. Buyers are buying more often and timing deliveries to allow for a continuous flow of merchandise because today's fashion customer wants to see something new each time she comes into the store.

Another factor influencing buyer trips is storewide or divisional promotions. **Promotion buying** involves such events as the store's birthday or anniversary sale, back-to-school, Easter, Christmas, or other important periods for the store. These events will influence the buyer's scheduling of market trips.

Where a buyer goes to market is determined by the type of merchandise to be purchased, and the relative importance and location of the various market centers. As discussed in Chapter 8, the most important domestic fashion market is New York City, with major regional markets in Los Angeles, Dallas, Chicago, and Atlanta. In addition, foreign markets are important for many fashion buyers.

The Buying Plan

Advance planning is necessary if the market trip is to be successful. Before the buyer goes to market to view vendors' merchandise offerings, the buyer completes a **buying plan**. This plan provides a general description of the merchandise to be purchased according to classifications, quantities, price lines, sizes, and other important elements. The plan limits the amount of money the buyer is to spend for each merchandise category. A plan is completed prior to going to market to guide the buyer while in the market. The plan tells the buyer what, where, and how much to buy.

The responsibility of market trip planning rests directly with the buyer. A detailed plan assists the buyer in making the most efficient use of time when visiting the market. A well-prepared plan can often make the difference between a profitable or an unprofitable operation. The primary purpose of the buying plan is to indicate to the buyer how much money to spend and how the store's money can be most profitably spent.

Before completing the plan the buyer needs to check current records and the performance of suppliers. The buyer should know which resources give the store the highest sales, the best markups, and the lowest markdowns. The buyer should also review the dollar merchandise plan and assortment plans and check current sales records.

In planning the market trip the buyer needs to determine the open-to-buy figure for each merchandise classification and each price line unit carried. Next, the buyer should determine what portion of the total open-to-buy should be reserved for local purchases, buying from sales representatives who visit the store, and reordering. The buyer should always reserve some open-to-buy to allow for reordering good sellers and taking advantage of opportunistic buys that may become available in the market. The buyer should never spend all of the available open-to-buy when in the market. Some money should be saved to use for purchasing merchandise at home and to provide for making adjustments required to meet changing customer demand.

The buyer should also plan how much money to spend with each key resource. This assures that all important resources will be adequately represented in the stock assortment. Since the key resources are those that are most profitable for the store, it is very important that sufficient funds be allotted for their purchase.

Buying trips should not be made to purchase staple merchandise. Purchasing staples can be done without going to market. The buyer should keep this in mind when preparing the buying plan.

The buying plan serves as a guide to the buyer when shopping in the market. It should not be viewed as rigid and unchangeable. Flexibility is important in a buying plan. Market conditions may require changes in the plan in order to obtain the types and quantities of merchandise needed for the store's customers. In department stores the buyer usually needs the approval of the divisional merchandise manager before changing the plan, especially if a change involves increasing the open-to-buy. The merchandise manager signs the plan when it is approved and a copy is sent to the resident buying office before the buyer goes to market.

Steps in Making a Market Trip

The buyer follows certain steps in making a market trip. The buyer must plan for the trip, carry out certain activities after arriving in the market, and follow through after returning to the store.

Planning the Trip

Prior to the market trip the buyer completes the buying plan and has it approved by the merchandise manager. Reservations must also be made for transportation to the market and lodging while there. Sometimes expense money can be drawn in advance from the store. The buyer will need to keep complete, accurate records of all business expenses incurred while in market, including transportation, meals, lodging, and business entertainment. The store's resident buying office should be notified in advance of the buyer's planned arrival in the marketplace, and the market representative should be sent a copy of the buying plan. The market representative needs to be informed of any assistance the buyer needs before coming to market.

The buyer may want the resident buyer to make appointments with vendors or to seek out possible new resources before the buyer comes to market.

Arrival in Market

Usually the first activity of the buyer after arriving at market is to register with the resident buying office and confer with the market representative concerning general market conditions, new resources, and any other pertinent information. The buyer can save considerable time in shopping the market by first talking with the resident buyer. Sometimes the market representative will accompany the buyer in visiting vendors. The buyer will also view any merchandise offerings assembled by the resident buying office before seeing vendors.

If appointments have not already been made with key resources, the buyer should contact them at this time and establish appointments. Making appointments is required by some vendors and is customary in certain markets. In any case appointments save time that may otherwise be wasted in waiting to see a vendor. Setting up appointments also forces the buyer to plan visits to vendors in a logical order.

Before visiting key resources a buyer should shop important market city stores looking for trends and merchandise ideas. This includes window shopping and visiting respective departments in stores. The buyer should also watch store advertisements in local newspapers while in market. Plans should be made to attend appropriate fashion shows, clinics, or seminars.

Visiting Resources

The buyer should list all resources to be visited and plan to visit first the resources most important to the store. Visits to resources should be organized on the basis of merchandise classification and price lines.

Some recommended guidelines for visiting resources are:

1. Know the buying plan fully. Have definite merchandise needs written down.

2. Visit better price-line resources first to develop fashion and quality standards.

3. Meet key executives at resources visited.

4. Visit factories and workrooms to learn more about manufacturers' capacity to produce and maintain quality control.

5. Wait to make a commitment until the market has been covered fully in a classification.

6. Don't overbuy. It is better to be safe than sorry. Buy in reasonable quantities.

7. Check and double-check buying plans, notes, and merchandise on order before writing orders.

8. Negotiate with vendor for best terms, discounts, and shipping arrangements.

9. Make notes about merchandise to share with store personnel responsible for selling the merchandise.

Completion of the Trip

After returning to the store, the buyer completes the buying plan and writes orders. The expense account should be completed and filed. The buyer may want to set up a schedule for checking on delivery of merchandise ordered to make sure that goods are received on schedule. If goods are not received, orders should be canceled. The buyer should also hold merchandise meetings with selling departments as the new merchandise arrives in the store.

Selecting Merchandise at Market

Selection of merchandise begins with a process of elimination. When a buyer views a vendor's merchandise offerings, the buyer eliminates from consideration the items that are wrong for the store and its customers. This process of elimination is called editing the line. The buyer views and edits the merchandise to meet the needs and wants of the store's target customer. In viewing the merchandise the buyer always maintains the customer's point of view. The buyer must ask the question: Is the merchandise the right price, style, fabrication, color, and fashion level for the store's customer?

The buyer must learn to be highly selective because of the many lines and items presented at each market by manufacturers. Many items are offered that are nearly identical in terms of styling, color, and fabrication. The inexperienced or unprepared buyer can easily be overwhelmed by the many offerings and by the enthusiasm of sales personnel for the lines they represent.

The buyer who is thoroughly prepared before going to market will make the best merchandise selections. Knowing the buying plan thoroughly and following it is the best way for the buyer to approach the market. The buying plan assists the buyer in making the right merchandise selections and in controlling expenditures. The buying plan provides the framework to narrow the factors that must be compared in the selection process. The plan tells the buyer what classifications, price lines, and brands need to be purchased. It deals with the quantitative aspects of buying by telling the buyer what, how much, and how many to buy.

The buyer must also consider the qualitative aspects of buying. Qualitative aspects relate to more intangible properties of merchandise selection such as quality, fashion level, and taste. The qualitative aspects of buying are not as easy to learn or identify as are quantitative aspects. Any buyer can be taught to study sales records and identify what sizes, price lines, and brands to buy, but to understand qualitative aspects of buying a buyer must have flair, good taste, and an understanding of fashion. The buyer must have a sense of what is right for the customer.

The Editing Process

In order to edit the vendor's offerings, the buyer must first have a clear picture of what is wanted. When selecting fashion merchandise this is not always easy to do. As we have seen, the buying plan will provide a guidepost for selection, but when planning to buy fashion merchandise not all factors can be determined in advance. The buyer must make certain decisions relating to fashion when viewing a vendor's offerings. It is impossible to determine exact styles, colors, and fabrications in advance of seeing the merchandise. When viewing the merchandise all of the buyer's knowledge about fashion trends and consumer demand come together to assist him or her in selecting merchandise.

A good buyer learns to say no quickly. By eliminating the items the buyer knows are wrong, the selection process is narrowed. A buyer tells the sales representative to remove immediately from consideration those items that are clearly unacceptable. The buyer takes notes while viewing the offerings. Most buyers develop their own system of rating merchandise to indicate how items rate for consideration. A simple system of checks and pluses is all that is needed. Often the vendor provides an order form that already has item numbers listed and sometimes even has sketches of the merchandise, facilitating the buyer's note taking.

Price is the first factor considered in eliminating merchandise. The buyer looks at the merchandise and immediately determines what his or her customers would be willing to pay for the item. If the wholesale price is too high to give the buyer the needed markup, the item is immediately eliminated from consideration. Regular-price fashion stores typically use a **keystone markup** on apparel. When keystoning, the retail price is determined by doubling the cost price.

The buying plan must always be kept in mind as the buyer views offerings. If the merchandise is not needed, it is not considered. When showing a line, a sales representative usually works with one buyer or store at a time. The buyer often sits behind a table so that he or she can take notes easily. The sales representatives shows the merchandise in groups. Ready-to-wear is on hangers and is often hung on a rack facing the buyer. This way the buyer can see and compare related items. Sometimes a model is available in the showroom who can try on merchandise at the buyer's request. Most ready-to-wear is purchased without the buyer seeing it on a model. Designer and more expensive lines of merchandise may be presented in fashion shows to groups of buyers, but this is not the way most merchandise is viewed by the buyer.

One style frequently comes in several colors or fabrications. When buying fashion separates, the buyer has many decisions to make. Tops and bottoms have to be balanced, colors coordinated, and size selections determined. A buyer purchases more tops than bottoms, but the possible combinations are considerable. Some styles work better in small sizes and others in larger sizes. The buyer must consider not only what is in fashion but customer preferences, ages, and figure types. Close-fitting straight skirts may be the hottest fashion item, but the buyer must remember that not every figure type can wear this style. Sleeveless tops and halters may be the rage, but if the store's target customer is the executive career woman or an older customer, such styles will not be appropriate. The buyer must always keep the customer and needs of the store in mind and not get carried away by a vendor's enthusiasm for a fashion. The buyer must also forget his or her own personal preferences and concentrate on the customer.

Vendors can provide assistance to the buyer in making selections. The buyer should ask which are key items in the line and which are **checking** (selling). The buyer should keep in mind that some items shown at market will not sell well enough to go into mass production, and should try to avoid selecting these items. Although the sales representative can provide the buyer with information helpful in making buying decisions, the buyer knows the store and its customers and should not let the vendor make the buying decision.

Buyers buy from resources in different ways. When buying from a key resource, the buyer selects merchandise in considerable breadth. Many items will be selected from the resource, and they may be purchased in depth. Because the store has enjoyed good business with these resources, the buyer usually schedules market visits with these vendors first.

Sometimes the buyer purchases only certain items from a vendor. For example, a vendor may have excellent sweaters or blouses, but may be weak in other merchandise classifications. The buyer refers to these vendors as **classification resources**.

A buyer may visit some resources and cherry pick. When **cherry picking**, a buyer selects a few good items from several vendors' lines without buying a complete line or classification from any one resource. This type of buying is time-consuming but is sometimes necessary in order to get the desired merchandise.

The buyer cannot always find in the market the merchandise that fits predetermined plans. In this case the buyer has to adjust the plan. A store must have fresh merchandise, and the buyer must make merchandise selections from available offerings.

Negotiating the Purchase

Negotiating the purchase is an important part of the buyer's job. The buyer and vendor must agree on the wholesale price, terms of the sale, transportation arrangements, and services to be included. Profit margin is one of the criteria used in evaluating the success of the buyer. Negotiating the best price and terms of sale will assist the buyer in improving the profit margin for the store.

Regular Price-Line Versus Special Promotion Buying

A distinction must be made between regular price-line buying and buying of special promotion merchandise. **Regular price-line buying** involves the buying of first-quality goods currently in demand. Wholesale prices in such goods are firmly established and the retailer has little opportunity to negotiate unless buying in large quantities. Discounts are often extended by the vendor when a retailer buys in large amounts.

When buying specials, price can often be negotiated. With special merchandise the main appeal is low price rather than fashion or quality. Specials may include end-of-season goods, excess production, canceled orders, and damaged or less-than-first-quality merchandise. Some stores specialize in off-price goods and actively seek out this kind of merchandise.

Robinson-Patman Act

All buyers should be familiar with the Robinson-Patman Act of 1936, which was designed to limit price discrimination and protect small businesses. The act prohibits vendors from providing excessive quantity discounts to large-volume retailers. It forbids a manufacturer engaging in interstate commerce from selling to similar customers at different prices if both sales involve products of the same quality and grade and if the resulting price difference serves to substantially lessen competition, create a monopoly, or prevent competition. Certain quantity discounts are allowed as are different prices for private and national brands. Vendors can offer lower prices when the method of buying reduces the vendor's cost of doing business, prices are reduced to meet a competitor's lower price, or the price is reduced on goods that are obsolete or becoming obsolete.

Elements in Price Negotiation

In negotiating the price buyers must always view the merchandise through the customer's eyes and first evaluate it in terms of what the customer would be willing to pay. Next, the buyer should determine if the markup obtained would be adequate and consider how the purchase would affect profit margin.

The buyer who knows the market and understands the cost of producing the merchandise is in the best position for negotiating price with a vendor. Buyers should keep aware of the availability of goods, prices being offered by vendors' competitors, and the probable salability of merchandise. Buyers should also learn all that they can about manufacturing and the costs of production.

Negotiating Terms of the Sale

Terms of sale include the amount of discount allowed on purchases, time allowed for taking the discount and paying the invoice in full, and transportation arrangements. Terms are fairly standard within each division of the apparel industry. For example, in women's ready-to-wear common terms of sale are 8/10 E.O.M. This means that an 8 percent discount may be deducted from the billed cost provided the invoice is paid within ten days after the end of the month.

Discounts

Buyers should understand the types of discounts whenever possible. Certain discounts are traditionally allowed, and the buyer should be familiar with the usual terms and percentage discounts allowed.

Discounts are reductions in the quoted price of merchandise that a vendor allows retail stores. **Dating** refers to the length of time the vendor allows the retailer to take the discount. Some of the types of discounts are cash, trade, seasonal, and quantity.

Cash discounts are percentage reductions allowed for paying invoices on or before a date specified by the vendor. Such discounts are offered as incentives to encourage retailers to pay invoices promptly. The cash discount terms consist of three elements: (1) a percentage discount, varying upward from 1 percent, (2) a time period in which the discount may be taken, often ten days, and (3) a net period indicating the date by which the invoice is due.

Among those cash discounts most often used are terms stated 2/10 net 30. The first figure indicates the discount rate; the second figure refers to the number of days the discount may be taken; and the third figure states the number of days within which the invoice must be paid. Thus, in the above example, the discount rate is 2 percent, the rate is available for ten days, and the full amount is due within thirty days from the date of the invoice. If the invoice is not paid within thirty days, it is past due and may be subject to interest charges.

Trade discounts are percentage reductions from a list price offered to wholesalers and middlemen and sometimes extended to retailers to compensate them for performing some marketing function. The price that the buyer pays for the merchandise is determined by deducting a certain percentage from the quoted list price. Trade discounts are usually quoted in series: less 35%, less 10%, less 5%.

Seasonal discounts are percentage reductions in price offered to encourage retailers to place orders for merchandise ahead of the usual buying season. This is called **advance buying.** Manufacturers offer seasonal discounts to encourage retailers to buy during slow selling periods. Retailers must have storage space and available money to take advantage of seasonal discounts. Retailers must also be able to predict merchandise needs well in advance of the selling season in order to do advance buying.

Quantity discounts are a price reduction offered by the vendor to the retailer for buying goods in large amounts. A buyer must have the ability to sell large amounts of merchandise in order to buy in quantities large enough to qualify for a quantity discount.

Price reductions may also be obtained by paying cash rather than following the usual pattern of buying on credit. Buying private brand merchandise is another way for the buyer to obtain a lower price.

Dating

Dating is the number of days the retailer is entitled to take a cash discount and to pay the invoice before it is considered past due. Examples of different types of dating are regular dating, E.O.M. dating, extra dating, and R.O.G. (receipt of goods) dating.

Regular dating is calculated from the date of the invoice. Terms of 8/10 net 30 mean that a discount of 8 percent is extended to the retailer provided payment is made within ten days from the invoice date. If the invoice is not paid within ten days, the retailer has thirty days to pay the bill before it is considered past due.

E.O.M. dating is calculated from the "end of the month" rather than from the date of the invoice. E.O.M. dating is commonly used in the apparel industry. An invoice dated July 18 with terms of 8/10 E.O.M. would entitle the retailer to an 8 percent discount if paid by August 10.

An invoice with E.O.M. dating on or after the 25th of the month is considered to be dated as of the first of the following month. This gives the retailer more than a month in which to take a discount. For example, an invoice dated July 27 with terms of 8/10 E.O.M. would be handled as if dated August 1 and would entitle the retailer to an 8 percent discount if paid by September 10.

Extra dating is another way for the retailer to receive a longer period of time in which to take a discount. An invoice with terms of 3/10-30 extra gives the retailer thirty extra days or a total of forty days from the invoice date to take a discount of 3 percent.

R.O.G. dating, which stands for "receipt of goods," allows the retailer to calculate the discount period from the date the merchandise is received at the store rather than from the date on the invoice. The buyer may want to negotiate for R.O.G. dating when delivery is slow or when a manufacturer tends to mail invoices in advance of shipping goods.

Delivery Terms

Retailers consider the cost of getting the goods to the store as part of the cost of the goods. The buyer must consider the available methods of transportation and specify on the order form the method to use. The buyer negotiates delivery terms with the vendor. The terms indicate where the title to the merchandise passes from seller (vendor) to buyer and where the risks of ownership begin. Thus delivery terms are important in determining the cost of the merchandise.

The location at which the goods change ownership is called the **FOB point**. FOB stands for "free on board" and indicates the point of origin where title to merchandise passes to the buyer. Most goods are bought FOB factory, which means that the title to the goods passes to the store at the factory with the store paying all transportaiton and insurance costs. If the buyer can negotiate with the vendor for delivery terms of FOB store, the seller will pay all shipping costs to get the goods delivered to the store. Obviously, FOB store provides the most advantageous shipping terms for the retailer.

The buyer should consider all aspects of shipping and select the method most advantageous for the store. The buyer decides whether to ship by truck, rail, air, parcel post, United Parcel Service, or other method. The buyer should consider cost and time involved in the transportation method selected. Packaging also influences shipping costs and should be carefully evaluated by the buyer.

Negotiating Services

Although negotiation tends to emphasize price and terms of the sale, the buyer must also negotiate for services to be provided by the vendor. The retailer should be aware of the services commonly available from vendors and should ask for those of value to the store. Examples of services that may be offered by a vendor include:

1. Packaging of merchandise for resale to the store's customers.

2. Preticketing and labeling of merchandise.

3. Point-of-purchase selling aids such as blowups of advertisements for store display, sample merchandise for display, posters, display fixtures, video tapes, and brochures.

4. Cooperative advertising money.

5. Advertising mats and radio and television scripts.

6. Training of store salespeople.

7. Money reimbursement for markdowns taken on merchandise that does not sell.

8. Assumption of inventory responsibilities for merchandise in the store.

9. Consignment selling, which allows for return of merchandise that does not sell.

Bargaining

It is the buyer's responsibility to determine whether or not negotiation is possible in making a purchase. The buyer must learn how to bargain. Bargaining is a system of negotiation involving the exchange of ideas between two parties, the buyer and the seller. A good bargain is mutually advantageous for both. The buyer should remember the importance of building an ongoing relationship with vendors and not ask for unfair prices, discounts, or services.

Writing the Purchase Order

The purchase order is one of the many forms the buyer uses. However, it is probably the most important document handled by the buyer. The buyer is responsible for the completeness, correctness, and legibility of the purchase order. Orders are written primarily to serve two purposes: (1) for the resource to use in filling the order, and (2) for the buyer's reference and to permit the buyer to summarize purchases.

The purchase order should be written by the buyer after the selection of merchandise is complete. Some buyers prefer to return to the store before writing orders where they are free from any vendor pressure and where it is easier to check store sales records, merchandise on hand, and committed orders. The buyer should always wait to write orders until all vendors within a classification have been viewed. It is also best to write firm orders away from the market showroom. Vendors will encourage a buyer to write an order while viewing a line and leave the "paper," as orders are called in the market, before leaving the showroom. After all, vendors want the buyer to see their lines only and do not want other lines considered.

Buyers should always write their own orders and never let a vendor write an order for them. The buyer is more familiar with the store's order form than is the sales representative and can write the order more accurately. The sales representative puts the vendor's needs first, not the store's need for reference. The buyer should be certain that all information provided on the order form is accurate, complete, and legible.

Large stores use their own order forms rather than those provided by the vendor. Stores design their own forms to provide the information the store needs to receive, distribute, and control the goods. Order forms usually consist of several copies so that all personnel who need a copy will receive one. Copies of orders are kept by the receiving department, merchandise manager, the buyer, and the vendor. It is easier for the store to work with its own order form since all merchandise orders are then placed on the same form. The buyer is less likely to leave off important information since he or she is familiar with the form and uses the same one to write all orders. Some stores today are writing orders by computer rather than on paper. This makes the order readily available to all store personnel who need to refer to orders.

Buyers from small retail stores frequently use the order blank provided by the vendor. This means that the buyer has to learn to handle many different formats and is more likely to make a mistake or leave off important information. The variety in format and size of order forms also makes it difficult for the buyer to read and file the orders.

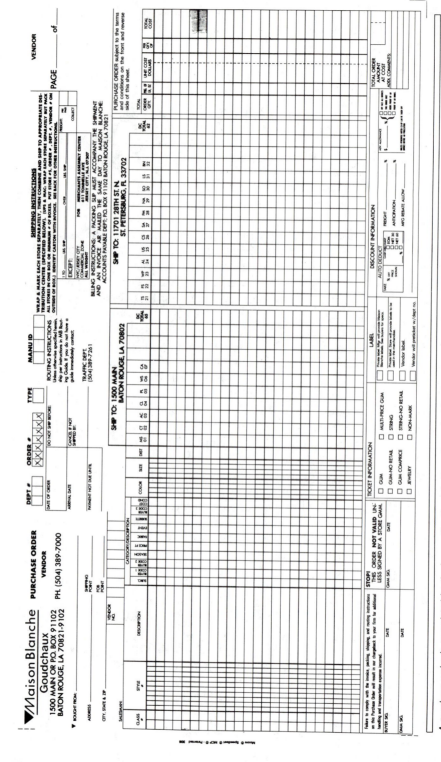

A purchase order is completed by the buyer after the selection of merchandise is made.
Source: Reprinted with permission of Maison Blanche.

Information on the Order Form

Order forms typically provide the following information:

1. Store name and address.

2. Where goods are to be delivered.

3. Order form serial number.

4. Store department number.

5. Date order is placed.

6. Name and address of the shipper.

7. Terms and dating: when payment is to be made and cash discounts allowed for early payment.

8. Delivery date.

9. Cancellation date: when buyer can cancel order if goods have not been received.

10. Method of payment.

11. FOB point: the point at which the buyer takes title to goods and assumes freight charges to destination.

12. Description of the merchandise: style number, colors, sizes, etc.

13. Quantity ordered.

14. Unit cost price of each item.

15. Total dollar estimate of the order.

16. Signatures.

17. Special instructions or agreements, such as any special services extended by the seller.

Signatures on the Order

In some stores the order form is binding with only the buyer's signature. The buyer is thus the store's legal representative and has the authority to place orders. In many large stores the signature of a merchandise manager is required in addition to the buyer's signature for the order to be binding. This enables the merchandise manager to keep a close check on the orders being placed by buyers.

The order form may also be signed by the vendor's sales representative. In some instances the vendor sends the store a signed confirmation or acceptance of

Nordstrom, Inc.

Nordstrom became the largest volume specialized department store in the United States in 1986, surpassing Saks Fifth Avenue. The company, which originated in Seattle in 1901 as a single-unit shoe store, was the fastest growing major specialty soft goods store of the eighties. In 1980 its sales in twenty-nine stores located on the West Coast totaled $346,269,000. By 1988 the company had grown to over 60 units with more than $2 billion in sales and was aiming at sales of $13 billion by 1990. Many department and specialty stores are trying to analyze Nordstrom's amazing success story. Although some of the factors responsible for its success are easy to identify, they are not so easily duplicated by other retailers.

Nordstrom opened its first stores in the eastern United States in 1988 with two stores in the Washington, D.C., area. The company plans to open additional stores throughout the country joining Saks Fifth Avenue, Neiman-Marcus, and I. Magnin as an upscale national specialty store chain.

An article in *Women's Wear Daily* described Nordstrom's new store at Tysons Corner Center in McLean, Virginia, as looking like most other upscale retailers, but went on to point out noticeable differences. For example, clothing at Nordstrom does not carry magnetic antishoplifting tags, and no limit is placed on the number of clothes the customer may take into a fitting room. Merchandise is displayed on furniture and on hangers, but mannequins are seldom used. Men's and women's restrooms are distinctly marked with foot-tall lettering, visible from a distance. Also, refreshments of cookies and juices are sold from a cart located near the dress department ("Nordstrom's Eastern Gold Rush," *Women's Wear Daily*, May 16, 1988, p. 5).

As a customer-oriented and entrepreneurial retailer, Nordstrom is considered a maverick in the retail industry. Most stores today promote heavily in December, but Nordstrom waits until the day after Christmas to put merchandise on sale, and the company's biggest volume day of the year comes in July when it holds its prefall sale. The company spends less on advertising than other major retailers but uses the money saved to improve customer service. The use of only a few mannequins in the stores is because management feels that it is difficult to remove the merchandise from them if the customer wants it. The stores are decorated with antique tables and armoires, which give them a homelike atmosphere suited to Nordstrom's target customer, who is traditional and career-oriented.

Much of Nordstrom's success is attributed to its emphasis on customer service. The commissioned salespeople are knowledgeable, attentive, and attractive. Although they are assigned to a department, they may sell merchandise throughout the store. The focus of the Nordstrom corporate structure is the sales force, and salespeople are highly motivated and have a sense of dedication to the company; in fact, 314 of the 506 clerks who opened the new Tysons Corner store in Virginia were veteran Nordstrom employees from the West Coast who paid their own expenses to move East.

Another reason for Nordstrom's success is its stock depth with stock levels 20 to 30 percent heavier than competitors. This means that the customer is more likely to find the desired size and color at Nordstrom than at other stores.

As a fashion leader, Nordstrom takes special care in selecting items for each store that specifically reflect the preferences of its customers in the surrounding area. At a time when most large retailers have moved to more centralized buying with fewer buyers, Nordstrom feels that decentralized buying provides the company with a merchandise mix different from its competitors and more suitable for its customers. Manufacturers say that Nordstrom buyers are the best in the industry at knowing what their customers want. This may be due in part to the company's requirement that each buyer visit the stores for which he or she buys at least once a week and spend time on the sales floor. Also, all Nordstrom buyers begin their company careers as members of the sales force, reflecting the firm's tradition of promoting from within.

Nordstrom believes strongly in self-improvement, and senior management has institutionalized its philosophy and motivational techniques through workshops and seminars, which are presented by an outside firm for employees. Such programs may be a prime contributing factor to the company's low shrinkage rate of only 1 percent.

Nordstrom is directed by the family management team of brothers of John and Jim Nordstrom and their cousin Bruce. The three Nordstroms serve as cochairmen, and the company does not have a chief executive officer. John McMillan, a cousin by marriage, is president of the firm. Decisions are made by the management team on a consensus basis, and merchandising and operational responsibilities are shared. Jim Nordstrom is responsible for better-priced women's apparel and sales promotion; Bruce Nordstrom handles shoes, finance, and accounting; and John Nordstrom oversees menswear, distribution, and store planning. John McMillan is responsible for merchandising moderate-priced women's apparel, clearance outlets, and Nordstrom's junior and young men's stores called Place Two.

In the 1960s and early 1970s Nordstrom made the transition from a shoe operation to an apparel specialist. In 1978 it moved from the Pacific Northwest to California where the primary expansion thrust remained until the company moved eastward in 1988. Nordstrom expects soon to have at least five stores in the Washington-Baltimore area and is looking to expand to Boston and northern New Jersey. Other possible locations for stores are Chicago and Atlanta, and plans for future stores have been announced for Minneapolis and Denver.

the order. Often no written acceptance is given by the vendor. The goods are simply shipped.

Types of Orders

The buyer places different types of orders. Most stores require that any order placed over the telephone must be followed with a written order to be binding. The different types of orders used by the buyer are listed below.

1. *REGULAR ORDERS* are orders for regular stock placed with vendors by the buyer.

2. *REORDERS* are orders for additional merchandise from a vendor to replenish depleted stocks; often placed for hot-selling items.

3. *OPEN ORDERS* are unrestricted orders placed with a resident buying office. They are used when goods are needed in a hurry. The resident buying office has the authority to seek out the merchandise and negotiate the best terms for the store.

4. *ADVANCE ORDERS* are placed well in advance of the specified shipping date. They are used with staple stock where the buyer can accurately predict needs far in advance. Such orders give the buyer a better price because the supplier receives business during a slack production period.

5. *SPECIAL ORDERS* are placed for merchandise not regularly carried in stock or temporarily out of stock. They are placed to meet requests of specific customers.

6. *BACK ORDERS* are placed for shipments or parts of shipments that were not filled on time by the vendor.

7. *BLANKET ORDERS* are preseason orders placed with a vendor to be delivered in several later shipments over a period of time.

Buyer-Vendor Relationships

The buyer acts as the store's agent in dealing with vendors and carries a strong responsibility to represent the store in an ethical manner. It is important for the buyer to develop good relations with vendors. A profitable business in the long run can be best achieved when a store and its suppliers have a feeling of mutual respect. Both retailer and vendor should be honest and ethical in their dealings with one another. Such behavior leads to a mutual feeling of confidence.

Store management often specifies rules the buyer is expected to follow in dealing with vendors. Such rules help guide the buyer and also protect him or her from being placed in a compromising position.

One problem area that often arises for a buyer is whether gifts should be accepted from a vendor. Because it is often difficult to distinguish between a gift and a bribe, the best policy to follow is for the buyer not to accept *any* gifts from vendors. Bribery is an unethical, illegal act that hurts everyone concerned. It increases the cost of doing business for both retailers and suppliers since suppliers must increase the selling cost of goods to cover the hidden cost of bribery. The cost is eventually passed on to the customer by the retailer who must also raise prices.

Many stores have a firm rule that buyers are not to accept gifts, and doing so may be considered justification for immediate dismissal from the company. Any buyer should know not ever to accept a monetary payoff as such behavior is not only unethical but illegal.

The buyer-vendor relationship is a two-way relationship. If retailers expect to be treated with respect, they should honor agreements with their suppliers. Vendors, of course, should do the same in return. Both parties should meet the agreements as specified on the order form in so far as possible.

To build good vendor relations, the buyer should follow these guidelines:

1. Keep appointments as scheduled to view a vendor's lines.

2. Make decisions quickly, especially when rejecting merchandise offerings. The buyer should not lead the vendor on if the merchandise does not fit the store's needs.

3. Charges for cooperative advertising should not exceed the cost of advertising.

4. Cash discounts should not be taken after the date allowed.

5. Purchase orders should be completed accurately and legibly.

6. Merchandise should be returned to the vendor only when returns are justified. For example, the store has the right to return merchandise received after the specified delivery date, merchandise that is damaged when received, merchandise sent by the vendor that is not what the buyer ordered, and merchandise shipped in excess of the buyer's order.

7. All verbal orders should be immediately followed by a written order.

Buyers as agents of retail stores should perform within the scope of assigned duties and according to store policies. The buying position entails responsibility. Good relationships are based on honesty, ethics, courtesy, and appreciation of the vendor's position.

Summary of Key Points

1. Buying through a market is the most common and the best way for fashion buyers to purchase goods. Markets offer buyers the opportunity to view and compare the greatest number of merchandise lines in the shortest amount of time.

2. Buyers also make contacts to purchase goods through sales representatives who visit the store, catalogs, resident buying offices, true wholesalers, and store-owned resources. Buying at the store away from the pressures of a market offers the buyer several advantages.

3. True wholesalers purchase goods from manufacturers in large quantities and then sell them to retailers in smaller quantities. Although purchasing from a wholesaler is more expensive than purchasing directly from a manufacturer or manufacturer's representative, it is sometimes advantageous for buyers to purchase from wholesalers. Both large and small stores may purchase convenience goods from wholesalers.

4. With consignment buying the vendor retains title to goods after they are in the retailer's possession. The retailer does not pay for the goods until after a sale is made.

5. A buyer seeks to select resources that will be most profitable for the store. In doing this the buyer must constantly analyze and evaluate vendors according to their merchandise offerings, policies, services, and performance.

6. A buyer may obtain exclusive merchandise through specification buying or by seeking confined merchandise.

7. Concentrating purchases with a few key resources enables buyers to qualify for the lowest prices and leads to the best services from vendors.

8. Buyers of fashion-oriented merchandise make frequent market trips because of the ever-changing nature of fashion.

9. The buyer completes a buying plan prior to going to market. It is a guide to what, where, and how much to buy.

10. Usually the first activity of the buyer after arriving in a market city is to visit the store's resident buying office and confer with the market representative concerning general market conditions and resources.

11. Buyers usually do not leave paper (place orders) during a market trip, but wait until after returning to the store to write orders.

12. Merchandise selection by the buyer is a process of elimination or editing the line.

13. The buyer negotiates with the vendor concerning prices, discounts, and transportation.

14. The buyer, as the store's agent, is responsible for dealing with vendors in an ethical manner.

15. The purchase order is the most important form handled by the buyer, who is responsible for its accuracy.

Key Words and Concepts

Define, identify, or explain each of the following:

advance buying	blanket orders
advance orders	buying plan
back orders	cash discounts

checking

cherry picking

classification resources

clearance merchandise

closeout goods

confined merchandise

consignment buying

convenience goods

cooperative advertising

dating

E.O.M. dating

extra dating

FOB point

irregular

job lot

key resources

keystone markup (keystoning)

memorandum buying

open orders

preticketing

promotion buying

quantity discounts

regular dating

regular orders

regular price-line buying

reorders

R.O.G. dating

seasonal discounts

seconds

special orders

terms of sale

trade discounts

trunk shows

wholesalers

Discussion Questions

1. Explain the difference between a sales representative and a market representative.
2. Buying through markets is the most common method for fashion buyers to make contacts for purchasing goods. What other ways for making buying contacts are available to buyers?
3. The buyer is responsible for identifying resources and for making contacts to purchase merchandise. Discuss the ways in which a buyer learns about resources.
4. Discuss the factors the buyer should consider in selecting a resource for merchandise.
5. How can a buyer obtain exclusive merchandise?
6. Outline the steps a buyer follows in planning and making a market visit.
7. Why do large stores prefer to design and use their own purchase order forms rather than using the vendor's order blank?

8. Discuss the importance of the purchase order. What rules should the buyer follow in writing orders?

9. When should buyers write orders and leave the "paper" with vendors?

10. Explain the difference between FOB store and FOB factory. Which shipping term is best for the retailer?

11. Discuss the difference between regular price-line buying and promotion buying.

12. Discuss the terms of sale, explaining discounts and dating. What are the best terms for the store?

13. Some stores carry irregular merchandise; others sell only first-quality merchandise. Which is the better policy? Should the policy vary depending upon the merchandise classification or department?

14. What are the buyer's responsibilities in maintaining ethical relationships with vendors?

15. What is meant by ROG, FOB, and EOM?

Note

Arthur Osborne, "Working Profitably with Resources," *The Buyer's Manual.* New York: NRMA, 1979. p. 129.

CHAPTER 16 _____

FASHION PROMOTION AND IMAGE

Buying the merchandise is only part of the retailer's job. Once the merchandise is selected and placed on sale within the store, the retailer must attract the customer to the store with the desire to purchase the available merchandise. The retailer does this through the various activities of sales promotion, including advertising, publicity, special events, fashion shows, visual merchandising, and personal selling. Before a company is ready to plan its sales promotion, its fashion image must be clearly defined. This chapter discusses the components of fashion image and how the activities of sales promotion are used to project the store's image to the public.

Creating a Fashion Image

No two stores or fashion manufacturers are exactly alike. Just like people, firms have their own individual personalities that set them apart. Sears Roebuck, Macy's, The Limited, and Neiman-Marcus have distinct, well-defined personalities or images. Each of these stores emphasizes different merchandise and appeals to a different customer type. Today it is very important for a store to develop a specific image. Stores that are not doing this are getting squeezed out of the marketplace. When the closings of Gimbels and Ohrbach's in New York were announced in 1986, retailing experts explained that the downfall of both of these stores was due in part to their inability to establish individual identities. These stores no longer had distinct personalities, and customers were choosing to shop stores that did.

_____ 485

A store's image is how the store is perceived by the public. The images perceived by the general public and by a store's customers are not always identical. For example, a high-fashion store may be perceived by its regular customers as presenting the latest fashions in an attractive and inviting atmosphere. Some customers who do not shop at this store may perceive it as offering the latest high-priced fashions in a snooty atmosphere that would make them feel uncomfortable. Such consumers feel intimidated by the store and choose not to shop there.

Components of Fashion Image

Fashion image is the perception people have of a store's fashion expertise. It is a store's fashion personality, which tells the public how well the store knows fashion. Several factors work together to determine this fashion image. Among the components are the store's merchandise, services, physical environment, employees, and sales promotion activities. How these components are combined projects a store's image to the public.

Merchandise

The most important component in projecting a store's fashion image is the merchandise carried by the store. The store's buyers select merchandise appropriate for the store's level of fashion leadership and at the right price, quality, and fashion level for the store's customers. Merchandise is generally classified in four fashion levels: (1) advanced, (2) updated, (3) traditional, and (4) classic. Some stores carry merchandise representative of all four fashion levels; others specialize in one or two levels.

Advanced fashion is for individuals who like to stand out in a crowd. Consumers accept fashions at varying rates of speed. Some want new fashions immediately and like to be first with a new look. Such individuals seek stores featuring advanced fashions. Some specialty stores and boutiques base their fashion images on selling the customer who wants forward-looking merchandise that expresses the latest fashion trends. These stores are considered trend-setters and often feature designer merchandise that may be high priced or offered at moderate prices. Some traditional department stores carry advanced merchandise as only a small portion of their merchandise assortment. They want to project that they understand fashion, but fashion-forward is not their only image.

Updated fashion is designed for the customer who wants to be in fashion but not ahead of it. Updated fashions are widely accepted by many consumers. Stores with an updated fashion image are important in today's retailing environment. The updated customer is likely to shop stores and departments that also feature advanced fashions.

Traditional fashion is designed for the customer who wants conservative fashion that is already firmly established. Stores featuring this kind of merchandise have fashion images that are generally considered ordinary and unexciting. Traditional fashion lacks newness and is described in the trade as "dumb" fashion. Traditional customers are slow to accept change and usually will not shop departments or stores featuring advanced fashions. Department stores often carry traditional fashion but are careful not to let it dominate their fashion image. Although these fashions lack excitement, they are easy to identify and may provide the "bread and butter" for a store.

Classic fashion is another level offered by retailers. The trend toward women working outside the home has led to an emphasis on investment dressing, which has made classic styles important in recent years. With investment dressing the customer seeks long-lasting styles that build on an existing wardrobe. Classic styles that remain in fashion for a long period of time are an important part of such wardrobe building. Today classics are often given an updated touch to make them current and add excitement. Some specialty stores feature this kind of merchandise exclusively.

Store Services

The services offered by stores also contribute to image. Services may include credit, merchandise returns, delivery, alterations, and gift wrap. In establishing a strong fashion image, selling service is also an important service. The customer expects to have salespeople available to assist with the selection of merchandise in fashion-oriented stores. In a bargain-image store self-selection with cashier checkouts at the front may be the method of selling service preferred, or at least accepted, by the customer.

Store services also include such amenities as restrooms, customer lounges, public telephones, restaurants, and parking. These services are important in large department stores where the customer is encouraged to spend the day shopping. The store provides all the needed services to make certain that customers have everything necessary to remain in the store for a lengthy time period.

Physical Environment

The physical environment or appearance of a store projects an immediate image to the customer. Appearance involves the store's architectural style, interior decor, fixturing, and housekeeping. Architectural style and interior decor vary greatly ranging from contemporary to traditional. The store's atmosphere may be homelike with antique furnishings and wooden fixtures, or a store may be highly contemporary with chrome and glass. Color and lighting are also important elements in creating an atmosphere for the store and a background for the merchandise. Dark cool colors suggest elegance and expense, whereas bright primary colors suggest youth and action. Lighting can create moods appropriate for selling the merchandise. Music may create the proper mood for viewing the merchandise.

Customers expect a store with expensive fashion merchandise to have an expensive decor and atmosphere to accompany it. Stores with bargain prices may convey a bargain look with simple fixtures and few if any decorative items.

A clean, neat, well-cared-for store says that the retail company cares about its image and values its merchandise by providing it with appropriate surroundings. A store in need of paint and cleaning projects an image that its merchandise may also be shopworn and dated.

Stores need to be concerned with the appearance of nonselling as well as selling areas. A store with poorly maintained restrooms, dingy stairwells, and unattractive back areas exposed to the customers' view will project a poor image.

Store interiors must be remodeled and updated frequently in order to keep a store fresh and new looking. Fashions change in store decor as well as in merchandise. A store that looks out-of-date with old, worn furnishings and fixtures suggests to the customer that it is not up-to-date with fashions either.

Employee Appearance and Attitudes

Store employees, particularly salespeople, are an extension of the store's image. For many customers the salespeople *are* the store. If a salesperson is rude, the customer may decide to never again shop in a certain store. Salespeople who are courteous, knowledgeable about the merchandise, and helpful to the customer project a positive image. Appearance of salespeople also says something about the fashion level of the store. The customer expects the salesperson to have an appearance appropriate for the merchandise being sold. At one time fashion saleswomen dressed in conservatively tailored clothing, always in a dark color. The idea was for the merchandise to stand out and be noticed, not the saleswoman. Today's sales personnel are likely to dress in a more fashionable manner in keeping with the fashion level they are selling.

Sales Promotion

Many customers have an image of a store even though they have never visited it. Much of this image is based on advertising and publicity. The look of an advertisement projects an image of a store as do articles or news items that appear in the newspaper or on radio or television. Advertisements tell the viewer the fashion level of the store. Advertisements crammed full of pictures and featuring price savings give a store a bargain image. Advertisements emphasizing fashion trends and designer names project a prestige image. The types of special events and fashion shows held by stores also project a store's image to the public. The activities of sales promotion are discussed later in this chapter.

Appropriateness of Image

A store must project an image that is appropriate in terms of attracting the store's target customer. First, a store must define who it is and what kind of customer it wishes to attract. The components of image should then be developed to appeal to the target customer. A store that wants to attract a traditional fashion customer should not have the same image as a store targeted toward the fashion-forward shopper. What is important is that the store image realistically project the kind of

Advertisements are used to project an image of a store.
Source: *Reprinted with permission of Terry Costa, Inc.*

merchandise and services provided in order to attract the right customer. A store does not benefit from increased sales if its image attracts the wrong customer. When a customer enters a store expecting to find one kind of merchandise and finds another, he or she usually leaves without making a purchase. A store should not strive for a high-fashion image if its target customer does not desire to purchase such merchandise.

Image should not be described as "good" or "bad." What is good for one kind of store would be bad for another. What is important is that the image projected be suitable to attract the desired customer.

Retailers need to know how their stores are perceived by the public. Image can best be determined by surveying both the store's actual and potential customers within the store's trading area. Such market research may be conducted by in-store personnel or by outside marketing firms. It is most important that the store know the image it is projecting. Sometimes a store learns that the image it thinks it is projecting is not the image perceived by the public. In such a situation the store needs to reconsider its target customer as well as all of the components of image. The store may be seeking the wrong customers or may be sending out the wrong message about its merchandise. In any case, an adjustment must be made. The store's image of itself and the customer's impression of the store should be identical.

Changing the Fashion Image

Sometimes it is necessary or desirable for a store to change its image. The need for a change may occur because the store is located in an area undergoing a change in socioeconomic background of the people living in the area. If the store is to survive in that area, it must adjust to its changing clientele. Sometimes a store wants to change its image to attract new customers it did not previously seek. Increased competition may lead a store to change its image as the store seeks a way to be different from other retail firms.

Changing an image is not an easy process, but many stores have succeeded in making such a change over a period of time. The greatest problem often faced is in retaining old customers while attracting new ones. In changing image a store must make adjustments in merchandise assortments. Quality may need to be changed and price ranges adjusted. In addition the store must make changes in the way sales promotion is used to attract customers. New visual merchandising techniques must be adopted and advertising approaches changed to appeal to the new target customer.

In recent years many stores have moved to upscale their fashion images, seeking to attract more fashion-conscious and higher-income customers. Examples of stores successful in upscaling include Bloomingdale's and Macy's in New York. Both of these stores upgraded the quality of their merchandise offerings, eliminated lower-priced goods, and created exciting visual environments for their customers.

Promoting and Selling Fashion

Sales promotion activities have become increasingly important in fashion today because of increased competition. Many stores offer the consumer similar merchandise assortments. The key difference is the way in which merchandise is presented to the customer. Stores use different means of sales promotion to bring customers into the store with the desire to buy the merchandise.

Definition of Sales Promotion

Sales promotion is any activity used to influence the sale of merchandise or services. The activities of promotion include advertising, publicity, special events, fashion shows, visual merchandising, and personal selling. Traditional department stores use all of these activities in various ways to disseminate information to the public about the store and its merchandise offerings. All stores make use of some of the sales promotion activities, but select those appropriate for the type of store and its customers. Some specialty stores rely heavily on visual merchandising and do little if any advertising. Such stores depend on highly visible locations where heavy customer traffic brings customers into the store.

Sales promotion is also an important tool used by manufacturers to sell their products to both the retailer and the consumer. Manufacturers advertise their products in order to establish name recognition among the public.

Organization for Promotion

In small companies all promotional activities may be planned and carried out by a single person, sometimes with the assistance of an outside promotion consultant or advertising agency. Large companies usually have their own sales promotion division, which is responsible for planning, preparing, and carrying out the activities of sales promotion.

In a large department store the typical sales promotion division has three departments: (1) advertising, (2) public relations, and (3) visual merchandising. The advertising department prepares and places ads in the various media. The public relations department is concerned with the store's relations with the public. It develops publicity and special events to promote goodwill for the firm. The visual merchandising department designs and installs displays and assists with arranging store merchandise in an attractive manner to attract customers. Figure 16.1 outlines the organizational structure of a retail sales promotion division.

The sales promotion director is responsible for overseeing and coordinating all

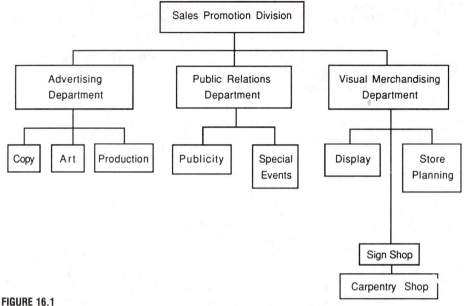

FIGURE 16.1
Organization of the sales promotion division in a retail store.

areas of sales promotion. This person works closely with the merchandising division to develop an effective promotional program for the store.

Many large stores have a fashion office that plans and coordinates fashion shows for the store. The fashion office, headed by the fashion director or coordinator, is often placed under the merchandising division rather than reporting to the sales promotion division. The basic function of the fashion office is to coordinate the fashion image of the store.

Planning and Budgeting for Promotion

In planning for promotion a firm must first define its target market and know what fashion image it wants to project. Only after these factors are determined is a store or manufacturer ready to plan promotional activities. Careful planning is necessary for effective sales promotions. Generally the larger a firm and the more employees involved with promotion, the greater the need for a structured plan. All firms, however, need to have some form of plan in order to achieve the best results and to spend the firm's promotion money most effectively. Some small firms make the mistake of spending money for promotion when they feel that they can afford it rather than planning promotion when it is most needed. A plan will help any firm produce more effective promotion and sell more merchandise.

The Sales Promotion Plan

The sales promotion plan serves as a guide in budgeting, planning, and conducting all promotional activities. A promotion plan usually covers a six-month period of time; thus two plans are prepared for the year correlating with a store's dollar merchandise planning. The typical promotion plan includes the following elements:

1. *GOALS AND OBJECTIVES TO BE ACHIEVED BY SALES PROMOTION.* Examples would be to increase sales a specified amount; attract new customers to the firm; present new designers or brand names to the public; reaffirm and strengthen the firm's fashion leadership.

2. *PROMOTION ACTIVITIES TO BE USED IN ACHIEVING OBJECTIVES.* Basic promotional themes and events are determined and scheduled.

3. *EXPENDITURES FOR PROMOTION.* Last year's figures for sales promotion for each month serve as a guide and are included in the plan. Expenses are determined for each month of the plan and distributed among the promotional activities. Ten to 20 percent of the budget is usually held in reserve to use for special promotions such as new items and special purchases that cannot be determined in advance.

4. *RESPONSIBILITY.* The assignment of responsibility for promotion is made to specific people and departments.

5. *EVALUATION.* The effectiveness of promotional activities must be evaluated to assist in planning future promotional efforts. Evaluation assists in repeating successes and avoiding unsuccessful activities.

The Promotional Budget

Part of the planning process involves determining the budget for promotion. The total amount of money to be spent for promotion must be determined and appropriations allocated to the various promotion activities. Usually the amount of money appropriated for sales promotion is based on a firm's anticipated annual sales. A retailer usually plans to spend from 1 to 5 percent of sales for promotion. A manufacturer typically allocates from 5 to 10 percent of sales for promotion.

Firms allocate their promotional budgets in very different proportions. For most retailers advertising receives the greatest share of the promotion budget, but this is not always the case. Whereas a department store is likely to spend the majority of its promotion budget for advertising, some stores emphasize other promotional activities such as special events and visual merchandising. A firm chooses the activities that will best sell its merchandise to its particular target market.

Cooperative Advertising

Cooperative advertising is a means by which retailers and manufacturers share the cost of advertising. In cooperative (co-op) advertising the manufacturer of a brand-name product reimburses the retailer for part of the cost of the ad placed by the retailer in local media. Co-op allocations cover a percentage of the cost of placing the ad in the media and often range from 40 to 60 percent of the media cost. Co-op advertising enables retailers to afford more advertising. The manufacturer benefits from lower local rates received by the retailer placing the ad in the media. Co-op advertising is mutually advantageous for both retailer and manufacturer. Both firms may benefit from the prestige of having their company names promoted together, and both receive additional exposure. The advertising dollars for both firms go further by sharing the advertising costs.

Although co-op advertising offers retailers several advantages, the retailer should consider some problems associated with this arrangement. Manufacturers often place rigid restrictions on retailers' ads in order to qualify for co-op money. Such restrictions may interfere with a retailer's image because the manufacturer's advertising style may conflict with the retailer's style. Retailers are sometimes tempted to purchase merchandise on the basis of available co-op allocations. The retailer should always remember that money for advertising is not as important as the quality of the merchandise. The buyer should always base buying decisions on the merchandise, not the advertising allowance.

Co-op advertising money is available from apparel and accessory manufacturers, textile firms, fiber producers, and certain trade associations such as the Wool Bureau and Cotton, Inc. Sometimes more than two parties share the cost of an ad such as the retailer, apparel manufacturer, and fiber producer.

The Robinson-Patman Act, discussed earlier, requires that advertising allowances be made available to all retailers within a marketing area on an equal basis. The small store owner should be aware of this and ask vendors about the availability of cooperative advertising money. Some retailers fail to receive such funds because they do not ask for them.

The Buyer's Role in Promotion

The buyer works closely with the sales promotion division, recommending merchandise to be promoted and making suggestions relating to advertising, displays, and special events. Buyers submit requests for ads based on their merchandise plans. Buyers are responsible for providing all of the necessary information for an ad. The buyer gives the art department a sample of the merchandise to use in preparing the artwork and completes an advertising fact sheet, which gives the copywriter the necessary information to write the ad. Typical information on an advertising fact sheet includes: (1) department name and number, (2) media in which ad is to run, (3) size of ad, (4) merchandise style number, (5) description of merchandise, (6) price, (7) list of features (selling points) in order of importance, (8) sizes, fiber content, colors, etc., (9) merchandise quantities available and at which locations, (10) method of payment for ad, (11) vendor requirements if co-op ad, (12) mail and phone orders, (13) buyer's signature, and (14) divisional merchandise manager's signature.

The buyer checks ad proofs and is responsible for verifying that all of the information is accurate and correct. If the ad is a co-op ad, the buyer checks to see that all vendor requirements have been met and completes appropriate forms for receiving co-op monies. The buyer is also responsible for seeing that the merchandise is available for sale in all stores as stated in the ad and requisitions signs as needed for the stores.

Advertising

Advertising is a paid communication of a sales message to actual or potential customers used to influence the sale of a product, service, or idea. Communication is established through space or time paid for by the advertiser in the print and broadcast media. The major media used by fashion advertisers include newspapers, magazines, direct mail, billboards, radio, and television.

Advertising is designed to provide consumers with information about firms and the products and services they offer. Retail fashion advertising is designed to enhance the image of a store and encourage current or potential customers to purchase merchandise through mail order or by visiting the store. Manufacturers direct their advertising both to the ultimate consumer and to the retailer in order to encourage the sale of merchandise.

An important premise of advertising is that it cannot sell unwanted merchandise. It cannot make people buy what they do not want. Retailers should keep this in mind when determining what items to advertise. Money should not be wasted advertising goods that consumers do not want to purchase. Advertising should feature merchandise with the best selling potential.

Types of Advertising

The purpose of fashion advertising is to sell specific items of merchandise or to promote the image of the company that produces or sells the product. All fashion advertising can be classified in two basic categories: institutional or promotional.

Institutional Advertising

Institutional advertising is designed to sell the image and reputation of the firm rather than to sell specific items of merchandise. Institutional ads seek to build a steady patronage of customers rather than bring immediate customer response. Institutional ads do this by focusing on fashion leadership, services offered, community involvement, and special events.

Promotional Advertising

Promotional or **product advertising** is designed to influence the sale of specific products or services. Most retail advertising is promotional advertising that seeks an immediate consumer response. Customers are encouraged to visit the store immediately to purchase specific items. Ads often have a sense of urgency built into them, letting the customer know that merchandise is available for sale for a limited period of time or that only a limited number of items is available.

Fashion ads are often designed to promote both specific items of merchandise and the image of a firm. In reality, a promotional fashion ad is also an institutional ad because all advertising contributes to building a company's image.

Media Selection

The media are the communications systems that carry advertising messages to actual and potential customers. Advertisers must choose the medium that will reach the desired target market most efficiently and effectively. The media most used to advertise fashion are newspapers, magazines, direct mail, radio, television, and outdoor signs.

Decisions must be made concerning which media forms to use and the specific media vehicles selected. The **media form** would be the type of media such as newspaper, radio, or television. The **media vehicle** refers to the particular newspaper, radio station, or television station. Specific media vehicles are read, viewed, or heard by different consumer groups. The advertiser must select the media that will reach the desired market.

The advertiser plans a media mix depending on the size and type of store, the target market, media availability, and cost of the media. The advertiser determines the best media combination, selecting media that will support one another and strengthen the overall advertising campaign.

A specialty store selling to college women might concentrate on spot announcements with a local radio station appealing to young adults, advertising in the campus newspaper, and using direct mailings. A department store needs to reach a wide market and might choose a daily newspaper, television, radio, and outdoor billboards.

Each advertising medium has certain advantages and disadvantages that should be considered by the advertiser. Table 16.1 summarizes the major strong points and weak points for various media.

Newspaper Advertising

Local newspapers have historically been the primary advertising outlet for fashion retailers. Although other media are now playing bigger roles, the newspaper still claims about 75 percent of the department store's advertising dollar. When looking through any local newspaper, it is obvious that department and other retail stores occupy most of the advertising space. In fact, department stores are the single

Table 16.1 Strong and Weak Points of the Various Advertising Media

	Strong Points	Weak Points
NEWSPAPER	Permits product illustration Frequent publication Flexible; can be changed on relatively short notice Regularly used as a shopping guide	Poor color reproduction Short life of individual issues Wasted circulation; everyone reads the newspaper
MAGAZINES	Excellent reproduction quality—shows fashion to its best advantage Specialty and regional magazines reach select audiences	Cost can be prohibitive May have considerable wasted circulation Long lead time required to place ad
DIRECT MAIL	Reach a select market with precision Can be used on a limited budget Flexible in timing and message	High cost per person per message May be viewed as junk mail Only as good as the mailing list used
OUTDOOR ADVERTISING (BILLBOARDS)	Low cost per impression delivered Frequent repetition of the message Good geographic selectivity	Copy limitations Considered offensive by some Considered wasted coverage
RADIO	Personal—human voice can often be more persuasive than print Flexible—permits sudden change Particular stations may appeal to selective audience because of program content	Audio only—may make less impact than visual media Message is short-lived Cannot show or demonstrate a product
TELEVISION	Combines sound, sight, and motion to convey message Some flexibility in responding to sudden change	Local television is not available in many small communities Message is short-lived Time and production costs are high

biggest users of newspaper advertising space. This domination by large stores is a disadvantage to the smaller store that must often accept a less desirable location and can only afford a small ad.

The small store in a large city is particularly at a disadvantage because the cost of buying newspaper advertising space increases with a newspaper's circulation. Newspapers price advertising space by the column inch. In comparing costs, a paper with a circulation of 17,500 was found to charge $4.25 per column inch; a major city newspaper with a circulation of 400,000 charged $54 per column inch.

Stores may contract for newspaper space on a yearly basis. The more space contracted for, the lower the price. Thus big users pay a lower rate than small users. Advertising rates for the Sunday editions are higher than weekly rates.

Large retailers often use special preprinted inserts in addition to their regular newspaper advertising. Some stores, particularly discount and highly promotional stores, do all of their newspaper advertising in this way. Such inserts are often printed in four colors on better quality paper and show merchandise to a better advantage than regular newsprint.

A number of major city newspapers print a weekly fashion section, which gives fashion-oriented stores an excellent vehicle for advertising. Fashion specialty stores may choose to advertise once a week in such a fashion section. Stores often contract with the newspaper to place their ads in the same location. This helps the store sell because the customer knows where that store ad is located.

Although smaller retailers may not be able to afford to advertise in costly large city daily newspapers, suburban and neighborhood weekly papers may provide a more reasonable outlet for ads. These publications also more nearly match the limited geographical trading areas of smaller stores.

Newspapers offer retailers the opportunity to advertise daily at a rate many stores can afford. Newspapers are read by many consumers to identify merchandise offerings before they go shopping. A newspaper ad can be clipped by the customer and taken to the store when seeking the merchandise. Some consumers even read newspapers primarily to look at the ads. Newspaper advertising tells consumers where merchandise is available and at what price. It brings customers into the store with the idea of buying specific merchandise.

Magazine Advertising

Larger retailers and manufacturers of nationally distributed brand-name merchandise advertise in magazines. Fashion magazines such as *Vogue, Harper's Bazaar, Mademoiselle, Glamour,* and *Gentlemen's Quarterly* provide a natural medium for establishing a fashion image. Fashion-conscious consumers turn to these fashion magazines for fashion trends; therefore, they provide an ideal setting for establishing fashion leadership for both retailers and manufacturers.

The cost of advertising in nationally distributed magazines is prohibitive for all but larger firms. A full-page ad in *Vogue* costs between $20,400 and $29,430, depending on whether the ad is in color or black and white. Also, retailers pay a lower rate than do other advertisers. Many regional and city magazines, however, are available offering much lower advertising rates, which may be affordable for smaller local area firms. For example, the cost of a full page ad in *D Magazine,* which is targeted to the Dallas/Fort Worth Metroplex, ranges from $3,300 to $5,000. Many specialized magazines appeal to specific consumer groups. They provide excellent advertising opportunities for specialty retailers. See Table 16.2 for advertising rates of selected periodicals.

Because of the length of production time, magazines are used primarily for institutional advertising. Many fashion retailers feel that national exposure in fashion magazines is important in building a store's fashion reputation.

Direct Mail

Direct mail includes any printed advertising matter delivered directly to the customer. The method of delivery most often used is the United States Postal Service, but direct mail may be hand delivered by some other means. Direct mail comes in many different forms, including postal cards, letters, self-mailing folders, fliers, bill stuffers, booklets, and catalogs.

The cost of direct mail varies greatly depending on the type of piece prepared and the method used for delivery. Bill stuffers or statement enclosures may be used at no cost to retailers. Such items are produced by manufacturers and provided to

Table 16.2 Advertising Rates for Selected Periodicals

Periodical	Full-Page Advertising Rate		Circula-tion
	Black & White	4-Color	
Architectural Digest	$11,215	$16,825	615,123
Gentleman's Quarterly	$13,780	$20,700	662,801
Glamour	$29,540	$41,630	2,386,150
House Beautiful	$20,275	$29,767	837,938
Mademoiselle	$18,840	$27,390	1,297,938
McCall's	$53,648	$63,300	5,275,428
Metropolitan Home	$19,665	$27,825	729,158
MGF, Men's Guide to Fashion	$3,380	$4,850	N/A
New York Times Magazine	$21,315	$32,210	1,645,060
Seventeen	$21,100	$30,575	1,853,314
Time	$77,010	$120,130	4,720,159
Town and Country	$13,390	$17,240	412,908
Vogue	$20,440	$29,430	1,281,597
W	$13,880	$17,910	225,608
Women's Wear Daily	$7,490	$9,970	64,278

Source: *Gale Directory of Publications, 1988.*

the retailer to be enclosed with monthly billings to charge customers. These enclosures typically include a mail-order blank to make it easy for the customer to buy the item. The retailer should never send a bill to a customer without enclosing such a direct-mail piece. If a stuffer is not enclosed with a bill, the retailer is missing a selling opportunity.

Manufacturers of better-priced sportswear produce mailers aimed at their target market that are sent out by retailers. As opposed to traditional bill enclosures, these mailers usually do not include an order form. If the customer wants to purchase the merchandise, he or she must go to the store whose name appears on the mailer. Manufacturers produce such mailers so that they can have creative control over what the consumer sees. The manufacturer usually pays creative costs and printing costs and the store pays for mailing. Some manufacturers split creative and production costs with the retailer.

Retailers like to use manufacturers' mailers because they serve as an educational tool and encourage stores to buy the merchandise in greater depth. The disadvantages to the manufacturer are the high cost of producing these quality mailers and the fact that store buyers may purchase only those items pictured in the mailer. Some stores do not use manufacturer-produced mailers because they interfere with projecting the store's image. Such stores say that they want to publicize the store, not the resource.

Direct mail offers the fashion retailer greater control than any other advertising medium. The retailer controls the design of the mailer and determines how many will be sent, to whom, and at what cost. A direct-mail piece can do whatever the

FASHION PROMOTION AND IMAGE _____ *499*

retailer wants it to do. It can sell merchandise, invite customers to visit the store, or tell customers about new merchandise lines, new departments, new store services or policies. Although direct mail is not inexpensive, it is highly accountable. The results of a mailing with a specific objective such as to invite customers to a fashion show are easily measured. Many specialty stores find that direct mail is their most effective form of advertising and devote a high percentage of their advertising dollar to this medium.

Broadcast Advertising

Radio and television are becoming increasingly popular **advertising media** with fashion retailers and manufacturers. Although radio cannot show the merchandise, it is amazingly visual. Through the use of words and sound effects, consumers can visualize the product. Radio is a medium that follows the consumer everywhere—indoors, outdoors, in the car, even jogging. Radio has the potential to deliver a sales message with repetition at far less cost than television or newspaper advertising. Radio also offers selectivity because of the range of station formats or programming styles. The advertiser selects the station to which the target customer listens.

Radio commercials are relatively easy to prepare and do not have to be expensive to be effective. Radio stations will provide assistance with preparing the commercials. Many retailers retain advertising agencies to prepare radio commercials; others prepare their own commercials in-house. Radio commercials vary in length from sixty seconds, thirty seconds, and ten seconds. Peak radio listening hours, such as morning or evening drive time, cost more than other times of the day. Radio stations will devise special packages to give the retailer a variety of time exposure of the firm's commercials. The most effective way to reach a radio audience is to schedule announcements evenly over a range of several days. Repetition is particularly important with radio because people listen at different times of the day, and radio is fleeting. Once the message is presented, it is gone. The customer cannot turn the radio back and hear it again.

Television is the fastest growing advertising medium with retailers. It offers the opportunity to show merchandise in use and gives retailers a way to reach mass audiences. The major drawback to television for many retailers, however, is the cost of time and production. Television commercials are usually prepared by outside advertising agencies, although some retailers are preparing their own commercials in-house.

As with radio, the cost of television time is determined by the length of the commercial and the time of day it is presented. Commercial lengths may be sixty, thirty, or fifteen seconds. The most expensive time for television is evening prime between 7:00 and 11:00 P.M. Some retailers find that they can reach their target markets at much less expensive broadcasting times.

Television has been very successful in selling designer and brand names such as Calvin Klein, Levi Strauss, and Jordache. Retailers have been slower than manufacturers to use television advertising. National retailers such as Sears, K mart, and J. C. Penney were the first to use television. Local department stores and national specialty chains are now allocating more time and money to television advertising.

Outdoor Advertising

Outdoor advertising consists of billboards, portable signs, and signs on public transit. Although not traditionally associated with fashion advertising, both fashion retailers and manufacturers are making greater use of this type of advertising today.

Billboards are expensive but effective, and their messages can reach many consumers with repetition. Billboards work best where traffic is high. Location is the most important factor in the choice of billboards. Advertisers choose location according to the consumer groups they want to reach. Advertisers lease space from billboard companies, which are responsible for painting the sign, attaching it to the desired board, and lighting it. Prices can vary from $500 to $6,000 per month. Usually the location is leased for a year with two or three sign changes over the period.

Messages must be brief but can provide direction to a store location or present a reminder message. Billboards make a good supplement to other advertising media. Most outdoor advertising is image advertising because of the need to be brief. Many billboards are viewed by motorists who may be driving at a high rate of speed; thus little time is available for the sign to make its impact.

Fashion billboards can make a strong visual impact. No one who saw the gigantic Calvin Klein underwear billboard in New York's Times Square could deny the impact of such advertising. The picture of a handsome young man wearing only his Calvin Klein briefs definitely attracted attention.

Special Events

Special events are designed by retailers to bring customers into the store or to create goodwill for the firm. Special events include a wide variety of activities ranging from a demonstration of a single product to a storewide festival involving many different exhibits, lectures, and celebrity visits. Special events may be institutional or promotional in nature. Macy's Thanksgiving Parade is an example of a totally institutional event. Other institutional events include art exhibits, flower shows, celebrity visits, educational lectures, and sponsorship of athletic teams. Institutional events build goodwill and image for a firm and are not designed to sell specific items of merchandise.

Many special events are promotional in nature and designed to sell particular items of merchandise. Examples of promotional events include product demonstrations, free merchandise samples, contests, designer visits and trunk shows, fashion shows, wardrobe planning clinics, and bridal fairs. Many special events consist of activities that are both institutional and promotional. Neiman-Marcus Fortnight, as profiled later in this chapter, is an example.

Special events have become increasingly important for retailers as they seek to differentiate themselves from their competition. Special events often serve to greatly increase store traffic and lead to developing retailing as a form of entertainment.

Neiman-Marcus Fortnight

Fortnight is a storewide special event held annually in the downtown Dallas Neiman-Marcus store. Originally held during the last two weeks of October, in 1984 the event was extended to three weeks. Neiman-Marcus developed Fortnight as a way to encourage sales during the usually slow selling period that occurs in October between fall and the beginning of the Christmas rush. Fortnight for Neiman-Marcus is the store's most expensive promotion outside of the Christmas catalog, but it is one that pays off financially. The first Fortnight in 1957, which featured France, cost $400,000 to produce and generated an estimated $2 million in sales, a 25-percent increase over the previous year's sales. Although Neiman-Marcus will not release more recent figures, Richard Marcus, chairman of the board, has said that the store does twice the level of business that it would do without Fortnight (Si Dunn, "Fabulous Fortnight '84," *D Magazine,* October 1984, p. 62).

Fortnight is both a promotional and an institutional special event. It has social, cultural, educational, and financial benefits for the store and the community. Each year Neiman-Marcus turns the downtown Dallas store into a celebration of culture, cuisine, and fashion. The store's decor is transformed to reflect the Fortnight theme. Special merchandise is purchased; exhibits, demonstrations, and entertainment are coordinated for the event. The community also becomes involved by scheduling appropriate cultural events to accompany Fortnight.

Stanley Marcus, former chairman of the store, got the idea for Fortnight in 1956 when he viewed a store window in Stockholm, Sweden, which featured a promotion of French merchandise. He learned from the store management that the store had received assistance from the French government through its Comité des Foires. Marcus went to Paris and approached this agency with the idea for a French promotion on a larger scale. He explained that he wanted to bring to Neiman-Marcus and Dallas the best of French merchandise and culture. He promised the Comité des Foires the support of the Dallas community and described his plans for transforming the store into a synthesis of France that would benefit French industry and French tourism. The cooperation of the French government was obtained along with financial assistance. Marcus then returned to Dallas and convinced business and civic leaders to help turn the idea into a citywide event to enrich the cultural life of the whole community. A number of community activities resulted. The Museum of Fine Arts scheduled an exhibition of Toulouse-Lautrec paintings never before shown in America. The largest exhibition of French tapestries ever shown in the United States was scheduled. French speakers were brought in for various luncheon clubs, and a French fashion show was scheduled for one organization. Hotel nightclubs even booked French entertainers.

French artists, writers, government officials, couturiers, and manufacturers were flown on an Air France plane to Dallas for the Fortnight opening. The Chambre Syndicale de la Couture presented a fashion show including the leading French designers at a gala ball preceding the formal opening of Fortnight. A local charity was the beneficiary of the ball. This custom continues with a Fortnight gala benefiting a different charity or organization each year.

For the first French Fortnight, the store facade was transformed to resemble the boutiques of the Fauborg St.-Honoré, and the interior of the store was decorated appropriately. To promote the event French merchandise was featured throughout the store.

The first Fortnight was a great success and it has been repeated each year since. In January or February the store announces the theme for the coming October Fortnight. Most Fortnights have featured a single country, emphasizing its culture or merchandise. Among those countries presented have been Great Britain, Ireland, Japan, Italy, Brazil, Spain, and Australia. Two Fortnights have combined countries thematically. "The Odyssey" combined Italy, Greece, and Yugoslavia, and "Orientations" featured Thailand, Japan, Singapore, and Hong Kong.

For a country to be featured for Fortnight, Neiman-Marcus reports that three criteria must be met: (1) the country must be newsworthy, (2) a large quantity of quality merchandise must be available, and (3) it must be possible to bring merchandise into the store and sell it profitably.

Two Fortnights have presented themes other than countries. "Fête des Fleurs" was a festival of flowers that had Prince Rainier and Princess Grace of Monaco as guests. "Ruritania" featured the mythical country from Anthony Hope's novel *The Prisoner of Zenda.* Ruritania came about because plans fell through with the country Neiman-Marcus had planned to feature. For the Ruritania Fortnight the store had to create the country's history and culture and design its currency and postage stamps. The coin of the realm was made in chocolate since "the reigning monarch preferred chocolate to silver." For the gala ball Victor Borge played the part of the prime minister, and Gloria Vanderbilt and her husband, Wyatt Cooper, appeared as the queen and king. Store buyers were allowed to buy anything that suited the theme for the event.

Planning a Fortnight begins eighteen months or more in advance of the event. Cooperation of the country being featured must first be obtained. Several buying trips are then made to seek exclusive fashion merchandise. All exhibits and demonstrations must be arranged and the designs determined for the visual transformation of the store.

Fortnight is both a promotional and an institutional event. It is a theatrical happening celebrating both merchandise and culture. Customers expect to be entertained and educated when they visit the store during Fortnight. Neiman-Marcus wants customers to enjoy what they see and do, as well as enjoy what they purchase.

In his book *Minding the Store,* Stanley Marcus reports that Fortnight has been widely copied by stores in the United States and in Europe. Although many stores have copied the idea of an import festival, no other store seems to have the level of community involvement that Neiman-Marcus has achieved with Fortnight (Stanley Marcus, *Minding the Store*. Boston: Little, Brown, 1974, pp. 199–224).

In 1986 following a Fortnight that featured Australia, Neiman-Marcus announced that it would no longer be held as an annual event. The company did not discontinue the special event entirely but rather left the door open to scheduling occasional Fortnights and indicated that they might be held in locations other than the Dallas flagship store.

They are often designed to bring customers into a store and increase sales at times of the year when sales are normally down. Thus special events help to balance sales throughout the year. Many special events serve to build the retailer's image and offer publicity value.

Manufacturers also use special events to increase showroom traffic and showcase the merchandise and services they offer. In addition, manufacturers sponsor special events in association with retail stores. The manufacturer may send a representative to the store to demonstrate merchandise and to assist with selling to customers. Cosmetics firms often provide gifts with purchase as a means of increasing in-store sales of their products.

Fashion Shows

Fashion shows are a special event of considerable importance in the fashion industry. Fashion shows are used by both retailers and manufacturers to communicate a total fashion story, build image, and sell merchandise. The fashion show incorporates all elements of theatre in its production. It combines lights, music, and live action to create an exciting fashion message. According to Winters and Goodman (1984), "Of all activities in the promotion mix, the fashion show stands out as the most dramatic and compelling. When it comes to presenting the excitement, immediacy and drama, no other form of promotion can compete with a fashion show."

Types of Fashion Shows

Fashion shows may be informal or formal. Formal shows are more structured and may be very elaborate, expensive events. Informal shows are produced on a much smaller scale and are within the realm of any retailer or vendor.

Formal Shows

Formal runway shows are held in an area where the audience is seated for the length of the show. Auditoriums, theatres, hotel ballrooms, and exhibition centers are typical locations for these shows, which are often held away from the store or showroom. Formal runway shows require considerable advance planning. Models must be booked, fittings scheduled, and physical arrangements made. Lighting, scenery, music, commentary, and programs all have to be arranged. A rehearsal is necessary to be sure the show will run smoothly. Advertising and publicity must be planned to attract an audience. In some instances special entertainment is included as part of the show. Many people are involved in producing a formal show. Such shows can cost thousands of dollars but can produce effective results.

Informal Shows

Informal shows are much easier and less expensive to produce. They may be held in a store selling department, restaurant, or showroom and are presented to a smaller audience. Often the audience stands for the show, so the show must be brief. Frequently, a few models wearing the clothes circulate among the customers showing and talking about the clothes. This is typical of tearoom modeling where customers may communicate directly with the models, and models answer customers' questions about the clothes.

Trunk Shows

Trunk shows are a popular way for manufacturers and designers to communicate with a store's customers. All or part of a line is brought into a store by a manufacturer or designer. Often a mini–fashion show is given or informal modeling held to show the clothes. Orders are taken by the manufacturer for future delivery to the customer. Such shows enable the store to offer the customer a wide merchandise selection without investing in inventory. Prestige is associated with trunk shows especially when the designer is present to show the line. Trunk shows are a popular promotional activity for fashion-oriented stores.

Trade Shows

Elaborate trade shows are often held during market weeks to give retailers an overview of market offerings and fashion trends. Thousands of retailer buyers may see one of these shows during market. Regional apparel marts have been designed with settings appropriate for such fashion shows.

Objectives of Fashion Shows

For retailers or manufacturers the primary purpose of a fashion show is to sell merchandise. For this reason it is best whenever possible to hold the show at or near where the merchandise may be purchased so that the customer may buy the goods immediately after seeing the show. Fashion shows have objectives other than to sell. Shows educate customers and help them adjust to new fashions by showing how they should be worn and accessorized. Fashion shows also are a form of entertainment. They build goodwill and contribute to the image of a firm as a fashion leader. Shows, too, can serve as a publicity device for retailers and manufacturers. Fashion shows become newsworthy when they introduce new fashions, benefit a charity, or showcase a celebrity.

Public Relations and Publicity

Public relations is a long-range program designed to influence favorable public opinion about a company. It involves the total image of a company and is concerned with everything a firm does to influence public views and attitudes. A public relations program helps establish criteria for sales promotion in order to help create a positive view of the company. Public relations is not a form of sales promotion. Publicity, special events, and advertising, however, are tools used by a public relations program.

Publicity

Publicity is an unsponsored and nonpaid message about a firm that appears in the public information media. What makes publicity different from advertising is that publicity must earn through its news value the space and time that advertising buys in the communications media; thus publicity must be newsworthy. It must be information of general interest to the public in order to get printed or broadcast by the media. A second way in which publicity differs from advertising is that it cannot be controlled by the firm it is written about. Whereas advertising says whatever the advertiser wants to say, publicity is at the mercy of the media editor. The editor can rewrite the story and delete whatever he or she sees fit, or the editor can decide not to feature the story at all.

Although publicity cannot be controlled, it can be created. Retailers and manufacturers often create publicity by planning events in a way to make them newsworthy. The Neiman-Marcus Fortnight in Dallas is an example of a special event created to have news value.

A large part of the public relations job is to create news. Knowing what makes news is the first step in developing publicity. The publicist, who develops publicity, must understand the needs of the various communications media and know how to get out the news about a firm. The publicist knows where to submit a story for consideration. Many possibilities are available such as daily newspapers, Sunday newspaper supplements, trade newspapers, consumer and trade magazines, and radio and television stations.

Press Releases

The news or **press release** is the primary means of making publicity material available to editors. The publicist writes the press release according to an accepted format and sends it to selected media. Press releases send out the news about a firm giving the important facts about a person, place, or special event. The press release begins by telling who, what, when, and where. It is written in order of diminishing importance, meaning that the most important information comes first. This is done to catch the editor's attention and because an editor often cuts the length of a story or news item. Photographs often accompany a press release. Sometimes a publication uses only the photo; therefore, a caption should be written so that a photo can stand alone. Many local newspaper fashion editors use press releases for much of the news printed in their fashion pages.

A well-planned public relations program can greatly assist a retailer or manufacturer in developing positive public opinion about the firm. Publicity is the primary tool of the public relations program; although space or time in the media is free, publicity is not "free." A good public relations program takes time and money to plan and produce but is well worth the effort. Publicity may be developed in-house or by an outside consultant or agency. Many publicity agencies specialize in fashion accounts.

Visual Merchandising

Visual merchandising is a strategy to make merchandise more appealing to the customer by showing it in the best possible way so that customers will be enticed to buy. Visual merchandising involves everything the customer sees in approaching the store and after entering it. Included are the exterior appearance of the store, the store sign, display windows, interior decor, store layout, fixturing, lighting, and, most importantly, the way the merchandise is presented and displayed within the store. Visual merchandising also includes activities that appeal to the customer's senses other than the visual, such as music or fragrance.

Although display is one aspect of visual merchandising, display and visual merchandising are not interchangeable terms. Visual merchandising is much broader than **display,** which is the impersonal visual presentation of merchandise and props. Displays are designed to build desire, to encourage impulse shopping, and, in many instances, to encourage self-selection. A good display becomes a silent salesperson. It attracts customers' attention, creates within them a desire to have the merchandise, and induces them to make a purchase.

Because of the trend in many stores to have fewer salespersons, visual merchandising and display must help sell the goods. Visual merchandising also sets stores apart and gives them individual personalities. Thus visual merchandising is an important part of creating image.

The Store as Theatre

In 1979 the *New York Times* published an article entitled "The Department Store as Theater." It described the phenomenon of visual merchandising, saying that it was responsible for "the biggest retailing boom in New York in 20 years." The article went on to state, "Visual merchandising in conjunction with status-conscious advertising, high-profile shopping bags and unconventional window displays has transformed the stodgy, family-oriented department store into a virtual amusement park" (Kornbluth 1979).

For some stores image appears to have become almost more important than the merchandise. Because many stores offer the same merchandise, stores have to develop a way to be different and to entice the customer to select their store. The answer that retailers have devised is visual merchandising. When visual merchandising is combined with special events, shopping truly becomes a form of entertainment.

Henri Bendel, a small exclusive specialty store, converted its first floor into a series of small shops in the late 1950s. The "Street of Shops," as it was called, was an immediate success and has been copied by many stores both large and small. During the 1970s Bloomingdale's set the standard for visual merchandising and excitement. In the 1980s Macy's entered the competition for presenting the most exciting, visually stimulating retail environment, and became the store to copy.

Edward S. Finkelstein, chief executive officer of Macy's New York, began transforming the image of the New York Herald Square flagship store in the late 1970s. The store had long promoted itself as the largest store in the world, but it had become faded, tired, and ordinary. Many in the Macy organization wanted to close off some of the store's one million square feet, but Finkelstein brought in a technique he had used as president of Macy's California. He used displays to showcase housewares as if they were designer dresses. The basement was turned into "the Cellar," a housewares arcade of shops. A wide red brick aisle divided it. On one side were pots and pans, housewares, and small appliances; on the other side were food-stuffs, including fresh fruits, vegetables, cheeses, bakery goods, and candy. At the end of the red brick aisle was a restaurant. The Cellar was an immediate success and brought customers in to see how Macy's had changed.

Macy's moved upward from the Cellar, redoing the store's fashion floors and restoring the first floor to its prior elegance. Gradually the whole store took on an exciting new look, and its image changed with the look. Visual displays filled the store, especially the fashion floors, and, more importantly, customers filled the store. Macy's by the mid-1980s became what many considered the most visually stimulating store in Manhattan.

Types of Display

Advertising motivates people to come to the point of sale, and display entices them to buy after they reach the store. Displays show customers the range of merchandise available, introduce new ideas, and suggest related merchandise. Display is the presentation of actual merchandise and is usually located at the point-of-sale. On occasion a display is located away from the store. For example, a store might set up a display in a case located in a hotel lobby, an airport terminal, or a convention center. This is called **remote display.**

Display located at the point-of-sale consists of three types: exterior, window, and interior display.

Exterior Display

Another name for **exterior display** is facade display. This type is located on the outside of the store building or on the street. Exterior display is used to promote seasonal themes and special events. Examples include flags, awnings, potted plants, or other decorative items on the exterior of the store. Exterior display is often used at Christmas when lights and ornaments are attached to the outside of the building. A Santa Claus figure sitting in a toy-laden sleigh on the roof of the store is an exterior display.

Window Display

Traditional window display, consisting of glass-enclosed windows facing the street, is more important for retailers located in downtown shopping areas than for those in shopping center locations. Many shopping centers, in fact, have no exterior windows. Even many downtown stores have deleted exterior windows as fewer people come downtown after store hours to window shop. In some cities, however, window displays still play an important function in catching the attention of passersby and drawing them into the store. In cities where people live in the downtown area and where people go downtown to shop, eat, or be entertained, window displays remain a form of entertainment and perform an important selling function even when stores are closed.

In shopping malls display windows are most often located inside the mall. The trend in recent years has been for store windows to be open-backed so that the whole store provides the background for the display. This has changed traditional window display. The visual merchandiser must consider the appearance of the total store when designing displays in open-backed windows. Department stores in malls frequently have no window display area at all; thus visual merchandising is centered on interior display.

Interior Display

The **interior display** has become increasingly important to many retailers as window displays have become less important. Interior display is an extension of window display and advertising and is most effective when correlated with these other forms of promotion. Good interior display greatly increases the customer's likelihood of purchasing. These displays help the customer find where the merchandise is located within the store, show the customer how to use the merchandise, and encourage the customer to purchase.

In some stores all display work is completed by members of the visual merchandising staff. In other stores the visual merchandisers do the window displays and major interior displays, but smaller displays within a department are planned and arranged by the department manager and salespeople.

There are several different kinds of interior displays, including vignettes, showcase displays and counter, wall, ledge, aisle, and island displays. Some stores use all of these kinds of displays.

Vignettes

A **vignette** may also be called an environmental or lifestyle display. It shows the merchandise in a realistic lifelike setting. Vignettes are used frequently to show fashion apparel, furniture, and tabletop merchandise such as china, crystal, and silver. The idea behind a vignette is to show the customer how the merchandise looks in use and to encourage customers to visualize themselves projected into the environment of the display. Vignettes are often set up within the store where they can be viewed from all four sides.

Showcase Displays

Various types of cases may be used to display or stock merchandise. Many small accessory items are effectively shown in this way. An enclosed glass case, called a **vitrine,** offers the advantage of protecting the merchandise display from customer handling.

Countertop Displays

Effective displays can be done on tops of counters. This type of display is called a point-of-purchase display because it offers merchandise on a self-selection basis. Because the customer can touch the merchandise, these displays require constant attention, but they can be excellent sellers. Some manufacturers design point-of-purchase displays to be used by stores.

Wall, Ledge, Aisle, and Island Displays

Stores with limited space can develop whatever unused space is available to show merchandise. Displays can be pinned to walls and hung from ledges about merchandise racks. Dead-end space at the end of aisles provides locations for island displays, which are free-standing display platforms. Even exterior doors of fitting rooms can be used for displays. One small store manager found her best selling displays were outfits she layered and accessorized on hangers and hung on hooks that faced out from plain white fitting room doors. These displays decorated an otherwise drab-looking area at the back of the store. Many customers were enticed to try on and buy an outfit hanging on one of the doors.

Elements of Display

The merchandise is the primary element used in a display. The major advantage display has over advertising is that it shows actual merchandise. The customer can see exactly what the merchandise looks like and sometimes can even touch it. In addition to merchandise, other important display elements are props, background, color, lighting, and signs.

Merchandise

Obviously the most important element in a display is the merchandise. Since that is what the store is selling, it should be the focal point of the display. The merchandise selected for display should be the merchandise customers want to buy. A store should display its best merchandise, not its dogs. In merchandising slang a **dog** is something that no one wants to buy. Such merchandise items are purchasing mistakes made by the buyer.

Display Props

Props include all the physical elements within a display that are not salable merchandise. Their purpose is to highlight the merchandise. Three types of props are used in completing displays: functional, decorative, and structural. Functional props include anything that holds the merchandise such as mannequins, body forms, or fixtures. Decorative props create a mood, provide a setting for the merchandise, and add to the attractiveness of the display. An example of a decorative prop would be a floral arrangement used in a mannequin fashion display.

Structural props support the functional and decorative props. They are architectural in design and may be a permanent part of the display area such as a stairway, shelves, or a window frame.

Background

The walls or backdrop used in the display form the background and may add a great deal to the effect of the display. A good background has been found to greatly increase the pulling power of a display, and the whole effect can be changed by adding a different background. A background may be a painted mural, a curtain, a painted wall, or the entire store.

Color

Color is a powerful element in display. Some visual merchandisers say that it is the most important element. It is effective in attracting and holding customer attention. When a display concentrates on a single vibrant color, the impact increases. When apparel is displayed, color is often the primary fashion story or theme.

Proper color combinations have a pleasing psychological effect, whereas jarring combinations may have a negative effect. Warm colors such as reds, oranges, and yellows are stimulating and encourage activity. Cool colors such as blues and greens are restful, relaxing, and more elegant in feeling. Neutral whites, grays, and beiges are more conservative and less dominating in a display.

Colors and color combinations suggest the season of the year, type of merchandise, age of customer, and even the price level of the store. For example, typical fall colors include darker earth tones such as browns, oranges, and golds. Spring colors run to brighter colors and pastels. Store displays must take the season into account as well as fashion trends when planning colors.

Color is a useful tool in projecting image and creating a mood. Color is extremely important in display, merchandise arrangement, and store decor. Merchandise fixtures are often organized according to color. A common color sequence used in arranging merchandise is white, yellow, orange, red, green, purple, blue, brown, and black. Merchandise that is colorized has a far greater visual impact than does merchandise organized by some other manner such as size, style, fabric, and brand.

Lighting

Color and lighting together do much to establish the mood for a display. The feeling of a display can be changed entirely with lighting. Colored lights intensify color, and spotlights can highlight the merchandise.

Interior lighting is important in creating the overall image for the store and in making it easy for the customer to see the merchandise. A brightly lit store helps convey an image of brisk activity and makes it easier for the customer to shop. Softly lit areas are more relaxing and create a calmer mood. Effective lighting increases the customer's shopping pleasure, cuts down on shoplifting, and makes merchandise selection easier. The kind of lighting used changes the perception of colors in merchandise. Fashion stores should be aware of this when planning lighting installations and select the lighting that makes both the customer and the merchandise look best.

Signs or Showcards

Signs or showcards are often used as part of a display, or sometimes a sign stands alone as a display in itself. The right selling sign can make a display more effective. Signs, by giving information, can provide the extra stimulation needed to cause the customer to make a purchase. Signs can do the talking for a display. A sign can state price, sizes, fabrics, colors, and tell where merchandise is located within the store. Signs can also tell customers how they will benefit from using the merchandise. Signs are often used to give information about a special event that is going to take place.

An effective showcard should do the following:

1. Be informative.

2. Be brief.

3. Use common words.

4. Relate to the merchandise in mood and appearance.

5. Look professional.

6. Be neat and clean.

7. Be timely.

8. Sell customer benefits.

9. Arouse interest.

Creating an Effective Display

An effective display is one that attracts the attention of shoppers and sells them the merchandise. A number of factors contribute to the effectiveness of a display. To produce effective displays, the visual merchandiser should do the following:

1. Plan the display in advance allowing sufficient time for installation.

2. Select the best merchandise to display. Merchandise should be in demand and should appeal to the store's target market. A store's stars should be displayed, not its dogs.

3. Change displays often. The frequency of change depends on the type of display, where it is located, and the type of traffic passing the display.

4. Make proper use of the elements and principles of design in arranging the display. Consider emphasis, balance, harmony, and rhythm. Also, color, line, texture, and form all influence effective display.

5. Provide for proper eye movement throughout the display. The viewer's eye should move through the display in a systematic fashion rather than jumping from one item to another.

6. Group merchandise so that the display has an organized rather than a cluttered appearance.

7. Keep the display in good taste and appropriate for the store's image. The store's image determines the kind and amount of merchandise used in a display. A strong promotional store wants to show many items of merchandise, whereas a prestige fashion store seeks simplicity in display.

8. Display timely merchandise using a current theme.

9. Use lighting to emphasize the merchandise.

10. Keep display area, merchandise, and props neat and clean at all times.

11. Use a showcard as part of the display when appropriate. Follow the rules for designing an effective showcard.

Loehmann's opened in 1921 in Brooklyn, New York, in an old automobile show-room that had been transformed into a conversation piece, with elaborate baroque furnishings. The store contained rows of clothes-laden racks topped with golden dragons. Decorations included marble lions, gilt angels, candelabra, and black columns with golden encrustations. Although the decor was elaborate and the clothes high fashion, the prices were bargain basement. Frieda Loehmann, the store's founder, was able to offer quality fashion apparel at lower prices because she purchased her merchandise off-price. In her previous position as buyer for a Fifth Avenue store, Loehmann had become acquainted with many New York manufacturers. With her access to their showrooms she was able to buy merchandise that vendors had been unable to sell for some reason. She acquired samples, overstocked goods, closeouts, and broken size ranges. She was willing to buy when it was too late in the season for vendors to wait for reorders from their regular retail customers. Whatever the reason, she offered to take the goods off their hands. Furthermore, she paid cash and agreed to remove the labels before selling the items in her store at reduced prices.

Frieda Loehmann is generally considered the originator of off-price purchasing in women's ready-to-wear. Today the number of off-price retailers includes several multiunit companies with stores located from coast to coast, but in the 1920s Frieda Loehmann was unique in her operation. Well known in the New York market, she provided a service to many vendors by purchasing merchandise that they could not longer sell.

Charles C. Loehmann was an active partner in the business with his mother for ten years before he opened his own separate store in the Bronx in 1930. He established firm merchandising and advertising policies, many of which are still followed by Loehmann's today. In order to keep prices low, no credit, refunds, or exchanges were given. Also, Loehmann's did not provide alteration or delivery service. Only institutional advertisements were used, which did not feature merchandise. Charles Loehmann's policies were extremely successful, and under his

Trends in Visual Merchandising

Fashions change in display techniques and visual merchandising trends just as they change in apparel and home furnishings. One reason techniques change is that direction the company expanded into a chain of more than seventy stores located in twenty-five states.

After Frieda Loehmann's death in 1962, the original store in Brooklyn closed, but the company continued under the direction of Charles Loehmann and George J. Greenberg who had joined the company in 1958 when there were only four stores in the chain. By 1964 Loehmann's operated seven stores, and in September of that year the company went public, which marked the beginning of its dramatic growth. By 1980 Loehmann's operated forty-nine locations in twenty-two states. Aggressive expansion continued with the company reaching a peak of ninety stores in 1986. It has since closed several stores, reducing its number to seventy-six in 1988 with total sales of $334 million.

During the 1980s, Loehmann's changed ownership four times. In 1981 AEA Investor Inc. bought the company and took it private again. Two years later the chain was purchased by the Associated Dry Goods Corporation, and in 1986 Associated Dry Goods was taken over by May Department Stores Company, which sold Loehmann's to an investor group in 1988.

Today Loehmann's continues to offer fashion merchandise at discounted prices, and although the labels are removed, customers can often decipher the manufacturer's code listed on the price ticket. Few services are offered, and the only amenity is restrooms. Large community dressing rooms with floor to ceiling mirrors are serviced by store personnel who return the rejected stock to the store's clothing racks. Merchandise ranges from moderate-priced to designer lines. The higher-priced designer merchandise is displayed in a separate area known as the Back Room where only female customers are allowed to enter because the merchandise is tried on in the same room.

Little advertising is done by the company. Loehmann's occasionally places institutional newspaper advertisements announcing the opening of a new store or inviting customers to a special event at the beginning of a fashion season. The company considers word of mouth its best form of advertising.

In recent years Loehmann's has had to face growing competition from other off-price retailers, factory outlet stores, and increased markdowns at department stores. The retailer has responded by extending store hours, permitting bank credit card sales, and launching a promotional campaign to attract young career women. Loehmann's has also closed some of its less productive stores. The company is now concentrating on placing its stores in the best locations rather than getting the lowest rent.

retailers copy one another. As soon as a new successful visual merchandising approach is presented by one retailer, others incorporate the approach into their stores. The stores that strive to be different are constantly seeking new visual merchandising approaches.

One way retailers keep up on trends in display and store design is by reading

Visual Merchandising and Store Design, a monthly publication designed for visual merchandisers and store planners. This magazine publishes an annual *Buyers' Guide,* which lists product suppliers, products and equipment, store designers' associations, and an event calendar for the year.

Another way to keep up on trends is by attending markets and exhibitions of products held for store planners and designers, visual merchandisers, and sales promotion personnel. The largest market is the NADI Visual Merchandising/Design Market, sponsored by the **National Association of Display Industries** (NADI), held in New York twice a year in June and December. Regional markets are scheduled in other locations that feature store fixtures, lighting, and display materials.

Video Merchandising

Video merchandising is another form of visual merchandising becoming increasingly important to retail stores. Videotaped fashion shows and interviews with designers play on video monitors throughout many stores. Some videos are produced by retailers, other by manufacturers.

Fashion videos have become important in selling. They first became important in designer showrooms, where tapes of runway fashion shows were shown repeatedly. These same tapes were then shown in designer departments in retail stores to attract passersby.

The emphasis in designer tapes is on image, excitement, and entertainment. Music is an important part of the tapes. They help set the mood and encourage the customer to remain in the department and look. The longer a customer looks, the more likely the customer is to make a purchase.

For designers, videotapes mean free advertising, which many of them could not otherwise afford. Designers have received thousands of dollars worth of free time on television news and cable programs (Bronson 1985).

Personal Selling

Personal selling is another activity of sales promotion. It differs from the nonpersonal sales promotion activities of advertising, publicity, and special events because it involves direct one-on-one contact between customer and salesperson. Thus personal selling is the only "personal" sales promotion activity. With personal selling the salesperson talks directly to the customer and is able to present the benefits and selling features of the merchandise. The salesperson has an opportunity to overcome objections the customer may have to the merchandise by demonstrating it and answering questions. The salesperson also may increase sales by trading up or suggestion selling.

Trading up is obtaining larger sales by (1) selling more than one of the same item, (2) selling a larger size of the same item as in a larger bottle of makeup or perfume, or (3) selling higher-priced, better-quality merchandise.

Suggestion selling is a method of increasing the sale by (1) suggesting related items that will go with the customer's original purchase, or (2) suggesting a substitute item.

Successful salesmanship is beneficial to both seller and customer. It leads to higher sales and greater profits for the seller, and to more satisfied customers. A customer who is satisfied with a sale is likely to return for future purchases. A satisfied customer is also likely to spread the word about the store or a product. Such word-of-mouth advertising is the best form of advertising for any firm.

Personal selling has deteriorated in many stores as they have reduced the number of salespeople and cut back on formal sales training for employees to reduce operating costs. Some stores set themselves apart from the competition by emphasizing personal selling.

Summary of Key Points

1. Fashion image is how people view a company's fashion expertise. The most important component in projecting a store's fashion image is the merchandise carried by the store. Other components of image are services, store appearance and decor, type of selling service, and sales promotion activities.

2. A store's image should realistically project the kind of merchandise and services provided in order to attract the target customer.

3. Fashion image can be changed by changing the merchandise mix, by using new merchandising techniques, and adopting advertising approaches to appeal to the new target customer.

4. Sales promotion is any activity used to influence the sale of merchandise or services. These activities include advertising, publicity, special events, fashion shows, visual merchandising, and personal selling.

5. Cooperative advertising allowances offer advantages to both retailers and vendors. Both parties benefit from increased advertising because of sharing costs. Whereas co-op advertising is generally desirable, the buyer should not be influenced to purchase from a vendor solely because of advertising allowances. The merchandise remains the most important consideration.

6. The buyer works with the sales promotion division recommending merchandise to be promoted and suggesting ways in which to promote it. Although buyers do not prepare ads, they are responsible for checking ad proofs and verifying that all information is accurate and correct.

7. Institutional advertising sells the image and reputation of a firm, whereas promotional advertising sells specific products or services. Fashion ads are often designed to be both institutional and promotional, building image and selling merchandise at the same time.

8. The primary purpose of fashion shows is to sell merchandise. Shows educate customers and help them accept new styles.

9. Each advertising medium has both strong points and weak points. The advertiser plans a media mix to meet the firm's target customer based on the available media, the cost of the media, and the appropriateness of the media.

10. Public relations is a long-range program designed to influence favorable public opinion about a company. It involves the total image of a company and is not a form of sales promotion. Important tools of public relations are publicity, special events, and advertising.

11. Publicity cannot be controlled, and it is not free. Companies spend a great deal of money creating events that will be newsworthy and provide publicity.

12. Visual merchandising is a strategy to make merchandise more appealing to the customer. It involves appealing to all of the senses and is concerned with not only traditional window and interior display but the total visual and sensual impact of the store and the presentation of its merchandise.

13. If fashion promotion is to be successful, all promotional activities should be coordinated to bring the customer to the point of purchase.

Key Words and Concepts

Define, identify, or explain each of the following:

advanced fashion	interior display
advertising	media form
advertising media	media vehicle
classic fashion	National Association of Display Industries (NADI)
direct mail	
display	press release
dog	promotional (product) advertising
exterior display	remote display
fashion image	sales promotion
institutional advertising	special events

suggestion selling

trading up

updated fashion

video merchandising

vignette

visual merchandising

vitrine

Discussion Questions

1. Why is it important for a store to develop its own fashion image in today's marketplace?
2. Discuss the components of fashion image. Which components are most important in retailing today?
3. Why is it sometimes necessary for a store to change its fashion image?
4. Why has sales promotion become increasingly more important in today's retailing?
5. Name and define each of the activities of sales promotion.
6. Describe the typical elements included in a sales promotion plan.
7. How is a sales promotion budget determined?
8. Compare the advantages and disadvantages of cooperative advertising.
9. What is the buyer's responsibility to sales promotion?
10. Compare and contrast institutional and promotional advertising.
11. What factors influence the advertiser's selection of a media mix?
12. Contrast the strong and weak points of the various advertising media.
13. Give examples of special events held by retail stores in your area.
14. Why did Neiman-Marcus develop Fortnight as a special event?
15. Why do retailers and manufacturers present fashion shows?
16. Compare and contrast public relations and publicity.
17. Define visual merchandising, and explain how display relates to visual merchandising.
18. Discuss the relative importance of the elements of display.
19. Describe the three types of props used in display.
20. Signs or showcards may serve as the silent salesperson in a display. What rules should be followed in designing effective display showcards?
21. Describe an effective display, and discuss the factors that contribute to effective display.
22. How may video merchandising be used as a promotional tool?

Notes

Gail Bronson, "Fashion Videos: Retailing Meets Show Business," *U.S. News and World Report,* September 30, 1985, pp. 68–69.

Jesse Kornbluth, "The Department Store as Theater," *New York Times Magazine,* April 29, 1979, p. 30.

Arthur A. Winters and Stanley Goodman, *Fashion Advertising and Promotion,* 6th ed. New York: Fairchild Publications, 1984, p. 301.

RECENT DEVELOPMENTS AND TRENDS IN RETAIL MERCHANDISING

OVER THE years retailing has changed with the times to satisfy the ever-changing wants and needs of consumers. New forms of retailing have emerged; older forms have evolved to suit consumers. Retailers who have not changed with changing demand have found themselves out of business, whereas those who have adapted to accommodate their customers have survived.

As social, political, and economic changes occur in the United States and the world, new challenges emerge for retailers. During the 1970s and 1980s uncertain economic times, inflation, energy shortages, and escalating operating expenses forced many retailers to adjust their ways of doing business. Shifting populations and changing consumer values had a strong impact on strategies followed by retailers in the 1980s. Retailing today has become more complex, requiring retailers to engage in strategic planning and to fight for market share in order to increase sales.

During the 1950s and 1960s opportunities for growth in fashion retailing seemed limitless. Today fashion retailing has become highly competitive as the number and kinds of retail distributors have increased, and many firms have expanded, building stores within overlapping trading areas. As retailers have sought increased business through expansion, one of the major problems facing them has become **overstoring.** Too many stores and shopping centers have been built, leading to strong competition in many geographic areas. Another problem facing fashion retailers is that many offer similar or even identical fashion merchandise. This redundancy has led to lack of differentiation among stores; thus retailers are developing new strategies to set themselves apart from their competitors. Changing roles have also occurred within the fashion industry. Retailers have entered manufacturing, and designer/manufacturers have become more involved in selling.

Discussed in this chapter are recent developments and trends in the retailing of fashion merchandise. Among the topics are retailers' responses to overstoring and competition, the identity crisis in retailing, specialty store expansion, growth in nonstore retailing, expansion of discount retailing, changing roles in the fashion industry, and the globalization of retailing. The chapter also presents consumer demographic and psychographic trends influencing fashion retailing.

Retailers' Responses to Overstoring and Increased Competition

Overstoring and increased competition are causing retailers to adjust their merchandising strategies to compete more effectively. Traditional department and specialty stores are feeling this competition keenly. Rather than adding new stores, many stores are focusing on renovation of existing buildings. Others are expanding by purchasing existing companies. Also, to improve efficiency stores are reallocating space; profitable departments are being increased in size and nonproductive departments are being phased out. Many budget fashion departments have been closed or integrated into other departments. Departments such as sewing goods, hardware, home electronics, and sporting goods are being eliminated by many department stores. Better utilization of space and elimination of nonproductive or wasted space have raised productivity for many retailers.

Growth Through Acquisition

Growth through acquisition has become the method used by many retail firms to expand their businesses. Buying existing companies is less expensive than building new stores and also eliminates some of the competition. Retail companies that have succeeded in expanding by purchasing other companies or stores include Dillard Department Stores, Maison Blanche, and The Limited.

As noted in an earlier chapter, Leslie Wexner, founder of The Limited, began to expand his empire in 1982 by purchasing existing companies, including Victoria's Secret, Lane Bryant, Sizes Unlimited, Roamans, Lerner Shops, Henri Bendel, and Abercrombie & Fitch. Two subsidiaries, The Limited and The Limited Express, were founded by Wexner.

Dillard Department Stores followed the same expansion pattern. In 1984 Dillard's purchased St. Louis-based Stix, Baer and Fuller, Oklahoma-based John A. Brown, and Arizona-based Diamonds. More recent purchases included Macy's Kansas

City stores, Joske's stores in Texas and Phoenix, Cain-Sloan in Nashville, Higbee Department Stores headquartered in Cleveland, Joseph Horne based in Pittsburgh, and New Orleans-based D. H. Holmes. Dillard's sold or liquidated some of the individual store locations and converted the remainder to the Dillard's name.

Baton Rouge's Maison Blanche (formerly called Goudchaux/Maison Blanche) followed a similar pattern of buying existing stores. Beginning as Goudchaux's in Baton Rouge the company expanded in the 1980s by purchasing Maison Blanche in New Orleans and Robinson's of Florida. With other stores following the same pattern of growth through acquisition, it has become difficult to keep up with changing store ownership.

Downsizing Stores

Competitive conditions and changing shopper habits and preferences are causing stores to reduce their square footage, or "downsize." Department stores typically are reducing store size by 20 to 30 percent (Bergmann 1986). An example of successful **downsizing** is May Department Store's G. Fox & Co. store in downtown Hartford, Connecticut, which was reduced in size from 1.2 million square feet to 400,000 square feet without any loss in volume. After remodeling, the company profitably leased out space no longer needed by the store (Standard and Poor's 1987).

Other examples of stores that have downsized include The Hecht Co., which built a new flagship store in downtown Washington, D.C., about half the size of the store it replaced. Sears and K mart are following expansion programs that emphasize building smaller stores. Sears's Small Store II prototype is 40,000 to 43,000 square feet and concentrates on men's, women's, and children's apparel, women's accessories, men's work clothes, and home textiles.

Department stores as part of the downsizing trend are eliminating or cutting back on nonprofitable merchandise areas. They are dropping categories that require large amounts of floor space, expensive handling and warehouse storage, tie up capital in inventory, or must be priced lower to meet competition. Departments that weaken a store's fashion image, such as budget apparel and accessories, are also being deleted as many department stores are seeking a more upscale customer.

Many retailers are eliminating entirely home-furnishings and hard-line categories. Some companies are eliminating furniture from their department stores but opening satellite furniture specialty stores in separate locations. Other merchandise classifications that many stores are eliminating are home electronics and major household appliances. Specialty stores such as Federated Group, Highland Superstores, and Sound Warehouse are taking over sales of these items in many cities. Book and toy departments are also being phased out as customers turn to specialty stores such as B. Dalton Bookseller or Toys "R" Us.

Many of the stores taking over the selling of merchandise categories being deleted by department stores are referred to as **category killers.** Such stores as those noted in the previous paragraph present dominant assortments at low prices. Many provide minimum service to their customers but have become popular because of their extensive merchandise offerings and competitive pricing.

Department store elimination of hard-line merchandise classifications has led to an increasing emphasis on fashion merchandise. Larger selections of women's apparel and accessories and expanded cosmetics areas are taking the place of eliminated merchandise categories. Department stores are emphasizing classifications or *market niches* previously overlooked by many retailers. Among these niches are petite clothing, large-size women's apparel, and more fashionable children's wear.

New Retail Formats

New retail formats have already appeared to supply consumers with home-furnishings and hard-good lines being eliminated by department stores. Companies that see a void in the marketplace and fill that void will continue to fill consumer needs. As department stores downsize and eliminate classifications, opportunities appear for new forms of retailing.

Category killers have seized market shares from both department stores and specialty retailers by using one of two approaches: (1) carrying heavy inventories of one merchandise category, or (2) organizing their merchandise into clearly recognizable lifestyle groups. Stores following the supermarket approach by carrying large inventories of products such as toys, children's wear, books, or sporting goods and activewear are Toys "R" Us, Kids "R" Us, Bookstop, and Sportsclub. Lifestyle merchandising is used by several home-furnishings stores such as Fortunoff's, Branden's, Lechmere, Crate & Barrel, Conrans, Stor, and IKEA. Offering customers what they want to buy, at prices they perceive as affordable, in an appealing setting has made these stores and others successful.

Category killers have become **destination retailers,** which attract customers to their location for the purpose of buying specific items of merchandise. Such stores are consumers' predetermined destinations when they go shopping. Destination retailers are found among all types of retailers, not just category killers. They are characterized by distinctiveness, exceptional merchandise presentation, and appropriate pricing. They are the retailers who are able to anticipate and accommodate changes in the environment that indicate changing customer demand. Among stores identified as destination retailers are Wal-Mart, The Limited, and Bloomingdale's.

The number and kinds of retail distributors have been increasing. New retail formats, such as electronic shopping, warehouse clubs, and hypermarts, have emerged to compete for the consumer's dollar.

Department and apparel specialty stores, too, are finding consumer groups that were not having their needs met and are merchandising to these groups. Examples include the woman executive, petites, and large-size women. Finding out what consumers need and want, and how and where they want to buy this merchandise, are secrets to success in retailing.

Store Restructuring and Consolidation

Another efficiency move among stores is an industrywide restructuring. Some major retailers have eliminated whole divisions; others have consolidated or sold divisions. Federated Department Stores combined Ohio-based Shillito's, Rike's, and Lazarus under the Lazarus name in Cincinnati. The two Texas-based stores, Sanger-Harris and Foley's, are now under the Foley's name. Allied Stores Corporation combined the company's two Florida divisions of Jordan Marsh and Maas Brothers. Dayton Hudson Corporation combined its two department store divisions, Minneapolis-based Dayton's and Detroit-based Hudson's, into one division called Dayton Hudson. Macy's merged its New York and New Jersey divisions, changing the name of its New Jersey Bamberger's stores to Macy's. Numerous other consolidations took place in the 1980s and more are anticipated. An industry trend of merging divisions within large retail companies has emerged.

Buyouts, mergers, and acquisitions, especially among department stores, are expected to continue and will result in further combining of store divisions, which will reduce competition. Such consolidation allows companies to cut expenses, eliminate duplication of jobs, and centralize many functions including buying. Costs are reduced in buying merchandise, advertising, and record keeping. Improved operating profit should result from consolidations.

Strategies to Control Expenses

Stores have taken steps to control expenses and thus improve profitability. Strategies have concentrated on reducing payroll, energy, and interest costs. Stores have installed electronic systems to control lighting, which typically accounts for 50 to 70 percent of total energy costs (Standard and Poor's 1985). Other means of controlling operating expenses include shrinkage control devices and improved management information systems to manage the store's inventory. More effective inventory management allows retailers to turn over their stock more often. Less stock is needed to meet demands, meaning that less money is invested in stock. Merchandise can be ordered closer to the selling seasons and buying mistakes are less likely to be made.

Rigorous cost-cutting programs have been followed by retailers seeking to operate more profitably during a time of decreased expansion and smaller sales gains. This is expected to continue as the pattern into the future. Fashion retailers are expected to see only limited sales increases over the next decade. This prediction is based on changing population characteristics and increased numbers and kinds of retail distributors. The decline in the teenage population coupled with an increased proportion of elderly will mean a reduced demand for fashion merchandise. Teenagers are quick to adopt new fashions and often set new fashion trends, which encourages the growth of fashion retailing. The elderly need and desire less clothing than do younger working people. They tend to spend a higher proportion of their income for necessities such as utility bills and medical care and spend more for travel and leisure-time activities. An aging population means less demand for fashion apparel, accessories, and home furnishings.

Specialty Store Point of View

Market segmentation, or **niche retailing,** is the leading strategy being followed by many retailers. They are realizing that no store can be all things to all people and are identifying a demographic, lifestyle, or shopping trend and designing stores and departments to sell to the desired customers. In department stores niche retailing follows a specialty store point of view in which departments are divided into a series of small boutiques, each appealing to a specific set of fashion tastes. Specialty stores that focus on a single type of product such as socks, quality bedroom linens, or modular clothing are niche retailers. Stores are seeking a narrower customer base and are looking for their particular "niche" in the marketplace. Many retailers are positioning themselves to attract the so-called baby boomers born between 1946 and 1964 as this is the dominant group within the population and many are entering their peak earning years.

Department stores are remodeling to project a specialty store ambience. Large department store chains are adopting a "store within a store" format, which divides the store into a series of small stores or boutiques, each appealing to a particular consumer type or taste level. This approach was pioneered and perfected by R. H. Macy and has been copied by many retailers.

Many department stores are narrowing their customer base by focusing on higher-income households with incomes above $50,000. Such households control approximately one-third of all personal income and purchase an even larger share of luxury goods. These stores seek to attract a more upscale customer by stressing service and fashion knowledge, and by creating a visual atmosphere that is consistent with a more exclusive image. As they reach for the more affluent customer, retailers are remodeling store interiors using expensive materials such as marble and mirrors. A trend is also emerging toward developing a consistent look for all stores in a chain. This is reflected as stores are remodeled following similar layouts and decor. In this way a store reinforces its identity.

Whereas department stores are copying specialty stores and narrowing their customer base, some ownership groups have entered other segments of the market by developing or purchasing specialty businesses. F. W. Woolworth Company entered the specialty store business with Afterthoughts, a costume jewelry and accessories store, and Herald Square Stationers, featuring greeting cards, paper products, and gifts. Both Macy's and Bloomingdale's have entered the specialty store business. Bloomingdale's opened Bloomie's Express stores in New York's Kennedy International Airport. The stores carry only items bearing the retail logo "Bloomie's." Macy's introduced several specialty formats selling the company's private-label merchandise.

Strategies for the Big Three General Merchandisers

The big three general merchandise retail chains, Sears, J. C. Penney, and Montgomery Ward, have developed their own strategies to compete. Sears is concentrating on its "Stores of the Future" concept and has branched out into financial services with its Discover Card. Introduced in 1986 the Discover Card combines retail charge card features with financial services. It may be used to charge purchases with airlines, hotels, restaurants, and with Sears and other retail stores. In addition the card can be used by holders of Sears Financial Network deposit accounts. Sears announced in 1988 a new strategy for everyday low prices, cutting prices across the board and relying less on sale promotions to build volume.

Montgomery Ward has closed its mail-order division and is concentrating on developing its "store within a store" format, which highlights the company's stronger merchandise areas, including apparel. It is expected to close many of its stores in its restructuring process. A new low pricing policy was adopted by Montgomery Ward in 1988. The policy was designed to offer Ward's customers lower prices all year long, not just during a special sale. The store also promised to match any other store's advertised sale prices on branded merchandise.

In 1983 J. C. Penney began a new strategy to emphasize fashion apparel and soft goods with the company's defined goal as "becoming the nation's department store." To do this, it introduced designer labels such as Halston, Mary McFadden, and Lee Wright, and stores were remodeled with an emphasis on visual merchandising to give them an updated, fashion-oriented appearance. Hard good lines, such as paint and hardware, large appliances, and lawn and garden equipment, were dropped. A nationwide television campaign was undertaken to give J. C. Penney a stronger fashion image to attract more affluent shoppers to its stores. It has since returned to an emphasis on moderately priced goods with the goal of attracting back its traditional, more price-conscious customers.

Identity Crisis in Retailing

An acute problem for retailers is look-alike stores, which are virtually identical in terms of merchandise carried and merchandise presentation. The National Retail Merchants Association has estimated that 80 percent of the merchandise in department stores is exactly the same (Bergmann 1985). Retailers are seeking ways to combat this redundancy of merchandise and lack of differentiation. Department stores in particular are turning to a renewed emphasis on fashion leadership, exclusive merchandise assortments, and personal service.

Private-Label Merchandise

Stores have become aggressive in seeking out new and fresh merchandise from suppliers and are making sure that this merchandise gets into stores early enough to impress fashion-conscious customers. Retailers also seek exclusive agreements with manufacturers to keep their competitors from having identical merchandise. However, it has become increasingly difficult for retailers to obtain merchandise exclusivity, and they have turned to developing private-label merchandise or **house brands** as a means of combating the problem of many stores carrying the same merchandise. Private-label merchandise carries the name of a retailer rather than the name of the manufacturer. Sometimes the name on the label is the name of the store, but more often it is another name developed by the store to sound like a status or designer brand. Private labels have been developed by both department and specialty stores. Examples of successful store brands are The Limited Store's Forenza and Outback Red; Saks Fifth Avenue's Real Clothes; and Dayton Hudson's Boundary Waters. Dayton Hudson uses its Boundary Waters label in men's, women's, and children's apparel as well as in gifts and housewares. Boundary Waters even has its own mascot character, Matthew Mallard. See Table 17.1 for examples of in-house labels used by department and specialty stores for fashion merchandise.

Private label usually refers to clothes manufactured specifically for a store according to the retailer's specifications. The retailer chooses the fabric, design, and

Table 17.1 Private Labels

In-house Label	Store
Boundary Waters	Dayton Hudson
Aeropostale	Macy's
Banker's Club	
Charter Club	
Christopher Hayes	
Jennifer Moore	
Morgan Taylor	
Amelia's	Marshall Field
Field Gear	
Field Manor	
Cambridge Classics	Mervyn's
Cheetah	
Classic Directions	J. C. Penney
Diversity	
Hunt Club	
Sakura	
Worthington	
Wyndham	
Real Clothes	Saks Fifth Avanue
Forenza	The Limited
Outback Red	

detailing; thus the seller becomes the creative force behind the design. Another way retailers purchase private-brand goods is by buying from manufacturers who develop goods specifically to be marketed and sold to retailers to sell under the store's label.

Private label was originally associated primarily with moderate-priced apparel and knock-offs, but many stores are now using private label in better ready-to-wear with a stronger fashion image. Private label can range from safe fashion classics to high fashion and from budget to upper price. Private labels are also found in fashion accessories, housewares, gifts, and household textiles.

Explosive growth in private-label sales was reported by *Women's Wear Daily* during the 1980s. However, the percentage of private-label goods in a store's merchandise mix varies greatly depending on the store and the merchandise classification. Some stores carry only private-label merchandise; others carry only manufacturer's brands. *Women's Wear Daily* has published estimates ranging from 10 to 40 percent for many traditional department stores. Industry analysts have estimated that many department stores have 20 to 25 percent of their women's apparel inventory in private label, and this percentage is expected to increase (Pagoda 1988). Macy's has been estimated to have 25 to 30 percent private label, and Federated Department Stores are reportedly aiming toward a range of 35 to 40 percent private label (Forman 1988).

Private-label merchandise offers retailers several advantages. Most importantly, it offers exclusivity, giving retailers something their competitors do not have. Another reason for retailers' interest in private labeling is that they often achieve a higher margin on it. Retailers can buy private label for less than branded goods because they are not paying for expensive advertising campaigns or covering manufacturers' selling expenses. The merchandise can usually be marked up more than branded merchandise because the consumer cannot compare prices directly with a competitor. Also, markdowns are controlled more directly by the retailer, who is not forced to lower prices because a competitor has marked down the merchandise.

Private label offers some disadvantages. With branded merchandise the retailer shares the risk with the manufacturer. Merchandise that does not sell can sometimes be returned to the manufacturer, or the manufacturer may give the retailer markdown money to compensate for lost sales. The cost of promoting goods is also often shared on branded merchandise. Manufacturers may do national advertising or cooperative advertising, sharing the cost of local advertising with the retailer. With private labeling the retailer carries all of the risk and assumes the total burden for advertising and promotion. In addition, developing private brands takes time. Producing a private label takes at least three to four months, but five to eight months is more common, according to *Women's Wear Daily* (Ginsberg and Born 1986).

Return to Customer Service

Department stores are returning to an emphasis on customer service as a way of differentiating themselves from other stores. The trend had been to cut back in service to reduce costs and remain price competitive with off-price stores; however, retailers are discovering that price alone does not bring in customers. Service is becoming more important in off-price and discount stores as well as in department and specialty stores.

Stores that cater to working women are finding that these women value time-saving services. Carson Pirie Scott and Company in its Chicago State Street store has converted its basement into a specialty store for professional women. Known as the Corporate Level, this "store within a store" offers services for the busy working woman. On this one level are found a dry cleaner, shoe repair, clothing, and accessories. To accommodate women's working hours, the department opens two hours earlier than the upstairs store and remains open two hours later.

Other stores are beginning to provide more service to satisfy time-conscious consumers. Macy's South has initiated a program to provide service for customers. More salespeople are being placed on the floor and more full-time salespeople are being hired. To motivate salespeople, they are being paid higher salaries and have been placed on commission sales. Nordstrom, based in Seattle, Washington, has found that providing personal selling service to its customers increases volume and profits.

Many stores are adding personal shoppers to advise customers on how to dress. Personal shoppers assist a customer by gathering apparel and accessories from throughout the store. A customer can make an appointment with a personal shopper who will search for appropriate apparel and accessories before the customer arrives. The customer benefits by saving time and by building a well-coordinated wardrobe. The store benefits from having a satisfied customer who is more likely to return for future purchases. Another major benefit to the store is that the customer is likely to buy more than if shopping alone.

Conventional stores are seeing that they cannot compete on the basis of price alone, and service is one way for these stores to attract customers in an overstored marketplace. It remains to be seen if these stores are successful in returning to a service emphasis.

Demise of Family Ownership in Retailing

Another change in retailing has been the demise of many old family dynasties. For years it was the practice for the ownership and management of a store to be handed down from the founder to the children and on to the next generation. Today few of the old retailing families remain in control. Stores that failed to compete effectively have gone out of business; others have been sold, many to large ownership groups. Few large stores remain under the ownership or leadership of the founding family. Two of the few still controlled by members of the founding families are Dillard Department Stores and Nordstrom. Maison Blanche is the largest department store still under family ownership.

Revitalization of Downtown Stores

During the 1950s and 1960s the major area for store expansion was the suburbs. For years the phenomenal growth of suburban shopping centers spelled the demise of downtown stores and many neighborhood retail centers. During the late 1960s and early 1970s a number of major downtown stores closed and some mid-size cities saw all of their larger downtown stores close as shopping shifted to outlying centers. Then in the late 1970s attention shifted back to downtown shopping in many cities. Downtown stores were revitalized. Stores were remodeled, updated, and new stores and shopping centers were constructed in several central city locations. All over the United States inner cities underwent restorative measures as part of extensive rehabilitation programs by private developers and city, state, and federal governments. This trend appears to be continuing as many cities have become aware of the importance of their downtown areas.

The Newspaper Advertising Bureau (NAB) presented a program entitled "City Alive" at the annual convention of the National Retail Merchants Association in New York in January 1986. Sound and film emphasized the rebirth of the "intown retail center." Downtown shopping was described as serving three groups of people: (1) those who live downtown, (2) those who work downtown, and (3) those who visit there. Three different approaches to downtown retail centers were presented by the NAB: San Diego's Horton Plaza, Washington, D.C.'s Hecht Metro Center, and the specialty store areas on New York's upper East and West sides and in Greenwich Village. The NAB emphasized that intown retailing is not suburbia replanted. It has its own character meeting the needs of the consumers who shop there.

Apparel Specialty Store Expansion

A major retail trend during the 1970s was the expansion of national apparel specialty chains. These chains operate stores of comparatively small size located in regional shopping malls throughout the United States. They feature highly selective lines of contemporary and often trendy fashions targeted toward a specific customer type. Although usually offering moderate to upper-moderate price ranges, some specialty chains feature budget-priced merchandise. The stores focus on a particular market segment or consumer group, such as juniors, misses, or young men. In the 1970s many of these stores marketed to the youth market. As their market grew older, many turned their emphasis to career women or contemporary misses. The stores have had to grow up with their market in order to retain their customers and continue to increase sales. The Limited and the Gap are specialty stores that have successfully repositioned themselves to attract an older customer base. The Gap stores originally sold primarily Levi's jeans. When jeans ceased to be a strong fashion item, The Gap responded by adopting a new merchandising strategy featuring fashion-oriented, colorful, casual apparel for men and women. The Gap has also gone upscale by opening Hemisphere shops with higher-priced merchandise aimed at a more sophisticated and more affluent customer.

A number of exciting new formats appeared in specialty store retailing in the 1980s as retailers sought to fill special marketing niches. Shops selling children's apparel became especially important and are expected to continue with strong growth throughout the 1990s. Prominent names in women's specialty retailing are opening specialty stores carrying children's wear. The Gap saw the potential for more fashion-oriented children's wear and opened GapKids. Other stores seeking this business are The Limited Too, Benetton's 012, for children 0 to 12 years of age, and Laura Ashley's Mother and Child shops offering infants' and children's clothing and bedroom furnishing with the romantic look.

Highly focused specialty stores are appearing, some of which carry only one product or specialize in one fiber. Examples of single-product stores are Sox Appeal, Something's Afoot, and Sock Shop International, all specializing in legwear. Interest in natural fibers has stimulated development and expansion of stores specializing in one fiber. Royal Silk, for example, grew from a catalog retailer specializing in silk blouses and tops. Cashmere-Cashmere carries products ranging from gloves or socks to blankets. Cashmere fashions for both men and women are sold including sweaters, dresses, robes, slippers, and scarves. Another chain of shops, Westminster Lace, originated in Seattle and sells lace items in all categories including home textiles and apparel plus trims and antique laces. Westminster Lace shops project a romantic nineteenth-century atmosphere similar to Laura Ashley but with different merchandise.

Specialty stores will remain an important form of retailing in the 1990s. The stores have continued to provide strong competition to department stores and, as previously discussed, have influenced many department stores to develop specialty store or "store within a store" concepts of their own.

Expansion of Discount Stores

Discount department stores appeal to consumers on the basis of price, convenience, and assortment. In recent years discount stores have become more like traditional department stores, offering more services, upgrading their merchandise, and upscaling the appearance of their stores.

Although discount stores have traditionally geared their merchandise to less affluent, less fashion-oriented consumers, many discount department stores have been upscaling to attract higher income, more fashion-conscious customers. They are remodeling stores, adding higher-quality, name-brand merchandise, and improving service. Both K mart and Target are repositioning their stores to attract the middle-income customer.

Standard and Poor's *Industry Surveys* (1985) predicted that discount department stores would grow more rapidly than traditional department stores over the next several years. *Chain Store Age* also sees full-line discount stores remaining a viable retail format. These stores, however, are facing increased competition from other forms of retailing and must adjust merchandising strategies if they are to compete effectively. Other forms of retailing having a strong impact on discounters are deep discount drug stores, wholesale warehouse stores, large grocery stores, specialty chains, off-price apparel stores, and category killers. Deep discount drug stores are offering customers bigger assortments and lower prices on health and beauty aids. Wholesale warehouse clubs offer a more limited assortment of goods than full-line discount stores, but their prices are lower. Large drug/grocery combination stores are presenting big assortments in general merchandise, which takes business away from discounters. Although prices are not as low, grocery stores are shopped more frequently by the customer and provide a convenient location to purchase many items carried by the discounter. Fashion specialty chains and off-price apparel stores have also taken business away from full-line discount stores. These specialty stores carry brands the customer recognizes as quality brands and are perceived as offering better style.

The future is brightest for the largest discounters. Small regional discounters are subject to consolidations, mergers, and bankruptcy. *Chain Store Age* predicted that by 1990 the discount department store industry might be reduced to less than "a dozen meaningful companies," such as K mart, Wal-Mart, Target, Caldor, Bradlees, and Zayre ("The Discount Lions" 1986).

Off-Price Stores

During the early 1980s off-price apparel specialty stores enjoyed extensive growth and became an important factor in the marketplace. Off-price stores appealed to customers by offering brand-name and designer merchandise at 20 to 50 percent below department store prices. These lower prices were available every day in contrast to department store patterns of inconsistent promotions. Off-price stores are able to offer lower prices because of the way their merchandise is purchased and because they operate their stores by low-cost means.

Department stores reacted to the competition from off-price stores by aggressively promoting lower prices and by developing private-label merchandise. An advantage of the department store was more complete merchandise assortments and, in some instances, better service. By the mid-1980s department stores had succeeded in slowing the growth of off-price retailers.

Off-price retailing underwent a period of consolidation in the mid-1980s. A number of off-price chains went out of business, whereas the more successful chains continued to expand. Standard and Poor's reported that off-price retailing is expected to peak at about 15 percent of total apparel and footwear sales. Earlier predictions had been 25 percent. The growth of off-price has slowed, and traditional retailers are less concerned about the future impact of these stores on their fashion business.

Growth in Nonstore Retailing

According to Maxwell H. Sroge, a pioneer in mail-order statistical analysis, by the year 2000 one-fourth to one-third of all consumer dollars will be spent via nonstore retailing channels such as direct mail and electronic home shopping (Feinberg 1988). Mail order at one time was associated exclusively with companies such as Montgomery Ward and Sears Roebuck, serving the needs of rural America where people lacked convenient access to retail stores. Today mail order has become big business both for companies offering goods exclusively through catalogs and for conventional retailers selling goods through both catalogs and stores. Mail order has also expanded to include other forms of nonstore retailing such as TV and computer shopping.

The offerings available through catalogs are extensive. Almost any merchandise category and fashion level imaginable are sold through general merchandise catalogs and highly specialized catalogs. Many catalogs feature fashion merchandise for very select target markets. For example, Talbots and Carroll Reed are known for preppy styles for women. L. L. Bean and Eddie Bauer feature sporting goods and apparel. The Gap-owned Banana Republic is known basically for the safari look. Lands' End has preppy styles and sports attire for men and women as well as canvas luggage. Department stores such as Bloomingdale's, Neiman-Marcus, and Saks Fifth Avenue offer more fashion-oriented merchandise.

In 1982 there were more than 4,000 catalogs in circulation. Sales by mail and telephone totaled more than $40 billion in 1982, and specialty catalogs accounted for $30 billion of this ("The Sale" 1984). By 1988 an estimated 6,500 catalogs generated estimated sales of $64 billion, up from $56 billion in 1987 (Feinberg 1988). Nonstore retailing is increasing at an annual rate of 10 percent as compared to 6 percent for in-store retailing.

Direct Marketing reported that mail-order apparel sales have grown in several categories including sportswear, career clothing, classic men's apparel, odd-size apparel, and lingerie (Fishman 1986). Odd-size retailing and career apparel have been important categories for mail-order apparel for many years. Career clothing includes blue-collar work clothing or uniforms, coordinated apparel for low and mid-scale women's office needs, and professional or executive career apparel for men and women. Catalog retailing offers odd-size apparel featuring large or small sizes for men and women in variety and depth not generally available in retail stores.

A growing trend in the apparel mail-order industry is for mail-order companies to open stores. Recognizing that some consumers will never order merchandise through mail order, some mail-order firms are seeking to expand their business by opening stores, such as Eddie Bauer or Royal Silk.

Another mail-order trend is the emergence of conglomerate ownership of specialty mail-order firms. The Limited has been a leader with its Lane Bryant and Victoria's Secret catalogs. Another is Arizona Mail Order, which features Old Pueblo Traders, Regalia, and Unique Petite and Tall catalogs.

The future of nonstore marketing appears bright because it meets the changing needs of many consumers. Catalog buying offers convenience to those who have limited time for shopping or are not able to visit certain retail outlets. Through catalogs, retailers are able to develop national sales without having to invest in expensive stores throughout the country. Catalogs also assist traditional retailers with building in-store sales.

The future is expected to bring exciting innovations to catalog retailing. Videotex and Teletext systems should be viable options for shopping in the future. With expected technological advances in computer graphics and improved quality of television video images, catalogs will be supplemented or possibly even replaced by video displays. **Videotex** is a computer service that displays graphic information through cable television or personal computers. It allows viewers to interact with the system; the viewer can give as well as receive information in the form of words or numbers. Other systems such as **Teletext** are one-way, over-the-air broadcast services transmitted via cable television.

Electronic shopping from the home is anticipated by some to replace both in-store and catalog shopping. This seems unlikely because consumers many times like to see, touch, and try merchandise before buying. Also, shopping is often a social activity and a form of entertainment for many.

Although a number of home shopping systems have been tested by computer and retailing companies, the technology has not yet reached the point of providing quality pictures of merchandise nor is it cost-effective for retailers and consumers. With improved technology, however, electronic shopping at home is likely to be used by many consumers in the near future.

Changing Roles in the Fashion Industry

Retailers and manufacturers have been changing their roles in the fashion industry. Traditionally, retailers have been the primary distributors of fashion merchandise to the ultimate consumer, whereas manufacturers specialized in producing these goods. Recently, however, many retailers have added in-house labels and are taking an active part in designing and manufacturing. At the same time that retailers have entered the manufacturer's area of expertise, manufacturers have increased their involvement with sales, and many designer/manufacturers have opened their own stores.

According to *Women's Wear Daily,* the practice of apparel designers or manufacturers entering retailing with their own freestanding boutiques or stores "is changing the landscape of American retailing" (Lockwood 1986). Although European designers have operated boutiques in the United States for some time, American designers have only recently opened their own stores. American designers include Ralph Lauren, Calvin Klein, Norma Kamali, Eli Tahari, Alexander Julian, Betsey Johnson, and Perry Ellis. Manufacturers with their own stores and franchised boutiques include Esprit, Liz Claiborne's First Issue stores, and J. G. Hook's Mickey & Co. Major locations of these boutiques are on New York's Madison Avenue and in Beverly Hills, California; Palm Beach, Florida; Dallas; and Chicago.

Designers and manufacturers have stated several reasons for opening their own stores—to reinforce their images and to show both consumers and their retail accounts how to correctly merchandise their lines. These stores also offer designers and manufacturers the opportunity to test new styles. Their own stores give designers and manufacturers complete control of the merchandising of their lines. They are able to present their entire line rather than an edited version as would be found in most department and specialty stores where the buyer edits the line in his or her selection of items to be carried by the store. Also, they are able to have constant window displays projecting their image to the public rather than competing with other lines carried by the department store. Designers also believe that they offer customers better service through their own stores than these customers would receive in department stores.

Esprit, a San Francisco-based manufacturer, is taking three approaches to retailing: (1) franchised Esprit boutiques located throughout the country limited to one category such as Esprit Kids or Esprit Sport, (2) freestanding flagship stores carrying all Esprit categories, and (3) shops located within department stores. Esprit mandates the visual merchandising and fixtures used in its shops located within department stores.

The burgeoning of designer boutiques is increasing the competitiveness of retailing. Opinions vary as to the effect such boutiques have on department and specialty stores that also carry their line. Some retailers believe that the department store attracts a different customer. The department store customer likes to look at a variety of merchandise and to do so without being intimidated by salespeople. Department stores edit the designer or manufacturer's line for their particular customer; therefore, this customer will continue to come to them to shop. Other retailers feel that designers and manufacturers should not compete with retail stores. They are concerned about losing business to the manufacturer and feel that manufacturers should stick to what they do best—manufacturing—and leave the retailing to the experts.

The Globalization of Retailing

The American economy has been replaced by a world economy, and the consumer marketplace is becoming international in scope. Foreign-based fashion retailers have opened stores in the United States in record numbers since 1980, and several American retailers have taken their retail concepts abroad.

Most foreign-based retailers come from highly developed areas including Europe,

Canada, Australia, and Japan. They are locating their stores in big cities and exclusive retail shopping areas through the United States, selling everything from fashion-forward clothing and unassembled furniture to shoes and accessories. Many international retailers license or franchise stores in the United States but still maintain tight control over store design and merchandising to ensure their own distinctive look.

Foreign-based retailers are expected to claim a larger share of the U.S. market, leading to an escalation of foreign competition in the 1990s (Standard and Poor's 1986). They have succeeded to a great extent because they offer merchandise that is different from that available in U.S. department stores. With their distinctive merchandise and innovative formats, imported retailers offer relief from the dull sameness of department store fashion merchandise.

Among the successful international fashion retailers with stores in the United States are Laura Ashley from England, Italy's Benetton, and Denmark's In-Wear Matinique. In the past, European fashion was confined primarily to the high-priced designer end of fashion as expressed by Gucci, Dior, or Saint Laurent. The foreign-based retailers that expanded in the U.S. market in the 1980s provided fashion at a more affordable price. They targeted the largest population segment: the maturing baby boomers and their children.

International home-furnishings retailers also successfully transported their merchandising concepts to the United States. IKEA, the Swedish retailer of ready-to-assemble furniture and other household goods, filled a void in the home-furnishings area. Conrans and Laura Ashley, both British-owned chains, also succeeded in establishing stores selling home furnishings in the United States.

A few American specialty chains are successfully taking their stores abroad, among them, the Gap, Brooks Brothers, and Tiffany. Esprit has also opened thirty-five franchises in twenty-five countries. Toys "R" Us, the largest toy chain in the United States, opened stores in Canada, Europe, and Asia.

American retailers and manufacturers have been reluctant to take their concepts abroad. Americans are not as familiar with operating in the international environment as Europeans are. They lack the language knowledge and the experience, and in the past have failed to understand the foreign customer. This is changing, however, and more American specialty chains may enter foreign markets in the future.

Changing Consumer Demographics and Lifestyles

Changing **demographic trends** and **consumer lifestyles** must be closely followed by retailers if they are to keep their merchandise assortments and store environments in line with consumer demand. Retailers need to be aware of changes in population size and age distribution, number and composition of households, consumer mobility, income, and employment patterns. Changing consumer tastes, values, and attitudes also must be concerns.

Population Shifts

The 1980 Census of the United States showed a population of 222,159,000. The population is growing at a slower rate than in the past, and zero population growth is projected sometime after the year 2000. In some states in the Northeast the population has already stopped growing, whereas in states in the South and West, population has increased. Obviously such geographical population shifts are important for retailers to consider. Areas where the population is increasing offer opportunities for retailers to build new stores, whereas stores may have to be closed in areas where the population is declining. Store expansion will naturally follow population growth.

Shifting age distributions have a major impact on retailing and offer many opportunities for new merchandise (Blackwell and Talarzyk 1983, p. 18). The population is growing older. In 1970 the largest age category was ages 5–13 at 18.2 percent; in 1980 the largest category was ages 25–34 with 16.3 percent of the population in this age group. The median age in 1960 was 29.4; in 1970 it was 27.9; and in 1980, 30.3. The median age of the population reached 32.3 years in 1988 and is continuing to rise.

Another expanding age group is over sixty-five. In 1960 the elderly comprised 9.2 percent of the population; by 1984 they were 11.8 percent. The number of older Americans is expected to increase from twenty-eight million in 1984 to thirty-two million in 2000. Also more older persons will be over seventy-five years of age. These older consumers have special needs, which retailers are slowly beginning to recognize. The large increase in sixty-five-year-old and older consumers offers opportunities to sell to people who have leisure time and who often still lead very active lives.

During the 1960s and 1970s teenagers and young adults were the age groups receiving retailers' primary attention. However, since 1978 when this population began to decline, retailers have shifted their attention to the older age group. The baby boom generation totaled seventy-six million people in 1985. These baby boomers have become the target group of many fashion retailers because they are the right age to be heavy consumers of apparel and home furnishings. Although the oldest baby boomer turned forty in 1986, many are still at the age where they are forming new households and having children. The baby boomers are more highly educated than any previous generation and are relatively affluent, thus making them prime targets for retailers' attention.

The growth rate of the U.S. population is expected to be slow on through the 1990s. Later marriages and preferences for smaller families have led to a lower birthrate. In spite of this, the United States enjoyed a baby boomlet in the mid-1980s, which is expected to continue in the 1990s because of the large number of women in the population who are in their twenties and thirties. Many of these women delayed having children while they were establishing their careers and are now having their first child. Many of these first-time mothers are over thirty years old. Older mothers are frequently working women and spend conspicuously on their children.

Between 1980 and 1984 the number of children in the United States under age five grew from 16.3 million to 17.8 million. This increase brought increased demand for children's apparel and many other related products, such as home furnishings for children and toys. Because many of these children are the first born and are born to two-income couples, a market for children's luxury items developed. As *Time* magazine reported, "a well-dressed child may be the ultimate status symbol" (Henry 1986).

Households and Family Composition

Family composition has been changing in the United States and the number of households is expected to rise significantly. Between 1970 and 1980 the number of households grew faster than the number of families, due primarily to the number of people living alone or with unrelated persons. More people were living alone due to the increased divorce rate, more young singles living away from home, and more senior citizens in the population. In 1980 the average household size was 2.8 persons; by 1989 it was down to just over 2.5. It is expected to decline even more in the 1990s (Berman and Evans 1983).

Families have grown smaller because people are having fewer children or having no children. More children are living in one-parent families because of the high divorce rate and society's wider acceptance of unmarried mothers' keeping their children. Another trend for nontraditional families is for nonmarried couples to live together, referred to as "mingles."

A shift from family to individual consumption is occurring in the United States because of the increase in nontraditional households such as singles, mingles, and career-oriented couples. Many products and services are being demanded and consumed at an individual rather than a household level (Sneth 1983).

Mobility

The U.S. population is mobile. About 17 percent of all Americans move each year (U.S. Statistical Abstract 1986). People in their twenties are more likely to move than any other age group. A mobile population likes to shop in familiar stores and buy merchandise brands they recognize. Therefore, national chain stores are expected to prosper in the coming years as well as nationally branded merchandise. Moves often lead to the need for purchasing new products. A change in climate brings about new clothing needs and any move, local or long distance, is likely to mean purchases of new home-furnishings products.

Employment

Changing employment patterns have had a major impact on retailers and will continue to be important. The United States is changing from an industrial society to an information society. This is creating new jobs at the same time that old jobs in industry are disappearing. Fewer workers are employed in blue-collar jobs and more employed in white-collar jobs.

One of the major changes in employment has been the increase in the number of women working and the prevalence of dual-income households in the population. Between 1947 and 1980, the number of women working increased from 16.7 to 45.6 million. During the same period the number of men in the labor force increased from 44.3 to 63.4 million. Women's participation rate increased from 34 percent in 1950 to 52 percent in 1980; men's fell from 87 to 78 percent (U.S. Bureau of the Census 1984).

The higher the level of education for a woman, the more likely she is to be employed. Such educated, employed women have become an ever-increasing market for retailers. In the early 1980s retailers began to seek the career woman as a customer by establishing special departments for her and adding services such as personal shopping to meet her special needs. The great number of working women with children created time-poor shoppers. Sunday openings and longer store hours have been added to service this customer who has limited time to shop. This customer is interested in purchasing products and services that will save her time. Also, she is willing to pay for better-quality goods and services (Blackwell and Talarzyk 1983).

Psychographic Trends

Psychographics relate to consumer lifestyles. How people live their lives and how they spend their time and money determine consumers' lifestyles. Demographic trends affect American lifestyles in many ways. Elderly consumers, for example, have more leisure time and when in good health are often interested in traveling and participating in leisure-time activities. The retired elderly are also interested in convenience and service as are singles and working wives who are time-poor. Retailers should continue to see a demand for increased shopping hours and time-saving products and services. Understanding psychographic trends and how they are influenced by demographics can help retailers target their merchandising to specific market segments. Psychographics are more important in describing customers than are demographics such as age or income.

Self-interest

The United States is a want-driven rather than a need-driven society (Sneth 1983). Consumers may buy because they want, not because they need something. Advertising appeals used by retailers and manufacturers reflect this. Advertisements for cosmetics tell consumers how they can look younger, and apparel advertisements often emphasize attractiveness or sex appeal.

In the 1980s "Yuppies" became the most popular target group for retailers. These Young Urban Professionals are a subgroup of the baby boomers born between 1946 and 1964. Yuppies are characterized as being affluent, sophisticated, free-spending, and innovative. They are eager to try new products and are demanding about quality and style. Constantly aiming for more, they have been called the "me generation." As Yuppies have become parents, many have turned their attention to dressing their children in the latest fashions.

The emphasis on self-interest and self-gratification provides many opportunities for retailers. The emergence of many stores selling quality merchandise reflects the importance of two-income, well-educated, self-oriented consumers.

Changing Sex Roles

Working women have impacted how Americans live in many ways. Dual-income families have meant that more money is available for consumers to spend. Much of this money is spent on services and time-saving products because working women are time-poor.

A myth exists that consumers today have more time than a few decades ago (Blackwell and Talarzyk 1983). The fact is that consumers who have money are likely to be dual-income families and therefore have less time. A reflection of shoppers with less time is the rise in mail-order sales. Increased operating hours of retailers is another example of retailers meeting consumers' needs.

Working women tend to be more concerned with fashion and dress than are women who have not worked outside the home. Working women also are more sophisticated in terms of traveling and dealing with the outside world. They are better educated and are concerned with improving themselves. They have become more cosmopolitan in taste and are more demanding consumers. (Berman and Evans 1983).

As more women have entered the work force and the two-income family has become the norm, men's roles are also changing. Today's male is more likely to share in performing household chores and in child rearing. In the 1980s both men and women tried to balance the often conflicting demands of home and job ("The American Male" 1985). As men's and women's roles change and become more similar, retailers will need to adjust their strategies.

Looking to the Future

Since the beginning of retailing, merchants have had to live with shifts in consumer preferences and buying patterns. Retailers must continue to adjust if they are to survive. Those companies that fail to look to the future and do not make adjustments in merchandise assortments, store decor, and services will go out of business. Those

Something different in fashion retailing surfaced in the United States with the spread of Italian Benetton shops specializing in vibrantly colored knitwear—particularly woolen sweaters, cotton T-shirts, and jeans—aimed at a young fashion-conscious customer. Merchandise is stacked and folded on shelves like a color chart for household paints. The vibrant colors draw customers into the stores and make it hard to resist carrying something away in one of the distinctive green-and-white bags.

The Benetton Group, based in Treviso, Italy, is controlled by four Benetton siblings. The business grew from a meager beginning in the early 1960s when Luciano Benetton and his sister, Giuliana, began producing brightly colored sweaters in the back room of their modest home and selling them to shops around the area. Later, their two brothers, Carlo and Gilberto, joined the business. Although no longer privately owned, the company is still family directed.

Today Benetton is one of the fashion world's greatest success stories, ranking as the world's largest knitwear manufacturer. It has grown into a major fashion company with distribution on a global scale. Benetton has become the Coca-Cola of the fashion industry. It has used the manufacturer-franchised shop concept to become the first global, mass-consumption, cross-cultural clothing retailer with stores in many locations, like McDonald's. The first Benetton shop opened in 1967. By 1982 there were 1,800 stores, and by 1988 more than 4,000 Benetton stores were located in sixty countries. Green-and-white Benetton stores have a strong presence in the United States, Great Britain, Canada, Western Europe, Japan, and South Africa. Stores are even located in Hungary, Czechoslovakia, Yugoslavia, and China.

Benetton sells only to authorized retailers who are overseen by agents on a regional basis. These agents earn commissions on all Benetton merchandise sold in their territory. A few stores are company-owned but most are franchised. Franchise holders pay the company a lump sum to open a Benetton store. In return they receive the promotional backing of the firm and agree to sell Benetton products exclusively and to follow the Benetton store format. The stores are designed with no back room storage. All merchandise is checked upon arrival and

retail firms that change to meet the needs, wants, and desires of consumers will find opportunity.

Retailing is constantly evolving, and new forms will appear to take the place of old forms and meet consumer demand. Only time can tell exactly what these new forms will be. Inventive fashion retailers will study and understand consumer de-placed directly on open shelves ready for sale, making short replenishment cycles a necessity. Merchandise varies in Benetton stores because store owners select their own merchandise assortments from the company's extensive offerings.

The Benetton formula for success is based on two factors: aggressive marketing and the use of bright colors, which appeal to the company's target customer who is fifteen to thirty-five years of age and interested in colorful fashion. A highly successful advertising program based on the slogans "All the Colors in the World" and "The United Colors of Benetton" has featured pictures of teenagers of all creeds and colors wearing Benetton apparel.

Benetton clothes appear under four labels: Benetton, a youthfully oriented sportswear line; Sisley, a more sophisticated and slightly higher priced clothing line; 012 for children; and Benetton UOMO for men. More recently Benetton entered the cosmetics market with makeup and perfume. Other products have been licensed such as sunglasses, watches, and shoes.

Benetton produces two main collections a year—spring/summer and fall/winter. Each collection has as many as 1,000 styles in hundreds of colors and patterns. A single garment may be produced in as many as forty shades. Two smaller collections of about thirty styles each are produced about a month after the primary collections to spotlight more forward looks.

Technology is a major contributor to Benetton's success. Designing takes place on video display terminals, and the clothing is manufactured in automated factories that operate twenty-four hours a day. The company follows a practice of dyeing assembled garments rather than dyeing the yarn. This allows Benetton to quickly meet changing customer demand. Technology is also important in the company's distribution center near Treviso, where much of the work is done by robots. In the stores, computerized cash registers give an instant read-out of how a particular style or color is selling so that production can be coordinated with sales.

Benetton's strategy for the 1990s is opening "better stores" (David Moin, "Benetton Expects to Shut 100 Stores in U.S. by 1993," *Women's Wear Daily,* September 15, 1988, p. 9). The company intends to close smaller U.S. stores and open more larger-size stores called United Colors. The prototype United Colors store owned by Benetton is located in Manhattan at 586 Fifth Avenue. United Colors stores are about four times larger than the typical 1,000-square-foot Benetton store and feature all of the Benetton lines. They carry about 350 styles as compared to the older smaller stores with 200 to 250 styles.

mographics and psychographics. They will be able to identify niches in the marketplace where consumer preferences are not being met and will fill those niches.

Successful retailers of fashion will become destination retailers carrying distinctive merchandise presented in an appealing manner and priced appropriately. They will provide an appropriate level of service and offer a proper balance of private-label and national brands. Such retailers will be able to anticipate and accommodate changes in the environment that will attract their target customers.

Summary of Key Points

1. Because of overstoring, retailers have had to adjust their merchandising strategies to compete more effectively. Strategies used to combat increased competition include acquisition of other retail stores, downsizing stores, elimination of nonprofitable merchandising categories, development of new retail formats, store restructuring and consolidation, greater control of expenses, and developing a specialty store point of view.

2. New retail formats have developed to supply consumers with merchandise categories eliminated by department and specialty stores. Opportunities exist for companies that respond to a need in the marketplace and fill a void.

3. Category killers have become destination retailers. They have seized market shares from both department stores and specialty retailers by either carrying heavy inventories of one merchandise category or by organizing their merchandise into clearly recognizable lifestyle groups.

4. Retailers are combating the identity crisis in retailing by turning to a renewed emphasis on fashion leadership, developing in-house labels, and stressing personal service.

5. Few large stores today remain under the ownership or leadership of the founding family. Two large stores still controlled by members of their founding families are Dillard Department Stores and Nordstrom.

6. Many central business districts are enjoying a revitalization of downtown shopping. Retailers located downtown serve three groups of people: those who live downtown, those who work downtown, and those who visit there.

7. Apparel specialty stores continue to provide strong competition to department stores for the fashion shopper and have influenced many department stores to develop specialty store concepts of their own.

8. New highly focused specialty stores are appearing in today's retail market. Some of these stores specialize in only one product or one fiber.

9. Discount department stores have become more like traditional department stores by offering more services, upgrading merchandise offerings, and upscaling store appearance.

10. An important trend in the apparel mail-order industry is the opening of retail stores. Other trends are the emergence of conglomerate ownership of specialty mail-order firms and the expansion of business by entering different apparel categories.

11. Retailers and manufacturers have changed the roles that they play in the fashion industry. Many retailers have become designers of products and manufacturers are becoming increasingly involved in selling.

12. Retailing is becoming increasingly global in nature. During the 1980s many foreign-based retailers franchised stores in the United States, and a few U.S. retailers have taken their stores abroad.

13. Retailers should be aware of changing consumer demographic and psychographic trends and how these trends will influence retail formats and merchandise sales.

14. Retailers must adjust and accommodate changing consumer needs, wants, and desires if they are to operate a profitable business.

Key Words and Concepts

Define, identify, or explain each of the following:

category killers	house brands
consumer lifestyles	niche retailing
demographic trends	overstoring
destination retailers	psychographic trends
downsizing	Videotex
electronic shopping	Teletext

Discussion Questions

1. How are retailers responding to overstoring and increased competition?

2. What strategies can retailers undertake to control operating expenses and improve profitability?

3. What is the identity crisis in retailing? What can retailers do to combat the tendency for all stores to look alike?

4. What advantages and disadvantages do private-label merchandise offer retailers?

5. Why are manufacturers and designers opening their own retail stores?

6. Why are some cities enjoying a resurgence of downtown shopping? What three groups of people are served by retailers in the central business district of a city? What is happening to fashion retailing in the central business district of your community?

7. Do you see electronic shopping replacing retail stores in the future? Explain why or why not.

8. What demographic trends affected retailing in the 1980s?

9. How will retailing be affected in the future by each of the following changing demographics: (1) increasing number of households, (2) shifts in age composition, and (3) increased numbers of working women?

10. What changes do you see taking place in the retail stores in your community? To what demographic and psychographic trends are these changes responding?

Notes

"The American Male," *U.S. News & World Report*, June 3, 1985, pp. 44–51.

Joan Bergmann, "*Stores* Editorial: Cookie-Cutter and Clones?" *Stores*, June 1985, p. 141.

Joan Bergmann, "*Stores* Editorial: Downsizing Is the Buzzword in Retailing This Year," *Stores*, March 1986, p. 6.

Barry Berman and Joel R. Evans, *Retail Management: A Strategic Approach*. New York: Macmillan, 1983.

Roger D. Blackwell and W. Wayne Talarzyk, "Life-Style Retailing: Competitive Strategies for the 1980s," *Journal of Retailing*, 59, Winter 1983.

"The Discount Lions Are Stalking the Future," *Chain Store Age*, May 1986, p. 14.

Samuel Feinberg, "Nonstop Growth for Nonstore Sales Channels," *Women's Wear Daily*, October 25, 1988, p. 14.

Arnold Fishman, "The Apparel Mail Order Marketplace," *Direct Marketing*, June 1986, p. 50.

Ellen Forman, "Campeau: More Private Label for Federated," *Women's Wear Daily*, April 7, 1988, p. 1.

Steve Ginsberg and Pete Born, "Private Label Sharpens Its Fashion Edge," *Women's Wear Daily*, January 13, 1986, p. 7.

Gordon M. Henry, "High Fashion for Little Ones," *Time*, June 2, 1986, p. 60.

Lisa Lockwood, "Fashioning a New Breed of Boutiques," *Women's Wear Daily*, January 13, 1986, p. 1.

Dianna M. Pagoda, "Private Label Crossing into RTW," *Women's Wear Daily*, March 1, 1988, pp. 6–7.

"The Sale Is in the Mail," *Chain Store Age Executive*, March 1989.

Jagdish N. Sneth, "Emerging Trends for the Retailing Industry," *Journal of Retailing*, 59, Fall 1983.

Standard and Poor's *Industry Surveys*, January 14, 1985, sec. 2, p. R117; July 4, 1985, sec. 2, p. R120; April 3, 1986, sec. 2, p. R62; January 22, 1987, 155, sec. 1, p. R84.

U.S. Bureau of the Census, Special Demographic Analyses, CDS-80-8, *American Women: Three Decades of Change*. Washington, D.C.: USGPO, 1984.

Glossary _____

Accessories: Items used to complete a fashion look. *See* Fashion accessories and Home accessories.

ACTWU: Amalgamated Clothing and Textile Workers Union, the major union in the menswear industry and the principal labor union of textile manufacturing workers.

Adaptation: A design that reflects the primary features of another design but is not an exact copy.

Adjustment: The settlement of a customer's complaint to the satisfaction of both the customer and the store. Often involves the resolution of differences regarding price or a refund. The lowering of price, as in the case of damaged or shopworn goods.

Advance buying: Buying merchandise well ahead of the desired shipment date. The buyer is usually given a lower price for the goods because of giving the manufacturer business during slack periods.

Advance order: An order placed well ahead of the desired shipment date.

Advanced fashion: Forward-looking fashion merchandise that expresses the latest fashion trends.

Advertising: Any paid, sponsored, nonpersonal communication of a sales message to actual or potential customers for the purpose of selling a product, service, or idea. Communication is established through such media as newspapers, television, direct mail, and magazines.

Advertising media: All of the channels employed to convey an advertising or sales message such as newspapers, magazines, television, radio, direct mail, and billboards.

American look: Casual, comfortable, functional way of dressing suited to the busy lifestyles of American women, introduced by American sportswear designers Claire McCardell, Clare Potter, Bonnie Cashin, and Vera Maxwell in the 1930s and 1940s.

Apparel: An inclusive term for clothing or garments; includes all categories of clothing from intimate apparel to outerwear for men, women, and children.

Apparel contractor: An independent firm engaged in sewing (and sometimes cutting) garments for other apparel producers.

Apparel jobber: A firm that handles all processes in apparel production but the sewing, and sometimes the cutting, and that contracts out these production processes to independently owned contractors. Middlemen who contract for the production of apparel that they then market.

Apparel manufacturer: A firm that buys materials and performs all of the functions necessary to produce a finished product; also called an inside shop.

Apparel pipeline: The process through which fiber evolves to completed garments in the retail store.

As ready: A term used by manufacturers to indicate that merchandise ordered by a retailer will be shipped as it is completed at the factory rather than on a specified delivery date.

Assistant buyer: A buyer-in-training position involving exposure to all phases of buying responsibilities, including the department budget, selecting and promoting merchandise, analyzing stock and sales reports, and summarizing information for the buyer.

Associate buyer: A position with greater responsibility than that of assistant buyer. Although not a full buyer, the associate buyer is often given the responsibility of buying a merchandise classification.

Associated buying office: A resident buying office controlled and financed cooperatively by a group of noncompeting, independent stores; also known as a cooperative buying office.

Assortment: The range of choice within a particular classification or category of goods, such as style, color, size, and price.

Assortment breadth: A description of the number of different categories or classifications available in a store or department without reference to the quantity available of any one style. A broad assortment has a large variety of different items within a classification.

Assortment depth: A description of the quantity of each item available in the assortment of goods offered the customer. An assortment containing an item in great quantities and many sizes is said to be "deep."

Assortment plan: A projection of the variety and quantity of merchandise in dollars or in units to be carried by a store or department to meet customer demand. Assortment plans may be developed through the basic stock list or model stock plan.

Atelier: A workroom where haute couture garments are made and duplicated.

Avant-garde: Original and unconventional designs, ideas, or techniques. Styles that are unusual and fashion-forward.

Back order: An order, or part of an order, to be shipped at a later date.

Balance of trade: The relationship between a country's imports and exports in foreign trade. When exports exceed imports, a country is said to have a favorable balance of trade. When imports are greater than exports, a trade deficit exists.

Balanced assortment: A stock assortment with sufficient breadth and depth to meet the demand of target customers while maintaining a reasonable investment in inventory. An ideal stock.

Basement store: Bargain store, often located in a department store's basement, which specializes in serving the needs of customers most concerned with low price.

Basic stock: Merchandise with a highly predictable sales history and a stable customer demand over an extended period of time. An assortment of merchandise that the retailer keeps available at all times; also called staple merchandise.

Basic stock plan: A method used to develop an assortment plan, which includes the names of each item to be carried in stock, brand name, physical description, cost and retail price, and other information that precisely identifies the merchandise.

Best seller: An item that consistently sells rapidly throughout a season or year at full price.

Big pencil: A term applied to buyers who represent large stores with considerable buying power. These buyers can write large orders and are said to have a "big pencil."

The Big Strike: 1909 strike of 20,000 shirtwaist makers in New York.

The Big Three: The three general merchandise chain department stores of Sears Roebuck, Montgomery Ward, and J. C. Penney.

Big ticket item: Any item of merchandise carrying a high price such as major appliances or furniture.

Blanket order: An order placed with the vendor in advance of a season to be delivered in several later shipments.

Bodywear: A merchandise category including coordinated leotards, tights, and wrap skirts.

Boutique: A freestanding store or shop within a larger store, featuring specialized merchandise selected for a special-interest customer, presented in an attractive unified manner. Boutiques often carry one-of-a-kind or few-of-a-kind merchandise.

Boutique merchandising: A form of store organization in which related merchandise from a number of departments is brought together in one shop to meet the needs of a specific customer.

Branch store: Retail units owned and operated by a parent store and often located in the suburbs or in metropolitan area shopping centers. An extension of a parent or flagship store, operating under the same name and ownership.

Brand: The name, trademark, or symbol that identifies the products of a specific manufacturer or distributor and differentiates the products from those of competitors.

Bridge: A fashion merchandise category priced between better and designer, offering a designer look at a more affordable price.

Bridge jewelry: A classification of merchandise that falls between costume jewelry and fine jewelry in terms of price.

Broad and shallow assortment: An assortment of merchandise with many styles but with limited sizes and colors carried in each style.

Brown goods: Radios, television sets, and other consumer electronic products.

Busheling: The tailoring and altering of men's garments after purchase and fitting.

Buyer: A line merchandising executive responsible for selecting and purchasing merchandise and for selling it at a profit.

Buying motives: The reasons people buy what they buy.

Buying plan: A description of the types and quantities of merchandise a buyer plans to purchase over a period of time. The plan tells the buyer what, where, and how much to buy.

CAD/CAM: Computer aided design/computer aided manufacturing.

Case goods: Term used in the furniture industry for pieces of furniture used for storage; usually made of wood.

Cash discount: A reduction in purchase price allowed by a vendor for payment before the due date of the bill. It is generally expressed as a percentage of the billed price. For example, a cash discount of 8/10 net 30 indicates an 8 percent price reduction given for payment within the first 10 days from the date of the invoice with a total of 30 days before the bill is overdue.

Catalog retailing: A form of selling in which the retailer provides the consumer with a merchandise catalog containing merchandise illustrations and descriptions and the consumer orders merchandise by mail, telephone, or in person at a facility maintained by the store for that purpose.

Category killers: Stores that have seized market shares from both department stores and specialty retailers by using one of two approaches: either carrying heavy inventories of one merchandise category, or by organizing their merchandise into clearly recognizable lifestyle groups.

Caution fee: French term for the admission or entrance fee charged to trade customers by haute couture houses. Often stated as a minimum number of garments.

Central buyer: A buyer responsible for the selection and purchase of merchandise for a group of similar departments or merchandise classifications in chain stores.

Central buying: The concentration of the authority and responsibility for merchandise selection for a chain of stores in the hands of the headquarters staff rather than in individual store units.

Chain store: A group of stores, usually twelve or more, commonly owned, each handling somewhat similar goods, which are merchandised and controlled from a central headquarters office.

Chambre Syndicale de la Couture Parisienne: The French trade association that represents the haute couture houses of Paris.

Cherry picking: The selection by the buyer from a vendor's line of only a few items that represent the best of the line.

Classic merchandise: Styles that have remained popular for an extended period of time; often considered fashion basics or investment purchases.

Classification: The breaking down of merchandise into categories called classes or groups of items similar in nature or in end-use. Classes are developed in direct response to the needs expressed by customers. They are fundamental merchandising units that change little from year to year even though the actual merchandise within each classification is in a constant state of change. Classifications provide a basic statistical structure to facilitate merchandise control.

Closed shop: An establishment where, by agreement, the employer hires only union members.

Collection: A group of garments shown by a designer to open a season.

Commissionaire: An independent foreign buying office that usually charges a commission for its services.

Community shopping center: A medium-size shopping center of 100,000 to 300,000 square feet selling both convenience and shopping goods. Generally consists of a variety or junior department store as an anchor tenant, smaller branch stores, and specialty stores. Trading area is usually limited to the community in which the center is located.

Confined style: A style that a vendor agrees to sell to only one store in a given trading area. *See* Exclusivity.

Conglomerate: A company consisting of a number of subsidiary divisions in a variety of unrelated industries.

Consignment buying: An agreement under which merchandise is shipped by a producer to a retailer with the understanding that the producer retains title to the goods until they are sold by the retailer. Unsold merchandise may be returned to the vendor after a specified time has elapsed.

Consumer advisory panel: Group of people brought together by retailers or manufacturers to secure opinion of different groups of consumers. Examples are boards of career women or a teen board.

Contemporary styling: An apparel classification distinguished by sophisticated, updated, and fashion-conscious styles.

Contracting system: Practice whereby outside shops are used to perform various tasks in the production process.

Contractor: One who operates an outside shop. *See* Apparel contractor.

Control division: A functional division of a retail store responsible for maintaining accounting records, credit management, inventory management, financial analysis, and merchandise budgeting; headed by the controller or treasurer.

Controller: An executive whose primary responsibilities include all of a company's fiscal and accounting operations; also spelled comptroller.

Convenience goods: Those items the customer purchases in small quantities, with a minimum of shopping and at the most accessible retail outlet; include daily necessities such as food, toiletries, and small hardware items.

Conventional department store: Traditional form of department store that emphasizes fashion and service; exemplified by such stores as Macy's, Marshall Field, and the May Company.

Converter: In the textile industry, a firm or merchant who purchases cloth in the greige from mills, contracts to have it finished, and sells the finished goods.

Cooperative advertising: Sharing of advertising costs by two or more parties such as the retailer and the manufacturer.

Cooperative buying office: *See* Associated buying office.

Corporate buying office: A resident buying office owned and operated by a department store ownership group or by a chain store organization; also known as syndicate buying offices.

Cosmetic, Toiletry, and Fragrance Association (CTFA): Trade association whose members are manufacturers and distributors of finished cosmetics, fragrances, and toilet preparations.

Cosmetics: Products designed to be applied to the face, skin, or hair for improving the user's appearance.

Cost price: The price at which goods are billed to a store, exclusive of any cash discounts that may apply to the purchase.

Costume jewelry: Jewelry made from nonprecious and relatively inexpensive materials; also called fashion jewelry.

Coty American Fashion Critics Award: Award founded in 1942 by the cosmetics and fragrance company, Coty, to encourage American fashion designers; discontinued in 1985.

Counterfeit goods: Unauthorized copies of products.

Couture: French term for sewing or needlework; now used to mean the top end of the fashion spectrum.

Couture house: An apparel firm headed by a designer who creates original designs.

Couturier (male) or Couturiere (female): French term for designers who create original designs that are presented in a collection each season primarily aimed at individual private customers.

Croquis: Fashion sketches.

CTFA: *See* Cosmetic, Toiletry, and Fragrance Association.

Custom made: Apparel made to the order of individual customers; cut and fitted to each customer's individual measurements.

Customs broker: A firm or individual who seeks permission from the U.S. government to bring goods involved in offshore production back into the country.

Dating: The time period during which discounts may be taken by the retailer, and the date on which the invoice becomes due.

Daywear: *See* Lingerie.

Demographics: Vital statistics of a population, including age, sex, marital status, family size, birth and death rates, location, income, occupation, race, education.

Department: A major subdivision in a store, either selling or nonselling, having a specialized function.

Department store: A large-scale retailing institution that sells a wide variety of goods, including home furnishings, household linens and dry goods, and apparel and accessories for the whole family. The department store takes its name from the units in which related kinds of merchandise are grouped for purposes of promotion, service, and control. Different kinds of department stores include conventional department stores, departmentalized specialty stores, chain department stores, and discount department stores.

Department store ownership group: A retailing organization in which the member stores (often once independent department stores) are centrally owned and controlled in terms of broad policymaking but are operated and merchandised autonomously. The individual stores often retain their own names, and the general public is seldom aware of their common ownership.

Design: A specific version or variation of a style. The arrangement of the visual elements of an object, including such considerations as color, texture, detail, and form.

Designer merchandise: Products actually created by a designer or with the approval of the designer whose name appears on the product.

Destination retailer: A store that pulls customers to its location for the purpose of shopping at that store.

Details: The individual elements that give a silhouette its form or shape.

Direct mail: An advertising medium that includes catalogs, mailers, and bill enclosures mailed to customers in an effort to sell merchandise.

Direct marketing: A term that embraces direct mail, mail order, and direct response; a process by which a message is conveyed directly to the customer and is designed to elicit a response.

Direct selling: The process whereby the firm responsible for production sells to the user, ultimate consumer, or retailer without intervening middlemen. At the consumer level direct selling includes the door-to-door approach or the in-home party plan.

Discount department store: A retail establishment that operates on low margins to offer merchandise at prices below the recognized market level. Discount stores emphasize self-service and are typically volume-oriented.

Discount merchandising: Retailing at less than manufacturer's list price with few customer services provided.

Display: The impersonal, visual presentation of merchandise or ideas. Types of display include window, facade, interior, and remote.

Diverted goods: Genuine trademarked products that are made abroad by legitimate manufacturers but imported into the United States and sold by unauthorized distributors; also called gray market goods.

Divisional merchandise manager (DMM): Executive responsible for operating a merchandising division who supervises a group of buyers in related departments.

Dollar merchandise plan: See Merchandise plan.

Domestic market: When referring to origin of goods, domestic means manufactured in one's own country as opposed to foreign made.

Domestics: Soft goods for the home including sheets, pillows, towels, blankets, bedspreads, and other textile products.

Doors: A term used in the cosmetics industry referring to the number of stores in which the company's product is offered for sale. The number of doors is the number of retail outlets.

Downsizing: Trend among retailers to reduce the size of stores.

Dry goods: Merchandise made from textile fabrics, including apparel, piece goods, towels, sheets, etc.; also called soft goods.

Dual distribution: Where a business organization uses two channels for the distribution of a product. A producer may combine the manufacturing and retailing segments of an industry by owning some or all of the retail outlets that sell the product. Common in menswear and in the shoe industry.

Duty: Tax or tariff paid on imported goods.

Editorial credit: The mention in a magazine or newspaper of a store name as a retail source for merchandise that is being editorially featured by the publication.

Electronic retailing: A form of in-home shopping by use of an electronic device such as computer or interactive cable television. *See* Videotex and Teletext.

Emotional buying motives: Reasons consumers buy based on feelings.

Entrepreneur: An individual who organizes, launches, and directs a new business venture and assumes the financial risks and uncertainties of the undertaking.

Entrepreneurial buyer: Retail buyer who is also the owner of a small store.

E.O.M. dating: In the dating of invoices, an agreement that cash discount and net credit periods begin at the end of the month. Invoices dated on the 25th of the month or later are generally treated as if dated on the first day of the next month.

Evolutionary fashions: Fashions that evolve gradually from one style to another rather than changing rapidly.

Exclusivity: Allowing a company sole use of a product within a given trading area.

Export merchant: Foreign wholesaler who specializes in exporting goods.

Export sales representative: A foreign source used by U.S. buyers for acquiring imported goods who represents selected manufacturers but does not maintain a wholesale inventory.

Exporting: Selling goods and sometimes services to other countries.

Extra dating: In the dating of invoices, an agreement that allows the purchaser a specified number of days before the ordinary dating of the bill begins.

Fabrications: Textile fabrics or other materials from which fashion products are constructed.

Facade display: Display on the store building or street; also called exterior display.

Factor: A financial institution that facilitates the flow of money between buyers and sellers by buying accounts receivable from sellers such as manufacturers and wholesalers. The factor assumes the risks and responsibilities of collection and charges a fee for this service.

Factoring: The selling of a retailer's accounts receivable to another party or factor.

Factory outlet: Manufacturer-owned store that sells company products at reduced prices.

Fad: A short-lived fashion.

Fashion: A style that is accepted and followed by the majority of a group at any particular time. A style becomes a fashion once it is accepted by the majority of a group.

Fashion accessories: Articles that complete or enhance a total look.

Fashion consultant: A person or firm that provides professional fashion advice or services.

Fashion coordination: Monitoring and analyzing fashion trends to ensure that merchandise sold in various apparel departments of a retail store is harmonious with regard to style, quality, and appeal.

Fashion cycle: A theory explaining the rise in popularity, acceptance, peak, and finally decline and disappearance of new styles.

Fashion director: The individual responsible for researching fashion trends, developing plans for the next season, and communicating this information to others within the organization.

Fashion forecasting: The prediction of future trends in fashion regarding color, fabric, styles, and other important elements.

Fashion goods: Distinctive merchandise possessing considerable current customer appeal.

The Fashion Group: A professional organization whose members are women executives in fashion and allied fields.

Fashion image: The impression people have of a company's fashion expertise and leadership. It is a store's fashion personality that tells the public how well the store knows fashion.

Fashion influential: An individual whose advice is sought by others regarding styles and trends and whose adoption of a new style promotes its acceptance by a peer group.

Fashion innovator: A person who assumes the leadership in accepting and adopting new styles.

Fashion look: The total accessorized appearance of a costume.

Fashion merchandising: The buying, selling, and promoting of fashion goods to target customers for the ultimate purpose of making a profit.

Fashion opening: Showing of new collections by apparel producers and designers at the beginning of a season.

Fashion press: Reporters of fashion news for print and broadcast media.

Fashion season: A selling period.

Fashion sense: An ability to detect what will capture the public's esthetic attention and develop into a respectable seller.

Fashion trend: The direction in which fashion is moving.

Fibers: The fundamental units used in the production of yarns and fabrics.

Findings: Sewing or trade term for all the small functional items that complete a garment, such as buttons, hooks, bindings, zippers, linings.

Fine jewelry: Jewelry made of precious metals such as gold, silver, or platinum; often set with precious or semiprecious stones.

Fixtures: Tables, counters, racks, furniture, or other items used in a store or showroom to stock and display merchandise.

Flagship store: The main store of a large retailing firm having several branches. The flagship store is often the original downtown store, which also houses the executive, merchandising, and promotional personnel responsible for the centralized operation of the firm.

Flatgoods: Another term for small leather goods.

FOB point: A term used in shipping agreements meaning that the buyer of goods pays the freight charges from the FOB point, which is the point of origin. Title to the merchandise passes to the buyer at the FOB point.

Focus group: A representative group of consumers brought together to share their views about a store and its merchandise or to discuss a manufacturer's products. Focus groups are led in discussion by a trained leader.

FOR results: Refers to Financial and Operating Results of Department and Specialty Stores, an annual statistical study published by the National Retail Merchants Association based on the financial statements and operating results submitted by participating store members; includes tables of performance used for purpose of comparison.

Ford: A fashion item that sells in great quantities and is widely copied at many price levels.

Foundation garments: A category of intimate apparel worn by women, including bras, girdles, corsets, garter belts, and body shapers.

Fragrances: Products that are applied to the body for the purpose of adding a pleasant scent, including such products as toilet water, cologne, perfume, and scented bath products.

Franchise: A contractual agreement between a wholesaler, manufacturer, or service organization (franchisor) and an independent retailer (franchisee) who buys the right to use the franchisor's products or service for a stipulated fee. In return, the franchisor provides its name, product line, services, and marketing and management expertise in exchange for an initial payment and often a share of the profits. The franchisee agrees to follow the guidelines and restrictions established by the franchisor.

Franchise distribution: A system of distribution in which manufacturers or their designated exclusive agents sell directly to retailers. No middleman is involved with franchise distribution.

Free trade: Allowing goods to flow freely among countries without the restraint of protectionism.

Freelancing: Working independently on an individual job or on a contractual basis for several clients.

Freight forwarding agent: A foreign agent who assists with handling shipping details in offshore production.

Full-line store: A retailer that carries all of the merchandise expected within a type of store.

Gallery programs: A merchandising program for furniture in which stores have exclusive displays of a particular company's line of furniture.

Garment center or district: The area to the east and west of Seventh Avenue in Manhattan running approximately from 30th to 40th Streets where much of the women's ready-to-wear industry is located; also referred to as Seventh Avenue.

GATT: *See* General Agreement on Tariffs and Trade.

General Agreement on Tariffs and Trade (GATT): International advisory organization, headquartered in Geneva, organized to reduce tariffs and other barriers to trade. GATT consults and negotiates on specific trade problems affecting individual commodities or member countries.

General merchandise manager (GMM): The merchandising executive responsible for total store merchandising operation. Supervises the divisional merchandise managers and interprets and executes the merchandising policies of the store. Acts as a liaison executive between the merchandise division and all other major store divisions and participates in major policymaking decisions.

General Merchandise Store: A store ranging in size from the rural general store to the large urban department store carrying a wide range of merchandise lines, often including food, apparel, hardware, furniture, and many other products, including department stores, mass merchandisers, variety stores, and general stores.

GMM: *See* General merchandise manager.

Grading: The process by which goods are compared in terms of quality, size, or some other factor. Standards may be set by governmental agencies, by the industry, or by an independent testing bureau. Also, process of sizing patterns up and down from the sample size.

Gray goods: Unfinished fabrics; also spelled greige goods.

Gray market goods: *See* Diverted goods.

The Great Revolt: Strike of 60,000 cloak makers in 1910, which ended in settlement known as the Protocol of Peace.

Gross margin: The amount of profit before selling expenses and other operating expenses have been deducted.

Group buying: A form of buying in which a number of noncompeting stores consolidate orders for goods in order to obtain a lower price through volume purchasing or to qualify for a minimum order size.

Haute couture: French term for high fashion. Actually translates as "fine sewing," but refers to firms whose designers create collections of original designs that are then duplicated for individual customers on a made-to-order basis.

Head of stock: The person who is responsible to the department manager or buyer and is charged with keeping stock on the selling floor in good order, maintaining merchandise in reserve, and monitoring inventory levels.

Hides: Animal skins that weigh more than twenty-five pounds when shipped to a tannery.

High fashion: Merchandise designed for the small percentage of consumers who want to be fashion leaders and are first to accept fashion change. Characterized by innovative and often high-priced designs.

Home accessories: Decorative items that complete the look of a residential interior, including lamps, pictures, tabletop merchandise, and domestics.

Homework system: Where production is performed at home rather than in a factory environment.

Horizontal integration: Merging with or purchasing other firms that produce and market the same type or similar types of merchandise, such as the merger of two fabric producers or one retail store with another store or store ownership group.

House brand: *See* Private label.

Hypermarket: A retail establishment that brings food and general merchandise together in a warehouse atmosphere. These stores originated in Europe and combine elements of the traditional discount operation with those of the supermarket.

ICSC: *See* International Council of Shopping Centers.

International Council of Shopping Centers (ICSC): Organization representing owners and developers of shopping centers that conducts research and gathers data on all aspects of the shopping center industry and compiles statistics. Sponsors courses on the industry.

ILGWU: *See* International Ladies Garment Workers Union.

Import commission house: Wholesale importer who represents foreign manufacturers and collects a commission from both the buyer and the manufacturer.

Import goods: Merchandise manufactured in one country and offered for sale in another.

Import merchant: Wholesale importer who offers a single classification or category of goods and sometimes carries domestic as well as foreign-produced goods.

Import quota allocations: Limits set by the government on the number of units of specific items that may be shipped from a particular exporting country over a period of time.

Import wholesaler: A middleman who purchases foreign merchandise and offers it to retailers. Three types of wholesale importers sell foreign-made goods in the domestic market—import merchants, resident sales agents, and import commission houses.

Impulse merchandise: Items that have immediate appeal to the customer who purchases them with little planning and consideration.

Independent store: A retail outlet owned and operated by an individual, family, partnership, or a local store that may be a publicly owned corporation not part of a larger chain or ownership group.

Initial markup: The difference between the cost price of merchandise and its first retail price.

Inside shops: Factories owned and operated by manufacturers who perform all the operations required to produce finished goods.

Institutional advertising: Advertising designed to sell the image and reputation of a firm rather than selling specific items of merchandise. Seeks to build a steady patronage of customers rather than seeking immediate merchandise sales.

Interior display: The presentation of merchandise within the store in such a way that the customer is encouraged to try the product.

International Ladies Garment Workers Union (ILGWU): Labor union for workers employed in the manufacture of women's and children's apparel.

Intimate apparel: Women's apparel in three categries: (1) foundations, which include bras, girdles, corsets, (2) lingerie, which includes daywear and sleepwear, and (3) loungewear, which includes robes, housecoats, and casual at-home wear.

Invoice: A bill or statement enclosed with a shipment of merchandise or mailed later by the seller.

Irregular: An item of merchandise with an imperfection that will not damage the serviceability of the goods. An irregular is closer to being perfect than is a second. *See also* Second.

Item merchandising: The planning involved in selling those specific articles of merchandise that, as best sellers, account for a significant portion of sales.

Jewelry: Articles of personal adornment made of precious, semiprecious, or nonprecious materials; includes items such as necklaces, rings, earrings, pins, chains, and bracelets. *See also* Costume jewelry and Fine jewelry.

Job lot: A broken lot, unbalanced assortment, or discontinued merchandise reduced in price for quick sale by the vendor.

Jobber: A firm or middleman who buys from manufacturers and sells to retailers. *See also* Apparel jobber.

Junior department store: Smaller than a conventional department store; offers a relatively wide variety of merchandise, including family apparel, housewares, gifts, and home textiles, in a departmentalized form of organization. Features moderate prices and does not carry major appliances and furniture.

Key resource: A vendor whose past dealings with the retailer have been excellent and from whom the retailer has consistently bought a substantial portion of its merchandise.

Keystone markup: Retail price is determined by doubling the cost price.

Keystoning: The practice of doubling the cost to determine the retail price; a common practice with fashion apparel.

Kiosk: An open sales pavilion often located in the open area of a shopping mall.

Kips: Animal skins weighing from fifteen to twenty-five pounds when shipped to a tannery.

Knock-off: A copy of another manufacturer's design, usually at a lower cost.

Landed cost: The total cost of imported merchandise, including loading, transporting, and unloading at destination.

Last: A form in the shape of a boot over which shoes are made.

LBO: *See* Leveraged buyout.

Leased department: A department within a store operated by an outside organization. Generally the store supplies the space and essential services in return for a fee or a percentage of the leased department's sales. Typical leased departments are shoes, fine jewelry, restaurants, beauty salon, and various repair services.

Leveraged buyout (LBO): The purchase of a public company's stock by a group of investors who borrow money from an investment firm using the company's assets as collateral.

Licensee: An individual or firm to whom a license is granted.

Licensing: An arrangement whereby firms are given permission to produce and market merchandise in the name of a licensor, who is paid a percentage of sales for permitting the use of his or her name or trademark.

Lifestyle: A distinctive mode of living centered around certain activities, interests, opinions, and demographic characteristics, especially as they distinguish one group from another.

Lifestyle merchandising: A form of merchandising in which the store continuously alters the merchandise mix to what the customer wants and will buy. Lifestyle merchandising recognizes that customers' lifestyles, demographics, value systems, and buying habits all play a role in determining their buying behavior.

Line: A group of new designs offered by a manufacturer usually at the beginning of a season. The term is also used to refer to a particular brand or class of goods offered by a manufacturer.

Line representative: Salespeople in retail stores who represent a particular cosmetic product line. They may receive their salaries from the cosmetic company directly and often are paid a commission on all cosmetics sold in the line they represent.

Line-for-line copy: An exact copy of an original design mass produced in standard sizes.

Lingerie: A category of women's intimate apparel that includes two general divisions of merchandise: daywear and sleepwear. Daywear includes slips, petticoats, camisoles, and panties. Sleepwear includes nightgowns, pajamas, and night shirts.

Longuette: Term coined by *Women's Wear Daily* to describe the radically longer lengths on coats, skirts, and dresses that reached from below-the-knee to ankle-length that were an abrupt change from the miniskirts of the late 1960s.

Loungewear: A category of women's intimate apparel that includes robes, housecoats, negligees, bed jackets, and other casual apparel for at-home entertaining.

Mail-order house: A nonstore retailing organization that generates business through catalogs. Customers select goods from the company's catalog by mailing or telephoning in their orders, which are then filled by mail or other delivery service.

Maintained markup: The difference between net sales and the cost of goods sold that represents the actual markup achieved for a selling period.

Man-made fiber: According to the Textile Fiber Products Identification Act: "any fiber derived by a process of manufacture from any substance which at any point in the manufacturing process, is not a fiber"; also called manufactured fiber.

Mannequin: The French term for a human model who wears and models clothing in a fashion show. In American usage a mannequin is a lifelike but nonhuman figure used to display clothing.

Mantilla: A short cape; one of the early garments mass produced for women.

Manufacturer's agent: *See* Sales representative.

Maquiladoras: Twin plants located on each side of the U.S.-Mexican border for the purpose of facilitating production of goods under Section 807. *See also* Section 807.

Markdown: A reduction from original or previous retail price.

Market: A place where buyers and sellers meet for the purpose of presenting, viewing, and ordering merchandise.

Market center: A geographical location where fashion merchandise is created, produced, and sold.

Market representative: An employee of a resident buying office who represents client stores in the marketplace. The market representative is often a specialist buying in a particular segment of the market; also called a resident buyer.

Market segmentation: The separation of the total consumer market into smaller groups or target markets. *See* Niche retailing.

Market trip: The buyer's visit to a wholesale market to view new lines of merchandise and write orders for future delivery of goods to the store.

Market week: Scheduled period when producers and their sales representatives present new lines for the upcoming season to retail buyers.

Marketing: Those activities that facilitate the exchange of goods and services as they move from producer to ultimate consumer. Marketing activities include product development, pricing, promotion, and distribution and are carried out with the objective of making a profit.

Markup: The difference between cost price of merchandise and its retail price. May be expressed in dollars or as a percentage based on either cost price or retail price. In retailing markup is usually based on the retail price of the goods.

Mart: A building or group of buildings designed to hold permanent and temporary showrooms for producers and their sales representatives.

Mass distribution: A system of product distribution in which goods are distributed from manufacturer to retailer by a middleman such as a wholesaler or rack jobber. Used in the cosmetics industry.

Mass fashion: Products designed to appeal to the majority of fashion consumers. These goods are mass produced in high volume and are widely distributed at popular to moderate prices; also called volume fashion.

Mass merchandiser: A large-scale retail establishment merchandising staple goods at prices lower than those commonly found in traditional department and specialty stores.

Mass merchandising: Retailing on a large scale of staple goods at prices lower than those commonly found in department and specialty stores.

Mass production: Production of goods in quantity rather than one or a few at a time.

Mazur Plan: A plan for departmentalization in which activities in large stores are divided into four functional groups: (1) merchandising, (2) operations, (3) promotion, and (4) accounting. The plan was first proposed by Paul Mazur in his book *Principles of Organization Applied to Modern Retailing* (1927).

Memorandum buying: An arrangement between vendor and retailer in which the retailer takes title to the goods upon receipt; however, unsold goods may be returned to the vendor after a specified time period. Retailer may also have the right to pay for the goods as they are sold.

Men's clothing: Tailored suits, overcoats, topcoats, sport coats, and separate trousers for men.

Men's furnishings: In menswear, ties, shirts, socks, underwear, sleepwear, robes, and accessories.

Merchandise broker: A type of independent buying office that receives its compensation from manufacturers as a percentage of orders placed with retailers. Used by small retailers and provides few services other than the purchasing of goods. Also called a commission buying office.

Merchandise plan: The dollar control budget for a store or department for a six-month period. The merchandise plan looks to the future, projecting the amount of merchandise needed to achieve planned sales. Also called the dollar merchandise plan or the six-month plan.

Merchandise selection factor: Any quality inherent in merchandise that helps determine the customer's decision to purchase.

Merchandising: The American Marketing Association's definition: "The planning involved in marketing the right merchandise at the right place at the right time in the right quantities at the right price." Merchandising is the buying and selling of goods to target markets for the purpose of making a profit.

Merchant: A person who buys and resells merchandise.

Merger: Combining of two or more organizations or businesses.

MFA: *See* Multifiber Textile Arrangement.

Middleman: An individual or firm acting as a marketing intermediary between producer or manufacturer and the ultimate consumer. The middleman may or may not take title to the goods handled and may operate as either a wholesaler or retailer.

Midi: Term coined in 1967 by *Women's Wear Daily* to describe mid-calf-length garments.

Millinery: Women's hats.

Misses: Size range in women's apparel in even numbers from 4 or 6 through 16 or 18; also called missy.

Model stock plan: A method for developing the assortment plan used in planning fashion merchandise. The model stock plan is less specific than the basic stock plan and lists information such as classification, price, color, size.

Mom-and-pop store: A small independent store often operated by a husband and wife.

MOR results: Refers to Merchandising and Operating Results, an annual statistical study published by the National Retail Merchants Association containing detailed information on the performance of the retail industry. Data is provided by NRMA member stores and is presented by store type and size, and by department and merchandise classification. Individual store results are not identified, only averages for all stores in a particular store category.

Multifiber Textile Arrangement (MFA): An international trade agreement governing trade in textiles and apparel. Its purpose is to allow foreign products to be exported to the United States and other developed countries at a growth rate that does not disrupt domestic industries.

NAB: *See* Newspaper Advertising Bureau.

National Retail Merchants Association (NRMA): A trade association composed of department, chain, and mass merchandise and specialty stores retailing men's, women's, and children's apparel and home furnishings.

Needle trades: Synonym for apparel industry.

Neighborhood shopping center: A planned shopping area including a line of stores held together by a covered walkway that runs along the front of the stores. The major tenant is often a single supermarket or a variety store. Other stores in the center tend to be convenience or service stores. Such centers serve the immediate needs of the surrounding neighborhood. Also called a strip shopping center.

Newspaper Advertising Bureau (NAB): A trade association that promotes the advantages of newspapers as an advertising medium.

Niche retailing: Following a specialty store point of view in which departments or stores appeal to a specific set of fashion tastes. Retailers identify a demographic, lifestyle, or shopping trend and design stores and departments to sell to the desired target customer. With niche retailing, stores are seeking a narrower customer base or looking for their particular "niche" in the marketplace. *See also* Market segmentation.

Nonstore retailing: A form of retailing in which a traditional store building is not involved.

Retail sales are made through such means as direct mail, door-to-door sales, vending machines, two-way television, and interactive computers.

NRMA: *See* National Retail Merchants Association.

Off-price retailing: The selling of brand and designer-name merchandise at lower than usual retail prices. Off-price retailers buy merchandise at cut-rate prices and pass the savings on to their customers.

Offshore production: Production of goods by a domestic manufacturer outside of the United States.

One price policy: A policy in which retail prices are fixed and uniform for all customers and are not subject to bargaining or negotiation.

Open order: An order placed with a resident buyer without any restrictions as to price, vendor, or delivery. The resident buyer has the authority to seek out the merchandise and negotiate the best possible terms for the client store.

Open-to-buy (OTB): The amount of merchandise in terms of dollars or units that a buyer is permitted to order for a specified period of time.

Openings: Fashion showings of new collections or merchandise lines by apparel producers at the beginning of a season.

Operating division: A functional division of a retail store responsible for such matters as merchandise receiving, store maintenance and housekeeping, security, and certain special services such as restaurants.

Opportunistic buy: An unexpected merchandise buy that offers good profit potential.

OTB: *See* Open-to-buy.

Outside shop: A manufacturing concern that does the sewing for other apparel producers; also called a contractor.

Outsizes: Sizes larger than the usual standard.

Over-the-counter selling: The sale of selected stock kept in display cases, drawers, or on shelves. A salesperson is needed to show the stock to customers and to complete a sale.

Overbought: A situation in which a store buyer has committed for purchases beyond the planned purchase allotment for the period.

Paper: A buyer's completed order form.

Patronage motive: The reason, rational or emotional, why a customer chooses to shop at one store rather than another.

Pelt: Skin of a fur-bearing animal.

Personal selling: Face-to-face contact between the seller and the customer.

Personal shopper: An employee or a retail store whose job is to select merchandise for shoppers in response to mail or phone requests as well as to accompany shoppers while in the store to help them select merchandise.

Personnel division: A retail store functional division responsible for hiring and training employees, maintenance of benefit plans, general record keeping, and evaluation of employees.

Piecework: System where production workers are paid a set rate for each piece completed.

Point-of-purchase selling aids: Promotional selling aids provided by the vendor for use at the point of sale or alongside displays of merchandise.

Policy: A clearly defined course of action or method of doing business that helps to define procedures and objectives for a company's employees and promotes consistency.

PR: *See* Public relations.

Press release: Publicity in the form of a written communication of a newsworthy story or information, distributed to the communications media. A press release is typewritten ready for an editor, complete in details, facts, and in a format that helps obtain acceptance in order to get the story into the media; also called a news release.

Prestige line: An item of merchandise at the top of the line and expensive in price.

Prêt-à-porter: French ready-to-wear apparel.

Preticketing: The practice of the vendor attaching price tags and labels to merchandise according to the retailer's specifications.

Primary markets: Producers of fibers, textiles, leather, and furs.

Prior stock: Merchandise that has been in inventory for the duration of the previous season. Considered to be old merchandise.

Private buying office: A store-owned resident buying office maintained in a market center by a large retail store. The office services only one retail company.

Private label: Merchandise that bears a retailer's own name brand rather than that of a designer or manufacturer; also known as house brand, private brand, store brand, or in-house label.

Product developer: An individual employed by retailers to create private-label merchandise for their exclusive use.

Production package: An agreement made between an American manufacturer and a production agent located in the country where merchandise is to be produced. The package agreement allows the foreign manufacturing plant to perform all the steps involved in production.

Profit: Total revenue less all costs and expenses.

Promotion buying: Buying goods at special prices for the purpose of offering reduced prices to the store's customers.

Promotional advertising: Advertising designed to influence the sale of specific products or services and to bring customers into the store immediately.

Prophetic styles: Interesting new styles that are still in the introductory phase of their fashion cycles.

Protection: The department responsible for protecting the store against losses from pilferage, shoplifting, robbery, and other crimes against persons and property; also called security.

Protectionism: Any attempt to protect American production by reducing, limiting, or excluding foreign goods.

Protocol of Peace: Settlement that ended the Great Revolt of cloakmakers in 1910. Granted workers a fifty-hour week, double pay for overtime, and higher wages. Also established a closed shop and a means for collective bargaining.

Psychographic segmentation: The division of a market into subgroups based on subjective or psychological factors such as lifestyle, attitude, interest, and values.

Public relations (PR): The total public image of an organization. PR programs are designed to create favorable public opinion about a company or its products.

Publicity: A nonpaid verbal or written message in the public information media about a company's merchandise, activities, or services.

Publicly owned: A corporation whose shares are available for sale by one of the major stock exchanges to any person who chooses to purchase them.

Push money: Bonus money paid by a vendor or a retailer to salespeople for selling specially designated merchandise.

Quality control or Quality assurance: Assuring that the merchandise corresponds to the quality requirements set by the company.

Quantity discounts: A reduction in price offered by the seller for purchases of larger amounts of goods.

Quick response (QR): An apparel industry strategy for fighting imports that uses new technology to reduce the time needed to produce goods and distribute them to retail stores.

Rack jobber: A wholesaler who provides, sets up, and maintains the merchandise as it is displayed in the store.

Rational buying motives: Factors explaining a consumer's decision to buy merchandise, based on logic, reason, and careful thought.

Ready-to-wear (RTW): Apparel mass produced in factories to standard size measurements.

Recurring fashions: Styles that enjoy popularity, decline in acceptance, and once again gain consumer acceptance.

Regional market or mart: Central location where manufacturers, importers, and other resources display their merchandise for store buyers from within that general area of the country, for example, the Chicago Apparel Mart, the Chicago Merchandise Mart, the Atlanta Apparel Mart.

Regional shopping center: The largest type of shopping center, anchored by one or more full-line department stores and complemented by fifty to one hundred or more smaller retail stores. Draws customers from a wide geographical area and requires 100,000 or more customers to support it.

Regular dating: An agreement that a cash discount may be deducted if the bill is paid within the discount period. Otherwise the full payment is due at the end of the period indicated. Both the cash discount and the net credit periods are counted from the date of the invoice, which is usually the date of shipment.

Regular price-line buying: Merchandise that is bought from vendors at regular price.

Remote display: Merchandise displays located away from the store location such as in an airport, a hotel lobby, or a convention center.

Reorder: A store's request for additional merchandise from a vendor to replenish depleted stocks of fast-selling merchandise.

Repricing: Includes markdowns and price increases necessary when the replacement cost of merchandise increases and prices on merchandise already in the store must be increased to correspond with prices on new merchandise.

Resident buyer: A buyer who works for a resident buying office; also called a market representative.

Resident buying office: A service organization located in a major market center that provides market information and representation to noncompeting client stores. Buying offices are either independent (salaried/fee/paid office) or store-owned (private office, associated/cooperative office, and corporate/syndicate office).

Resident sales agent: Wholesale importer who represents a group of foreign manufacturers and may or may not carry stocks.

Resource: *See* Vendor.

Resource analysis: The continuous evaluation of vendors to determine those from whom the store should buy merchandise.

Retailing: The business of buying goods from a variety of resources and assembling these goods in convenient locations for resale to ultimate consumers. Includes all activities necessary to sell to the ultimate consumer.

Revolutionary fashions: Styles that are an abrupt change from the styles currently in fashion.

Returns to vendor (RTV): Goods shipped back to a supplier by a store.

Road buying: Purchasing of goods through traveling sales representatives.

R.O.G. dating: An invoice agreement specifying that the discount period allowed by the vendor to the retailer does not begin until the goods are actually received by the retailer.

RTV: *See* Returns to vendor.

RTW: *See* Ready-to-wear.

Rubber-banding: A return agreement for cosmetic products that allows the store to return the merchandise to the manufacturer if not sold within a specified period of time. The merchandise is replaced with current products.

Runner: An item that consistently sells through a season or a year at full price; also called a best seller.

Salaried, fee, or paid buying office: An independent resident buying office that is paid a fee on an annual contractual basis by the stores it represents in the market.

Sales promotion: Any activity that is used to influence the sale of merchandise, service, or ideas; includes advertising, special events, display, fashion shows, publicity, and personal selling.

Sales representative: A salesperson who represents a manufacturer or several manufacturers' lines and sells products often within a limited geographical area.

Salon: A room where a designer's collection is shown. In a retail store, an area devoted to expensive and sometimes exclusive merchandise.

Sample: The model or trial garment shown to the trade.

Secondary markets: Producers of finished consumer fashion products.

Second: Factory reject having defects that may affect wearability.

Section 807: Section of the Tariff Classification Act that allows an American apparel manufacturer to design and cut garments in the United States and ship the materials out of the country for sewing. The goods are then sent back for finishing and packaging.

Seventh Avenue: An expression used as a synonym for New York City's women's apparel industry. The street on or near which the showrooms of many of the city's garment manufacturers are located.

Shopping goods: Merchandise the consumer is willing to exert considerable effort to find in an attempt to compare price, quality, and style.

Silhouette: The outline or shape of a costume.

SKU: Stockkeeping unit. In inventory control and identification systems, the stockkeeping unit represents the smallest unit for which sales and stock records are kept.

Slop shop: Name given to the first men's ready-to-wear shops, which were known for carrying shoddy merchandise.

Small leather goods: Small leather items that are usually carried in a briefcase, a woman's handbag, or a man's pockets. Includes such items as wallets, billfolds, coin purses, and cases for cosmetics, credits cards, glasses, cigarettes, keys, and business cards. Also called flatgoods.

Soft goods: Merchandise made from textile fabrics; also called dry goods.

Sourcing: The process where a retailer, manufacturer, or jobber seeks a contractor to produce goods to specifications.

Special events: Activities held both inside and outside the store to increase customer traffic or to enhance the store's image. Special events include such activities as visits by celebrities, parades sponsored by the store, fashion shows, exhibits, and demonstrations.

Special order: An order placed by the retailer with a vendor for merchandise not regularly carried in stock.

Special purchase: Merchandise bought by a retailer at a lower than regular price.

Specialty store: A store that deals either in one category of merchandise or in limited categories.

Specification buying: Where buyers submit definite specifications to the manufacturer detailing how goods are to be made rather than shopping the market for goods already designed.

Staple stock: Merchandise that is always in demand and retailers always keep on hand.

Stock depth: The amount of merchandise kept on hand to meet projected sales.

Stock shortage: When the book inventory is greater than the actual physical inventory.

Stock turnover: The number of times the average inventory has been sold and replaced in a given period, usually a year. It is calculated by dividing net sales in dollars by average inventory at selling price in dollars. Also called stock turn.

Store ownership group: A retailing organization consisting of a group of stores that are centrally owned and controlled in terms of broad policymaking but are operated autonomously.

Style: A characteristic or distinctive way of doing things; also a type of product with distinctive characteristics that distinguish it from another type of the same product.

Style number: A number a manufacturer uses to identify an individual design. Retailers place orders by style number, which are also used for stock identification.

Style piracy: The act of using a design without the permission of the originator.

Stylist: An individual who advises concerning styles in clothes or home furnishings. A stylist organizes the look of a particular garment for show or photography by choosing and arranging such factors as accessories, backgrounds, and lighting.

Suggestion selling: A method of increasing a sale by suggesting related items to go with the customer's original purchase or suggesting a substitute item.

Sumptuary laws: Laws regulating extravagance in dress.

Sweatshop: A garment manufacturing plant that employs workers under unfair, unsanitary, and often dangerous conditions.

Sweetener: New items added to a manufacturer's line in between seasons.

Syndicate buying office: See Corporate buying office.

Synthetic fiber: Noncellulosic chemically made fiber; more often referred to as man-made synthesized fiber.

Tabletop merchandise: China, glassware, flatware, and textile products such as tablecloths and napkins.

Tanning: The process of transforming animal skins into leather.

Target customers or market: Those persons whom a company would most like to attract as customers and toward whom it directs its marketing strategy.

Tariff: A schedule of duties imposed by a government on imported or in some countries exported goods.

Taste level: The subjective level of individual preference, which includes a sense of quality, beauty, and appropriateness. The recognition of what is and is not attractive and appropriate.

Teletext: A form of electronic shopping that consists of a one-way, over-the-air broadcast service transmitted via cable television.

Terms of sale: The conditions governing a sale as set forth by the seller. Terms include amount of discount, payment period, date of delivery, point of transfer of title to the merchandise, allocation of transportation costs, and any other specific conditions of the sale.

Textile fabric: Cloth made from fibers by weaving, knitting, braiding, felting, crocheting, knotting, laminating, or bonding.

Texture: Refers to the tactile surface characteristics and appearance of a material; the look or feel of a fabric.

Tobé Associates: Fashion consultant firm founded by Tobé Collier Davis.

Toiletries: Products used in grooming oneself. Category of products produced by the cosmetics industry, which includes personal care items such as antiperspirants, toothpaste, shaving creams, shampoos, and hair care products.

Trade association: A nonprofit voluntary professional association of businesses having common interests. Provides a means for exchange of information and may attempt to form public opinion and influence the passage of legislation related to the field.

Trade deficit: When a country imports more goods than it exports, a trade deficit occurs.

Trade discount: A reduction in price offered to wholesalers, middlemen, and retailers by manufacturers to compensate them for the performance of some marketing function.

Trade publication: Newspapers or magazines published for professionals associated with a particular line or trade.

Trade show: Merchandise exhibitions staged periodically in various trading areas by groups of producers and their sales representatives for the purpose of selling to retailers. Enables buyers to view many lines of merchandise in one place and to gain an overview of what is available in the market.

Trademark: A word or symbol or combination of the two used by producers to distinguish their products from others. Exclusive right to use a trademark is granted by the federal government.

Trading area: The surrounding area from which most of a store's or shopping center's customers are drawn.

Trading up: Obtaining larger sales by (1) selling more than one of the same item, (2) selling a larger size of the same item, or (3) selling higher priced, usually better quality merchandise.

Traditional fashion: Styles that change little from year to year.

Traffic: The number of customers or prospective customers who either pass by or enter the store or department within the store.

Triangle Shirtwaist Fire: Fire that occurred in the Triangle Shirtwaist factory, New York City, in 1911, taking the lives of 146 young women. The tragedy rallied public support, which led to improved conditions in the garment industry.

Trickle-across theory: A theory explaining fashion adoption in which new styles are seen as gaining acceptance across socioeconomic strata at a number of levels simultaneously. Each level of society contains persons who act as influentials and innovators and transmit new styles laterally. Sometimes called the horizontal flow theory or the mass market theory.

Trickle-down theory: A theory explaining fashion adoption in which upper classes are the fashion innovators, with subordinate classes acting as followers or imitators. Styles are seen as trickling down the social strata.

Trickle-up theory: A theory explaining fashion adoption in which fashion adoption begins among young people or lower socioeconomic groups and then moves upward.

Trimmings: Items used to decorate merchandise. Examples include buttons, topstitching, lace edging, piping, appliqués, and embroidery.

Trunk show: When all or part of a producer's or designer's line is brought to a store or exhibition space and shown to the public. Customers may place orders for future shipment either through the store or directly to customer's home.

Turnover: *See* Stock turnover.

Twig store: A small branch store that carries a selection of its parent store's merchandise, generally targeting a specific customer.

Updated fashion: Styles that are made current by revising lines, colors, fabrics, details. The styles are new, but not so fashion-forward as avant-garde.

Upscaling: The changes made in a retailing organization leading toward upward movement in the store's level of fashion sophistication and price. The objective is to attract the upscale customer who is well educated, sophisticated in taste, and has a high disposable income.

Variety store: A store that stocks a wide range of merchandise classifications in a limited number of assortments and at relatively low prices. The original "five and ten" or "dime store."

Vendeuse: French term for saleswoman.

Vendor: A person or firm from whom a retailer buys goods; also called resource or supplier.

Vertical integration: Acquisition by a business organization of firms that are engaged in a variety of operations, marketing different types of merchandise.

Videotex: A form of interactive electronic shopping through cable television or personal computers. A two-way form of communication in which graphic and written material is sent via telephone or cable TV hookup from an originating source to a video screen. This permits the user to receive and transmit information.

Vignette: A display that uses props to suggest realism and to create an atmosphere; also called an environmental display.

Visual merchandising: Everything appealing to the senses that is done to, with, or for a product and its surroundings to encourage its sale. This includes display, store decor, store layout, and merchandise presentation.

Vitrine: A glass-enclosed display case, used to display small items or accessories.

Volume fashion: *See* Mass fashion.

Want slip: A form on which is recorded the items requested by shoppers that were out of stock or not carried by the store.

Warehouse club: A retail store that specializes in bulk sales of nationally branded merchandise at discount prices.

Wholesaler: A true wholesaler is a marketing middleman who buys merchandise from a producer and sells it to an industrial user or retailer.

Winner: An item that sells quickly but may not have a long period of acceptance.

Winnie: The original Coty Fashion Critics Award for women's wear design given from 1943 to 1985.

Women's Wear Daily: Newspaper trade publication covering the women's and children's fashion industries, published by Fairchild Publications.

Wrapper: Robelike dress worn by women at home during the nineteenth century, the forerunner of the housedress.

Yarn: A continuous thread formed by spinning or twisting fibers together.

Bibliography

Abend, Jules. "Widening the Gap." *Stores* (November 1985).

Adams, Muriel J. "Hot New Retail Formats." *Stores* (February 1988).

Anderson, Patricia M., and Leonard G. Rubin. *Marketing Communications*. Englewood Cliffs, N.J.: Prentice-Hall, 1986.

Anspach, Karlyne. *The Why of Fashion*. Ames: Iowa State University, 1967.

Arnold, Pauline, and Percival White. *Clothes and Cloth: America's Apparel Business*. New York: Holiday, 1961.

Ballard, Bettina. *In My Fashion*. New York: McKay, 1960.

Bannon, Lisa. "Bernard Arnault: New-Style Tycoon." *Women's Wear Daily* (July 22, 1988).

Barmash, Isadore. *More Than They Bargained For: The Rise and Fall of Korvettes*. New York: Chain Store Publishing, 1981.

————. "Strategies for Private Brand Growth." *Stores* (April 1986).

————. "The Warehouse Clubs." *Stores* (September 1985).

"Batus Aims at $4 Billion in Sales for 1985." *Women's Wear Daily* (April 18, 1984).

Beasley, Norman. *Main Street Merchant*. New York: McGraw-Hill, 1948.

Beaton, Cecil. *The Best of Beaton*. New York: Macmillan, 1968.

————. *The Glass of Fashion*. New York: Doubleday, 1954.

Bell, Judith A. *Silent Selling: The Complete Guide to Fashion Merchandise Presentation*. Cincinnati: ST Publications, 1988.

Bender, Marilyn. *The Beautiful People*. New York: Coward, McCann & Geoghegan, 1967.

Bennington, Richard R. *Furniture Marketing From Product Development to Distribution.* New York: Fairchild Publications, 1985.

"Bergdorf Shuts Custom Shop." *Women's Wear Daily* (May 13, 1969).

Berman, Barry, and Joel R. Evans. *Retail Management.* New York: Macmillan, 1983.

Binder, Pearl. *The Peacock's Tail.* London: George G. Harrap, 1958.

Birmingham, Nan Tillson. *Store.* New York: G.P. Putnam's, 1978.

Blackwell, Roger D. and W. Wayne Talarzyk. "Life-Style Retailing: Competitive Strategies for the 1980s." *Journal of Retailing,* 59 (Winter 1983).

Blake, Nelson Manfred. *A History of American Life and Thought.* New York: McGraw Hill, 1963.

Blythe, LeGette. *William Henry Belk: Merchant of the South.* Chapel Hill, North Carolina: The University of North Carolina Press, 1950.

Bogart, Anne. "How Lacroix Created His Own House." *Women's Wear Daily* (July 9, 1987).

Bohlinger, Maryanne Smith. *Merchandise Buying.* Dubuque, Iowa: William C. Brown, 1983.

Born, Pete. "Lauren NY Store: Million-dollar Baby." *Women's Wear Daily* (April 30, 1986).

———. "Lauren Store Tops $30 M in First Year." *Women's Wear Daily* (July 14, 1987).

———. "Limited Expects $10B in Volume by Early 1990s." *Women's Wear Daily* (May 24, 1988).

———. "Macy's Tops Post-LBO Projections." *Women's Wear Daily* (December 29, 1986).

———. "Overstoring is Cited As Top Problem." *Women's Wear Daily* (January 13, 1986).

———. "Private Label Makes Climb Up Price Scale." *Women's Wear Daily* (September 26, 1983).

Boyes, Kathleen. "Ralph Lauren Telling Stories." *Women's Wear Daily, Best of New York* (October 24, 1988).

Brady, Maxine. *Bloomingdale's.* New York: Harcourt, 1980.

Brumberg, Elaine. *Save Your Money, Save Your Face.* New York: Facts on File, 1986.

Burggraf, Helen. "Fur Business in 1986: Nearly $2 Billion and Purring Nicely." *Stores* (March 1987).

"Buying Offices: The New Retail Consultants." *Retail Week* (May 15, 1981).

Cahan, Linda, and Joseph Robinson. *A Practical Guide to Visual Merchandising.* New York: John Wiley, 1984.

Calasibetta, Charlotte. *Essential Terms of Fashion.* New York: Fairchild Publications, 1986.

———. *Fairchild's Dictionary of Fashion.* New York: Fairchild Publications, 1975.

Callison, Charlene G. "The Apparel Markets in Chicago and Dallas with Emphasis on Development." Ph.D. dissertation, Texas Woman's University, 1977.

Cash, R. Patrick, ed. *The Buyer's Manual.* New York: NRMA, 1979.

Chase, Edna Woolman, and Ilka Chase. *Always in Vogue.* London: Victor Gollancz, 1954.

Cobrin, Harry A. *The Men's Clothing Industry: Colonial Through Modern Times.* New York: Fairchild Publications, 1970.

Colborne, Robert. *Fundamentals of Merchandise Presentation.* Cincinnati: ST Publications, 1982.

Contini, Mila. *Fashion: From Ancient Egypt to the Present Day.* New York: Odyssey, 1965.

Cooper, Grace Rogers. *The Invention of the Sewing Machine.* Washington, D.C.: Smithsonian Institution Press, 1968.

Corinth, Kay. *Fashion Showmanship*. New York: John Wiley, 1970.

Crawford, M.D.C. *The Ways of Fashion*. New York: G. P. Putnam's, 1941.

Cumming, James C. *Making Fashion and Textile Publicity Work*. New York: Fairchild Publications, 1971.

Curry, Jill. "Catering to Women Who Work." *Stores* (October 1985).

Daria, Irene. "Rising CFDA Throws Shadow on Coty." *Women's Wear Daily* (January 22, 1985).

Daves, Jessica. *Ready-Made Miracle*. New York: G.P. Putnam's, 1967.

Davidson, William R., and Alice Rogers. "Changes and Challenges in Retailing." *Business Horizons* (February 1981).

Davis, Marian L. *Visual Design in Dress*. Englewood Cliffs, N.J.: Prentice-Hall, 1987.

deMarly, Diana. *The History of Haute Couture, 1850–1950*. London: B.T. Batsford, 1980.

dePaola, Helena, and Carol Stewart Mueller. *Marketing Today's Fashion*. 2nd ed. Englewood Cliffs, N.J.: Prentice-Hall, 1986.

"Department Stores: Threats and Opportunities," *Chain Store Age, General Merchandise Trends* (January 1986).

Diamond, Jay, and Gerald Pintel. *Retail Buying*. Englewood Cliffs, N.J.: Prentice-Hall, 1989.

A Dictionary of Textile Terms. New York: Dan River Mills.

Dior, Christian. *Dior by Dior*. London: Weidenfeld and Nicholson, 1957.

———. *Talking About Fashion*. New York: G.P. Putnam's, 1954.

"The Discount Lions are Stalking the Future." *Chain Store Age, General Merchandise Trends* (May 1986).

Donovan, Carrie. "The Swagger of Christian Lacroix." *New York Times Magazine* (September 6, 1987).

"Downtown St. Louis: Awake Again." *Women's Wear Daily* (September 30, 1985).

Dubinsky, David. *David Dubinsky: A Life with Labor*. New York: Simon and Schuster, 1977.

Duka, John. "Tradition and Change on Madison." *New York Times Magazine* (November 4, 1984).

Dunn, Si. "Fabulous Fortnight '84." *D Magazine* (October 1984).

Easterling, Cynthia R., and Marian H. Jernigan. "Careers in Fashion." *Forecast for Home Economics* (October 1985).

Easterling, Cynthia R., Ellen Flottman, and Marian H. Jernigan. *Merchandising Mathematics for Retailing*. Englewood Cliffs, N.J.: Prentice-Hall, 1984.

Edwards, Charles M., Jr., and Carl F. Lebowitz. *Retail Advertising and Sales Promotion*. 4th ed. Englewood Cliffs, N.J.: Prentice-Hall, 1981.

Ettorre, Barbara. "Buying Offices in N.Y.: A Matter of Change or Die." *Women's Wear Daily* (April 10, 1977).

Evans, Derro. "Camelot on Main Street." *Dallas* (October 1978).

Fairchild Fact File. *The Textiles/Apparel Industries*. New York: Fairchild Publications, 1987.

Fairchild, John. *The Fashionable Savages*. New York: Doubleday, 1965.

Fairchild's Financial Manual of Retail Stores. New York: Fairchild Publications, annual.

Fairchild's Market Directory of Women's and Children's Apparel. New York: Fairchild Publications, 1985, revised periodically.

Fairchild's Textile and Apparel Financial Directory. New York: Fairchild Publications, annual.

Fashion Group. *Your Future in Fashion Design*. New York: Richard Rosen, 1966.

"Fashion's New Regional Look." *Business Week* (November 6, 1978).

Feinberg, Samuel. *What Makes Shopping Centers Tick*. New York: Fairchild Publications, 1960.

"Finkelstein Puts Forth the Gospel of Private Label." *Women's Wear Daily* (March 23, 1988).

Finley, Ruth E. *The Lady of Godey's Sarah Josepha Hale*. Philadelphia: Lippincott, 1931.

Fishman, Arnold. "The Apparel Mail Order Marketplace." *Direct Marketing* (June 1986).

Fitzgibbons, Bernice. *Macy's Gimbel's and Me*. New York: Simon and Schuster, 1967.

Flugel, John C. *The Psychology of Clothes*. New York: International Universities Press, 1966.

"Focus: Economic Profile of the Apparel Industry." Arlington, VA.: American Apparel Manufacturers Association, 1987.

Forman, Ellen. "Campeau: More Private Label for Federated." *Women's Wear Daily* (April 7, 1988).

————. "Surge Seen for Electronic Shopping." *Women's Wear Daily* (May 21, 1987).

Francese, Peter. "Vital Consumer Trends for Retailers." Presentation at National Retail Merchants Association meeting (January 13, 1987).

Frank, Bertrand. *Progressive Apparel Production*. New York: Fairchild Publications, 1953.

————. *The Progressive Sewing Room*. 2nd ed. New York: Fairchild Publications, 1958.

Frey, Nadine. "Benetton: Between Armani and Coca-Cola." *Women's Wear Daily* (June 26, 1985).

Fried, Eleanor L. *Is the Fashion Business Your Business?* New York: Fairchild Publications, 1970.

Frings, Gini Stephens. *Fashion From Concept to Consumer*. Englewood Cliffs, N.J.: Prentice-Hall, 1987.

Garland, Madge. *The Changing Form of Fashion*. New York: Praeger, 1970.

George, Leslie. "Paris Couture is Alive and Well." *Women's Wear Daily* (March 3, 1987).

Ginsberg, Steve. "Nordstrom: A Maverick Takes Aim at $2 Billion." *Women's Wear Daily* (February 19, 1986).

Ginsberg, Steve, and Pete Born. "Private Label Sharpens Its Fashion Edge." *Women's Wear Daily* (May 15, 1984).

Ginsberg, Steve, and Joanna Ramey. "Nordstrom's Eastern Gold Rush." *Women's Wear Daily* (May 16, 1988).

Glosling, David, and Barry Maitland. *Design and Planning of Retail Systems*. New York: Whitney Library of Design, 1976.

Glynn, Prudence. *In Fashion: Dress in the Twentieth Century*. New York: Oxford University Press, 1978.

Gold, Annalee. *How to Sell Fashion*. New York: Fairchild Publications, 1978.

————. *75 Years of Fashion*. New York: Fairchild Publications, 1975.

Grace, Evelyn. *Introduction to Fashion Merchandising*. Englewood Cliffs, N.J.: Prentice-Hall, 1978.

Grass, Milton N. *History of Hosiery*. New York: Fairchild Publications, 1955.

Greenwood, Kathryn Moore, and Mary Fox Murphy. *Fashion Innovation and Marketing*. New York: Macmillan, 1978.

Guerin, Polly. *Creative Fashion Presentation*. New York: Fairchild Publications, 1987.

Guppy, Alice. *Children's Clothes 1939–1970 The Advent of Fashion*. New York: Blandford Press, 1978.

Hackett, Donald W. *Franchising: The State of the Art.* American Marketing Association Monograph Series #9, 1977.

Hall, Max, ed. *Made in New York.* Cambridge, MA.: Harvard University Press, 1959.

Hamburger, Estelle. *Fashion Business: It's All Yours.* San Franciso: Canfield Press, 1976.

Hamilton, I.T. "Linen." *Textiles,* 15 (1986).

Harriman, Margaret Case. *And the Price is Right.* New York: World Publishing, 1958.

Harris, Leon. *Merchant Princes.* New York: Harper & Row, 1979.

Hartlein, Robert E. "Hemisphere: The Gap Goes Upscale." *Women's Wear Daily* (August 19, 1987).

Hawes, Elizabeth. *Fashion is Spinach.* New York: Random House, 1938.

————. *It's Still Spinach.* Boston: Little, Brown, 1954.

————. *Why Is a Dress.* New York: Viking Press, 1941.

Haynes, Kevin. "Private Label Makers: Pushing More Than Price." *Women's Wear Daily* (January 19, 1987).

Henry, Gordon M. "High Fashion for Little Ones." *Time* (June 2, 1986).

Hendrickson, Robert. *The Grand Emporiums.* New York: Stein and Day, 1979.

Herndon, Booton. *Satisfaction Guaranteed.* New York: McGraw-Hill, 1972.

Hess, Max. *Every Dollar Counts.* New York: Fairchild Publications, 1952.

Horchow, Roger. *Elephants in Your Mailbox.* New York: Truman Talley, 1980.

Horn, Marilyn J., and Lois M. Gurel. *The Second Skin.* Boston: Houghton Mifflin, 1981.

Howard, Tammi. "Spiegel Adds Extra Beef to Sportswear Mix." *Women's Wear Daily* (June 22, 1988).

————. "Ward's Chief Focusing on Apparel." *Women's Wear Daily* (March 10, 1988).

Hudson, Peyton B. *Guide to Apparel Manufacturing.* Greensboro, N.C.: Mediapparel, Inc.

"In the Matter of Buying Office Closings." *Clothes* (June 1, 1977).

Jabenis, Elaine. *The Fashion Directors: What They Do and How to Be One.* New York: John Wiley, 1983.

Jarnow, Jeanette A., Miriam Guerreiro, and Beatrice Judelle. *Inside the Fashion Business.* New York: Macmillan, 1987.

Joseph, Marjory L. *Essentials of Textiles.* New York: Holt, Rinehart and Winston, 1984.

Kacker, Madhav. "Coming to Terms with Global Retailing." *International Marketing Review* (Spring 1986).

Kaikati, Jack G. "Don't Discount Off-Price Retailers." *Harvard Business Review* (May-June 1985).

Kaplan, David G. *World of Furs.* New York: Fairchild Publications, 1974.

Kelly, Katie. *The Wonderful World of Women's Wear Daily.* New York: Saturday Review Press, 1972.

Kidwell, Claudia B., and Margaret C. Christman. *Suiting Everyone: The Democratization of Clothing in America.* Washington, D.C.: Smithsonian Institution Press, 1974.

Klapper, Marvin. "Washable: Silk's Newest Wrinkle." *Women's Wear Daily* (September 8, 1987).

Koepp, Stephen. "Selling a Dream of Elegance and the Good Life." *Time* (September 1, 1986).

Kolodny, Rosalie. *Fashion Design for Moderns.* New York: Fairchild Publications, 1967.

Kornbluth, Jesse. "The Department Store as Theater." *New York Times Magazine* (April 29, 1979).

Kowinski, William Severini. *The Malling of America.* New York: William Morrow, 1985.

LaFerla, Ruth. "Soviet Chic." *New York Times Magazine* (July 31, 1988).

Lagner, Lawrence. *The Importance of Wearing Clothes.* New York: Hastings House, 1959.

Lambert, Eleanor. *World of Fashion.* New York: R. R. Bowker, 1976.

Langer, Judith. "The Baby Boomers: Target Market of the '80s." *Product Marketing* (August 1985).

"Lauren Launches NY Flagship." *Women's Wear Daily* (April 21, 1986).

Laver, James. *Modesty in Dress.* Boston: Houghton Mifflin, 1969.

————. *Taste and Fashion.* New York: Dodd Mead, 1938.

Lee, Sarah Tomerlin, ed. *American Fashion.* New York: Quadrangle, 1975.

LeVathes, Christine, ed. *Your Future in the New World of American Fashion.* New York: Richard Rosen, 1979.

Levin, Phyllis Lee. *The Wheels of Fashion.* New York: Doubleday, 1965.

Ley, Sandra. *Fashion for Everyone: The Story of Ready-to-Wear.* New York: Scribner's, 1975.

Lockwood, Lisa. "Fashioning a New Breed of Boutiques." *Women's Wear Daily* (January 12, 1986).

Lynam, Ruth, ed. *Couture.* New York: Doubleday, 1972.

McCardell, Claire. *What Shall I Wear?* New York: Simon and Schuster, 1956.

McDowell, Colin. *McDowell's Directory of Twentieth Century Fashion.* Englewood Cliffs, N.J.: Prentice-Hall, 1987.

McNair, Malcolm, and Eleanor May. "The Next Revolution of the Retailing Wheel." *Harvard Business Review* (September-October 1978).

Mahoney, Tom, and Leonard Sloane. *The Great Merchants.* New York: Harper & Row, 1974.

Man-Made Fiber Guide. Arlington, Va.: Man-Made Fiber Producers Association.

Marcus, Stanley. *His and Hers: The Fantasy World of the Neiman-Marcus Catalogue.* New York: Viking Press, 1982.

————. *Minding the Store.* Boston: Little, Brown, 1974.

————. *Quest for the Best.* New York: Viking Press, 1979.

Marketing—Sales Promotion—Advertising Planbook. New York: NRMA, annual.

Mauger, Emily M. *Modern Display Techniques.* New York: Fairchild Publications, 1964.

May, Eleanor G. "Trends in Retailing." Paper presented to the American Collegiate Retailing Association (April 19, 1985).

Mazursky, David, and Jacob Jacoby. "Exploring the Development of Store Images." *Journal of Retailing,* 62 (Summer 1986).

Mendelson, Nathaniel H., and Herbert S. Walker. *Children's Wear Merchandiser.* New York: NRMA, 1979.

"Merchandise Marts Are Getting Contagious." *Business Week* (September 28, 1981).

Messenger, Carol. "The Retail Buyer At the Hub of the Wheel." *Stores* (June 1975).

Meyers, William H. "Ray-Trade Revolutionary." *Business World, New York Times Magazine* (June 8, 1986).

Milbank, Carolyn R. *Couture: The Great Designers*. New York: Stewart. Tabori and Chang, 1985.

Mills, Kenneth H., and Judith E. Paul. *Create Distinctive Displays*. Englewood Cliffs, N.J.: Prentice-Hall, 1982.

Mitchell, Jan. "First Show Opens at Infomart." *Dallas Morning News* (January 22, 1985).

Moin, David. "A Passive Power at Mercantile." *Women's Wear Daily* (March 30, 1988).

————. "Benetton Expects to Shut 100 Stores in U.S. by 1993." *Women's Wear Daily* (September 15, 1988).

————. "Limited, Mast to Shift Bases on RTW Sourcing." *Women's Wear Daily* (April 20, 1987).

————. "Where is Bendel's Going?" *Women's Wear Daily* (February 16, 1988).

Molloy, John T. *Dress for Success*. New York: P. H. Wyden, 1975.

Montgomery, M. R. *In Search of L. L. Bean*. Boston: Little, Brown, 1984.

Morgenstein, Melvin, and Harriet Strongin. *Modern Retailing*. Englewood Cliffs, N.J.: Prentice-Hall, 1987.

Morris, Bernadine. "Fashion Uptown and Down." *New York Times Magazine* (November 4, 1984).

Morris, Harvey F. *The Story of Men's Clothes*. Rochester, N.Y.: Hickey-Freeman Co., 1926.

Morton, Grace Margaret. *The Arts of Costume and Personal Appearance*. New York: John Wiley, 1955.

"New York: Fashion Capital of What?" *Clothes* Magazine (October 15, 1974).

Newman, Edwin David. "Retailers Need Great Designers." *American Fabrics and Fashions,* No. 133 (1985).

Nystrom, Paul H. *Economics of Fashion*. New York: Ronald, 1928.

————. *Fashion Merchandising*. New York: Ronald, 1932.

Ocko, Judy Young. *Retail Advertising Copy: The How, the What, the Why*. New York: NRMA, 1971.

————, and M.L. Rosenblum. *Advertising Handbook for Retail Merchants*. New York: NRMA, 1974.

————, and M.L. Rosenblum. *The Specialty Store and Its Advertising*. New York: NRMA, 1976.

O'Leary, Sean. "Les's Successes." *Visual Merchandising and Store Design* (June 1986).

Ostrow, Rona, and Sweetman R. Smith. *The Dictionary of Retailing*. New York: Fairchild Publications, 1985.

Packard, Sidney. *The Fashion Business Dynamics and Careers*. New York: Holt, Rinehart and Winston, 1983.

————, Arthur A. Winters, and Nathan Axelrod. *Fashion Buying and Merchandising*. New York: Fairchild Publications, 1983.

Pagoda, Dianne M. "Private Label Crossing into RTW." *Women's Wear Daily* (March 1, 1988).

Paul, Marla. "Kelley Seeking Rx for Apparel Center Problems in Chicago." *Women's Wear Daily* (December 14, 1983).

Pegler, Martin M. *Visual Merchandising and Display*. New York: Fairchild Publications, 1983.

Perna, Rita. *Fashion Forecasting*. New York: Fairchild Publications, 1987.

Picken, Mary Brooks, and Dora Loues Miller. *Dressmakers of France*. New York: Harper & Brothers, 1956.

Pistolese, Rosanna, and Ruth Horsting. *History of Fashions*. New York: John Wiley, 1970.

Poiret, Paul. *King of Fashion: The Autobiography of Paul Poiret*. Philadelphia: Lippincott, 1931.

Pope, Jesse. *The Clothing Industry in New York*. New York: Burt Franklin, 1905, reprinted 1970.

Purtell, Joseph. *The Tiffany Touch*. New York: Random House, 1972.

Quant, Mary. *Quant by Quant*. London: Cassell, 1965.

"The Rag Business." *Forbes* (July 1, 1964).

Reichele, Diane. "Wholesale Center Thrives in 20th Year." *Dallas Morning News* (August 12, 1984).

Reilly, Philip J. *Old Masters of Retailing*. New York: Fairchild Publications, 1966.

Retail Terminology. Dayton, Ohio: NCR Corporation.

"Retailers Ready to Berth at Pier 17 in New York," *Women's Wear Daily* (August 28, 1985).

Richards, Florence S. *The Ready-to-Wear Industry 1900–1950*. New York: Fairchild Publications, 1951.

Riche, Martha Farnsworth. "Demographic Trends in the Work Place." Paper presented at National Retail Merchants Association annual meeting (July 13, 1987).

Riley, Robert, and Walter Vecchio. *The Fashion Makers*. New York: Crown, 1967.

Roach, Mary Ellen, and Joanne B. Eicher. *Dress, Adornment and the Social Order*. New York: John Wiley, 1965.

———. *The Visible Self: Perspectives on Dress*. Englewood Cliffs, N.J.: Prentice-Hall, 1973.

Rogers, Dorothy S., and Lynda R. Gamans. *Fashion: A Marketing Approach*. New York: Holt, Rinehart and Winston, 1983.

Rosenblum, Anne. "SA's Move Into Its Own Stores Gains Momentum." *Women's Wear Daily* (March 29, 1988).

Roshco, Bernard. *The Rag Race*. New York: Funk & Wagnalls, 1963.

Rutberg, Sidney. "Benetton: A Maker with Its Own Market." *Women's Wear Daily* (May 23, 1985).

———. "Sale of Stock Rakes in Lire for Benettons." *Women's Wear Daily* (July 10, 1986).

Ryan, Mary Shaw. *Clothing: A Study in Human Behavior*. New York: Holt, Rinehart and Winston, 1966.

Saint Laurent, Yves. *Yves Saint Laurent*. New York: Metropolitan Museum of Art, distributed by Crown, 1983.

Saunders, Edith. *The Age of Worth*. Bloomington: Indiana University Press, 1955.

Schiaparelli, Elsa. *Shocking Life*. New York: Dutton, 1954.

Schulz, David P. "Retail Expansion." *Stores* (August 1985).

Segal, Marvin E. *From Rags to Riches: Success in Apparel Retailing*. New York: John Wiley, 1983.

Shapro, Dana. "New Team Out to Hone Chicago Center Image." *Women's Wear Daily* (January 9, 1985).

Sheldon's Retail Directory of the United States and Canada and Phelon's Resident Buyers and Merchandise Brokers. New York: Phelon, Sheldon and Marsar, 1988.

Sheth, Jagdish N. "Emerging Trends for the Retailing Industry." *Journal of Retailing* 59 (Fall 1983).

Sixty Years of Fashion. New York: Fairchild Publications, 1963.

Sloane, Carole. "Time to Re-examine the Changing Role of the Buying Offices." *Stores* (July 1977).

Snow, Carmel. *The World of Carmel Snow*. New York: McGraw-Hill, 1962.

Solomon, Michael R. *The Psychology of Fashion*. Boston: D.C. Heath, 1985.

Sones, Melissa. *Getting Into Fashion*. New York: Ballantine, 1984.

Standard & Poor's Industry Surveys. Retailing Basic Analysis; July 4, 1985; April 3, 1986; July 30, 1987.

Stegemeyer, Anne. *Who's Who in Fashion*. New York: Fairchild Publications, 1980.

Stevens, Mark. *The Inside Story of Bloomingdale's*. New York: Ballantine, 1979.

Stone, Elaine. *Fashion Buying*. New York: McGraw-Hill, 1987.

———, and Jean A. Samples. *Fashion Merchandising: An Introduction*. New York: McGraw-Hill, 1985.

Summers, Teresa Anderson. "Buyer and Vendor Perceptions of the Importance and Use of Support Services of the Dallas Apparel Mart." Ph.D. dissertation, Texas Woman's University, 1983.

Thomas, Evan. "The Baby Boomers Turn 40." *Time* (May 19, 1986).

Tolman, Ruth. *Selling Men's Fashion*. New York: Fairchild Publications, 1982.

Tortora, Phyllis. *Understanding Textiles*. New York: Macmillan, 1982.

Trachtenberg, Jeffrey. "You Are What You Wear." *Forbes* (April 21, 1986).

Troxell, Mary D., and Elaine Stone. *Fashion Merchandising*. New York: McGraw-Hill, 1981.

U.S. Bureau of the Census, Special Demographic Analyses, CDS-80-8. *American Women: Three Decades of Change*. Washington, D.C.: USGPO, 1984.

U.S. Congress, Office of Technology Assessment. *The U.S. Textile and Apparel Industry: A Revolution in Progress—Special Report*. OTA-TET-332, Washington, D.C.: USGPO, 1987.

U.S. Department of Commerce, Bureau of the Census. *1982 Census of Manufacturers*.

U.S. Department of Commerce. *U.S. Industrial Outlook, 1988*.

Vance, Stanley. *American Industries*. New York: Prentice-Hall, 1955.

Visual Merchandising. New York: NRMA, 1976.

Waldinger, Roger D. *Through the Eye of the Needle: Immigrants and Enterprise in New York's Garment Trades*. New York: New York University, 1986.

Walz, Barbara, and Bernadine Morris. *The Fashion Makers*. New York: Random House, 1978.

Watkins, Josephine Ellis. *Who's Who in Fashion*. New York: Fairchild Publications, 1975.

Webster, Bruce. *The Insider's Guide to Franchising*. New York: Amacom, 1986.

Weishar, Joseph. "The Business of Product Priority." *Visual Merchandising and Store Design* (March 1986).

Wendt, Lloyd, and Herman Kogan. *Give the Lady What She Wants*. New York: Rand McNally, 1952.

Wilcox, Ruth Turner. *The Mode in Costume*. New York: Scribner's, 1983.

Wilson, Kax. *A History of Textiles*. Boulder, Co. Westview Press, 1979.

Wingate, Isabel B. *Fairchild's Dictionary of Textiles*. 6th ed. New York: Fairchild Publications, 1979.

Wingate, John W., and Joseph Friedlander. *The Management of Retail Buying*. Englewood Cliffs, N.J.: Prentice-Hall, 1978.

Winters, Arthur A., and Stanley Goodman. *Fashion Advertising and Promotion*. New York: Fairchild Publications, 1984.

Women's Wear Daily. New York: Fairchild Publications, various articles.

Woodward, Helen. *The Lady Persuaders*. New York: Obolensky, 1960.

Worth, Jean Philippe. *A Century of Fashion*. Boston: Little, Brown, 1928.

INDEX